W9-CLG-165

COLLECTED WORKS OF ERASMUS

VOLUME 11

Victory column designed by Albrecht Dürer as a satiric comment on the Peasant
War. The spoils are domestic articles, farm produce, and captive animals,
with a peasant at the top transfixed by a sword.
Albrecht Dürer, 1525
Courtesy of the Robarts Library, Toronto

Phillips

COLLECTED WORKS OF
ERASMUS

LETTERS 1535 TO 1657

January–December 1525

translated by Alexander Dalzell

annotated by Charles G. Nauert jr

University of Toronto Press

Toronto / Buffalo / London

The research and publication costs of the
Collected Works of Erasmus are supported by the
Social Sciences and Humanities Research Council of Canada.
The publication costs are also assisted by
University of Toronto Press.

© University of Toronto Press 1994
Toronto / Buffalo / London
Printed in Canada

ISBN 0-8020-0536-5

Printed on acid-free paper

Canadian Cataloguing in Publication Data
Erasmus, Desiderius, d. 1536
[Works]
Collected Works of Erasmus

Includes bibliographical references.
Partial contents: v. 11. Letters 1535 to 1657, January–December 1525 /
translated by Alexander Dalzell; annotated by Charles G. Nauert.
ISBN 0-8020-0536-5 (v. 11)

1. Erasmus, Desiderius, d. 1536. I. Title.

PA8500 1974   876'.04   C74-006326-X rev

Collected Works of Erasmus

The aim of the Collected Works of Erasmus
is to make available an accurate, readable English text
of Erasmus' correspondence and his
other principal writings. The edition is planned
and directed by an Editorial Board, an Executive Committee,
and an Advisory Committee.

Contents

Illustrations

Preface

Throughout the year 1525, which is precisely the period covered by the contents of this volume, Erasmus sat uneasily at Basel, apparently not even venturing outside the city to make the sort of social calls he had made to Porrentruy and Besançon in the spring of 1524. No doubt part of his immobility resulted from ill health, for he still suffered from kidney stones, which had nearly killed him in the preceding year. But the greater cause of his staying close to home was the German Peasant War, which reached its peak in the spring and early summer of 1525 and which directly and deeply affected regions in the immediate vicinity of Basel. Especially when writing to friends and patrons in the Netherlands who wanted and expected him to return to Louvain or Brussels or some other place in his native region, he frequently mentioned both his poor health and the dangers of travelling through a countryside torn by social revolution.[1]

The Peasant War was the greatest social upheaval of the century, and though Basel itself was secure, much of the most violent conflict occurred near-by. The rebellion grew mainly out of long-standing grievances against aristocratic and clerical landlords. Local peasant uprisings had been endemic for more than half a century, but the excitement caused by Luther's reform contributed to the gigantic scale of the rebellion of 1525. The violence began at Stühlingen (not far from Basel) in June 1524 and spread rapidly. By early 1525, peasant armies were springing up in many localities. Ultimately all of south Germany and German-speaking Switzerland was affected except Bavaria and the three forest cantons of central Switzerland. The peasants extended their control not only to country districts but also to several cities. A number of towns (including Basel and Strasbourg) sought a peaceful resolution, but the princes had no intention of yielding. In April the Swabian League disbanded the peasant armies near Lake Constance and by

* * * * *

1 Eg, Epp 1545, 1553, 1554, 1585

early June had crushed rebellion in Württemberg and Franconia. On 15 May the duke of Hesse led another army which slaughtered some 6,000 peasants at Frankenhausen and ended the war in Thuringia. Just two days later, the duke of Lorraine retook the Alsatian city of Saverne, slaughtering 18,000 rebels and ending the rebellion west of the Rhine. But while western Germany was under control by June, the rebellion was just reaching its peak in the archbishopric of Salzburg and the Hapsburg provinces of Tyrol, Styria, and Austria, where violence continued for several months. In March 1526 the archbishop had to face a second rebellion. The uprising in East Prussia did not begin until early September 1525. Even after all organized resistance was over, large parts of southern Germany and many towns in the Rhine valley remained unsettled.[2] Thus Erasmus was not being unduly cautious when he hesitated to venture outside of Basel.

Yet at the same time he felt restless in Basel. True, he had excellent relations with his great printer, Johann Froben, and with other important persons and groups in the city, including the city council, which twice explicitly sought his advice on questions of religious policy.[3] Part of his restlessness about staying in Basel was his clear realization that unless he returned to the Netherlands, his imperial pension, which was charged against the revenues of Charles V's Dutch provinces, would never be paid despite all his entreaties.[4] But the major problem was his accurate perception that the local Reformation party, led by his former associates Johannes Oecolampadius and Conradus Pellicanus, was growing in numbers and influence and might soon get control of the city.[5] Erasmus could live com-

* * * * *

2 The standard older authority, which surprisingly was never translated into English, is Franz. An influential recent interpretation is Blickle. Pages xi–xxvi of this volume offer a clear, succinct account of the war by the translators. See also the collection of essays, *The German Peasant War 1525: New Viewpoints* ed Bob Scribner and Gerhard Benecke (London 1979), and the historiographical essay by Robert W. Scribner 'The German Peasants' War' *Reformation Europe: A Guide to Research* ed Steven Ozment (St Louis 1982) 107–33. Older English-language works still often cited are Friedrich Engels *The Peasant War in Germany* trans David Riasanov (New York 1926; original German ed 1850), E. Belfort Bax *The Peasants' War in Germany* (London 1899; repr New York 1968), and Jacob Salwyn Schapiro *Social Reform and the Reformation* (New York 1909; repr New York 1970); the first two of these were influential in establishing a socialist interpretation of the Peasant War. But all three older books are now superseded by modern studies, including the Blickle book and the collection of essays edited by Scribner and Benecke.

3 Epp 1539, 1636

4 On the pension see Ep 1380 introduction; cf Epp 1545, 1553, 1554, 1621, 1645.

5 Cf Epp 1545, 1554, and most poignantly, perhaps, his sense of isolation and

fortably enough in a religiously divided and fairly tolerant city. But his open break with Martin Luther, marked by the publication of *De libero arbitrio* in 1524, was an affirmation of his determination to remain true to the old religion despite his deep dissatisfaction with many aspects of it. Better to leave Basel in good time, before both conscience and concern for his reputation might force a hasty departure.

If he left Basel, however, the question of where to move remained unanswerable. In a few of the letters written in 1525 to friends at Rome or elsewhere in Italy, he expressed a desire to move to Rome;[6] and he knew well that Pope Clement VII would welcome his settling there. But at Rome he would at least be perceived as belonging body and soul to a curial establishment which he regarded as corrupt and in part even as unchristian.[7] Furthermore, the rising influence of Girolamo Aleandro, a former friend whom Erasmus quite rightly perceived as a malevolent secret enemy,[8] must have made Rome unappealing. In the period 1522–4 he had been hotly courted by Francis I of France, who offered him a lucrative sinecure if he would move to France. But for many and complex reasons, Erasmus had never maintained truly intimate friendships with his French acquaintances, not even with leading humanists like Jacques Lefèvre d'Etaples and Guillaume Budé.[9] The disastrous French defeat at Pavia in February 1525, which left the French king a prisoner in Madrid until the spring of 1526, removed the one patron whose favour might have made Erasmus feel secure against the attacks of conservative French theologians and law courts, the two groups that had direct responsibility for repression of real or alleged heresy. The evangelical reform sponsored by Guillaume Briçonnet, bishop of Meaux, was smashed. Lefèvre d'Etaples, the elder statesman of reformist French humanists, fled to Strasbourg for fear of prosecution.[10] So France in 1525 hardly seemed an appealing place to settle. The only other

* * * * *

entrapment in Ep 1586: 'I have been caught, as the saying goes, between the altar and the sacrificial knife, in a position of some considerable danger.'
6 Epp 1586 (to Jacopo Sadoleto), 1621 (to Pierre Barbier), 1631 (to Paolo Bombace)
7 Epp 1581, 1586
8 Cf the discussion below at Ep 1553 n9.
9 André Stegmann 'Erasme et la France (1495–1520)' in *Colloquium Erasmianum: Actes du Colloque International réuni à Mons...* (Mons 1968) 275–97.
10 In fact, Ep 1650A provides reasonably clear evidence that Erasmus intervened with friends at the curia to protect Lefèvre from prosecution. Lefèvre prudently stayed out of France from October 1525 to the spring of 1526. On his return cf Ep 1713.

likely option (for though he had friends aplenty in England, in 1525 he never mentions moving there to stay), to go back to his native Netherlands, meant returning to the daily friction of life among the theologians at Louvain, an existence which he had assayed from 1517 to 1521 and had not found pleasant. Or else as a person bearing the title (and vainly claiming the pension) of an imperial councillor, he would be drawn into the activities of the court at Brussels, where he would not only be made to live the tiresome and insecure life of a courtier but beyond doubt would be drawn directly into the government's effort to suppress heresy in the provinces.[11] So, despite his uneasiness at Basel, he sat out the whole year there. In fact, he stayed there until the definitive triumph of the Reformation in 1529 made his conscience compel him to retire to the safely Catholic city of Freiburg in the Hapsburg-ruled Breisgau.

In terms of literary productivity, the year 1525 did not match the remarkable achievements of the period covered by the preceding volume of letters published in CWE.[12] Under Erasmus' direction as general editor, the Froben press produced an important edition of the *Naturalis historia* of Pliny the Elder; but much of the detailed textual work was done by his associate Beatus Rhenanus, who the following year published his own far more valuable commentary on the text of Pliny.[13] His *Lingua*, dedicated to the Polish nobleman Krzysztof Szydłowiecki, came from Froben's press in August.[14] This dedication solidified his close contacts with several politically and intellectually important figures in that remote kingdom;[15] and the young Polish nobleman Jan Łaski lived in his house at Basel for about six months, from spring to early October 1525.[16] But despite its warm reception in Poland and elsewhere, *Lingua* never attained the status of a major work or had a lasting influence. The year 1525 opened with the dedication of a minor work, his oration on Psalm 4, to his friend John

* * * * *

11 In 1523 the first burning of Lutheran heretics, two Augustinian friars, occurred in the Netherlands. As both an imperial councillor and a member of the Louvain theological faculty, Erasmus could hardly have avoided being drawn into the emperor's policy of active repression.
12 See James M. Estes' preface in CWE 10 xi on the productivity of the period covered by that volume of letters.
13 Charles G. Nauert, jr 'Caius Plinius Secundus' in *Catalogus Translationum et Commentariorum* ed Paul Oskar Kristeller et al IV (Washington 1980) 312, 367–9.
14 Ep 1593
15 On the Polish connection cf Epp 1572, 1593, 1602, 1615, 1629, 1652.
16 For discussion of his dates of residence with Erasmus see Ep 1593 n18.

Longland, bishop of Lincoln.[17] There were two small patristic editions: the revised Greek-Latin edition of St John Chrysostom's *De orando Deum* in April, and Chrysostom's *De sacerdotio* in May, the latter work dedicated to his old friend Willibald Pirckheimer of Nürnberg.[18] The letters for 1525 also include one dedication for a Greek-Latin edition of two treatises of Plutarch;[19] and one work of theological controversy, *Adversus Petri Sutoris ... debacchationem Apologia*, published in August and dedicated to Jean de Selve, *premier président* of the Parlement of Paris.[20] The year also yielded a revised and enlarged edition of what is surely one of the least typical of Erasmus' works, a mass written by him in honour of Our Lady of Loreto, dedicated to Thiébaut Biétry, parish priest at Porrentruy, the habitual residence of Erasmus' good friend the bishop of Basel. This work was favoured by another friend, the archbishop of Besançon, with an indulgence for all who made use of this mass within his diocese.[21]

In many respects, the most significant literary product of Erasmus during 1525 was none of these published books but his voluminous correspondence with the most influential of the Paris theologians, Noël Béda, who had revived the defunct office of syndic in 1520 and had transformed it into a vehicle for his personal dominance over the whole faculty of theology.[22] If Erasmus ever dreamt that his open break with Luther in 1524 would silence his most aggressive Catholic critics, the continuing attacks by Latomus and other Louvain theologians and by the Spanish theologian Diego López Zúñiga should have disabused him quickly. But Paris was the most authoritative centre of traditional scholastic theology; and Erasmus' informants there, including friends within the Parlement of Paris and within the theological faculty itself, informed him that for many months Noël Béda had been compiling a list of articles, or alleged errors, found in Erasmus' paraphrase on the Gospel of Luke and his exposition of the Lord's Prayer. His *parlementaire* friend François Deloynes had received a copy of these articles from Béda and shortly before his own untimely death had sent

* * * * *

17 Ep 1535
18 Epp 1563, 1558
19 Ep 1572
20 Ep 1591
21 Ep 1573
22 Within the time covered by this volume these were Epp 1571, 1579, 1581, 1596, 1609, 1610, 1620, 1642; the correspondence continued down to November 1527 (Ep 1906). On the office of syndic and Béda's dominance over the faculty, see Farge *Orthodoxy* 41–2.

Erasmus a copy.²³ Also at the beginning of 1525 an equally hostile but much less competent Paris conservative, Pierre Cousturier, had published an open attack on both Erasmus and Lefèvre d'Etaples, *De tralatione Bibliae*, to which Erasmus felt compelled to respond with the *Apologia* mentioned above, published in August.²⁴

Far more important for an understanding of Erasmus' theological opinions than this and his other publications against Cousturier, however, were his letters to Béda. Contrary to the conventional opinion that Erasmus lacked candour and strength of character, his reaction to the news that Béda was preparing the grounds for a formal inquiry into his orthodoxy was forthright and bold. At the end of May he initiated contact by writing directly to Béda, politely but firmly expressing both his concern at the rumours he had heard and his determination to uphold his own status as an orthodox Catholic theologian. He also lodged complaint against what he presented as the grossly incompetent and extreme attack by Cousturier.²⁵ He claimed that he was not offended by Béda's notes on his work and even urged him to send further critical notes that he could use in preparing the next edition of his Greek New Testament. The degeneration of their correspondence from this polite beginning to a thinly concealed hostility can be traced in the subsequent letters between them, extending down to 1527. What is most striking is Erasmus' blunt assertion of his own orthodoxy and theological competence. He attempted to co-opt the powerful Béda into the role of mediator between Erasmus and supposedly more conservative theologians like Cousturier. This was similar to a tactic he had used in 1518–20 at Louvain, where despite continuing mistrust Erasmus did succeed in co-opting the most influential of the Louvain theologians, Jan Briart of Ath, as a mediator whose influence allowed Erasmus to maintain civil, personal, and professional relations with most members of the theological faculty. But at Paris the plan did not work. Erasmus was not present to employ his very considerable personal charm in winning the trust of the conservatives. And Béda was more narrow, more arrogant, and more independent of external political pressures from Erasmus' friends than Briart had been. He was, in fact, remarkably unimpressed by Erasmus' attack on Luther and seems to have regarded Erasmus' reformist opinions on questions like mandatory fasting, private confession, and clerical celibacy as far more weighty matters than the freedom of the will or the preservation of

*****

23 Ep 1571
24 Ep 1591; cf Rummel II 61–73.
25 Ep 1571

unity within the church. So while Erasmus' direct approach led to an exchange of letters which set forth two fundamentally opposed conceptions of sound Catholic theology, it accomplished little more than delaying the formal censure of his theological works by the Paris faculty, an event which occurred in December 1527.[26] The delay, in fact, was caused more by pressure and intervention from the royal court than by Erasmus' appeals to rational discourse.[27]

If the encounter with Béda and his fellow theologians was Erasmus' most significant activity during 1525, his problems with the Protestant leaders in Basel were also important. Although the city council was still predominantly Catholic and opposed radical theology (especially the Sacramentarian view of the Eucharist) firmly, it had made concessions to the reformers, including the appointment of both Johannes Oecolampadius and Conradus Pellicanus to the theological faculty of the local university in 1523. Erasmus faced the problem of separating himself from the Sacramentarian theology of his former colleagues. Both Oecolampadius and Pellicanus were able, well-educated humanists. Both had been closely associated with Erasmus in his scholarly work on the scriptural and patristic editions of the Froben press. He had relied on their expert advice in his own editorial decisions, a point he candidly admitted in one of his letters to Béda.[28] Both men had defected to the Reformed cause, and this close friendship was now an embarrassment, especially as both of them sincerely believed that their new religious doctrines were the inevitable consequence of what they had learned from Erasmus' scholarly work. In January 1525 Erasmus confronted Oecolampadius directly in a letter that emphasized his disagreement with Oecolampadius' opinions and actions and that objected strongly to attempts to associate his own name with the new heresy.[29] The break with Pellicanus, whose gentle personality and devotion to study made him especially attractive to Erasmus, was even more harsh. The exchange of letters initiated by Erasmus in October 1525 ended in a total severing of relations by 1526 or 1527, and Erasmus repeatedly rebuffed Pellicanus' efforts to restore friendly relations. He felt betrayed by a friend, and not till 1535 did Pellicanus (by then located at Zürich) succeed in his efforts to restore communication, culminating in his personal visit to Erasmus on 25 June 1536, just a

* * * * *

26 Rummel II 49; Farge *Orthodoxy* 194–6
27 For a general account of the censure of Erasmus, see Rummel II 29–59 and Farge *Orthodoxy* 170, 186–96.
28 Ep 1581
29 Ep 1538

few days before the latter's death.[30] Perhaps there was an added edge to Erasmus' hostility because he found Oecolampadius' defence of the Sacramentarian position highly persuasive, admitting even in a formal letter of advice to the Basel city council that one of Oecolampadius' publications on the Eucharist was 'learned, well written, and thorough. I would also judge it pious, if anything could be so described which is at variance with the general opinion of the church, from which I consider it perilous to dissent.'[31] To Pierre Barbier, one of his principal contacts at the Roman curia, he wrote candidly that Oecolampadius' *De genuina verborum Domini 'Hoc est corpus meum' expositione* (September? 1525) was 'a book so carefully written and so buttressed with argument and supporting evidence that even the elect could be led astray.'[32]

Erasmus had already made his own personal choice, in favour of the authority of the institutional church, when he broke with Luther in 1524. Yet despite his loyalty to the old religion and his hostility to many former friends who defected to the Protestant side, he still defended the wisdom of his long delay in openly opposing Luther,[33] and he described with remarkable equanimity the restriction or liquidation of monastic communities by many town governments in Germany, including Basel itself.[34] He could also still ignore obvious Protestant sympathies in a man whose talent and personal character he approved, such as the evangelical preacher Pierre Toussain, whom he provided with valuable introductions to Jean de Guise, Cardinal of Lorraine, Michel Boudet, bishop of Langres, and Guillaume Budé when Toussain went to France, ostensibly to study but actually to propagate heresy.[35] In the long run, what distressed Erasmus most about the work of the Reformers was the conflict, disunity, and social disorder which it produced; and the letters in this volume are full of laments about these sad events, including the slaughter of the peasants.[36] On several occasions he admonished critics (and friends) living outside of Germany that they simply had no idea of the real problems faced by Catholics living in Germany, where order and stability had collapsed.[37]

* * * * *

30 Ep 1637 introduction; cf Epp 1638, 1639, 1640, 1737, 1792A.
31 Ep 1636
32 Ep 1621. Erasmus used almost the same words in a letter to Béda, Ep 1620.
33 Ep 1634 to Alberto Pio
34 Eg Ep 1547
35 Epp 1559 to Jean de Lorraine; 1618 to Bishop Boudet; 1619 to Budé
36 Eg Epp 1584, 1597, 1601, 1603, 1606
37 Ep 1576 to Celio Calcagnini; Ep 1608 to Nicolas Coppin and the Louvain theological faculty; Ep 1620 to Noël Béda

Having clearly made the choice for Rome, and being well aware that he had dangerous opponents there, Erasmus had to make sure that he had well-placed and influential patrons at Rome itself and elsewhere in the papal bureaucracy. Twice in 1525 he sent his most trusted confidential agent, Karl Harst, to Italy on business. Harst's most important task was his successful effort to secure a papal brief issued by Clement VII authorizing Erasmus to dispose of his properties by will (having taken monastic vows in his youth, Erasmus normally would not have had such a right).[38] But beyond this private business, Harst had the duty of renewing personal contact with Erasmus' friends at the curia, and in particular securing papal action to silence the Louvain theologians who continued to attack Erasmus even while he was engaged in controversy with the followers of Luther. Harst succeeded in this part of his mission also, for in July two informal but very clear papal commands were sent ordering the theological faculty to stop open attacks on Erasmus by its members.[39] Thus Clement renewed earlier attempts by Leo X and Adrian VI to impose silence on Erasmus' critics, though the attempt was far from completely successful. In addition, through Harst and through other couriers Erasmus carefully solicited the favour of influential curial officials: Floriano Montini (Ep 1552), secretary to Cardinal Lorenzo Campeggi, papal legate to Germany, Hungary, and Bohemia; Jacopo Sadoleto (Ep 1555), secretary to Pope Clement; Felix Trophinus (Ep 1575), former chaplain and secretary to Clement before his election and an influential adviser; Fridericus Nausea (Ep 1577), a colleague of Montini in the household of Cardinal Campeggi; Antonio Pucci (Ep 1580), an influential papal diplomat; Francesco Minuzio Calvo (Ep 1604), the official printer to the Holy See; Pierre Barbier (Ep 1605), who had been very close to Pope Adrian VI and continued to have influence at Rome until his departure (not yet known to Erasmus) to enter the service of the viceroy of Naples; Jacobus Apocellus of Bruchsal (Ep 1630), an official of the confraternity of Germans resident in Rome; and Paolo Bombace (Ep 1631), another secretary to Pope Clement. Other curial figures who helped Erasmus at this time were Albert Pigge (Ep 1589), papal chamberlain to both Adrian VI and Clement VII, and Gian Matteo Giberti (Ep 1589A), datary to Clement VII. These two men were active in admonishing the Louvain theologians to silence attacks on Erasmus. Through Montini, Erasmus also struck up correspondence with Celio Calcagnini, an influential humanist of Ferrara who had compiled a work, *De libero animi motu*, in support of Erasmus' *De*

* * * * *

38 Ep 1588
39 Epp 1589, 1589A

libero arbitrio. Erasmus arranged for publication of Calcagnini's book by Froben in June 1525.[40]

Despite all these valuable contacts at Rome (including many native Italian humanists), Erasmus was never fully comfortable with curial society, and his failure to leave Basel for Rome resulted not just from his ill health or his desire to avoid being perceived as the papacy's kept man, but also from a deep-seated mistrust. Part of this mistrust arose from Erasmus' perception that as a group the curial humanists were far more attracted by the literary, secular, and pagan values of ancient civilization than by its Christian aspects. He frankly told Noël Béda that one of his major goals was 'to give literary studies a Christian voice, for up to that time ... humanists in Italy concentrated on pagan themes.'[41] With Sadoleto, whom he admired as a notable exception to this irreligious tendency, he was somewhat less open but still clear enough, warmly praising his recent commentary on Psalm 50, while contrasting his union of humanistic and theological studies with the pagan tone that dominated the publications of most Roman humanists.[42] The other source of Erasmus' mistrust of the curia was his concern about the growing influence of Girolamo Aleandro, whom he correctly identified as a secret enemy who consistently worked to raise suspicions at Rome about Erasmus' orthodoxy, and who in fact had recently composed and privately circulated at the curia an unpublished work attacking Erasmus as a heretic.[43] Aleandro seemed so powerful and so skilled at curial politics that Erasmus did not dare force the issue to public attention, though he did complain privately.

Among his Italian critics, the most outspoken was the aristocratic and learned Alberto Pio, prince of Carpi. As early as 1524, Erasmus complained that an unnamed person was circulating charges of heresy against him at the curia;[44] and in May 1525 he complained in a letter to Celio Calcagnini, a mutual friend, that Pio was slandering him at Rome.[45] Despite Calcagnini's reassuring reply,[46] the reports were true. Pio was one of a number of curial humanists who seriously maintained that Erasmus was the source of Luther's heresies and bore ultimate responsibility for the religious up-

* * * * *

40 Epp 1552, 1576, 1578, 1587
41 Ep 1581
42 Ep 1586
43 Ep 1553 n9; cf Epp 1549, 1605, 1621.
44 Ep 1479
45 Ep 1576
46 Ep 1587

heaval in Germany. Pio was a formidable figure, whose blue blood as heir
of a ruling family was matched by his gilt-edged humanistic credentials:
nephew of the famous Giovanni Pico della Mirandola and educated under
his direction by the future publisher Aldo Manuzio; one of the early financial backers of Manuzio's famous humanistic press at Venice; student of
Pietro Pomponazzi at Ferrara; close friend of Celio Calcagnini, Pietro
Bembo, Jacopo Sadoleto, and Ludovico Ariosto. His diplomatic service to
both the French and Spanish kings and to the papacy further enhanced his
influence among Italian intellectuals and policy-makers. Finally, in October
1525, Erasmus wrote directly to Pio, telling him of the rumours he was
hearing about his defamation of Erasmus at Rome. The result was a bitter
literary controversy which continued down to, and even after, Pio's death
in 1531.[47] Indeed, the friction between Roman humanism and Erasmian
humanism exemplified by this conflict is the prelude to the subsequent
controversy aroused by publication of Erasmus' *Ciceronianus* in 1527.

For the rest, Erasmus' correspondence for 1525 continued many of the
themes noted in earlier volumes of this series. His complaints about the
injustice of being attacked from the rear by Catholic critics while he was
engaged in opposing Luther's followers appears in many of these letters,
notably those addressed to Béda and the Louvain theologians. He assiduously cultivated contacts with archbishops, bishops, and other high clerics
in transalpine Europe and of course with secular rulers and nobles from
England to Poland and from the Netherlands to Italy; and he just as assiduously advertised to others the closeness of his relations with these powerful
figures.[48] Amidst all his controversies, he persistently worked away at
future scholarly editions for Froben, not only the next edition of his Greek
New Testament, for which he even sought Béda's advice, but also his
projected edition of the works of St Augustine, for which he sought and
received the assistance of the Dutch scholar Maarten Lips.[49] He even continued some activity on editions of pagan authors, seeking to trace a manuscript of Seneca through his English friend Robert Aldridge.[50] But although
pure scholarship continued, religious controversy and the concerns of mere
survival dominate the contents of his letters. One development of 1525
whose significance Erasmus himself at first did not realize was the emergence of his admirer Erasmus Schets, merchant of Antwerp, as a far more

* * * * *

47 On this letter and the ensuing controversy see Ep 1634 introduction.
48 Eg Epp 1559, 1571, 1581, 1608
49 Ep 1547. This edition was finally published by Froben in 1528–9.
50 Ep 1656

effective replacement for Pieter Gillis as his chief financial agent. Although Schets' Latin was not very good, his admiration for Erasmus was unmistakably sincere, as was his eagerness to help. In January 1525 he wrote to forward letters from Spain and to express his admiration, but within six months he had become Erasmus' confidential business agent in the Netherlands, collecting his revenues from ecclesiastical sources in England and the Netherlands, efficiently transmitting funds from Antwerp to Basel, and transmitting letters – all very much to Erasmus' advantage and apparently at no profit to himself. Erasmus carefully preserved most of this correspondence but regarded it as wholly private and published none of it.[51]

The present volume contains 126 items, whereof 123 are letters to or from Erasmus, one is the letter from Albert Pigge to the Louvain theologians, one is a letter of Gian Matteo Giberti to Theodoricus Hezius about the same matter, and one an appendix to Ep 1634A, which was discovered and published after publication of Allen VI in 1926. One letter, numbered 1644 by Allen, has been redated to March 1527 and renumbered 1792A; it will appear in CWE 12. The surviving letters are heavily weighted in favour of letters written by Erasmus to others, eighty-nine by him as against thirty-four addressed to him. Sixty-three of these letters were first published by Erasmus himself: fifty-four of them in his *Opus epistolarum* (Basel: Froben 1529), and nine as dedications to works by him or edited by him. Five were first published by Noël Béda in his *Apologia adversus clandestinos Lutheranos* (Paris: Josse Bade, February 1529), and two of these appeared again shortly afterward in the *Opus epistolarum*. One letter first appeared in Alberto Pio's treatise attacking Erasmus, *Responsio accurata et paraenetica* (Paris: Josse Bade, 7 January 1529) and was soon reprinted in Erasmus' *Opus epistolarum*. Three letters, Epp 1637, 1638, and 1639, appeared in two rare pamphlets probably printed early in 1526 (see the introductions to these letters below), and one of these (Ep 1637) also found broader circulation by appearing in the *Opus epistolarum*. His letter of January 1525 advising the Basel city council on religious policy (Ep 1539) first was printed as an unauthorized pamphlet in 1526. Of the other letters, five were published in Melchior Goldast's edition of the *Opera* of Willibald Pirckheimer (1610), ten were first published at Leipzig by Förstemann and Günther in 1904, and ten first saw print in Allen's edition (1926). The one letter not found in Allen, Ep 1634A, and its appendix, were published by Ida Calabi Limentani in *Acme* (1972). In order that readers may know when each letter became accessible in print, the

* * * * *

51 Ep 1541; cf Epp 1583, 1590, 1647, 1651, 1654.

introduction to each cites the place where it was first published and identifies the manuscript source if one exists.

All of the letters in this volume were translated by Alexander Dalzell, and as annotator I wish to acknowledge the remarkably thorough help he provided in tracing classical references in the letters. The index to this volume, prepared by Penny Cole, contains references to the persons, places, and works mentioned in the volume, following the plan for the correspondence series. When that series of volumes is completed, the reader will also be provided with an index of classical and scriptural references. Because the three volumes of the CEBR are now available, the biographical annotation of this volume has been kept to an absolute minimum, as has the citation of biographical sources. Although I have cited articles in CEBR only rarely, I have found them of great value. Wherever information is supplied without the citation of a source, the reader is tacitly referred to the appropriate article in the CEBR and to the literature there cited.

I wish to acknowledge the debt that I owe to colleagues who have given me expert assistance and advice, especially A. Mark Smith, A.S. Bradford, and Lawrence Okamura of my own department at the University of Missouri-Columbia, Jill Raitt of the Department of Religious Studies, and Victor Estevez of the Department of Classical Studies. The editors and collaborators on this project at the University of Toronto and elsewhere have been both helpful and patient. The support of the Research Council of the University of Missouri-Columbia for several other projects related to this one permitted me to accumulate notes, printed and manuscript sources, and secondary literature from many places; and these were frequently helpful to this work. And of course, none of us could do scholarship without our librarians: I wish to thank the reference and interlibrary loan staffs of Ellis Library at the University of Missouri-Columbia, and in particular Anne Edwards, who at the time when most of the work on this volume was done was our divisional Humanities librarian. Finally, as a person living outside Canada, I wish to express my admiration to the University of Toronto Press and to the Social Sciences and Humanities Research Council of Canada for their courage and persistence in undertaking such a vast and valuable enterprise.

I also wish to express my appreciation to my wife Jean and our sons Paul and Jon, who have long shared their home and my attention with the 'Erasmus project.'

CGN

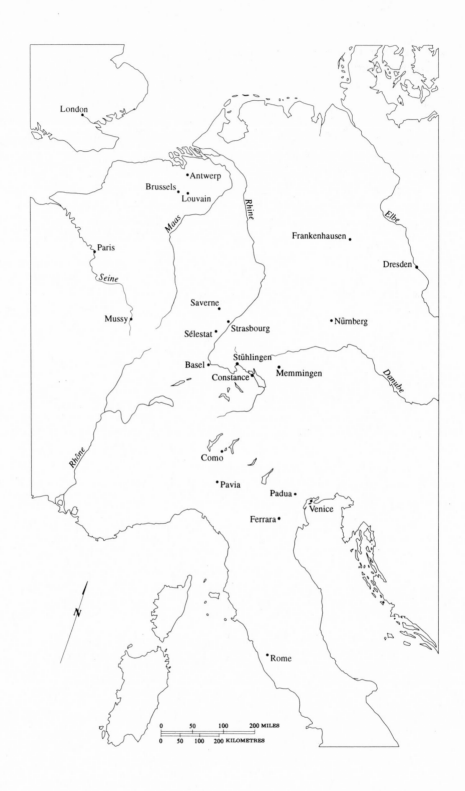

London

Antwerp

Brussels
Louvain

Maas

Rhine

Elbe

Paris

Frankenhausen

Dresden

Seine

Saverne

Mussy

Nürnberg

Sélestat
Strasbourg

Basel
Stühlingen

Constance
Memmingen

Danube

Rhône

Como

Pavia

Padua
Venice

Ferrara

N

Rome

| 0 | 50 | 100 | 200 MILES |
| 0 | 50 | 100 | 200 KILOMETRES |

THE CORRESPONDENCE OF ERASMUS

LETTERS 1535 TO 1657

1535 / To John Longland   Basel, 5 January 1525

This letter to John Longland (1473–1547), bishop of Lincoln, one of his best
friends among the English bishops, is the dedication for Erasmus' *In Psalmum
quartum concio* (Basel: Froben, February 1525) and was first printed there. In
Ep 1570 Longland acknowledged this dedication. Though he was considerably
more conservative than Erasmus, he remained friendly and in later years
frequently sent him gifts of money (Epp 1758, 1769, 2072, 2159, 2227, 3104,
3108). His interest in the Psalms was genuine: he was a distinguished
preacher, and his Lenten sermons at court were based on five of the penitential Psalms. Erasmus later dedicated to him his treatise on Ps 85 (Ep 2017) and
his translation of Athanasius (Ep 1790). Cf J.W. Blench 'John Longland and
Roger Edgeworth, two forgotten preachers of the early sixteenth century'
Review of English Studies n s 5 (1954) 123–43.

TO THE MOST REVEREND FATHER JOHN, BISHOP OF LINCOLN IN
ENGLAND, FROM ERASMUS OF ROTTERDAM, GREETING
Several years ago at Calais,[1] most honourable bishop, you were the first to
encourage me to produce a commentary on the Book of Psalms and in
frequent letters since then you have returned again and again to the same   5
theme. Later others made the same request, not only men of learning but
even princes. When I saw that my excuses, though I thought them perfectly
justified, were not well received, I tried repeatedly to look into this holy of
holies of the divine Spirit. But whenever I tried, other obligations turned my
attention elsewhere or a feeling of awe and reverence for the grandeur of   10
the work frightened me off from the attempt. Some time ago, as a sort of
prelude, I wrote something on the first Psalm;[2] then I added a regular
commentary to the second;[3] for the third I tried a paraphrase. Now I am

* * * * *

1535
1 In July 1520. See Ep 1118 introduction. His visit to More and Warham at Calais
  occurred between 6 and 30 July, probably while he was travelling in the
  retinue of the emperor Charles V, who was at Calais 11–14 July. Longland was
  already a friend of long standing, and during their conversation invited him
  to undertake a commentary on the Psalms, of which this publication is one
  result.
2 Cf Ep 327 introduction.
3 Cf Ep 1304 introduction. Erasmus' own commentary on Ps 2 was appended to
  his edition (Basel: Froben, September 1522) of the *Commentarii in Psalmos* of
  Arnobius Junior. In his introduction to that letter, Allen V 100 lists all of
  Erasmus' commentaries on the Psalms: in all, Pss 1, 2, 3, 4, 14, 22, 28, 33, 38,
  83, and 85, for a total of eleven. Cf Ep 1581 n12.

sending you a homily on the fourth,[4] leaving nothing untried in the hope
of discovering the right road to success. But I am not yet satisfied. The work   15
by its nature scarcely admits of paraphrase, and yet I realize that, where
there is such a host of commentaries, if I am to hold the reader's attention,
there must be some novelty in the treatment. I shall press on if you approve
this sample of my work and if you remember my efforts in your prayers to
God. Farewell.   20

Basel, 5 January 1525

1536 / To Willibald Pirckheimer   Basel, 8 January 1525

This letter continues Erasmus' friendly relationship with the eminent Nürnberg
patrician and humanist Pirckheimer (see Ep 318 introduction), a friendship
based entirely on correspondence, since they never met in person. It also
reflects their common admiration of the artist Albrecht Dürer. It was first
printed in Melchior Goldast's edition of *Pirckheimeri Opera* (1610).

Cordial greetings. You reached me, my dear Willibald, first in the form of
a medallion,[1] accompanied by a ring and a letter, and now as a portrait[2]
painted by our own Apelles.[3] I sent a reply some time ago through a most
impudent vagabond:[4] the world is full of such people nowadays. I gave

* * * * *

4 That is, the publication to which the present letter served as preface and letter
  of dedication.

1536
1 Cf Ep 1480, a letter from Pirckheimer enclosing a medallion bearing his own
  likeness.
2 Allen Ep 1536:2n notes the existence of a well-known engraved portrait of
  Pirckheimer by Albrecht Dürer but observes that no painting of this period is
  known. Perhaps a drawing made preparatory to the engraving is involved
  here, since the nearly contemporary engraving of Frederick the Wise was
  preceded by a silverpoint drawing now in Paris, Ecole des Beaux-Arts. See
  Walter L. Strauss *The Complete Drawings of Albrecht Dürer* (New York 1974) IV
  2252, and the facing plate, for that drawing. For Dürer's engravings of both
  Pirckheimer and Frederick the Wise see F.W.H. Hollstein *German Engravings,
  Etchings and Woodcuts, ca. 1400–1700* (28 vols to date, 1954–80) VII no 103, no
  102. Cf Ep 1376 nn1 and 2.
3 Dürer is frequently called an Apelles, a reference to the famous ancient Greek
  painter.
4 An unidentified fugitive Franciscan; the letter he carried seems to have been
  lost. Cf Allen Ep 1536:3n.

Willibald Pirckheimer
Portrait medal by Albrecht Dürer
Victoria & Albert Museum, London

him seven plappards[5] (may they bring him no luck!) and promised more if   5
he delivered the letter as he undertook to do, but I see I have been cheated.
What is happening in your part of the world will soon be repeated everywhere unless some deity takes care of us. The Evangelicals are doing all
they can to encourage this state of affairs even in spite of Luther's protests.
Some are evidently bent on destroying everything and putting an end to all   10
learning. How I wish for a happy issue out of our present turmoil! As for
Luther, now that he has become more moderate, he is being treated with
absolute contempt.

I should like to be painted by Dürer,[6] for he is such a splendid artist.
But is it possible? He made a start at Brussels with a charcoal sketch, but,   15
I imagine, he has forgotten me long since. If he can manage anything with
the help of the medallion[7] and his own recollections of me, I hope he will
do for me what he did for you; that is, he gave you a little extra weight. I
have not yet worked up the courage to take the medicine[8] you recommended.   20

I shall write soon to let you know how things are with me. I have been
informed that the coachman who brought your letter and who was supposed to leave tomorrow morning is leaving after dinner. So I decided not to
risk a long letter. Farewell.

The octave of the Circumcision 1525   25
Erasmus – you will recognize the hand.
To the honourable Willibald Pirckheimer

1537 / From Pieter de Corte   Louvain, 21 January 1525

This letter proves that Erasmus continued to have influential admirers as well
as hostile theological critics at Louvain. On de Corte, who had been regent of
the College of the Lily since 1522, see Ep 1347:66n. This is the only surviving
letter between him and Erasmus. Despite de Corte's rise to high position in the
theological faculty, he remained a strong defender of Erasmian humanism.
Active in the work of Catholic reform in the Netherlands, he became the first

* * * * *

5 See Ep 1543 n2.
6 Dürer never painted Erasmus but did execute a woodcut portrait. See Hollstein
   VII no 105; cf Ep 1376 n2.
7 A reference to the famous medal of Erasmus made by Quinten Metsys in 1519;
   cf Ep 1092 n2.
8 The reference is to a remedy for kidney stones, from which Erasmus suffered.
   Cf Ep 1558 for further discussion.

bishop of Bruges in 1561 under the new system of dioceses instituted by Philip II, which he helped to create. This letter was first printed in LB but also survived to Allens time in MS Rehd. 254.57 at Wrocław.

Greetings, illustrious Erasmus. It might appear that I lacked a proper regard for your high distinction if, when your man Lieven[1] volunteered his services, I did not send at least a word of greeting, even if there was nothing else which particularly needed to be said; I am sure, too, that you enjoy hearing now and then of absent friends and of places which were once close 5 to your heart. So, as I am not the least of the admirers of your learning, I thought it right to present my compliments and to commend to you our whole family here at the College of the Lily. I know how sincerely you have always cherished this garden of lilies and how in turn it looked up to you when de Neve[2] was regent. So I pray that your feelings towards us will not 10 alter now that I am in charge. For in the college itself the respect in which you have long been held, far from declining, has in fact greatly increased. Nothing takes place here, either in religion or education, which is not influenced by Erasmus; there is no one here who does not think himself indebted to Erasmus for whatever knowledge he possesses. 15

Many in this place have been turned into scholars by reading your works, just how many and to what degree I would rather you learned from others than from me. But perhaps you will be able to draw your own conclusions from the following incident. A few months ago the enemies of every kind of good literature were in a high state of jealous fury and the 20 theologians were moving heaven and earth to have your books banned from the arts schools by public decree and already they had persuaded most of the old guard to side with them. But it became clear that those who understood what Erasmus had done for letters – and there were many – would never allow that to happen; so their opponents lost heart and abandoned 25 their plan. That was a shaft aimed particularly at us: for in other schools nothing of Erasmus is studied except the *De octo partibus*.[3] Subsequently

* * * * *

1537
1 Lieven Algoet had been a *famulus* of Erasmus for six years, one of his most widely travelled couriers. Cf Ep 1091 introduction.
2 Cf Ep 298. Erasmus was the guest of Jean de Neve at the College of the Lily from 1517 to 1521. Under de Neve's direction the Lily became an important center for the diffusion of humanism at Louvain.
3 Erasmus' *De octo orationis partium constructione libellus* (Basel: Froben, August 1515) was a brief work on Latin syntax based on the work of his English friend William Lily. Cf Ep 341.

they tried by different methods to tear from our students' hands the
Colloquia,[4] the *Enchiridion*, and many other works of yours, exercising their
influence either publicly in sermons or privately in the hearing of confes-   30
sions. But the harder they try, the less they succeed; for, as the saying goes,
they are swimming against the tide.

For our sake and for the sake of all those who love learning may God
in his goodness and power keep you safe and sound for many years to
come and not just safe and sound but fruitful also, so that by your labours   35
we may daily become richer and better men.

College of the Lily, Louvain, 21 January in the year of our Lord 1525
Your devoted servant, Pieter de Corte of Bruges
To that consummate and eloquent theologian, Master Erasmus of
Rotterdam. In Basel   40

1538 / To Johannes Oecolampadius   Basel, 25 January 1525

Erasmus took care to publish this letter himself in his *Opus epistolarum* of 1529
in order to distance himself publicly from the religious views and actions of
Oecolampadius. Such action was important not only because of Oecolampadius' printed references to Erasmus as his friend but also because of his
close association with Erasmus' scholarly work on the first Greek New Testament in 1515 and again on the collected works of St Jerome. Precisely because
of their intimate association in humanistic scholarship and their many published expressions of mutual esteem, Oecolampadius' increasingly open endorsement of Luther and his emergence as a leader of the Protestant cause in
Basel proved an embarrassment to Erasmus, as this letter clearly states. On
Oecolampadius cf Ep 224:30n.

ERASMUS OF ROTTERDAM TO JOHANNES OECOLAMPADIUS,
GREETING
I pass no judgment on you and your friends, leaving you to our Lord, by
whose judgment you will stand or fall. But I ask myself what does the
emperor think of you, and the pope, and Ferdinand, and the king of Eng-   5
land, and the bishop of Rochester, and the cardinal archbishop of York and
several others whose authority it would be imprudent of me to despise and
whose favour it would be pointless to resist. I say nothing of that horde of

* * * * *

4 De Jongh 49* prints an extract from the acts of the theological faculty of Louvain, dated 1 April 1524, showing that at Eastertide some confessors had
refused to absolve students who admitted reading Erasmus' *Colloquia*.

Johannes Oecolampadius
Contemporary copy of an original portrait attributed to
Hans Holbein the Younger
Collection of Mrs Carl J. Burckhardt-de Reynold, Switzerland

monks and theologians who are ready for another hysterical outburst on
any excuse, however flimsy. These men, as you well know, consider all of 10
you arch-heretics and promoters of schism: what will they say when they
read in your preface[1] 'our friend the great Erasmus,' especially since the
subject of your work offered no occasion for mentioning my name? If I had
written on Isaiah or you on the freedom of the will, there would have been
some reason for your mentioning me. 15

But, you say, some people suspect a lack of accord between us. There
is no accord between us, except that I have never refused anyone my personal friendship. Must I, then, in order to allay the suspicions of these
nameless critics of yours, rekindle a dangerous suspicion against myself in
the minds of the most powerful princes and my most implacable foes, who 20
after the publication of my *De libero arbitrio* were at last beginning to take
a more sympathetic view of me? The very reasonable anxiety which I feel
on such an important matter you describe as 'peevishness.' But, my dear
Oecolampadius, as a sensible man you should have avoided an action which
can do you no good, but is certain to increase even further the intolerable 25
burden of hostility which I now suffer. Many will suspect that this is no
innocent action of yours, but that you are either attempting to shore up
your own cause by taking advantage of an unfounded suspicion about me
on the part of princes and people or are playing this sort of trick out of a
desire for revenge. I do not suspect you of such malice, and yet I cannot fail 30
to regret your lack of prudence, at least on this occasion. In the present state
of things, what I should like best would be to receive from you and your
friends neither praise nor blame; but if that is too much to ask, then I would
prefer a lambasting to a eulogy and especially to a eulogy addressed to 'our
friend.' 35

I reject no man's good will, and I trust that in my own actions thus far
I have been guided by such feelings of good will that not even the most
partisan of Luther's followers could complain that I had violated the laws
of a long-standing friendship. But good will untimely differs not from

* * * * *

1538
1 Allen Ep 1538:8–9n identifies this as a reference to Oecolampadius' commentary
In Iesaiam Prophetam (Basel: Andreas Cratander, March 1525), of which Erasmus
seems to have learned while it was still in proof. In published form, the preface lauds Erasmus as the leading figure among the learned men of Basel but
does not specifically refer to him as 'our Erasmus.' Allen concludes that either
Erasmus was misinformed about the exact contents of the preface or the word
'our' was omitted at his request, a request at least implied here.

hate.[2] If, as you claim, your other friends are pleased to be celebrated by   40
your pen, well and good. But you were under no illusion as to how I felt,
since I warned you against embarrassing your friends. For myself, I make
it a practice to avoid making things difficult even for those friends of mine
who would welcome such treatment. Some people ask me to mention their
names among those of my friends, but I take more thought for their inter-   45
ests than they do themselves. So if you wish me to believe that your feelings towards me are such as you say, please delete 'our friend Erasmus' and
keep your praise for another occasion.

I am not so suspicious as to think that whatever is said against the
Pelagians is aimed at me.[3] I have now boiled down my remarks on 'so   50
many worlds': yet anyone who has read as far as my preface will understand it was Erasmus you were attacking.[4] Apparently you did not want
to modify what you presented in public. I admire your consistency, but
surely, if something had slipped out on that occasion, you ought to have
corrected it in the written version.   55

It was a silly error which brought my man Karl[5] to your house when
he had been told to go to Pellicanus'[6] to inquire if the reports we got were

* * * * *

2 Quoting *Adagia* I vii 69
3 Oecolampadius had recently published an anthology of patristic texts on free
   will, *De libero arbitrio* (Basel: Thomas Wolff, 4 December 1524); and in the
   preface he had denounced contemporary Pelagians, a group that in the opinion
   of some might include Erasmus, especially now that he had upheld freedom
   of the will against Luther. Erasmus was aware that Oecolampadius had criticized his own *De libero arbitrio* in sermons: cf Ep 1526:243.
4 Allen Ep 1538:41n shows that this is a reference to Erasmus' *Argumentum* to
   1 John, where he notes that the apostle repeated the word *mundus* 'world' six
   times in three verses and remarks, 'How many worlds are here!' Oecolampadius had criticized grammarians who were offended by such repetitions in
   Scripture, attributing to them precisely the words used by Erasmus. Thus the
   point of this whole paragraph is to say that while he is not so thin-skinned as
   to think that any and all attacks on contemporary Pelagians are aimed at him,
   neither he nor any other reader of Oecolampadius' anthology on free will
   could fail to perceive that Erasmus was an object of Oecolampadius' attack on
   modern Pelagians, not only in sermons but also in a published work.
5 Karl Harst, whom Erasmus frequently used as a confidential courier. On him,
   cf Ep 1215 introduction.
6 Conradus Pellicanus, a former Franciscan, like Oecolampadius a former colleague in Erasmus' work on Jerome and other patristic editions, and also like
   him an emergent leader of the Protestant cause in Basel. Since 1523 he was one
   of the new 'advanced' professors of theology appointed by the city council. Cf
   Ep 1637 introduction.

true. He had no message about Farel,[7] nor do I care how close he is to you, except that it is friendships of this sort which are getting many people into trouble these days, including that fine young man 'X'[8] and that honest 60 fellow at Constance, 'Y,'[9] both of whom you now seek to help. If they had heeded the warnings they received, they would not have fallen into such danger. But I cannot serve their cause with the pope or the princes if these men are convinced that I am one of you.

Every blessing in Christ 65

Basel, 25 January 1525

1539 / To the Town Council of Basel   Basel, January 1525

This letter exemplifies Erasmus' effort to adopt a moderate position on contro-versial questions of religious practice, making concessions to the reformers but still upholding what he regarded as the essentials of tradition. The city at this period was still officially Catholic but was under strong pressure from a well-placed group of reformers led by Johannes Oecolampadius and Conradus Pellicanus. Apparently written at the council's request, the letter was private advice; but it was printed as an unauthorized pamphlet in 1526, *Consilium Erasmi Roterodami in caussa evangelica*, without name of place or printer. On account of the extreme inaccuracy of this text, Allen Ep 1539 introduction preferred the authority of a late sixteenth-century manuscript copy now in the University Library at Basel, MS Ki. Ar. 23a f 17 (*a*).

TO THE TOWN COUNCIL OF BASEL, GREETING
Distinguished sirs and honoured patrons, I do not think that I need a long preamble to tell you what I am sure you already know, that I am deeply conscious of the extraordinary kindness you have shown me and am eager to prove my gratitude should an opportunity arise to serve your interests. 5

You are not asking me, I think, to pass a general judgment on the merits of Luther's case, nor have I the learning or the authority for such a task, to say nothing of my age or my health or the demands of the studies

* * * * *

7 Guillaume Farel's radicalism in promoting religious change at this delicate period was a problem even for the Basel Protestant leaders who sheltered him; and Erasmus, who detested him as a troublemaker, had played an important part in encouraging the city council to expel him in 1524. Cf Allen Ep 1407:92n, and CWE Epp 1341A n305, 1477A.

8 Johann Zwick, parish priest at Riedlingen; cf Allen Ep 1519:21n.

9 Johann von Botzheim, canon of Constance. For his troubles there, cf Epp 1519 introduction, 1574 introduction.

on which I am now engaged. God will grant you in your wisdom an abundant counsel. If more is needed, you have, among others, your townsman   10
Ludwig Baer,[1] a man of great integrity, learning, and judgment, whose one
finger is worth more to you than my whole body. Such is the nature of this
problem that it cannot be resolved without the agreement of great princes
and many cities and regions. If I interfere, I shall only make the trouble
worse compounded. One should not fear danger where there is some   15
prospect of success, but I do not see such a prospect here. Neither side is
acting prudently. So if I offer a moderate opinion, I shall offend both; and
yet I would rather offend both than give unqualified support to either.

Moreover some of the advice you seek depends on circumstances, and
these I cannot know, first because I am a stranger here with very different 20
interests and secondly because I am not even familiar with your language.[2]
Nor is it proper for a stranger to meddle in the affairs of another city. If I
had been a troublesome visitor, then I should have to endure my share of
criticism. But as it is, although I have brought neither praise nor profit to
your city, at least I have lived a quiet and peaceful life, using my own   25
means and devoting myself since I came here to the general cause of learning. So even if I could accomplish something in the present situation – and
I see no hope of real success – I do not think that I deserve to be called to
so invidious a task. To say nothing of the schism which divides the world,
think of the flaming antagonisms within your own Switzerland and of the   30
controversies which tear this city apart; and in your own council too I hear
there is much divergence of opinion. So whatever course I urge, I am likely,
if not to cause, at least to exacerbate the trouble and to bring upon myself
much unpleasantness. So far I have excused myself before emperors and
prelates, and with good reason. I do not think you will be so unkind as to   35
reject my appeal to be excused. There can be no secret about something

* * * * *

1539
1 Cf Ep 488 introduction. Baer was not only a good friend of Erasmus but also
  professor of theology at the University of Basel who had compiled an outstanding academic record during his studies in the theological faculty at Paris.
  Erasmus had used Baer as his principal theological consultant during the
  preparation of his *De libero arbitrio* in early 1524, and he later made repeated
  use of Baer's name in his controversy with Noël Béda to demonstrate that
  theologians of acknowledged orthodoxy and talent regarded his own theological views as sound: cf Epp 1571, 1581.
2 Erasmus repeatedly claimed inability to read German, but he could when he
  wanted to; cf Ep 1313 n16.

which many people already knew before it began to happen – and once I had given an undertaking, I would be obliged to honour it – but sometime next Lent, whether I like it or not, I shall have to leave here unless I am willing to forgo my imperial pension, which is already more than three 40 years in arrears. I think that your kindness and good sense will find these reasons adequate for my not involving myself in so tangled an affair.

Nevertheless, to show how sincere is my devotion to your city, whose hospitality I have enjoyed for several years, I shall offer you some advice; it may not be good advice, but at least it is given in a friendly and loyal 45 spirit. I shall confine myself to the problem of maintaining the peace, which is your proper function. There are three points to be considered: the publication of books, the eating of meat, and the marriage of priests and monks.

Article 1   50
First, there is no need to worry about the printing of ancient texts even if they contain error, for in that case not even Jerome could be printed; in fact no book would appear except the Scriptures. Yet even with these texts one needs to be on one's guard about prefaces and commentaries to ensure that no dangerous material is added. It is the duty of magistrates, in accordance 55 with the principles of universal law, to prevent the publication of libellous or seditious books. For if we punish the slanderer or the speaker who delivers himself of a seditious speech, there is all the more reason to punish those who disseminate such things in the form of books. There should be a general ban on books which make no mention of author, publisher, or 60 place and those who import, print, or sell such works should be punished. There should be stiffer penalties for those who give false information on the title-page. But even if a book has these three pieces of information, if it is openly libellous or seditious, those who print or import it should be punished, not by introducing some new regulation, but in accordance with 65 universal law.

It is very difficult to prevent every abuse. First, who will read everything produced by so many publishers? Then after it has been read, unless a copy is kept, what is to prevent some pages being changed and others inserted at will? And then the odium would fall on those who permitted the 70 book to be published: some people would say, 'This book was approved.' I should certainly find this an intolerable burden, since I can hardly tolerate the unpleasantness which my own works stir up. On the other hand much of this criticism would fall on the printers, importers, and booksellers, if they ventured to bring out libellous or seditious books on their own respon- 75 sibility without a title-page or with false information on the title-page, and this would be true, even if no one gave or withheld approval in your name.

I do not know what you have decided about Luther's views. If you do not want to see them in print, then you should not publish the commentaries of many others, Bugenhagen and Oecolampadius,[3] for example, who introduce such doctrines into their writings at every turn. But then much valuable work would be lost. Perhaps it would be better to turn a blind eye towards all these works, especially where they merely engage in argument and discussion and avoid inflammatory and abusive language. For what is most likely to cause sedition is a sudden and unexpected attack upon some established practice or deeply held belief. Any innovation which seems more likely to stir up trouble than to promote piety should be particularly avoided. In this category I would place all discussion of images, the tonsure of priests and their vestments, the rite of the mass, sacred music, and other practices which are good, or at least tolerable, if properly used; for it is less painful to put up with these things than to apply the remedy. Moreover if some difficulty remains, it can be relieved by other measures. For, however radically it changes, the world will never reach so happy a state that it will not have to overlook many faults. At present there are some who dislike everything – vestments, music, bells, the tonsure, anointing, ordination, all rites and ordinances, even the holy sacraments; and there is no end of it, for always some new controversy follows on the heels of the old. Men are wrong to put too much trust in human ordinances; but it is equally dangerous to despise utterly all regulation and tradition, for without these the peace of the state cannot be preserved.

If the people of Zürich could be persuaded to put back the images, to restore the formulary of the mass, which has served us well enough, and to return to the old way of receiving communion until a decision on these matters was taken at a general council, this would have great significance for the peace of all Switzerland. But if they cannot be persuaded, I should not wish to see a war break out on this account; it would be better to await a more favourable turn of events. On the manner of receiving communion, if a petition is made in loyalty and affection on behalf of the whole region, it will take only a word or two from the pope and you will obtain what you want. His authority is at least strong enough here to prevent civil war.

* * * * *

3 Johann Bugenhagen by this time was clearly committed to Luther's cause and published commentaries on Deuteronomy and on the Psalms in 1524. Oecolampadius was Basel's leading Protestant theologian and was active as a commentator, publishing commentaries on Isaiah and Romans later this same year.

Article 2

On the eating of meat my opinion is the same.[4] If the pope is approached officially in the name of the whole region, there will be no difficulties. In the meantime you can do what is done throughout Italy. There meat is sold openly even in Lent with no objection from the pope and therefore, we may   115
infer, with his silent approbation. For it is not the pope's wish that anyone should become ill or die through eating fish. In this matter I should leave everyone to his own conscience and not interfere, unless someone, by flaunting his views, encourages discord or tries to persuade others to disregard the general practice. If a man distrusts his own conscience, let him   120
seek a dispensation from his priest or bishop.

Article 3

Speaking for myself, I do not think that monks who thoughtlessly abandon the cowl or priests who marry deserve your forbearance. But there are some   125
who at an early age were forced into the cloister or the priesthood through pressure from their parents or in some other way; these I should like to see helped by a superior authority. There are many who need the cloister to save them from committing graver sins. Many are weak, and for these discipline is helpful and freedom perilous. But there is no reason to tolerate   130
those who not only change their way of life without serious reflection, but persuade others to do the same, as though it were wrong for a monk to abide by his vows or celibacy in a priest were itself a sin. It is hardly likely that one who has led a turbulent life within the monastery will live a good life when he is free again. Nor is it probable that a priest who, as a celibate,   135
had several mistresses will settle down with one wife; one would fear rather that a debauched celibacy would be followed by a worse marriage. It is difficult to contain oneself when monks and priests who have hypocritically entered into the honourable estate of holy orders venture to criticize the regulations of the church authorities, when they have dishonoured their   140
vows by the shamelessness of their lives, supporting their lusts on the stipends of the church when they should have been confessing their sins. Yet even in these cases I should like some consideration to be given; for it is better that a man be bound to a wife than live with a concubine. But this course is hardly possible without the support of the princes or the authority   145

* * * * *

4 Erasmus' permissive views on the Lenten fast had already been published in his *Epistola apologetica de interdicto esu carnium deque similibus hominum constitutionibus* (Basel: Froben, August 1522), a work dedicated to the reformist bishop of Basel, Christoph von Utenheim. See Ep 1274 n7 and LB IX 1197–1214.

of a council. If you undertake to protect these people on your own, you will receive from all quarters a flood of men of loose or even criminal character who will do little to preserve the peace of your city. If several bishops joined with the magistrates or, supposing the bishops to hold back, if the magistrates acted together and agreed to petition the pope for authority to   150 regulate this matter by decree, then the problem could be controlled, each case being considered on its merits before the magistrates. As for those ignorant priests who are unworthy of their office, if they were unable or unwilling to restrain themselves, I would allow them to turn a mistress into a wife, but they should have to leave the priesthood and be treated as   155 laymen. On the other hand men who entered the priesthood in good faith and have the ability to serve the church by their learning, but cannot re- strain themselves because of the weakness of the flesh, though otherwise of good and honest character, these should be allowed to marry without being required to abandon the priesthood. I hold the same opinion about monks,   160 that each case should be examined and consideration given to those who deserve it.

So much for the problems which face us now. But for the future we should be on our guard against filling the world with monks and priests who are ignorant, idle, and depraved. Meanwhile all who have changed   165 their mode of life on their own authority, or rather on a reckless impulse, should be left to their bishops and abbots to deal with, unless they have committed an offence against the good order of the state. In all other cases I think you should continue to act prudently and moderately, as you have done in the past, until experience teaches us whether what is happening   170 now is of God or not. In the meantime everything which encourages sedi- tion must be assiduously rooted out.

1540 / From Johann von Botzheim   Constance, 25 January 1525

On the troubles which led to Botzheim's being cited to Rome on charges of heresy and on his appeal to Erasmus and other friends with influence at Rome for help in getting the case quashed, see Ep 1519 introduction. This letter, preserved in autograph at Leipzig, remained unprinted until the edition by Förstemann and Günther (1904). Since Erasmus himself published other parts of their correspondence which dealt with humanistic learning and his conflict with conservative monks and theologians (eg Ep 1103), his failure to publish this one probably results from his belief that Botzheim's troubles were a private matter, not to be publicized.

Greetings. I have received an apostolic brief,[1] which I must deliver to the
Right Reverend the Bishop of Constance. I am sending a copy to you. As
soon as I received it, I showed it to my brothers in the chapter and asked
them if they would be kind enough to deliver it to the bishop in my name
and to commend me to him. My request was granted and the members of   5
the chapter appointed two men from the order to deliver the brief to the
bishop with their commendation and this was duly done. The bishop is
allowing himself some time to consider the matter, but he promises a reply
shortly and gives me grounds for hope. Now some matters have intervened
which are delaying a decision on my case. I have friends who have influ-   10
ence with the bishop and they offer me great encouragement.

Yesterday the courier arrived (ordinary people talk nowadays about
'the post').[2] He brought us the news, in a letter from Prince Ferdinand, that
the pope is siding with the king of France;[3] this has made him very unpopular with our leaders.   15

Several delegations are here in Constance in connection with the
Waldshut affair,[4] representing Prince Ferdinand, the greater Swabian

* * * * *

1540
1 Cf Ep 1519 introduction. Allen Ep 1540:1n identifies the bishop of Constance
  as Hugo von Hohenlandenberg.
2 This new term was in current use throughout western Europe by this time. In
  1516 Maximilian I authorized Franz von Taxis to conduct regular postal service
  between Vienna and Brussels, and the word *Post* began appearing in German
  texts. See Jacob Grimmm and Wilhelm Grimm *Deutsches Wörterbuch* ed Mat-
  thias von Lexer (Leipzig 1889) VII col 2018. The French *poste* appears in documents of the 1480s. See Frédéric Godefroy *Dictionnaire de l'ancienne langue
  française* (Paris 1889) sv 'poste.' The English usage is attested from 1506: OED[2]
  sv 'post.' The Italian equivalent *posta* was used in the modern sense in the
  works of Marin Sanudo (1466–1536), a Venetian nobleman, historian, and
  humanist who was an associate of Aldo Manuzio; and in the broader sense of
  a relay station for couriers, the word is found in Italian versions of the works
  of Marco Polo. Cf *Grande dizionario della lingua italiana* ed Salvatore Battaglia
  (Turin 1961–) sv 'posta.'
3 After drifting hesitantly away from the pro-Spanish policy of his predecessor,
  in December 1524 Pope Clement VII joined Venice in making a peace treaty
  with Francis I of France. On 2 January 1525 he formed an alliance with him.
  Pastor IX 253–70.
4 Led by their parish priest, Balthasar Hubmaier (c 1480–1528), the people of
  Waldshut had openly adhered to the Evangelical movement of Huldrych
  Zwingli by the end of 1524 and that summer had given support to the rebellious peasants of Stühlingen. In April 1525 Hubmaier and several hundred of
  his parishioners, influenced by Conrad Grebel and Wilhelm Reublin, were
  rebaptized, and the city also gave military aid to rebellious Swabian peasants

League, and the princes of our own country; the Waldshut people are here themselves, accompanied by delegates from Zürich, Basel, and Schaffhausen. There is no news of a settlement. The men of Waldshut will not listen to any argument that would require them to dismiss their priest, since he has not been convicted by Holy Scripture; but this is what the other side most desires. Everywhere in this country the peasants are in a violent mood. The princes are marshalling five hundred armed cavalrymen and a thousand infantry to defeat the peasant party, if what I am told is true.

Bishop Sadoleto[5] has written to Master Bonifacius.[6] He is a very close friend of Bonifacius' and could settle my business if he chose. My opponent,[7] from all I hear an honest man, takes his lead from Bishop Sadoleto and he in turn is well disposed to you. Soon you will know what the bishop of Constance has done with me. I await his reply. Farewell, and spare a thought for your friend Botzheim.

Constance, 25 January 1525

Your devoted Botzheim

To Master Erasmus of Rotterdam, prince and restorer of true theology and of all humane studies and our most respected mentor. In Basel

1541 / From Erasmus Schets   Antwerp, 30 January 1525

This opens a correspondence that continued for the rest of Erasmus' life. Erasmus Schets (d 13 May 1550) had become a successful merchant and banker at Antwerp. His connections with Spain gave him this occasion to write his learned namesake while forwarding a packet of letters from Spain. Despite Schets' rather defective Latin, Erasmus reacted positively to his sincere enthusiasm; but the friendship endured because Schets proved both willing and

* * * * *

in 1525. In early December, Austrian troops occupied Waldshut, forced Hubmaier to flee, and restored Catholicism. See Thorsten Bergsten *Balthasar Hubmaier, Anabaptist Theologian and Martyr* trans Irwin J. Barnes and William R. Estep (Valley Forge, Pa 1978). For an earlier reference by Erasmus to the turmoil there cf Ep 1522:64. On the peasant movement of 1525, see Preface, pages xi–xii.

5 Sadoleto was involved in the efforts to quash the charges of heresy against Botzheim. Cf Ep 1519 introduction and Richard M. Douglas *Jacopo Sadoleto* (Cambridge, Mass 1959) 47.

6 Amerbach, a close friend of Erasmus and of Sadoleto, also involved in efforts to bring influence to bear at Rome in favour of Botzheim. Cf Epp 1555 n1, 1586 n7.

7 Allen Ep 1519 introduction conjectures that this person may be an informant named Johannes de Milis, a cleric of Cremona. Cf AK II Ep 989.

able to solve difficulties Erasmus long had faced in transferring funds to Basel
from his English pension (cf Ep 1583). In a short time, Schets replaced Erasmus' old friend Pieter Gillis as his confidential business agent in the Netherlands, a task he handled very much to Erasmus' advantage and with apparently no profit to himself. Erasmus preserved their correspondence carefully but
did not publish it since it involved his private financial affairs. Allen VI 12–14
first published this letter, based on the autograph at Basel. On Erasmus'
business relations with both Gillis and Schets, see Eckhard Bernstein in
Erasmus of Rotterdam Society Yearbook 3 (1983) 130–45, who surmises that
despite his continued friendship with Erasmus, Gillis was somewhat offended
at being supplanted by Schets in the management of Erasmus' business affairs;
and Bernstein 'Erasmus' Money Connection: The Antwerp Banker Erasmus
Schets and Erasmus of Rotterdam, 1525–36' *Erasmus in English* 14 (1985–6) 2–7,
a useful survey of the whole course of Erasmus' relationship with Schets and
also of the obscure question of Erasmus' finances.

Distinguished sir, you may perhaps wonder who is this person who is
writing to you now! My name is Erasmus, but I am a very different
Erasmus from you – though, with the sort of name I bear, people often treat
me with great respect, the name being rare among us in Brabant and
known and esteemed because of the excellence of your learning. I have   5
often had the experience, in the course of a meal or a conversation, of being
addressed by several people as Erasmus and being taken by those present,
who did not know either of us in person, as the great Erasmus whose
famous intellect and impressive erudition are adding lustre to the name.
But you, and you alone, are that Erasmus and certainly there is no one with   10
whom you can be compared: your *Paraphrases*, with their immense learning
and true piety, have brought the wisdom of heaven and the message of the
gospel within range of our human frailty. Now whoever wishes to read and
savour these works will find himself drawn from darkness into light, from
weariness to rest, and from the burden and stain of sin to freedom and   15
purity of heart. Is there anyone, I wonder, who would not rejoice in that
noble mind of yours, which has brought forth such things for us? Is there
anyone who would not take pleasure in works of such heavenly inspiration? You have shown us what is meant by true Christian gentleness and
the religion of the gospel. When, under the guidance of the Spirit, we   20
embrace this religion in faith and hope, we are seized with a burning love
of God and are carried into the paths of righteousness; we are set free and
made strangers to every evil thought and to all those troubles which prey
upon our age.
    But I stray too far from the point and risk wearying your ears with   25

this long preamble. What I meant to explain to you was that my friends in Spain have given me a sort of excuse for writing by sending me the attached letters to be forwarded to you;[1] I hope you will duly receive them along with this of mine: that at any rate is what I have in mind. I am addressing them to my very close friend, Johann Paumgartner at Augsburg,[2] to be sent on to you. I hope he will not delay in forwarding them to Basel. Please let me know when you receive them: I should like to be able to assure my Spanish friends that I have taken good care of the letters.

But there is something else which I cannot pass over, something which has been remarked on by several of my friends in Spain, one of whom is Francisco de Vaylle,[3] who is dearer to me than a brother. In their individual letters they tell me how much you are talked about and how widespread is your reputation – and believe me, there is nothing grudging or undeserved about their praise. Nearly everyone in that country – princes, scholars, and persons of repute – think so highly of you that, if you were to arrive at their borders, they would rush out to meet you halfway. On points of doctrine and on Scripture they read nothing, and consider nothing worth reading, except the books which you have written: they regard you as someone unique in the world. For, more than anyone before you, you know how to reveal, through your remarkable writings, that divine wisdom which brings peace and consolation to pious hearts; their greatest and most pressing hope is that, before you die, you will expound the songs of David. That is what I am told by Francisco de Vaylle, a man of no small learning, who is deeply devoted to you, as are many of my other friends.

I have asked Pieter Gillis[4] many times about your health. He has assured me often about it, though I know you have to suffer the constant agony of the stone. I wish with all my heart, as do many others, that you were here with us. I have often asked what enchantment keeps you there when you could be here with us. Pieter himself suggested one possible reason, that we have no Burgundy, which is the wine that best agrees with

* * * * *

1541
1 Not extant
2 Like Schets, Paumgartner (1488–1549) of Augsburg was a wealthy merchant-banker with strong financial ties to the Hapsburg dynasty, a good choice for forwarding letters from Antwerp via Augsburg to Basel. Cf Epp 2602, 2603.
3 Identified by Bataillon (Fr) 173–4, 176 as a businessman of Spanish origin, perhaps from a Marrano family but for a generation established in Antwerp, where he held public office. He and Schets were married to sisters. He visited Spain in 1525 and may have eventually resettled in that country.
4 Cf Ep 184 and introduction to the present letter.

your constitution. But you should have no fears on that score. If nothing else stands in your way, you need not hesitate to return; we shall see to it that you are provided not only with Burgundy, but with wine from Persia or India if you desire or need it.   60

In conclusion, I send you my good wishes and ask you to be charitable towards these lines from the pen of an ignoramus; for I do not often write except from the labyrinthine maze of my business office.

Antwerp, from that same office, 30 January in the year of our Lord 1525   65

Your devoted servant, Erasmus Schets
To the learned Master Desiderius Erasmus of Rotterdam
In Basel

1542 / From Lorenzo Campeggi   Buda, 2 February 1525

This letter, first published by W. Vischer *Erasmiana* (Basel 1876) 32 from the original sealed document in Basel, is a dispensation permitting Erasmus to eat meat in Lent on grounds of poor health (but not the first such: cf Ep 1079 n1). On Campeggi, cf Ep 961 introduction. At this period, he was papal legate to Germany, Hungary, and Bohemia.

LORENZO, BY THE MERCY OF GOD CARDINAL-PRIEST OF THE
HOLY ROMAN CHURCH OF THE TITLE OF SAINT ANASTASIA AND
LEGATE OF OUR LORD THE POPE AND OF THE APOSTOLIC SEE
THROUGHOUT ALL GERMANY AND THE KINGDOMS OF HUNGARY
AND BOHEMIA AND POLAND AND SUCH OTHER LANDS AS HE   5
MAY CHANCE TO VISIT, TO OUR BELOVED FRIEND IN CHRIST
DESIDERIUS ERASMUS OF ROTTERDAM, PRIEST OF THE DIOCESE
OF UTRECHT, GREETING AND ETERNAL SALVATION IN THE LORD
The feelings of deep devotion which you are known to bear towards our
most Holy Father Pope Clement VII and towards the Roman church are   10
sufficient reason for our looking favourably, so far as we may, upon your
requests, and especially where our actions may be beneficial to your health.
Hence, being provided with a letter from the Holy See with the necessary
authority over the matters set out below, and being desirous, out of regard
for your past services, to attend you with our gracious favour and being   15
well disposed towards your request in this particular, since you assure us
that you suffer from certain physical infirmities which make the eating of
fish especially harmful,[1] we grant you and three other persons who eat at

* * * * *

1542
1 From early youth Erasmus experienced digestive difficulties which made him

Lorenzo Campeggi
Courtesy of the Trustees of the British Museum, London

your table and whom you have thought fit to select, a licence and dispensation, during Lent and at other times of the year when the eating of meat   20
and of all dairy foods is prohibited by law or custom, to eat and consume
not only meat, but also eggs, butter, cheese and other dairy foods, this
dispensation to apply to you without the report of a doctor, but to the
others who dine at the said table, with respect to the said meat, only on the
advice of two doctors, and this we grant through the authority of the Holy   25
See which we here exercise, all laws, ordinances and other interdictions,
apostolic or synodical, notwithstanding.

Given at Buda in the diocese of Veszprim on 2 February 1525 in the
second year of the pontificate of our most Holy Father, Pope Clement VII
Eremita[2]   30
February. Without charge and on the orders of the Right Reverend
Cardinal and Legate
Floriano Montini
D. de Paternina

1543 / To Willibald Pirckheimer   Basel, 5 February 1525

This letter, first printed in *Pirckheimeri Opera*, continues the discussion
launched in Ep 1536 between Erasmus and Nürnberg's leading humanist. It
also mentions Erasmus' conflict with his former associate Eppendorf and his
recurrent suffering from kidney stones.

Greetings, my distinguished friend. I have already written twice, though
briefly.[1] I assume that my first letter was not delivered. The messenger was
a Franciscan who had got rid of the cowl without getting rid of his deprav-

* * * * *

unable to eat fish, a condition that was especially oppressive during his years
in the monastery. On these infirmities see Johan Huizinga *Erasmus of Rotterdam*
trans F. Hopman (London 1952) 22; M.M. Phillips *Erasmus and the Northern
Renaissance* (London 1949) 27, and Roland H. Bainton *Erasmus of Christendom*
(New York 1969) 33, 82. Cf his reminiscences of the harsh diet at the Collège
de Montaigu in his colloquy 'A Fish Diet' in *The Colloquies of Erasmus* trans
Craig R. Thompson (Chicago 1965) 312–57.
2 Allen Ep 1592:23n identifies this as the name of the scribe. The other signato-
ries are D. de Paternina and Floriano Montini, secretaries of Cardinal Campeggi.

1543
1 The first letter, an answer to Ep 1480 from Pirckheimer, was never delivered
and is now lost; the second is Ep 1536, which contains references to the ring,
medallion, and portrait (by Dürer) of Pirckheimer.

Willibald Pirckheimer
Engraving by Albrecht Dürer
Kupferstichkabinett, Staatliche Museen, Berlin

ity. I gave him seven plappards[2] and promised a larger sum if I had proof
of the fellow's good faith. Nowadays the world is full of such itinerant   5
rogues. I sent a second letter by a merchant. I received the ring and also the
medallion with your likeness on it; shortly afterwards your portrait arrived,
painted by Dürer's skilful hand. These now adorn two walls of my bedroom
so that, wherever I turn, Willibald meets my eye.

I wish you had said something in your letter about the contents of   10
those silly publications which you mentioned.[3] I suspect they emanate from
Strasbourg. Eppendorf even boasts to everyone he meets that he has written
attacking me.[4] You know what a madman Otto is.[5]

This is all I am able to write at present, dear Willibald. I have barely
escaped death, or I should say rather that my life has been spared for another   15
bout of torture. I was in labour for fully ten days; then, when I had given up
all hope of being rid of the thing, I brought forth a huge stone. The illness
keeps changing its course, making relief impossible. I shall write at greater
length soon. I wrote some time ago to Rudbert von Mosham[6] and to Joachim
Camerarius,[7] who I hear is now at Bamberg. If you can do anything from   20
where you are, see that my letters reach them. Best regards to Dürer.

Basel, 5 February 1525
To the honourable Willibald Pirckheimer

* * * * *

2 Latin *plapardos*: shilling or *Schilling* silver coins, also known as *Plapparts* and
  Blaffarts, in the Austrian-South-German-Swiss *Rappenmünzbund* monetary
  system, based upon the Basel pfennig (more commonly called the *Stäbler* = 0.5
  Rappen); thus the plappart was worth 12 pfennigs.
3 This vague reference is probably to publications emanating from Strasbourg
  and related to the machinations of Heinrich Eppendorf. Erasmus does not
  point to a clearly definable body of literature. Miriam Usher Chrisman *Bibliog-
  raphy of Strasbourg Imprints, 1480–1599* (New Haven 1982) contains only two
  items which could be involved, P3.2.16: *Ulrichi ab Hutten cum Erasmo Roterodamo ... Expostulatio* (Johannes Schott 1523; repr 1524) and P3.12.6: an anonymous *Pro Ulricho Hutteno, vita defuncto, ad Erasmi Roterodami Spongiam responsio*
  (n pr 1524).
4 Cf Ep 1122 n5. Eppendorf was then living in Strasbourg, working for printers
  there, and Erasmus constantly suspected him of conspiring against himself. For
  a succinct account of both the quarrel and the probable reasons for Erasmus'
  unremitting hostility, see Barbara Könneker in CEBR I 438–41.
5 Otto Brunfels, who upheld Ulrich von Hutten in his controversy with Erasmus.
  Cf Ep 1405 introduction.
6 Epp 1450, 1512. He was an ardent admirer of Erasmus and in his later ecclesiastical career an outspoken but rather erratic agitator for church reform and
  reconciliation between Protestants and Catholics.
7 Cf Ep 1501 introduction. Erasmus thought highly of him despite his open support of Luther. In 1526 he became the first rector of the new town school at
  Nürnberg.

1544 / To Stanislaus Thurzo   Basel, 8 February 1525

This is the preface to an edition of Pliny's *Naturalis historia* published at Basel by Froben in 1525 and edited by Erasmus. Erasmus had already contributed some notes to an influential edition of Pliny published at Paris in 1516 under the direction of Nicolas Bérault. Although the present edition was issued under his name, much of the textual work was done by Beatus Rhenanus, who published a set of annotations on Pliny with the same press in 1526, and by Sigismundus Gelenius, who took editorial control of subsequent Froben editions of the work even though Erasmus' preface remained in place. On Thurzo, bishop of Olomouc in Moravia, see Ep 1242 introduction.

TO THE ILLUSTRIOUS PRINCE, THE RIGHT REVEREND STANISLAUS
THURZO, LORD BISHOP OF OLOMOUC, FROM ERASMUS OF
ROTTERDAM, GREETING

Most honoured bishop, the finest works of great artists have this quality in common, that they bring fame not only to those who inspired them – that   5
is, to those under whose auspices or at whose expense they were created and those to whom they were dedicated – but also to those who have devoted some of their energies to completing and restoring them. Sometimes the desire to excel others, however unfortunate its consequences may be, has left its mark on history. For who would know today of Mausolus,[1]   10
the petty tyrant of Caria, or of his wife Artemisia or of Scopas or Bryaxis or Timotheus or Leochares or Pithis, were it not for the wide repute of the Mausoleum, which, though it could not protect itself against the gnawing ravages of time, yet brought all these undying fame. Of the sumptuous tabernacle which Moses built or of that famous temple which Solomon   15
erected in Jerusalem and Esdras restored, no trace remains today; and yet the names of the famous Bezaleel[2] and of Hyram, king of Tyre, will live for ever in the minds of men. Solomon himself, though he has other claims to fame, yet owes much of his renown to that remarkable building.

But monuments which have some special usefulness for the life of men   20
bring a truer and more lasting fame than the massive pyramids of Egypt,

* * * * *

1544
1 On him, Pliny *Naturalis historia* 36.30–1. His widow Artemisia completed his splendid tomb (the Mausoleum) after his death. Scopas, Bryaxis, Timotheus, and Leocharis were sculptors who worked on the monument, and the architect was Pythius of Priene. Erasmus spelled the latter name 'Pithis,' following the spelling used in manuscripts of Pliny (*Naturalis historia* 36.31).
2 Exodus 31:2. By his craftsmanship he made the tabernacle.

which are nothing but a vain and foolish display of barbaric wealth. They are more lasting, too, than labyrinths, or colossal statues, or intricate knots, or tiny chariot groups no bigger than the wings of a fly, or the cauldrons of Dodona, or the sevenfold echoing porticos, or other subjects of this sort which delight by their marvellous skill and ingenuity, but are otherwise without value.[3] Such works bring notoriety rather than renown to their creators. Perillus[4] won fame for himself with his brazen bull, but it was a fame he would have been better without. Real distinction belongs to those who, by building bridges, harbours, baths, and aqueducts, have created works which combine grandeur with utility. But if you were to select from all such things the one which stands out above all others, could anything compare with this work which Pliny left us as the living and breathing monument of his genius? In fact it is not simply a work, but a treasure house, a veritable encyclopaedia of all that is worth knowing.[5] It should not surprise us, therefore, if this single work has made, and continues to make, many a man's reputation. For however obscure a man may have been, once he puts his hand to Pliny's text, people take notice. 25 30 35

This marvellous gift would have been lost to us, had not some men of great ability taken the trouble to rescue it from the almost hopeless state into which it had fallen, each attempting to go beyond the other. There can be no question that our greatest debt is to Ermolao Barbaro,[6] not just because he was the first to tackle this noble task, but because none of the others improved the text in so many places. It is not my intention to put together a long list of names, but among the many who followed Barbaro's example I must mention the sterling labours of Guillaume Budé,[7] a scholar 40 45

* * * * *

3 All of the works of ancient art referred to are discussed in Pliny *Naturalis historia*: on labyrinths, 36.84–93; on colossal statues, 34.39–46; on tiny chariots, 7.85, 34.83, 36.43; on the cauldrons of Dodona, 36.92 (where they are barely mentioned, but cf Strabo VII frag 3 [Loeb ed III 325]); on the echoing portico at Olympia, 36.100.

4 According to Pliny *Naturalis historia* 34.89, he was an artist who made for the tyrant Phalaris of Akragas a brazen bull in which a man could be roasted to death, and was himself the first victim of his device. The story appears in many other classical texts: PW 19 (1937) 797, sv Perilaos 9.

5 Renaissance authors did indeed regard *Naturalis historia* as a treasure-house of knowledge about the ancient world. For a survey of the many humanistic commentaries on this author, see Charles G. Nauert, jr 'Caius Plinius Secundus' in CTC IV (1980) 297–422.

6 Cf Ep 126:150n and CTC IV 308–9, 338–44. His *Castigationes Plinianae* (2 vols, Rome: Eucharius Argenteus [Silber] Germanus 1492–3) were the first really extensive and important Renaissance commentary on Pliny.

7 He produced no full commentary on Pliny, but his influential *De asse et*

of consummate learning and scrupulous attention to detail. After him there
is Nicolas Bérault,[8] who in addition to his vast learning in the humanities
is an expert mathematician and, what is more important in this field, a man
of sound judgment; he devoted himself to this subject with an enthusiasm   50
matched only by his scrupulousness. Finally there is Johannes Caesarius,[9]
a man accomplished in every branch of literary study, who has recently
turned his attention to this author with happy results. It is due to the
assiduous efforts of all these men that we now possess a Pliny much freer
from error than at any time before.   55

Whenever we look at certain pictures of great artistic merit, there is always
something new for us to admire; similarly, for those engaged in the correction
of Pliny's text there will never be any scarcity of passages to be repaired. Plautus
was of course joking when he said, 'Whoever wants to acquire a deal of trouble
for himself should acquire two things, a boat and a wife; for no two things   60
cause more trouble than these.'[10] But the same could be said in all seriousness
of the man who chooses to work on the emendation of Pliny, that he will never
be out of trouble. For, if nothing else, there is always the carelessness of printers
to contend with. Because of them scholars working on the best writers must
constantly unweave Penelope's web;[11] for every day these people by their   65
slovenliness introduce more errors into a text than can be put right by the
industry of scholars. Some works by the inimitable quality of their art have
inspired such reverence that craftsmen have been discouraged from supplying
what was missing or repairing what was damaged. Among the works of Apelles
two Venuses in particular are praised by critics:[12] one shows her emerging   70
from the sea and is hence known as 'Venus anadyomene'; the other, which he
undertook for the people of Cos but left unfinished, would have surpassed the
first if Death had not become jealous of the work as it took shape. When the
lower part of the earlier work was damaged, no one could be found to repair
it, and similarly with the later one, which was incomplete, no one was able to   75
finish it along the lines sketched out in the drawings.

If we respect such modesty in an artist, then we should be all the more

* * * * *

partibus eius (1515) discusses many passages from that author. Cf Ep 403
introduction.
8 Cf Ep 925 introduction and CTC IV 311–12, 358–61. His edition of Pliny (Paris
1516) incorporated notes from many humanists, including Erasmus.
9 Cf Ep 374 introduction and CTC IV 363–7.
10 Poenulus 210–13
11 Cicero Academica 2.95
12 The source for this story, as for most of what the postclassical world knows
about Apelles' paintings, is Pliny Naturalis historia 35.91–2.

ready to condemn the recklessness, or should I say the irreverence, of those copyists and printers who have disfigured Pliny's text, a work which deserves to be honoured beyond anything which painters or sculptors have produced; one might imagine they had sworn to destroy this remarkable writer. To prevent such a thing from happening was a task worthy of a king, since no work is more fit for the hands of a king and from no other will he gain more rapidly a comprehensive knowledge of the world. Nothing is more becoming to a monarch than excellence in learning. But knowledge which comes from experience, as Pliny himself has rightly said, is not just a lamentable thing, since it is purchased at the expense of others, but is difficult and costly to acquire and so generally arrives too late.[13] The state can no more endure these delays than a ship in peril on the sea can wait for an incompetent captain to learn his trade. Pressing dangers require immediate and expert solutions. So rulers cannot afford to waste any part of their lives: it is not possible for them to act as children and even in adolescence they must manifest the maturity of their elders. There is no source from which that quality can be so readily acquired than from this work, which presents all knowledge with remarkable conciseness. Pliny's subject is the world. Could you imagine anything more absurd than to rule the world and not know what it is? Nor can one excuse oneself by pleading the pressure of public business; for Pliny was occupied with just such business when he compiled this work from a reading of thousands of volumes. At the very least some of the time now wasted on dice should be spent on reading so valuable – and enjoyable – a work.

But to resume, just as the recklessness of those who have corrupted the text is to be condemned, so the greatest possible restraint should be shown by scholars in their efforts to restore it. Granted it is blind conservatism to reject every bold conjecture when we know that boldness has often produced excellent results. But it is reckless folly to substitute a new reading for an old on the basis of some feeble conjecture. A true respect for the text demands that we provide a separate note wherever we have made a judgment on grounds of plausibility; in this way we lay a foundation for further investigation by other scholars. I wish that all the leading men in literary studies would join together in this noble cause, each sharing his discoveries with all the others, until we had a Pliny free from fault. The reward which is held before us is not insignificant. The restoration of even a single pas-

* * * * *

13 Pliny *Panegyricus* 66.4 – a work, however, of the younger Pliny, not by the author of *Naturalis historia*. Erasmus seems here to confuse the two Plinys, or to attribute the *Panegyricus* to the elder, as was often done in the Middle Ages.

sage will win for a man an honourable place among the learned, for such
is the splendour of Pliny's name and such the attraction and usefulness of   11
his work. Your Excellency will serve the world of learning well if you
encourage your friend Velius,[14] or any others who have his abilities, to
work in this field.

With the help of a manuscript[15] which is very old but badly corrupted (as such manuscripts generally are) I have restored several passages   120
which could not otherwise have been corrected and which had not been
noticed by any previous editor. You will not doubt this claim if you consider this passage from book 12, chapter 4: *Aethiopiae forma, ut diximus, nuper
allata* etc. [the geography of Ethiopia which, as we have said, has lately been
reported on ...]; also in book 13, chapter 24: *Apes quoque nunquam defore* etc   12
[that the bees too will never fail ...]; again in book 18, chapter 6: *Verumque
confitentibus latifundia* etc [if the truth be told, large estates ...] and chapter
25: *Omnesque eae differentiae fiunt in octavis partibus signorum* etc [and all
these changes occur at the eighth degree of the zodiacal signs ...] But it
would be silly to list all my corrections. I mention these passages simply so   130
that the reader, by comparing my text with that of all other editions, will
see that very many passages which could not have been restored by conjecture have been restored on the authority of this ancient manuscript.
Throughout I have spent such pains on the work that I am ready to stake
my reputation on the claim that no better text of Pliny has ever appeared.   13
It has also benefited from the glorious and splendid workmanship of the
Froben press. Froben himself seems to me to have been intended by nature
for the embellishment of letters.

That my Pliny may be launched upon the world under still more
favourable auspices, I have decided to dedicate the work to you. I know   14
how much I owe to your incomparable brother, Thurzo, late bishop of
Wrocław,[16] who, though I was so far away, sent me splendid gifts and the
most affectionate letters and invited me to accept his friendship. From such

* * * * *

14 On the Silesian humanist poet Caspar Ursinus Velius, a protégé of Bishop
   Thurzo, cf Ep 548:5n.
15 Allen Ep 1544:113n identifies this as the Codex Murbacensis, an old and
   apparently excellent manuscript of Pliny borrowed from the Alsatian monastery of Murbach by Froben for use in this edition. Despite Erasmus' claim here,
   the principal use of this source was not by him but by Beatus Rhenanus in his
   commentary of 1526, which is still important textually because it preserves
   readings from this manuscript, which is now lost. Cf CTC IV 367–9.
16 On Johannes Thurzo, cf Ep 850 introduction. Like his brother Stanislaus, he
   was a patron of humanism.

a debt the death of the creditor does not set me free. What could not be
paid to him must be paid to his memory. You have inherited your brother's   145
place and have called me more than once your friend. You are dealing, my
lord bishop, with a man as fragile as glass. I live under the constant threat
of death. If God grants me a longer life, you may consider this a mere token
which, far from discharging my debt, puts me under a tighter obligation;
but if it should not turn out so, this will be proof that what I lacked was   150
opportunity and not a grateful and thankful heart. May the Lord Jesus keep
your Excellency safe.

Basel, 8 February in the year of our redemption, 1525

1545 / To Frans van Cranevelt   Basel, 10 February 1525

Cf Ep 1145 introduction. This letter survives in a manuscript of Louvain from
which portions have been lost. Henry de Vocht first published it in his edition
of Cranevelt's *Literae* in 1928. The principal theme is Erasmus' chronic difficulty in securing payment of the pension promised by the Emperor Charles v.
Here he seeks the support of his influential friend. For the complicated story
of Erasmus' unpaid imperial pension, see Ep 1380 introduction.

Cordial greetings. My congratulations to our friend Maximilian,[1] for I
suppose it was the abbot of Middelburg to whom you were referring.
Congratulations also to Noviomagus.[2] I have never met anyone with a
more delightful or more modest disposition than the abbot.

The petitions you mentioned are simply an appeal for money. Unless   5
you have some reason for acting differently, I should be happy if you
would take an interest in this affair of mine. Some time ago the emperor
wrote from Spain to the Illustrious Lady[3] to ask her to make a special

* * * * *

1545
1 Cf Ep 1164 n11. The reason for these congratulations remains unclear, but
  Bietenholz (CEBR I 227) notes that later the same year, he received the endorsement of Charles v for his candidacy (which was ultimately unsuccessful) to
  become coadjutor to the abbot of Saint-Ghislain in Hainaut. Maximilian was
  abbot of Middelburg.
2 On Noviomagus, also known as Gerard Geldenhouwer of Nijmegen, cf Ep 487
  introduction. Geldenhouwer, who was an intimate friend of Cranevelt, had
  become secretary to the abbot of Middelburg in 1524 but before the end of
  1525 defected to the Lutherans.
3 Margaret of Austria, aunt of the emperor Charles and of Ferdinand, was
  governor of the Netherlands from 1515 down to her death in 1530. Since

payment of my annuity, which is now more than three years overdue. I had
entrusted this business to the archbishop of Palermo,[4] who is agreeable and   10
all smiles. He sent me the Illustrious Lady's reply, that, if I returned, not
only would the pension be waiting for me, but I might expect other preferments besides. I have just written to the archbishop of Palermo again on this
matter now that Ferdinand[5] has sent a letter to the Illustrious Lady since
the emperor is in distant parts. Could you spur the archbishop into action?   15
Otherwise he is likely to take his time. Or if it is convenient, could you take
up the business yourself? I left with the permission of the court. It was not
just my work which kept me here all this time – my health was also part of
the reason. And what I have published for the honour of the emperor and
of Ferdinand, the record itself clearly shows. I have resolutely refused all   20
offers from France: the latest was the treasurership of Tours, a great plum,
with an income of six hundred crowns;[6] and there were bishoprics too.
Budé wrote me about these on the king's authority.[7]

Now whether I wish it or not, I am being forced to leave this place: for
one thing war seems to be imminent and then I am afraid that the   25
Lutherans may get the upper hand here. I wrote to Ruffault.[8] I hesitate to

* * * * *

Erasmus' pension was payable from the emperor's treasury in those provinces,
her support for payment was of special importance.

4 Jean Carondelet; cf Ep 803:12n. Because he was very influential at the Hapsburg court in the Netherlands and was friendly, Erasmus frequently wrote to
   get his help in securing payment of the imperial pension.
5 Ferdinand of Hapsburg, younger brother of the emperor and imperial regent
   in Germany. Erasmus had known Ferdinand personally since the latter's
   residence in the Netherlands (1518–21), had dedicated to him his paraphrase
   on the Gospel of John (Ep 1333), and subsequently had established a cordial
   and enduring relationship that made Ferdinand a helpful ally within the ruling
   dynasty. The specific letter sent by Ferdinand on Erasmus' behalf is not extant,
   but Epp 1553, 1581, and 1585 contain evidence that he did write to his aunt
   Margaret, governor of the Netherlands, to support Erasmus against his critics.
6 Latin *sexcentorum coronatorum*. For the reasons noted in Ep 1434 n3, these
   'crowns' were probably *écus d'or au soleil* (3.296 g fine gold), the French gold
   coin that displaced the *écu à la couronne* in 1475, and was now worth 40s
   tournois in France and 76d gros in the Hapsburg Netherlands (CWE 8 350).
   Thus this income would have been worth £1,200 tournois, or exactly £190 gros
   Flemish, or £128 5s 0d sterling.
7 Guillaume Budé, the leading figure among French humanists, played the role
   of intermediary in the repeated attempts of King Francis I to persuade Erasmus
   to settle in France. Cf Epp 1439, 1446.
8 On Jean Ruffault, treasurer-general to Charles V, cf Ep 1287 n10. He was
   repeatedly helpful to Erasmus, though not always successful.

write to the count of Hoogstraten since I am not sufficiently sure of his attitude towards me.[9] The same goes for the bishop of Liège.[10] I should prefer to live close to all of you ... Everything is now up in the air. I shall have to make my plans on the spur of the moment.   30

Whatever you can do for me in this affair will be much appreciated. But if there are reasons why you should refuse, Cranevelt will still be Erasmus' friend. I wish Dorp were as steady as he is brilliant:[11] he must have the courage to press on if he is not to expose himself to attack by scoundrels with malice in their blood. Farewell.   35

Frans,[12] who is the bearer of this letter, is a canon at Antwerp, a young man of great ability and warmly attached to me. He can be trusted to deliver anything you may care to send or write.

Basel, 10 February 1525

To the most learned Frans van Cranevelt. In Mechelen   40

1546 / To Frans van Cranevelt   [Basel, 10 February 1525]

This short note on a small strip of paper accompanied a number of letters (probably copies) demonstrating that the pope and the Hapsburg princes were favourable to Erasmus. It is probably a postscript to the preceding letter and like it was first published in de Vocht *Literae*.

I am sending a packet of letters which show you my good relations with the pope and the princes. When you have made use of them, you can keep

* * * * *

9 On Antoine de Lalaing, count of Hoogstraten, cf Ep 1038 n7. That letter shows that Erasmus feared that attacks by the monks had turned the count against him.

10 Erard de la Marck, prince-bishop of Liège, had been a strong supporter of Erasmus and a reforming bishop but moderated his criticisms of curial policy after being appointed cardinal in 1520. While monkish attacks may have been one source of Erasmus' uncertainty about his continued support, Erasmus' own indiscreet letter of 30 May 1519 to Martin Luther (Ep 980) also embarrassed their relations. Cf Ep 738 introduction.

11 Maarten van Dorp was probably Erasmus' closest friend and best supporter among the Louvain theological faculty, but Erasmus still feared that his early criticisms of *The Praise of Folly* and of the plan for an edition of the Greek New Testament, expressing his susceptibility to the influence of his colleagues, would cause him to drift away. Cf Ep 304 introduction.

12 Frans van der Dilft, who at this period was living in Erasmus' home at Basel and serving him as secretary and courier. Cf Allen Ep 1663 introduction, and Bierlaire *Familia* 64–7.

them for yourself or send them back with this young man, Frans van der
Dilft.

1547 / To Maarten Lips   Basel, 11 February 1525

> On the recipient, Ep 750 introduction. Lips, a distinguished patristic scholar,
> was helping Erasmus with the edition of St Augustine's works that Froben
> eventually published in 1528–9. The letter survived only in a single manuscript
> copy (Rotterdam MS Erasmus III 102, page 136) until published by Adalbert
> Horawitz *Erasmus von Rotterdam und Martinus Lipsius* Sitzungsberichte der
> kaiserlichen Akademie der Wissenschaften, philosophisch-historische Classe
> (Vienna 1878) 80.

DESIDERIUS ERASMUS OF ROTTERDAM TO HIS FRIEND LIPS,
GREETING
Neither the *De doctrina christiana*[1] nor the *Commentary on Genesis*, with your
corrections, has reached me, nor the material which you gave to Goclenius.[2]
I have received only what you gave Lieven.[3] The world is now filled with   5
rogues and vagabonds whom the freedom of the new gospel is letting loose
upon us. All the more reason to be careful. Everything is now opened and
intercepted. I already have the *De musica* and the *Commentary on Genesis* and
some other works, all with corrections, but apparently from a different
manuscript from the one you used. So your trouble has not been for noth-   10
ing. Dorp is holding on to the *De Trinitate* with corrections entered on my
manuscript. I cannot persuade him to send even the notes which he made
on the basis of the Gembloux manuscript which was lent me.[4] Please take
this up with Goclenius. You are aware of the *De civitate* which Vives has
published.[5] I have corrected the *In Faustum*. Will you work on all the rest?   15
Do not send me individual fragments: in fact send me nothing before Easter,

* * * * *

1547
1 Lips had borrowed this manuscript of Augustine's treatise from a monastery
  at Groenendaal for the textual work he was doing in collaboration with
  Erasmus. The other titles in this paragraph are all texts of St Augustine on
  which the two men were working for the planned edition.
2 On Conradus Goclenius (d 1539), cf Ep 1209 introduction.
3 Lieven Algoet; cf Epp 1091 introduction, 1537.
4 On the difficulties which Erasmus had in recovering this manuscript from
  Dorp and on Goclenius' role in eventually recovering it for him after Dorp's
  death, cf Epp 1890, 1899.
5 Edited by Juan Luis Vives (Basel: Froben 1522), with a preface by Erasmus.

for I may be with you next spring, and Froben can do nothing without my
direction. If you produce any notes on the *Paraphrases*, I shall be deeply
grateful, for I should like that work to be perfect in every respect.[6] If you
are interested in books, Froben is always more willing to part with books   20
than with money. If you prefer money, I shall see to it that your labours do
not go unrewarded.

Here is news for you. In this town we have a college of the regulars
of Saint Leonard.[7] Just before the Feast of the Purification all the monks
along with the prior abandoned the habit; but all who chose to do so still   25
live there, though with different clothes. Each man receives from the magistrates sixty florins,[8] the prior a little more. No one seems surprised at this
and I fear that the same thing will happen everywhere. The bishops have
put their heads together to control the situation by strong measures; but I
am afraid they will have little success. Different remedies would be needed.   30
I am constantly issuing warnings; some day people will recognize that my
warnings were not lightly given.

I was delighted by the pledge of mutual good will which your prior,
Jan Aerts, sent me.[9] Please tell Walter, the Dominican,[10] not to write without due caution, for we live in most perilous times. If you need money,   35
Goclenius will give you four philips:[11] in the meantime I shall have a talk
with Froben. Farewell.

Basel, 11 February 1525

* * * * *

6 The preceding summer, Erasmus had instructed Goclenius to buy Lips a set
 of his own *Paraphrases* if he did not have them. Cf Ep 1473.
7 This community of Augustinian canons surrendered its properties to the city
 of Basel on 30 January 1525 and on 1 February completed an agreement by
 which the prior, Lukas Rollenbutz, and the six canons received lifetime pensions.
8 Latin *florenus sexaginta*. If this reference meant the local gold coins, then they
 were almost certainly Rhenish or Electoral gold florins (Rheingulden), currently worth 57d gros Flemish and thus in total £14 5s 0d gros Flemish, or £9 12s
 4½d sterling, or exactly £90 tournois. See Epp 1362 n2; 1651 n5.
9 Cf Ep 1190 n2.
10 At this time, Erasmus regarded Walter Ruys OP as a friend because he had
 expressed favour for the *Paraphrases*, but later in 1525 he seems to have been
 one of four Dominicans who published a hostile *Apologia* against Erasmus'
 Exomologesis and *De esu carnium*. Cf Allen Ep 1472 introduction and the subsequent letters cited there.
11 Latin *quatuor philippicos*. Not the Burgundian gold Philippus, struck from 1433–
 54, but the St Philip florin, struck from 1496 to 1520 in the Burgundian-Haps-
 burg Netherlands, and currently worth 51d gros Flemish; thus a sum worth
 about 17s gros Flemish. See CWE 1 317–18, 321 (plate), 327, 336; CWE 8 349.

1548 / To Jan de Hondt   Basel, 11 February 1525

Erasmus here discusses two perennial topics in his correspondence, his own ill health and the complex arrangements involved in securing payment of the annuity he received from a prebend at Courtrai. De Hondt was the actual holder of the prebend against which this annuity was charged, and his promptness and good will in paying it gained him Erasmus' trust. Cf Ep 751 introduction. The letter also reflects Erasmus' growing uneasiness at the religious changes going on around him in Basel. It was first published in *Magni Erasmi vita* (Leiden 1615) and again in the 1642 London edition of Erasmus' correspondence.

TO THE HONOURABLE MASTER JAN DE HONDT, CANON OF
COURTRAI, GREETING

I came very close to freeing you from the burden of my annuity.[1] Even now my recovery is slow, if it can be called recovery to be spared for new tortures or to face death again and again. But blessed be the Lord who has   5
been pleased to purge me in this way, scourging me in this world that he may spare me in eternity.

Bentinus, whom you mentioned in your letter, has taken a wife here.[2] I remonstrated with him for casting a stain on his young years; he admitted the charge and laughed in a good-natured way. He expects to be called to   10
some of the neighbouring French towns, as Farel was called to Mont-béliard,[3] to preach this new gospel which is enjoying such a remarkable success here. Already many have repudiated baptism and revived the practice of circumcision. A great number will have nothing to do with the

* * * * *

1548

1 That is, his death would relieve de Hondt from payment of the life pension due from the income of the prebend at Courtrai.
2 Michael Bentinus, cf Ep 1433 n2. Bentinus had worked for the Froben press on several occasions from 1520; but by 1524, as he became increasingly committed to the Reformation, he not only married, as here reported, but also found employment at the presses of Valentinus Curio and Andreas Cratander, whose output included Protestant works not acceptable to Froben. He became particularly interested in spreading the Reformation to France and cultivated friendships with Guillaume Farel and other French reformers.
3 Farel had lived in Basel after fleeing Meaux in 1523 but was expelled from that city in 1524 because of his open agitation for the Reformation and also because of his slanderous attacks on the integrity of Erasmus (Epp 1496, 1510). He then transferred his activities to Montbéliard, beginning his lifelong dedication to the evangelization of what is now French-speaking Switzerland.

mass: some teach publicly that in the Eucharist there is nothing but bread   15
and wine. The veil and the cowl are being abandoned everywhere. Monks
and nuns are marrying. It is not safe for me to live here any longer. The
behaviour of the men who teach in this place troubles me more than their
doctrine. Bentinus will visit you again in Lent to confirm his flock in the
faith.   20

Barbier[4] has left for France in the company of Aleandro, who is now
archbishop of Brindisi;[5] he was driven to it, I imagine, by poverty and so
has decided to live in future by what he can get his hands on. His manner
towards me, I must say, was exceedingly offhand. If I am not mistaken, he
once stole forty florins from my imperial pension.[6] Since I suffered in   25
silence because of our friendship, he now has designs on this pension too,
relying on some further indulgence on my part. As usual I am sending a
blank form of receipt. Please be good enough to pay the sum to Pieter
Gillis[7] or to Dean Marcus Laurinus[8] or to Frans, canon of Antwerp,[9] if he

* * * * *

4 On Pierre Barbier, cf Ep 443 introduction. He was an admirer of Erasmus, but
his association with Aleandro, whom Erasmus distrusted, and his role in the
complex arrangements for the ecclesiastical (Courtrai) and imperial pensions
granted to Erasmus in the Netherlands made Erasmus suspicious of him.
5 Girolamo Aleandro, formerly a close friend of Erasmus during his residence
in Venice, had risen high in curial service and became archbishop of Brindisi
and papal nuncio to Francis I on 8 August 1524. Barbier, who had lost two
promising patrons with the unexpected deaths of the chancellor Jean Le
Sauvage in 1518 and Pope Adrian VI in 1523, spent 1524 and 1525 in the
service of Aleandro, whom Erasmus deeply and justifiably distrusted as a
barely hidden enemy, a distrust that he confessed candidly to Barbier in Ep
1605. On his troubles with Aleandro see Ep 1553 n9.
6 Probably Rhenish florins (Rheingulden), currently worth 57d gros Flemish (see
Ep 1651 n3); and if so, a sum worth £9 10s 0d gros Flemish, or £6 8s 3d sterling,
or £60 7s tournois. Allen Ep 1548:20n suggests that this may be a reference to the
complex arrangements by which Erasmus received partial payment of his pension in August 1517. In any case Barbier seems to have been permanently
involved, in some way that the documents do not make clear, in the transmission
of de Hondt's payments to Erasmus; and the latter blamed him, rather than de
Hondt, for problems which frequently arose in securing what was due him.
7 Cf Ep 184 introduction. At this point, Gillis was still the person in charge of
receiving and transferring Erasmus' revenues from the Netherlands to Basel,
though Erasmus Schets (cf Ep 1541) was soon to replace him.
8 His vernacular name was Mark Lauwerijns; cf Ep 651 introduction. He was
another friend involved in Erasmus' financial affairs, including the collection
and transfer of de Hondt's payments for the Courtrai annuity; cf Ep 1458.
9 Frans van der Dilft, who was then serving Erasmus as secretary and courier.
Cf Ep 1545 n12.

happens to deliver this letter in person. Farewell.   30
    Basel, 11 February 1525

1549 / To Johann von Vlatten   Basel, 11 February 1525

> This letter reflects Erasmus' ambivalent relationship with the prince-bishop of
> Liège, Erard de la Marck, and also his deep-seated mistrust of Girolamo
> Aleandro. On the recipient, see Ep 1390 introduction. Jean Leclerc first pub-
> lished this letter in LB III pt 2 cols 1705–6 (Appendix no 330).

ERASMUS OF ROTTERDAM TO THE HONOURABLE MASTER JOHANN
VON VLATTEN, HEADMASTER, GREETING
Some friendly deity must have arranged your meeting with my man Lieven[1] so that he could bring me your most welcome letter. Being the warm-
hearted person you are, you are even willing to shower on the servant of   5
an undeserving friend the same kindness which you always show to me;
and in depriving yourself of your cloak to cover him, you went one better
than St Martin, for he kept half of his cloak for himself – the lesser part, as
I recall.
    In the world of learning, things are much as you describe them. But   10
no court has more Midases than ours. I cannot quite remember what I wrote
about the cardinal,[2] but I can guess. Although he was friendly, I got nothing from him but words. Aleandro,[3] who is now bishop of Brindisi, is consumed with jealousy at my reputation, though he conceals it. The fame
which he envies is something I would gladly do without. He has a brother   15
in the service of the cardinal who is more deadly than himself:[4] for Alean-

* * * * *

1549
1 Lieven Algoet, Erasmus' *famulus* and courier; cf Ep 1537 n1.
2 Erard de la Marck, prince-bishop of Liège; cf Ep 1545 n10. The uncomplimen-
  tary remark about his failure to express his friendship in anything but words
  had already appeared in Erasmus' *Catalogus omnium Erasmi lucubrationum*,
  originally written as a letter to Johann von Botzheim and published by Froben
  in 1523 and again (in considerably expanded form) in 1524 (cf Allen I
  43:38–44:2 / CWE Ep 1341A:1716–24).
3 Cf Ep 1548 n5 for Erasmus' mistrust of him. Aleandro had formerly been
  secretary to Cardinal de la Marck.
4 Giambattista Aleandro (documented 1500–22), who appears to have lived as
  a dependent satellite to his elder brother's brilliant career. For the little that is
  known about him, see M.J.C. Lowry in CEBR I 28.

dro allows his feeling to break out, but Giambattista can hide all. I hear too that the dean of Louvain is up in arms against me,[5] doubtless relying on the cardinal's support; for he is confident that the cardinal has changed his customary attitude towards me. But all this makes little impression on me. 20

I have an adequate supply of Burgundy here. But there are other reasons which almost make it necessary for me to leave this place. For the present, however, my health does not permit my leaving, for I am suffering a serious attack of the stone. You continue to harp on the flattering remarks I made about you; if my life is spared, I shall show you that this was noth- 25 ing. I have received from Heresbach a very Heresbachian letter.[6] I do not have time to reply at the moment. Perhaps I shall see you both in the spring. In the meantime my best wishes.

Basel, 11 February 1525
Your friend, Erasmus of Rotterdam 30

1550 / From Duke George of Saxony   Dresden, 13 February 1525

A reply to Erasmus' letter of 12 December 1524 (Ep 1526). Duke George (1471–1539; ruled from 1500), second ruler of the Albertine line of Saxon dukes, was friendly to humanistic learning and to reform but was one of the most outspoken and persistent opponents of Luther among the German princes. Despite the excuses offered in Erasmus' letter, the duke here urges Erasmus to take the lead in defending the Catholic faith and chides him, though in a friendly way, for his hesitation. The letter, which survived in Dresden MS Loc 10299 f 135, was first published in Adalbert Horawitz *Erasmiana* I Sitzungsberichte der kaiserlichen Akademie der Wissenschaften, philosophisch-historische Classe (Vienna 1878) 9.

* * * * *

5 Nicolas Coppin, a theologian of Louvain who served repeatedly as rector and as dean of the faculty. Cf Ep 1162 n18. He had become dean of the chapter of St Peter's of Louvain, and hence vice-chancellor of the university, in 1525. He had originally been well disposed to Erasmus but turned against him at about this time. Ep 1585 shows that Dorp was the source of Erasmus' knowledge of his change of attitude.

6 On Konrad Heresbach cf Ep 1316 introduction. At this period he was serving as tutor to young Duke William V of Cleves and hence would have been close to Vlatten. Although the following remark sounds derogatory, he was in fact a great admirer of Erasmus, who had done much to promote his career, and subsequently was one of the leaders of Erasmian church reform in the principality of Cleves.

Duke George of Saxony
Portrait by Lucas Cranach the Elder, after 1537
Bayerische Staatsgemäldesammlungen, Munich

GEORGE, BY THE GRACE OF GOD DUKE OF SAXONY, LANDGRAVE
OF THURINGEN AND MARGRAVE OF MEISSEN

I send you my greetings, most learned Erasmus, and the assurance of my
support. I learned from the letter you sent me from Basel on the fourth of
December[1] how many of my letters have reached you and how many   5
replies you have sent; it also contained a summary of all our correspondence and a long series of excuses for not taking a greater part in the
Lutheran affair. With regard to the number of my letters, you did not
include one which I sent recently and which I suppose has reached you by
now. When you claim that I too was impressed at first by the Lutheran   10
charade, I shall not deny it; for I thought Luther offered some prospect of
correcting the abuses and corrupt practices which had become far from
uncommon among us. But when he decided to revive the Hussite heresies,
the hand of Satan could be seen; and eventually he reached the point where
there was nothing in the whole of the church which he left untouched and   15
undefiled, beginning with the supreme pontiff and reaching to the traditions
of the most revered Fathers, which he distorted and befouled. I never
counted you a member of that band of conspirators which Luther formed
to accomplish these ends; rather it was your exceptional eloquence and
learning which made me urge you to attack and crush this Philistine who   20
was trying to violate and dishonour the bride of Christ. For this, in my
opinion, is a task for all Christians, not just for theologians, but more particularly for anyone who claims to be both theologian and Christian, and most
of all, if he excels everyone else in influence and authority.

I see that you are upset because, in arguing as I did, I used rather blunt   25
language which failed to pay you proper respect, but there is no reason for
you to take this in bad part. Indeed I continue to appeal to you and to beg
and implore you to disregard the unjust and stinging criticisms of the theologians and to be staunch in defending the Catholic faith. For you must see
that however wise and prudent your advice may have been, it has not taken   30
us very far; but if you turn your pen against Luther now, you may be able
to make good what has been lost by your procrastination and win a greater
victory than St Hilary's,[2] since Luther is a greater heretic than Arius –

* * * * *

1550
1 Either a letter has been lost or this is a slip for 12 December, the date of Ep
   1526. The present letter certainly responds to many specific points mentioned
   in that one, such as the difficulty of replacing Petrus Mosellanus as professor
   of Greek at Leipzig and Josse Clichtove's work *De votis* (ie, his *Antilutherus*).
2 St Hilary of Poitiers (315–67) was an outspoken opponent of the Arian heresy,
   suffered several years of exile for his refusal to condemn Athanasius of Alex-

though I am well aware that you are the least likely of men to be swayed by pride and that you seek rather the glory of Christ. There is no reason to be deterred from the task by the mountain of abuse which has been piled up and hurled at our Holy Father the pope and at our invincible emperor and other princes. In this company I too find a place, like Saul among the prophets;[3] for because of our sins we Israelites have all deserved the insults hurled at us by this Goliath. One day we shall be defended from such abuse by some puny David who trusts not in arms or intellect, but places his hope in the grace of God; he will not tolerate that man's insults and, though unarmed, he will defeat his well-armed foe; the pious and humble man will prevail over the impious and proud. But, tell me, why does the example of Uzzah frighten you?[4] Your writings are sufficient proof that you are not only a Christian (and Christians too have a duty to support the Ark when it is in danger of falling), but also a true theologian and from the tribe of those whose special duty it is to care for and protect the Ark. For there can be no doubt that if Uzzah had been of the tribe of Levi and if he had thoughtlessly placed the Ark upon the oxen instead of placing it on his own shoulders, things would not have turned out so disastrously for him.

About the matters which you thought too sensitive for a letter, I know nothing. But I completely agree with you on this, that our present woes are the price we must pay for our sins: we want to measure everything by our own human wisdom, placing all our trust in our own powers and none in God. It is the same with Luther; had he not relied on his own wisdom and aspired to greater knowledge than is proper for a man to have, he would not have made the mistakes he made nor led others so far astray that now they do not even draw the line at revolution, though this is an offence punishable by death. Likewise the other side, for all its ability and hard work, has made little headway, since in everything they do they are too much a prey to their passions and desires. What is needed now is to return to God with all our hearts and pray for someone who can steer a middle course and bring the ship back to harbour. That you are just such a man I have no doubts. So keep up your courage, Erasmus, and press on with the fight in the way you have begun. You have the pope, the emperor and all

* * * * *

andria, and produced, in his *De Trinitate*, the first extensive Latin work on the doctrine of the Trinity.
3 Cf 1 Sam 10:10–12.
4 A reference to God's killing Uzzah (2 Sam 6:6–7) because he had touched the Ark of the Covenant though he was not a member of the priestly tribe of Levi. Cf also 1 Chron 13:11.

the princes of the Christian faith helping and supporting you; and our holy mother church, the bride of Christ, will smile upon your efforts; she will be watching and applauding when you enter the fray, and at the end you will receive from Christ himself the victor's palm. He will finish the fight which 70 you have so splendidly begun and will always stand beside you to give you his aid. This is the vision which I see in my mind.

. If the letters you receive from the pope, the emperor, Ferdinand, and the king of England are in very different vein from mine, that is because I am no Oedipus.[5] But if anything I write vexes you, put it out of your mind 75 and look at my heart, not my words; for in my heart I am totally dedicated to this one object, the service of the Christian commonwealth, and I find it hard to tolerate anything which changes or perverts what has been firmly established in the past. No, you were wide of the mark when you thought my letters were written under someone else's influence or guidance, for 80 there was no one here to advise or influence me. But let us forgive and be friends and let us drop these ungrounded suspicions. I have never found fault with that modest and courteous manner of yours, which has won the admiration of many of our princes. But it has always been among my dearest wishes to see an end to this tragedy in our time: I believe that no one but 85 you can bring this about and I hate the thought of any further delay.

You are right about Mosellanus' successor.[6] Luther has ruined everything, and we have reached the point where one can scarcely depend on the just and the elect to be faithful and stay the course. Still, if someone suitable occurs to you, let me know, for the post has not yet been filled. Your book 90 on prayer is being read everywhere:[7] it shows the quality of your mind and proves you are a real theologian – and a theologian by no means unarmed for the fight. I have not seen Clichtove's *De votis*.[8] Farewell, and remember you can always count on my good will.

Dresden, the eve of St Valentine's day AD 1525

* * * * *

5 A reference to Terence *Andria* 194, implying that Duke George claims to be only an ignoramus, not an expert.
6 In Ep 1526 Erasmus lamented the recent death of Mosellanus, professor of Greek at Leipzig, and warned that finding a suitable successor would be difficult because most persons who had sufficient mastery of Greek did not satisfy the duke's insistence that the successor should be firmly opposed to Luther. Indeed, Mosellanus himself had felt sympathetic to Luther but realized that in ducal Saxony he had to exercise discretion in expressing his opinions. On him see Ep 560 introduction.
7 *Modus orandi Deum* (Basel: Froben 1524).
8 On him, Ep 594:15n. Duke George appears to have misunderstood Erasmus'

1551 / From Hieronymus Emser   Dresden, 16 February 1525

This letter no doubt was dispatched with the preceding one, since Emser was then a councillor to Duke George. On his earlier life, see Ep 553. He was one of the earliest German humanists to abandon his initial favourable reaction to Luther, and for a time he regarded Erasmus as a Lutheran. Erasmus suspected him of being the real author of Duke George's blunt letter of 21 May 1524 challenging him to do his duty by openly opposing Luther's heresies (Ep 1448; cf Ep 1521); but after the publication of *De libero arbitrio*, Emser became more friendly and resumed direct correspondence with Erasmus. Preserved in a Leipzig manuscript, this letter was published by Förstemann and Günther in 1904.

Greetings, thrice mighty Erasmus! Your advice is good: we should avoid insulting language and when we do battle with the heretics, our weapons should be moderation, not abuse. So I have adopted a more conciliatory tone in my reply to Zwingli's insolent *Antibolon*,[1] though I could not overlook the lying charges which he brought against me. For, as you know, it is only the barbarian who is indifferent to his own reputation.[2] I hope you will approve of my response – whatever its merits may be. Our illustrious prince has very warm feelings towards you, as is evident from his most recent letter. What he wrote earlier was not intended to cast doubt on your good faith or honesty, but to spur on the horse which is already running strongly on its own.

* * * * *

letter. The work *De votis*, which he criticizes as 'very wordy,' was by Martin Luther (Wittenberg 1521); Erasmus excused himself from any obligation to respond to it by pointing out that the Paris theologian Josse Clichtove (cf Ep 594:15n) had already done so. This reference is to Clichtove's *Antilutherus* (Paris: Simon de Colines 1524), of which part 3 bears the title 'Contra enervationem votorum monasticorum.'

1551
1 Zwingli's work was a reply to an earlier work by Emser attacking Zwingli's *De canone missae epichiresis* (1522). The reply was *Apologeticon in Uldrici Zuinglii Antibolon* (n p 1525), edited by Theobald Freudenberger in Corpus Catholicorum 28. As he here claimed, Emser in this Latin treatise moderated the crude and scurrilous style of his popular pamphlets against Luther. On this controversy, cf G.R. Potter *Zwingli* (Cambridge 1976) 153–4.
2 *Auctor ad Herennium* 4.20.28

H.E. is not important enough to damage your reputation;[3] he was born in a peasant hut in our part of the world. You have long passed the point where the malice of such nonentities can reach you. He threatens the gibbet and the sword, but it is his own neck which will discover what they   30
feel like. My hope is that you will rise, like some luxuriant palm, to even greater heights and that you will not forget my deep devotion to you. A friend of mine has made a most careful translation into the vernacular of your *Paraphrase on St John's Gospel*:[4] this winter I have had it printed at my printing house. Already it is finding its way into the hands of scholars and   35
you are receiving great praise. In return perhaps you will spare a thought from time to time for your friend Hieronymus. Farewell, bright and shining star of letters.

From Dresden on the feast of Juliana the virgin in the year 1525
Your reverence's devoted friend, Emser   40
To the celebrated high-priest of every branch of learning, Master Erasmus of Rotterdam, theologian and his most respected friend

1552 / From Floriano Montini   Buda, 22 February 1525

This letter from the secretary to Lorenzo Cardinal Campeggi expresses strong approval of Erasmus' *De libero arbitrio* by him and his friends at Ferrara and encloses a manuscript copy of a work written in support of it, *De libero animi motu*, an anthology of authorities collected by Montini's friend Celio Calcagnini which Erasmus arranged to have published (Basel: Froben, June 1525), with his own letter to Montini (Ep 1578) serving as an introductory essay (cf also Epp 1576, 1587). The present letter also reflects the interest of Montini and Calcagnini in the Neoplatonist Proclus and their hope that Erasmus could help them obtain a better text of his works. Even though it reflected approval of Erasmus' treatise among influential Italian scholars and churchmen, Erasmus never published it, and it first appeared in a collection of Erasmus' letters from Leipzig manuscripts edited by Förstemann and Günther in 1904. Montini (d 1533), a native of Ferrara and secretary to Cardinal Campeggi during his

* * * * *

3 A reference to Heinrich Eppendorf, Erasmus' former secretary, with whom he had a protracted and bitterly personal controversy. Cf Ep 1122 introduction.
4 Erasmus' Latin original was published by Froben at Basel in February 1523. The German translation here mentioned was the work of Michael Risch, with a preface dated from Pirna, 10 November 1524. This edition was without place or date, but the publisher used by Emser to bring it out would have been Wolfgang Stöckel of Munich, who had recently set up shop in Dresden.

legation in Germany, Hungary, and Bohemia and his more famous mission to England regarding the divorce question, was useful to Erasmus as a link to Calcagnini and other Italian humanists.

Cordial greetings. I should like, if you will allow me, to apologize for the laconic brevity of my earlier letter which accompanied the documents[1] you asked for and to make amends by writing this time at greater length, for now I have more time at my disposal and there is more to write about. So here is something which may amuse you during your afternoon walks if   5
someone will read it to you or you may use it to prolong the pleasures of conversation after dinner; at the same time it will show you what my countrymen at Ferrara think of you and of your defence of the freedom of the will. For in recent months, since your *De libero arbitrio* came into my hands, I have persuaded everyone to read it whom I knew to be closely   10
attached to you by old ties or a common interest in the Muses. I am thinking particularly of Pistofilo,[2] whose subtle mind and experience of law and politics have deservedly earned him the post of private secretary to our prince,[3] and also of Celio,[4] who stands out like a bright light in the church and indeed in the whole of the country because of the brilliance of his gifts   15
and the versatility of his scholarship and learning. The more conspicuous these men become among us for their own achievements, the better they are known as supporters of your fame and learning.

The gratitude they felt for this good turn will be evident, I think, from a letter which Celio wrote to Pistofilo and which Pistofilo lately passed on   20
to me. I thought it only proper that you should read it too, so that you would have the pleasure of sharing our interests and discovering what we

* * * * *

1552
1 Cardinal Campeggi's dispensation relieving Erasmus from the church's dietary laws (Ep 1542), which Montini had countersigned and dispatched in his role as secretary.
2 Bonaventura Pistofilo of Ferrara (d 1535) was secretary to Alfonso I d'Este, duke of Ferrara, and was also a poet and an historian who wrote an important biography of his patron. At the University of Ferrara, he had studied medicine under Niccolò Leoniceno and had taken a degree in law. He was a noted collector of ancient coins and a student of philosophy and was a special patron of Celio Calcagnini, who dedicated to him his work supporting Erasmus' position on free will (cf introduction to this letter).
3 Alfonso I d'Este, duke of Ferrara (1505–34).
4 Celio Calcagnini. Cf Ep 611:27n. On his *De libero animi motu* (1525), see the introduction to this letter.

said about you, for it was you who gave us a good excuse for getting in
touch with one another and you hold us together in a common bond despite the distances which separate us. What delights me particularly about   25
Celio's letter is the sympathy he shows not just for your achievement, but
also for your motive, in publishing this book. For I do not think we need
praise your teaching or your erudition, any more than we need praise the
light and radiance of the sun, which even the blind can feel and experience
as all men do. But if with this little work you have relieved your dearest   30
friends of so much worry and freed good Christian folk from the suspicions
they have had about you, what will happen, I wonder, if you unfurl your
banners and descend into the field of battle with all those forces which you
maintain at home and marshal by lamplight? But it would be foolish to put
pressure on you to do this, for, as we ought to realize, you are a man in   35
whom great piety is joined to learning and great learning to piety. Even so,
this is precisely what all good and learned men would now be demanding
of you and pressing with all the eloquence at their command, if only such
a request did not look like applying force to the great champion and defender of the freedom of the will! Nevertheless we hope to enjoy in due   40
season all the rich fruits of your piety and learning when questions of this
kind arise; and they will be all the more welcome because the enemies of
the faith will be able to see they were given freely and not produced to
please one person or another.

But I have gone on too long on this subject. I have an urgent request   45
to make of you. Will you let me know if you have a copy of Proclus?[5] He
is cited by Celio, and a long time ago I read a volume with the title *De
decem dubitabilibus circa providentiam et De fato et De eo quod in nobis est*. Or
better still, will you have a copy made for me and I shall send you the
money for the copyists? The text which I found at Rome was full of errors.   50
As his essays show, Proclus was a man of wide learning with a deep interest in religion. In the essay which he wrote for Theodorus on the working
of providence, which (as I just said) contains a discussion of the problem of
free will and destiny, he put forward many subtle arguments and clarified
many points, though the subject is generally perplexing and difficult. So I   55
would appreciate it greatly if you would help me to read these essays in a

* * * * *

5 Lycian Neoplatonist philosopher (d 485). Allen VI 31:63n observes that the use
   of the Latin *millesies* (a thousand times) in line 63 of his edition demonstrates
   that Montini was using the thirteenth-century Latin translation of Proclus by
   William of Moerbeke, a Dominican pupil of St Thomas Aquinas. Obviously he
   was seeking an improved text.

more accurate text. I know of course how far the teachings of the Platonists and other philosophers fall short of the true Christian faith. But we do not utterly despise and reject this human wisdom as something which is completely at variance with that wisdom which we drank in from the Scriptures   60
with our mothers' milk. Often we see that it gives wings to the soul and raises it up towards God.

Such studies draw us to them by a natural and spontaneous attraction; the soul itself pants with a deep desire to know and understand all that concerns itself and seeks better and more thoughtful answers, as Proclus   65
says, to questions which have been posed a thousand times before; yet the present age exercises a powerful influence too, for it has brought us to such depths of godlessness, superstition, and anxiety that we feel a heavy cloud of confusion covering everything; we can scarcely trust our eyes or our senses or the traditions of our fathers, and every reality, sacred and profane,   70
is insolently and stubbornly twisted in accordance with some individual whim or ridiculous philosophy.

This is what I have been discovering these past months among those benighted sects which have recently formed in Germany, as I accompanied the legate on his mission. Among these people I see many in such miserable   75
straits that it is scarcely comprehensible how such madness could have arisen: they heed no laws, submit to no one's authority, and tolerate no opinion which is in conflict with their own; at the same time they believe that they alone are entitled to be called good and learned and wise; and there is no poultice in the way of sound advice which you could apply to   80
them to make them better. In this they are like men who are ill with a raging fever and who at the crisis and turning-point of the disease cannot quench their thirst or find any measure of relief from the burning heat, not even by drinking the waters of the icy Danube; but the more they complain of the heat and fan themselves, the more the fever increases and their   85
temperature rises, until either the natural vigour of the body asserts itself and their temperature drops or it loses the battle and life and fever both depart together.

This situation makes your proposal for curing such lunacy very convincing; you advise us not to use excessively violent or elaborate threats but   90
to remove and eliminate only those things which could exacerbate the illness or make it worse. In this category you include anything from the lecture halls, booksellers, and preachers which might spill over and lodge in those parts of the body which have been seriously weakened by the disease. No one who understands the principles of medical science and has   95
examined the illness and the condition of the patient would quarrel with this diagnosis.

Your advice is now being strongly reinforced by news reaching us from reliable sources in Bohemia and by recent events in that country. It has been in a constant state of frenetic agitation for about a hundred years, but now, largely on its own initiative (for I shall say nothing for the moment about the legate's efforts in this direction) it is returning to the bosom of the church and seeking to be reconciled with the Holy See. On the fifth of February last, this was ratified in a public decree of all the estates, couched in the most impressive language.[6] Before this, no courtesy, no promise of favours, no threats or show of force by king or emperor could influence them. It would be tempting to conclude that Germany's devotion to the faith had somehow been swept away by the movement of sea and tide and deposited on the borders of Bohemia. Now the Bohemians are receiving it everywhere with open arms and words of welcome, as though it were an exile returning home. But if it is nature's plan that everything should change in accordance with its own fixed laws, and if the evils which exist and flourish in the world can be justified in so far as they allow us to practise whatever good and virtuous qualities we possess, should we not conclude that your German countrymen must one day change in the same way, that, struck with the light of truth and wearied by a life which brings little satisfaction, they will at last return to the place from which they stumbled in their folly and bewilderment?

When the good news of what had happened in Bohemia reached the legate, his delight was a measure of the great effort he had put into the case. With the same thoughtfulness he sent a personal messenger to report to the pope; after that he thought it right to inform all men of good will, yourself among the first, for I am sure you will have many reasons for being pleased by the news. So now – and I hope this will be a bright and happy omen for the future – the Bohemians are supporting the unity of the church. Every day we await their envoys so that the whole business may be properly concluded. In the meantime those who harbour unfriendly, not to say un-christian, thoughts about the apostolic see will have time to reflect on this, that its authority has not been so fatally weakened that no one will follow it any longer or that it fails to give first place to that faith without which we are nothing.

But I have already trespassed too long upon your kind attention and

* * * * *

6 The agreement, which was intended to reunite the more conservative wing of the Hussite movement, the Utraquists, with Rome was signed on 9 February, not the fifth. Allen Ep 1552:98n, citing F. Palacky *Geschichte von Böhmen*, 5 vols (Prague 1836–67) vol 5 pt 2, 537–41, especially 538n.

I am keeping you from more serious work, thus 'sinning against the public
good.'[7] But I am both your friend and your ardent supporter, so please
forgive me; I could not in all decency omit the first part of this letter and   135
I would be at fault if I passed over the second. I shall be happy to learn that
it has been safely delivered. The cardinal is your devoted friend and places
himself at your disposal. Do look after yourself.
Buda, 22 February 1525
Your friend, Floriano Montini   140
To that great scholar and distinguished theologian, Erasmus of
Rotterdam, my much respected friend. In Basel

1553 / To Maximilianus Transsilvanus   Basel, 24 February 1525

This is another of Erasmus' efforts to get the help of well-placed persons at
court for payment of his imperial pension. For an account of his problem, see
Ep 1380 introduction. Unlike most such begging letters, this one was published
by Erasmus himself in his *Opus epistolarum*. Maximilianus Transsilvanus (d
1538) was in a good position to help, for following service to Maximilian I and
Cardinal Matthäus Lang, bishop of Gurk, in 1519 he became secretary in the
imperial chancery of Charles V. He was the person who read aloud the titles
of Luther's books at the famous hearing at the Diet of Worms. By the end of
1523 he had entered the service of Margaret of Austria, governor of the Netherlands. There is substantial evidence (the present letter and Epp 1585, 1645,
1802, 1897) that he did use his influence at court to support Erasmus' cause.
Allen Ep 1553 introduction reports that he was a natural son of Bishop Matthäus Lang, but Albrecht Luttenberger chose not to repeat this claim in CEBR
III 339–40. Maximilianus studied under the Italian humanist Pietro Martire
d'Anghiera and wrote Latin poems, but his most important publications were
historical, including an account, based on personal interviews, of the circum-
navigation of the globe by the survivors of Magellan's expedition, *De Moluccis
insulis* (Cologne: Eucharius Cervicornus, 1523). Whether the name Transsilvanus indicates an origin in Transylvania is uncertain, but he spent most of his
career in the Netherlands.

ERASMUS OF ROTTERDAM TO MAXIMILIANUS TRANSSILVANUS,
GREETING
The letters which our friend Beat brought from Spain were late in reaching

* * * * *

7 Cf Horace *Epistles* 2.1.3.

me.[1] This happened because Beat was so thoroughly fed up with the journey by sea that he took the overland route and forgot to remove from his   5
trunk the things which were intended for me. So the letters were taken to
Brabant; from there by many twists and turns they eventually reached
Sélestat. Nevertheless, in spite of the delay, I wrote to everyone my friends
suggested. I sent letters to Nürnberg to be taken on to Spain by Michiel
Gillis,[2] whom you know. But I have not been able to find out what hap-   10
pened to all these letters. The distance is considerable and, especially in
these times, people have no sense of honour about opening, intercepting,
and suppressing mail. I do not think that we ever had a chance to get to
know each other, though when I was in Brussels (I believe it was four years
ago), many people spoke warmly of your remarkable kindness and of the   15
exceptional generosity of your nature. But your letter painted such a clear
and revealing portrait of an honest heart in which the Muses and Graces are
evidently at home, that nothing which I have read for many a long year has
brought me greater pleasure. So felicitous was the style that I was almost
afraid to reply. However, I covered up my blushes and dashed off a note   20
in this hurried manner. I gather from Beat's letter that it was not delivered.

What remains to be said can be put briefly. The emperor had given
instructions for a special payment to be made to me. In reply the illustrious
Lady Margaret promised that, if I returned, not only would my pension be
paid, but better things would await me. I fear, however, that if I did return,   25
I should soon hear, 'Come back tomorrow. Where were you before?' The
king of France is remarkably devoted to me: he has made me some very
generous offers, most recently the treasurership of Tours, which has an
annual income of 600 crowns.[3] I have refused everything and in the process
have given offence to many of my friends. Pope Clement, who is well   30
disposed towards me, as I know from past experience, is most profuse in

* * * * *

1553
1 On Beat Arnold (Arnolt) cf Ep 399:7n. On the packet of letters from Spain cf
   Allen Ep 1467:28n.
2 On this young imperial councillor who travelled frequently between Spain and
   Germany, see Ep 1432 n3.
3 Latin *sexcentorum coronatorum annui census*. See Ep 1545 n6. This offer, part of
   a sustained effort to persuade Erasmus to settle in France, is frequently mentioned in the correspondence for 1524 and early 1525. Cf two letters from
   Guillaume Budé explaining its advantageous terms, Epp 1439:31–35, 1446:48–
   50; Francis I's own letter of invitation, Ep 1375; and also Epp 1434:23–5, 1471:
   15–16; 1484:7–11, 1487:18–20, 1488:22–4, 1529:7–9, and 1545:21–4.

his promises of support. You will say 'Why don't you come back here?' but
my scholarly work has made this impossible and even if it had been possible, my health would not permit me to travel. The attacks of the stone are
now considerably less frequent, though much more dangerous, so that it is   35
not so much a matter of being ill as of facing death again and again. In
Germany the stoves are lit all the year round, June and July scarcely except-
ed: it is a choice between putting up with them, although their odour
almost chokes me, or enduring the heat of June or July or even August. I
have been thinking longingly of Italy because of the large number of doctors   40
and druggists to be found there, but my health has not allowed me to
return. And yet the situation here is now so bad that I have no choice but
to move somewhere else.

You know how deeply I am hated by certain theologians in your
monasteries, whose ringleader is the Carmelite Egmondanus.[4] Adrian[5]   45
silenced him by a special decree, but he had difficulty in holding his
tongue. After Adrian's death he made up for his silence by a torrent of
abuse. If things turn out for Luther as those people would wish, no one will
be able to tolerate them in their hour of victory. If the emperor were here,
there would be nothing to fear; but as it is, I don't know what protection   50
can be expected from the court, especially for someone like myself, who is
not a practised courtier. If only our distinguished prelate were as obliging
with his help as he is lavish with his praise![6] As for the illustrious count
of Hoogstraten,[7] I have never been very close to him. And it appears that
he has a wife who pushes piety to the point of superstition. Such people are   55
an easy prey to sanctimonious hypocrites. I am told that the bishop of Liège

* * * * *

4 Nicolaas Baechem of Egmond, O Carm; on this conservative theologian, one
  of Erasmus' harshest critics at Louvain, cf Epp 878:15n, 1254 n6, and Rummel
  I 135–43.
5 Pope Adrian VI, himself a former professor of theology at Louvain, ordered
  Egmondanus to stop his attacks on Erasmus (cf Allen Ep 1359:2n), but this
  prohibition lapsed upon Adrian's death in 1523.
6 Jean de Carondelet, archbishop of Palermo, one of the closest advisers to
  Margaret of Austria, governor of the Netherlands, was generally a reliable
  supporter of Erasmus' claim to his pension, though Ep 1434 suggests that both
  he and Margaret were pressing Erasmus to move back to Brabant as a condition of payment. In January 1523 Erasmus had dedicated to him the edition of
  the works of St Hilary of Poitiers (Basel: Froben, February 1523). Cf Epp 803,
  1334.
7 For the suspicion that this adviser to Margaret of Austria had turned against
  Erasmus, cf Ep 1545; for his career, Ep 1038 n7.

is a doubtful ally,[8] the problem being Aleandro.[9] He is a flatterer to one's face, but behind one's back, I hear, he is quite a different person. He has a brother in Leiden more deadly than himself since he knows how to disguise his feelings, which is something Aleandro cannot do.[10]

I am sending this letter by a young man called Frans van der Dilft,

60

* * * * *

8 See Ep 738 introduction. Erasmus' doubts about his support also appear in Epp 1467, 1545, 1549, and 1585. The real source of Erasmus' suspicions was that his rapprochement with the Roman curia when he was made cardinal in 1521 brought him into closer touch with Aleandro, who had served him as secretary from 1514 to 1516.

9 For Erasmus' earlier friendly relations with him, see Ep 256 introduction. But as Aleandro rose in curial service from 1517 and began dealing with the Lutheran crisis as papal legate from 1520, Erasmus not only became concerned about his harsh, repressive stance but became increasingly (and correctly) convinced that despite his outward show of friendship, Aleandro regarded him as a supporter of Luther. In fact from about 1520, after the publication of Erasmus' indiscreet letter of 30 May 1519 to Martin Luther (Ep 980), Aleandro seems to have concluded that Erasmus was dangerous and began denouncing him in private to friends. Erasmus soon learned of this; and although they behaved as friends when they met by chance at Louvain in 1521, and Aleandro even proved helpful by using his influence to silence open attacks on Erasmus, the undercurrent of hostility grew. In a letter of 1524 (Ep 1482) Erasmus directly accused him of having written to the bishop of Liège from Rome to bring to that bishop's attention Erasmus' indiscreet remark that the bishop sympathized with Luther (cf Ep 980). Indeed, Erasmus had already published such a charge against Aleandro in his treatise against Hutten, *Spongia* (1523): ASD IX-1 148–52 / LB X 1645A–1646D. In 1524 Aleandro composed (but never published) a work attacking Erasmus as a heretic, commonly known as the *Racha* and privately circulated at the papal curia. Eugenio Massa, 'Intorno ad Erasmo: Una polemica che si credeva perduta,' in Charles Henderson, jr (ed) *Classical, Mediaeval, and Renaissance Studies in Honor of Berthold Louis Ullman* (Rome 1964) II 435–54 describes a manuscript containing part of this tract, though he was inclined to attribute it to the former general of the Augustinian order, Cardinal Egidio Antonini of Viterbo; cf Chris L. Heesakkers 'Erasmus's Suspicions of Aleander as the Instigator of Alberto Pio' in *Acta conventus neo-Latini Torontonensis: Proceedings of the Seventh International Congress of Neo-Latin Studies, Toronto ... 1988,* ed Alexander Dalzell, Charles Fantazzi, and Richard J. Schoeck (Binghamton, NY 1991), 371–83. But Rummel II 108–13 concludes that Erasmus was probably right about Aleandro's authorship. Erasmus heard rumours of this tract and eventually received a copy from a friend (cf Allen Ep 2443:289–97). When Alberto Pio, prince of Carpi, openly attacked Erasmus (cf Ep 1634), he initially thought that Aleandro was the source of that attack.

10 Cf Ep 1549 n4.

who is a canon at Antwerp.[11] He is returning here, so you can safely write anything you wish. I don't know what hope there is of my annuity. I have put the matter in the hands of the archbishop of Palermo and of Cranevelt,[12] whose kindliness is unmatched among our people. I don't want to trouble you with my affairs, but if an opportunity arises, I know you will lend your support to the present negotiations. Ferdinand writes to me frequently in the most affectionate terms.[13] He has now written to the illustrious Lady Margaret, asking her to silence the Carmelite who continues his slanderous attacks upon me by name; that fellow will stop at nothing. When Frans returns, I shall decide what to do after I have seen your letter. Farewell.

Basel, the feast of Matthew the Apostle, 1525

1554 / To Jean Lalemand   Basel, 24 February 1525

Jean Lalemand (d 1560), a native of the Franche-Comté, was secretary to Charles V from 1519 and until he fell from favour in 1528 was extremely influential at court. At this time he was with the emperor in Spain and thus was well placed to help Erasmus both with his pension and with his desire for a firm order fom the emperor requiring the Louvain critics to stop their attacks. The letter remained unpublished (Munich MS Heine XI) until the appearance of Allen VI in 1926.

Cordial greetings, most honoured sir. A year ago I sent you my good wishes in a letter which I wrote on the prompting of Beat Arnold,[1] who will deliver this. Whether that letter ever reached you I have not yet been able to find out for certain. So many mountains and plains and seas separate us that you seem to live in a different world! Arnold, who never tires of speaking about your kindness and generosity, has again urged me to write to you. I wage a perpetual war against the stone, which keeps up such a fierce assault upon

* * * * *

11 On this young man, whom Erasmus frequently used as a courier, see Ep 1663 introduction.
12 On Frans van Cranevelt, cf Ep 1145 introduction and Ep 1546.
13 Archduke Ferdinand of Hapsburg, brother of Charles V. His letters included the one mentioned here, addressed to his aunt, Margaret of Austria, urging her to silence the attacks on Erasmus by the Carmelite theologian Nicolaas Baechem, known as Egmondanus.

1554
1 Cf Ep 399:7n.

this poor fragile frame of mine that those who have to face death only once seem to me the most fortunate of men. But in all things we must give thanks to the Lord, who knows what is best for each of us and gives us the strength   10
we need to endure even a thousand deaths.

My annuity has been paid from the imperial purse only once.[2] Now it is more than three years overdue. Some time ago the emperor wrote to authorize a special payment to be made, but so far I have received nothing but kind words. Now Ferdinand has written on the same subject to his   15
aunt;[3] he is a frequent, and indeed a most friendly, correspondent. I have refused all offers from the king of France – and his offers were most generous and assured. I decided to be content with the emperor's bounty – if only I could have it to enjoy. I hope you will rekindle his interest in me by some words of commendation.   20

So far I have been tethered to this place by various compelling circumstances, but mainly by the demands of my work and by my health, which on the one or two occasions when I ventured abroad drove me back to the nest. Now, whether I like it or not, I shall have to crawl out and go somewhere else, for the duke of Württemberg is openly preparing for war, and   25
I am afraid that the contagion will spread.[4] Moreover I live within a cluster of regions where the Lutheran faction is especially influential, Zürich being on one side and Strasbourg on the other. Before I wrote a word against Luther, the most violent attacks were being made upon me; now that I have published my *De libero arbitrio* and my *De modo orandi*, it is not safe for me   30
to stay here any longer. I am thinking of moving to Brabant, if my pension will be paid, which now accounts for more than half my income. There are

* * * * *

2 This pension had last been paid in the summer of 1522 (Epp 1273 n4, 1302:29). Any reader of this or the two preceding volumes will soon learn that Erasmus spent much time and effort seeking support for a resumption of payment, which had been stopped on the excuse that he was living in Basel rather than in the Netherlands. For the history of this pension issue, see Ep 1380 introduction.
3 Cf Ep 1553:68–70.
4 Erasmus had received a report on these preparations in a letter of 26 November 1524 from Johann von Botzheim (Ep 1519:100–3). Duke Ulrich had been driven out of Württemberg in 1519 by the Swabian League, and the Hapsburgs had taken control of the territory. But from his county of Montbéliard he continually schemed to regain his duchy. An invasion attempt of February 1526 failed, and not until 1534, with the aid of Philip of Hesse and financial support from Francis I, did he succeed. Cf Hajo Holborn *History of Modern Germany* I (New York 1959) 51, 218.

still at Louvain two monastic theologians, the Carmelite Egmondanus[5] and
the Dominican Vincentius of Alkmaar[6] who never cease their impudent and
lying attacks upon me by name, both in public and in private. Pope Adrian   35
silenced them, but after his death the frogs returned to their croaking.
People like this could be muzzled once and for all by a word or two from
the emperor to the university;[7] for these rabble-rousers are few in number
and they are derided and hated by everyone. They are now moving heaven
and earth to destroy the Collegium Trilingue, which is the crowning glory   40
of our dominion.[8] I derive no profit from it personally, but it has immense
value both for the prince and for the state. It is a sort of Trojan horse, from
which men leap forth to serve the imperial court – fine secretaries, eloquent
councillors, diplomats with the gift of words, leaders who know how to act
firmly and speak brilliantly, and citizens who are true human beings. For   45
men who are ignorant of letters (which are not called the humanities for
nothing) scarcely deserve the name of men.

I wanted you to know these things so that, if ever the occasion arises,
you will be better equipped to plead my cause before the emperor and the
cause of literature in general. Farewell.   50

Basel, the feast of the Apostle Matthew 1525

Erasmus of Rotterdam by my own hand, in haste

To the honourable Doctor Jean Lalemand, distinguished member of the
Imperial staff. In Spain

55

1555 / To Jacopo Sadoleto   Basel, 25 February 1525

This letter thanks Sadoleto for his successful intervention, in response to pleas
from Erasmus, Bonifacius Amerbach, and others, on behalf of Johann von

* * * * *

5 See Epp 878:15n and 1254 n6 for his life; cf Ep 1553 n4.
6 On Vincentius Theoderici of Beverwijk, another of Erasmus' most persistent
   foes at Louvain, see Ep 1196 and its introduction.
7 In other words, Erasmus wanted from the emperor a flat order to desist from
   the attacks on Erasmus. In fact the emperor did intervene and demanded an
   end to the attacks (cf Epp 1643, 1690), but the monks and theologians persisted; and in 1527 the imperial chancellor had to make (with similarly limited
   success) another attempt to impose silence: Ep 1784A.
8 This famous humanist institute, founded by a legacy from Erasmus' friend
   Jérôme de Busleyden (d 1517) of which Erasmus was one of the trustees, was
   a recurrent concern in this correspondence. As in this case, Erasmus repeatedly
   claimed that the attacks on him were really intended to destroy or weaken the
   college and the whole humanist program of study. See de Vocht CTL.

Botzheim, canon of Constance, who had been cited to appear at Rome on charges of supporting Luther. Although Botzheim did at first sympathize with Luther, like Erasmus he refused to break with Rome and eventually joined the rest of the Constance cathedral chapter in going into exile when the Reformation triumphed in Constance in 1527. Ep 1518 introduction summarizes the whole sordid story of Botzheim's prosecution. In a word, the real cause seems to have been the resentment of Bishop Hugo von Hohenlandenberg because Botzheim had privately admonished the bishop to break off his notorious and adulterous involvement with a woman of Constance. On Sadoleto, bishop of Carpentras and a distinguished humanist who at this time was secretary to Pope Clement VII, cf Ep 1511 introduction, to which this letter is a reply. Erasmus published it in his *Opus epistolarum* of 1529, but Allen also had available two original manuscripts in the Vatican Library (MSS Reg Lat 2023 ff 150, 153, 154).

Cordial greetings. I cannot imagine anyone so depressed, reverend bishop, as not to be cheered by your kind and affectionate letter. It enabled me to see as clearly as in a mirror the full reflection of your honest character, which I had previously known only in hazy outline from hints which I had pieced together and from the enthusiasm of your many admirers. For all   5 this I am as much indebted to Bonifacius as you modestly profess yourself to be.[1] I could only wish I had something to offer in return for the favour you have shown me. Certainly you have every reason to be fond of Bonifacius, for there is no one in Germany who surpasses him in integrity and honour. He would rise to a position of great authority if he did not find   10 princely courts and political office so uncongenial; and yet he may some day be dragged into public life whether he likes it or not, for Plato, who believes that only a philosopher should hold the reins of state, says that no one is fit for office except one who assumes it reluctantly and under protest.[2]

    I recognize how good the pope is to me and I shall more than repay   15 his kindness as soon as I escape from here to some safe place, as I am now planning to do. My heart is torn by the present conflicts among our rulers, which prevent me from enjoying the friendship of the pope and the emper-

   * * * * *

1555
1 Bonifacius Amerbach, youngest child of the famous Basel printer and recent recipient of a doctorate of laws from Avignon, had probably been the inspiration for Erasmus' intervention with Sadoleto in behalf of Johann von Botzheim. Cf Ep 408 introduction. His own correspondence with Sadoleto and Botzheim in this matter appears in AK II Epp 970, 991, 992.
2 *Republic* 7.519B–520A.

or and the king of France. After such fierce storms Christ will surely bring
us some peace and calm.   20

The secret of that leisure on which you congratulate me is a mind
which despises honours and is content with little. You are kind enough to
reject the word 'failure' as applied to me. How future generations will think
of me or whether they will think of me at all is a matter which I leave to
the powers above. It is evident that my poor body is failing; yet it could   25
serve my mind for some years to come if it were not constantly under
attack from the stone, a malady so painful that it makes even the ultimate
terror of death seem preferable. If it is hard to die once, how much harder
it is to die again and again and be nursed back to life only to endure fresh
torments. To face such troubles I need a strong and unshakeable philos-   30
ophy. Let us give thanks to the Lord in all things, for he so moderates our
human miseries that they can be borne and turned to blessing for the
sufferer.

It is only right that I should add my thanks for the help you gave
Botzheim,[3] for I felt that in some way I too was on trial in that case, not   35
just because he was my friend but because I had dedicated to him a catalogue of all my writings. This is something I would never have done had
there been the faintest odour of suspicion that he supported the party which
the pope condemns. Two years ago[4] I spent a whole month as his guest
and during all that time we talked to one another in the most open fashion.   40
Since then he has come to see me often in Basel. Being a straightforward
sort of person, entirely innocent of any kind of deceit, he never concealed
from me any of his secret thoughts; yet not a word escaped his lips to
support the accusation which some are now bringing against him. It is
obvious that he was intended by nature for the service of the Muses and the   45
Graces. I doubt if he has ever given a thought to any of Luther's doctrines
nor has there ever been any gossip of that kind about him. Some may
perhaps have had their suspicions, but such people were hardly unbiased.
He has some friends of long standing whom I regard as admirable in every
way except that they lean towards Luther's point of view: with these he has   50
kept up his old association without, however, involving himself in their
campaigns. Sometimes he has welcomed Lutherans to his home, but more
often it has been Luther's bitter enemies whom he has entertained. As

* * * * *

3 See introduction to this letter. On Botzheim cf Allen Ep 1519 introduction and
  AK II Ep 991 introduction.
4 Actually in September 1522, when Erasmus spent about three weeks as Botzheim's guest at Constance. Cf Ep 1316 introduction.

things now stand in Germany, it is impossible to avoid an occasional intimacy with persons of this sort. In my own case by similar acts of courtesy   55
I have rescued not a few from that benighted sect. Now people are writing
to me from every part of the world to tell me that my *De libero arbitrio* has
won them over and that they no longer accept what Luther teaches on this
point.

To speak frankly, neither Botzheim's bishop[5] nor his chapter is very   60
sympathetic to him. His bishop is hostile for the very reason which ought
to make Botzheim more precious in his eyes – unless nature has so arranged
it that even among good and powerful men emotion sometimes gets the
better of reason. It is generally true of the cathedral chapters in Germany
that men who hunt and feast and devote their energies to making money   65
are better regarded than those who have dedicated their lives to the cause
of learning.

I could name the persons responsible for this intrigue, but it would be
a long story and there is nothing to be gained by pointing the finger at
someone now that the pope's sense of fairness and your own prompt   70
actions have cleared our friend of a false and dangerous charge. If I were
convinced that someone was a member of some perverse sect, I would not
utter a word to help him. This will always be my attitude as it has been my
attitude in the past. But if anyone considers the state of things today,
especially in Germany, he will realize that it is better to try to win over   75
those who may have strayed a little from the proper path than to alienate
them when the infection they have caught is so slight that it can easily be
cured. Moreover, given our human frailty, I think we need to be on our
guard that, while pretending to support religion and defend the faith, we
do not cause innocent men to suffer, and that those who wish someone   80
mischief or who covet another man's wealth do not employ the alluring
pretext of the public interest to cloak their own sinful and selfish ends.

Bonifacius has returned to us from Avignon, resplendent with the rank
of doctor.[6] The council here has offered him a public chair in law and he
has accepted it. I understand he plans to write you himself to express his   85
thanks. Before I seal this letter, here is a little extra to amuse you. My
friends frequently tell me that the name 'Jacobus' is not very lucky for me
since three Jacobi have published books which are wildly insulting. First

* * * * *

5 See introduction above and Ep 1519 introduction.
6 Amerbach's doctorate had been conferred at Avignon on 4 February. He soon
  returned to Basel and taught law in the local university, though he did not
  officially assume the chair of Roman law until 1530.

there is Jacobus Faber Stapulensis[7] – though in his case, since he acknowledges he was wrong, our friendship has never been interrupted, and cer-   90
tainly he has not renewed the fight. Then came Jacobus Latomus[8] and after
him Jacobus Stunica,[9] a man with a natural talent for this sort of scandalous abuse. But I reckon that my good fortune in knowing Jacobus Sadoletus
outweighs all the misfortunes I might suffer, even if ten such Jacobi should
take up their pens against me.   95

I bid your Lordship farewell.

Basel, 25 February 1525

I subscribe myself, in my own hand, your Lordship's most obedient
servant, Erasmus of Rotterdam

To the reverend father in Christ, Jacopo Sadoleto, lord bishop of   100
Carpentras and secretary to our most Holy Father

1556 / To Jan Sucket   [Basel, February] 1525

The addressee of this puzzling letter was a man who had died in 1522 and
whose death had been reported to Erasmus (Ep 1351). Apparently Erasmus
had forgotten. Sucket had been a member of the Grand Council of the Netherlands at Mechelen and so would have been a useful protector of the Collegium
Trilingue if he had been alive. Antoon Sucket, the brother whose death is
lamented here, had died on 31 August 1524 and had been a patron of Erasmus, a member of the privy council, and a knight of the Golden Fleece. On his
part in the founding of the Collegium Trilingue, cf Ep 1331 n11, and De Vocht
CTL I 55–9. Erasmus published the letter in *Opus epistolarum*.

ERASMUS OF ROTTERDAM TO JAN SUCKET, GREETING

Distinguished sir, your brother Antoon Sucket has been taken from us, the
most generous of my patrons and an indomitable champion of the humanities. I have many reasons to feel his death most keenly, but my sorrow is
much easier to bear because I am aware of your good nature and have   5
every confidence that you will take your brother's place. I should be constantly urging you to do this if I were not convinced that you had already
assumed that responsibility without my asking you.

* * * * *

7 On Jacques Lefèvre d'Etaples, one of the leading French humanists, see Ep 315
   introduction. For his controversy with Erasmus, which left a permanent residue of diffidence despite their reconciliation, cf Ep 597:37n, 44n.
8 Cf Ep 934:4n; de Vocht CTL I 324–34, 338–48; and Rummel I 66–93, II vii, 7–14.
9 Cf Ep 1128 n2 and Rummel I 145–77, II vii.

It appears that several people at Louvain have formed a conspiracy to destroy Busleyden's college,[1] which is the special glory of our land and   10
indeed of the whole of the emperor's dominion. They are devising some remarkable schemes to bring about its ruin, though the benefits, both public and private, which it will confer on all will be enormous; it will provide the imperial court with trained secretaries, judicious councillors, eloquent ambassadors, nobles whose claim to distinction does not rest on pedigree   15
alone, and leaders who, if they chose, could reply to foreign envoys without the help of an interpreter; and finally it will lend a new splendour and dignity not just to the training needed for these important responsibilities but to all the liberal arts in general.

If such a college had not been established, the emperor would have   20
had to found it at his own expense as a matter of the greatest urgency. And now some men are trying to destroy a splendid institution bequeathed to us by another's generosity. Some have been led to do this by sheer stupidity, some by greed and some by spite, and others are the slaves of someone else's will. So I beg and implore you to use your authority and influence at   25
the court, where you have rightly earned for yourself a strong position, and to complete what your brother so happily began, so that the college may enjoy the enthusiastic support of all the leading figures of the court. Its revenues are still slender, scarcely enough to support the professors. But they will be increased through the generosity of the powerful and wealthy   30
if you and men like you give the project your support.

But, distinguished sir, I am counting on you not just for this, but I confidently expect that you will be a second Antoon Sucket to me in all respects. I can think of no one more upright in character than he was, more warm-hearted towards his friends, more willing to serve, more dependable   35
in his counsel, more staunch in a just cause, or more vigorous in his opposition to injustice and to every kind of treachery and deceit. He was deeply religious without being credulous, a man of clear and balanced judgment, independent of the crowd, and possessed of remarkable skill in the conduct of affairs. Who knows what talent and distinction the imperial court has lost   40

* * * * *

1556
1 On hostility to the new Collegium Trilingue at Louvain, see De Vocht CTL I
  324–34, 418–532; II 249–81. The most persistent 'conspirators' were the theologians Jacobus Latomus, Nicolaas Baechem, O Carm, known as Egmondanus, and Vincentius Theoderici (Dierckx) OP. These attacks were often explicitly directed against Erasmus, but he insisted that the real target was the new college and the program of trilingual humanism which it embodied.

in the death of this one man? And what remarkable dedication he showed
to the education of his family, so that from their earliest years they might
be trained in the most honourable fields of learning. He had several children, and they had inherited their father's abilities to a remarkable degree.
The eldest he had marked out for theology, the second for law, and the   45
third, while still a child, was destined for the study of the humanities. Here
too you will have to take your brother's place.

   At a convenient moment please give my greetings to your neighbour,
my old friend Johann the gunsmith,[2] with whom I once exchanged
weapons as a token of friendship, though the exchange was no more apt   50
than that between Glaucus and Diomedes.[3] I gave him my *Enchiridion*[4] –
I am sure you are familiar with the work since it has been circulating for
some time now in every quarter of the globe, in Latin, French, German,
Spanish, or Italian. In return he gave me a dagger, for which I have found
no more use than he has for my book! Farewell.   55

   1525

1557 / From Caspar Ursinus Velius   Vienna, 12 March 1525

On Velius' earlier career, see Ep 548:5n, 6n. He had taught Greek at Vienna
from about 1517 to 1521, went to Basel in November 1521 to meet Erasmus,
and after periods at Freiburg im Breisgau and Stuttgart, had gone to Rome,
returning in 1524 to take the chair of rhetoric at Vienna. Erasmus assumed (Ep
1514) that this appointment provided a large salary, a notion which the present
letter corrects. Subsequently he became historiographer to King Ferdinand and
from 1532 tutor to the king's children. This letter was first published in the
Appendix to LB, but Allen also discovered the original manuscript at Wrocław
(MS Rehd 254.163).

* * * * *

2 Johann Poppenruyter of Nürnberg, later a citizen of Mechelen and a neighbour
  of Jan Sucket there, had become an internationally famous gunsmith. In *Apologia contra Latomi dialogum* (LB IX 85D–E) Erasmus mentioned him as representative of his trade. For Otto Schottenloher's demonstration that Poppenruyter
  was the man for whom in 1501 Erasmus wrote his *Enchiridion militis Christiani*,
  see Ep 164 introduction. The reference to the *Enchiridion* in line 51 of the
  present letter is one of Schottenloher's principal pieces of evidence.
3 Two heroes in the *Iliad* (6.119–236), who declined to fight because of old family
  ties. They exchanged armour as a token of friendship, but Glaucus' armour
  was made of gold while that of Diomedes was only of bronze.
4 See introduction to this letter. There is a play on words here: the Greek word
  enchiridion means both 'handbook' and 'dagger.'

Greeting. When you wrote that you first heard of my unfortunate return to Germany[1] from a letter of Landavus',[2] I realized that the one which I sent you before leaving Rome had gone astray. Everybody thinks that I have struck it rich when in fact I have scarcely ever in my life been closer to destitution. High-sounding but empty promises and, worse still, the threat   5
of plague drove me from Rome and brought me back here from the very heart of Italy. There is no prospect of fame and fortune from this tiresome profession of teaching. You think you have 'left the band and turned gladiator,'[3] but I feel I have been demoted from the harp to the flute;[4] and please don't call this disgusting sweatshop 'an elegant sphere of oper-   10
ations.'[5]

Moreover I have neither sufficient learning nor a keen enough mind to be able to help the failing cause of letters, especially against those ferocious Evangelicals who claim such a monopoly of the heavenly Spirit that we may as well be dead. My friends think, and I share their opinion, that   15
I have not been fairly treated by certain influential persons who are fitter company for a vegetable than for a bear![6] And to speak frankly (as I always

* * * * *

1557
1 It is not quite clear whether he calls his return unfortunate (Latin 'parum foelici reditu') because he regretted leaving Rome or because of the disappointment of his financial expectations by the position in Vienna to which he returned; probably the latter. In the sixteenth century (indeed, until the nineteenth century), Vienna or any place in Austria would have seemed an integral part of Germany.
2 Jakob Ziegler of Landau; cf Ep 1260; also CTC IV 375–8. A noted astronomer and geographer, he lived in Italy from about 1521 to 1531 and conducted what must have been an extensive correspondence with Erasmus, of which only two letters survive.
3 Ursinus quotes back to Erasmus the phrase in Erasmus' letter of 14 November 1524 (Ep 1514) in which he describes his entry into active theological combat with publication of De libero arbitrio.
4 In antiquity, flute players held lower status than harpists and were sometimes said to be musicians who could not learn the harp (Cicero Pro Murena 29). Because of its association with revelry (see Plato Theaetetus 173D5) and ecstatic dancing (Proclus In Alc. 198.5), the flute was generally distrusted by Greek philosophers. Plato excluded it from his ideal republic (Republic 339D), and the Pythagoreans condemned it as vulgar (Iamblichus Vita Pythagorae 111).
5 Despite this complaint about the University of Vienna, Ursinus Velius had repeatedly served as a teacher there, beginning in 1515. In Ep 1514, Erasmus refers to that university as 'an elegant sphere of operations,' a label that Ursinus here rejects.
6 Ursinus is punning on his own name: the Latin for 'bear' is ursa.

do), I have been worried by the rumblings of our lord Hephaestus.[7] So I have made up my mind to move from here. I have received a generous offer from Hungary,[8] and now I hear that the Silesians are coming to their senses again.[9] In either place I could lead a pleasant and agreeable life.   20

My friend, the right reverend the bishop of Olomouc,[10] thinks that I have played him false because I told him several times, both in person and by letter, that you were promising him a special volume with a dedication to himself and that the book was about to appear.[11] I was quite sure that   25 you would make good your promise conscientiously and without delay, but apparently this was the furthest thing from your thoughts. The valuable gift which I was to send on to Beatus[12] took a long time to reach me because of the inefficiency of the merchants. I shall forward it as soon as I find someone honest and reliable to whom it can safely be entrusted. It is en-   30 closed in a rather large wooden box. From the appearance of the case I imagine it is a handsome cup. Please give Beatus this news when you write so that he won't think I was responsible for his not receiving the gift along with the letter. I was slow to discover that it had arrived.

You may be amused to know that I am giving public classes to tolerab-   35 ly good audiences on Cicero's *Orator*, though I have no facility with words

* * * * *

7 The context does not make it clear whether the god of fire (and armaments) here mentioned is the Emperor Charles v or his brother Archduke (later King) Ferdinand; but since Charles spent most of this decade in Spain, the reference is probably to Ferdinand. The phrase is of Homeric origin (*Iliad* 18.137) and is quoted in Greek. This may refer to preparations for war against the Turks; in fact, after Ursinus became royal historiographer in 1527, he accompanied Ferdinand on campaigns against the Turks.
8 For this offer, cf Ep 1662.
9 Ursinus was himself a Silesian by birth and had previously benefited from the patronage of Johannes Thurzo, bishop of Wrocław (d 1520). He was still in touch with that patron's brother, Stanislaus Thurzo, bishop of Olomouc, and perhaps had hopes of preferment in his homeland.
10 On Stanislaus Thurzo, see Ep 1242 introduction.
11 In this case, Ursinus and his patron were too impatient. Erasmus was about to publish his edition of Pliny's *Naturalis historia* (Basel: Froben, March 1525), with a dedication to Bishop Stanislaus dated 8 February 1525 (cf Ep 1544).
12 Bishop Stanislaus sent this gilt cup to Beatus Rhenanus to acknowledge the dedication of Beatus' edition of *Auctores historiae ecclesiasticae* (Basel: Froben 1523). Cf BRE 234. Beatus (Ep 327 introduction) spent most of the period 1511–26 in Basel and became a major member of the scholarly team that assisted the publisher Johannes Froben in the publication of humanistic works and also a close friend of Erasmus. In 1526 he moved permanently to his home town, Sélestat in Alsace, but remained in close touch with Erasmus.

myself. I am giving private lessons on Homer's *Iliad* – imagine a Greek poem expounded by a barbarian! Farewell.

Vienna, 12 March 1525

1558 / To Willibald Pirckheimer   Basel, 14 March 1525

This letter is both the dedication of Erasmus' edition of the Greek text of St John Chrysostom's *De sacerdotio* (Basel: Froben, May 1525) to his friend, the eminent Nürnberg humanist, and a reply to Ep 1480 (there had been three earlier replies, two of which [Epp 1536, 1543] were very brief and one of which seems to have been lost in transit). On Pirckheimer see Ep 318 introduction. Not until line 185 does he turn from personal news, such as the exchange of gifts and discussion of the ill health and remedies which both ageing humanists enjoyed, to the topic in hand, a discussion of the work of Chrysostom. St John Chrysostom (c 347–407), patriarch of Constantinople, was the author of numerous homilies, treatises, and letters, and was particularly important as a preacher and a practical interpreter of Scripture. *De sacerdotio* was one of his major works. Erasmus edited and translated several works by him and was eager to see a complete edition of the Greek text, but his dream of a full edition was not fulfilled until the next century with the edition in eight folio volumes by Sir Henry Savile (Eton 1610–12).

DESIDERIUS ERASMUS OF ROTTERDAM TO THE HONOURABLE
WILLIBALD PIRCKHEIMER, GREETING

Dear Willibald, glory of our age, from every side our ears are assaulted with talk of 'faith,' yet creditors complain that those who owe them money are no more trustworthy than they ever were. For myself, I see little evidence of good faith, at least in the way letters are carried back and forth. Everything is examined, intercepted, and unsealed, just as one would expect in time of war. You know the old joke about the crooked servant from whom nothing was sealed or locked away![1] The story fits this age of ours perfectly. I have often sent my letters with couriers who solemnly swore that they would deliver whatever they were given without fail. When they had repeated these assurances several times, I gave them a few coins to seal the bargain. But I see from your letter that I was duped. So this time I have decided to send you a thousand copies in the hope that at least one will get through to you.

* * * * *

1558
1 Cicero *De oratore* 2.248; cf *Adagia* II iv 99.

The handsome ring which you wanted me to have as a keepsake   20
reached me safely.[2] I know that precious stones are valued because they are
thought to give protection in a fall. It is also believed that if the fall is
severe enough to cause death, the disaster is transferred to the stone and
this is the reason why it can be seen to be broken after the accident. Once
in Britain I fell with my horse down a very steep bank. There was no harm   25
done either to me or to the horse and yet the ring which I was wearing
remained intact. It was a gift from Alexander, archbishop of St Andrews,
whose name, I think, is known to you from my writings.[3] When I was
leaving him at Siena, he pulled the ring from his finger and handed it to me
and said: 'Take this as a pledge of the friendship between us which will   30
never die.' I kept my vow, even after he had passed away, by celebrating
the memory of my friend in my works. There is no aspect of our lives into
which a superstitious belief in magic has not penetrated. If there really were
some special power in precious stones, what I would want most of all these
days would be a ring with an effective remedy for the stinging insults of   35
malicious slanderers.[4] As for the danger of falling, I shall follow your
advice and believe the story rather than put the matter to the test!

You are right that the portraits are not of the highest quality – I have
received one in bronze and a second on canvas – but they do give a reasonably faithful likeness of your good self.[5] Alexander the Great forbade any-   40
one but Apelles to paint him. You are lucky to have your own Apelles,
Albrecht Dürer,[6] who is not only recognized as pre-eminent in his own art,
but is no less admired for his uncommon good sense. I wish you had been
as lucky in finding a Lysippus[7] for the bronze work. The medallion hangs
on the right-hand wall of my bedroom and the painting on the left. Whether   45
I write or walk about, Willibald is always before my eyes – so much so that,

* * * * *

2 Cf Ep 1480:116–20, Epp 1536:1–2, 1543:6.
3 At Siena in 1509, Erasmus was tutor to Alexander Stewart, son of James IV of
  Scotland and archbishop of St Andrews. He cherished the ring given him by
  his pupil when they parted. Cf Ep 604:4n.
4 A reminiscence of Pirckheimer's reference to Aristophanes in Ep 1480:116.
  Erasmus uses the Greek word ($\delta\hat\eta\gamma\mu\alpha$ 'bite,' 'sting'). For the ineffectiveness of
  charms against the stings (or stinging insults) of slanderers, cf Aristophanes
  Plutus 883–4.
5 For earlier references to Pirckheimer's disappointment with his likenesses in
  paintings and medallions, see Ep 1480.
6 See Ep 1536 n2.
7 Fourth-century Greek sculptor from Sicyon. Like Apelles he was employed by
  Alexander the Great.

even if I wanted to forget you, I could not. But in fact there is nothing which I hold so firmly in my mind as the memory of my friends. Certainly I could never forget you, Willibald, even if there were no souvenirs, no portraits and no letters to keep my memory of you alive. And there is something else which pleases me greatly: when my friends come to visit me we often begin to talk about you because the portrait is there. If only the letters which we send one another arrived safely, would anything else be needed to bring you to me and me to you? You already have a medallion of Erasmus.[8] Speaking of Dürer, I should not object to being painted by so fine an artist, but I don't see how it could be managed. He once did a sketch of me at Brussels, but the work was interrupted when callers arrived from the court to pay their respects.[9] I know of course that for some time now I have been a sorry sight for any painter and each day it grows worse.

At this point, my dear Willibald, I should be offering you my thanks, but we are such close friends that I thought we could dispense with these ordinary courtesies. Then you are always so unfailingly generous to me that the arrival of some new kindness has no longer any novelty about it. You are obviously very concerned about my health since you have armed me with so many remedies against the stone. I had some difficulty in getting used to the oil of turpentine, but I take it now from time to time. I have not yet made use of Ricius' cure since it has been impossible to get the prescription because of a bad storm.[10] I did have something very like it, but more medical, that is to say less simple; though there is probably truth in the advice which I once received from some competent doctors, that diuretic drugs should not be administered except after the body has been purged so that they can clear away whatever remains of the old trouble; otherwise they will carry undigested food into the bowel. I am so well supplied with doctors' prescriptions that I could set up as a veritable Aesculapius for the treatment of this ailment. But my illness fights an insidious action against all cures by constantly changing itself: sometimes I imagine I am dealing with a different disease.

The pain is torture – I can hardly bear it when it plays the tyrant and

* * * * *

8 At Pirckheimer's request, Erasmus sent to Nürnberg the matrix of a medal made by Quinten Metsys in 1519 so that additional copies could be struck. Cf Allen Ep 1408 n17.
9 Cf Epp 1136, 1376 n2, 1536.
10 Paulus Ricius was an eminent physician, at this period physician to Archduke Ferdinand. See Ep 548:16n. On the success of his prescription for kidney stones, which Pirckheimer had sent to Erasmus (cf Ep 1536:19–20) cf Ep 1603:128.

moves, with its cruel escort, from the back through the abdomen into the region of the spleen, only to burst forth into the bladder, causing pain, injury, and distress wherever it goes; it is like some barbarous prince who would rather be feared than liked.[11] I used to have a remedy which never failed me until that last attack; it came on me without warning just before the beginning of February and was so severe that I began to hope for an end to my miseries and an entry into a more tranquil life. It is not that I am tired of this life, if it should please God for my soul to live on in the protection of my poor body, but like Paul I should like to be free and be with Christ.[12] I shall say nothing about the remedy until I tell you who was responsible for it. It was Thomas Linacre, chief physician to the king of England, an accomplished scholar in every branch of learning, whose thoroughness might almost be called obsessive.[13]

But more about its discoverer later; now let me tell you about the cure. The stone, which had developed from drinking beer, had lodged for six weeks in a crevice somewhere in the body. The pain was not then too severe, but a general feeling of anxiety and depression warned me that trouble was brewing. For I was not certain myself what the trouble was. It is part of my nature to be shy about asking for help and Linacre was not the sort of man who would concern himself with a case unless invited to do so. A friend advised me to address a few ingratiating words to him to catch his interest. I did so. No one could have been more attentive. A druggist was called. The medication was heated in my bedroom and applied in the presence of the doctor himself. Two applications were made, and shortly after I had had some sleep, I passed a stone as big as an almond. The Germans use hot baths for the same purpose; but Linacre's method is equally effective and much simpler. I wrap camomile and parsley in a linen cloth and heat them in a clean pan, approximately half full of water. When the cloth is hot, I squeeze out the liquid as quickly as I can and apply it to my side. If the heat is too great to bear, I wrap the bag containing the herbs in a dry cloth in such a way as to form handles which can be held at either end. If at first my side cannot stand direct contact with the cloth because of the heat, I hold it above the spot so that the heat can have its effect on the

* * * * *

11 A traditional characteristic of a tyrant; cf *oderint dum metuant* 'let them hate us provided that they fear us,' Accius fr 168.
12 Phil 1:23
13 Cf Ep 118:27n. Erasmus repeatedly expressed his high opinion of Linacre's medical skill and also closely followed his translations of Greek medical and scientific works, notably Galen.

body until the temperature becomes bearable. Shortly afterwards I settle down to sleep, after which, if the pain returns, I reheat the cloth and apply it a second time. I never followed this procedure twice without the stone descending into the region near the bladder where the pain is less intense. 115 But in my latest travail the method failed me for the first time.

I am sorry to hear that this same trouble has paid you a visit too. Doctors tell us that gout and stone are sisters. It was enough to have this wretched bond between us of being wedded to two sisters, but I resent my wife rushing off to you every now and then without at the same time desert- 120 ing me! There is truth of course in the proverb that shared misfortunes bring men together.[14] But I should not want our friendship to be based on this when you have so many fine qualities to endear you to me and indeed to all good men. Pliny mentions among the wonders of nature certain lakes, streams, and springs which turn to stone anything that is thrown into 125 them.[15] I think this wretched body of mine has a similar capacity to turn even the most fluid material into stone. It has this remarkable quality too, that, while women become sterile with advancing years, old age makes me more fertile. For I bring forth with ever increasing frequency, though with greater danger to myself; it is just like the birth of vipers.[16] 130

If a comparison of these two dreadful diseases would interest you, I should say that the agony of gout is less severe though its attacks are no less frequent. Moreover with gout one can generally find some relief in telling tales about it, for it is always accompanied by wit and humour. Then again hardly anyone dies of it. On the other hand, every attack of the stone 135 is not just an illness, but death itself or perhaps something worse than death. Nor does it come alone, but arrives like a tyrant with a large and cruel retinue. Besides the deadly pain there is also vomiting, which ruins the digestion and causes a frightful headache. The result, at least in my case, is that the risk from starvation is greater than from the stone. It is often 140 associated with pleurisy and with griping pains in the stomach and abdomen, so that, by treating one illness, you exacerbate another. So while gout is not an embarrassment in social life, the stone, like mental disorders, keeps

* * * * *

14 *Adagia* II i 71
15 *Naturalis historia* 2.226
16 Pliny *Naturalis historia* 10.170 reports that the eggs of the viper are hatched inside the body and are released one each day to a total of about twenty. The young held in the mother's body sometimes break their way out, causing great distress and even death to the mother. Here he refers to the pain of passing kidney stones.

everyone at a distance. It shares one advantage, however, with gout: it is not contagious; so, though it may not be particularly pleasant to associate with a sufferer, it is perfectly safe.

Nevertheless it is not impossible to find something good to say about this dreadful illness. If we believe what Plato said, philosophy is nothing but a rehearsal for death.[17] Now if philosophy is a noble enterprise, as indeed it is, then the glory of philosophy must be shared with the stone, since it is truly a rehearsal for death. For just as, in the opinion of the rhetoricians, there is no better way to learn how to speak than by speaking, so there is no quicker way to learn how to die than by facing death again and again. Moreover philosophers generally agree that human happiness depends in large measure on being free from the fear of death and they have tried by various ways to remove this fear. One tells us that it is useless to fear what cannot be avoided, another that only what is morally wrong need be feared and that death, being natural, is neither an evil nor something to be dreaded; another holds that since no part of a man survives the pyre, death brings an end to all those countless ills to which human life is heir, while yet another says that death is a crossing over to a better world and is therefore something which good men should even pray for. It does not take long for the stone to teach us this great lesson, and far from making us fear death, it even makes us long for it. But you will say, 'The stone is a cruel teacher.' I agree, but the lesson it teaches is the bravest we have to learn. Think how many blows a gladiator must bear before he learns not to fear the sword, and how much pain a boxer must endure before he steps boldly into the ring. But to box with death is the most manly sport of all.

But, dear Willibald, we may joke in the midst of our troubles, but I fear our laughter has a hollow ring to it.[18] I wish that you and your gout would get a divorce, for after all these years you have won the right to a long period of good health in compensation for all those excellent qualities of yours and for the great service you have done to scholarship and to the state. Let her take herself off to those who deserve this kind of misfortune. 'But to whom?' you will ask. My choice would fall on those Carians[19] who

* * * * *

17 *Phaedo* 67
18 Erasmus' Latin is *risus Sardonicus* (Sardonic laugh), an expression of doubtful origin which goes back to Homer (*Odyssey* 20.302). The ancients associated it with a Sardinian herb which was said to cause the face to be distorted as in bitter laughter. Cf *Adagia* III v 1.
19 A warlike people from the hilly country of south-western Asia Minor, often employed as mercenaries, especially by the Pharaohs. Here they stand for the Swiss and other mercenary soldiers of Erasmus' day.

forsake their wives and children and abandon the duties they owe to their
masters to fly off at the first scent of war and hire themselves out for a
paltry sum to kill or be killed. Don't you think these men deserve to be tied
to their homes by the fetters of gout? But with regard to the stone, it is too
awful a disease to be wished on anyone, even a cutthroat. This poor body   180
of mine, frail though it is, could stand up to the drudgery of study for some
years yet, if it were not being constantly battered by this frightful disease.
For, once the mind has surrendered itself totally to the heavenly will, it can
face death even a thousand times.

Up to now we have been discussing the most dismal of subjects; now   185
for something more pleasant. I am sending you six dialogues of John
Chrysostom in which he discusses with remarkable eloquence the proper
respect which is owed to a bishop and also how difficult it is for a bishop
to carry out the duties of his office properly.[20] You will ask, 'What has this
to do with me?' Well, several scholars have written to ask me to prepare for   190
students a specimen of Chrysostom's work in his own tongue. For they
recognize in his work (however good or bad the translations may be) a
wonderful felicity of style and from this they infer how much greater their
pleasure and profit would be if they could drink from that glorious stream
which flows from his truly golden lips[21] as from a rich and abundant   195
fountain. For the study of Greek has made such progress everywhere that
many men no longer need the help of a translator – even if we had a good
translation of Chrysostom. But not only is the translation incomplete, but
what we have is full of mistakes because of the carelessness of the copyists;
and it is not felicitous enough to do justice to the author's learned eloquence   200
and pious charm.

Here is an example of what I mean. The *Homilies* which he left us on
St Matthew begin like this:

Ἔδει μὲν ἡμᾶς μηδὲ δεῖσθαι τῆς ἀπὸ τῶν γραμμάτων βοηθείας, ἀλλ' οὕτω   205
βίον παρέχεσθαι καθαρόν, ὡς τοῦ Πνεύματος τὴν χάριν ἀντὶ βιβλίων γενέσθαι
ταῖς ἡμετέραις ψυχαῖς, καὶ καθάπερ ταῦτα διὰ μέλανος, οὕτω τὰς καρδίας τὰς
ἡμετέρας διὰ Πνεύματος ἐγγεγράφθαι. Ἐπειδὴ δὲ ταύτην διεκρουσάμεθα τὴν
χάριν, φέρε κἂν τὸν δεύτερον ἀσπασώμεθα πλοῦν, ἔπει ὅτι τὸ πρότερον
ἄμεινον <ἦν>, καὶ δι' ὧν εἶπε καὶ δι' ὧν ἐποίησεν, ἐδήλωσεν ὁ Θεός.   210

The general sense of these words is as follows: 'Indeed we ought not to

* * * * *

20 See introduction to this letter.
21 A pun on the name Chrysostom, which means 'with golden mouth'

require the help of books, but should lead so pure a life that the grace of
the Spirit itself would take the place of books within our souls; and just as
the precepts of God are written in books in ink, so they are inscribed on our   215
hearts through the Spirit. But since we have rejected this grace, then let us
try to follow the second-best course. For God has shown, both by word and
deed, that the former was the better course.' Now listen to the translation
of Anianus:[22] 'It had been right to have no need of the help of books, but
to lead a life so pure in all things that in place of them we would use the   220
grace of the Holy Spirit, and just as pages are inscribed with ink, so our
hearts would be inscribed by the Spirit. Because we excuse this grace from
ourselves, then we await even the second riches. But God is showing us,
both by his words and actions, that the first course had indeed been the
more sublime.'   225

I do not propose to argue about points of details – the addition of 'in
all things' for the sake of the rhythm of the sentence, the statement about
our using the Holy Spirit, where 'Holy' is his own insertion, the reference
to the inscribing of 'pages,' the translation of πρότερον [former] as 'first,'
and of ἄμεινον [better] as 'more sublime,' and the gratuitous interpolation   230
of 'indeed.' For it is not my purpose to bring a case against the translator,
to whom I am personally and properly very grateful, but I want to make
clear to students how much of Chrysostom one misses if one knows him
only in a Latin version. But there is a more significant error, the translation
of δεύτερον πλοῦν [second course] as 'second riches.' It was, I think, his   235
unfamiliarity with the old proverb[23] which led him astray; for he came to
the conclusion that the passage did not make sense and this led him to
suspect that πλοῦν [voyage] was a corruption for πλοῦτον [wealth]. But the
Greeks use the expression ἐξ οὐρίας [sailing before the wind] for the first,
or most desirable, course when a ship is moved forward by favourable   240
winds and currents. But when it is necessary to tack or use the oars, they
called this δεύτερον πλοῦν [the second best course]. See Eustathius[24] on

* * * * *

22 A younger contemporary and translator of Chrysostom, identified by Allen Ep
   1558:202n as the Pelagian deacon of Celeda in Campania (fl 415). Allen notes
   that in his Latin edition of Chrysostom published in 1530 (Basel: Froben) III 5,
   Erasmus gave a corrected text of Anianus' translation. The Latin text quoted
   in this letter does not make very good sense, and not all of these difficulties
   can be blamed on Anianus, since, as Erasmus admits, his text of Anianus was
   seriously corrupt. Although Erasmus criticizes Anianus for adding to the
   original, his own version is not free of this fault. The same passage is discussed in much the same terms in Adagia III iv 71.
23 Adagia III iv 71; cf I iv 18.
24 Twelfth-century compiler of a huge commentary on Homer. His commentary

book 2 of the *Odyssey*, citing Pausanias as his authority. There is also a clear allusion to the proverb in the *Orator ad Brutum* of M. Tullius.[25] He writes, 'But if a man lacks natural ability or a vigorous and brilliant intellect, or if   245
he has had an inadequate training in the liberal arts, he should hold none-theless to the best course he can. For so long as one aspires to gain the first place, there is no disgrace in ending up in the second or third.' As for the fact that the Latin manuscripts have *excusemus* [excuse] for *excussimus* [rejected], and *expectamus* [we await] for *expetamus* [let us seek], it would   250
surely be as unjust to accuse the translator of this as to excuse him for turning 'course' into 'riches.' Is this not a real case, as the proverb has it, of 'running aground in the harbour'?[26]

At this point someone may protest: 'Surely Anianus is not the only person who has run aground? Do you not often run aground yourself?' I   255
admit it. Ermolao Barbaro too made an equally spectacular error, and right at the very beginning of his work, when he was translating Themistius' commentary on Aristotle's *De anima*.[27] Far from refusing to make allow-ances for human error – and often I have to crave such indulgence for myself – I frankly admit how very much I owe even to fallible translators   260
like this. But beginners should be given a taste of something better, some-thing which will make them eager to drink, wherever they can, from the fountain-head itself rather than from the water-holes of the translators. For if there are so many errors at the very beginning of the work, what do you think we would find if we collated the rest? I could cite innumerable   265
examples of the same kind, but I would rather work for the advancement of learning than criticize men who have given all they have to this same end.

What made me more sympathetic to the present task was not just the fact that Chrysostom is a useful model for Christian eloquence, since he has   270
a unique talent for combining pious learning with an appealing style, but I also felt that he is particularly suitable for those who want to acquire a good command of Greek. He has Lucian's facility, clarity, charm, and

* * * * *

on *Odyssey* 2.434 cites the Greek geographer Pausanias, but vaguely and without a specific reference: *Eustathii commentarii ad Homeri Iliadem et Odysseam* ed Gottfried Stallbaum 7 vols (Leipzig 1825–30; repr 7 vols in 4 Hildesheim: G. Olms 1960).
25 Cicero *Orator* 1.4
26 *Adagia* I v 76; III iv 71
27 In the first and second editions of Themistius' commentary (Treviso 1481 and Venice 1499), one of which Erasmus must have used, Barbaro's translation has *quo* or *quomodo* in place of *quum*.

wealth of vocabulary, but many passages in Lucian, while they improve the
mind, corrupt the soul, whereas Chrysostom is as helpful in promoting   275
godliness of soul as eloquence of tongue. He is very fond of developing
commonplaces and might be thought to go too far except that in his hands
this fault (if fault it is) produces such happy results. I have chosen the
present volume in preference to many others because I am writing for the
young and this work is closer in style to the rhetoric of the classroom – it   280
reads like the work of a young man. Yet everyone will learn more from it
than from any other book about the dangers which beset those who seek the
office of a priest or the high rank of a bishop and do not reflect on the risks
involved in shouldering such a burden. I hope it will be read henceforth
with greater care and attention, now that it has been separated from the   285
mass of material with which it has been buried up to this point.

I hope also that this sample will prompt young scholars to call for the
rest of Chrysostom and encourage our leading men to respond generously
to the widespread and reasonable demands of students to have this valuable
resource made available to them. In the meantime here from Johann Froben   290
and myself is a first offering: he has covered the costs and I have given my
time in copying and collating the text. Just think how much money our
princes lavish on worthless trash and how much is wasted by our bishops
in the same way. If only they devoted a small portion of this amount to the
purposes I have just mentioned, they would acquire a solid reputation   295
among men and greatly commend themselves to God.

If you want to know why I decided to dedicate this first offering to
you, it was my hope that you would support this project, either by helping
yourself or by using your influence with others. You could help by retrans-
lating those of the author's works of which we have only poor translations,   300
so that Chrysostom, who in the Greek text is clearly 'golden-voiced,' would
seem to Latin readers equally worthy of the name; for in his present form
he often stutters and makes mistakes in grammar. Or, if this is too much to
ask, you could collate the Greek texts and correct errors made by copyists
or careless translators. Finally you could discuss the matter seriously with   305
men of rank, so that by their interest and support these important studies
might flourish increasingly; at present, like all the humanities, they seem to
be reeling from the effects of some dreadful storm. I know the extent of
your influence and the acclaim which you have won among the best of the
German princes. I know too how effective are your powers of persuasion.   310
Now is the time to use these powers more fully, for we see two factions,
which are generally at each other's throats, uniting in a surprising coalition
to destroy all that is elegant and refined in literature. One side has the
impudence to proclaim that the sects are the children of the humanities, and

the other includes among its members many who detest everything that has 315
been a part of our human existence in the past. So that nothing may remain
unchanged, they want to suppress all humane learning. But without this the
life of man would be a poor and shabby thing.

It is right then that you and men like you, who have spent all your
lives in the service of the Muses, should accept the responsibility of defend- 320
ing literature against the impious schemes of wicked men. The Collegium
Trilingue at Louvain is flourishing beyond all expectations – so much so
that it has now earned the hostility of these miserable sophists. There is a
man at Tournai who is following in the same path.[28] Francis, the most
Christian king of France, attempted the same thing and this was the main 325
reason why he invited me so frequently to France. He has not changed his
mind, but you know how difficult the situation is. This is why all who
favour sound learning are praying for a happier future for the prince,[29] so
that he may lend his support to the humanities, as he has long desired to
do. They are nowhere in greater danger than in France. 330

So I appeal to you, most honoured sir, as a German to play your part
in this enterprise; and as for me, if there is anything I can do, I shall not fail
in my duty.

I read with great delight your wise and witty remarks about the
commotion caused by a group of people who are wrecking the Evangelical 335
cause by their stupidity while all the time they believe they are supporting
it valiantly![30] I could match your story with many similar instances from
my own experience. But that will have to wait till we have more time to
spare. Farewell.

Basel, 14 March 1525 340

* * * * *

28 Pierre Cotrel; cf Ep 1237 n8. On his attempts to found a humanistic college at
   Tournai, see de Vocht CTL I 521–3.
29 Doubtless an allusion to the defeat and capture of Francis I at Pavia on 24
   February 1525. Erasmus could already see that the involvement of the French
   king in Italian wars distracted him from the promotion of humanistic learning,
   and perhaps he already suspected what the near future actually produced, that
   the king's captivity would encourage foes of humanism such as Noël Béda and
   Pierre Cousturier to increase their attacks on all of the humanist reformers,
   including not only Erasmus himself but also Lefèvre d'Etaples and Guillaume
   Briçonnet, bishop of Meaux.
30 Cf Allen Ep 1480:45–9. Pirckheimer's actual remarks, however, were rather
   more sympathetic to the Evangelical cause (or at least to Luther himself), and
   rather more inclined to blame conservative Catholics, than Erasmus' words
   might imply.

1559 / To Jean de Lorraine   Basel, 22 March 1525

Considering the hostile position which by this time Erasmus had taken
towards Luther, Oecolampadius, Farel, and other reformers who had broken
with Rome, this defence of Pierre Toussain (1499–1573), a close associate of
Oecolampadius and Guillaume Farel, is perhaps surprising. The addressee is
Jean de Lorraine (cf Ep 997 introduction), of the house of Guise, cardinal and
bishop of Metz and several other dioceses. Although well-disposed to Erasmus
and other humanist reformers, Jean was a remarkable pluralist, even for the
aristocracy of that age. Toussain had become canon of Metz in 1515 but had
spent most of his time studying at various universities and had come under
the influence of Oecolampadius and other leaders of the Reformation. Even
though he was living in Oecolampadius' house, he seems to have convinced
Erasmus that he was not a follower of Luther. His fellow canons had demanded that he return to Metz, but when he did so and attempted to preach his
Reformed doctrines in the cathedral during Lent, the chapter forbade him to
preach. He then returned to Basel and persuaded Erasmus to write this appeal
to the (absentee, of course) bishop. In June, accompanied by Farel, Toussain
renewed his attempt to preach in Metz, but both of them were driven out.
Again Erasmus provided him with letters of recommendation (Epp 1618, 1619)
when he relocated in Paris, ostensibly to teach Greek. After being sheltered
from persecution by Margaret of Angoulême, sister of the French king, for
several years, he eventually returned to Basel. From 1535 to the end of his life,
he was the Reformed pastor at Montbéliard. This letter survived only in an
autograph rough draft at Copenhagen (MS G.K.S. 95 Fol f 241) until Allen
discovered it, identified the recipient, and published it in 1926.

Cordial greetings, right reverend bishop and most illustrious prince. I have
been waiting for a happier occasion on which to address your Eminence, of
whose kindly interest in me my good friend Dr Cantiuncula[1] has so often
spoken at length; but chance has forestalled me and brought me an occasion
quite different from what I had hoped for, since it arises from necessity   5
rather than pleasure. A friend of mine is in danger and I am therefore
constrained to ask for your protection against the behaviour of your own

* * * * *

1559
1 Claudius Cantiuncula (Claude Chansonnette), humanist doctor of laws and
  native of Metz, was chancellor to the cardinal of Lorraine. On him see Ep
  852:85n.

canons, which, if not unjust, is certainly harsh and unreasonable. I write of
Pierre Toussain,[2] a young man of great promise, who was summoned home
by your canons and immediately called to account in a most offensive   10
manner and subjected to insulting remarks, confiscations, and imprisonment. In the end the young man withdrew at the request of the magistrates
so as not to cause a riot in the city, though he was ready to answer any
charges which could be brought against him.

First of all I trust your Eminence will believe that, if I had good reason   15
to suspect anyone of being a member of the Lutheran faction, I would
refuse to take him under my protection, though I would try to cure him of
his folly if I could. But although I have had many frank conversations with
Pierre Toussain, I have never detected a hint of sympathy on his part for
those whose opinions are condemned by the Roman pontiff. At first he took   20
lodgings with Oecolampadius – it was Cantiuncula who suggested it – not
from any sympathy with the sect but because of his love of learning.[3] His
first idea was to stay with me, whom the Lutherans regard as an enemy;
but when that proved impossible because I was preparing to move, he took
Cantiuncula's advice and boarded with Oecolampadius, whom he did not   25
know personally. My disagreement with Oecolampadius is well known and
it is evident also from my published works. The friendship which I once
enjoyed with him has turned into an open quarrel, which is better in my
opinion than a bogus friendship. Yet, though he is no friend of mine, I must
concede that he has considerable competence in theology and the three   30
ancient tongues. But in spite of these qualities Pierre Toussain took the
advice of his friends and removed himself from Oecolampadius' house. He
did attend an occasional lecture of his, for no one else teaches theology here.
Sometimes he has associated with people who are not hostile to Luther, but
this is something which no one who lives here can avoid since the whole   35
place is full of Lutherans. Sometimes in the interests of learning I too listen
to those whose opinions I do not entirely approve. St Cyprian used to call
Tertullian his master and took pleasure in his writings.[4] Jerome was fasci-
nated by Origen's mind though he rejected his opinions. He was also proud

* * * * *

2 See introduction to this letter.
3 Despite his growing alienation from Oecolampadius over eucharistic doctrine
  and other issues (cf Allen Ep 1523:35n, 112n), Erasmus retained respect for the
  reformer's learning and personal character. But here of course he had to
  attempt to excuse Toussain's intimate association with the principal leader of
  the Reformed party in Basel.
4 Jerome De viris illustribus 53 (PL 23 698). In his later years, Tertullian, the first
  great Latin theologian, adhered to the Montanist heresy.

of his teacher Didymus, but rejected his philosophy, and he studied with a   40
Jewish teacher, whose heretical views he detested.[5] Paul bids us put all
things to the test but hold to that which is good.[6]

When Toussain's books were examined, some notes were found in the
margin which it would be wrong to regard with suspicion. For a note is not
intended to express what we feel but to point to something which needs   45
further consideration. For example, when I was preparing to write on free
will, I marked in Scripture all those passages which told against the freedom of the will. Similarly, if I were preparing a work on the primacy of the
pope, I would also note whatever seemed to argue against the primacy of
the pope. Yet with feeble arguments like this they raised an outrageous fuss   50
against a young man whose intelligence, honesty, and love of knowledge
should have drawn forth their deepest respect. The colleges of canons are
extremely unpopular with the laity because so many of the canons live for
their bellies and their appetites with little thought for sacred learning of any
kind. But this unpopularity would fade if they began to attract more men   55
like Toussain. If he continues in his studies as he has begun, he will be a
great asset and adornment not just to his own community but to the whole
country. How rare it is to see a young man turning aside from all the
pleasures which his contemporaries pursue so madly, poring night and day
over the noblest authors and finding his greatest delight not in girls and   60
drink and dice, but in the sacred texts! It is priests like this whom we need
today, not men who impose their faith on others by imprisonment and
threats of violence, but who follow St Peter's advice and trust to the power
of persuasion, being ready at all times to give an answer to any man who
asks.[7] Otherwise is there any difference between a priest and a murderous   65
bully?

This does not mean that I condemn measures to suppress the incurable
heretic; my point is rather that we should follow the example of a good
doctor who resorts to cautery or the knife only after other remedies have
been tried in vain. So even if we grant (which I do not) that this young man   70

* * * * *

5 For Jerome's debt to Origen, cf Jerome Ep 84. He had studied very briefly with
   Origen's disciple Didymus at Alexandria; cf his Ep 84:3, also *Commentarii in
   Osee* prol (CCL 76 5), *Commentarii in Zachariam* prol (CCL 76A 748), and Rufinus
   Apologia contra Hieronymum 2.15 CCL 20 94. Jerome's Jewish teacher, with
   whom he studied Hebrew, was Baraninas, cf Ep 84.3. Although Origen was
   one of the greatest theologians (if not the greatest) among the Greek church
   Fathers, certain of his opinions were condemned in later centuries.
6 1 Thess 5:21
7 1 Pet 3:15

had somehow been infected with the same malady which has taken possession of men's minds almost everywhere in the world, we should nonetheless have treated him with every kindness and ministered to his sickness
with gentle remedies, as Christ taught us by his example, for he did not
break the bruised reed nor quench the smoking flax;[8] and if something had   75
been said or done by this young man without due reflection, we should
have pardoned him because of his outstanding abilities and the promise
which he showed of great things to come. But nowadays some people are
so carried away by their own prejudices that they condemn even what is
helpful to religion; in fact they call everything heretical which has anything   80
to do with good literature or polite learning. Sometimes they do not even
read what they condemn. I hear that your canons have been attacking me
with wild stories that I am a Lutheran when I am fighting Luther with
considerable risk to my life. Many bishops, the emperor, Ferdinand, the
king of France, the king of England, and many cardinals, notably Cardinal   85
Campeggi, all judge me a fit correspondent and write frequently and in the
most complimentary terms. They are well enough satisfied with me, but to
swine of that sort I am a heretic.

But I shall speak about myself on another occasion. For the moment
I should like to appeal to your Eminence most sincerely to restrain the   90
lawlessness of your canons and help a young man who deserves every
consideration and whom you will one day be glad to have rescued. When
Alcibiades was summoned to face trial before his fellow Athenians, he chose
to leave the country; and when he was advised to trust his fate to the jurors,
he said he would not trust himself to his own mother for fear she might   95
substitute the black pebble for the white by mistake.[9] So it is not surprising
that Toussain refuses to trust those who show such obvious signs of hostility towards him and who want to ruin him, not to bring about his rehabilita-
tion. Toussain is confident that he can give a satisfactory account of himself
to any fair-minded person. But to have a clear conscience and yet to suffer   100
disgrace, excommunication, and imprisonment, that is surely unjust. Christian charity requires us to care for those whose sickness can be cured; it is
completely incompatible with the loving nature of Christ to attack the
innocent and, because of a prejudice against humane studies, to trump up

* * * * *

8 A favourite verse of Erasmus (Isa 42:3), usually cited, as here, in the form
  baculum fractum non comminuit, literally 'he will not crush the broken staff.'
9 Plutarch *Alcibiades* 22. The use of black pebbles (for condemnation) and white
  (for acquittal) was one of several systems adopted in the Athenian courts to
  record the votes of jurors.

a charge and destroy a brilliant and gifted person who could bring great 10
distinction and support to his country and to the church of Christ. Moreover
he now has an additional claim on our support since he departed at the
request of the magistrates to avoid a disturbance in the city. This in itself
is proof of his loyalty; but the fact that he acted in the interests of those
very people who were attacking him shows his true Christian charity. For 1:
it seems probable that, given any excuse, an attack would have been made
on the canons. Monks and priests have stirred up enough hostility against
themselves even without the addition of any further incidents. So we shall
have to try all the harder to lessen the unpopularity which we have caused
through our behaviour by a radical change in our way of life. If we wish to 1:
be loved, we must make ourselves lovable.[10] The world now detests
priests because of their ignorance of Holy Scripture and their enslavement
to lust, extravagance, and money, but it will begin to love and respect them
when they change their ways and become learned, chaste, sober, and generous. But if we try to check this deadly evil by applying only the common 1:
remedies – confiscations, excommunications, imprisonment, and the stake,
I am afraid that the outcome will be less happy than many people imagine
who believe that severe measures are all that is necessary. Certainly experience so far has shown us that such remedies simply spread the disease and
make it worse. 1:

I have expressed myself rather bluntly, but remember that, while this
is going on, I am fighting a battle of words with those whose cause I am
supposed to be defending! To conclude, my most reverend lord, if you help
my friend Toussain now – and two or three words from someone in your
position is all that is needed – you will show that generosity which every- 1:
one admires in you and you will help a man who not only deserves your
support, but will one day repay it with interest. Finally by this action you
will bind to you even more closely than before someone who has long been
your illustrious Highness' most devoted servant. I am sending you now my
De libero arbitrio, which I wrote to counter the views of Luther. If I hear that 1,
this effort of mine pleases you, I shall send you later my *De modo orandi
Deum*, in which, in opposition to Luther, I defend the doctrine of the invocation of the saints. I wish your Eminence well and I pledge to you my sincere devotion.

Basel, 22 March 1525 1,

* * * * *

10 Ovid *Ars amatoria* 2.107

1560 / To Willibald Pirckheimer   Basel, 25 March 1525

This letter accompanied a gift copy of Erasmus' edition of the Greek text of St
John Chrysostom's *De officio sacerdotis*, which had just come off the press and
which he had already promised to Pirckheimer in Ep 1558, which is the
preface to the book. The letter remained unpublished until Allen included it
in his edition (1926), using British Library MS Arundel 175 f 18v.

ERASMUS TO WILLIBALD PIRCKHEIMER

Sincerest greetings, my honoured friend. I sent you a letter by a carrier and
attached another for the dean,[1] about whom you had written. I imagine
they have been delivered. Here now is a work of Chrysostom in Greek, 'On
the responsibilities of a bishop.' A long time ago someone made a tolerable   5
translation of it. I had nothing else at hand with which to repay your kindness, since I lost almost two months through illness. Shortly, however, two
or three little volumes will appear. Please give my kind regards to Ricius[2]
and to Dürer.[3] Farewell.

Basel, feast of the Annunciation 1525   10

If you knew the sort of person Froben is, you would realize that he deserves
the support of all honest men.[4] His associates are not quite straight with
him. One of these is Koberger, whom I have reason to regard as a close
friend because of the faithful services he rendered me in the past.[5] I am
aware that he is a businessman and that he has a partner from Gelderland,   15
called Franz Birckmann, who is the greatest scoundrel on whom the sun
ever shone.[6] There is a character called Pseudocheus in my *Colloquies*.[7]

* * * * *

1560
1 Rudbert von Mosham, dean of Passau. Cf Allen Epp 1450 introduction, 1512.
2 Cf Ep 1558 n10.
3 Cf Epp 1136, 1536, 1558.
4 High praise for the Basel printer who for a decade had been Erasmus' principal publisher. Cf Ep 419 introduction.
5 Johann Koberger (d 1543), the prominent Nürnberg publisher and bookseller;
   cf Ep 581:23n. Although Erasmus here acknowledges his many helpful acts, he
   also complains that he and his business partners treated Froben unfairly in
   financial matters.
6 Cf Ep 258:14n. Birckmann (d 1530) learned the book trade in Cologne and in
   partnership with his brother Arnold became a large-scale distributor of books
   in the international market, being based at various times in Antwerp and
   Cologne but also active in London and Paris and having business dealings

Although the work was not written with him in mind, he fits the role so completely that no one is likely to rob him of the distinction. I shall have more to say about this monster on another occasion, for it is a long story. He has played the trickster for all of twelve years now. In the meantime please take any chance which offers to talk to Koberger and try to persuade him to be more civil to Froben, who has done so much for the cause of letters. Farewell again.

1561 / To Duke George of Saxony Basel, 26 March 1525

A reply to Ep 1550, but also to an earlier letter (Ep 1520) which had welcomed Erasmus' open break with Luther and urged him to be more outspoken in opposing heresy in the future. It also responds to the duke's request for help in finding a successor to Petrus Mosellanus as professor of Greek at Leipzig. Erasmus published it in his *Opus epistolarum*.

ERASMUS OF ROTTERDAM TO GEORGE, DUKE OF SAXONY,
GREETING
Most illustrious prince, I received your Highness' most recent letter, written on the eve of St Valentine's day, and nothing could have given me greater pleasure. True you are spurring on a willing horse,[1] but still I am delighted to have the encouragement of such valiant heroes as yourself. Your previous letter had reached me a little earlier and a few days ago I wrote a brief reply and gave it to Haubitz[2] to deliver.

* * * * *

with printers in many northern European cities, including Froben at Basel. Although Erasmus himself had long had dealings with Birckmann and used his services to transmit mail, books, and even money, he did not trust him; and this mistrust seems to have grown more pronounced from about 1523–4. In September 1523 he sternly warned his agent Conradus Goclenius not to entrust any of Erasmus' business affairs to Birckmann (Ep 1388:27–8).
7 The colloquy 'Pseudocheus and Philetymus' was first printed in the 1523 Froben edition of the *Colloquies*. Pseudocheus is depicted as an arrogant liar and cheat, especially in financial matters.

1561
1 *Adagia* III viii 32; cf Cicero *De oratore* 2.186.
2 Cf Allen Ep 1522:99n. A young man from Haubitz in Saxony had visited Erasmus at Basel late in 1524, one of two recommended by Heinrich Stromer, professor at Leipzig. He carried a brief letter acknowledging Ep 1550 on his return to Saxony. Erbe and Bietenholz suggest (CEBR II 168–9) that this may have been Valentin Albert von Haubitz, a nobleman who had matriculated at

I am expecting a professor of Greek to be here by Easter.[3] He did not write a word to me on the matter, but another scholar, who is a close 10 friend of both of us,[4] tells me that he is not reluctant to accept the post. In his mastery of Greek he is more than a match for three Mosellani and he is no less fluent, I understand, in Latin. I cannot be sure of this until he arrives.

As for myself, although I have reached the age at which I should 15 already have been pensioned off, I shall not fail in my duty. I only hope your Highness and the other princes will ensure that our recent victory will not be used to further the mad ambitions of certain people who are hardly human, but will redound to the glory of Christ and the salvation of Christ's people. For that cause I shall be glad to give even my life. I wish your 20 Lordship well.

Basel, the day following the feast of the Annunciation 1525

I enclose letters for Pistoris[5] and Emser[6] in the hope that this way they will get there more safely. For I do not have a courier whom I can trust. But I am sending these to Frankfurt, where they will be handed over 25 to someone else.

* * * * *

Leipzig; but since three other students carrying the name of the village matriculated at Leipzig in the same period, the precise identity of this person remains uncertain.

3 Epp 1564–8 show that the person recommended by Erasmus for this vacancy on the Leipzig faculty was Jacobus Teyng of Hoorn, known as Ceratinus, whose career he had repeatedly sought to advance. On his early career, see Ep 622:34n. In 1524 Froben had published his revision of Craston's Greek dictionary. Ceratinus took up his position at Leipzig in the summer of 1525 but by September had already left for his native Netherlands, where he spent the rest of his career. Apparently at Leipzig he soon was suspected of being a sympathizer with Luther and so decided to leave. His subsequent history, which included ordination as a priest in 1527, indicates that these suspicions were unfounded. Erasmus continued to think highly of his abilities and recommended him for other positions. Cf Ep 1611 n2.

4 Allen Ep 1561:7n surmises that this was Conradus Goclenius, whom Erasmus probably would have consulted before recommending a candidate who had been living in and near Louvain, as Ceratinus had been.

5 This letter is not extant. On Simon Pistoris cf Ep 1125 n6. He was now serving as chancellor to Duke George.

6 This letter also has not survived. Presumably it was a reply to Ep 1551. On Emser cf Ep 553 introduction. He had been secretary and chaplain to Duke George since 1505.

1562 / To Cornelis of Bergen   Basel, 26 March 1525

This letter is evidently to an old friend from the Netherlands whom Erasmus
had not heard from in many years and who seems to have written expressing
anxiety at reports that Erasmus was in grave personal danger and about to go
into hiding. Aside from the present letter, there is no information about Cornelis. Allen Ep 1562 introduction speculates that he may have been the Burgomaster of Bergen, William Conrad, who is a character in the *Antibarbari*, but
this identification is by no means certain. Erasmus published it in his *Opus
epistolarum*.

ERASMUS OF ROTTERDAM TO CORNELIS OF BERGEN, GREETING
Truest of friends, what is all this about flight and bolt-holes and labyrinths?
Every day I am swamped with the most flattering letters from the pope and
from cardinals, bishops, the papal legate Campeggi, the emperor, Ferdinand,
the king of England, dukes, and barons. I receive invitations on the most   5
generous terms; benefices and bishoprics are offered me. If I were a young
man, I would doubtless be king. So why do you believe those abominable
drones who can do nothing but hurl abuse? And they tell such impudent
lies that sensible men regard them as mad.

Your note was very welcome, if only because it brought me the news   10
that my dear Cornelis, the oldest and truest of my friends and companions,
is still in good health. If I return this spring, as I think probable, we shall,
God willing, enjoy a drink together.[1] In the meantime I have asked Pieter
Gillis[2] to send you some of my books. May the Lord keep you in good
health, dearest Cornelis, and all your family too. How is our friend Joost?[3]   15

* * * * *

1562
1 In several letters of this period, all of them addressed to persons connected
  with the Netherlands and holding influential positions in the service of Charles
  V (Epp 1545:28-9; 1553:24-6; 1554:31-2), Erasmus hints that he is considering
  a return to the Netherlands. If he really was doing so, this was probably
  because Margaret of Austria, governor of those provinces, was insisting that
  if Erasmus wanted his imperial pension paid, he should return there. Cf Ep
  1380 introduction.
2 For his connection with this friend of long standing, see Ep 184 introduction.
  He was town secretary of Bergen-op-Zoom, where Cornelis lived.
3 Probably Joost of Schoonhoven, the 'Joost the physician' who appears as a
  character in the *Antibarbari* (ASD I-1 41), which (in its second recension) was
  written about the time which Erasmus spent living in Bergen, c 1492-5. Although this man had died in 1502, Erasmus had had little contact with Bergen
  since leaving there and may not have known of his death.

Is he still working the same old hide?[4] We shall enjoy a good laugh together.

Basel, the day following the feast of the Annunciation 1525

1563 / To Maximilian of Burgundy   Basel, 30 March 1525

This is the dedicatory preface to the first edition of St John Chrysostom's *De orando Deum libri duo* in Erasmus' Latin translation with accompanying Greek text (Basel: Froben, April 1525). Froben had also published a less complete edition in October 1524. Since one aspect of Chrysostom's text is its defence of invocation of the saints, the publication seems in part to be associated with Erasmus' desire to distance himself from Luther. On the recipient, see Ep 1163 n11.

TO THE REVEREND FATHER IN CHRIST MAXIMILIAN OF
BURGUNDY, ABBOT OF MIDDELBURG, FROM ERASMUS OF
ROTTERDAM, GREETING

Among the many good things which we owe to the practice of writing letters, reverend father, not the least in my opinion is the fact that we can be in touch with our friends even though we live, so to speak, in another world. Recently I published a little work entitled *De modo orandi Deum*. Subjects like this which do not involve much work and are useful for the spiritual life are the sort of thing with which I occupy my old age; for, like an athlete who is beginning to feel the weight of years, I am eager to retire. My book was already in circulation and was enjoying some success, when I discovered among the works of Chrysostom two discourses on the same subject which had not yet been translated into Latin.[1] I could hardly wait to find out how far we agreed in our treatment of the same theme. Painters, I believe, often react in the same way when they discover that an artist of considerable talent has worked on the same subject as themselves; when this occurs, they want to compare the two canvases and see where they are

* * * * *

4 Although this sounds like a proverb, none of the possible classical parallels seems likely.

1563
1 Altaner *Patrology* (1960) 383 cites an unpublished dissertation demonstrating that these sermons on prayer are not genuine. Allen Ep 1563 introduction observes that at the end of the volume Erasmus himself added a note suggesting that the second one was not by Chrysostom.

equal in artistic skill and where one is superior or inferior to the other. In
my case I was so disillusioned by the comparison that, had it been possible,
I would gladly have destroyed my work altogether. The competition, you   20
might say, was between a Rutuba and an Apelles;[2] for who could match
Chrysostom's more than golden eloquence[3] even if he had the model before
him and was trying to copy it? As a rule competition is a great incentive to
men of talent; but, having nothing to spur me on and rouse me from my
torpor, I felt more like an ant confronting a camel![4] But I prefer to hear   25
what you have to say on the matter. To help you reach a better verdict, I
am including the Greek text so that no one may accuse me of producing a
poor translation to make my own work look less unattractive.

But however the comparison turns out, I shall consider myself victorious if as a result of my efforts I see a great number of people beginning to   30
pray frequently or becoming more conscientious about their prayers. I knew
of course there was no need of such encouragement for a man with your
pious nature and that the devout and godly spirit which others can acquire
only with difficulty and after long and arduous effort seems to have come
naturally to you. As a young man, when you were suddenly transferred   35
from the court to the cloister, you conducted yourself so well in this new
mode of life that in modesty, sobriety, chastity, and devotion you surpassed
even those who had grown old in the discipline of the religious life. There
was nothing in your conduct to remind us of your earlier years, no trace of
your familiarity with the life of the court, no pride in that illustrious family   40
which you trace back to Philip, duke of Burgundy, who, we are told, was
given the nickname 'Philip the Good.' Here was clear evidence of the integrity of your nature, an integrity which not even daily contact with the court
could corrupt, although so many men of humble background and modest
upbringing are corrupted not just by elevation to the rank of abbot, but   45
even by the style and manner of a monk. When the pure whiteness of one's
character matches or surpasses the whiteness of one's vestments, there is a
special pleasure to be felt in such harmonious concord. You entered this life
reluctantly because you knew you could not be a simple monk before
becoming an abbot. To men like you the responsibilities of a bishop, the   50

* * * * *

2 Although Rutuba was one of two gladiators mentioned in Horace *Satires*
  2.7.96–7 and Erasmus appears to have known this, he frequently uses the name
  in contrast to that of a talented painter like Apelles, as if Rutuba were an
  unskilful painter. Cf Ep 999 n5, *Adagia* IV v 1.
3 A pun on Chrysostom's name, which means 'golden-voiced'
4 *Adagia* I v 47

most sacred office which this world can bestow, can safely be entrusted; for
such men claim no distinction for themselves by right of office: on the
contrary they lend distinction to any office which they undertake by the
upright manner of their lives. Farewell.   60
     Basel, 30 March 1525

1564 / To Heinrich Stromer   Basel, 8 April 1525

> This is the first of three letters (cf Epp 1565, 1566) which Erasmus wrote to
> recommend the Dutch humanist Ceratinus, whom he strongly and successfully
> backed as a candidate for the Leipzig chair of Greek left vacant by the prema-
> ture death of Mosellanus (cf Epp 1550, 1561). Ceratinus himself delivered this
> and the other letters of the same date. Stromer was a suitable recipient because
> he was dean of the medical faculty at Leipzig, a member of the city council
> there, and (despite his open though moderate support of Luther) personal
> physician to Duke George of Saxony, patron of that university. On his earlier
> career, cf Ep 578 introduction. Erasmus published this letter in *Opus episto-
> larum*.

ERASMUS OF ROTTERDAM TO HEINRICH STROMER, PHYSICIAN,
GREETING
You were very attached to Mosellanus; it was natural to be fond of him and
equally natural to feel his death keenly as you did. I imagine that time and
reflection have now eased or wiped away your sorrow, but in case a trace   5
of it remains, here is a new remedy for your pain. Jacobus Ceratinus is with
me now:[1] I wrote on the prince's orders to invite him to take Mosellanus'
place. I hardly expected him to accept the terms which we offered, for he
was being pressed to take the chair of Greek at the Collegium Trilingue, and
although the salary is the same, the reputation of Louvain is scarcely   10
equalled anywhere except possibly at the University of Paris, and Paris is
now controlled by sophists and barbarians and true learning languishes in
the cold. But it is something to be in a place with magnificent buildings and
to have hundreds of students, at every lecture too, and the sons of great
princes among them.   15
     From the friendly talks we have had and from his writings I have
gained a very thorough idea of Ceratinus' abilities. Without this I would not

* * * * *

1564
1 Epp 622:34n, 1561 n3

be so confident in recommending him to such an astute judge as yourself, especially since I have often been embarrassed in the past by being too free with my praise. Ceratinus is so genuine and has such a friendly disposition   20 that I believe he is as much at home among the Graces as among the Muses. I have no doubt you will become very fond of him – if there is any truth in the proverb about birds of a feather.[2] Since heaven does not allow us to meet, Ceratinus will have to take my place and through him you will show your affection for me and I shall be bound more tightly to you. I trust the   25 prince will be generous and that I shall have no cause to regret having lured Ceratinus away and he will not repent having given in to my solicitations. If he is treated more generously, it will be largely due to your kindness and influence. I hope the prince will take account of the length of the journey here and the heavy expenses which he has already incurred – and   30 now he is faced with another long journey to reach you. Admittedly he was given the usual travelling allowances; and yet if brigands relieve him of his purse or anything else happens to put him in need of help, you have only to ask Froben or myself and anything you lend him will be paid at once wherever you choose.   35

The sophists are working with all their might to destroy the humanities utterly. It is up to us to use every tactic to counter their impious designs. In this, you may be sure, I shall act like a man. A few days ago I went into labour and brought forth a veritable viper's brood![3] I am afraid to trust my poor body to these Swiss doctors (if that is the right name to   40 call them by); my friend Antonin, who was the only one in whose hands I was able to feel safe, has left for his native Hungary.[4] I could hope to be well again if someone like your good self were here. Farewell.

Basel, 8 April 1525

1565 / To Duke George of Saxony   Basel, 8 April 1525

This formal recommendation of Jacobus Teyng of Hoorn, called Ceratinus, to fill the chair of Greek at Leipzig fulfils the promise made in Ep 1561 and responds to Duke George's request for a nomination, made in Ep 1550. On Ceratinus, see Ep 1561 n3. Like the preceding and following letters, this was first published in Erasmus' *Opus epistolarum*.

* * * * *

2 Literally, 'like is drawn to like.' Cf Homer *Odyssey* 17.218, Plato *Gorgias* 510B. Erasmus here gives the phrase in Greek.
3 Cf Ep 1558 n16.
4 On this physician, whose medical advice Erasmus regarded highly, cf Epp 1602 introduction, 1512:53–5.

ERASMUS OF ROTTERDAM TO GEORGE, DUKE OF SAXONY,
GREETING

Most illustrious prince, the commission your Highness gave me in regard
to the professorship has turned out much better than I dared hope. Jacobus
Ceratinus,[1] about whom I wrote to you, has come here in response to my   5
invitation. He has such a fine knowledge of Greek that there are scarcely
two or three scholars in all Italy with whom I should be hesitant to compare
him; in Latin too he maintains the same high standards; nor is he any
stranger to philosophy and, to top it all, his youth and intelligence make it
reasonable to hope that, if God grants him years, he will do much to further   10
and enhance all sound and honourable learning. Since your Highness
showed such exceptional kindness in encouraging and supporting Petrus
Mosellanus, you should do even more for Ceratinus, since he is a better
scholar than Mosellanus, especially in those subjects on which he will
lecture for you. Mosellanus was a man of great learning and greater prom-   15
ise and I loved him dearly for the talents which he possessed; I know too
that comparisons are odious.[2] But honesty compels me to say: here is something very different.

I had made up my mind to be more circumspect in my testimonials
since I was once shamefully deceived in someone you know.[3] But in intro-   20
ducing Ceratinus, I feel there is no need for such qualms. I have experienced his warm nature at close quarters, and from our intimate conversations as well as from his copious writings I have been able to test the thoroughness of his scholarship, the originality of his mind, and the sharpness
of his judgment. So I congratulate your Highness on having found a man   25
who fully deserves the benefit of your natural generosity and kindness. I
send my congratulations also to the University of Leipzig, for our friend
Ceratinus, if the Muses prosper his efforts, will pump new vigour into its
intellectual life, which I hear has suffered badly because of Mosellanus'
death. I have no doubt about the result, that Leipzig will make other univer-   30

* * * * *

1565
1 See introduction.
2 This well known proverb seems not to have a classical source. OED cites it in
  English from Lydgate *Hors, shepe and Gosse* 526; it also appears in Fortescue *De
  laudibus legum Angliae* chapter 19 and in other, later, English texts, but not in
  any source likely to have been known by Erasmus.
3 A reference to Erasmus' former secretary, Heinrich Eppendorf, whom Erasmus
  had warmly commended to Duke George in 1522 (Ep 1283) but from whom
  he had subsequently become bitterly estranged.

sities jealous or, as I should prefer to think, eager to follow its example. All
the distinction which that man will bring and all his services to learning
will be credited to your illustrious Highness; for, to conceal nothing from
you, our friend Ceratinus has this one fault – he is excessively modest, so
shy in fact as to be almost embarrassing. So it is fortunate for him that he   35
has fallen in with a prince whose good sense is founded on sound personal
judgment and who does not wait for the outstretched hand before showing
his kindness, but makes the first generous approach when he sees someone
worthy of his favour.

Enough about Ceratinus. I replied in a word or two to your Highness'   40
last letter and enclosed letters for Pistoris[4] and Emser,[5] to give them a
better chance of arriving safely. Now I have nothing to add except to
express this wish, that from now on, as you put it so courteously in your
letter, there may be an end to all differences and suspicions between us. I
am, and I profess myself to be, your most humble servant. Farewell.   45

Basel, 8 April 1525

1566 / To Hieronymus Emser   Basel, [c 9 April] 1525

Another of Erasmus' letters recommending the Hellenist Jacobus Ceratinus to
persons influential at the Saxon court and the University of Leipzig (cf Epp
1561, 1564, 1565). On Emser, see Epp 553 introduction, 1561 n6. By this time,
Emser was known not only as a humanist but also as an outspoken opponent
of Luther. Erasmus published the letter in his *Opus epistolarum*.

ERASMUS OF ROTTERDAM TO HIERONYMUS EMSER, GREETING
I recently sent you a long and probably tiresome letter; now I have nothing
to write except to tell you that the bearer of this letter is a man called
Jacobus Ceratinus, who is such a fine Greek scholar that he could hold a
chair even in the heart of Italy, and he does not let himself down in Latin   5
either. On top of all this he is modest almost to a fault and is blessed with
a very open nature which is completely free of any kind of affectation. On
the prince's orders I invited him here with more hope than confidence that
he would accept the offer. So far my efforts have been crowned with success; now it is up to you to see that I don't regret having obliged the prince   10
in this affair.

* * * *

4 Cf Ep 1125 n6. The earlier letter to Duke George is Ep 1561, but the letters
  enclosed for Pistoris and Emser are not extant.
5 Ep 1561 n6

I have finished reading your book[1] and am delighted with everything in it except that I don't understand why you credit that man[2] with an agreeable style. I can imagine nothing more unattractive than the way he writes. At the end you lay down rules for monks and priests to help them improve their lives. I only wish they would take what you say to heart. At present neither side is ready to patch up a peace: both prefer to widen the grounds of conflict. I have written several times to the emperor and to Ferdinand and the other princes as well as to the pope and the legate Campeggi and given my opinion that things would improve if they would strike at the root of the trouble. But it seems that my words still fall on deaf ears.[3] In fact anyone who wants to see pontiffs, bishops, priests, and monks better than they are at present is just about branded a Lutheran. Farewell.

Basel, 1525.

1567 / To Martin Hune   Basel, 9 April 1525

The recipient was a physician of Erfurt who had carried letters of Erasmus to Heinrich Stromer and Duke George in the spring of 1524. See Allen Ep 1462 introduction for his career. Erasmus included the letter in *Opus epistolarum*.

ERASMUS OF ROTTERDAM TO MARTIN HUNE, PHYSICIAN,
GREETING
I learned in a letter from that kind man Stromer what trouble you took to deliver my letter, to say nothing of the heavy expense you incurred.[1] I know what I owe to your generosity and I shall not forget it. I would have sent you a small gift with Ceratinus, who is Mosellanus' successor and a brilliant scholar in both Greek and Latin, but it was not clear if he would pass your way. If he does visit you and if you feel like getting to know him,

* * * * *

1566
1 Emser's *Apologeticon*. On this controversy between Emser and Huldrych Zwingli, cf Ep 1551 n1.
2 Huldrych Zwingli, who had been an active humanist and an enthusiastic admirer of Erasmus until his conversion to a strongly evangelical faith and his emergence as the leader of the Reformation in Zürich
3 *Adagia* I iv 87

1567
1 Cf introductions to Epp 578, 1564. The letter mentioned here, probably a reply to Ep 1522, is not extant.

you will find him a man with high scholarly standards and one whose
character is totally free from affectation and whose only fault is an excessive   10
modesty.

I must write some day to Eobanus, but it takes a year for a letter to
reach him, if it ever does reach him.[2] Everything is opened and unsealed
on the way. This is where the Evangelical faith has brought us! I am waiting
for Eobanus' work. Today Beatus Rhenanus finally returned from Sélestat.[3]   15
He sends you his very best wishes. Farewell, my dearest Hune.

Basel, 9 April 1525

1568 / To Willibald Pirckheimer   Basel, 9 April 1525

This is a sequel to Ep 1560, which accompanied the presentation copy of
Erasmus' edition of the Greek text of St John Chrysostom's *De sacerdotio* to
Pirckheimer. The occasion for writing again so soon was the opportunity of
dispatching the letter with Jacobus Ceratinus, who was going from Basel to
Leipzig to become professor of Greek. Melchior Goldast first published this
letter in *Pirckheimerii Opera*, but Allen based his Latin text on a manuscript in
the British Library (MS Arundel 175, f 18v).

Cordial greetings. I imagine that by now you have received the volume of
Chrysostom in Greek to which I added a preface addressed to you. If
Jacobus Ceratinus brings this letter, please greet him like a second Erasmus.
He is such a fine Greek scholar – and equally accomplished in Latin – that
he could teach with distinction in any region of Italy. He is also a man of   5
impeccable character, though modest almost to the point of causing embarrassment; but this is his only fault, if indeed it is a fault. It was at the
request, or rather on the insistence, of Prince George that I wrote to invite
him, though I scarcely dared to hope that he would not reject the proposi-

* * * * *

2 Helius Eobanus Hessus was generally regarded as Germany's leading humanist poet. On him, see Ep 874 introduction. It is unclear why Erasmus thought
Eobanus to be so remote, since he was still living and teaching at Erfurt, where
he had become professor of Latin in 1518. Previously, he had spent several
years in the service of a bishop far away in East Prussia and then had studied
at Frankfurt an der Oder and Leipzig, but he had returned to Erfurt in 1514,
long before Erasmus met him in 1518, when he made a trip to Louvain specifically to meet Erasmus.
3 Beatus remained one of Erasmus' closest collaborators at the Froben press in
Basel, but from about 1519 he made frequent visits to his native town of
Sélestat (Schlettstadt), and in 1526 he moved back there permanently.

tion out of hand. For he was offered a public appointment with a large   10
salary in his own country. He will succeed Petrus Mosellanus, though as a
scholar he is worth more than ten of Mosellanus; not that I did not have the
highest regard for Mosellanus' learning and abilities. Another man might
perhaps resent it when an old man is overtaken by the young; but I am
delighted when I see younger men make such progress (with a little help   15
also from my own writings) that they are now able to teach those who once
taught them. So whatever you do for Ceratinus will please me more than
if you had done it for myself. He is not short of travelling money and
should not run short, unless by some mischance he is robbed on the way.
If that happens (which God forbid!), you can be assured that I shall guaran-   20
tee anything you lend him.

I would write more, but it is far from certain if Ceratinus will pass
your way, though he seems keen on doing so for the pleasure, I am sure,
of seeing you. Give my regards to Ricius[1] and Dürer.[2] A short time ago I
brought forth another viper's brood,[3] and my health is still unsettled. Fare-   25
well, most honoured sir.

Basel, 9 April 1525
To the honourable Willibald Pirckheimer
You will recognize the hand of your friend Erasmus.

1569 / From Johann von Vlatten   Aachen, 9 April 1525

A reply to Ep 1549, first published by Förstemann and Günther on the basis
of a Leipzig manuscript. On Vlatten see Ep 1390 introduction.

Greetings, most learned Erasmus. If you are well and everything goes as
you would wish, then I am most happy for you, and not just for you but
also for myself, for I am always affected by the troubles and triumphs of
my friends as though they were my own. I am sorry I was absent when our

* * * * *

1568
1 On this prominent imperial physician, cf Epp 548:16n, 1558 n10.
2 Cf Epp 1376 nn1 and 2, 1536 n2. Since Dürer was a Nürnberger and a good
  friend of Pirckheimer, Erasmus often sends greetings to him in his correspondence with Pirckheimer.
3 Cf Ep 1558 n16; as in that place, the reference here is to the painful passing of
  kidney stones, an ailment from which Erasmus suffered acutely.

friend Frans was here with your most welcome letter.[1] But it always seems   5
to turn out that my travels take me abroad on some pressing business just
when I would like to be at home. Frans called on his way back and that has
amply made up for my former disappointment, for he brought me happy
news of you – it seems that all my prayers for you are being answered.

Your arrival is being eagerly awaited here by all men of good will; for   10
the most intelligent people here are so impressed by the integrity of your
life and by your exemplary learning and moderation that they are praying
to Christ that the sacred person of Erasmus may soon be here among us.

You once honoured me with an immortal gift[2] which I did not deserve and now you are trying to outdo yourself. You were so kind to me   15
that every day I ask myself how I can repay you properly and yet you are
promising even greater things if your life is spared. In return for all this, if
you think I could be of some help to you, I am yours to command. Your
friend von Vlatten is ready to be used, or used up, in your service in any
way you please. Farewell.   20

Aachen, Palm Sunday 1525
Your friend, Johann von Vlatten
To the most learned Desiderius Erasmus of Rotterdam, my revered
and respected friend

1570 / From John Longland   London, 26 April 1525

On both the writer, bishop of Lincoln, and the homily on the fourth Psalm by
Erasmus, see Ep 1535 introduction. The letter, of which the original survived
at Leipzig, was first printed by Förstemann and Günther (1904).

Dear Erasmus, on the last day of March I received your homily on the
fourth Psalm, though I was not able to meet the man who brought it. I have
read, and carefully reread, this new work of yours and it has given me
great pleasure; for, while everything you write is marked by great learning
and distinction – and this is not just my own opinion, but the opinion of all   5

* * * * *

1569
1 Frans van der Dilft, who was living as a paying boarder and secretary in
  Erasmus' household, frequently carried letters for Erasmus between Basel and
  the Netherlands. Cf Ep 1663 introduction and Bierlaire 64–7.
2 Erasmus dedicated to Vlatten his edition of Cicero *Tusculanae quaestiones* (Basel:
  Froben, November 1523). On him see Ep 1390 introduction.

the best scholars – this new volume, unless I am prejudiced by my affection
for you, must surely be the equal of anything you have done, if it does not
deserve an even higher commendation. You remembered what I said long
ago at Calais and repeatedly urged in my letters, that you should produce
a commentary on the Psalms. I do not know how I can thank you properly   10
for the honour you have done me in dedicating this work to me. But I do
know this, that I have many reasons for feeling a deep indebtedness to you,
for you are trying to make me immortal through the lasting fame of your
writings. I am not so hard to please as to reject what everyone I know will
approve of nor so ungrateful that, when I see a friend engaged upon a holy   15
task for the glory of God and the strengthening of the faith and of the
church, I should deny him the support of my prayers to God. In my prayers
and petitions I shall commend my dear Erasmus to the protection of Christ
our glorious Lord: may he be pleased to aid your efforts and fill your mind
with saving thoughts; may he send you his sacred inspiration and the   20
breath of his spirit; may he guide you and direct your pen to his own glory
and the profit of learned men who will welcome your work, and may he
grant you a long life. Farewell and best wishes.

London, 26 April 1525.
Your friend, John Lincoln   25
To Desiderius Erasmus of Rotterdam, his special friend. In Basel

1571 / To Noël Béda   Basel, 28 April 1525

This letter opens a series of direct communications with Noël Béda, the conservative syndic of the faculty of theology at Paris, who was the most formidable,
though perhaps not the most extreme, of Erasmus' French antagonists. Since
January 1524, with the permission of the theological faculty, but essentially on
his own initiative, he had been conducting a search for errors in Erasmus'
Paraphrase on Luke and his *Exposition of the Lord's Prayer*. Béda himself first
published most of the ensuing correspondence, including the present letter, in
his *Apologia adversus clandestinos Lutheranos* (Paris: Josse Bade, 1 February 1529).
The materials published by Béda were also reprinted by Charles du Plessis
d'Argentré in *Collectio judiciorum de novis erroribus* 3 vols (Paris 1728–36,
reprinted Brussels 1963) III, part 2, pp 2–80. His preface to this book observes
that Erasmus received a copy of his *censurae* directed against the Erasmian
works even though Béda had communicated it only in private to the late
François Deloynes, a counsellor in the Parlement of Paris. Deloynes had been
approached by the German-born publisher Konrad Resch, who was established
at Paris, doing business under the sign 'à l'Ecu de Bâle,' and who in 1523
sought through Deloynes the approval of the theological faculty for a Paris

edition of Erasmus' *Paraphrase on Luke*. Allen VI 66–7 prints much of the Latin text of Béda's preface to his book of 1529, setting forth the circumstances of his first official encounter with Erasmus' biblical scholarship. On this entire correspondence and the resulting attack on Erasmus' orthodoxy, see Farge *Orthodoxy* 186–96 and Rummel II 29–55, 58–9.

Béda (c 1470–1537) studied at the Collège de Montaigu in Paris, where he also taught and where Erasmus as a young theological student who resided in that college probably knew him. From 1495 he was a member of the strict reformist group centered around Jan Standonck, whom he succeeded as principal of Montaigu in 1504. Although he retained control of Montaigu until 1535, he studied theology and took his doctorate in 1508. In his early years as a theologian he seems not to have been very active in the faculty, but from about 1519 he began publishing attacks on the orthodoxy of Erasmus, Lefèvre, and other humanists, maintaining that the critical exegetical methods used by them undermined the authority of the hierarchy and the unity of the church. He soon became the principal watchdog for orthodoxy in the faculty; and in 1520, after concluding that the deans of the theological faculty were not providing strong leadership, he persuaded the faculty to re-establish the old office of syndic, to which he was then repeatedly elected, gradually establishing the dominance of that office (and of himself) over the affairs of the faculty. Although his own extremism and harshness alienated even many of his fellow theologians, he remained unassailable until his injudicious attacks on the Lenten sermons of a preacher favoured by the king's sister, Margaret of Angoulême, caused him to be exiled for several months in 1533 and then, after he added open attacks on the professors of King Francis' nascent *collège royal* to his many other offences, permanently in 1535. He was the principal force behind the attacks on Erasmus by Paris theologians in the 1520s, and the present letter shows that Erasmus' initial reaction was to confront him and firmly maintain his own claim to orthodox status. For a biographical outline, full list of publications, and survey of older and modern scholarship, see Farge *Biographical Register* 31–6 (no 34) and the unpublished work of Walter F. Bense, 'Noël Beda and the Humanist Reformation at Paris, 1504–1534' (PhD dissertation, Harvard University 1967). Béda's reply is Ep 1579.

TO THE EXCELLENT MASTER NOËL BÉDA, CORDIAL GREETINGS
The late lamented François Deloynes[1] sent me a list of passages which you

* * * * *

1571
1 On his early career cf Ep 494 introduction. He had been a member of the

had marked in my *Paraphrase on Luke*.[2] Far from being offended by the   5
trouble you took, I would like you to do the same for the rest of the *Para-*
phrases and more particularly for my annotations. For nothing would please
me more than to have my books purged of error and of anything which
might cause offence.   5

When I was preparing the second edition of the New Testament,[3] I
made a strong and pressing appeal to the late Jan Atensis of blessed memory,[4] who was then chancellor of the University of Louvain, to let me know
if anything in my work might cause offence. He promised to do so. He read
it through and approved it unreservedly as a pious and scholarly work.   10
When I replied that what I wanted was criticism, not praise, since that was
more useful, he repeated again and again his favourable opinion. I asked

* * * * *

Parlement of Paris since 1500 and had risen to a position of great influence. He
was also the centre of a learned humanist circle at Paris, probably the main
reason why the printer Konrad Resch approached him for help in obtaining
authorization for an edition of Erasmus' *Paraphrase on Luke*, though as *Président*
de la chambre des Enquêtes of the Parlement of Paris, he was also important to
Resch, since under French law the publisher had to secure from the Parlement
or the *prévôt de Paris* a copyright (*privilège du roi*) before a book could be
published. In response to Deloynes' request for advice from the faculty of
theology, made in conformity to a law of 21 March 1521 giving the faculty the
duty of judging the orthodoxy of any book concerning religion, Béda provided
him with a copy of his own *censurae* on Erasmus' biblical scholarship, which
Deloynes transmitted privately to Erasmus shortly before his own death, which
occurred no later than 27 July 1524.

2 Since Resch's request for approval involved chiefly this work, Béda's inspection of Erasmus' biblical scholarship concentrated on this paraphrase, which
was published by Froben at Basel on 30 August 1523. For a modern evaluation
of Erasmus' work as textual scholar and translator of the Bible, see Bentley
161–73.

3 The Froben press dated the first edition of the Greek New Testament February
1516, and the colophon of the annotations is dated 1 March. The colophon of
the second edition is dated March 1519.

4 Jan Briart of Ath (d 1520), commonly known as Atensis, had been the most
influential theologian at Louvain after the departure of Adrian of Utrecht in
1515 into the service of the future Charles v. Although Erasmus often suspected him of hostility, he made a point of maintaining officially correct and
even friendly relations with him and of trying to win him over to the side of
humanistic textual scholarship. Thus the present narrative, though it emphasizes the positive, is essentially true. On Briart, see Ep 670 introduction; and for
a more nearly contemporary account of Erasmus' efforts to court his favour,
cf Ep 1225; also Rummel I 59–60.

the same question of Latomus,[5] who is now tearing to shreds what he could have corrected at the time if there was anything which displeased him. I also approached Ludwig Baer,[6] Christoph, bishop of Basel,[7] John,   15
bishop of Rochester,[8] and many others. I received nothing but praise. Nevertheless in spite of this chorus of approval from such distinguished men I removed and corrected many passages on my own and toned down many more.

I am now preparing the fourth edition.[9] If it is not too much trouble   20

* * * * *

5 On Jacques Masson, called Latomus, see Ep 934 introduction and 4n, and Rummel I 63–93, II vii, 6–15. Even in the period of Erasmus' residence at Louvain, he had been openly hostile to the Erasmian program of biblical studies and had published a direct repudiation of the humanistic plan of trilingual studies, *De trium linguarum et studii theologici ratione* (Antwerp: Michaël Hillen 1519; NK 1326), though this was formally directed against a work by Petrus Mosellanus and did not mention Erasmus by name. These attacks had continued (though he still avoided attacking Erasmus by name), and already by 1520 Erasmus described Latomus as his principal opponent in Louvain (Epp 1088, 1113).

6 On him see Ep 488 introduction. Baer was sympathetic to Erasmus' biblical and patristic scholarship and had also assisted him while he was preparing his *De libero arbitrio* against Luther (for evidence of Erasmus' consulting him before publishing this work against Luther, see Epp 1419, 1420). He was particularly useful in Erasmus' attempts to defend his own orthodoxy because he had been professor of theology at Basel since 1513 and had received his doctorate in theology from Paris with a distinguished academic record, ranking first among the theological graduates for the year 1512. At Basel he served as rector and vice-chancellor of the university and dean of the theological faculty. Despite his openness to Erasmian scholarship, he personally adhered to the scholastic tradition in which he had been educated and consistently upheld the authority of the papacy, choosing exile over conformity when Basel became officially Protestant in 1529.

7 On Bishop Christoph von Utenheim, see Ep 598 introduction. Although he was no doubt too sympathetic to humanistic reform for the taste of a conservative like Béda, his support was of special value to Erasmus because he was bishop of the diocese in which Erasmus lived and in which most of his books were published.

8 In Ep 432, dated about 30 June 1516, Bishop John Fisher warmly acknowledged receiving a copy of Erasmus' Greek New Testament. He had long been one of Erasmus' principal supporters in England. On his early career see Ep 229 introduction. Erasmus regarded him as one of the few exemplary bishops of his time.

9 The third edition of Erasmus' Greek New Testament was published in February 1522 and the fourth in March 1527, both by Froben at Basel. This fourth edition was in fact the definitive version of Erasmus' work on the scriptural text, and the last one (1535) made only minor changes.

to point out anything which could rightly give offence to good and learned men, you will put me under a heavy obligation; and I shall be sure to acknowledge in my writings my very deep appreciation of your kindness. If you are frank and forthright in this matter, I shall welcome your honesty as the true mark of a Christian theologian; but even if you choose to act in   25
a more severe and critical spirit, I shall nonetheless take it in good part.

The moderation of which I spoke is important also for the reputation of theology, which has now been tarnished for many men by the hypercritical and insulting attitude of some theologians and the insolent manner in which they condemn everything. I wonder what intelligent men will say   30
when they read that pamphlet of Pierre Cousturier's,[10] who was formerly a theologian at the Sorbonne and is now a Carthusian monk. What a farrago of abuse, arrogance, stupidity, and ignorance is to be found there! On every page he rattles on about half-baked theologians, bogus rhetoricians, dilettantes, jackasses, incompetent translators, aberrations, follies, errors, scandals,   35
heresies, and blasphemies; and all the time he is treating a subject about which he is totally ignorant. He reminds me of the old proverb that the

* * * * *

10 At the end of 1524 or early in 1525, Cousturier (known in Latin as Sutor) had published an attack on all new translations of the Bible, including that of Erasmus: *De tralatione Bibliae* (Paris: Pierre Vidoue for Jean Petit 1525). Cf Ep 1591, the dedication to Erasmus' rebuttal, *Adversus Petri Sutoris, quondam theologi Sorbonici, nunc monachi Cartusiani, debacchationem apologia* (Basel: Froben, August 1525). A lengthy controversy ensued, involving at least two additional publications by Erasmus and three more by Cousturier, who regarded Erasmus and all humanist reformers as heretics; in addition, from this letter onward, Erasmus filled his correspondence with repeated complaints about the malevolence and incompetence of Cousturier. His general line of attack was that while theologians might disagree on many points, Cousturier's positions were so extreme and so incompetently argued that they put him beyond the limits of acceptable academic controversy or traditional Catholic theology and merely brought discredit upon the cause which he claimed to defend. Cousturier (c 1475–1537) had been educated in arts and theology at Paris, where he completed his doctorate in 1510 and then entered the Carthusian order, one of a considerable number of men attracted to reformed monastic orders through the influence of Jan Standonck. He naturally stood by Standonck's disciple Béda in his opposition to the humanists. He was never a prominent member of the Paris theological faculty and indeed was at least twice officially corrected by the faculty for doctrinal statements judged to be unsound. Yet during the 1520s he emerged as an outspoken critic of the reformers, both humanist and Lutheran. On him and his attacks on Erasmus cf Bentley 205–6; Farge *Orthodoxy* 179, 189–90; Farge *Biographical Register* 119–21 (no 123); Rummel II 61–73.

cobbler should stick to his last.[11] He assumes as true what is evidently false
or controversial: he thinks that the translation of the New Testament which
we use is Jerome's, that it was written under the inspiration of the Holy   40
Spirit, and that it was accepted as such by the church. He assumes it was my
aim to have my translation read as authoritative to the exclusion of the old.
Setting out from these assumptions, which he believes to be established
beyond doubt, he reaches the conclusion that all later translations are dangerous to faith, heretical, and blasphemous. But he does not realize that this   45
charge applies also to Thomas, Bede, and Nicholas of Lyra,[12] who frequently cite a different reading, simply translating it without adverse comment.
For whatever is blasphemous in the whole must also be blasphemous in the
part. Nor does he understand that, when he says these things, he is slandering the pope, who approved my work in an official brief. Need I mention   50
Adrian VI, who far from condemning my efforts encouraged me to do for the
Old Testament what I had done for the New, or the bishop of Rochester, who
expressed his gratitude more than once and assured me that he had derived
much profit from my work, or Tunstall, the bishop of London,[13] or countless others who are as distinguished for their virtue as their learning.   55

It is plain to me that Cousturier has not read my work. Could anything be more high-handed than to rail against another man's work without
reading what one is denouncing with such angry abuse? He challenges me
to produce even a single authority who has adopted the reading *In principio
erat sermo* [In the beginning was the statement]; but I explained that clearly   60
in my *Apologia*. He asks if I can cite one passage where a scholar has gone
astray as a result of a mistake on the part of the translator; but I pointed out
many such errors in my annotations.

* * * * *

11 The proverb 'the cobbler should stick to his last' (Latin *ne sutor ultra crepidam*)
   is from Pliny *Naturalis historia* 35.85 and here involves a pun on the Latin form
   of Cousturier's name (*Sutor* 'cobbler').
12 That is, three authorities respected and acknowledged even by conservative
   Paris theologians: St Thomas Aquinas, the leading theologian of the Dominican
   order; the English Benedictine monk Bede, whom Erasmus had commended
   in a letter to Cardinal Wolsey in 1520 (Ep 1112) as 'a man who lacked neither
   learning nor industry by the standards of his time' and who was a major
   source of the twelfth-century *Glossa ordinaria*, the standard scholastic gloss to
   the text of the Vulgate Bible; and the Franciscan Nicholas of Lyra (c
   1270–1349), the best known and most authoritative biblical commentator of the
   later Middle Ages, whose work Erasmus had already cited (Ep 182:182) as
   justification for Lorenzo Valla's humanistic *Annotationes in Novum Testamentum*.
13 Cuthbert Tunstall, bishop of London, another of Erasmus' loyal supporters
   among the higher English clergy; cf Ep 207:25n.

You will find scores of people everywhere who bear no animus against Erasmus and yet are men of sane and sober judgment. What will these   65 people say, I wonder, when they read works like this emanating from the Sorbonne? I know of course that the best scholars among you disapprove of such things; yet all the while, because of the stupidity of a few, fine theologians have to face contempt and resentment.

A book has also appeared in Brabant, written by a Dominican,[14] but   70 it is so silly and unscholarly that one would expect a higher level of scholarship from a pig; it is so packed with blatant insults that no sneering toady could do worse. Theologians turn a blind eye to this sort of thing and don't realize the ridicule and hostility they are bringing down on their own heads.

I sent Nicolas Bérault[15] my reply to your *Annotationes* and asked him   75 to make it available to you. Farewell.

Basel, 28 April 1525

Erasmus of Rotterdam

I signed this with my own hand.

* * * * *

14 *Apologia in eum librum quem ab anno Erasmus Roterodamus de Confessione edidit, per Godefridum Ruysium Taxandrum theologum. Eiusdem libellus quo taxatur Delectus ciborum sive liber de carnium esu ante biennium per Erasmum Roterodamum enixus* (Antwerp: S. Cocus and G. Nicolaus, 21 March 1525; NK 1840). The name Taxander, which appears in a preface addressed to Erasmus' English antagonist Edward Lee, is a pseudonym, as Erasmus suspected from the beginning. The work is an attack on Erasmus' treatises *Exomologesis sive modus confitendi* and *Epistola apologetica ad Christophorum episcopum Basiliensem de interdicto esu carnium*. Erasmus initially blamed the attack on the Louvain theologian Vincentius Theoderici (or Dierckx) OP (cf Ep 1196) but subsequently learned from friends in the Netherlands that other Dominicans had participated also: Cornelis of Duiveland, Walter Ruys of Grave, and Govaert Strijroy of Diest (cf Epp 1598, 1603, 1608, 1621, 1624, 1655, 2045 for the gradual unravelling of the mystery). The pseudonym Godefridus Ruysius Taxander appears to have been compiled from the names of Vincentius' three co-conspirators. On Vincentius and his co-conspirators cf de Vocht *Literae ad Cranefeldium* Ep 148 introduction; de Vocht CTL I 464–5, II 260–2; and Rummel II 1–4, 28. The book by 'Taxander' is mentioned again in Erasmus' next letter to Béda, Ep 1581, and is discussed at length in Ep 1581A, which has recently been redated by Erika Rummel but is also printed as Ep 1436, where Allen had placed it on the strength of his conjectural dating of c 2 April 1524, a date which Rummel shows to be impossible.

15 On Bérault, a humanist and for a time a printer at Paris, who had himself crossed swords with the Paris theologians, see Ep 925 introduction. Since at this time he was living in Paris, had been the protégé of Etienne Poncher, the recently deceased archbishop of Sens, and was very well connected with other

1572 / To Alexius Thurzo   Basel, 30 April 1525

This is the dedication of Erasmus' Latin translation of two treatises of Plutarch, *De non irascendo* and *De curiositate*, printed with the Greek text by Froben at Basel in May 1525. Alexius Thurzo (d 1543) and two of his brothers, Johannes (II), bishop of Wrocław, and Stanislaus, bishop of Olomouc, all became corre-spondents and patrons of Erasmus and of many humanists in eastern Europe. Unlike his brothers, Alexius followed a secular career in the mining business and in public office. After the death of King Louis II of Hungary in the battle of Mohács (1526), he became an important supporter of the Hapsburg dynasty's claims in the parts of Hungary not conquered by the Turks. Like his brothers the bishops, however, he was an active patron of humanistic learning. This dedication was offered at the urging of Jan Antonin of Košice, a young physician educated at Padua who had treated Erasmus for kidney stones while visiting Basel in 1524 and who after returning to Hungary and Poland pro-moted contact between his wealthy patrons and Erasmus.

TO THE RIGHT HONOURABLE ALEXIUS THURZO, TREASURER TO
HIS SERENE MAJESTY THE KING OF HUNGARY, FROM ERASMUS OF
ROTTERDAM, GREETING
You must not think, most honoured sir, that only witches have prying eyes[1] and that no one but Midas has long ears:[2] here am I, separated from   5
you by such a distance, yet my eyes and ears can reach right to your part of the world and hear what all good men are saying about you and see and

* * * * *

members of the French hierarchy, with courtiers and members of the Parle-ment, and even with members of the university, he was a suitable channel for transmission of Erasmus' response to Béda's *Annotationes*. Even Bérault, how-ever, had been the object of an attack by the faculty of theology because of his critical remarks about scholastic theology in his preface to his own edition of Johannes Oecolampadius' Latin translation of John Chrysostom's *In totum Genesaeos librum homiliae sexaginta sex* and *Psegmata* (Paris: Pierre Gromors for Jean Petit 1524) and had been required to modify his introduction. See Farge *Registre* 44–5 (no 36A). On Bérault see CTC IV 358–61. The letter of Erasmus here mentioned is lost, though there is other correspondence between Erasmus and Bérault.

1572
1 Plautus *Aulularia* 41
2 Legendary king of Phrygia in ancient Asia Minor, noted for his curiosity. He gave judgment against Apollo in a musical contest and was rewarded by the god with ass's ears.

admire the rare qualities of your mind. With these qualities you are far
richer than if you owned the king's treasure or even if everything which has
passed through your hands was yours. And yet it is not from any sharpness   10
of ear or eye that I know you without having met you; but, just as a crack
of thunder in the distance is heard even by those who are hard of hearing
and a flash of lightning dazzles even the half-blind, so the brilliance and
fame of your achievements have made themselves felt in every corner of the
world. I am by nature something of a sluggard, but the harsh realities of the   15
times are rousing me from my slumbers and making me anxious to meet
men of outstanding merit and enlist them in our cause; for we are like
soldiers beleaguered by a powerful enemy and fearful of disaster, who
welcome help from any quarter, however distant, and turn their eyes and
ears in every direction in the hope of finding assistance somewhere.   20

So when I see certain men – if such creatures deserve the name of
'men' – conspiring in deadly earnest to destroy the humanities (which
acknowledge that they owe something to me as I readily admit the enormous debt which I owe to them) – when I see this happening, I am not
ashamed to seek out gallant warriors wherever I can and to beg for help   25
against the wild assaults of these Goths and Vandals; for it is clear that
there is no future for languages and letters or indeed for any discipline
worthy of a civilized man unless we find not just a single Camillus,[3] but
a whole host of champions whose intelligence, virtue, and influence will
match the folly, villainy, and insolence of our enemies, these being the   30
qualities in which they indisputably excel. If studies of this sort are snuffed
out, how, I wonder, will our life differ from that of cattle or fish or creatures of the wild?

I could not refuse this mission, distinguished sir, on behalf of the common cause of learning, for I was prodded into action by that warm and   35
honest man Jan Antonin of Košice.[4] You cannot doubt that I at least have
proved my faith in him since I was willing to trust him with this poor body
of mine, which is more fragile than glass, and no older physician has inspired more confidence or treated me with happier results than this young
man. While he was here he talked constantly of your readiness to support   40

* * * * *

3 M. Furius Camillus, distinguished military and political leader of Rome in the
   early part of the fourth century BC. His career was much embroidered in
   history and legend. He was noted especially for the refounding and recovery
   of Rome after the Gallic invasion of 387–386 BC (Livy, book 5) and thus was
   an appropriate parallel to Erasmus' dream of the rebirth of 'good letters.'
4 See introduction above and Ep 1602 introduction.

those who cherish true learning; he spoke also of your influence with the illustrious king of Hungary and of the authority you enjoy in every part of Hungary. In short he convinced me that my mission would turn out well both for myself and for the cause of learning. So I come as an ambassador of literature and I bring you, as a little gift from the world of literature   45 itself, two of Plutarch's essays. I hope that as a result of my efforts they may speak as eloquently to Latin ears as they have spoken so far to those who understand Greek.

It was certainly no easy task to convey the subtlety of Plutarch's language and reproduce those recondite expressions which he called up   50 from the secret stores of every author and every discipline and put together in his work. The result was not so much a composition as a patchwork, or better still, a mosaic[5] composed of the most exquisite pieces. All this was easy enough for him since his mind was stored with literary works of every kind, but it is very difficult for the translator to discover what he borrowed   55 and from what source, especially as we no longer possess many of the authors from whose meadows he picked the blooms for the weaving of his garlands. But this is not the only difficulty: there is also something terse and abrupt about his writing which sends the reader off suddenly in a new direction. Not only must Plutarch's reader be a man of good all-round   60 education, but he must also be alert and vigilant. Plutarch may himself be a Boeotian,[6] but no one with a Boeotian ear or a Boeotian mind is qualified to read him. As for the errors imported by the copyists, I shall say nothing about these except that, like ruts in the pavement, they often impeded my progress. I have solved many of these difficulties; but in some (not very   65 numerous) cases it would be truer to say that I skipped over the problem than that I found a solution.

But the importance of the subject amply compensates for all these difficulties. Socrates[7] brought philosophy down from heaven to earth: Plutarch brought it into the privacy of the home and into the study and the   70 bedroom of the individual. This is a field which interests me more these days because things have reached such a state of confusion throughout the Christian world that it is hardly safe to speak of Christ whether what one says is true or false. Under every stone there sleeps a scorpion.[8] The sub-

* * * * *

5 *Adagia* v ii 20
6 Plutarch was born and passed most of his life at Chaeronea in Boeotia. Boeo-
   tians were supposed to be slow-witted.
7 Cicero *Tusculanae disputationes* 5.10
8 *Adagia* I iv 34

jects which Plutarch discusses in these essays are such as anyone at any time would find immediately applicable to the ordinary concerns of life. Indeed it is hard to understand why this author's moral treatises are not constantly in people's hands and not studied by the young. I have perused these volumes with some care in the past, but I feel I have derived consider-   75
able profit from reading them more carefully and examining them in greater detail.

    Some human failings disappear or at least grow weaker with age. But anger,[9] which is intense among the young because of their hot blood and inexperience of life, takes on a new vigour among the old, doubtless be-   80
cause of the infirmities of age, unless experience and philosophy provide an effective cure. Inquisitiveness too is a vice familiar to both periods of life, to the young as well as to those who are entering their second childhood, except that when we encounter it among children we call it 'foolishness,' while among the old it is 'suspicion.' If we believe the Peripatetics, this   85
quality has been given to children to inspire them with a thirst for knowl-edge and to the old as a remedy for apathy and depression or, more import-antly, as a defence against fraud. For myself, I have never been curious about other people's affairs: indeed I am more careless than I ought to be about my own. But I am 'to anger prone, yet easily appeased.'[10] Some-   90
times feelings of anger overtake and subvert my real intentions, especially when the fault is compounded by impudence and malice. Yet I believe I belong to that small minority who do not lightly or quickly abandon a friendship or bear a grudge even when they have been bitterly wronged on more than one occasion. Perhaps a man of your wisdom and gentleness has   95
no need of these remedies, though anyone who shoulders such heavy burdens must sometimes find it difficult to control his feelings. Certainly no ordinary mortal is so perfect that he cannot improve, even if he has no faults to correct. Farewell, most noble sir.

    Basel, 30 April 1525   100

1573 / To Thiébaut Biétry   Basel, 4 May 1525

This is the preface of a second and enlarged edition of *Virginis matris apud Lauretum cultae liturgia* (Basel: Froben, May 1525), a mass written by Erasmus at Biétry's request in honour of Our Lady of Loreto. The earlier edition (see

* * * * *

9 Cicero mentions the view that old age is prone to anger, though he disagrees: *De senectute* 65; cf Seneca *De ira* 2.19.4.
10 Horace uses these words of himself in *Epistles* 1.20.25.

Ep 1391 for its dedication to the same person) was also by the Froben press. Allen Ep 1440 records a visit by Erasmus in April 1524 to Porrentruy, where Biétry was parish priest, in order to spend time with his friend and patron Christoph von Utenheim, bishop of Basel. During that trip, Antoine de Vergy, archbishop of Besançon, granted an indulgence to all persons who made use of the Erasmian mass in his diocese (Ep 1391 introduction). The archbishop's diploma granting the indulgence was printed in the second edition, and Erasmus also added a sermon for the revised version. Allen Ep 1391 introduction notes that it is highly unlikely that Erasmus could have visited the Loreto shrine during his time in Italy and speculates that Biétry may have made a pilgrimage there. In this mass, Erasmus makes no allusion to the story of the miracle, according to which the home of the Virgin Mary at Nazareth, having been made into a church by the apostles, was miraculously transported by angels after the fall of Jerusalem in 1291, first to Tersatto near Fiume in Istria, and then three additional times until it reached its present location at Loreto in southern Italy in 1295.

DESIDERIUS ERASMUS OF ROTTERDAM TO THIÉBAUT BIÉTRY,
PARISH PRIEST OF PORRENTRUY, GREETING
I have played the fool so often to please you, dear Biétry, that I think I would even do the rope dance[1] in the centre of the town square or the Cyclops' jig[2] if you told me to. I am not asking you in return to transform   5
yourself from an old musician into a new preacher. From every quarter of the world music of every style rises from every kind of instrument to assault the ears of the Blessed Virgin, who hears every day the song of the angelic choirs – unless I am mistaken, a far sweeter song than ours. It is only because men listen often to the din of voices and the noise of instru-   10
ments and never or rarely to the message of the gospel that in our villages and even in some of our towns there is such naïveté and such ignorance of the Christian faith. Yet it is the music of the gospel which casts its spell upon us and frees us gently from the spirit of this world and implants within us the spirit of Christ. If Amphion[3] could work such wonders with   15

* * * * *

1573
1 Terence *Adelphi* 752, a figure dance in which the dancers were joined together by a rope
2 Horace *Satires* 1.5.63 refers to dancing the role of the Cyclops in the mime.
3 He drew the stones together by the magic of his music to build the walls of Thebes. Apollodorus *Bibliotheca* 3.5.5 is one of several classical sources.

the sound of his lyre and if Orpheus' lute had such power that it could move rocks and oaks, how much more powerful must be David's lyre, whose music drove the evil spirit from Saul![4] And how much more effective must be the music of the gospel!

To be sure a priest has fulfilled a good part of his duty if, by living a pure and sober life, he provides a light for the guidance of his flock. But although I have no fault to find with you on this score, remember, my dear Thiébaut, that when we make allowance for priests who compensate for their lack of eloquence by the special saintliness of their lives, it is because they are unable to be competent in both, and the conduct of one's life has, so to speak, an eloquence of its own. Thus allowance was made for Valerian, the bishop of Hippo,[5] who delegated half his duties to Augustine because he spoke a language which the people did not understand. But I shall not allow you to be half a priest, since you can perform both functions well; and the Virgin Mother will think that her cherished Loreto is crowned with success only if you use your persuasive powers to draw as many men as you can to the love of her Son. But perhaps all along you have been doing what I am now urging you to do.

I have added a short homily[6] to make the liturgy complete. Farewell.
Basel, 4 May 1525

1574 / From Johann von Botzheim   Constance, 5 May 1525

Botzheim, canon of Constance, was the central figure of the humanist circle in that city and a close friend of Erasmus, who visited him there in 1522 (Epp 1103, 1342). He was also deeply committed to reform of the church and had at first been attracted to Luther and had written him an enthusiastic letter in 1520. But as the present letter shows, he was distressed by what he regarded as the sectarian spirit and extremism of the Reformation. In 1524 he was accused of heresy and summoned to Rome but managed, with the aid of Erasmus and others,

* * * * *

4 1 Sam 16:14, 23
5 Valerian (in other texts, the name appears as Valerius) was an elderly Greek bishop who spoke Latin but not the local Punic vernacular. See Augustine Ep 31.4 and cf Peter Brown *Augustine of Hippo* (Berkeley 1967) 139. Because he saw the need to uphold the Catholic faith in the presence of a Donatist majority and an active Manichean minority, he relied on Augustine as a preacher. The reference is especially suitable because one of the revisions made in this second edition was the addition of a *concio* or sermon.
6 Cf the preceding note.

to have this prosecution dismissed (Epp 1519, 1540, 1555). In 1527, when the city of Constance adopted the Reformation, he joined the other canons in exile. The original letter survived in a manuscript collection at Leipzig and was first edited by Förstemann and Günther in 1904.

Cordial greetings. The rumour that I have taken a wife[1] is as true as the story that Zwick has been arrested.[2] I can recollect no such event and he has manifested no signs of fear. Both of us are free of the chains which we are supposed to bear. So please tell Froben to thank the imbecile who told him these tales with such positive conviction.   5

I cannot make up my mind about Oecolampadius[3] and his followers. I look at his writings, but I cannot see into his mind. How few people there are who can sort out their own thoughts! I see many sects springing up, even among those who glory in the one gospel. To what extent this is Christ's will is a question I leave to others to decide: I shall not listen to any   10 of these people or take any notice of what they say, for I am content with my own simple faith in Christ. I do not intend to torture myself trying to puzzle out which of them has the finer arguments. There are so many different theories to explain what takes place when we partake of the body and blood of our Lord. One man holds it is merely a commemoration and   15 wishes it to be administered by officers of the state; another angrily protests that beneath the elements lie the real body and blood of our Lord just as they were when Christ was on the cross and insists that the sacrament be administered by a priest. Some reject both these views and propose a different theory. One man wishes to hold the elements in his own hands, another   20

* * * * *

1574
1 That is, the rumour is false. At that period, getting married was often one of the first overt evidences that a priest had adhered to the Reformation. Botzheim had only recently been subject to a formal accusation of heresy (cf introduction).
2 Johann Zwick (cf Allen Ep 1519:21n) apparently ran no danger of arrest, though he was becoming openly favourable to the Reformation and in fact was already secretly married despite being in holy orders. Though he was cited to Rome along with Botzheim, unlike him he simply ignored the citation.
3 By this time Oecolampadius was openly the leader of the Protestant party in Basel, a change to which Erasmus reacted more negatively than Botzheim, perhaps because Erasmus resented what he regarded as Oecolampadius' exploitation of their earlier relationship to imply that he himself favoured the reformer's opinions (cf Ep 1538).

to receive them from the hands of a priest. One is satisfied to communicate in one kind, another fights like a gladiator for both. One wishes to receive the blood from a silver chalice, another from a cup made of pine or ash. One wants the bread which has always been used for this purpose, another, not wishing to seem deficient in imagination, introduces some new kind of   25
wafer. So the quarrels continue with no end in sight. And the commotion over infant baptism is just as heated. I hear there are places in the district of Zürich where the peasants rebaptize one another out in the open in lakes and rivers.

Here where I live there is nothing but fighting and bloodshed. The   30
princes are armed and in a violent mood. The peasants are out of control[4] and act like raving madmen, though many here have accepted the terms offered[5] and are staying out of the conflict. In Württemberg,[6] I am told, the pent up fury of the peasants has exploded with terrible consequences for some of the princes there. The armed forces of the princes have regrouped   35
with the object of crushing these fanatical rebels. May Christ bring to pass whatever seems to him to be best!

I have no information about the pamphlets written against you.[7] If you take my advice, you will deal with these theological charlatans as they deserve, but I fear your inherent decency has sapped your will completely.   40
You ought to point out that there is no affinity between a Cousturier[8] and a real theologian, that there is a vast difference between the Carthusian rule

* * * * *

4 Although there had been preliminary outbreaks of violence around Lake Constance in the autumn of 1524, the peasant rebellion in general was just reaching its climax at this time. On the German Peasant War of 1525, see Preface, pages xi–xii.
5 Although some peasant bands broke and ran when faced by the army of the Swabian League, the so-called Lake Army, composed from peasants around Lake Constance, was so large and well armed, and so obviously stiffened by experienced mercenaries, that the League's general, Georg Truchsess von Waldburg, negotiated a settlement (Treaty of Weingarten, 17 April 1525) based on arbitration of grievances, and the peasant army disbanded. Cf the useful introduction by Brady and Midelfort to Blickle xvi.
6 The revolution in Württemberg was complicated by an abortive attempt of the deposed Duke Ulrich to regain his lands from the occupying Hapsburg administration. On learning of the French defeat at Pavia on 24 February 1525, which involved disastrous losses for Swiss mercenaries, Duke Ulrich's Swiss troops hastened home, leaving the Württemberg peasants exposed to the army of the Swabian League (Brady and Midelfort, introduction in Blickle xvi).
7 A reference to the works of Pierre Cousturier; cf Ep 1571 n10.
8 Ep 1571 n10

which they profess to follow and the vitriolic abuse which pours from their tongue and pen, and that though they claim a monopoly over all theology, they have no conception what true theology is. I wonder if there will ever   45 be an end to this brawling.

The letter which you sent me to be forwarded to Rome[9] will be dispatched with one of my own. Nothing is holding up my visit to Basel except my duties at the church. Many of the canons have departed because of the peasant uprisings and I am left to sing the office at every service. But   50 I expect some relief within three days and shall then get myself ready for the road. Please give my regards to the members of your household and to Froben's family. Farewell.

Constance, 5 May 1525

Your friend, Botzheim   55

To the most learned Master Desiderius Erasmus of Rotterdam, distinguished theologian and eloquent spokesman, his beloved teacher. In Basel

1575 / To Felix Trophinus   Basel, 13 May 1525

This letter commending Erasmus' former secretary, Johannes Hovius, to his new employer was probably written at Hovius' request. Felix Trophinus of Bologna (d 1527) had accompanied Cardinal Cajetanus to the diet of Augsburg in 1518 and subsequently had become chaplain and secretary to Cardinal Giulio de'Medici. The election of Giulio as Pope Clement VII in 1523 resulted in Trophinus' appointment as bishop the following year. Erasmus published this letter in his *Opus epistolarum*.

ERASMUS OF ROTTERDAM TO FELIX, BISHOP OF CHIETI, GREETING

Reverend bishop, I have long admired your generous and gifted nature. Now I am delighted that through the good offices of the pope, your circumstances have caught up with your merits. I also congratulate my friend Hovius[1] on his good luck in finding a place in your household. Had he   5

* * * * *

9 Not extant. Allen Ep 1574:39n suggests that it is probably related to Ep 1588, Clement VII's letter authorizing Erasmus to make a will, a privilege for which he deployed the influence of many persons having connections at the curia. The other possible subject, Botzheim's citation to Rome on charges of heresy, seems to have been fully resolved long before.

1575
1 On this former secretary of Erasmus, cf Epp 857 introduction, 867:189n, 1387 n3.

stayed with me, there was no possibility of his advancement except perhaps in learning. I hope he will show by his loyal service that he is worthy of your favour. I shall certainly encourage him to do so.

About the state of things here, it will be better if you inquire from the courier,[2] whom I am sending to Rome at my own expense on a small mat-   10
ter of business; there is no one in my household whom I trust more. So please look after him if he should need help. He has become embroiled in some sort of difficulty, though he is a good fellow who deserves a quieter life. Please add the name of Erasmus to the list of your protégés: you may be sure that no one will easily surpass him in loyalty and devotion. I pray   15
you may have every blessing, so that you may continue to be everything that people say you are.

Basel, 13 May 1525

1576 / To Celio Calcagnini   Basel, 13 May 1525

Although this is the first surviving letter between Erasmus and Calcagnini, they had met at Ferrara in 1508. This letter, like others sent to Italy with Karl Harst at the same time, is part of Erasmus' campaign to defend his reputation for orthodoxy against critics at the papal curia. Hence Erasmus included it in his *Opus epistolarum* of 1529. Calcagnini was an important member of the circle of humanists at Ferrara who admired Erasmus' scholarship (cf Ep 1552:10–18); and his own book *De libero animi motu* was inspired by Erasmus' work against Luther. Erasmus wrote a preface (Ep 1578) for it and had it published by Froben.

* * * * *

2 Karl Harst; cf Ep 1215 introduction, and Bierlaire *Familia* 61–4. In April 1524 he moved to Basel and became Erasmus' secretary. Erasmus placed great confidence in him, and in 1525 he made two important trips to Italy as a courier, delivering this and many other letters and also managing Erasmus' request for a papal dispensation and his relations with the Venetian publisher Gianfrancesco Torresani. At the end of 1525 and in 1526 he conducted another important mission to the Low Countries and England, again dealing with Erasmus' literary and business affairs. Another indication of Erasmus' reliance on his judgment is that in this letter Erasmus commissioned him to give a confidential oral report on the religious situation in Germany to a rising figure in the curia such as Trophinus. Since Harst planned to marry, Erasmus released him from service in June 1526, and he returned to the Netherlands. His later years were spent as one of the circle of Erasmians serving the duke of Cleves.

ERASMUS OF ROTTERDAM TO CELIO CALCAGNINI, GREETING
I was so delighted, dear Celio, by your book *De libero arbitrio* that, but for
a single passage which gave me some offence, I was ready to have it printed to promote the splendour of your name. In this passage you refer to
suspicions which certain people have about me and you give the impression   5
of being sympathetic to their views. These people keep on saying that I
derive some satisfaction from the present spectacle, because up to this
moment I have 'looked on in silence with my arms folded while that boar
is laying waste the vineyard of the Lord.'[1] The passage could have been
put right by altering a word or two, but I felt some compunction about   10
allowing myself even this small liberty with another man's work. I shall
make the change, however, if you say the word.
    It seems to be my fate that, whenever I try to do my best for both
parties, I have stones thrown at me from both sides. In your country and in
Brabant I am taken for a Lutheran, while here in Germany where I live I am   15
considered so anti-Lutheran that there is no one whom Luther's supporters
attack so savagely. They consider me principally to blame for the fact that
they are not now celebrating a triumph over the pope. You would soon
realize how true this is if you were here to witness the threats and insults
to which I am subjected and could examine the malicious caricatures and   20
defamatory (or should I say lunatic?) pamphlets which are constantly being
fired off against me. It was not just recently with the publication of my
diatribe *De libero arbitrio* that I began to earn this hostility. Three years ago
in every letter and every book which I produced I made it clear that I had
no sympathy with the fantasies of Luther. Yet it is still being said of me that 25
I am satisfied 'to look on with my arms folded.' Luther himself,[2] to say
nothing of the others, has now replied to my diatribe – his book has not yet
reached me, but I am sure its tone is highly offensive. While all this goes
on, I am the target of persistent and mindless attacks from monks and
theologians whose implacable hostility I have brought upon myself through   30
my support of the humanities, for these swine detest the humanities more
than they detest Luther himself. If my will had not been as hard as crystal,
their antagonism might well have driven me into the arms of Luther. Perhaps you consider this whole affair ridiculous, but no one could credit how

* * * * *

1576
1 Ps 80:14 (79:14)
2 Luther's *De servo arbitrio* was published at Wittenberg in December 1525, but
  Erasmus must have heard rumours that it was in preparation.

far it has spread and what inroads it has made in almost every country. I   35
used to enjoy the friendship of many learned men and thought myself more
fortunate than Croesus;[3] but I have willingly given up that happy fortune
and exposed myself, naked, defenceless, and alone, to the fury of a host of
enemies, whose tyranny the world cannot and will not endure for long. And
yet these men know well enough what a defeat I could have inflicted on   40
them, had I been willing to lift even a finger on behalf of the Lutherans.
Now, when the merits of theologians are being discussed, Erasmus is dismissed as a dullard; but when someone wants to damage his reputation,
then it is he and he alone who could have put out this whole conflagration
if he had chosen to lift his pen.   45

    And now Pio of Carpi[4] has launched a campaign of vilification. Peo-
ple write to tell me that at every meeting and every dinner-party at Rome
he belittles me, claiming that I am no philosopher and no theologian and
that I possess no genuine scholarship at all. Why does he 'look on in silence
with his arms folded while this wild boar is laying waste the vineyard of   50
the Lord?' Why is there no one at Rome with the courage to do what I did
in the very heart of Germany with no thought of reward except that of a
clear conscience? For, since I am shortly to leave this world, neither the
emperor nor the pope can do anything to improve my lot. Indeed they
cannot even guarantee that I shall not be cut to pieces by cruel and defama- 55
tory pamphlets, even from those pot-bellied gluttons who boast of their
support for the pope, though the truth is that nobody does greater damage
to the prestige of the papacy.

    If you wish to know how we are faring here, the man who brings
this letter[5] will give you a reliable account; he has authority from me to   60
tell my friends some news which it would be tedious and imprudent to
commit to a letter. You can safely trust him to bring me back a letter
in reply. I have given him a commission in connection with my own
work. Please don't hesitate to express your own opinion about this if
he asks. I am eager to know how Dr Leoniceno is getting on,[6] also Paniz-   65

* * * * *

3 King of Lydia, proverbial for his wealth. According to Herodotus (1.30–33) he
  inquired of Solon who was the happiest of men.
4 Alberto Pio, prince of Carpi, became Erasmus' principal Italian critic. Cf Ep
  1634.
5 Karl Harst; cf Ep 1575 n2.
6 On Niccolò Leoniceno, whom Erasmus regarded as a great restorer of ancient
  medical learning, see Ep 541 (especially l 61 and note), Erasmus' famous
  'Renaissance' letter of 26 February 1517 to Capito. Leoniceno was a famous
  professor of medicine and a highly controversial figure because of his critical

zato;[7] I met both of them at Ferrara. I am very fond of Rhodiginus too,[8] although he criticized me in several places in his miscellany. But I am not one to gag at the least criticism. I do not think we are acquainted unless, as I suspect, you are the person who welcomed me at the house of Richard Pace[9] with such an eloquent and graceful speech that I felt myself reduced   7(
to silence. Farewell.

Basel, 13 May 1525

1577 / To Fridericus Nausea   Basel, 13 May 1525

Fridericus Nausea (d 1552) was a colleague of Floriano Montini in the service of Cardinal Thomas Campeggi, the papal legate to Germany, Bohemia, and Hungary. Educated at Leipzig and Pavia, where he took a doctorate in law, he entered Campeggi's service in 1524. Appointed cathedral preacher at Frankfurt in 1525, he was forced out by a popular uprising in favor of the Reformation. His strong resistance to the Reformation attracted the attention of Johannes Fabri, bishop of Vienna, who brought him to the notice of King Ferdinand and whom he eventually succeeded as bishop. Already in 1525 he was a person of some importance both because of his humanistic publications in Italy and because of his connections to persons at the papal curia. Erasmus included this letter in his *Opus epistolarum*, but Allen Ep 1577 introduction gave preference in text and dating to the version printed in a collection of Nausea's letters, *Epistolae miscellaneae ad Nauseam* (Basel: Johannes Oporinus 1550).

* * * * *

evaluation of Pliny's *Naturalis historia* as a source for medical knowledge. See CTC IV 310–11 and the literature cited there.
7 Niccolò Mario Panizzato (d 1529), teacher of Latin and Greek at the University of Ferrara since the 1480s and a court poet whose verses celebrated Lucrezia Borgia at the time of her marriage to Alfonso I d'Este. Celio Calcagnini was one of his faculty colleagues. The poet Ludovico Ariosto was his student.
8 Cf Epp 469:10n, 1587 n53. Perhaps Erasmus is referring to Rhodiginus' *Antiquae lectiones* (Venice: Aldus 1516), though in criticizing Erasmus' *Adagia* there, Rhodiginus avoided mentioning Erasmus by name – to such an extent, in fact, that Erasmus' main complaint was not that he had been critical but that he had borrowed from the *Adagia* without acknowledgment.
9 Erasmus met Pace at Ferrara in 1508 and regarded him highly though regretting his decision to abandon scholarship for politics. As a diplomat serving Henry VIII he made several trips to Italy and remained in touch with Calcagnini. Cf Ep 211:53n.

DESIDERIUS ERASMUS OF ROTTERDAM TO THE MOST LEARNED
FRIDERICUS NAUSEA, CORDIAL GREETINGS

Your little book reached me safely,[1] which pleased me greatly, if only
because it came from someone who is very dear to me. Yet I could have
wished you had spent your time on a more profitable subject, and I should   5
still say the same even if your plan had turned out as you conceived it. But
now that it has failed, your efforts seem all the more pointless. Those who
have sailed the seas with little success themselves are generally more successful at warning others of the danger. The most important thing in establishing a reputation is to choose a subject which is attractive and has possi-   10
bilities, so that, however it is treated, it may interest the reader through its
intrinsic merits.

Cochlaeus[2] wrote me a letter which showed throughout how fond he
is of you. I have no time at present to write more. But soon I shall do something to let future generations know that it was no ordinary friendship   15
which joined Erasmus and Cochlaeus together. Meantime take good care of
your health and please give my best wishes to your colleague.[3]

Basel, 13 May 1525

* * * * *

1577
1 Although a firm opponent of the Reformation, Nausea took a conciliatory
   approach to dealing with it and published an open appeal for Erasmus' support for his efforts, *Ad magnum Erasmum Roterodamum, ut is proximo in Spira
   sacri Rhomani imperii principum statuumque conventui intersit oratio* (Vienna: J.
   Singriener 1524), which Erasmus here acknowledges. Nausea's plan, proposed
   in this book and here rejected by Erasmus, called for Erasmus to attend the
   imperial Diet already summoned for 1526 and to put himself forward as the
   leader of a comprehensive program of reconciliation and reform that would
   end the religious conflict. Nausea had already brought together several south-
   German leaders in order to enforce the edict of Worms against Luther, but this
   preliminary step had already failed to restore order, and Erasmus remained
   doubtful even though he respected his friend's good intentions. As a moderate
   Catholic reformer, he remained openly loyal to Erasmus' memory even when
   it was becoming unfashionable to do so. See Bruce E. Mansfield *Phoenix of His
   Age: Interpretations of Erasmus c. 1550–1750* (Toronto 1979) 8–11.
2 The letter is lost. On Cochlaeus, one of the most outspoken Catholic pamphlet-
   eers against the Reformation, see Allen Ep 1863. Cochlaeus was a close associate of Nausea.
3 Floriano Montini, who like Nausea was in the service of the papal legate,
   Cardinal Campeggi. Cf Epp 1552 introduction, 1578.

1578 / To Floriano Montini   Basel, 16 May 1525

> This letter was written as an introduction to the edition of Celio Calcagnini's
> *Libellus elegans de libero arbitrio ex philosophiae penetralibus*, a short work (essen-
> tially an anthology of texts) inspired by Erasmus' *De libero arbitrio* and pub-
> lished by Froben (June 1525) on Erasmus' recommendation. Cf Epp 1552, 1576.

DESIDERIUS ERASMUS OF ROTTERDAM TO THE MOST HONOURED
FLORIANO MONTINI, GREETING

Here is another example of laconic brevity,[1] shorter even than the previous
one, although you put me on my mettle by writing such a generous, eloquent, and amusing letter; its effect was to chase away most of those   5
gloomy thoughts which crowd in on me these days because of the present
state of the world. The situation would be depressing enough even if the
stone were treating me kindly and I suffered none of the vexations which
come from old age or from the incessant drudgery of my work and were
free of those other miseries with which this life of ours is beset. The plea- 10
sure which your letter gave me was increased by Celio's book *De libero
arbitrio*, a short but elegant work which shows the dedication with which its
author devotes himself to the sacred mysteries of philosophy. Before this I
had not had the good fortune to see any of his work. In fact, unless I am
mistaken, I met the man only once – at Ferrara in the home of Richard   15
Pace.[2] He greeted me most kindly, but with such a flood of eloquence that
I felt myself completely tongue-tied.

     I admit that I hesitated some considerable time before deciding
whether to hand over the book to the printers, who were clamouring for it,
or to hold it back. I see, dear Floriano, that there are people with dangerous 20
suspicions in your part of the world too, like those I have to put up with
here. I would have nothing to worry about, however, if the plot of the play
were completely reversed. If only the suspicions of your countrymen would
migrate to Germany, and the malicious caricatures and fanatical pamphlets
which are constantly being discharged against me here would take up their   25
abode with you! As it is, I am in danger here because I am an 'opponent'
of the sect in question, while in Italy and Brabant I am in even graver

* * * * *

1578
1 A reference to Montini's apology (Ep 1552) for the brevity of an earlier letter,
  now lost.
2 Cf Ep 1576 n9.

danger as its 'supporter.' Some censure me for treading a middle course. To
tread a middle course between Christ and Belial[3] is, I admit, a heinous sin,
but to steer midway between Scylla and Charybdis is in my view simple   30
prudence. Throughout my life I have hated nothing so much as schism, nor
have I said one thing and believed another. I refuse to commit myself to
anything which I do not comprehend or about which I am uncertain or to
which I cannot give intellectual assent. These gentlemen never mention me
as a theologian except when there is an opportunity to run me down; when   35
it is a question of distributing the honours, my name is not on the list. But
it is the fate of kings to be abused on every hand while serving the interests
of all.[4] Christ, our judge in the race of life, is alive! May he keep you safe,
dear friend!
Basel, 16 May 1525   40

1579 / From Noël Béda   Paris, 21 May 1525

A reply to Ep 1571, and like it first published by Béda in his *Apologia* of 1529.
Although this reply is an unflinching defence of traditional scholastic learning
and concedes nothing to Erasmus' opinion that the church is seriously corrupt,
assuming instead that any general criticism of the church is disloyal, it is quite
clear that he took Erasmus' direct challenge seriously and felt obliged to at
least pretend to be open to rational discourse even while threatening to bring
formal charges of heresy against Erasmus unless he retracted his previously
published opinions. The evidence for this is not only the great length of this
letter but also the author's obvious attempt to put on the dog: ie, to write in
a manner that he thought would impress a humanistic rhetorician. The letter
is composed in a convoluted and pompous style, though marred by occasional
lapses in grammar.

IHS
TO ERASMUS OF ROTTERDAM FROM NOËL BÉDA, GREETING
Over the past few years, beloved brother in Christ and fellow priest, I have
heard many different opinions expressed by learned men about your work;
so I finally decided to sample it for myself when I had the leisure, and this   5
I have done. I must tell you that I have begun to feel some considerable
anxiety for your soul, though I could see from the brilliance of your writings that you possess a soul endowed with great natural gifts. Indeed I

* * * * *

3 2 Cor 6:15
4 *Apophthegmata* LB IV 199E; cf Plutarch *Alexander* 41.

recall often saying in our solemn assembly: 'Erasmus is a man of more than
human ability with a rare capacity to say precisely what he wants to say   10
and a unique elegance of style.' When I read your work, I discovered that
much of your argument (so far as I could judge it in the fear of God) was
based on the dubious teaching of Origen[1] and of certain other writers who
(providentially, in my opinion) are less well known; at the same time you
have rejected the sound teaching of the accepted Doctors of the Catholic   15
church, whose ideas, because they needed clarification in the interests of
consistency and intelligibility, were systematized by Gratian,[2] Lombard,[3]

* * * * *

1579

1 Erasmus had long acknowledged the greatness of Origen (c 185–c 254), probably the ablest theologian among the Greek church Fathers, who was especially
attractive because of the central role of Scripture in his theological work. Errors
(or at least extremely speculative views about the ultimate salvation of all
souls) had eventually caused Origen's name to fall from favour, but many of
his works survived because of their influence on other patristic theologians,
both Greek and Latin. The revival of interest in patristic writings among Italian
humanists in the fifteenth century had already attracted attention to Origen,
and in 1512 Jacques Merlin, himself a Paris doctor of theology, published a
Latin edition of the complete works of Origen in four volumes (Paris: Jean Petit
and Josse Bade), accompanied by a long apology upholding Origen's sanctity
and greatness. A decade after its appearance, this edition and its *Apologia* for
Origen became the object of attack by Béda, who saw in Origen a source of the
theological errors which he indiscriminately attributed to Luther, Erasmus, and
Lefèvre d'Etaples. For Origen's influence on Erasmus and the resulting conflicts, see André Godin *Erasme, lecteur d'Origène* (Geneva 1982).
2 This twelfth-century Italian Camaldolese monk compiled the *Decretum*, or
Concordantia discordantium canonum, a collection of ecclesiastical laws which by
the end of that century had become the principal text used in the teaching of
canon law. He was, therefore, one of the founders of the medieval academic
tradition which Béda here upholds against humanist critics.
3 Peter Lombard (1095–1160), an Italian by birth, went about 1134 to study at
Reims and Paris and settled in Paris as a teacher of theology, becoming bishop
of Paris toward the end of his life. His *Book of Sentences*, completed c 1157–8,
represents the triumph of the dialectical approach to the study of theology and
became the standard textbook for study of scholastic theology in all universities, a dominance which was not seriously challenged until the revival of
Thomist theology by Cajetan, Konrad Köllin of Cologne, Pieter Crockaert of
Paris, and especially Crockaert's pupil Francisco de Vitoria, who in 1529 at
Salamanca became the first to break away from lecturing on the *Sentences* and
to base his lectures on Thomas Aquinas, and of course the flat rejection of the
whole scholastic approach to theology by Luther and his supporters. Lombard
is here cited as another founder of the scholastic tradition which Béda is
defending.

and those of our school whom we call the 'scholastics,' men who were truly
needed by the church at a period when it was in decline. No one should
believe that chance led these men to use a new and simpler style; on the   20
contrary it was the Spirit of God who wished it so and made this special
concession to our times, for He guides the church along different paths
according to the needs of each particular age.

So, dear brother, these things have made me grieve for you. I have no
doubt that everyone would have been delighted by your pen, if only your   25
intellect had not repudiated the ideas of Ambrose, Jerome, Augustine,
Gregory,[4] and all those saintly Doctors of the faith who came after them,
and please remember that it was these teachings which were scrupulously
followed in all matters pertaining to the divine law by William of Auxerre,[5]
Alexander of Hales,[6] Thomas,[7] Bonaventure,[8] and all the other acknowl-   30
edged masters of this school. It is not a valid objection that the afore-mentioned schoolmen disagree among themselves on certain issues which have
not yet been resolved and are in no way essential, so that even now one
need have no fear about investigating them. But since, as the saying goes,
'the die is cast'[9] and 'the word once gone forth can ne'er return,'[10] I pray   35

* * * * *

4 These were the four greatest Latin church Fathers, and Béda's charge that
  Erasmus repudiated their ideas was all the more offensive because Erasmus
  was the principal figure in the humanists' effort to restore patristic theology
  as an alternative to the medieval tradition. Erasmus himself was deeply involved in editorial work on these authors whose opinions he is accused of
  rejecting, editing Ambrose (4 volumes, 1527), Jerome (9 volumes, 1516), and
  Augustine (10 volumes, 1528–9), all from the Froben press. In fact he had
  produced, or was soon to produce, the most authoritative edition of each of
  these authors except Pope Gregory the Great.
5 Noted scholastic theologian (c 1150–1230) active both at Paris and at the papal
  curia, author of *Summa aurea*
6 English-born Paris theologian (1185–1245), a leader of the reorganization of the
  university in 1231, who as a mature man became a Franciscan, thus gaining a
  theological chair in that university for his order
7 St Thomas Aquinas (1225–74), the authoritative theological doctor of the Dominican order, and probably the most influential of all medieval scholastic
  theologians; also a central figure in the assimilation of Aristotelian philosophy
  into scholastic theology. His *Summa theologiae* is only the best known of many
  works.
8 Italian-born but Paris-educated theologian (1217–74), noted for mystical as well
  as theological writings, and the most influential doctor of the Franciscan order
  in the high scholastic period
9 Suetonius *Divus Iulius* 32; cf *Adagia* I iv 32.
10 Horace *Ars poetica* 390

you, dear brother, by the unfathomable goodness of God, listen to the advice of your poor friend Béda in the spirit which, I hope, inspires this response to your letter – for it was God who ordained that you should write to me first. I shall feel all the more free to say what I feel I ought to say for the good of your soul (whose salvation I desire with all my heart) because   40
you proclaim[11] your eagerness to learn by every possible means and to have everything which is false or erroneous removed from your books and you expressed the hope that 'you would always have Béda at hand when you were preparing to publish a book,' etc. I trust in the Lord that it has turned out to your advantage that you received my criticisms of your   45
paraphrase on Luke's Gospel, which were passed on to you without my knowledge: it was at the instigation of the supreme senate that I marked certain passages which made me uneasy, some less so than others.[12] So listen to me, my good brother, and humble yourself with me before God.

First, I cannot help suspecting trouble in the fact that you are constant-   50
ly exerting yourself, for what you claim is the good of others, in writing an unending stream of new books which the church does not need. It can scarcely ever be possible for you, I imagine, to deepen your knowledge through the refreshment of your spirit, that is to ponder in your own heart the vanity of this world and to taste the joyous security of the world to   55
come. For we should listen to the words of the Apostle, who says, 'If I speak with the tongues, etc' and 'if I have all knowledge, etc'[13] and 'thou that teachest another, teachest thou not thyself.'[14] When our Lord was teaching those who were soon to teach others, he said,[15] 'Whosoever shall break one of these least commandments and shall teach men so, etc.' In a   60
similar vein St Augustine wrote these words in the third *quaestio* for Dulci-tius (volume 8, section C in the edition I am using):[16] 'Here is something

* * * * *

11 Ep 1571:2–7
12 The supreme senate here mentioned is the Parlement of Paris, which was the supreme judicial court of France, not a legislative assembly like its English homonym. Under French law, the Parlement had the authority to issue the copyright (*privilège du roi*) which was required before publication of a book; and in the case of any book concerning religion, the Parlement was legally required to secure the judgment of the faculty of theology on the book's orthodoxy. This is why the book came into Béda's hands.
13 1 Cor 13:1,2
14 Rom 2:21
15 Matt 5:19
16 Augustine *De octo Dulcitii quaestionibus* 1–3 (PL 40 156–61). Allen Ep 1579:51n demonstrates from the wording of the citation that Béda was using the Amer-bach edition of Augustine's *Opera* (Basel 1506).

I must confess to your good nature: I prefer to learn rather than to teach. This is the lesson which the apostle James teaches us, when he says: "Let every man be swift to hear, but slow to speak."[17] So we are drawn to learn 65 by the beauty of truth, but compelled to teach by the obligations of charity; and when these obligations fall upon us, we should rather pray to be delivered from the necessity which makes one man the teacher of another.'

This is the view of Augustine, and he repeats the same sentiment more than once. So make up your mind to stop publishing new books, so that 70 you may find yourself again and prepare for the judgment of God, which, given our age, cannot be far away for you or for me. You have had your fair share of the glory of this world; now listen to me and devote the last part of your life to the glory which is eternal. You will not be on sure ground on theological matters until you unlearn many things, humbling 75 your spirit in the eyes of God, and trusting no more in your own judgment. Those who are trying to persuade you to act otherwise should consider by whose spirit they are being led and remember the words of Isaiah: 'And there will be some,' he said, 'who will call the people blessed, leading them astray, and those who are called blessed shall be cast down' and again: 'O 80 my people, those who call you blessed, lead you astray.'[18]

Then, unless I am misled by some human weakness, you would find no small profit both for your soul and for the church, if you followed the example of your mentor St Augustine[19] and, beginning with the earliest of your many and varied writings, subjected them to a critical examination, 85 and after considering them in the light of experience and with the help of the criticisms of others, rejected completely and utterly anything which you found at odds with faith or morals. To strengthen your mind for such a task, I suggest you read the letter to Marcellinus by this same Augustine whom you admire (it is number 7 in the collection).[20] I do not think – and 90 I speak as a friend – that you should set too much store by the general approval which, you tell us, has been accorded to your work by men of great learning and character, nor should you be too impressed (though this seems more significant) by formal communications from the pope. For you

* * * * *

17 James 1:19
18 Isa 9:16, 3:12
19 St Augustine frequently reconsidered his earlier position on certain issues and also explicitly revoked his earlier errors (as Béda expects Erasmus to do) by writing his *Retractationes* (PL 32 583–656 / CSEL 36). Presumably Augustine is 'your mentor' because Erasmus was technically still a member of the Augustinian canons regular at Steyn.
20 Augustine Ep 143 (PL 33 585–90 / CSEL 44 250–62)

know very well that it is one thing to scan a friend's work uncritically,   9
however honest one's intentions may be, and quite another to examine it
with the eye of an experienced critic and carefully weigh what one reads.
As Jerome says, our enemies do not listen with the same ears as our
friends.[21] A hostile reader looks for a knot in the bullrush,[22] but to a
friend even the crooked is made straight. This is clear even on your own   1C
evidence; for you admit[23] that after these great men had passed a favourable verdict on your *Annotationes* (and we may suppose that they read them),
you removed many passages, corrected others, and toned down more. So
I tell you with all the passion I feel for the salvation of your soul that you
have treated many matters in a manner which is dangerous and likely to   1C
cause grave scandal to Christ's people, matters such as the celibacy of the
clergy, monastic vows, fasting and the interdiction against the eating of
meat, the observance of feast days, the evangelical counsels, the translation
of Holy Scripture into the vernacular, human laws and the canonical hours,
the divorce among Christians, the creeds of the church, and many other   1:
issues of this sort. All this gives me cause to be anxious about you and
especially because of your reaction when some of your claims were challenged by men like Lee[24] and Zúñiga,[25] who are neither ignorant nor stupid and inarticulate. It is unlikely that all of their statements were without
foundation – indeed, unless I am mistaken, a good deal of what they said   1:
was true and to the point. Yet you refused to admit that you had nodded
or taken the wrong turn. Such behaviour makes one suspect a sin. Holy
Scripture is not silent on this point.[26]

Furthermore, with respect to the articles which are the occasion for this
present correspondence, it hurts me to think, dearly beloved brother, that   1:

* * * * *

21 *Contra Ioannem* 3 (PL 23 373). But Béda rather overlooks Jerome's main point
   here, that it is difficult to pass judgment on another person's intention (ibidem
   1 PL 23 371).
22 *Adagia* II iv 76; cf Terence *Andria* 941.
23 Ep 1571:19–21
24 Edward Lee, who engaged in a bitter controversy with Erasmus over the
   latter's editions of the New Testament, and whom Erasmus suspected of acting
   on orders of conservative theologians at Louvain; cf Ep 765 introduction, and
   Rummel I 95–120.
25 Diego López Zúñiga (known in Latin as Stunica), intellectually one of the most
   formidable of Erasmus' conservative critics. On him see CWE 8 336 and the
   literature there cited; also Rummel I 145–77. Allen IV 622 lists the ten controversial tracts exchanged betwen these two men.
26 Béda may be thinking of passages like Ps 32:5 and Prov 28:13 on the need to
   confess one's sins, but this is not a reference to a specific biblical passage.

those who are engaged in this debate should use such astringent, arrogant, ill-tempered, sneering, and abusive language when they write on these most sacred subjects, and I include myself in this criticism (if I have ever been guilty of the offence) and you too, and anyone else you may care to mention; such behaviour achieves nothing and poisons what might otherwise be   125
a more agreeable atmosphere. Nevertheless since those who are engaged in such disputes regard themselves as defenders of the truth and believe that their motives are pure and that they are inspired by a hatred of falsehood, perhaps their intemperate outbursts will find a ready forgiveness in the eyes of the Lord. You ask me to examine the rest of your works (especially your   130
Annotationes) with the same thoroughness with which I examined your paraphrase on Luke, and you suggest to our mutual friend, Master Bérault[27] (who was responsible for my receiving what in all charity you wrote) that, provided that I added nothing to what you had already seen, you would prefer your letter to him to be suppressed,[28] since it had been   135
written largely in the dark. Let me say in reply that it is my dearest wish that the Lord make it possible for us to enjoy such mutual converse; for I hope you will gain some profit by it.

I must tell you (and I know you will take it in good part) that I marked some passages in your paraphrases on Matthew, John, and the   140
apostolic Letters where I cannot agree with what you say; the occasion was given me by the Parlement of Paris[29] on the authority of our president

* * * * *

27 Cf Epp 925 introduction, 1571 n15.
28 The letter here discussed was one from Erasmus to Bérault which Erasmus did not want to be published unless the articles extracted by Béda from the *Paraphrase on Luke*, which Deloynes had revealed to Erasmus, were themselves published beforehand. This letter is now lost. Béda clearly refers to it in the preface to his edition of Ep 1571 in his *Apologia adversus clandestinos Lutheranos*, reprinted in Allen VI 66–7, especially lines 43–7. The Latin phrase here translated as 'written largely in the dark' means literally 'replying, so to speak, to uncertain things,' and implies either that Béda's criticisms were themselves incomplete or (more likely) that the material sent by Deloynes to Erasmus included only the extracted articles and did not represent the full range of Béda's critical annotations. Unfortunately, none of Erasmus' surviving correspondence with Bérault is from this period.
29 This is not an entirely accurate statement. Indeed the faculty, in the face of a warning from the king's confessor that the king was angry because of the faculty's hostile intentions toward Erasmus, specifically decided on 3 November 1523 not to take further action against him in its own name; but it authorized Béda, acting on his own personal responsibility, to write to the royal confessor and to send him any articles against Erasmus that he might have collected. Cf A. Clerval (ed) *Registres des procès-verbaux de la Faculté de Théologie*

Deloynes, of blessed memory.[30] I touched nothing in the *Annotationes*, since I understood that others had been through them before. For that matter, even on those texts which I did mark I wrote no comments of any 145 kind, but I have held on to my work and here it remains, on little sheets of paper, without additions of any kind. In other words I have written nothing at all by way of refutation of your ideas, nor have I yet made up my mind to do so. All I did was to extract certain statements, in the form of articles,[31] which caused me to be concerned. It would be quite pointless 150 to hand these over to you now. But if I discover later, on the advice of Master Bérault or other friends of mine, that it would be helpful for the advancement of the faith to add some words of explanation, and if the Lord will grant me his aid, I shall be in a position to do what is requested. If God in his mercy grants me this privilege, I shall aim for such moderation as 155 becomes an ageing priest who stands in awe of the judgment of God and I shall do everything possible to give you an opportunity to express your opinion before the material is published. If, however, you were to accept my advice and retract voluntarily whatever errors you have made in your writings, I would be most happy for your sake and would give thanks to 160 God because, through your action, he had relieved me of this burden.[32]

To make you more receptive to my words and to convince you that you have gone astray in many passages, I should like you to read the twenty-eighth sermon which the blessed father Augustine wrote on the words of the apostle [James],[33] also letter 154 of the same author,[34] 165 addressed to Publicola, along with his reply to the fourth Question of Hilary, in volume 11 of his works.[35] Then read volume 22, question 1 in

* * * * *

de Paris I (Paris 1917) 402. In 1524, Béda had quite appropriately been involved in the examination of Erasmus' *Paraphrase on Luke* because the printer Konrad Resch had requested permission to publish that work, and French law required the Parlement to secure the opinion of theological faculty before issuing the necessary *privilège*. See n12 above. But Béda's examination of these other *Paraphrases* was done as part of his broader campaign against Erasmus, conducted despite the king's opposition.

30 Cf Ep 1571 n1.
31 Ibidem
32 Cf Virgil *Eclogues* 9.65.
33 Augustine *De verbis beati Iacobi*, 'ante omnia nolite iurare' [James 5:12], in *Sermones* 180 (PL 38 972–9).
34 In modern numeration, Ep 47 (PL 33 184–7 / CSEL 34 129–36), not a very apt citation except perhaps for the fourth paragraph (col 186): 'Neque enim non licet corrigere cogitationes a falsitate in veritatem,' and the following warning that error of belief is a sin.
35 Hilary's letter to Augustine is in Augustine's *Opera* as Ep 156 (PL 33 674 / CSEL

the collected works of Gratian,[36] and you will understand that, like Luther and Lefèvre, you were wrong in following Origen,[37] when he wrote in the last of his homilies on Matthew (folio 82B in my copy) that all oaths were prohibited by Christ as unlawful. This was a manifest error and for that reason was condemned at the Council of Constance.[38] You were also mistaken to argue on grounds of piety that it is an advantage to the church to have all the Scriptures, even including the Song of Songs and Ezekiel, translated into the vernacular. You have been busy propagating this view with great frequency and persistence, not noticing the spiritual dangers and disastrous disturbances which the church has suffered time and again as a consequence; for this reason she banned the practice on more than one occasion.[39]

170

175

* * * * *

44 448); Augustine's reply, Letters 157:40–1 (PL 33 693 / CSEL 44 487–8). Allen Ep 1579:141n observes that the form of Béda's reference shows that he is using the Amerbach edition of Augustine's works (Basel 1506).

36 Causa 22.1: Quod iuramentum praestandum non sit. Cf Corpus iuris canonici 2nd ed, ed Emil Friedberg (2 vols Leipzig 1879–81) I 861–6.

37 Allen Ep 1579:144n shows that the form of the reference proves that Béda is citing the 1512 edition of Origen's Opera edited by Jacques Merlin (cf n1 above). The apparent confusion arising from the absence of any evidence that Origen wrote homilies on Matthew is cleared up by this edition, which labels these commentaries as homeliae both in the table of contents and in the running titles for that portion of volume III. Origen's commentary is not directed at the obvious passage on whether Christians may take oaths, Matt 5:34, which is cited only in passing, but at a section near the end of that Gospel, Matt 26:63–4 (cf Patrologiae cursus completus, series graeca ed J-P. Migne [161 vols, Paris 1857–91] 13 1757). That text also shows that Béda has thoroughly misunderstood (or deliberately distorted) what Origen wrote, as well as the position of Luther, who essentially accepted the position of the medieval church on the licitness of oaths.

38 See Mansi XXVII 634, Articuli Joannis Wiclef, no 43 (Sessio VIII, 4 May 1415); cf ibidem XXVIII 153–4 (Theologorum Constantiensis Concilii Diffusa condemnatio XLV articulorum Vicleffi, art XLIII).

39 In their court case against Bishop Briçonnet (see n40), the Parlement and faculty of theology cited in this regard Pope Innocent III's letter to the bishop of Metz, 'Cum ex iniuncto' (PL 214 695–8; cf Denzinger-Schönmetzer Enchiridion symbolorum et declarationum de rebus fidei et morum 36th ed [Rome and Freiburg im Breisgau 1973] 245–6, no 770–1). They also cited the condemnation of the Waldensians in 1179 and 1184, as well as Tertullian De praescriptione haereticorum 38 1–10 (CCL 1 218) and Origen Peri Archon (De principiis) 4.2.2 (9) Werke 5 in Die griechischen christlichen Schriftsteller der ersten drei Jahrhunderte 22 (Leipzig 1899–) 308–9. On these matters see James K. Farge Le parti conservateur au XVIe siècle: Université et Parlement de Paris à l'époque de la Renaissance et de la

I hope you will allow me to say that my Lord Bishop of Meaux[40] has   180
just been finding out to his cost what benefit an illiterate peasantry has
derived from the exertions of Jacques Lefèvre in this field.[41] And you will
know better than I if the translation of the Scriptures into the German
tongue has increased piety among peasant men and women in that country.
I wish you had been willing to read what the eminent doctor Gerson said   185
about this in various places in his works.[42] You will find them in volume
I, *De scriptoribus ecclesiasticis*, consideration xi; and in the same volume, *De
communione laicorum sub utraque specie*, xvii M; volume III, tractate 8 on the

* * * * *

Réforme Documents et inédits du Collège de France (Paris: Collège de France
/ Les Belles Lettres, in press 1992) p 75–6, nn51–7. Dr Farge kindly provided
the reference on this point.

40 Guillaume Briçonnet (1472–1534), patron of the reforming humanist Jacques
Lefèvre d'Etaples, in 1518 began a program of reform in his diocese and in
1521 called Lefèvre and several younger reformers to his aid. His reforms
quickly came under attack as heretical, an attack begun by the mendicant
orders and continued by Béda and other members of the Paris faculty of
theology. The capture of Francis I at Pavia removed his most powerful protector and enabled the faculty and the Parlement of Paris to secure warrants for
the arrest of several of his assistants. The bishop himself was fined by the
Parlement for allowing heresy to spread in his diocese. Although the return of
the king from captivity in 1526 ended such direct attacks, Briçonnet henceforth
administered his diocese much more cautiously. See Henry Heller in CEBR I
199, Farge *Orthodoxy* 169–98, 255–64, and Michel Veissière *L'évêque Guillaume
Briçonnet (1470–1534)* (Provins 1986).

41 In the opinion of Béda, one of Bishop Briçonnet's principal errors was encouraging the publication and distribution of Lefèvre's French translation of the
New Testament (2 vols, Paris: Simon de Colines 1523). A third volume, containing the Psalms in French, came out the following year, 1524. See *The
Prefatory Epistles of Jacques Lefèvre d'Etaples* ed Eugene F. Rice jr (New York
1972) 563–5. On Lefèvre see Ep 315 introduction. For similar parallels between
social unrest in Germany and manifestations of religious unrest in Meaux, as
well as Briçonnet's own apprehensions about the consequences of the reforms
he had introduced in his diocese, see Veissière (as in n40) 318–21, 358–63, 375.

42 Allen Ep 1579:163n observes that the following citation, employing 'the anti-
quated division of Gerson's works into numbered alphabets,' shows that Béda
was using one of the fifteenth-century editions rather than the recent one
published by Jean Petit and François Regnault (Paris 1521). In the modern
edition by Palémon Glorieux, *Oeuvres complètes de Jean Gerson* (10 vols, Paris
1960–73), the passages cited by Béda are: *De laude scriptorum* (formerly known
as *De scriptoribus ecclesiasticis*) IX 432; *De communione laicorum sub utraque specie*
X 57–8; *Collectorium super Magnificat, tractatus octavus* VIII 350. On Gerson's
prestige cf Ep 224:16n. For Erasmus' own rather reserved attitude toward the
much-admired Gerson, cf Ep 1581:91–8.

Magnificat, lxxxvii Z; volume IV, xiii L; the same volume IV, xlvi G; the same
volume again, lxvi I.   190

My brother, if you dismiss this doctor as simple-minded and common-
place, it will be hard for you to receive the help you need, however deep
my desire for your salvation. I venture to say that what you need before all
else is to read the work of this humble doctor so that you may humble
yourself in your own eyes; for there is no other way whereby you will find   195
favour with God. If, after reading the passages to which I refer you, you
conclude that in those two articles I have made my case to your satisfaction,
then I hope you will realize that I have grounds for what I said about the
rest, and could produce convincing testimony to prove my point.

Now to conclude this letter, let me tell you what was proposed yester-   200
day about some of your books when we met in solemn conclave.[43] An
admirer of yours has translated into French the following works: the *Encomium matrimonii, Oratio dominica*, and the *Symbolum*.[44] If there were others,
I don't remember them now. In accordance with the current practice in
Paris, the translations were presented to our faculty to find out if it was   205
proper to print them or not. The men appointed to this commission, following the usual practice of the faculty, read out from the actual translations
anything which they had discovered to be unsound. On hearing these, the
whole assembly was dumbfounded – they certainly showed no sympathy
with your views. I think, dearest brother, that the translator (whom some   210
suspect to be Louis de Berquin) did you no good by his zeal. It is to be
feared that you and Lefèvre may share a common fate at the hands of our
Masters,[45] for there is no doubt that both of you are the target of frequent

* * * * *

43 For the record of this session, see 'Notice sur un registre des procès-verbaux
de la Faculté de Théologie de Paris pendant les années 1503–33' ed Léopold
Delisle in *Notices et extraits des manuscrits de la Bibliothèque Nationale* 36 (Paris
1899) 378; also *Collectio judiciorum de novis erroribus* ed Charles du Plessis
d'Argentré 3 vols (Paris 1728–36; repr Brussels 1963) II–1 42, and now Farge
Registre 96–7 (no 94A).

44 Although the name of the translator did not appear in the editions, the faculty
already suspected that the translator was Louis de Berquin (cf line 211 below,
and Ep 925:17n), whose lack of discretion not only troubled Erasmus but also
led to his execution in 1529 on charges of heresy. On him cf Margaret Mann
Phillips *Erasme et les débuts de la Réforme française* (Paris 1934) 113–39 and Farge
Orthodoxy 173–7, 186–7, 198, 264. Béda is mistaken about the Latin title of the
second Erasmian work translated, which was *Brevis admonitio de modo orandi*.
But the faculty had authorised three doctors to examine Erasmus' *Oratio
dominica* in January 1524. See Farge *Registre* 6 (6A); cf ibidem 14 (13B). The
Symbolum is the colloquy *Inquisitio de fide*.

45 This is a threat. The Paris faculty had been waging a relentless campaign

and widespread criticism. In saying farewell, I pray you once more to pay
attention to the advice of your friend Béda so far as it is possible for you to   22
do so. If you do, all will be well with you.

Montaigu, Paris, 21 May 1525
Your friend, Béda, who is ready to serve you as you wish

1580 / To Antonio Pucci   Basel, 7 June 1525

This letter was written as a favour to Erasmus' friend Ludwig Baer, the Basel
theologian, who seems to have sent a petition of some sort to the papal curia.
On the recipient, see Ep 860 introduction. Since their previous correspondence
in 1518, Pucci had continued to be influential at Rome through his service as
a papal diplomat. The letter was published in *Opus epistolarum*.

ERASMUS OF ROTTERDAM TO ANTONIO PUCCI, BISHOP OF
PISTOIA, GREETING

My Lord bishop, although your extraordinary kindness to me is etched
deeply in my memory, I have thus far resisted the temptation to write to
you, for I thought I could best show my kindness by not interrupting your   5
Lordship in the midst of your many pressing duties with a superfluous
correspondence. But a courier became available and when I asked Provost
Ludwig Baer,[1] who is a great supporter of mine, if he had a message for

* * * * *

against Berquin since 1523. The Parlement of Paris authorised the arrest of
Berquin on 8 January 1526, and by 24 January he was a prisoner in the Con-
ciergerie in Paris. See Farge *Registre* 128 nn14, 15, and the references there
given. The king's captivity in 1525 removed his protection by the royal court,
and despite repeated royal intervention, he was speedily retried and executed
in April 1529 while Francis I was away from Paris and unable to intervene.
Indeed, by 1528–9, King Francis seemed less inclined than previously to shelter
persons accused of heresy and may well have 'written off' Berquin (Knecht
205). Romain Rolland 'Le dernier procès de Louis de Berquin (1527–1529)' *Ecole
française de Rome. Mélanges d'archéologie et d'histoire* 12 (1892) 324 suggests that
after the destruction of his army in the kingdom of Naples in the late summer
of 1528, the king needed to cultivate the support of the papacy and so abandoned his resistance to the legal process against Berquin, a conclusion endorsed by Knecht 205. Nevertheless, those conducting the process against
Berquin took care to act rapidly during the king's absence from Paris, perhaps
fearing that he would change his mind.

1580
1 See Ep 488 introduction.

Tomb of Johannes Thurzo
At the cathedral church in Wrocław
Courtesy of the Institute of Art, Polish Academy of Sciences

Rome, your name came up in our conversation and he insisted that I send you a few words of greeting. I am delighted to learn that you are well. We both of us cherish the hope that Fortune, which has begun to raise your station in the world,[2] will one day do justice to your true worth, and indeed that is sufficient to make you a great man in your own right, whether Fortune smiles or not.

Until recently the stone and the yapping of my enemies have exhausted all my energies. But now such a storm has blown up as almost to make me forget my former troubles. When it is the Lord's will and we deserve his mercy, the present upheavals will give way to some measure of peace. Already there has been a faint glimmer of hope that our rulers will patch up their differences. If that happens, perhaps I shall visit you in the autumn. I would be asking you to be kind towards your poor friend Erasmus, if I were not confident of your continued support without my asking for it.

Baer, I believe, is planning to write you a letter, though he is ashamed of his long silence and is overawed by your Lordship's magnificence. But there is no doubt of the sincerity of his respect and affection.

I wish your Lordship every blessing and happiness.

Basel, the fourth day after Pentecost 1525

1581 / To Noël Béda   Basel, 15 June 1525

This lengthy and blunt reply to Ep 1579 did not reach Béda until early autumn although it was dispatched in June. When it reached Strasbourg, no courier to Paris was available; and so it was returned to Erasmus, who dispatched it again together with the shorter and more conciliatory Ep 1596. It is a direct response to the critical, even menacing tone taken by Béda in Ep 1579. This is one item in their correspondence that Béda did not choose to publish in his *Apologia* of 1529, but Erasmus included it in his own *Opus epistolarum* of that same year. Allen Ep 1581 introduction concludes on the basis of irregularities in the number of lines per page that Erasmus must have deleted several sentences after typesetting for his 1529 publication had been completed, but the text provides no clue to where the excision was made or what it concerned. See also Epp 1571, 1581A introductions.

ERASMUS OF ROTTERDAM TO NOËL BÉDA, GREETING
Excellent sir, I am not one to form an adverse opinion of anybody unless

* * * * *

2 Whatever rumoured promotion Erasmus may be hinting at, it was not promotion to the cardinalate, a position Pucci did not achieve until 1531.

the plain facts of the case compel me to look at the matter in a different light. Vulgar tattle has no effect on me; suspicions do not bother me at all; even unjust treatment does not upset me if it is not too harsh or inhuman. 5 These things I disregard and ignore; I find excuses for them or suspend judgment until there is repeated evidence of obvious malice and I am forced to say 'I never thought it possible.'[1] Nothing, in my opinion, is more unbecoming to a Christian than to cling to a hastily formed suspicion of a neighbour and after attacking the reputation of an innocent man with repeated 10 abuse, to discover in the end that he was very different from the picture one had formed of him – and then to say, 'I never thought it possible.' So although for several years now I have been receiving a stream of letters which mention you in terms that are hardly flattering, these did not prevent me from believing that Béda was a good theologian and an honest man. 15 That opinion was backed up in a letter from my friend Bérault,[2] whose judgment I greatly respect.

So although there were occasional remarks in your letters which hinted at a less than favourable opinion of me, I was quite sure that your purpose in writing was sincere and honest. So your criticisms did not offend me at 20 all or lower you the least bit in my regard. Often in your letter I am your 'beloved brother,' but you never acknowledge me as your colleague: I am your fellow priest, but not your fellow theologian, although neither Leo nor Clement hesitated to give me that title, nor Adrian either, and he was indisputably a great theologian himself.[3] If you acknowledge no one as a 25 fellow theologian unless he is exceptionally learned, then you will not acknowledge anyone as a fellow priest unless he is extraordinarily devout.

* * * * *

1581
1 Cicero *De officiis* 1.81. Cf Epp 447:713 and 1161:16–17.
2 Cf Ep 1571 n15. Bérault was acting as a sort of middleman, keeping Erasmus informed of actions by the university and the Parlement of Paris that might endanger him, but the particular letter here referred to is lost.
3 Pope Leo X addressed Erasmus as theologian in Ep 864; Clement VII, in Ep 1588:67 and presumably in earlier letters as well; Adrian VI (himself the leading theologian of Louvain in his earlier career) presumably did so in the addresses of letters such as Epp 1324 and 1338, though the addresses of those letters do not survive. Adrian, a native of the Netherlands, appears to have been friendly to Erasmus and to humanism in general despite his own personal commitment to traditional scholastic theology. See Ep 171:16n for Adrian's earlier life, and Ep 1324 for a long and friendly papal brief urging Erasmus to come to Rome and put his scholarly talent at the service of the papacy, a letter which Erasmus took care to print in his *Exomologesis* (1524) and in subsequent collections of his letters.

Yet I have less claim to holiness than to learning, though my natural inclinations are more towards religion than scholarship. God welcomes the unlearned, but the godless he will not own. There are other passages in your   30
letter which seem to bear a double meaning, but I convinced myself that such sophistries were completely alien to your nature; if this is not the case, then my estimate of you is wide of the mark. Even if I had a penchant for such insinuations myself, I don't think a man of your good sense would adopt such a style towards someone who had written you a plain and   35
simple letter, nor would you wish to appear so different from what your correspondent imagined you to be.

You seem to have convinced yourself that I am the sort of man who thirsts for this world's glory, that I am stubborn and obstinate, and because of an obsession with writing worthless books, have little time to reflect on   40
the things which belong to the life to come. You know without my telling you, excellent sir, how difficult it is to judge another man's character; Paul refused even to pass judgment on himself.[4] But perhaps some scandalmonger has put these notions into your head, for nowadays the tongue of slander is everywhere supreme. It may be true that, without my knowing   45
it or being aware of it, I do harbour some of the vices which you find in me. Your scolding has had an effect, for I have begun to look at myself critically to see if such deadly weaknesses are lurking somewhere in my character. 'I am a man, and nothing that concerns a man / Deem I alien to myself.'[5] As for ambition, I admit that long ago when I was young I did   50
think it a glorious thing to be praised by famous men; but as soon as I realized what a tedious burden fame was, my one desire was to be free of it completely or banish it, as the saying goes, to where the stags drop their antlers.[6] Moreover why should one covet this kind of glory when it is marred by perpetual abuse, disparagement, and incrimination? I must be the   55
most pitiable creature alive if, after completing all my labours, I have nothing to show for it except the glory of this world, a glory which has less honey in it than bitter aloes[7] (if indeed you will find any honey there at all).

No one, I admit, is a good judge of himself;[8] but, although I have a   60

* * * * *

4 1 Cor 4:3
5 Terence *Heautontimorumenos* 77
6 *Adagia* II v 71, citing Aristotle *Historia animalium* 9.6.1 and Pliny *Naturalis historia* 8.115
7 *Adagia* I viii 66; cf Juvenal 6.181.
8 Cf Seneca *De beneficiis* 2.26.2.

profusion of other faults, I don't think that I am particularly prone to the failing we have just mentioned. Consider this, for example: before the appearance of Luther on the scene, when liberal studies flourished in a general atmosphere of peace, I was proud, to be honest, to enjoy the friend-ship of many learned men, but I never took much pleasure in their compli-   65
ments and indeed I was embarrassed when they were excessive. Had I enjoyed the plaudits of the Germans and been delighted when they ad-dressed me as the 'prince of letters,' 'high-priest of learning,' 'champion of the true theology,' 'the glorious shining star of Germany,' now that I have been robbed of these titles, I ought to be writhing on the rack. But the truth   70
is I am not at all unhappy although to these men I am now just plain Erasmus. I might almost say that I am glad to be free of those invidious compliments. Indeed I think I have borne up tolerably well so far against hysterical and libellous attacks from the very people who were once so enthusiastic in trumpeting my praise.[9] I knew of course that there would   75
never be peace between me and some malign persons who have always hated me because of my interest in the liberal arts; nevertheless I chose to expose my defenceless body to attack from both sides when I might have been a great nabob in the faction which dominated so many courts and regions; and so far, neither coaxing nor threats nor insults has been able to   80
make me change my ground. Someone perhaps will see this as caution rather than conviction. This is not so: I knew I would have been safer if I had thrown myself into the arms of Luther's friends, for I was aware of things which many people did not know. It was not fear that held me back, but conscience. Far from courting preferment, I even refused those offers   85
which came my way. And yet this attitude, which I have maintained stead-fastly to the present day, seems to you to show a craving for worldly glory? Nevertheless I take your advice in good part and I shall not let your warn-ing go unheeded.

You urge me to read Gerson[10] and other unpretentious writers of the   90
same kind as a way of humbling my pride. Now it is not my habit to

* * * * *

9 Notably *Cum Erasmo Roterodamo presbytero theologo expostulatio* (Strasbourg: Johann Schott 1523) by his formerly all-too-ardent admirer, Ulrich von Hutten. Cf Hajo Holborn *Ulrich von Hutten and the German Reformation* (New Haven 1937) 189–97, and Roland H. Bainton *Erasmus of Christendom* (New York 1969) 175–9.

10 The recommendation is in Ep 1579:185–90. Erasmus' rejection of him and of all the scholastic doctors in the following lines neatly defines a major area of disagreement between himself and Paris theologians who upheld the scholastic tradition. On Gerson cf Ep 224:16n.

despise any writer, but with regard to these so-called scholastics of yours
I find nothing unpretentious about them except the quality of their style. On
every page they parade their knowledge of the philosophy of Aristotle and
Averroes (which Scotus developed with pretentious additions of his own).   95
As a young man I read a few of Gerson's works and found something in
them to admire. But, for some reason which I cannot explain, whenever I
take up these modern writers, I begin to feel my own inadequacy less;
indeed there are no books which humble and mortify my pride so effectively as those of the evangelists and the apostles. I know it is a hard and   100
difficult struggle to get the better of human pride – it is something which
I have long striven to achieve, even if you suspect me of having no time to
reflect on anything which has to do with true religion because I am always
bringing out new books. I am not surprised you have gained this impression, since perhaps you have not had the same practice as a writer yourself 105
and think it difficult and time-consuming to do what is quite simple for a
practiced hand. For years now I have worked with heart and soul to clear
my conscience before Christ my judge and I am preparing myself, as best
I can, for that day which my age and health tell me cannot be far off. I
believe that through Christ's mercy, which I never cease to ask for in my   110
prayers, I have made some progress. For I await that day with a mind
which is more and more at peace, and no talk is more welcome to me than
that which fosters or excites such feelings in my heart.

So I am devoting myself almost entirely to subjects which further my
purpose, certainly not to anything which might thwart it. I refer to works   115
like *De misericordia Domini, De modo orandi, De moderanda lingua*,[11] which
is now in the press, and two short commentaries on certain of the
Psalms.[12] I am planning to wean myself away from the writing of books,
like a veteran athlete who retires gradually from the field, and I am concen-

* * * * *

11 Three of Erasmus' most recent works, *De immensa Dei misericordia, Modus orandi
   Deum*, and *Lingua*, all published at Basel by Froben, the first two in 1524, and
   the third about to be published (August 1525).
12 His first commentary, on Ps 1, was printed in his *Lucubrationes* (Strasbourg:
   Schürer, September 1515); cf Ep 327, the preface. His commentary on Ps 2 was
   apppended to his edition of the commentaries on Psalms by Arnobius the
   Younger, dedicated to Adrian VI (Ep 1304) and published by Froben in Sep-
   tember 1522. His paraphrase on Ps 3 appeared in his *Exomologesis* (Basel:
   Froben 1524); cf Ep 1427. His *In Psalmum quartum concio*, dedicated to John
   Longland, bishop of Lincoln (Ep 1535), was published by Froben in February
   1525. He also subsequently wrote commentaries on seven other psalms. On his
   Psalms commentaries in general, cf Charles Béné in ASD V-2 1–17.

trating on revising and polishing my earlier work, especially those of my   120
books which deal with Christian faith and piety. It has always been my aim
to inspire a renewed interest in the liberal arts and to bring about a marriage between them and those subjects with which you and your colleagues
are concerned. Part of my purpose was to give literary studies a Christian
voice, for up to that time, as you are aware, humanists in Italy concentrated   125
on pagan themes. But I also hoped, by adding an interest in languages and
fine literature, to bring something valuable and illuminating to the existing
curriculum of the schools. Both sides, I believe, have been at fault in this
controversy: the devotees of literature bitterly attack those whose interests
are different from their own, while the other side refuses to accept the   130
humanities into partnership, although they could have profited greatly from
them; instead they dismiss them unceremoniously and condemn and reject
what they do not understand.

    With regard to the teaching of the scholastics, I have always kept away
from it as much as possible, for I am very conscious that a person of my   135
modest abilities should not enter this difficult field of dogmatic theology,
which could only result in peril alike to myself and many others. What
success I might have had in this field I do not know, but certainly my
natural abilities took me in a different direction. I have always detested
factions, so much so that I have been more inclined to discourage my   140
supporters than rebuff my critics. So if I have erred or put myself at risk,
the error and the risk are mine alone. My sole purpose in the New Testament was to establish a pure text and to shed some light on problems which
had clearly caused many to run aground. Nothing was further from my
thoughts than to displace the Vulgate; in fact I would have given the old   145
translation beside the Greek text in spite of the discrepancies, if some of my
learned friends had not put pressure upon me and overridden my objections: it was not sound advice which they gave me nor happy in its outcome. As for the comments which I made from time to time, I swear before
God that I honestly thought I was doing something which would be pleas-   150
ing to him and vital to the Christian faith. I thought too that I had carried
out my plan in such a moderate spirit as to give no possible cause for
discord; certainly I worked hard to achieve that end. I saw much evidence
of decline and it was a time of peace. Could anyone have foreseen that the
whole world would soon be engulfed in this fateful storm?   155

    You suggest in your charity that my writings, unless amended, are
dangerous to Christian faith: but I was equally convinced that it would be
dangerous for the Christian faith if I held back the criticisms I wished to
make. If this was wrong, it was an error of judgment, not of design. And
yet I never relied upon my own judgment in the matter, nor was I swept off   160

my feet by the world's applause. Far from refusing to humble myself before God, as you kindly advise me to do, there was hardly anyone to whom I did not defer. Indeed this practice sometimes led me into error, which I could have avoided had I put more faith in my own judgment than in that of others. You can guess how ready I was to listen to advice by the fact that, when I was making a hurried revision of my work on the New Testament, I appealed for help not just to Briart,[13] Latomus,[14] and Dorp,[15] but even to Lee,[16] who had a very elementary knowledge of theology as I afterwards discovered, and it was because of this experience that I allowed a close and friendly association to develop between us. The result, as you know, was less than happy for me. Yet you appear to suspect me of obstinacy and as evidence for this charge you say that, in spite of having the considered advice of two articulate men, who are neither ignorant nor stupid, I nowhere acknowledge that I went astray.

Zúñiga[17] and Lee, I admit, are not inarticulate; in fact I would go further and acknowledge their extraordinary loquacity. But how true is it that they are 'neither ignorant nor stupid'? That is a question their own writings will answer for you if you read them without prejudice, though I imagine you have been too occupied with more serious business to condescend to such frivolities; and yet, my dear Béda, a man with your sense of decency should have read them before forming such a horrible suspicion about me. Zúñiga is a scurrilous buffoon of the worst sort. In passage after passage I demonstrate that he does not understand what he is talking about. Yet in not a few places I thank this impostor for his advice, though there is no reason to be grateful, even for good advice, if it is inspired more by spite than good judgment.

Lee is less of a scholar then Zúñiga, but more venomous; yet when his advice is sound, I acknowledge his help. If you imagine I have never done so, you cannot have read my book, or if you have read it, you must have done so with other things on your mind. To be frank, I am surprised that

* * * * *

13 Cf Ep 1571 n4.
14 Cf Ep 1571 n5.
15 Despite Erasmus' ambivalence about him, Dorp was the most friendly of the Louvain theologians and even at his most negative was willing to advise him about revisions for the second edition of the New Testament. See Ep 496.
16 Unlike the others, it is doubtful that Erasmus ever welcomed active participation by Lee in the revision of his edition of the New Testament. In fact, his coolness to Lee's eager suggestions was the source of their subsequent conflict. See CWE 6 xv and 7 xi–xii (prefaces by Peter G. Bietenholz) and cf Ep 1579 n24.
17 Cf Ep 1579 n25.

you approve of writers like that. When they write something unusually rancorous, you say the fault is pardonable. Your circle may find such things easy to forgive, but I am sure God will not easily forgive those who attack the reputation of a neighbour with a flood of falsehoods, slanders, fabrications, and conceited airs. I have shown that in his attacks on me Lee makes 195 several assertions which are plainly heretical; nor has he any friends in England sympathetic enough to stand up for these views of his. England in fact has imposed a ban of silence on him and no one has been more offended by his book than those who were his close friends and kindred spirits.[18] Had he published that feeble pamphlet as he first wrote it – the one he 200 prepared in twenty copies for private distribution among his friends – you can imagine what snorting and sneering there would have been! There were things in it which were undoubtedly blasphemous. What he published later was largely the work of others. You will say that this is all my imagination, but I had the book in my possession before I completed my reply. 205

Zúñiga is regarded in Spain as a vain and stupid man, as indeed he is. How his calumnies went down with the pope is clear from the fact that he was silenced several times,[19] first by Leo, then by the college of cardinals, after that by Adrian, a second time by the cardinals and finally by Clement, who seriously threatened to throw him into prison if he did not 210 hold his tongue.

Let me say for a start that neither Zúñiga nor Lee was the right person to take it upon himself to criticize me. Even if their scholarship had been up to it, they lacked credibility because of the violence of their prejudices and the enormity of their conceit. I know one should listen to advice, but only 215

* * * * *

18 Erasmus certainly had worked upon his English friends, such as Bishop John Fisher, Thomas More, Richard Pace, and John Colet, to bring pressure on Lee (Epp 936, 1061, 1074, and Ferguson *Opuscula* 250:279n) and had complained directly and indirectly to Henry VIII (Epp 1098, 1126) but had never completely succeeded in silencing these persistent criticisms. If Lee's stubbornness had ever deeply offended their many mutual friends in England, it did not harm his standing for very long. At this very time he was appointed ambassador to Spain, the first long step in a court career which by 1531 made him archbishop of York. On the whole controversy see the references cited above in n16.

19 By Leo X: Ep 1213:37–9, cf n9; by the college of cardinals: Epp 1302:68–71, 1305:6–9; by Clement VII: Epp 1431:14, 1433:19–20, 1488:18–20; as for Adrian VI, Allen Ep 1581:194n found no record of an order by this pope silencing Zúñiga but thinks that Erasmus had in mind the actions reported in Ep 1433:16–17, which appear to deal only with silencing the Louvain theologians (but which Erasmus links with the cardinals' silencing of Zúñiga by mentioning that incident in the very next line).

if it comes from someone who is capable of giving good advice and only if the advice is helpful. Would anyone entrust himself to a surgeon, with a scalpel and branding-iron in his hand, who showed every sign of wanting to murder his patient if he could? Or who would swallow a dose of medicine from a doctor who was clearly bent on killing the invalid, not curing   220
him? But it would take a much bigger fool to trust himself to someone of that sort who in addition knew nothing about surgery or medicine. On my own initiative I corrected many passages which had been praised by others: what do you think my response would have been if some scholar had criticized my work in a friendly spirit? To show you how far I am from   225
being obstinate, let me tell you that I was forced to delete certain passages which I had previously altered on Lee's advice. If I had heeded him throughout, the reader of my book would be exposed to heresy plain and simple, and I am not speaking of the arguments of the schoolmen but of the central doctrines of the faith. Not to make a long story of it, the very point   230
which you criticize, that Jesus owed obedience to no mortal man, was something I learned from Carranza[20] and Zúñiga, although they force it down our throats in a much more offensive way. And you will find other ideas, more heterodox than this, if you can spare the time to read their scurrilous polemics and my replies.   235

You attach great weight to the vituperative writings of these men, although many bishops and theologians and the Roman pontiff himself judge them of slight importance. It is one thing, you say, to win the approval of one's friends, quite another to face the judgment of one's critics, for they are looking for the knot in the bullrush.[21] I know that passionate love is   240
blind,[22] but hate is blinder still, and the heart of man is much readier to hate than to love. Why should those who have commended my work be blinded by their love for me, since it is my work and nothing else which is the reason for their love and there is nothing which they need from me? Am I then to distrust these men, who know more about theology than   245
scores of Lees and Zúñigas, and submit to the judgment of those friends of yours, who make their violent and irrational hatred of me so plain to see? If we are to put our faith in theologians, my supporters too are theologians.

* * * * *

20 Cf Ep 1277 n8, also H.J. de Jonge in ASD IX-2 24–5, 42; CWE 8 346 n4 (on page 460), and Bataillon (Fr) (also Bataillon 1991 vol 1) 131–3, who notes (131 n2) that at the theological conference held at Valladolid in 1527, Carranza spoke in defence of Erasmus' scholarship; cf the Spanish edition, Bataillon (Sp) 122–4.
21 Cf Terence *Andria* 941; *Adagia* II iv 76.
22 Cf Plato *Laws* 731E; Theocritus 10.19.

But, you say, some of these have turned into enemies and are now condemning what they had approved as friends. Which opinion then is to weigh more heavily with me? Or rather, why should anyone respect the judgment of those who alter their opinions with their moods and from the selfsame lips blow hot and cold?[23]

When I was producing the first edition of my New Testament, Capito[24] and Oecolampadius[25] were always at hand, both of whom struck me at the time as godly men and learned theologians, however much the situation may have changed since then. My neighbour Baer,[26] whom you too, I believe, consider a theologian, came to see me frequently. He read my work with considerable care: why then did he not notice those pernicious doctrines which cause you such great concern? I know he is a friend of mine, but he is an outspoken friend and he is well aware that I like friends who speak their minds.

After the appearance of the first edition I moved to Louvain, where the theologians welcomed me into their circle, although this was the least of my ambitions. When the work appeared, the Carmelite Egmondanus raised a great fuss,[27] claiming that I was the Antichrist. When we had a chance to talk in private, I asked him to tell me what needed correction and assured him that there was no greater service he could do me. His answer was that he had not read the work! I pleaded with Atensis[28] more than once to let me know if there was anything which caused him offence, for my aim was to serve, and not to hurt, the cause of Christ. I made the same request of Latomus and Dorp. Atensis agreed to do what I asked. Just before my departure[29] he invited me to dinner. After dinner I broached the subject once more. He said he had read my work right through and found it both

250

255

260

265

270

* * * * *

23 *Adagia* I viii 30
24 Cf Ep 459 introduction.
25 Cf Ep 224:30n.
26 Cf Epp 488 introduction, 1571 n6.
27 Cf Ep 878:15n, and Rummel I 135–43. Erasmus consistently ridiculed this Carmelite theologian as the most benighted of his enemies at Louvain. His admission in an interview with Erasmus that although he repeatedly denounced Erasmus' New Testament in his sermons, he had never read or even seen it is reported in Epp 948, 1196, 2045. Erasmus did, however, make this same accusation against other critics, although not naming names: cf Ep 1200.
28 Cf Epp 670 introduction, 1571 n4. The specific incidents mentioned here are recorded in Ep 1225.
29 Erasmus left the Netherlands for Basel about 1 May 1518 in order to supervise final revision of the second edition of the New Testament, the subject of these conversations with the theologians of Louvain.

learned and devout. I asked him to tell me frankly what he thought and I   275
made it clear that I preferred criticism to praise since criticism would be
helpful but eulogies would not. He repeated his earlier comments over and
over again and encouraged me to serve the Christian faith with my holy
endeavours (for this was the way he talked in those days). Then to leave
himself a loophole, he added this reservation, 'I don't know what you are   280
going to write, but what you have written so far pleased me very much.' I
replied that I hoped to make improvements everywhere in the work, and
unless I am mistaken, this is what I have done. And this man, whether you
consider his influence or his learning, was the leading figure in the university there.   285

    I returned with a case of the plague, or so the doctors thought, and
certainly there was no doubt about the three buboes on my body. In spite
of my protests Atensis and some other theologians came running to pay
their respects. There was no trouble until Lee started up his song and dance.
When my health permitted, I invited him to talk with me. I made three   290
proposals which were eminently fair: he could show me his notes or, if he
had misgivings about that, he could come and talk to me about it, or finally
he could put his views into print. None of these proposals satisfied him.
Then I suggested that Atensis should be judge between us, though he was
already showing signs of prejudice against me. Lee would agree to nothing.   295
He had made up his mind to enjoy the spurious satisfaction of having made
hundreds of criticisms of my work which he claimed he was suppressing
as a favour to my friends. I had a private meeting with Atensis and I asked
him to let me know if he found any serious problem in my work; I told him
it was not yet quite ready to appear and that rather than suffer a loss of   300
reputation I would prefer to lose the cost of redoing several pages. I had
brought the *Annotationes* with me from Basel, amounting to half the total
work, and I gave these to Dorp to read. He read them through and made
some comments, none of which had to do with matters of faith. Later I
handed them to Latomus. No one raised any objections.   305

    When all this was going on, the work came out, since it could no
longer be held up without serious financial loss to the printer. Meanwhile
Lee's hysterical opposition was growing worse and, as one might expect,
rumblings began to be heard from other quarters. When there seemed no
end to these strictures, I approached Atensis again and suggested that he   310
commission a group of scholars – Dorp, Latomus, and men like that – to
identify any passage which might properly cause offence; for I was not
prepared to take seriously the criticisms of some half-educated novice. It
was agreed. Atensis found fault with some passages and Dorp with a few
others. I exercised my right of reply (for this was part of the bargain) and   31

satisfied them on all points but one: they complained that I had omitted to
state that the current practice of confession was instituted by Christ. I
replied that it was not my habit to assert what I could not prove, but that
I submitted my judgment to the authority of the church; this for the present
was good enough for me.   320

Later a third edition was being prepared for publication.[30] I approached everyone who seemed to have any critical ability and asked to be
told of anything in the text which troubled them, especially in regard to the
essentials of the Christian faith. Many have expressed approval, no one has
mentioned any difficulties so far. Adrian,[31] who was then a cardinal, sent   325
me a message by his friend Barbier[32] to urge me to do for the Old Testament what I had done for the New. He said nothing about any serious
problems. I do not think he would have acted in this way, if he had felt as
you seem to feel about my work.

Now a fourth edition is in preparation and I am ready to accept advice   330
from anyone, even from the half-educated. You will say that it is the opinion of theologians which counts. Well then, do you not think that John,
bishop of Rochester,[33] is a theologian? I recognize the pre-eminence of
your university in theology, but I have always held that there are theologians in other institutions as well. Ludwig Baer, Gillis van Delft,[34] and   335
Herman Lethmaet[35] are among the leading figures of your school. I have
had thorough discussions with all of them. I wrote to Prierias[36] to ask him
to point out any passages which worried him. He had nothing to say. And
yet you think my attitude stubborn and inflexible.

* * * * *

30 Published in 1522 by Froben at Basel
31 Adrian of Utrecht, the future Pope Adrian VI. Allen Ep 1225:1n suggests that
    Pierre Barbier's advice to maintain good relations with the Louvain theologians
    was inspired by Adrian.
32 Cf Epp 443, 1216. Since Barbier had been in Adrian's circle both in Spain and
    during his pontificate and had always been an outspoken admirer of Erasmus,
    he was a likely channel for the transmission of a suggestion for an edition of
    the Old Testament.
33 John Fisher; cf Ep 1571 n8.
34 A distinguished Paris theologian; cf Ep 456:98n.
35 Cf Ep 1320; of particular relevance here is that Lethmaet was not only a recent
    (1520) Paris doctor of theology but also had ranked first in his graduation
    class. See Farge Biographical Register 278–9 (no 307).
36 Ep 1412; cf Ep 872:19n. Prierias had died in 1523, but the use of his name here
    seemed appropriate because from 1514 he was professor of Thomistic theology
    in the curial university and was the personal theological advisor to Pope Leo
    X. He was also one of the earliest theological opponents of Luther.

But you say, 'Even when your errors are pointed out, you don't admit   340
that you are wrong.' Do you expect me then at the first hint of criticism
from anyone to cry out like a child who is threatened with a beating, 'Forgive me, I know I've done wrong'?[37] Do you want me to admit to a fault
where no fault exists? Or does someone who is doing all he can to serve
others seem to you to be beneath the attentions of a theologian? My princi-   345
pal reason for wanting to visit Paris was to have private talks with some of
your colleagues. There were many obstacles in the way, especially the war
between the emperor and the king of France, which was becoming more
and more savage every day. I was offered a post with a large and assured
income – there was even a letter from the king. But I suspected that, no   350
matter what was said, the invitation amounted to a call to war, which
would break out at the first opportunity. So I turned my back on fortune,
preferring a quiet life. I have had my fill of controversy already. Berquin[38]
I know only from his letters, but to judge from these, he seems a wise and
temperate man. Yet I have never ceased to urge him to steer clear of contro-   355
versy. I am deeply sorry if the bishop of Lodève[39] has run into trouble. He
struck me as having the qualities I should like to see in many of our
bishops.

No bishop has ever been placed under a cloud because of me or led
from the straight and narrow path.[40] You were good enough to express   360
concern that I might end up like Lefèvre,[41] but I am more concerned, my
good Béda, that you and your colleagues may share the fate of the German
theologians,[42] whose influence has now reached the point where anything

* * * * *

37 Cf Cicero *Pro Ligario* 30.
38 Cf Epp 925:17n, 1579 n44.
39 Apparently Erasmus means Guillaume Briçonnet, the reforming bishop of
   Meaux, whom Béda had treated as a reckless promoter of heresy and disorder
   (Ep 1579:180–2 and n40). He had been bishop of Lodève from 1489 to 1516,
   when he was translated to Meaux and was succeeded at Lodève by his brother
   Denis. In fact the see of Lodève was vacant in 1525.
40 Allen Ep 1581:320n concludes, probably correctly, that Erasmus was obliquely
   referring to Erard de la Marck, prince-bishop of Liège, who must have been
   embarrassed by Erasmus' indiscreet letter of 30 May 1519 to Martin Luther,
   where the bishop is mentioned as one who favours Luther's opinions (Ep 980).
   Cf Ep 1127A:84–6, also to Luther. The incident seems to have caused no lasting
   difficulty either for Bishop de la Marck or for Erasmus.
41 In Ep 1579:182 Béda refers to this leading French humanist negatively as an
   associate of the unwise Bishop Briçonnet. Cf ibidem n41. In fact, Lefèvre was
   even more directly an object of attack by Béda and his associates than Erasmus.
42 Erasmus means that ultra-conservative German theologians (such as Jacob of

they disapprove of is supported for the very reason that they have opposed
it. I do not say this in any threatening spirit: I should like learning to flour-   365
ish in all its forms, with theology in the forefront. But what I see at present
is a depressing and general collapse with the whole of Christendom sinking
into a state of Turkish barbarism. There can be no doubt that many people
have a low opinion of theologians; indeed, one could hardly believe the
contempt with which the very mention of theology is greeted everywhere,   370
and this is not just the attitude of ordinary people, but also of men of rank.
The cause of the trouble (to be frank about my feelings on the matter) is the
vindictiveness and want of principle of some of our theologians. I concede
that it is very unfair to judge a whole profession by the habits of a few, but
men commonly react in this way. The depravity of the few leaves a deeper   375
impression than is left by all the rest, and of these some pretend that nothing is amiss, while others simply smile, or refuse to take a stand, or give
secret support, or let themselves be dragged into the same lunacy as though
smitten by a contagious disease.

No one could have convinced me that there were such nauseating   380
creatures among our theologians if I had not experienced the reality for
myself. Who would have credited Standish[43] with such stupidity as he
himself exhibited for everyone to see, when in front of the king and queen
of England and before a crowd of noblemen and scholars, he knelt down on
bended knee and with hands raised to heaven, accused me of denying the   385
resurrection, of wishing to abolish marriage and of holding unorthodox
views on the Eucharist. When asked to provide evidence for these assertions, he talked such utter nonsense that the king himself was embarrassed
on his behalf. Then there was the fierce outcry over the passage *In principio
erat sermo*; you will understand what it was like if you have the time to read   390
my *Apologia* on the subject,[44] which has now gone through more than one
edition.

For some time now the Carmelite Nicolaas of Egmond has been making furious attacks on me in my own country and there seems no end or
limit to it. I could not tell you how often he made the pulpit ring with his   395

* * * * *

Hoogstraten) were so completely out of touch with reality and so thoroughly
despised in their country that their attacks on Luther actually attracted people
to his cause.

43 Henry Standish, a Franciscan theologian of Oxford and bishop of St Asaph,
who (according to Erasmus) had embarrassed only himself by making emotional public attacks on Erasmus. Cf Epp 608:15n, 1126, 1127A.

44 *Apologia de 'In principio erat sermo'* (Louvain: Dirk Martens, February 1520; NK
780); cf Ep 1072 introduction.

charges that there was nothing to choose between Erasmus and Luther, except that Erasmus was the greater heretic; or warned his hearers at a public meeting or a lecture to steer clear of the false teachings of Luther and Erasmus; or asked them to pray for us that we might be restored to our senses, or, when he was at a dinner-party or travelling by coach or ship, 400 called Erasmus a 'heretic,' a 'heresiarch,' or an 'impostor.' When I asked him in the presence of the rector of the University of Louvain to mention a single proposition in Luther which had been condemned as heretical, but which I had defended even in jest, he quoted from a letter of mine to the cardinal-bishop of Mainz,[45] in which I had written that he himself had 405 publicly condemned something he had not understood. For Luther had written that only 'manifest sins' need be confessed, meaning sins which are clearly mortal, such as murder and adultery. He interpreted the passage differently, as though Luther had been thinking of crimes which were common knowledge. This was not a case of defending Luther, but of con- 410 victing Nicolaas himself of mindless scurrility for pontificating about something he did not understand. I know what Luther subsequently wrote about confession, but at this point he had published nothing on the subject except this. If you are interested in learning more about the matter, read my *Apologia* on the disputed passage of Paul, *Omnes quidem dormiemus*.[46] Read also 415 the second edition of my *Catalogus*.[47] Yet every day this fellow continues to set new records for stupidity, impudence, and abuse. Adrian VI issued a brief to silence him. But it was not easy for the fellow to hold his peace, and soon after the pope's death he returned to his old ways. Recently Ferdinand wrote an urgent letter to his aunt, asking her to shut the noisy blockhead 420 up.[48] He is ridiculed by everyone and treated as a madman, as indeed he is, but nothing brings him to his senses.

During the time when I was at Calais for the meeting of princes, a Dominican at Louvain launched a personal campaign against me from his

* * * * *

45 This is Erasmus' remarkably candid letter of 19 October 1519 to Albert of Brandenburg, partly excusing Luther and bluntly denouncing the scholastic theologians and the friars (Ep 1033).
46 On Erasmus' *Apologia de loco 'Omnes quidem'*, cf Ep 1235 n5. In this letter he discusses an attack by an ignorant and malicious Carmelite theologian, obviously Egmondanus, on his translation of 1 Cor 15:51.
47 His *Catalogus omnium lucubrationum*, first published as a letter to Johann von Botzheim in 1523 and reprinted in a much expanded form in 1524. It is printed in CWE as Ep 1341A.
48 Archduke Ferdinand's letter urging his aunt, Margaret of Austria, governor of the Netherlands, to silence Egmondanus is also reported in Ep 1553.

pulpit,[49] which went on for a month and a half and was particularly offen-   425
sive. When the rector[50] eventually succeeded in restraining him, a second
Dominican[51] was put up to deliver a violent and quite unexpected attack
upon me in St Peter's. A search was made for him after lunch, but he had
already decamped. The former returned while I was staying at Louvain and
made a strong attack on me in the morning and threatened to say more   430
after lunch; and he would have done so, but Aleandro was present at the
time and, on hearing from me, he shut him up.[52]

     The suffragan bishop of Tournai[53] ranted against me in Bruges for
hours at a time, linking my name with Luther's and calling us both chatter-
ing cranes and wild beasts, and denouncing certain passages in my books   435
as heretical. On one occasion a person with some education[54] intercepted
him as he left the pulpit and asked him to point to anything heretical in my
books. He admitted he had not read them; he said he had wanted to read
the *Moria*,[55] but the style was so grand he was afraid I might have slipped
into some heresy. It is buffoons like this who have given theologians a bad   440
name among the people at large. Good theologians of course do not approve of such foolishness, but they continue to tolerate these men and even
give them encouragement, not realizing that the obloquy reflects upon
themselves.

                    * * * * *

   49 Laurens Laurensen; cf Ep 1166 n6. The attack would have occurred in the
      summer of 1520, when Erasmus went to Calais to attend the famous diplomat-
      ic conference known as the Field of the Cloth of Gold, at which he saw More,
      Henry VIII, and other English friends.
   50 Godschalk Rosemondt, a theologian, tried repeatedly but in vain to reconcile
      Erasmus and his theological critics. Cf Epp 1153, 1164.
   51 The identity of this person is unknown; cf Epp 1172 n1, 1173 n24.
   52 Cf *Spongia adversus aspergines Hutteni* in ASD IX-1 152:753–6, which describes an
      intervention by Aleandro in Erasmus' behalf even though, as Erasmus' corre-
      spondence for the early 1520s repeatedly shows, relations between Erasmus
      and Aleandro were not particularly friendly at that time. On Aleandro's
      persistent hostility cf Ep 1553 n9.
   53 The Franciscan Nicolas Bureau; cf Ep 1144 n12.
   54 Allen Epp 1967:140–6 and 2045:150–63 make it possible to identify this defend-
      er of Erasmus as Frans van Cranevelt, at that time pensionary of the city of
      Bruges. On this close friend of Erasmus cf Ep 1145 introduction.
   55 Thus also in Epp 1967 and 2045, but in earlier tellings of this oft-repeated
      story, Erasmus said that it was his *Paraphrases*, not the *Praise of Folly* (or *Moria*)
      into which Bishop Bureau had barely glanced because he found the Latin so
      difficult: cf Epp 1144:51, 1192:43.

There is a certain Vincentius van Haarlem at Louvain,[56] a Dominican, a downright stupid man, totally lacking in judgment. I met him once when he was jabbering away about me, saying whatever occurred to him, whether it made sense or not; I asked him to tell me what it was that bothered him. I had great difficulty in coaxing him to respond. When he did, God save us!   45 no donkey would produce such nonsense as he produced on that occasion. Of all the passages which he criticized he did not understand a single one. He has now issued a little book against me under an assumed name,[57] but with enough hints that it is clear he does not want to forego the glory of the enterprise. I had a very low opinion of the fellow beforehand, but no one   45 could have persuaded me there was anyone in the entire order as stupid, dull-witted, ignorant, untruthful, and insolent as he has proved himself to be with this book of his. I am sure it has already made its way to you.

And what was Latomus[58] up to when he poked fun at me in his dialogues in such a sly and devious manner? This was to behave more like a   46 mountebank than a theologian. When theologians are involved in schemes like this, is it any wonder that the reputation and influence of theology are declining?

That fellow in Paris who published a travesty of my *Colloquies*,[59] with

* * * * *

56 Cf Ep 1196 introduction.
57 Cf Ep 1571 n14, and Ep 1581A introduction.
58 See n14 above. Allen Ep 1581:408n plausibly concludes that the reference here is not to Latomus' antihumanist dialogue *De trium linguarum et studii theologici ratione* (1519) but to several works of this immediate period, especially *De confessione secreta* and two other treatises published with it (Antwerp: Michaël Hillen 1525; NK 1325), even though these works are not dialogues. *De confessione secreta* is ostensibly directed against Oecolampadius, but Oecolampadius himself wrote that although Latomus 'does not dare' to mention Erasmus by name, *De confessione secreta* 'often accuses Erasmus.' (Quoted in Allen Ep 1585:80n.)
59 Although no copy survives, modern scholars believe Erasmus' charge that late in 1523 or in 1524 a false edition of the *Colloquies* appeared at Paris from the press of Pierre Gromors. Erasmus first made this charge in the second edition of his *Catalogus lucubrationum* (Ep 1341A:307–412; cf nn72, 85, 86). The forged edition suppressed passages critical of monks, vows, pilgrimages, and indulgences and added an apocryphal preface in which 'Erasmus' supposedly declared his readiness to purge his writings of numerous errors. On the Dominican forger, Lambertus Campester, see Alphonse Roersch 'Un contrefacteur d'Erasme: Lambertus Campester' in *Gedenkschrift zum 400. Todestage des Erasmus von Rotterdam* (Basel 1936) 113–29 and M.-H. Laurent 'Autour de la controverse luthérienne en France: Lambert Campester' *Revue d'histoire ecclésiastique* 35 (1939) 283–90. The forgery is also mentioned in other letters (Epp 1591,

a preface under my name, would be capable of anything. Those who know   465
the facts are convinced it is the work of a Dominican called Lambertus
Campester. It was printed by someone who gets his name from his 'great
bite' [*grosso morsu*] or 'large haul' [*grandi bolo*].⁶⁰ If you are too busy to look
at this nonsense, read the second edition of my *Catalogus* and you will be
astounded at the monumental lunacy of the fellow. And these things hap-   470
pen in your university, where it is forbidden to print the *Paraphrases* of
Erasmus!

    Now we have this book by Pierre Cousturier,⁶¹ which is clearly the
work of someone who has more need of an exorcist than a doctor. Yet,
unless the statement on the title-page⁶² is false, it was printed with your   475
approval. Are you prepared to excuse such things, while making a mountain out of a molehill,⁶³ as many of you do, when I make a mistake? Do
you imagine that books like Cousturier's have no effect on the reputation
of your university? Moreover I am aware of the insults and venomous
attacks which certain members of your fraternity have been aiming at me   480
for some time now. There is no need to mention names, for these are well
known to you and are all too familiar to many others. Can you expect a fair
verdict from men who are totally dominated by a blinding prejudice? If they
took the same attitude to the epistles of St Paul, they would find more to
object to in them than in my writings. People like this cannot endure some-   485
one else's pride because they are full of pride themselves. When Dioge-
nes⁶⁴ set his foot on Plato's mattress and said that he was stepping on his
pride, he got this response: 'You may be stepping on my pride, but yours
is pride of another sort.' So it is when these men attack me for vanity and
obstinacy and impatience – there is more vanity and obstinacy and impa-   490
tience involved than mine.

    So, just as we can err as writers (for we are all human), they can err
as critics; in fact men who are prompted by prejudice cannot fail to go

* * * * *

1598, 1603, 1655, 1686, 1697, 2728), which add further information, some of it
unconfirmed and improbable gossip about his evil character.
60 A pun on the name of the Paris printer Pierre Gromors (active c 1517–45), who
   published the forged *Colloquies* as well as genuine works of Erasmus. Cf Ep
   1598:13–14 for a clearer demonstration of his link to the false edition.
61 Cf Ep 1571 n10.
62 The verso of the title-page bears a *privilège* from the Parlement of Paris, dated
   5 December 1524, and granted after certification by the faculty of theology that
   the book was suitable for publication.
63 Literally, 'an elephant out of a fly': *Adagia* I iv 59
64 The Cynic philosopher. Cf Diogenes Laertius 6.26.

astray. There are some, especially among the older generation, who can
accept nothing that has the slightest odour of the humanities about it or   495
departs at all from the preferences they acquired as children. They don't
realize that times change and that we must change with them. Then there
are others, naturally peevish and weak in judgment, who arrive in the
classroom straight from the goat-pen and because of a lack of means are
deprived of good books and of leisure and so learn only what is offered by   500
the schools – and you know how wretched much of that is. They spend
their lives among children where they reign like kings, giving orders as they
please with a nod or a shake of the head and browbeating those who don't
obey. No one opposes them, so they come to believe that whatever they
want is right, and they carry this attitude into ordinary life; they lack any   505
kind of refinement and know almost nothing of the feelings of ordinary
men, for they always imagine that they are dealing with children or their
own students. When on top of this they bring to the task of criticism a
general feeling of resentment, it is unlikely they will find anything to approve of. And of course there are so many reasons for finding fault: a work   510
may detract from the honour due the saints, or show disrespect for our
rulers, or criticize some laudable practice, or smack of the Waldensian
heresy, or come close to the error of the poor Catholics of Lyons.[65]

   I need not go through the whole list; there are hundreds of possibilities. When a critic has so many ways of snaring his opponent and is pos-   515
sessed of a severe and censorious nature with a rooted dislike of good
literature and the author, how will anyone escape his net? Ordinary human
feelings of vanity often play a part; so, to gain a reputation for cleverness,
these people fasten on quite trivial details or distort what is in fact correct.
There is no need to say more. This endless and interminable passion for   520

* * * * *

65 The Poor Catholics (or Poor Men) of Lyons were in fact the Waldensians, a
   heresy that originated at Lyons about 1176 under the leadership of the lay
   preacher Peter Waldo. The distinctive deviations which led ultimately to their
   condemnation as heretics were their refusal to recognize the restraints that the
   clergy imposed on preaching and other ministerial functions by lay persons,
   and their strict ideal of poverty, which directly challenged the wealth of the
   clergy. Though persecuted and driven underground, they survived as small
   sectarian groups down to the Reformation. See Gordon Leff *Heresy in the Later
   Middle Ages: The Relation of Heterodoxy to Dissent, c 1250–c 1450* 2 vols (Man-
   chester 1967) II 452–85, and more briefly, art. 'Waldenses' in *The New Schaff-
   Herzog Encyclopedia of Religious Knowledge* 12 vols (New York 1908–12) XII
   241–55 and also in NCE XIV 770–1.

compiling 'articles' has developed into a bad case of the articular disease.[66]
You people are not trying to prevent heresy, but to create heretics. This was
how the Arian heresy burst into flame and how Tertullian left the church.
And think of the furore stirred up by a few people over that obscure little
book of Reuchlin's.[67]   525

I have nothing to do with Berquin.[68] But (if you will let me share
with you a little truth) was there any need to include among your criticisms
his statement that preachers should invoke the Holy Spirit rather than the
Virgin Mary? This, you say, is to insult a commendable practice. Commendable it may be today, but the Fathers knew nothing of this commendable   530
practice. In almost all of the prefaces to his commentaries on the prophets
Jerome speaks about invoking the aid of the Holy Spirit, but not of praying
to Mary. And supposing the practice is commendable, is it a sin to point out
something that is more commendable? It is strange behaviour to endanger
the life and reputation of a man like Berquin with petty objections of this 535
sort. It would surely have been more sensible to let such matters pass. You
people are disliked by almost everyone and those whom you attack have
their supporters. The result is discord and unrest. If the pope approved of
this pedantic scrutiny, he would not have silenced Zúñiga and Prierias and
their like. At the height of the excitement over Lee, the theologians at   540
Louvain compiled various articles from my books and sent them to Adrian,[69] who was then a cardinal and soon to be pope. I have no doubt that
they acted out of spite since, even in their review of Luther's teaching, they
construed certain passages differently from the way they appeared in the
written text. Yet Adrian, though not too well disposed towards me at the   545
time, judged the complaints too insignificant to justify raising a fuss.

When we pull too hard on a rope,[70] it will often break. Unless I am
completely mistaken, more could be accomplished by courtesy and consideration. At present neither party will concede an inch of its authority to the
other; each grimly defends its own position and bitterly attacks the other   550

* * * * *

66 A pun on *articuli* (articles of belief) and *morbus articularis* (arthritis)
67 Ie, his *Augenspiegel*, which became the specific target of the prosecutors in the
   notorious conflict between Reuchlin and the Cologne theologians
68 Cf Epp 925:17n, 1579 n44.
69 Probably in November 1519, when the Louvain theologians were consulting
   Cardinal Adrian of Utrecht about their pending condemnation of Luther. Since
   Adrian encouraged Erasmus' biblical studies (Epp 1324, 1338), he seems not
   to have shared the hostility that many of his former colleagues at Louvain felt
   towards Erasmus.
70 Cf *Adagia* I v 67.

side. The result is confusion and disorder. What began with theological argument and noisy protestations soon turned into a matter for papal bulls; then it came to the burning of books and finally to the burning of men. What, I should like to know, has been gained by all this? Here at this moment a bloody drama is being played out – and it is not without danger to myself. How it will end I do not know.   55

I am touched by your kindness and your deep concern for the salvation of my soul. But at least on moral questions and on matters of faith, I have no misgivings about my writings, for I still see nothing in them which is improper or irreverent or seditious. It is possible I may have gone astray   56 somewhere without knowing it. But if you worry about the salvation of a man who, despite a genuine desire to help others, occasionally goes astray, why are you not more worried about those who attack a brother who has done them no harm with malicious slanders, manifest lies, and deadly insults? You have a mild term for such mad and diabolical behaviour – you   56 call it 'zeal.' Why, then, are you not equally understanding about me? You excuse them because you consider them champions of the truth. Why don't you find the same excuse for me, for I too am fighting for the truth, and with more restraint than they. Consider that pamphlet of Cousturier's: what do you see there but vanity, pride, obstinacy, a man who is inordinately   57 pleased with himself and whose rudeness knows no bounds. A man like that who is completely puffed up with pride – why don't you advise him to humble himself? Perhaps someday he will learn how far he is from the truth. He is your colleague; why don't you show the same anxiety for him as you show for me? I am obliged to you for your concern, but cannot   57 understand why you are not worried on his account. I write books, it appears, which bring no benefit to the church: would the house of God, then, collapse in ruins without such books as Cousturier writes? You worry that I may not have leisure to attend to heavenly things – and the men who write that sort of stuff dwell, I suppose, in the third heaven![71]   58

You have something to say in your letter about people who pore over the poets, but the scribe has so corrupted the passage that it is incomprehensible.[72] As a young man I loved poetry, which I consider perhaps the most important element in a liberal education. I do not repent of this attitude of mine. I only wish I had been more successful in my own attempts.   58

* * * * *

71 2 Cor 12:2
72 See Ep 1579:51; cf Allen Ep 1579:42. In fact Béda said nothing about poetry, but in the form in which his letter reached Erasmus, the scribe had written *poetas* for *putas*, making the passage meaningless. Cf Allen Ep 1581:523n.

But now I am no longer interested in the poets, as, I think, my books make abundantly clear. If we are afraid that those who include polite letters among their scholarly interests may not have time to care for their souls, why are we not more concerned about those who waste a good part, or indeed all, of their time on the labyrinthine intricacies of Aristotle or Averroes or Scotus and on sophistical hair-splitting and trivial questions which serve no useful purpose? But this is the way men are. We are kind towards our own interests and greatly undervalue anything which we believe offers us no prospect of success. It is easy to pardon this attitude in others, but I don't think it is becoming in a theologian, whose very title implies a concern with the divine and with that which transcends our human failings. 590

595

You urge me to follow the example of St Augustine. I shall say nothing here about the sort of work his *Retractationes* is; but he certainly passed over many things which he ought to have retracted, but did not. Yet my own views are completely in line with the advice you are giving me. All I need is a rule to guide me in the revision of my work. You send me off to read Gerson and Gratian[73] and the rest of the scholastic doctors, whose work, I assure you, I have never rejected *in toto*. But many errors are coming to light in their work also – even supposing they were in substantial agreement with one another. In fact their disagreements are striking, though you pass over this fact as of little consequence. It is not my view that we should repudiate the teachings of the schoolmen, especially where they have won conciliar approval; for certain controversial issues raised by the schoolmen were referred to councils for decision. But neither do I think we need defer to their authority to the point of not feeling free to discuss these issues in an uncontentious spirit, especially if the occasion arises naturally. If no one had ever argued about these matters, official approval would not have been obtained. 600

605

610

Suppose someone should appear with a more precise and careful analysis of these same problems: provided the argument is made soberly, is there any reason not to permit it? Perhaps discussion will lead to official approval. I am speaking here of ideas which are not directly concerned with the substance of the faith. If through the gift of the Spirit certain insights, which had escaped for centuries many of the great luminaries of the church, have been revealed to men of relatively recent date, that is, if Gerson and Ockham[74] saw what Chrysostom and Basil and Ambrose and Augustine 615

620

* * * * *

73 That is, traditional scholastic authorities. Cf Ep 1579 nn2 and 42.
74 In other words, if the Paris theologians believe that there is theolgical insight found in recent scholastic doctors like Jean Gerson and William of Ockham

and Jerome[75] did not see, is there anything to prevent this same Spirit from revealing to someone of our time a truth which no one had noticed before? Why do we not respect St Paul's injunction on this subject,[76] that if another receive a revelation, the first should hold his peace and listen. But   625
nowadays the dogmas of the schoolmen are brought out from the trenches, like the axe of Tenedos,[77] and no one thinks fit to instruct the erring soul in simple language; indeed it often happens that someone is criticized for expressing an idea which is part and parcel of scholastic teaching, yet because he has not reproduced it in identical language and in the same   630
number of words, he is vilified by some of these uncharitable theologians.

Some men are so ill-natured that they are unable to approve of any-thing except what they do themselves. Peter gave an answer in all meekness and fear to every man who asked him about the lessons he had learned from Christ,[78] and yet the theologian thinks it beneath him to explain the   635
teachings of the schoolmen; indeed he will not abide any argument on this subject, however moderately it is presented. There is no authority more weighty than the canonical Scriptures, and yet, although there has always been controversy over their interpretation, we may still discuss them today. But must we keep our lips sealed about the teaching of the schoolmen,   640
though it is important to know by whom, when, and in what circumstances their ideas were produced? For some doctrines, like drugs, need to be changed to suit the circumstances of the case. If we must avoid reading the old authors because there are occasional passages in their works which have been shown, upon careful examination by later scholars, to be mistaken,   645
then we should not read Peter Lombard or Thomas or Duns Scotus because later authorities have detected a considerable number of errors in their works too.[79] Perhaps those who come after us will find in the works of

* * * * *

that was not to be found in the ancient church Fathers, why is it thought wrong for a contemporary writer to offer his own insights which go beyond the scholastics? William of Ockham (d 1349) was the acknowledged founder of the nominalist tradition in late medieval scholasticism.

75 That is, the leading Greek and Latin church Fathers. Erasmus omits Origen and Tertullian, the two other Fathers of comparable rank, probably because each had been accused of teaching heresy.

76 1 Cor 14:30

77 *Adagia* I ix 29. The axe of Tenedos symbolizes a rough-and-ready decision on a controversial issue.

78 1 Pet 3:15

79 These were probably the three most authoritative theological writers of medi-eval scholasticism, but none was free from accusations of error on some points. Lombard's *Book of Sentences* became the standard textbook of theology from the

Tartaret[80] and Cousturier[81] some notions which they will have reason to
condemn.   650

Shall we take refuge, then, in the doctrines of the schoolmen, clinging
to them as to a holy anchor? I would agree if their doctrines were consistent
with one another and did not change with time and party. Once it was
Alexander of Hales who was the reigning authority; then came Thomas and
after him Duns Scotus; Albert dominated his age, as Gerson did his;[82] for   655
a time the so-called realists flourished, but now by and large it is the
nominalists who hold sway.[83] You will say, 'Let the Fathers be read by all
means, but let them be read with discretion.' Personally I have never read
Jerome in any other way. But is there any reason why we should not use

* * * * *

early thirteenth century, but there were many lists of articles in which it was
not permitted to follow him (cf NCE XI 222). As for Aquinas, the official theologian of the Dominican order and canonized saint, some propositions from his
works were included among the 219 theses condemned by the bishop of Paris
in 1277, and subsequently *correctoria* were appended to copies of his books sold
at Paris. Cf Etienne Gilson *History of Christian Philosophy in the Middle Ages*
(New York 1955) 405, 410–11. There were also attacks on the orthodoxy of John
Duns Scotus, for example by Petrus Aureoli and William of Occam (cf Gilson
477, 489–98).
80 Pierre Tartaret (d 1522), a leading theologian of Paris, known as the most
   prominent Scotist of his generation. His works were published and used not
   only at Paris but at many other universities.
81 Cf Ep 1571 n10.
82 Major scholastic doctors, most of whom are mentioned favorably in Béda's
   letter of 21 May 1525 (Ep 1579). Erasmus' point here is that the influence of all
   these scholastic doctors was ephemeral. Allen Ep 1581:590n points out that if
   Erasmus is following chronological order (as he usually does in such lists),
   Albert is not Albertus Magnus, the teacher of Aquinas, but Albert of Saxony
   (d 1390), first rector (1365) of the University of Vienna and an important figure
   in the introduction of the nominalist tradition into the first German universities.
83 A telling allusion to the recent history of Béda's own university. In 1474 a
   royal decree forbade the teaching of nominalist logic at Paris, but the decree
   was rescinded in 1481, and a flurry of interest in the fourteenth-century nominalist doctors followed, extending into the time when both Béda and Erasmus
   were students at Paris. See Kretzmann *Cambridge History of Later Medieval Philosophy* (Cambridge 1982) 789. There had, indeed, been an earlier royal ban on
   nominalist teaching at Paris in 1407, which also proved ephemeral but helps
   to explain the migration of many nominalist masters to the newly founded
   German universities. Whether Erasmus and Béda knew of the earlier ban is
   uncertain, but the later one occurred within living memory and well illustrated
   Erasmus' contention that scholastic learning was not unchanging but experienced its own cycles of fashion.

the same discretion when we read the teachings of your school? Even when 660
those teachings are supported by the authority of a council, so that it would
be heresy to argue against them, discussion will at least have this merit, that
it will challenge scholars to provide a reasoned defence. This is not to say
that there is any place for obstinate and factious wrangling. But to set up
a law which one cannot or will not explain even when someone is willing 665
and eager to learn is to act like a tyrant. If the teachings of the theologians
are solid and unshakeable, why are we so timid and anxious about them
that we are suspicious of everything?

But, to tell you the truth, most learned sir (and I shall conceal nothing
from so true a friend), I am afraid that there are men in our universities 670
who are more interested in sparing themselves trouble than in worrying
over the church of Christ. For there are not a few theologians, especially
among the older generation, who are not only unfamiliar with the great
authorities of the past, but have never read through Peter Lombard or the
canon of Scripture. And yet these men preside over our universities. If a 675
young scholar brings up something from Augustine or Jerome or Cyprian
or from the Greek commentators, they are upset because they realize the
danger to their own reputation if they are called to fight on unfamiliar
ground; here their inexperience would be apparent, though in their own
field they are great experts. Consequently they prefer to condemn what they 680
do not know rather than appear ignorant of something worth knowing. In
some cases there is not only embarrassment, but deep reluctance to learn
these lessons, and I mean not just the new discoveries of our own age but
those old ideas which have now come back in the regular ebb and flow of
history. Those who adopt such an attitude naturally find this short-cut most 685
attractive, since it allows them to abandon all study of language and literature, to neglect the ancient authors, and to teach in the schools only what
they have learned themselves and taught for several years, and no discussion is permitted within their institutions unless it is based on the received
opinions of that school. In my opinion there is no need to conduct our 690
public institutions on the same principles as govern games of drafts or cards
or dice. In the latter case, if one does not abide by the rules, there will be
no game. But in literary discussion there is no call for alarm if someone
proposes a new idea which is worthy of our attention. In fact universities
have been established for this very purpose, that we may approach ever 695
closer to the truth. Just as the young should not despise the authority of the
old and it would be wrong to throw all men over sixty off the bridge,[84] so

* * * * *

84 *Adagia* I v 37

old men should not be jealous of the success of the young; they have no more reason to be upset than parents who see their children surpass them in beauty and strength.   700

But let us return to the matter before us. If I cannot trust the accepted authorities of the past or of the present or of the period between the two, what rule shall I follow to correct what I have written? Your first advice is that I abandon writing. Indeed, even if I were disinclined to take this advice, old age and infirmity are forcing me to do as you suggest and I have   705 no personal objection to the idea of retirement. I should prefer to be a spectator at someone else's show rather than an actor in the play myself. The trouble is that I am always receiving urgent appeals from people who wish me to continue on my present course. At this point I imagine you singing that old refrain from the prophets: 'My people, those who call you   710 blessed are leading you astray.'[85] If it was ordinary people who are urging me to write and thanking me for the books I have produced, even if my supporters were numerous (as indeed they are), it would nevertheless be proper for me to give more weight to the judgment of the few. But as it is, not only are my supporters numerous, but they are learned, honest, and   715 distinguished men. I have boxes stuffed with letters from great scholars. I wrote my *Paraphrase on Matthew* against my own inclination at the urging of the cardinal-bishop of Sion.[86] The cardinal-bishop of Volterra wrote more than once to encourage me to press on with my work,[87] and he is a learned man. The cardinal-archbishop of York has written often, and he too   720 sings the same song.[88] I also receive frequent letters from John, bishop of

* * * * *

85 Isa 3:12
86 Matthäus Schiner, on whom see Epp 447:660n, 1155 n1. In his dedication of the *Paraphrase* to Charles v, Erasmus attributed his making the *Paraphrase* to the urging of Cardinal Schiner: Ep 1255:26–31.
87 Cardinal Francesco Soderini, who became bishop of Volterra in 1478 but had resigned the see in 1509 (see Ep 1424 n3). There is not much record of his association with Erasmus, but Mario E. Cosenza *Biographical and Bibliographical Dictionary of the Italian Humanists* 2nd ed, 5 vols (Boston: G.K. Hall 1962) IV 3291 shows that he had friendships with a number of Italian humanists, and in Ep 1424 Erasmus mentions having written to him.
88 Erasmus is referring to Cardinal Thomas Wolsey, who could hardly have been counted among the learned, but with whom Erasmus had presciently begun a correspondence as early as January 1514 (Ep 284), on the eve of Wolsey's obtaining his first major ecclesiastical promotion, the bishopric of Lincoln. Wolsey had certainly encouraged the growth of humanist learning in England.

Lincoln[89] and Cuthbert, bishop of London;[90] Cuthbert, as well as possessing great saintliness of character, is also a man of exceptional erudition and intelligence. This is not to mention that great patron of mine, the archbishop of Canterbury, himself a man of uncommon learning.[91] Not long ago I   72
received a letter from the king of England,[92] insisting strongly that I write on the Psalms, and another from the queen, requesting the *Institutio matrimonii*.[93] At not infrequent intervals I hear from Cardinal Campeggi, the present papal legate, and the tune he plays is very different from yours.[94] And more than once I have had a letter of encouragement from the pope –   73
I mean, from Clement, our present pope.[95] But I shall not go on with this list of eminent people, though I could add to it greatly. Some, I imagine, would not be eager to be named in this absurd discussion, and there is no need to mention them. I suppose you will insist that I include some theologians; otherwise you will continue to intone the same old text, 'My people,   73
etc.' I could mention several bachelors of theology who are nevertheless men of considerable learning, but you will discount their opinion as coming from a lower court. I hesitate to mention doctors, for I know that some of them have such violent prejudices that they will not tolerate even men of their own rank who have a higher opinion of me than they have them-   74
selves. Several names I have already mentioned, though with considerable reluctance. John, bishop of Rochester, has been pressing me repeatedly for

* * * * *

89 Cf Ep 1535 introduction.
90 On Cuthbert Tunstall cf Ep 207:25n.
91 Archbishop William Warham was a patron and protector of long standing. Cf Ep 188 introduction.
92 This letter from Henry VIII is not extant; in fact, only one letter to Erasmus from Henry as king (Ep 1878) and one written before his accession (Ep 206) survive.
93 Although this letter does not survive, Erasmus' dedication of *Christiani matrimonii institutio* (Basel: Froben, August 1526) to Queen Catherine, dated 15 July 1526, states that her request for the writing of this treatise had reached him 'more than two years ago.' Cf Allen Ep 1727.
94 Most recently in February (cf Ep 1542), though this letter involved merely granting Erasmus a dispensation from observance of the Lenten fast and did not deal with his scholarly works. In 1519, however, Campeggi warmly praised Erasmus' work on the New Testament and explicitly endorsed his orthodoxy. Cf Ep 995.
95 In Ep 1443B (1438 in Allen) Clement VII assures Erasmus that he has intervened to silence the attacks of López Zúñiga.

a work on preaching,[96] threatening me, begging, and almost compelling me to comply. In this one man you have, if I may say so, three persons – a man of great integrity, a devout bishop, and, unless I am mistaken, a theologian of more than common learning. You will not deny that Pope Adrian had these same qualities – except that in learning and in rank he was superior. As I have said, when he was a cardinal, he went out of his way to encourage me to do for the Old Testament what I had done for the New; later when he became pope, he had kind words for the time and trouble I had spent on Arnobius and urged me to continue my efforts.[97] Until this moment no one in this mortal world has told me to put down my pen except you alone.

But suppose for a moment that I were the most modest and compliant of men: whom should I listen to? On the one hand are all those distinguished men, including even some theologians, and on the other Béda by himself (whose judgment, let me be clear, I do not at all despise). But I do not suppose you attach so much importance to your own opinion that you will demand it be given precedence over the verdict of all the others. Yet even this I am prepared to do if you will convince me with rational argument that yours is the better plan. For to set aside the general view and accept so readily the authority of one man would give the appearance of frivolity rather than modesty.

Now you will tell me perhaps that I should speak directly to the theologians. But, my good sir, I have already done this wherever it has been possible. I have always submitted my work to the judgment of the church: you will not ask me, I think, to emend it in accordance with rules laid down by Zúñiga and Lee! And who would ever have guessed that Cousturier, who was previously unknown to the world, would start up such an awful barking from his cave?

It is kind of you to point out those places where you think the views I have expressed dangerous: on the celibacy of the clergy, monastic vows, fasting and the interdiction on the eating of meat, the observance of festal days, the evangelical counsels,[98] the translation of Holy Scripture into the

* * * * *

96 Cf Epp 229, 1571 n8, and for another report on the request for a book on preaching, Ep 1332:41–4. The eventual product was *Ecclesiastes sive de ratione concionandi*, published in 1535 by Froben.

97 For Erasmus' dedication of his edition of Arnobius' commentary on the Psalms to Adrian VI, see Epp 1304, 1310; for the pope's friendly acknowledgment, Ep 1324.

98 Although the Latin text accepted by Allen reads *conciliis*, the variant in N, *consiliis* (which is also the reading in the corresponding passage at Ep 1579:

vernacular, canonical hours, the divorce of believers, the creeds of the   77
church, and many matters of a similar kind. I do not understand what your
objections are. Certainly when I read the passages again, I see nothing to
repent of and I would say so (as God is my witness) even if my life were
near its end. In fact what troubles me is the reverse of this, that in making
the criticisms which I thought necessary, I may not have been as forthright   78
as the situation required. But if you read what I wrote with an open and
unprejudiced mind, you will see that I do not condemn the teaching of the
scholastics on any of the points which you have been kind enough to enu-
merate. The world was in a deep and drugged sleep.[99] Pharisaism held
sway everywhere and went unpunished. Material gain was considered the   78
highest form of religion and superstition took the place of true belief. The
conduct of the monks had become such a scandal that the world could no
longer tolerate it. Learning had suffered a serious decline. I shall say nothing of the collegiate churches, or the bishops, or of those who have the
distinction of belonging to the Roman curia, but a man with your knowl-   79
edge of the world must know what I mean. Perhaps the situation needed
someone else to give advice. That may be true. But those whose responsibility it was shut their eyes to the utter ruin of the church and, for fear of
causing offence, chose rather to stir up a fuss over the *Salve regina* and the
Regina coeli, laetare. You may wonder at the moderation which I showed in   79
all those discussions when everywhere else there was no limit to the acri-
mony of the debate.

   With regard to my letter to the bishop of Basel, in which I discuss
some similar problems,[100] Ludwig Baer read it through carefully twice at

* * * * *

   108), seems preferable; however, the distinction between *conciliis* and *consiliis*
   was not always clear in current Latin. The reference is to the 'evangelical
   counsels,' also called the 'counsels of perfection,' namely chastity, poverty, and
   obedience.
 99 Literally, 'was sleeping on mandrake,' a drug often mentioned in antiquity as
   a soporific, eg Celsus 3.18.12; Pliny *Naturalis historia* 25.150
100 Erasmus' *Epistola apologetica de interdicto esu carnium deque similibus hominum
   constitutionibus* (Basel: Froben, 6 August 1522) had been addressed to the
   prohumanist bishop of Basel, Christoph von Utenheim. According to the
   present letter and also the notes that Erasmus added to a new edition by
   Froben in 1532, the work was published at the bishop's request and only after
   careful inspection by the Basel theologian Ludwig Baer and after revision to
   incorporate Baer's suggestions. But the treatise did offend many conservative
   Catholics because of its endorsement of relaxing the laws on fasting and other
   disciplinary restrictions (including permission for priests to marry). See the
   introduction by Cornelis Augustijn to his edition, ASD IX-1 3–13.

my request before it was published. I made all the changes he recom-   800
mended. I asked him, when he was examining the letter, to put aside the
feelings of a friend and assume the attitude of a critic. He promised to do
so. The bishop is a man of high character and more than ordinary learning.
The letter was published at his request: for I had no intention of publishing
it myself. I had not written it with a general audience in mind; my purpose   805
rather was to cool down the passions which were boiling up at that time on
account of the 'Evangelicals,' as they are called.

I have not seen what Lefèvre and Luther wrote about oaths,[101] nor
do I know precisely what it was that the Council of Constance condemned;[102] but in my discussion of the issue I take no position myself.   810
Certainly the proposition that anyone who takes an oath is committing a sin
is something which I have never said and never believed. What I did write
was this,[103] that where an oath is necessary, there you have evidence of
human weakness, a view which, I think, you do not deny yourself. Since
you were prepared to read the profanities of Zúñiga, I hope you will not   815
refuse to read my *Apologiae* also. There is one on celibacy. I was not aware
of any decree of the church forbidding the translation of the Scriptures into
the vernacular. If this is true, the rule has been broken everywhere and continues to be broken up to this day. For when I was a boy, the Scriptures
were being read in French and German translations. Moreover I think that   820
regulations of this kind should be prescribed, like drugs, to fit the needs of
the time. The pope published an edict forbidding anyone to read the works
of Luther; yet you people continue to read them. I have not myself translated any of the Scriptures into the vernacular nor encouraged anyone to do
so. But in the note which I placed at the head of my paraphrase on Mat-   825
thew, I explain very clearly with what sensitivity I should like to see the
task performed. As for your view that the revolt of the peasants was caused
by books of this sort, the facts, my dear Béda, certainly do not bear you out.
A few radical preachers were partly to blame, but much greater responsibility rests with certain scandalmongers who were born to make trouble. There   830
are additional causes of a more fundamental kind which it would not be
safe to put in a letter.

* * * * *

101 Although some radical Protestants interpreted Matt 5:33-7 as an absolute
    prohibition of swearing oaths, Luther in general upheld the medieval approba-
    tion of the use of oaths in judicial proceedings and other solemn acts. Cf TRE
    IX 388.
102 Cf Ep 1579 n38.
103 *Annotationes in Novum Testamentum* sv 1 Cor 7:39 (LB VI 698B).

I am surprised that you bring up the question of translating the Song of Songs and Ezekiel since, so far as I remember, there is no such discussion in my writings. You also express the fear that Berquin's enthusiasm may be   835
doing me harm. But since he translated my books without my knowledge, I do not think it fair that a faculty, which ought to exercise the greatest moderation in their judgment of others, should allow their dislike of some-one else to injure me. Moreover was there any need to judge my work from another man's version, when the books from which he made his translations   840
were available? The translator might have added something of his own to enlist me as a partner in his cause. I wish that when he translated my *Encomium matrimonii*, he had also translated a work which I wrote from the opposite point of view, which advises against marriage. In the *Precatio dominica* and the *Symbolum fidei* I doubt if there is a single word at which   845
anyone might reasonably take offence. And since he was pleased to translate my *Enchiridion militis christiani*, I wish he had also decided to translate my diatribe *De libero arbitrio* and my little book *De modo orandi Deum*.

The *Enchiridion* was first published at Louvain twenty-two years ago. At that time Adrian was enjoying great success there and was head of the   850
university. He read the book and gave it his blessing. No one in fact found anything to criticize in it until recently, when a few people in Spain wanted to print a Spanish translation; then a Dominican (I don't know who) raised an objection:[104] he drew attention to two passages, arguing that in one I had denied the fires of Purgatory, and in the other I had written that mo-   855
nasticism and piety were not the same thing. To both of these criticisms

* * * * *

104 Allen Ep 1581:768n suggests Pedro de Vitoria, the probable name of a brother of the noted Dominican theologian Francisco de Vitoria who also belonged to the order. Unlike his famous brother, who was moderate, Pedro was a determined opponent of Erasmus and his Spanish admirers. Cf Juan Luis Vives' letter of 13 June 1527 (Allen Ep 1836), where Pedro is named as a foe of Erasmus, and also Epp 1902, 1903, 1909 (Erasmus to Francisco de Vitoria), 2205, 2371. On the problem of verifying this identification cf Bataillon (Sp) 245n, Bataillon 1991 vol 1 262 n5, 293 n1, 481 n1, and vol 2 97, and Carlos G. Noreña *Studies in Spanish Renaissance Thought* (The Hague 1975) 37–8, 47–9, 55, who does not essentially go beyond Bataillon in clarifying the identity and name of Francisco's brother. Bataillon cites evidence that the Dominican brother of Francisco de Vitoria was named Diego and that Pedro de Vitoria, whose relationship (if any) to Francisco remains undefined, was a member of the secular Colegio de Santa Cruz and so could not have been a Dominican. On the other hand, Vives, who clearly refers to Pedro as a Dominican, was a well-connected native Spaniard and should have known.

Luis Coronel made a most elegant reply,[105] which I have by me now. With regard to the preface which I wrote for Abbot Volz,[106] I am told that certain people have raised objections. Since the *Encomium matrimonii* is just a rhetorical exercise which deals with a particular question of current inter-   860
est, and since I cannot think of a single word in the other works which could offend anyone, I wonder what it was which, as you put it in your letter, caused a solemn meeting of your faculty to be 'dumbfounded'; for these are your own words: 'Everyone was dumbfounded.'[107] You understand, I hope, that there is an immense difference between Lefèvre and   865
myself: he boldly asserts his position, I merely put the case and leave the decision to others. But what am I to do when faced with these widespread suspicions? Where there is such a multitude of forbidden doctrines, such a host of scholastic dogmas, so many pitfalls, so many cliques, so much suspicion, so many sects, so much partisanship, so much hatred, so many   870
madmen, it would be impossible to please everyone. You would acknowl-
edge this yourself if you were here.

If I were as eager as some suspect to win an empty name, or to put it more precisely, if I did not detest cliques and heresies with all my being, I might have been lured by all the flummery of Luther's friends, or ensnared   875
by their tricks, or intimidated by their threats and hysterical pamphlets, or I might have been driven into the Lutheran camp by all the bitterness, malice, and misrepresentation of the other side and their equally hysterical pamphlets. If I had joined the Lutheran side, things would now have reached the point where the censure of theologians would have little signifi-   880
cance. You will say, I am sure, that this is too proud a claim to make; but I could make an even prouder claim and still speak nothing but the truth. I see no need to apologize for the position I have taken, and I hope with

* * * * *

105 On this Spanish theologian, a fervent admirer of Erasmus' biblical studies, cf Ep 1274 introduction.
106 Paul Volz, abbot of Hugshofen near Sélestat and one of the humanist circle in that town, received the dedication for a new edition of the *Enchiridion* pub-lished by Froben in 1518. That long letter (Ep 858), which was reprinted in subsequent editions of the *Enchiridion*, set forth many of Erasmus' opinions on religious and social conditions and hence gave offence to some. On Volz cf Ep 363 introduction.
107 Erasmus quotes Béda's own words; cf Ep 1579:208–9. Béda and the faculty were referring not to Erasmus' original Latin texts but to Berquin's French translations. The official proceedings that prohibited publication explicitly affected only the works 'translated in this way' ('*sic translata*'). See Farge *Registre* 96 (94A).

God's help to maintain it as long as I live. If you think such a position deserves the unfair ridicule of Cousturier and the denunciations of men of his ilk, on your own head be it! You will be doing something which will be as painful to many scholars and bishops and to the princes and the pope as it will be welcomed by the partisans of Luther. What advantage that will bring to your order, only time will tell. But if you remember the role which every theologian ought to play and pay no attention to the demands of a spiteful few, you will not find wanting in Erasmus, I warrant you, any of the qualities of a Christian or a man of peace.

I have not yet reread those passages which you kindly suggested I should reread, but I shall do so shortly, and if there is time, I shall add a note to let you know what I have gained from the exercise. If you are planning to send me anything in writing, don't do so unless you can find someone who is completely reliable; for everything is opened on the way and even copied. Your letter had no trace of wax on it or of a seal. Even the secretaries who write out our letters make copies available to the public. So please take care since we are conducting this discussion in a spirit of genuine friendship. If a reliable courier does not turn up, I should prefer to send a man at my own expense to bring your comments here. Or if there is a change in the course of events, I shall go and visit you myself. Since my works cannot now be suppressed, nothing would please me more than to have them so perfected that they could be read with profit to the Christian faith. You will not upset me with your criticisms, however outspoken they may be. My only worry is, human nature being what it is, that some of your students or admirers may fashion a melodrama out of our disagreements, when neither of us would wish it. There will be no lack of honesty or moderation on my side. But the Cousturiers of this world I will not endure. Farewell, beloved brother in Christ.

Basel, the feast of Corpus Christi 1525

If it is convenient, give my regards to Gervasius.[108] Baer is very well, if any of us can be well when things are as they are.

1581A To X   [Basel, spring 1525]

This fragmentary letter, without indication of addressee, was discovered in 1906 by Helen Mary Allen in a Basel manuscript; and P.S. Allen Ep 1436 introduction dated it c 2 April 1524 on the basis of his conjecture that it might

* * * * *

108 Probably Gervasius Wain, a pupil of Ludwig Baer when he taught at Paris; cf Ep 1884 introduction.

have been addressed to Gerard Geldenhouwer. It appears in Allen and in CWE
10 as Ep 1436. Recently, however, Erika Rummel in 'Nihil actum est sine au-
thoritate maiorum: New Evidence Concerning an Erasmian Letter Rejecting the
Accusation of Apostasy' Bibliothèque d'Humanisme et Renaissance 54 (1992)
725–31 has demonstrated that it refers explicitly to a book published at
Antwerp on 21 March 1525, thus proving that Allen's date was incorrect and
establishing a new terminus post quem, the date of the Antwerp publication.
The work in question is Apologia in eum librum quem ab anno Erasmus Roterodamus de confessione edidit. Its title-page bears the name 'Godefridus Ruysius
Taxander' as author. Erasmus knew of it by 28 April 1525, when he referred
to it in his initial letter to Béda (Ep 1571:72), already identifying it as a Dominican product. In Ep 1581:446–54 he attributed authorship to an old enemy,
Vincentius Theoderici, a Louvain theologian; and he gradually uncovered the
identity of the other members of the group of four Dominicans who compiled
it. On the identity of the authors and Erasmus' success in identifying them see
Ep 1571 n14. Rummel dates this letter-fragment (which lacks not only address
but also any introductory or concluding section) late spring to early fall of
1525; and Alexander Dalzell has suggested that it must antedate 25 August,
since in a letter of that date (Ep 1598) Erasmus shows himself aware that the
authorship of 'Taxander' involved several persons. Rummel also argues that
this fragment may represent a portion of Ep 1581 which Erasmus removed at
some time between the first draft and the eventual first publication of that
letter in his Opus epistolarum of 1529. We cannot know whether it was actually
part of the letter which Erasmus sent to Béda on 15 June 1525 and then dispatched a second time (because it had been returned undelivered for want of
a courier from Strasbourg to Paris, and perhaps after revision of the text),
together with Ep 1596, on 24 August 1525, since Béda chose not to include Ep
1581 among the materials which he published in his Apologia adversus clandestinos Lutheranos (cf Ep 1571 introduction). Rummel has even suggested a place
in Ep 1581 (immediately after lines 453–8, where Erasmus describes the book
to Béda) where the present text may have been located. Although there is no
conclusive proof of Rummel's theory about the origin of the present text, her
case for redating it to 1525 is irrefutable. Late spring seems a likely date, and
on that basis it is inserted here after Ep 1581. The subject also links it closely
to Ep 1582, dated 1 July. The text survived only in the Basel manuscript used
by Allen Ep 1436, and his edition (1924) was its first publication. The notes to
the following translation incorporate those provided by James Estes in his
edition of the letter for CWE 10 and references to 'Taxander' based on Rummel's article. Rummel's discovery came at a time when it was too late for the
editors to withdraw the text of Ep 1436 from CWE 10, though the introduction
was revised to indicate the new date. The quotations and references to

'Taxander' in the notes to this translation rest on Rummel's article, but the
annotator has translated her Latin quotations into English.

... A man who is not afraid to tell such manifest lies,[1] and who may be
refuted at any moment out of his own writings, which mean something
quite different, will be capable of inventing anything. The old story of my
changing my style of dress he keeps on repeating with emphasis,[2] adding
plenty of falsehoods – the first of which is that Luther never got quit of his   5
monkish cowl,[3] though Luther himself in that book dedicated to his father
admits that he laid aside his monastic status while he was at Patmos.[4]
Another is to call anyone an apostate who has changed his dress, although
the word apostate is used by the orthodox of those who have abandoned
the profession of the name of Christ. If one wants to distort the word apos-   10
tate and apply it to monks, it would be better to use the word of those who
pile up money, the fornicators and adulterers, the gluttons and greedyguts,
who vilify their bishops and attack their own official superiors not only
with scandal but with fisticuffs and poison; these are the men who break

* * * * *

1581A
1 This is the precise title (*Manifesta mendacia*) of a reply to 'Taxander's' *Apologia*
   which Erasmus wrote but never published. The work survives in MS Gl Kgl
   Samling 96 fol, fols 207–14, of the Royal Library at Copenhagen and has
   recently been edited by Erika Rummel, 'An Unpublished Erasmian Apologia
   in the Royal Library of Copenhagen' *Nederlands Archief voor Kerkgeschiedenis* 70
   (1990) 210–29. Her translation has now appeared in CWE 71. See also Rummel's
   article '*Manifesta mendacia*: Erasmus' Reply to "Taxander"' RQ 4 (1990) 731–43.
2 See lines 121–8 below. The accusation is that by abandoning use of his monastic habit, Erasmus became a runaway monk, an 'apostate' from his order (and
   by implication, from the church as a whole).
3 Cf Taxander, fol G viii: 'he [Luther] in that matter goes one further than his
   teacher [allegedly Erasmus] because he [Erasmus] did not consistently reject
   the cowl which he consistently condemns.' In other words, Erasmus is worse
   than Luther because he does not openly reject monastic dress and so is more
   hypocritical. But the pronoun references in Taxander's Latin are obscure; and
   as Rummel has noted in the essay cited in the introduction to this letter, it
   appears that Erasmus misunderstood the sentence and read it to claim that
   Luther was the one who had not rejected monastic dress.
4 In the preface, dated 21 November 1521, to the *De votis monasticis*; WA 8 573–6.
   The treatise was written during Luther's confinement in the Wartburg, which
   he often called his 'Patmos' (as, for example, in the dedication of *Rationis
   Latomianae confutatio* of 1521; WA 8 44).

their vows. The least important thing about a monk is his habit. Every day   15
they are guilty of the faults I mentioned, but when a monk changes his style
of dress or place of abode, there are endless cries of 'Apostate!'[5] – as
though it were not the commonest thing among them for a man to abandon
his habit and go off to the wars or wherever he pleases.

Then again, let us grant that canons living under a rule are monks; let   20
us grant that the man who has changed his form of dress can rightly be
called an apostate; none of this in any case applies to me, for I never was
a monk. It is voluntary, not enforced profession that makes the monk.
Consequently, profession made before the age of puberty has no binding
force, because will without judgment is worth no more than will which is   25
not free.

Our guardians, looking for an easy way to get quit of our affairs,
which they had managed so badly, determined somehow to drive us into
a monastery. Perhaps they thought they would offer God a highly acceptable service if they had made two proselytes. With this in mind they bought   30
us board and lodging with the brothers who are called Collationers;[6] for
they know how to break a boy's spirit, and it is here that monks pride
themselves on finding young stock to continue the race, which will otherwise die out. When we were preparing to leave them, I was urged to stay
in the same place. My answer was that, being of an age that did not yet   35
know its own mind, I wanted to take no decisions about my way of life.
When we had returned to our own country,[7] they again purchased a lodging for us in a similar community. I had already been suffering for more
than a year from a quartan fever. The elder of our two guardians (the third
had died of the plague) began to look about for a permanent place for us.   40
When I realized this, I asked my brother, who was three years older than
I, whether he was so minded, and whether he thought it a good idea to get
involved in a way of life from which we could not possibly extricate ourselves if we changed our minds, though in what was left of our inheritance
there still remained enough to keep us for some years at the university. He   45
did not attempt to conceal that he acted as he did out of fear, and entirely
approved my idea, only on condition that I should speak to our guardians
on behalf of us both, for he dared not do so himself. 'I'll do it,' I said,

* * * * *

5 Erasmus defends himself against this charge in Ep 809:119–81.
6 See Ep 447:108.
7 Gouda, home of Pieter Winckel (Ep 1), the principal guardian of Erasmus and
   his brother

'provided you don't change your mind later and let me down.' And he
swore he would be loyal.   50

Our guardians arrived. The elder opened with a long discourse on the
trouble he had taken, and how it was only with the greatest difficulty he
had secured an ideal situation for both of us; and he congratulated us on
our great good fortune. And I, though I was a child scarcely out of my
sixteenth year,[8] replied that we were grateful for the energy and zeal he   55
had shown in doing so much without being asked. At the same time, I said,
it did not seem to us a good idea to tie ourselves down to a form of life like
that, before we knew our own minds better and had a much clearer notion
what the religious life really was. In the meantime we would devote ourselves for two or three years to liberal studies, and after that, at the proper   60
time, would take advice about our way of life. At that point that educated
and sensible man (for such he was thought to be), whose duty it was, if we
were disposed to tie ourselves down in too much of a hurry, to say the sort
of things that would discourage us, took offence at a reply which was so far
from childish, flew into a rage, and called me a rascal with no proper spirit,   65
threatening to abandon us and leave us to find a livelihood for ourselves.
'From this moment,' he said, 'I renounce the undertaking I have given for
your boarding fees.' I replied that for my part I accepted his resignation of
the trust; but that I had not lost my devotion to honourable studies, and
was passionately anxious to learn; it would be time enough after that to   70
take advice on the kind of life we wanted. He went away as angry as if he
had been beaten black and blue. He then put forward a succession of other
people to drive us, when he saw we were likely to refuse, into the net.

For my part, being ruled by reason and not by my feelings, I was
unable to change my mind. In the end my brother, who had always been   75
my evil genius, surrendered and was dragged into the opposite camp; he
abandoned me, his younger brother, and was beguiled into the net. It was
all right for him. He was physically strong, skilful in handling money, a
powerful drinker, and pleasure-loving. In a word, in their society he was in
heaven. From now on, I, who was only a boy, in poor health and alone and   80
lacking all experience of ordinary life (for I had always lived in a school),
was daily belaboured with threats; nor was there any lack of people to piece
out the threats with blandishments. My brother, who had always managed

* * * * *

8 This conflicts with Ep 447:167–8, where Erasmus states that he had scarcely
  entered his sixteenth year. Allen suggested that perhaps *īgressus* should be read
  here for *egressus*, but Erasmus was always vague and often misleading about
  the dates of his birth and his early life.

our financial affairs by himself, carried off with him what little remained,
being much given to thieving anyway. To finish the story, I did not change   85
my opinion; I gave in, and entered a monastery.

There at first life was all smiles, and we were given our own way in
everything. The day came for assuming the sacred habit. I protested afresh,
and again my protests were rejected with more cruel threats, and all hope
of livelihood was taken from me should I change my dwelling-place. So I   90
took the habit, or rather, had it forcibly put upon me. Even now there were
blandishments to lure me on; and yet the miseries of that way of life began
to taint the air. The year was up for my profession, from which I had the
greatest possible aversion. At that stage they attacked me with every kind
of weapon, internal and external. Among the arguments they used what   95
moved me most was the disgrace, which they grossly exaggerated, if I were
to lay aside my sacred habit. They threatened me with immense dangers
from the wrath of Augustine himself, if I were to abandon a garment he
held so dear, nor was there any hope of help from my friends if I did
anything so rash. Was this not an outrageous use of force against an adoles-   100
cent shy by nature and without experience, deprived of support of every
kind and betrayed even by his own brother? If this was not 'fear falling on
the man of constant heart,'[9] it was at least fear falling on a youth despite
his constancy. And so your Erasmus became a canon. And in later days that
Judas of a brother confessed the sin he had committed in pushing me into   105
that trap; but when he came to his senses, it was too late for me.

Once the halter was round my neck, the mysteries of that life began
to be revealed. Though I had no hope of making my escape from that kind
of life, yet secretly and against objections from the fathers, I found as much
time for study as I could. And while in my heart I had never accepted this   110
kind of life, I endured it all for fear of scandal, which at that time would
have been almost insuperable. This superstitious feeling had taken such
deep root in men's minds that a woman suffered a miscarriage because she
had seen a canon who was chaplain to a nunnery walking about in the
neighbourhood in a linen frock not covered by a black cloak. And an elderly   115
man seriously confessed to me that he was afraid, if he slept without the
protection of a linen frock, of being carried alive by the devil into hell.

Meanwhile an opportunity arose by chance, and none of my seeking,
and I was summoned to Brabant, and thence to the bishop of Cambrai.[10]

* * * * *

9 Cf *Digest* 4.2.6.
10 These words seem to imply that there was an intermediate stage between the
     monastery and employment by the bishop of Cambrai. But in Ep 447:496–7

In this regard nothing was done without the authority of my superiors. I   120
went to Paris nor did I change my habit, from a kind of pious respect for
it, until when I was in Italy I was compelled to change it, having twice been
put by my habit in peril of my life.[11] At first I concealed it, but did not lay
it aside. Later I obtained permission from the pope to wear it or not wear
it.[12] On returning to England I resumed it,[13] but was obliged to change   125
again by my friends. And so at length, as it seemed to be God's will that I
should give it up, and constant changing would have been more objectionable, I continued to dress as a priest. The rest I have set out clearly enough
in a letter to Servatius,[14] which certain people stole from him and made
public, though it was written to him alone, and in the first book in which   130
I reply to the calumnies of Lee.[15]

My first point is then that, if I had on occasion changed my style of
dress without papal authority, I should not be an apostate,[16] for I have
never accepted this kind of life. Had I wholeheartedly accepted it and later
changed my life for good reason, I should not be an apostate, unless per-   135
haps the supreme pontiff, who sets many people free from this serfdom, is
doing something that he has no power to do. Furthermore, when he says
that I am trying to persuade all monks to abandon their profession, I will
admit the truth of this if he can produce one single monk whom I have
encouraged to change his way of life. I on the other hand can produce a   140
certain number who were wavering, and I strengthened their resolve not to
do so. It is true, I am sorry for many of them; but as things are now, I can
see no less unhappiness awaiting them if they abandon their vows.

The facts being as I set them out in my letter, what object can they
have in so zealously ensuring that no one is ignorant of something that is   145
already very widely known? Do they wish to encourage more people to do

* * * * *

and in the *Compendium vitae* (Ep 1437:339–46) Erasmus states that the invitation
came from the bishop. The meaning here, as Allen suggests, may be that
Erasmus was summoned to Brabant, likely Brussels or Mechelen, before
learning that the bishop was the person whose service he was to enter.

11 That is, he feared being physically attacked by those who feared the plague,
since his monastic habit resembled the costume worn by persons who cared
for victims of the disease. See Epp 296:185–202, 447:514–45.

12 See Ep 296:197n.

13 See Epp 296:202–18, 899:15–25.

14 Ep 296:181–218

15 The *Apologia qua respondet* (1520); see Ferguson *Opuscula* 294–5.

16 A reference to Taxander, H iv verso–H v: 'what weight does the criticism of an
apostate carry?'

without due thought what I did lawfully and under compulsion? I cannot
foresee any other result. Personally I have never condemned any form of
life, but not every form of life is suitable to just anybody. For me at least,
no way of life was less suitable, whether one considers body or mind, than   150
the one into which I had been driven. Finally suppose someone wishes to
paint me falsely as a young man determined to get free somehow or other,
while I had never wholeheartedly accepted my servitude, what sort of
civilized behaviour is it to publish this in print? – unless perhaps they are
ready to approve if someone publishes the things that are perpetrated   155
among them every day. This is like their pretense that they approve of
confession among themselves, as though they have nothing to confess to a
priest. I only hope their misdeeds remain unknown at least to the outer
world.

We see the same common sense in his denial that there is any hope of   160
making our peace with Christ,[17] if there are no celibates – as though all
celibates were chaste, and as though married people cannot make their
peace with God through prayer, and as though nuns and monks need no
one to intercede with God on their behalf. He accuses me of having a
ferocious spirit,[18] though I have never mentioned anyone except under   165
savage provocation; he accuses me of a lust for revenge, though several
people have attacked me like madmen to whom I have not replied. He has
doubts about my chastity,[19] as though I had ever boasted of it or everything on their side was pure and chaste. And here is this hangman ranting
about prisons: I suppose by prison he means monastery.[20] It is the writers   170
of such crazy pamphlets who are ripe for fetters, shackles,[21] and prisons,
not those who win the approval of all men by their labours for the public
good.

But enough of this nonsense.

* * * * *

17 Cf Taxander, A iii: 'who will bring us back to peace with the Son when he is
  angry?'
18 Cf Taxander, H iv: 'in ferocity of mind he yields to no living person.'
19 A reference to Taxander's statement insinuating unchastity without making a
  direct charge: 'I won't say anything about his chastity since everyone may be
  considered a good man as long as nothing to the contrary is known.' Cf Epp
  296:54–7, 1347:380–1.
20 Taxander, H iii verso: 'What hangman has covered Erasmus' eyes? ... Let him
  return to the prison whence he has come forth.'
21 Taxander, H iv verso: 'Such impudent preachers ought rightly to be fettered
  with Jewish shackles,' a phrase by which he probably means externally imposed restraints analogous to the rules of Jewish law.

1582 / To the Theologians of Louvain   Basel, 1 July 1525

The book with which this letter is concerned is *Apologia in eum librum quem ab anno Erasmus Roterodamus de confessione edidit* (Antwerp: Simon Cocus, 21 March 1525; NK 1840). Although the title-page gives the author's name as Godefridus Ruysius Taxander, Erasmus immediately recognized that as a pseudonym and concluded that the real author was the Louvain Dominican Vincentius Theoderici (or Dierckx), who had been openly hostile to him since at least 1520. He later unravelled the whole mystery of its collective author-ship. On the book and its principal author Theoderici see Ep 1571 n14. Erasmus included this self-defence in his *Opus epistolarum*.

TO THE THEOLOGIANS OF LOUVAIN FROM ERASMUS OF
ROTTERDAM, GREETING
Vincentius' book has come out at last: it had a long period of gestation, for the vicar-general[1] would not give permission for the birth. The false name on the title-page achieved nothing: no one but Vincentius could have writ-   5
ten such a dull and stupid book. They say he received help from a Domini-
can, a refugee from England.[2] In spite of the outrageous attacks on myself, I could not read the book without laughing – in fact I read only passages here and there. The thing (God help us!) is a pack of transparent lies. It claims that I 'condemn the veneration of the saints,' although I have pub-   10
lished two books defending the veneration and invocation of the saints against the opinions of Luther. I 'wish to venerate no one but Luther,' but the truth is that I am engaged in a running battle with him. I 'am trying by

* * * * *

1582
1 De Vocht *Literae* Epp 148 introduction, 172:12n concludes that this was Johannes Faber of Augsburg, Dominican vicar-general for (Upper) Germany from 1511 to 1524, who had studied in Venice and Padua and was sym-pathetic to humanistic learning. On Faber cf Epp 1149 introduction and 1196:139–51.
2 This English connection appears also in Ep 1585:72–3. In Ep 1603:48 and else-where, Erasmus names Cornelis of Duiveland as one of the Dominican con-spirators, but there is no firm evidence to prove Allen's suggestion (VI 107:5n) that he was the 'refugee from England' whom Erasmus had in mind. In any case, the *Apologia* was dedicated to Edward Lee (who, however, had studied at Louvain and had drawn close to Erasmus' other enemies there); and it circulated almost immediately in England. On 16 May Thomas More wrote to Frans van Cranevelt, who had written to him about it, that it was available in London: De Vocht *Literae* Ep 151 and Rogers Ep 138.

every means to undermine the practice of confession,' but I wrote a book
'on the proper manner of confession' (*De recte confitendo*); I am supposed to   15
'come out openly against confession' in my *Colloquia*, but in that work I
defend two types of confession, confession to God and confession before a
priest, and I approve both. I 'am Luther's mentor,' I 'condemn celibacy,' I
want priests to 'go straight from the bedsheets to the mass' (for that is the
sort of language the fellow uses).   20

Nothing in this book from one end to the other makes sense. You
might say it was written in the heat of a fever. But it also has pretensions
to style, since there are even quotations from the poets. What can one say
about the indecency of the language, the unbridled malice, the undisguised
jealousy? If such men brought down the world's resentment and ridicule on   25
no one but themselves, it might be tolerable, but the whole profession is
discredited by the idiocy of a few. And some of this resentment (if I may
speak frankly) is rubbing off on you. Some time ago, when the Dominicans
were causing an uproar, most of you turned a blind eye; now you are
tolerating a Carmelite who acts like a madman; and I have no doubt that   30
this book is circulating among you, since it has the word 'theologian'
on the title-page and mention is made of Louvain. Clearly Vincentius did
not wish to lose all credit for his work, for there are frequent laudatory
references to the distinguished theologian Vincentius of Haarlem[3] and to
Jacobus Latomus.[4] How splendid to tie together these two theologians of   35
Louvain so as to create the impression that Latomus is in the same
class as Vincentius! That (as the saying goes) is to compare a camel with an
ant.[5]

There are still many learned and intelligent men in the world whose
unspoken judgments you should not discount. What do you think is their   40
reaction when they read such books as these? It is fools like that who are
destoying the monasteries everywhere and ruining the universities. The
world could not tolerate these monsters any longer. Sins committed by a
few evil men are being laid at everyone's door: I know it is most unfair, but
that is the way people are. They suspect that you support those whose   45
excesses you do not control when it is within your power to do so. Pope

* * * * *

3 That is, references to Theoderici himself, who was born at Beverwijk near
  Haarlem and was sometimes called Vincentius Haerlemus.
4 On this leading theologian of Louvain see Epp 934:4n and introduction, 1571
  n5.
5 *Adagia* I v 47

Adrian[6] put a stop to Egmondanus' stupid tirades:[7] you pretend nothing
happened. When I was at Louvain, Aleandro[8] silenced Laurens, the
Frisian,[9] at my request: you took no action. The college of cardinals and
three popes stopped Zúñiga's wicked tongue,[10] though there was more   50
sense and moderation in his ravings than in those of Egmondanus or
Vincentius or that awful Frisian. I do not know how secure your own
position is, but I very much fear that the storm which has broken over us
may one day move to you. I can think of nothing sillier or more absurd
than that book of the theologian Pierre Cousturier.[11] Did it offend you, I   55
wonder; it certainly offended the fathers of his order, not because they were
worried about Erasmus, but they realize the shame and peril which
threatens them from one man's folly.

Perhaps there are some among you who think that I would not be
capable of hurting anyone, even if I wished to. You would change your tune   60
if my mind were as twisted as the minds of these men clearly are. I am
concentrating now on making myself ready for that final day and I shall do
nothing knowingly which might burden my conscience as I prepare to leave
this world. Your institution too bears a heavy burden – the burden of some
ignorant and stupid men. A Vincentius attracts a Vincentius and a Carmelite   65
another Carmelite. You enjoy their company now, but I am afraid you will
also reap the harvest they are sowing. I should like to see your university
famed for its learned and honest men and for its success in every branch of
learning. But what we see everywhere these days is the plundering of the
monasteries, the complete destruction of theology and the ruin of the uni-   70

* * * * *

6 For Erasmus' claim that Adrian VI intervened directly to silence the attacks by
  Egmondanus see Ep 1359:2–3. Adrian had special standing at Louvain not only
  as pope but also as the leading member of the theological faculty before he left
  the university to enter the service of Charles V.
7 On this ultra-conservative Carmelite theologian see Ep 879:15n. Erasmus'
  letters from 1516 down to Egmondanus' death in 1526 are full of complaints
  about his malevolent and unremitting hostility, which not even direct orders
  from two popes could silence for very long.
8 Although Erasmus rightly perceived his old friend Aleandro as hostile, when
  the two met at Louvain in 1520 he did prevail on him to prohibit the Dominican Laurens Laurensen of Friesland from publicly accusing Erasmus of heresy
  in his sermons. See Ep 1342:131–66 for Aleandro's prohibition; cf Epp
  1166:25–33, 1553 n9, 1581 n52.
9 See the preceding note and Ep 1166 n6.
10 On official efforts to silence his attacks see Ep 1581 n19; on the man himself
   see Ep 1579 n25 and the references given there.
11 Cf Ep 1571 n10.

versities. And the poison spreads from day to day along its inevitable course.

Suppose you found in my work some statement which had slipped in through a careless error. Would it not have been better and more courteous to warn me privately by letter or to let it pass, since you must be aware of   75
the hostility and danger with which I am faced? Are you not afraid I may join some sect? When a man is under attack from one side, to throw stones at him from the other is the surest way to drive him into heresy. But no behaviour, however outrageous, will have this effect on me. I ignored the preface which Latomus attached to his polemic against Luther;[12] and I   80
knew well enough what he was saying about me at dinner-parties and in lectures, but I ignored that too. Now he has issued some new works in which he cleverly tries to represent my writings as heretical and ingeniously associates my recent work with the ideas of Luther. But I have only just sampled his latest efforts, since they reached me a short time ago. What, I   85
should like to know, is the point of this systematic attempt to blacken reputations? If I had not had more than enough of such controversies, he would soon see that I would not be stuck for an answer. Some people are doing all they can to crush the ancient tongues and the humanities in general. But time will show them that, when the humanities collapse, so do   90
those studies which they wish to see acclaimed to the exclusion of all others. How much more sensible it would be to welcome the liberal arts to your company! Believe me, they would lend an added grace to the essentials of your discipline and would win many of the princes to your cause.

I hear that my *Exomologesis* displeases certain people.[13] But it dis-   95
pleases Oecolampadius' disciples even more.[14] Several scholars, some even from England,[15] have written to thank me for it, because I have re-estab-

* * * * *

12 Allen Ep 1582:71n observes that it is not clear precisely which passage of the preface Erasmus thought to be directed against himself. Latomus' work is *Articulorum doctrinae fratris Martini Lutheri per theologos Lovanienses damnatorum ratio* (Antwerp: Michaël Hillen, 8 May 1521; NK 1329). The preface is also in de Jongh 69*–80*.
13 Erasmus' *Exomologesis sive modus confitendi* (Basel: Froben 1524) offended conservative Catholics because even though it endorsed confession, it candidly admitted that confession was not instituted by Christ and that in the early church it involved not private communication to a priest but public humiliation before the congregation.
14 Extreme Protestants (eg Guillaume Farel in a letter quoted in Herminjard I 224 n32) took offence at Erasmus' endorsement of the traditional practice of private confession.
15 No such letters survive, but Erasmus had several friends in the English episco-

lished the practice of confession, which was then on the brink of collapse. I do not claim, however, that it was instituted by Christ. I shall do that when I am convinced beyond doubt that this is true. King Henry of Eng- 100 land attempts to do so with some appealing arguments and I can follow him so far as to agree that the case is plausible.[16] What a commotion I would have caused if on this and other issues I had simply laid down the law and not supported my case with argument. But to provide proof, even supposing it were within my powers, would have been a lengthy task, and 105 I had already started on another project. I attempted only what I hoped I could accomplish. And remember where I was when I wrote it: I was living between Zürich and Strasbourg, in a city where Oecolampadius teaches openly that confession is unnecessary and where some assert that it is pernicious. 110

     If these doctrines are so certain that we should be ready to die in order to defend them, why, then, do none of you come here and bravely proclaim what you believe? If you understood how things are in these parts, you would admit that, in the circumstances, I wrote with great courage; I only wish I had written with comparable success. As for my learning, you will 115 decide as you please. I have made it clear that I am a man of peace and that I am happy in the company of moderate men. Those who fight tooth and nail[17] to protect their rights are likely to break the rope by pulling too hard.[18] I never liked this wrangling and my advice has always been on the side of peace. But what is one to do with those pseudo-monks who act like 120 madmen? There is no limit to what they will do. They are exempt from all good laws. They are vagrants and never stop in any one place. It was no longer possible to put up with them or to cure them with ordinary remedies. This is the point to which they have brought us.

     So, relying on your good sense, I appeal to you, distinguished dean,[19] 125

* * * * *

pate, plus the layman Thomas More, who defended traditional religious practices while still endorsing humanistic criticism of the traditional justification offered for those practices.
16 Henry VIII *Assertio septem sacramentorum adversus Martinum Lutherum* (London 1521) fols K4v–L4v. The king did attempt to provide scriptural evidence for confession, but nearly all his citations were from the Old Testament, and his clearest authorities were patristic. In the modern bilingual edition by Louis O'Donovan (New York 1908), this chapter on confession is pages 326–43.
17 *Adagia* I iv 22
18 *Adagia* I v 67
19 Nicolas Coppin; on him cf Ep 1162 n18.

and to you, van Vianen[20] and to you, Rosemondt[21] and to you, Turnhout[22] and to all of you whose sense of fair play I have experienced in the
past. Do what has to be done to bring about that tranquillity which our
studies need and to defend your own reputation, and put an end at last to
all this noisy agitation. You will find me zealous for Christian harmony and   130
true piety. Farewell, respected masters and teachers.

Basel, 1 July 1525

1583 / To Erasmus Schets   Basel, 2 July 1525

> Like most letters dealing with Erasmus' personal finances, this letter remained
> unpublished until modern times. Allen first printed it from a manuscript in the
> British Library (MS Add 38512 f 6). On Schets and his emergence as Erasmus'
> principal financial agent in the Netherlands and England, see Ep 1541 intro-
> duction. The present letter is the first from Erasmus to Schets to have sur-
> vived. Allen Ep 1583 introduction argues that there must have been one or
> more earlier letters intervening between this one and Schets' initial contact
> with Erasmus in Ep 1541, but Eckhard Bernstein disagrees and regards this as
> Erasmus' first (though rather tardy) reply to Ep 1541; see his 'Erasmus' Money
> Connection: The Antwerp Banker Erasmus Schets and Erasmus of Rotterdam,
> 1525–36' *Erasmus in English* 14 (1985–6) 2–7, esp p 2.

Cordial greetings. If my name has been some help to you in Spain, perhaps
in return your name could be of use to me in England. I receive an annuity
from the archbishop of Canterbury,[1] but I lose heavily on it, partly because

* * * * *

20 On Willem van Vianen cf Ep 650:7n. He was at least moderately favourable to
   Erasmus, who never mentions him among those Louvain theologians who
   were his enemies.
21 Godschalk Rosemondt was another reasonably friendly Louvain theologian; cf
   Ep 1153 introduction.
22 Jan Driedo of Turnhout; cf Ep 1163, especially n3. As that letter shows, Erasmus had a high opinion of his ability.

1583
1 On this pension, derived from the revenues of the parish of Aldington in Kent
   and granted in 1512 through the good will of Archbishop William Warham,
   see Ep 255 introduction. For an estimate of its value, see Allen Ep 255 introduction. Samuel Knight *The Life of Erasmus* (London 1726), Appendix XV, pages
   xli–xliii, prints an extract from Archbishop Warham's register in which he
   declares that it is his policy never to burden a benefice with such a pension

of the rate of exchange and partly because of the charges made by the
bankers. I am sure you have business connections in England. So if, with   5
the help of some acquaintances of yours, you could arrange for my pension
to reach me with fewer deductions, I should be most grateful.

As for my going back, the times are so uncertain that I cannot make
a decision one way or the other. Please answer this letter by the next courier. My best wishes to you and your good wife and the other members of   10
your household.

Yours truly, Erasmus of Rotterdam
Basel, 2 July 1525
To the honourable Erasmus Schets, merchant. In Antwerp

1584 / To Adrianus Barlandus   Basel, 2 July 1525

This double lament over the death of Maarten van Dorp, Erasmus' best friend
among the Louvain theologians, and over the ruin of scholarship associated
with the religious and social upheaval in Germany is addressed to Adrianus
Barlandus, the noted humanist and first professor of Latin in the Collegium
Trilingue at Louvain. On him see Ep 492 introduction. Dorp had died on 31
May 1525. Erasmus included this letter in his *Opus epistolarum.*

ERASMUS OF ROTTERDAM TO ADRIANUS BARLANDUS, GREETING
Dorp's passing is a loss to the world of learning:[1] I would show how deeply I feel it, if my sorrow could bring him back. But it is we who must soon
join him: he will never come back to us. He died at the height of his
powers, and surely this is the best time to die, when it is sweetest to be   5
alive. He was destined for great things, had he lived, but now, I trust, he
is enjoying a greater glory with Christ. He stood almost alone in his support
of the humanities, which some are now desperately trying to destroy. I do
not think they realize what effect this will have upon their own studies,
whose success alone interests them; for, as events will prove, once the   10
gentler forms of learning have been destroyed, the things which they are

* * * * *

but that he makes an exception in this case because of Erasmus' outstanding
scholarly attainments.

1584
1 Maarten van Dorp had died at Louvain on 31 May 1525, aged about forty, and
  this letter is probably Erasmus' prompt response to a lost letter from Barlandus
  reporting the death.

defending with more zeal than wisdom will perish also. Everything would turn out better if the doyens of the old learning graciously welcomed the humanities into a friendly partnership, like exiles returning home to resume their rightful place. As friends, they could bring us something of value: what we may expect from them as enemies, I do not know; and on the other side the humanities would make their civilizing presence felt within that fellowship of disciplines which dominate the universities at present. But now both sides are losing the benefits which might be theirs because of the disreputable behaviour of a few.

Throughout Germany, not just the humanities, but almost every form of learning has crumbled into ruin. Theologians have lost all authority and monks and priests are openly reviled. For these are the evil consequences which the good must also suffer because of the actions of evil men. I see our civilization sinking into a state of barbarism worthy of the Turks. Perhaps some of the princes would not be displeased by this state of affairs. In this region a bloody tragedy is being played out among the peasants;[2] what the final scene will be I do not know.

Your devoted friend, Adrianus a Rivulo,[3] coaxed this letter out of me. He will give you all the news from Germany. Farewell my dear Barlandus. Give my greetings to Jan van Borssele if he is with you.[4]

Basel, 2 July 1525

1585 / To Maximilianus Transsilvanus   Basel, 2 July 1525

This is a sequel to Ep 1553, in which Erasmus enlisted the support of Maximilianus in his efforts to secure payment of his imperial pension. On the recipient see Ep 1553 introduction. Erasmus included it in his *Opus epistolarum*.

* * * * *

2 Although the peak of the peasants' rebellion (*Bauernkrieg*) came between February and May 1525, the uprising lasted until 1526 in some regions. Even in areas near Basel, the bloody reprisals which followed the defeat of the rebels were still going on. For a concise summary of the course of the uprisings in various regions, see Brady and Midelfort 'Translators' Introduction' in Blickle xiii–xx. Cf Preface, pages xi–xii, for a short account of the Peasant War.
3 This pupil of Barlandus at Louvain had travelled to Basel in 1524 and lived in Erasmus' household for about a year before returning to Louvain with this letter. His vernacular name was probably Adriaan van der Beken, and Etienne Daxhelet *Adrien Barlandus, humaniste belge, 1486–1538* (Louvain 1938) 298–9 states that he came originally from Antwerp. Cf Bierlaire *Familia* 64.
4 On this humanist teacher, also known as Jan Becker, whom Erasmus regarded highly, cf Ep 291 introduction.

ERASMUS OF ROTTERDAM TO MAXIMILIANUS TRANSSILVANUS,
GREETING

A short time ago, my kind and cultivated friend, I replied to your two letters, which were identical in content and delivered together by the same person. I can hardly say how much I appreciate your kind attentions and how fortunate I count myself in having acquired such a warm-hearted friend. You say you won't be outdone in friendship. Well, if I have no hope of victory, at least I shall not let it appear that you won without a fight! But of this another time.

You write that you happened to be present when there was a dis-cussion about me in council,[1] but I suspect that what you heard is ancient history. I received a letter some time ago from her illustrious Highness with news of the decision which you say was taken on that occasion. The emperor had written to his aunt from Spain to request that a special pay-ment be made to me. Ruffault,[2] the treasurer-general, had suggested it, stating that he was ready to pay the money if Lady Margaret said the word. On 1 September eight hundred gold florins will be owing,[3] that is the

* * * * *

1585
1 As the following text shows, this discussion in council must have occurred upon receipt of the emperor's letter of 22 August 1523 (Allen Ep 1380), in-structing his governor in the Netherlands, Margaret of Austria, to ensure that Erasmus' pension and the arrears on it were paid. Although the letter from Margaret here mentioned does not survive, Ep 1408:11–12 shows that the council's decision implied that Erasmus must move back to the Low Countries as a condition of being paid, even though a letter of Maximilianus to Alfonso de Valdés (15 December 1525, quoted in Allen VI 226) shows that the formal position was that he must be paid so that he could afford to live in the Low Countries, where he would be free to write against Luther in a way that was not possible while he lived 'in Germany.' Two years later, the demand that he must return to the Low Countries as a condition of being paid was more open; cf Ep 1871. Indeed a letter from the privy councillor Jean de Carondelet had already made that expectation clear in 1524, as Erasmus acknowledged in his reply, Allen Ep 1434:12–15. That Erasmus acknowledged this condition is also evident from the long list of excuses in the next paragraph for his failure to return north.
2 On Jean Ruffault cf Epp 1287 n10, 1545 n8.
3 Latin *octingenti floreni aurei*. See Ep 1380 introduction. Since this is evidently the pension that Margaret of Austria (1480–1530), regent of the Netherlands, offered to pay Erasmus, but only on his return to Brabant, these florins are undoubtedly Charles V's new gold Carolus florins (14 carats), first struck in 1521, and currently worth 42d gros Flemish apiece (CWE 8, Table B, 350). That would have been a sum worth exactly £140 gros, or £94 10s 0d sterling, or about £884 4s 6d tournois.

amount due for four years. What good this belated payment is supposed to do me, I do not know – unless there is need of money in the Elysian Fields! For this poor body of mine, which has been so often battered by the stone, is growing thinner and more desiccated every day. I do not think it will be long before I slough off the old skin and rise anew, like a cicada.

The only thing which kept me from rushing off to join you was the problem I have about eating fish and the fact that the stoves have not yet been put out. I would have had to travel during Lent, and even the smell of fish is enough to make me desperately ill. I have a dispensation from the pope, but I prefer not to give offence when staying at a public inn. After Easter, when I was ready to move, this dreadful revolt of the peasants broke out here without warning. So I am stuck in this place, between Scylla and Charybdis,[4] as the saying goes, though how safe it is I do not know. Throughout this business the town council has acted with great discretion, particularly the burgomaster,[5] who is a close neighbour of mine. I would not have been safe from attack by some of Luther's party if I had not been on good terms with several members of the council and friendly with the bishop. A meeting of representatives of the princes and the peasants will take place at Basel.[6] They will see if this bloody uprising can be settled by moderate measures.

Amid such uncertainties I can make no definite plans. I asked Lieven,[7] a former servant of mine, to deliver a packet of letters which had been addressed to me by cardinals, kings, and princes. Cranevelt thought this would be some protection against malicious criticism.[8] But the letters were

* * * * *

4 *Adagia* I v 4
5 Allen Ep 1585:27n observes that since the term of Basel's chief magistrate began and ended on 24 June, it is not clear whether the old burgomaster Heinrich Meltinger (who lived just opposite Erasmus) or the new one Adelberg Meyer (who also lived nearby) is meant. But he reports that Meyer, acting as a former burgomaster, conducted negotiations with the peasants in the first half of 1525.
6 Allen Ep 1585:29n reports that this meeting took place 4–14 July. Paul Burckhardt *Geschichte der Stadt Basel* (Basel 1957) 12 notes that the city's government, having pacified its own peasants by making limited concessions, actively adopted the role of mediator in near-by regions of Alsace and the Breisgau. On the Peasant War as a whole, see Preface, pages xi–xii.
7 Lieven Algoet had left Erasmus' service but still occasionally carried letters for him. Cf Epp 1091, 1537 n1.
8 Cf Ep 1145 introduction. As a member of the Grand Council at Mechelen, Cranevelt was a useful source of advice on dealing with the government of the Netherlands.

stolen by peasants whom my servant met on the way. The journey through the various regions of France would be costly; it would have to be covered entirely on horseback, and I do not ride any more, although I used to find riding an effective remedy against every kind of disorder.   45

I do not doubt the bishop of Palermo's kind feelings towards me,[9] though I wish he were as good a patron as he is a *beau parleur*. I don't have any serious doubts about Leontinus'[10] attitude either, although I do know that at the Diet of Worms he made some remarks about me which were unambiguously disparaging. You will easily guess who put him up to it.   50 They have associates in his entourage to whom they are closely related. Then a theologian, who is in charge of things at Louvain,[11] let slip certain remarks in Dorp's hearing which clearly showed that Leontinus was far from friendly;[12] but he is said to be the sort of fellow who knows how to invent a story to fit the occasion. I was never very close to the count of   55 Hoogstraten.[13] He seems a kind and reasonable man; nevertheless some words of his which were reported to me were hardly flattering. But I know better than to believe every talebearer who comes along, although I have no doubts about the cases which I mentioned earlier; and I am well aware that

* * * * *

9 Jean de Carondelet, titular archbishop of Palermo, was one of the closest advisers of Margaret of Austria and hence a useful patron in this effort to secure payment. The pseudonym used in the Latin text, *Omniportuensis*, is a Latin equivalent of the more usual Greek *Panormitanus*, 'of Palermo.'

10 Allen Ep 1585:41n suggests that the prince-bishop of Liège, Cardinal Erard de la Marck, is meant, though as Ep 1482 shows, Erasmus no longer regarded him as a reliable friend, thanks (or so he thought) to Aleandro's hostile influence on him. Girolamo Aleandro is the person whose identity Maximilianus 'will easily guess,' and the 'associates in his entourage to whom they are closely related' is almost certainly Girolamo Aleandro's younger brother Giambattista, who by 1515 had followed his brother into the service of the bishop of Liège and whose later history is so obscure that he may well have remained in the bishop's service. These identities are rather obvious (cf Allen Ep 1585:44n), despite Erasmus' use of plural verbs and pronouns.

11 Nicolas Coppin, not only professor of theology but also, as dean of St Peter's at Louvain, the chancellor of the university, and so 'in charge of things at Louvain.' Cf Epp 1162 n18, 1549 n5.

12 This is good evidence that the recently deceased Maarten van Dorp, Erasmus' best friend among the Louvain theologians, was a useful source of inside information on who his enemies there were and what they were saying. On his life see Ep 304 introduction.

13 Antoine de Lalaing (cf Ep 1038 n7) was the most influential member of the court of Margaret of Austria, and hence someone whose hostility Erasmus would regret.

men change their minds from one hour to the next. I would not lack confi-   60
dence in the protection of the court if my health and years permitted me to
serve its interests in any way. But this poor body of mine is so fragile that,
unless I am mistaken, it is likely to fall apart in the near future if exposed
to even the slightest of risks.

One cannot live without money. Nevertheless the scandalous behav-   65
iour of certain monks and theologians worries me more than the state of my
finances. You say in your letter that they can easily be restrained. But Pope
Adrian did not succeed when he sent off an official letter to silence the
Carmelite.[14] The fellow had difficulty holding his tongue, and after
Adrian's death he made up for his silence with a vengeance and every day   70
his tirades grow more and more demented. Recently at Antwerp a wretched
Dominican theologian called Vincentius,[15] with the help of a fugitive from
England,[16] published a book under the name of Taxander;[17] it was a dull,
false, stupid, misleading, impudent, and lunatic work, the like of which no
one could have written except this great Coroebus.[18] He had tried to pub-   75
lish it several years earlier, but was prevented by his vicar-general.[19] No
educated person at Louvain doubts that the work is his brainchild.

Since in your country the greatest blockheads can escape punishment
for such outrageous behaviour, what is this protection which you promise
me from the court? The illustrious prince Ferdinand[20] wrote to his aunt to   80
ask her to see that my pension was paid and also to silence the Carmelite
and other loud-mouthed individuals of the same character. He had taken
some pains with the letter, which was delivered to the archbishop of
Palermo. If he suppressed it for some good reason, I am not aware of it. We
have lost Maarten van Dorp,[21] who was the only person who gave   85
wholehearted support to the humanities. He did not have the same aversion
as the others to anything with the remotest resemblance to Luther's views

* * * * *

14 On Adrian VI's intervention to silence Erasmus' relentless critic Nicolaas
    Baechem, or Egmondanus, cf Epp 1359:2–3 and 1582 n6.
15 Cf introductions to Epp 1196 and 1582 and Ep 1571 n14.
16 Cf Ep 1582 n2.
17 The pseudonym used by Vincentius Theoderici and his collaborators in their
    Apologia, an attack on Erasmus' *Exomologesis*. Cf the references given in n15.
18 One of the young heroes in Virgil's *Aeneid*. But in the later classical tradition
    he represents youthful folly and arrogance; cf Quintus Smyrnaeus 13.168–77
    and Servius on *Aeneid* 2.341.
19 Cf Ep 1582 n1.
20 Cf Ep 1553 n13.
21 Cf Ep 1584 n1.

(which means that his support did not count for much), nor did he have much time for these pseudo-monks. Latomus[22] also has published three short works which poke fun at me in a sly and underhand way. I have just dipped into them. I can easily guess where all this is leading. At Paris a work has been published by a certain Pierre Cousturier,[23] a theologian from the Sorbonne and a Carthusian monk, which for sheer lunacy goes beyond anything I have ever read. At Rome various popes[24] have imposed a ban of silence on Zúñiga.[25] It is people like these who are raising such a fuss against me, and they care nothing for anyone else.

I wish all monks deserved the respect of decent people everywhere.[26] But some are insufferable and as a consequence the majority, including even the respectable, are becoming objects of public scorn. Throughout this whole region monasteries are being plundered and set on fire, monks scattered and nuns ravished, and no distinction is made between good and bad. The more moderate states have taken the monasteries under their protection on the following conditions: that they obey the authorities, that they do not maintain anyone who has taken his vows elsewhere, that they do not admit novices without the knowledge of the authorities, that they do not hold anyone who can give good reasons for wishing to leave, that they do not keep the belongings of those who leave, that they do not involve themselves with parishes or convents. Itinerants who move continually from place to place, with forged documents purporting to come from their priors, are forbidden to enter the city. I say nothing about the soundness of these measures from a religious point of view, but at least they are more humane than what other monasteries are suffering. The people whom we deal with here are the most tolerant you could imagine, but they are still sitting on the fence and waiting for some Ezra to help them.[27]

* * * * *

22 Cf Ep 1581 n58.
23 Cf Ep 1571 n10.
24 Cf Ep 1581 n19.
25 Cf Epp 1128 n2, 1579 n25; also CWE 8 336.
26 The following paragraph not only describes the measures taken by various German and Swiss cities to either suppress or reform and control the monasteries but also reflects Erasmus' personal sympathy with at least some of the moderate reformers' measures against the monks, at least when judged from a secular and social point of view.
27 Ancient Jewish priest and reformer. For Ezra's code of laws, see Neh 8:1–12. Erasmus' point here is that a decisive reform leader, but one remaining within traditional bounds like Ezra, is needed to direct well-intentioned but indecisive persons at Basel to undertake the necessary reforms.

But more of this on another occasion: perhaps, if it is God's will, we 115
shall be able to discuss these matters face to face. Guy Morillon[28] has
already written once or twice from Spain and gives the impression that he
will soon be back in Brabant. Please let me know if he has returned. I have
heard nothing from Cranevelt. I shall not move a step from here until I hear
from my friends. If necessary, I shall hire my own courier. I wish you and 120
More would get acquainted.[29] Cranevelt will tell you the sort of man he
is. I have already written and told him something about you. True friends
are a rarity in these times; so good men must tighten the ties of friendship
which bind them together. My best wishes, dearest Maximilianus, to you
and yours. Give my greetings to the lord of Halewijn[30] and all my other 125
friends.

Basel, 2 July 1525

1586 / To Jacopo Sadoleto   Basel, 2 July 1525

This letter, which Erasmus included (twice, for some reason not now clear) in
his *Opus epistolarum*, acknowledges receipt of Sadoleto's commentary on Psalm
50 (Rome: Franciscus Minutius Calvus 1525), while at the same time contrasting Sadoleto's successful union of humanistic and theological studies with the
pagan tone that Erasmus found and deplored in most contemporary Roman
humanism. On the recipient, who at this period had resumed his position as
an influential papal secretary, see Allen Ep 1511 introduction.

Cordial greetings, most reverend father. I have not yet finished reading your
commentary on Psalm 50. So far I have been too busy to do more than
nibble at it here and there, but soon I shall devour the whole of it avidly.
Right from the first bite I was captivated by the clarity, ease, and simplicity

* * * * *

28 Allen Ep 1585:102n reports that these letters are not extant. On his early life cf
   Ep 532 introduction. At this period he was living in Spain in the service of the
   Emperor Charles V.
29 Although Maximilianus may not have known Thomas More, they had a
   mutual friend in Cranevelt, who corresponded frequently with More in this
   period. Cf Rogers Epp 135, 138, 139, 142, 155, 163, or de Vocht *Literae* Epp 115,
   151, 156, 177, 242, 262.
30 Joris van Halewijn, a nobleman unusual among the court aristocracy of the
   Low Countries for his humanistic learning and literary activity. Cf introductions to Epp 641, 1115. In Ep 1269 he reports the emperor's positive reaction
   to the presentation of the dedication copy of Erasmus' *Paraphrases* on Paul's
   Epistles and on Matthew by himself and Jean Glapion.

First page of an autograph letter from Erasmus to Jacopo Sadoleto, Ep 1586
Biblioteca Apostolica Vaticana, Reg Lat 2023 f 156(a)

of the style as well as by the tone of deep spiritual devotion. You have   5
omitted nothing important for the understanding and elucidation of the
prophet's meaning, even to the point of consulting Greek, and occasionally
Hebrew, sources. If Rome sent us a steady stream of books like this, people,
I am sure, would soon form a higher opinion of your city: they would
realize that you have scholars there who know how to write eloquently   10
about the mysteries of Scripture, and not just eloquently, but with reverence
and pious devotion. For up to the present time those of you who are interested in literature, although excellent in your own field, have contributed
little to the understanding of theology.

I am very eager to have your book published by the printers here so   15
as to assure it a wider circulation and inspire a greater number of people
with religious zeal. But the penalty of excommunication which is attached
to the book has given me pause, though I suppose this is intended simply
to protect Calvo in Italy against financial loss.[1] But since Calvo's publishing
house cannot supply copies to all parts of the world, it would be a serious   20
blow to scholarship, in my opinion, if a book of such importance could be
obtained only from a single Roman publisher.

I think my man Karl[2] has completed his mission successfully and is
preparing to return. Here a terrible and bloody tragedy is being played
out.[3] I pray the Lord may give it a happy ending. As for myself, I have   25
been caught in this sudden squall and am stuck, as the saying goes,
between the altar and the sacrificial knife,[4] in a position of some considerable danger. How I should like at this moment to be drinking the waters of
the Tiber![5] Some monastic clowns are continuing their scurrilous attacks on

* * * * *

1586
1 On the printer Francesco Giulio Calvo cf Ep 581:33n. Since 1524 he had been
  the official printer to the Holy See and in order to protect his financial interest
  in his edition of Sadoleto's commentary had obtained a papal *privilegium* or
  copyright. Erasmus had met Calvo at Louvain in 1518 (Ep 832:32) and had a
  high opinion of his learning and his work as a publisher.
2 Karl Harst, Erasmus' secretary and trusted courier. Cf Ep 1215, Epp 1538 n5,
  1575 n2.
3 Another reference to the peasant uprising, which in most regions was now in
  its terminal phase of bloody repression by the victorious princes. On the
  Peasant War, see Preface, pages xi–xii.
4 *Adagia* I i 15, citing Plautus *Captivi* 616–7
5 In letters addressed to persons at the curia, Erasmus sometimes expressed the
  intention of going to Rome in connection with his scholarly work, and even of
  settling there permanently (eg Epp 1143:85–6, 1236:200–2, Ep 1580:20), but he
  never went.

me in fanatical pamphlets, some of which are even anonymous. As for my   30
imperial pension, I have no hope of receiving it unless I return to Brabant.
But because of the wind which blows here[6] I can neither set sail nor drop
anchor. I place great hopes in the goodness of our Holy Father Clement. I
send your Lordship my best wishes.

Basel, 2 July 1525   35

Bonifacius holds a public professorship here in civil law.[7] He is highly
regarded by all his friends. He sends you his very best wishes.

To the most reverend father Jacopo Sadoleto, doctor of theology and
bishop of Carpentras

1587 / From Celio Calcagnini   Ferrara, 6 July 1525

This is a reply to Ep 1576 and like it was printed in Erasmus' *Opus epistolarum*.
On the writer and on Erasmus' role in the publication of his *De libero animi
motu* against Luther see Ep 1576 introduction. The letter gives eloquent testimony to Calcagnini's mastery of both Greek and Latin classical literature, most
remarkably in Allen lines 139–42, where he elegantly patches together and
adapts two passages from Lucretius.

CELIO CALCAGNINI TO THE MOST LEARNED ERASMUS OF
ROTTERDAM, GREETING
When I wrote to Pistofilo[1] about the freedom of the will, nothing was
further from my thoughts than that my jottings would ever see the full light
of day, much less that they would fall into your hands. My only purpose   5
was to show my gratitude to someone who had been very kind to me and
who had sent me your *De libero arbitrio diatribe* as soon as it reached him
from Germany through the good offices of that distinguished man, Floriano
Montini.[2] He knew I was interested in all your scholarly writings and that
I particularly enjoyed those which were intended to check or blunt Luther's 10
arrogance. Many had attempted this before, but in a half-hearted manner,

* * * * *

6 *Adagia* II v 21, citing Aeschylus *Philoctetes* fr 250 (Nauck)
7 Bonifacius Amerbach, son of the Basel printer, was a mutual friend of Sadoleto
   and Erasmus. Although he did begin teaching law at Basel soon after receiving
   his doctorate at Avignon in February 1515, he did not accept the city's offer of
   an official chair of Roman law until 1530. Cf Epp 1519 introduction, 1555 n1.

1587
1 Cf Ep 1552 n2.
2 Cf Ep 1552 introduction.

as though their thoughts were elsewhere: all they accomplished by their efforts was to make a naturally rebellious man even more insolent. As a consequence he came to believe that he alone held the truth; he systemati- cally rejected all the established authors of the past; he became the sole   15 arbiter of everything that was written on sacred themes; he restored opin- ions which were long ago condemned and repudiated by the decrees of the Fathers of the ancient church and he defended them and hammered them into people's heads. We have now reached the point where it seems better not to touch this stinking shrub rather than provoke it by contact.[3]   20

When Hercules did battle with the hydra, he must have realized there could be no respite until he had dispatched the creature with fire and sword. I too have always thought it best either to ignore Luther altogether or to vanquish him completely, for I saw no middle course. At the begin- ning he had gained a reputation for himself by the fearless and unblushing   25 way in which he attacked the manners of our age and by the vicious insults which he heaped upon the scarlet-robed fathers of the cardinalate and the noble office of the supreme pontiff, uncovering (so to speak) his father's shame,[4] like some wicked and ungrateful child. This behaviour caught the attention and the interest of many people: it appeared as though a virtuous   30 man was being carried away by a love of goodness and truth and a strong desire to help mankind; and this seemed all the more plausible because up until then he covered his character with a cloak of modesty. In fact, far from offering a stubborn defence of the ideas which he was then bringing forth (though much more horrible and shocking things were yet to come), he   35 submitted his thoughts to the judgment of his betters and of pious people within the holy church.

I shall tell you the truth, my dear friend: I was almost taken in by that lying hypocrite (as we later discovered him to be); I had convinced myself that Luther was a good man, someone less likely to deceive than be   40 deceived, but too violent and emotional in his moral strictures – though, I admit, the morals of the age were almost more than anyone could bear. I attributed this attitude to something in his nature, which manifested an

* * * * *

3 Literally the 'anagyris' or bean-trefoil, a plant which gave off an offensive odour. 'To touch the anagyris' is a proverbial expression whose origin was disputed in antiquity (see *Adagia* I i 65). It usually refers to people who bring trouble upon themselves.
4 Cf the story of Noah, Gen 9:20–7, and Nahum 3:5, both of which have the concept, though this passage is not a verbal reminiscence of either Vulgate text.

extravagant zeal for the cause of Christ and for our faith; he seemed to be
consumed with such a passion for religion and such fervour for the worship   4!
of the Lord that he forgot the precepts of the evangelists[5] and apostles[6]
and gave in to anger more readily than he should. But when he rang up the
curtain on that new and terrible scene and began spewing forth that old sad
stuff of John Hus[7] and all that perverse nonsense of the Bohemians and
tried to bring back those worn out fantasies of the past, believe me, he cut   5(
a very different figure from that which we had known before. Suddenly
where there had been modesty there was obstinacy, and where there had
been piety and innocence there was ambition and fanaticism. His attack
upon religion began, so to speak, with the shrine of Vesta:[8] he first made
an assault on the gospel and tried to discredit all the commentators, so that   5!
there would be no place for anyone but himself. He weakened the authority
of the sacraments to the point where there were hardly more than one or
two which he respected. He wished all the priestly orders to be equal, so
that there would be no one to whom appeal could be made against Martin's
sovereign will. He taught that it was useless and silly to remember the   6(
dead, that the will of man is bound by necessity, and countless other doctrines of the same sort which the mind shudders to recall.

I know that Luther can always support his teaching with false and
specious arguments drawn from Sacred Scripture; these he regards as
irrefutable, like the Achilles argument of Zeno.[9] No one should be surprised   6!

* * * * *

5 Matt 5:22
6 Eph 4:26, 31; Col 3:8; 1 Tim 2:8; James 1:19; 1 John 3:15
7 The charge of merely reviving old, discredited heresies had been used for
  centuries against heretics; and in Luther's case, the accusation that he was
  reviving the errors of the Bohemian heretic John Hus (1370–1415) was used
  against him with great effect by Johannes Eck in the famous Leipzig debate of
  1519. Cf Roland H. Bainton *Here I Stand: A Life of Martin Luther* (New York
  1950) 115–20.
8 The Greek goddess Hestia, who corresponds to the Roman Vesta, was entitled
  to receive the first sacrificial offerings. Hence the proverb 'from Hestia' or
  'from Vesta' came to mean 'from the beginning'; cf *Adagia* I vi 83.
9 Zeno of Elea, a fifth-century Greek philosopher, is described by Aristotle as the
  inventor of dialectic. For the 'Achilles argument' see Aristotle *Physics* 239b and
  Diogenes Laertius 9.23, 9.29. At 9.23 Diogenes Laertius attributes the argument
  to Parmenides rather than to Zeno, but at 9.29 he attributes it to Zeno. Cf
  Adagia I vii 41. Philip H. Wicksteed and Francis M. Cornford, in their introductory note and argument to chapter 9, book 6, of the *Physics*, provide a clear
  account of the objections that Aristotle raised to Zeno's discussion of motion,
  including the Achilles argument. See *Physics*, Loeb edition, II 176–80.

by this, for the heretics of old never lacked a bandage with which to cover
up their sores. And what do you make of this story which I have from
reliable and trustworthy witnesses? They told me that, to make a name for
himself, Luther resorted on more than one occasion to the following trick:
he would make a secret agreement or contract with certain people to pres-   70
ent themselves as adversaries (or should I say 'conspirators'?); then, when
the battle was joined, they would haul down the flag, and professing themselves routed by the force of his arguments, willingly accede to Luther's
point of view. This, I suppose, was the sort of boast which Alexander,[10]
the false prophet, made: he used to pride himself on the fact that, however   75
bitter his adversaries may have been, after a single tête a tête, he always
sent them away pacified and in a better frame of mind.

I know that some say it is easy to make a verbal assault on Luther and
insult him with wild abuse, to call him a rebel, a barbarian, and a monster
and use other foul names to discredit him, but that it is not easy to van-   80
quish him with rational argument. I believe that this is far from being the
case. For 'the tale of truth is simple, but deceit has many forms.'[11] Suppose
that it is Proteus[12] I have to deal with and that he turns himself miraculously into every shape; it is enough for me to hold on firmly to this fact,
that he is Proteus and so slippery that he cannot easily be tied down with   85
a knot. Or suppose that Chrysippus is teasing my mind with one syllogism
after another,[13] to which I can find no satisfactory solution; imagine even
some sophist fastening three heads on me or at least a set of horns:[14] must
I for that reason imagine that I am Geryon[15] or Cipus?[16] When someone
devised an argument to prove that Diogenes was not a man and the philos-   90

* * * * *

10 Lucian *Alexander* 65.
11 This line, which is cited in Greek, is an amalgam of Euripides *Phoenissae*
   469–72 and Aristotle *Eudemian Ethics* 1239b12; cf Aeschylus fr 176 (Nauck) and
   Erasmus *Adagia* I iii 88 and *Lingua* ASD IV-1A 60:121 (this is the revised text
   edited by J.H. Waszink and published in 1989; the corresponding passage in
   the original ASD edition, ASD IV-1, is 268:64 [LB IV 678], but it is defective).
12 Virgil *Georgics* 4.411, 441
13 One of the founders of Stoicism, distinguished especially for his work on logic
14 A reference to the famous sophism of the 'man with horns,' which goes as
   follows: 'What you have not lost, you still have. You have not lost horns ...'
   See Quintilian 1.10.5; Gellius 18.2; Diogenes Laertius 7.187; Jerome *Letters* 69.2.
15 A legendary giant with three bodies; cf Lucretius 5.28; Virgil *Aeneid* 8.202;
   Apollodorus *Bibliotheca* 2.5.10.
16 Roman commander on whose head horns sprouted miraculously; cf Ovid
   Metamorphoses 15.565–621.

opher could find no way of resolving the contradiction, he said 'Begin with me.'[17]

So, if Luther, the great logician, has been throwing dust in my eyes and playing tricks on me, that is no reason why I should regard him as a greater or better person. When one of Callipides' admirers was telling Agesilaus[18] how highly he regarded his skill, the king said, 'O I know him all right: he is Callipides the *deilelistes*' (for this is the Spartan word for a 'mime-actor').[19] Certainly there would be no reason why I should think any better of 'Luther the sophist' or 'Luther the trickster.' And surely these are the right names for someone who is trying to trick us into bringing back old discredited beliefs and who is tearing down those which have been approved and supported for generations by great defenders of the faith and passed down, one might say, from hand to hand? Is it not abundantly clear that Luther is an impostor, for he rejects Nazianzen, Gregory of Nyssa, Damascene, Basil, Chrysostom, Jerome, Gregory, Augustine and sets himself up as the sole interpreter of the gospel and wishes us to put our trust in him alone as if his lamp puts their light into the shade? Yet inasmuch as those men were closer to the church in the days of its glory, they could drink more deeply from the fountain of the Holy Spirit, without which no one can aspire to the truth. Suppose that all these great princes of the holy faith are on one side, and suppose that they say 'Yes' when Luther says 'No,' would anyone be such an utter blockhead as to think we should believe Luther and refuse to trust them?

But someone may say: 'Luther holds the same views as they do: they are not saying something different, just expressing it differently.' But what troubles me about him and makes me uncertain and suspicious is precisely that he does not seem to be expressing himself differently, but to be saying something quite different. He creates a fog to confuse me and disguises his ideas by wrapping them in a veil of words, so that one might apply to him

* * * * *

17 LB IV 177E. The argument went as follows: 'You are not the same as I am; but I am a man; therefore you are not a man.' To which Diogenes replied, 'Begin the argument with me.'
18 King of Sparta (399–360 BC), whose career is narrated in Plutarch. The story about Callipides is given as an example of his lack of interest in matters other than athletic contests.
19 The story about Callipides, the tragic actor, is told by Plutarch (*Agesilaus* 21). The insult lies in the choice of a rare Doric word, used to refer to an actor in the primitive mime. The Loeb translator renders *deilelistes* (or *deikeliktas*) as 'buffoon.' Mime-actors were despised by actors of tragedy and comedy; cf Athenaeus 14.621d–e, 622a–d.

the words of Euripides, 'What I understood was impious and what I did not   115
understand, I fear, was impious too.'[20] There is also that witty remark of
one of the old writers: 'Don't be so clever, so I'll understand you!'[21] We
should have been warned against trusting men of that sort by the words of
the Apostle: 'If an angel from heaven,' he said, 'preaches any other gospel
unto you than that which you have heard, let him be accursed.'[22] Does he   120
think that I have forgotten how the Arians cleverly deceived the Council of
Rimini[23] with a similar verbal trick when these vile men were considering
the issue whether Christ was consubstantial (homoousios) with the Father?
The good but innocent fathers were asked this question, 'Do you think we
should put our trust in Christ or in homoousios?' The strange expression   125
puzzled them and they expressed their hatred of homoousios and professed
their faith in Christ as God. Because of this, the proceedings of the Council
of Rimini were repealed at a larger and more vigilant meeting of the fathers.
Tradition records that one of the Arians could not be defeated in argument
by any of those who challenged him with human reason or the science of   130
logic, but readily submitted when he encountered someone with little
learning and a deep faith, who had no trust in himself, but trusted greatly
in the Lord.[24]

* * * * *

20 The line quoted here in Greek does not appear in the known works of Euripides. Allen Ep 1587:108n cites *Iphigenia in Aulis* 1255, but the parallel is weak.
21 Aristophanes *Frogs* 1445
22 Gal 3:8–9
23 This council of 400 western bishops was convoked by the Emperor Constantius
   II at Rimini in 359 in order to endorse a compromise formula on the Trinity in
   which both *homoousios* and *homoiousios* were omitted as unscriptural. Cf Karl
   Joseph von Hefele *A History of the Councils* 5 vols (Edinburgh 1883–96, repr
   New York 1972) II 251–61.
24 The annotator has been unable find an exact parallel to this tradition concerning arguments between followers of Nicene orthodoxy and the Arians, but
   Sozomen *Historia ecclesiastica* 1.18 recounts two incidents in which sophisticated
   pagan philosophers were overwhelmed and converted by the vehement profession of faith made by a sincere Christian who lacked the refined skills of
   dialectical argumentation. In the first case, it is 'a simple old man, highly
   esteemed as a confessor,' who does this; in the second case, it is Alexander,
   bishop of Constantinople. The source places these events at the Council of
   Nicaea. A more likely direct source is Rufinus *Historia ecclesiastica* 1.3 (PL 21
   469–70), which also deals with the conversion of a sophisticated pagan philosopher by the fervent declaration of faith made by a simple, unlearned, and also
   unnamed bishop. This is also presented in the account of the actions of the
   Council of Nicaea against the Arians. Socrates *Historia ecclesiastica* 1.8 tells the
   same story as an event that took place shortly before the opening of the coun-

In this way, I believe, Luther's sophistries and paradoxes can easily be
undermined. He will be forced to admit defeat, and all the confusion which   13
he has been provoking right up to the present day will vanish in an instant.
But if the shameless effrontery of the man continues along its present course
and flares up at critical moments, I have no doubt that eventually he will
repudiate the Gospels as something written by uneducated men and
accepted by simpletons and will assert with Muhammad that Christ himself   14
was not a real man, but a ghost or vision,[25] deceiving our eyes and cheating our senses. For Cicero put it well when he wrote: 'Once a man has over-
stepped the bounds of modesty, he may as well be utterly and completely
shameless.'[26] And yet (would you believe it?) this man who teaches such
a diabolical doctrine has his followers, indeed his disciples, especially   14
throughout Germany, who are ready to acclaim Luther in the language
which Lucretius used of his master Epicurus:

> He was a god, a god, dear Memmius,
> Who freed our souls from all   1
> the horror and terror of the gods.
> Religion in turn is trampled underfoot:
> His victory makes us equal to the heavens.[27]

Since that remarkable province has always produced brilliant and talented   1
men and true religion has reaped its greatest harvest there, it is hard to
understand how it turned so quickly from the long-established and proven
teaching of the Fathers to the absurdities of a madman, who, so far as I can

* * * * *

cil. In this version, as logical contests were being carried on, a simple layman,
a confessor, reproved the theologians for relying on dialectics and emphasized
the value of simple faith and good works. But in this version, there is no
conversion of either a pagan or a heretic, but merely general approbation
followed by greater moderation in the debates.

25 This is apparently a reference to a docetic interpretation of the Crucifixion. The
Koran firmly upholds Christ's real human existence but denies that he was
really crucified or killed by the Jews; the crucifixion was only an appearance
(IV 157). Some Islamic interpreters construe this to mean that only a likeness
of Christ underwent crucifixion; others, that before that event he was replaced
by a double; cf The Encyclopaedia of Islam, new ed IV (1978) 83–4.

26 Ad familiares 5.12.3

27 These lines of verse are a very skilful pastiche of Lucretius: the first line comes
from 5.8, with optime 'excellent' or 'dear' substituted for inclyte 'famous'; the
last two lines are from 1.78–9; the rest is largely Calcagnini's invention, but the
second line contains a verbal reminiscence of 5.49–50.

see, is neither learned nor particularly bright. I suspect the cause lies not so
much in their love and enthusiasm for Luther as in something which I   160
know you have often spoken of, the hatred which they bear towards certain
monks and theologians, who under the guise of religion established a
tyrannical empire for themselves, and whose aim it was to prey upon men's
souls and property alike. So, in seeking refuge from the avarice of the
monks in the heresies of Luther, they went from the frying pan into the   165
fire,[28] choosing the more perilous course, since the one endangers the blessings of fortune, but the other the blessings of the mind and even of the
soul.

In my opinion what attracted certain people to Luther's platform was
his invitation to abandon all duties and obligations to the pope and other   170
princes; in some sense he was setting mankind free. Who would not be glad
to shake off the yoke and embrace his freedom, especially when freedom
was linked with self-indulgence? For if Luther had his way, no one need be
greatly troubled by his actions, since faith and the blood of Christ are all
that is necessary for salvation and eternal life. So off with all restraint, gorge 175
yourself, be as merry as a Greek,[29] give yourself up, if you feel the urge, to
lust and violence and larceny – heaven and everlasting happiness are
assured if your faith is still unshaken and you maintain an unwavering
hope in the blood of Christ. What a schemer the angel of wickedness has
found for himself, how clever and persuasive! This was the argument which   180
Muhammad used to turn a large part of the world upside down.[30] We are
told that Epicurus,[31] who attracted a larger following than any other philosopher, never lost any of his students with the exception of one called
Metrodorus.[32] As the great exponent of pleasure, he offered inducements
for men to come and join him, and when they came, he retained their   185

* * * * *

28 Literally 'from the charcoal burner into the lime kiln'; cf Tertullian *De carne
   Christi* 6.
29 The Latin is *pergraecari*, a favourite word of the Roman comic writers, meaning
   'to carouse.'
30 It is difficult to imagine what teaching of Muhammad he has in mind; perhaps
   the permission of polygamy, or perhaps the doctrine of *kadar* (predestination
   or fate).
31 Diogenes Laertius 10.9
32 There is confusion here between Epicurus' disciple and successor, Metrodorus
   of Lampsacus, and a later philosopher, Metrodorus of Stratonicea. It was the
   latter who defected from the Epicureans to Carneades, the founder of the New
   Academy, but he was never a pupil of Epicurus. Cf Diogenes Laertius 10.9 and
   Cicero *De oratore* 1.45.

loyalty by offering a constant stream of new pleasures, giving each man whatever delights best suited the cravings of his own nature. Men are naturally eager for something new,[33] but they also tire easily, and unless I am much mistaken, these men too will soon tire, for anything which is evil cannot please for long. Once when that famous orator[34] who roused the   190 people of Athens was warning a patriotic citizen that he would be severely punished if ever the people lost their wits, he replied, 'But you will be punished if they ever find them.' I think one could apply this very appropriately to Luther; the German nation has already paid too heavy a price for the new doctrines he has introduced.   195

Germany sent us this monster to destroy religion and morals; but fortunately at the same time she has given us Erasmus to restore religion and morals, and he is a man whose intellectual and literary gifts are so outstanding that they will cast their light on ages beyond our own. He is capable of providing not just a counterweight to Luther, but an answer. So   200 it is all the more scandalous, in my opinion, that there are people who unblushingly condemn this good and learned man as a sympathizer with Luther and a sort of standard-bearer and partner in the same sect. I have often protested bitterly against these people and have earned their hostility, which was perhaps deserved. I did the same in some incidental remarks in   205 my *De libero animi motu*; I felt happier about doing so because, after the publication of your *De libero arbitrio*, I saw that there was no longer any excuse for the suspicions which these wretches harboured. They could no longer pretend that you were enjoying the spectacle which Luther provided since you were engaged in an attack upon it, nor that you were secretly   210 supplying the enemy with arms since you were making a frontal assault upon his position. For by saying in your letters and other writings that you disapprove of all this nonsense of Luther's while at the same time making clear your desire to help both sides, you had given the impression you were offering bread with one hand[35] and concealing a stone in the other; you   215 seemed to be whitewashing two walls from the same bucket in the hope of winning applause from both sides.[36] Gentler and more moderate critics accused you of being a procrastinator because, although you saw that a

* * * * *

33 *Adagia* II ix 85
34 Demosthenes, a political opponent of the 'patriotic' Phocion; see Plutarch *Phocion* 9, and cf Erasmus *Apophthegmata* (LB IV 219D).
35 Plautus *Aulularia* 195; Jerome *Letters* 49.13.1
36 This lively Latin proverb is roughly the equivalent of our 'killing two birds with one stone.' Cf Cicero *Ad familiares* 7.29.2; and *Adagia* II vii 3.

great fire was raging which no one but Erasmus could extinguish, you acted
as though it were a joke or something which did not concern you and you   220
looked on, with arms folded,[37] while flames encircled the shrines and
altars of the gods.

I have introduced these feeble charges into my book to show the
character of your critics, not because I have the slightest suspicion on this
score myself. For heaven has given me more brains than to think such evil   225
of so unreservedly honest and warm-hearted a man, whose reputation I
have defended in many a bitter battle, or, if any such suspicion ever came
to me, to mention it to others. So, my dear Erasmus, be assured of this, if
there is anything I regard as established beyond doubt, it is your integrity
and honesty and piety. But if you find something in the book which offends   230
your ears or appears to give a captious critic an opening for attack, erase it,
delete it, blot it out, alter it as you see fit. Make sure there is no hiding
place for any blemish to lie unnoticed.

I am sorry that it seems to be your destiny to be harried from both
sides, and that Luther's followers and Luther's opponents are both raging   235
against you. But don't lose heart; be content with the prize of a good conscience and think how fine it is to be famous here on earth and receive from
God your heavenly reward. The great Hercules, who was born at the third
rising of the moon, did not leave this world for heaven until he had completed his destined tasks and overcome the monsters.[38] And I am sure you   240
know the saying, 'It is the fate of kings to serve others and be derided for
their pains.'[39]

Your remarks about Pio of Carpi were as unexpected as they were

* * * * *

37 Apuleius *Metamorphoses* 9.5.5
38 That is, Hercules was taken up to heaven to live as one of the immortals only
   after his long series of difficult labours. Cf Apollodorus 2.7.7. The reference to
   his being born at the third (rather than the fourth) rising of the moon appears
   to reflect confusion on Calcagnini's part. His error may stem from an uncon-
   scious recollection of the three nights spent on Hercules' conception, so that
   he mistakenly changed 'fourth' to 'third.' According to that legend, Zeus, in
   order to extend his night of love with Hercules' mother Alcmene, made the
   night three times its normal length (cf Diodorus Siculus 4.9.2). The correct
   reference here is *Adagia* I i 77: *Quarta luna nati*, a translation of a Greek proverb, applied to Hercules, and referring to those who were born to suffer for
   others. For the pertinent Greek proverb, see Philochorus *Fragmente der griechischen Historiker* ed Felix Jacoby (3 parts, Berlin and Leiden 1923–58) 1.413, 177;
   Suidas sv τετράδι γέγονας; and Eustathius on *Iliad* 24.336 and *Odyssey* 5.262.
39 Plutarch *Alexander* 41.1; cf Erasmus *Apophthegmata* (LB IV 199E). Calcagnini
   gives the quotation in Greek.

distressing.[40] I have enjoyed a long-standing friendship with him ever
since he was a young man and I a mere boy, and we sat at the feet of Pietro   245
of Mantua,[41] a first-rate philosopher, who was then giving classes in logic.
Prince Pio was the kindest and most unassuming person I have ever met;
far from denouncing honest and worthy men, he would help, out of the
goodness of his heart, those who were quite unlike himself, that is, men
who were unworthy of his help. So I find it strange that he has deteriorated   250
so far in character as to make this bitter and undeserved attack on you.
Anyone who does not love you must be jealous of you, or does not understand what the true object of our affection ought to be. Although I am as
sure of your good judgment as of your honesty, yet my deep affection for
you prompts me to sound this note of warning: 'Do not be too ready to   255
lend an ear to gossips and talebearers.' For, as Domitian[42] rightly observed, 'not to rebuke someone is to encourage him.' Remember, too, that
if once in a while these people do whisper something in your ear which is
true, they always embellish it and make it more offensive by adding something of their own. Men of great distinction have never escaped jealousy   260
and criticism. For, just as there are birds of ill omen which always portend
disaster, so there are men of little talent and worse education who never
cease to vent their rage against the good.
　　　So let us allow the rhetoric of these men to flow over us and leave it

* * * * *

40 Erasmus had been receiving reports that the influential humanist Alberto Pio,
　 prince of Carpi, was denouncing him at Rome on charges of heresy and had
　 complained to Calcagnini, who was a friend of both men. Cf Epp 1576, espe-
　 cially introduction and n4, and 1634.
41 Pietro Pomponazzi of Mantua (1462–1525), the most famous Aristotelian
　 philosopher of Italy in the High Renaissance, is now best known for his *De
　 immortalitate animae*, though Allen Ep 1587:231n did not identify him by sur-
　 name and knew him only as the author of *Logica* (1492). Originally educated
　 as a Thomist, he became an extreme defender of secular Aristotelianism during
　 a long and highly successful career of teaching at Padua, Ferrara, and Bologna,
　 and with the support of Pietro Bembo and Pope Leo X easily withstood attacks
　 on his orthodoxy based on his denial that the immortality of the soul can be
　 proved by reason. Calcagnini and Pio probably studied under him during the
　 five years (1510–15) he spent at Ferrara, though Calcagnini was no 'mere boy'
　 but rather a young lecturer on Greek and Latin in the university. Erasmus
　 nowhere mentions Pomponazzi by name, but his description of radical Aristo-
　 telian opinions on immortality in a letter of 1519 (Ep 916:315–8) shows that he
　 was aware of what some Italian Aristotelians were teaching, even if he did not
　 know the name of Pomponazzi.
42 Suetonius *Domitianus* 9

to be tossed about in its own backwash. For if we spend time on such   265
things, we shall accomplish nothing else. The kindest way to treat these
people is to let them rejoice in secret and celebrate an imaginary and blood-
less triumph. You would certainly appear too quick-tempered, or at least too
prickly, if you lunged out against these boorish critics of yours who have
taken up their dull pens to attack you. By that sort of argument, if an ass   270
brayed in your ear, you would feel entitled to respond in kind! I hope you
will forgive me and accept my apologies if I speak in too familiar or perhaps too blunt a manner. But many insults must be suffered in silence or
'swallowed,' as you put it. Often we have to close our eyes to things if we
are not to be always on full alert and ready for battle.   275

Your letter was not delivered by the messenger you claim to have sent
to Italy,[43] but by somebody whom nobody knows from Adam.[44] I
thought he had dropped down from heaven because he performed such a
delightful and welcome task. Of course I was sorry to miss the chance to
inquire after you and find out about your work and personal circumstances.   280
For I would have left no question unasked, I would have omitted nothing
which seemed to concern my dear Erasmus. Believe me, your messenger
would have received a most courteous, friendly, and gracious welcome. I
can tell you that neither his hat nor his cloak would have been safe,[45] if
that would have kept him here a few days longer! But some god begrudged   285
me this pleasure and so I shall have to make good the loss by reading and
rereading your letter and sending you mine in return.

A few months ago the physician Leoniceno,[46] a man made for eternity, rang down the curtain on this sorry life.[47] I used to call him the last
of the heroes and a relic of the golden age.[48] He was the last survivor of   290

* * * * *

43 Karl Harst, Erasmus' usual courier to Italy at this time; cf Epp 1575 n2, 1586
    n2, and (for his early career) 1275 introduction.
44 Literally 'I know not what child of earth.' The expression 'child of earth' (*filius
    terrae*), which goes back to Cicero, was used to describe someone of unidenti-
    fied or dubious origins. Cf *Adagia* I viii 86 and Cicero *Ad Atticum* 1.13.4.
45 A variation on the proverb 'To tear a cloak,' that is, to urge a guest to stay by
    rendering his travelling cloak useless; cf *Adagia* I i 99.
46 Erasmus had met this famous professor of medicine at Ferrara late in 1508 or
    early in 1509. Cf Epp 216A:21n, 541:61n. In Ep 1576:13 he had inquired about
    him, and this news of his death is Calcagnini's reply. Erasmus regarded him
    as Italy's outstanding medical writer, who together with Guillaume Cop in
    France and Thomas Linacre in England had effected a renaissance of medical
    learning; cf Ep 862:20–4.
47 Literally, 'finished life's comedy' or 'life's mime'; cf Seneca *Epistulae morales*
    80.7.
48 Calcagnini is applying to the preceding generation of Italian Renaissance

an era that was rich in talent, with men like Ermolao, Poliziano, Pico, Merula, and Domizio;[49] he was almost a hundred years old, but still, surprisingly, with all his wits about him. He wrote much and translated much 29 from the Greek and restored many places in the corpus of medicine,[50] which was then in a sorry state. He waged an unending battle with barbarian doctors;[51] even Pliny was constantly attacked without mercy, in spite of my frequent and vain attempts to dissuade him. In the end he achieved something which few men succeed in doing: he lived to see the future 30 which he had helped to create. His passing affected me deeply, for both private and public reasons, private because he had been my teacher, and

* * * * *

humanists the classical myth of the golden age, given its standard formulation in Greek literature by Hesiod *Works and Days* 108–12 and in Latin literature by Ovid *Metamorphoses* 1.89–112.

49 These are leading humanists of the preceding generation whom Calcagnini lists as representatives of the golden age of Italian humanism – in fact, a well-chosen list. The persons are: Ermolao Barbaro (1453–93), on whom see Ep 126:150n; Angelo Poliziano (1343–94), cf Ep 61:154n; Giovanni Pico della Mirandola (1463–94), Calcagnini's maternal uncle, who had guided his education, cf Ep 126:150n; Giorgio Merula (c 1424–94) of Alessandria; and Domizio Calderini (1446–78). Merula, a distinguished humanist teacher active for long periods at Venice and Milan and more intermittently at the University of Padua, wrote historical works, made translations and commentaries on classical authors, and was especially significant as an early humanist editor of classical authors for the press. Calderini was educated at Verona and Venice but spent his most productive years at Rome, first in the circle around Cardinal Bessarion, to whom he was secretary, and then under the patronage of Cardinals Pietro Riario and Giuliano della Rovere.

50 Leoniceno's most influential translations from Greek were in medicine and natural philosophy, including the *Aphorismi* of Hippocrates, several treatises of Galen, Aristotle *De animalibus* and *De partibus animalium*, and Ptolemy *Inerrantium stellarum significationes*. He also made vernacular translations for the dukes of Ferrara, including texts of Cassius Dio, Arrian, Diodorus Siculus, Procopius, and Flavio Biondo.

51 This reference is to Leoniceno's lifelong hostility to medieval Arab authorities in medicine. In a famous commentary on Pliny *Naturalis historia*, he maintained the superiority of Dioscorides over Pliny, and in general of Greek over Latin and Arab medical authorities. On his anti-Arab opinions, see Heinrich Schipperges *Ideologie und Historiographie des Arabismus, Sudhoffs Archiv für Geschichte der Medizin und der Naturwissenschaften*, Beiheft 1 (Wiesbaden 1961) 14–26; on his attack on the authority of Pliny (*De Plinii aliorumque in medicina erroribus* [Ferrara 1497]) and his emphasis on the value of Greek sources see CTC IV 310–11 and the literature there cited.

public, because I realized that his death meant an enormous loss to Latin studies.

There was one thing which consoled me, the fact that Giovanni Manardo,[52] who is an excellent scholar in both Greek and Latin, is following in Leoniceno's footsteps both as a student of medicine and an explorer   305
of the mysteries of the natural world. The *Epistulae* which he published recently will give you some idea of his work. I imagine it has already reached you, but if not, just tell me and I shall see that a copy gets to you without delay. He wrote many other works which deserve an abiding fame, but, being a man of little ambition, he has not yet made them public. He is   310
still with us, and that makes the loss of Leoniceno easier to bear.

Rhodiginus too has bidden the world a long farewell.[53] When he heard that the French army was almost wiped out at the Ticino and that his most powerful Majesty, on whom all his hopes depended, had fallen into the hands of the enemy, he became so despondent that the distress was too   315
much for him. I wish that in his writings he had been as judicious as he was hard-working: he would have caused you less offence and scholars would have found his work more acceptable. There is no doubt he was a good man and a true Christian. We had a close personal friendship, as you might infer from the fact that he dedicated to me a volume of his *Antiquae*   320
lectiones; but he kept his own counsel and was reluctant to take the advice of his friends. There was something almost penitential in his dedication to

* * * * *

52 Manardo (1462–1536), born and educated at Ferrara, where Leoniceno was one of his teachers and where he succeeded to Leoniceno's chair in the medical faculty on the latter's death in 1524, was a close friend of Calcagnini, through whose influence he became physician to Ladislas Jagellon and Louis II, kings of Hungary. He was also a close friend of Giovanni Francesco Pico della Mirandola and helped him edit the works of his famous uncle, Giovanni Pico. He continued the Galenic and anti-Arabic medical tradition of Leoniceno but differed from him in accepting the venereal nature of syphilis. His *Epistolae medicinales* in twenty books (first six books, Ferrara 1521) were his principal medical work. Cf Juliana Hill Cotton in *Dictionary of Scientific Biography* IX 74–5 and Peter Dilg *Der Kommentar in der Renaissance* (Boppard 1975) 225–52, especially 245–6.
53 Lodovico Ricchieri (1469–1525), known in Latin as Caelius Rhodiginus. A native of Rovigo, he studied philosophy at Ferrara under Leoniceno and also studied law at Padua, and he taught Greek and Latin in several cities. Francis I appointed him to the chair of Greek at Milan, a position he occupied only when the French were in military control of that city. Hence the following explanation of his death as the result of dismay at the disastrous French defeat at Pavia, 24 February 1525. Cf Epp 469:10n, 1576 n8.

research and writing. Panizzato,[54] a good man and a fine scholar, is alive
and well. I have greeted him on your behalf and he reciprocates your good
wishes.   325

I could not help being surprised at the remark at the end of your
letter, about remembering what I had said at the house of Richard Pace[55]
when you paid a brief visit to Ferrara. When the conversation turned to the
harpist of Aspendos and the question was raised as to what was meant by
playing 'inside'[56] and 'outside,' you immediately produced from your   330
wallet a copy of your *Adagia*, which had then been printed at Venice for the
first time. My admiration for the abilities and learning of Erasmus dates
from that point; and since then the name of Erasmus has hardly ever come
up in learned company without my recalling that conversation: it has
become a kind of ritual with me! Richard Pace will confirm this, a fine   335
scholar himself and an ideal patron of those with similar talents; I have
often acknowledged the great debt I owe him for all his services to me.

I think I have now answered fully almost all the main points of your
letter. It only remains for me to remind you that you have a friend in Italy
who is most solicitous for your good name and reputation. You may rely   340
on him to respond most generously and liberally to any request you make,
whatever it may be. Farewell.

Ferrara, 6 July 1525

I had finished these foolish scribblings and was waiting for a reliable
courier to whom I could safely trust my letter, when your man[57] suddenly   345
appeared on his way back from the City. No one could have been more
welcome. When you see him, he will give you a better account than I could
compress into a few words or would dare to commit to a letter: he will tell
you how delighted I was to receive him, what I think about the uprising in
Germany, how much I would like to see you out of range of that conflagra-   350
tion, and what I felt about bringing out a new edition of your *Adagia* (provided the matter has not yet been settled). Be assured that I myself and
everything I possess, whatever it may be, are at your disposal, leaving aside
all legal impediments and exclusions. Farewell again.

* * * * *

54 Cf Ep 1576 n7.
55 Cf Epp 211:53n, 1576 n9.
56 Cicero *In Verrem* 2.1.20 and *De lege agraria* 2.68; cf *Adagia* II i 30. 'Playing
   inside,' according to Erasmus, is to act for one's own advantage.
57 Cf n43 above.

1588 / From Clement VII   Rome, 8 July 1525

Erasmus' illegitimate birth rendered him legally ineligible to hold benefices, and his membership in the order of Augustinian canons subjected him and his property to the prior of his home monastery of Steyn in the Netherlands. As early as 1506 with much effort he had secured a papal dispensation permitting him to hold benefices and releasing him from the authority of the prior so that he could live permanently outside the monastery. He had supplemented this limited grant by Julius II (Ep 187A) with a much broader dispensation from Pope Leo X (1517; cf Epp 517, 518). But the circumstances of his birth and his monastic vows still raised questions about his right to dispose of his property freely by will; and in May 1525 he sent his trusted secretary, Karl Harst, to Rome, partly to carry letters but chiefly to secure the present dispensation, which explicitly grants Erasmus full powers to dispose of his properties (by this time, fairly substantial) by will. Of course Erasmus kept this document confidential, but he carefully preserved it among his papers, and it is now at Basel (Öffentliche Bibliothek of the University of Basel). L. Sieber discovered it and published it in *Das Testament des Erasmus* (Basel 1889).

POPE CLEMENT VII

My beloved son, greetings and apostolic benediction. You have lately made known to us your wish to make a testimentary disposition in anticipation of the close of your earthly pilgrimage. Being well disposed towards this request of your Reverence, and holding you in special regard because of the   5
excellence and distinction of your learning, especially in sacred letters, we grant you, by the authority of these presents, the full and unrestricted right, both during life and by any last will, to dispose of, bestow, devise, and bequeath all property, real and personal, inherited from your family both in the male and female line, or acquired as a result of your own efforts and   10
the success of your affairs; likewise all property obtained by you from churches, monasteries, priorships, provostships, headships, dignities, parson-ages, administrations and offices, canonries, prebendaryships, and all other ecclesiastical benefices, with or without the cure of souls, whether secular or regular from any order whatsoever; likewise property which you have   15
possessed, do now possess, or will possess in the future from any papal grant or dispensation, whether held in title, commendam, or for administra-tion, or upon any other condition; likewise all annuities paid from ecclesias-tical revenues, and all ecclesiastical income, receipts, and revenues set aside for you, or to be set aside, in lieu of an annuity, and anything acquired by   20
reason or cause or right of these provisions, or in consideration of these provisions, or by any other lawful means, whatever the value or amount

may be. We permit you to dispose of all such property in order to provide for the reasonable and proper expenses of your funeral, and for the rewarding of those who served you during your life, whether related to you or otherwise, even in an amount exceeding the just recompense of their services, as also for the benefit and advantage of any persons, related or unrelated, and for the support of colleges and universities, both secular and religious, and of holy and other places, and for all other purposes provided they be honourable and legitimate; excepting that deduction shall first be made from the said property to discharge your debts and to pay whatever costs are necessary for the repair of houses and buildings standing on church lands or on land belonging to any of your benefices, where these have been destroyed or allowed to decay through your fault or negligence, or through the fault or negligence of your agents, and also to pay the costs of restoring other entitlements of the same churches and benefices lost through fault or negligence aforementioned.

These dispositions shall not be rendered invalid by any apostolic constitutions or ordinances nor by those of churches or monasteries or those respecting lands of the regular orders in which such regular or secular benefices may be situated or to which the regular benefices themselves may be attached, nor by those of orders to which these benefices belong, though such constitutions and ordinances have been sanctioned by oath or confirmed by apostolic decree or by some other confirmatory act; nor shall they be rendered invalid by any statute or custom, or any privilege or papal dispensation granted to the Augustinian order or to the monastery of which you are a canon and in which you may have taken vows, or to other monasteries, lands, benefices, and administrations, whatever the conditions may be under which these dispensations were granted, even when they were several times renewed, approved, and reaffirmed by us and the Holy See, and even if these provisions may not properly be set aside unless full, precise, special, specific, and individual mention is made of them and of their full signification, using the exact words of the documents and not expressions of a general nature having the same sense, or unless some other statement is made or some other precise formula adopted; we considering the sense of such provisions to be sufficiently defined, on condition that such provisions remain in force in all other cases, specifically and expressly set them aside in this case only, along with all other impediments whatsoever. It is our wish, however, that in the disposition of property derived from the church, you show yourself generous, in proportion to the amount of the residue, towards those churches and benefices from which you received the same, as your conscience will dictate and as you will consider expedient for the salvation of your soul.

Given at Rome at St. Peter's under the ring of the Fisherman, on the
eighth day of July 1525, in the second year of our pontificate   65
   Benedetto, bishop-elect of Ravenna[1]
To our beloved son, Erasmus of Rotterdam, master of theology

1589 / From Albert Pigge to the Theologians of Louvain

Rome, 12 July 1525

Erasmus had long complained bitterly about the slanderous public attacks on
him by certain Louvain theologians, especially the Carmelite Nicolaas Baechem
of Egmont (Egmondanus). He had already obtained papal intervention to
silence various ultra-conservative critics (cf Epp 1438, 1571, 1581). This letter
represents an effort by his friends at Rome, including Albert Pigge, to intervene by sending a private letter to Louvain in lieu of a formal papal brief of
admonition, which would have been an embarrassment to the faculty if it had
become known. The plan also involved sending a confidential papal emissary,
Theodoricus Hezius, directly to Louvain to confer with the offending theologians. Pigge (c 1490–1542), a native of Kampen, studied at Louvain, where he
ranked first among MA graduates in 1509, and then studied theology under
Adriaan of Utrecht, the future Pope Adrian VI. He received a bachelor of
theology degree in 1515. He may have accompanied Adriaan to Spain in 1515
but in any case lived at Paris (1518–22), publishing *Astrologiae defensio* (Henri
Estienne 1519) and other astrological works. When Adriaan became pope in
1522, he became papal chamberlain; and thanks to the influence of Girolamo
Aleandro, he retained this position under Clement VII. In his later years,
required by the terms of a valuable benefice to reside in the Netherlands, he
became an active defender of Catholicism; and his theological and ecclesiastical tracts of the 1530s and 1540s are of some significance in the definition of
the authority of tradition that prevailed at the Council of Trent, while his
opinions on papal infallibility were influential at Vatican Council I in 1870.
This letter survives in autograph at the British Library (MS Add 38512 f 8) and
was first printed by J. Le Plat in *Recueil de quelques pièces pour servir à la con-
tinuation des Fastes académiques de l'université de Louvain* (Lille 1783).

* * * * *

1588
1 Benedetto Accolti (1497–1549) of Florence signed this letter in his role as papal
   secretary. He was at this point archbishop-elect of Ravenna. In 1527 Clement
   VII raised him to the cardinalate. Cf Eugenio G. Massa in DBI I 101–2.

Greetings, worshipful and learned masters, my most respected teachers. That revered and venerable faculty of yours is gaining a very bad reputation here because of the malicious tongues of a few troublemakers among you; every time they address the people from the pulpit, they launch a loud and bitter attack on Erasmus of Rotterdam, a man who is surely the most   5
eloquent and erudite that this age has seen and who enjoys the favour and respect, not only of the pope and of all men of rank, but of everyone who has made a name for himself in literary studies. These men know that the troublemakers are accomplishing one thing and one thing only: by branding Erasmus at one moment as a heretic and at another as a Lutheran and by   10
publicly labelling him with any number of other insulting names, they are alienating a man who has recently taken a public stand against Luther on our behalf and in support of the Catholic faith, someone whom the pope is trying to win over by every kind of inducement; for the pope is wise enough to recognize how much influence a single individual can wield on   15
one side or the other. But those men are likely to raise up a whole host of Luthers in place of one, as if we did not have all we needed of controversies and schisms.

Some time ago his Holiness commissioned the Reverend Theodoricus Hezius,[1] on his departure from Rome, to talk to these men privately on his   20
behalf and advise them courteously to try to be more restrained in their language and to speak as befits theologians and men who have taken vows, for the accusations against them expressly referred to them as such. But the complaints continued without interruption, and it was not just from Erasmus that they came, but from many influential people as well, whose   25
letters were shown me by the Most Reverend, the datary.[2] Luckily at this

* * * * *

1589
1 Cf Ep 1339 introduction. Unfortunately for Erasmus, although Hezius had been favourable to Erasmus and encouraged his patron Adrian VI to uphold him against his theological critics (Ep 1331), upon returning to Louvain in 1525 with this charge from Pope Clement VII to warn the critics against continuing their attacks, he seems to have been won over to their opinion that Erasmus' writings fostered heresy. Hence in this business he played a double game, formally fulfilling his commission to impose silence but secretly speaking and writing against Erasmus in Louvain and in his private letters to Rome. By June 1526 Erasmus was aware of this betrayal but could do little about it (cf Epp 1717, 1875). Subsequently Hezius blocked the use of Erasmus' books by schools at Liège and still later managed to have several of his works put on the Index published there in 1545 (Epp 2369, 2566).
2 The papal datary at this period (1523–7) was Gian Matteo Giberti (see Allen

point I happened to come on the scene, otherwise Erasmus would have been given a strongly worded papal brief, directed against his detractors, the theologians of Louvain. I realized the damage this would do to the reputation of your faculty; so I opposed it with all my powers, for I did not 30 doubt that once it left here, it would quickly make its way to every corner of the globe. It took a great effort, but I succeeded with some difficulty in having it stopped. In place of the brief, however, I was instructed to write to your university to request that you do everything possible to see that no further complaints reach us on this subject. I was also ordered to write to 35 Erasmus and set his mind at rest.

So I thought it my duty, reverend fathers, to write to you and advise you to consider your reputation, which we have tried by every means to raise above the ordinary and have always taken great pains to promote. But it has suffered dreadfully because of the obstinacy, the name-calling, and 40 the supercilious behaviour of a few, as well as by the continual complaints which are made about you by others.

In my judgment the best thing which you can do is to compel those who are still causing these complaints to be more moderate in their speech; you should also write to Master Erasmus as soon as possible and make your 45 peace with him, so that he will understand that he has nothing to fear in future from those men and that the instructions of the Holy Father on his behalf have had some effect on you. If you do this, Erasmus will be quick to pardon you, and indeed to commend you in his letters to the datary and other friends of his in Rome, so that the wrongdoing of a few may not cast 50 a shadow over a distinguished faculty. Erasmus is a civilized man: I am confident that, if you write, he will respond in the most generous way. For my part I shall not cease to do all I can to protect and defend your honour, which I consider to be linked with my own.

My best wishes. Please don't be too critical of this letter, which was 55 tossed off in great haste: I was swamped with a lot of business which had to be attended to at the same time, since the courier was in a hurry and I had several other letters to write.

From the apostolic palace, 12 July 1525

* * * * *

Ep 1443A introduction). Giberti, who became a noted reforming bishop after 1527, had encouraged Erasmus to speak out against Luther and hence had a lively interest in preventing renewed challenges to his orthodoxy by the Louvain theologians. On the office of datary, see Ep 1589A introduction. Cf also Ep 1589A.

Your most devoted pupil, Albert Pigge of Kampen, chamberlain to his   60
Holiness

To the reverend fathers and learned doctors, the dean and faculty of
theology of the distinguished University of Louvain

1589A / Gian Matteo Giberti to Theodoricus Hezius

Rome, 21 July 1525

This letter from the datary of Pope Clement VII aims to reinforce the verbal
instructions given by himself and by the pope for Hezius to impose silence on
Erasmus' critics at Louvain. See Ep 1589 on the mission; Epp 1443A introduction and 1589 n2 on Giberti; and Epp 1339 introduction, 1589 n1 on Hezius.
The letter remained unpublished until the appearance of Allen VI in 1926,
where the text is based on a Vatican manuscript (MS Particolare 154 f 102). The
office of datary, founded in the fourteenth century to supervise the conferring
of benefices granted by the papal power of reservation, had also acquired a
major role in the official dating (and hence authentication) of apostolic letters.
Thus it was a powerful curial office, involving frequent contact with the pope
and considerable influence on policy.

Reverend sir, etc. When you were leaving here, I enjoined you in the name
of our most Holy Father to rescue our friend Erasmus from his detractors
at Louvain. I now wish to repeat that message in writing. It is not that I
imagine that anything of interest to his Holiness or to Erasmus himself
could have slipped your memory, but I wanted to assure Erasmus through   5
a member of his own household,[1] who is with me now, that I had con-
veyed these instructions to you, and at the same time seize the opportunity
which the occasion affords of sending you a letter. For I am most eager (as
I ought to be) to retain your affection and regard. His Holiness will be
grateful if, with the tact which you know is essential in this case, you will   10
discuss the issue with the appropriate people and tell them to leave
Erasmus in peace and quiet, for he has accomplished much in the past and
promises to accomplish even greater things in the future. When you have
done this, please write to me here and to Erasmus himself.

* * * * *

1589A
1 Karl Harst, Erasmus' confidential courier, who was returning with letters from
   Rome, including the papal brief authorizing Erasmus to draw a will (Ep 1588).
   On Harst, cf Ep 1587 n43 and the further citations given there.

Gian Matteo Giberti
Portrait by Bernardino India
Museo di Castelvecchio, Verona

His Holiness will be much in your debt, and so indeed shall I, though   15
in my case I must thank you also for that other commission which I gave
you on behalf of my servant Julian – if, that is, without causing yourself too
much trouble, you can bring it to a satisfactory and successful conclusion.
Farewell.

Rome, 21 July 1525   20

To the Reverend Theodoricus Hezius, canon of Liège, a friend as dear
to me as a brother

1590 / From Erasmus Schets   Antwerp, 23 July 1525

This letter illustrates how a respected and well-connected merchant like Schets
could develop a network of business correspondents and use it for the rapid
and efficient transfer of funds from one country to another. Especially striking
is the clear and simple procedure he outlines for transferring Erasmus' English
revenues to Basel. On Schets' emergence as Erasmus' principal agent for such
business matters cf Ep 1541 introduction. The letter remained among Erasmus'
private papers at Basel, unpublished until the appearance of Allen VI in 1926.

I received the letter which you were kind enough to send me. I understand
the measures you want me to take in connection with your pension from
Canterbury.[1] There is no wish of yours which I would not willingly satisfy
provided it was in my power to do so. Be assured that it is my desire that
whatever authority or influence lies within my humble competence should   5
be at your disposal to serve you. I only wish I could do more to help.

I have no business in England myself, since the English, by imposing
tariffs at an excessive and crippling rate, are discouraging merchants from
abroad. But I do have some close and trusted friends there who send me
daily bulletins with all the gossip and the business news. Among these I   10
would give pride of place to Alvaro de Castro,[2] who is Spanish by birth,

* * * * *

1590
1 Cf Ep 1583 n1.
2 Both Alvaro and his brother Luis were Spanish merchants from Burgos who
settled in England. Their business connections with Schets caused him to
suggest Alvaro as a suitable person to collect Erasmus' English income on the
spot and transfer it to Schets for further transmission to Erasmus in Basel.
Although he knew no Latin, Alvaro favoured humanism and was a friend of
the Spanish-born humanist Juan Luis Vives, who composed his De officio mariti
(Bruges: H. de Crook 1529; NK 2171) while living in Alvaro's house at London.

but is now resident in London. If you will write to my Lord the archbishop
and ask him to deposit the money for your pension with this man, I shall
see to it that whatever is paid will be transferred to you, at home or elsewhere, without any added charges. You should also ask Canterbury to   15
require a receipt from Alvaro for the amount transferred; he should then
have his secretary send this on to me with a covering letter, indicating also
the type of currency in which payment was made. If you do this, everything
will be carried out in proper order. I am anxious to do what I can to help
you.   20

You are putting off your return, I am sorry to hear, and you offer me
no hope. The problem, I know, is the turbulence of the times, which abates
in one province only to emerge somewhere else. Violent disturbances have
broken out in Austria and Hungary.[3] If God does not intervene, every
mark of decency will disappear; the course of justice will be obstructed, and 25
a godless tyranny will reign everywhere. It is plain to see that we are
receiving a just recompense for all our sins.

I send you my best wishes, dear Erasmus, for your happiness and
success. Antwerp, 23 July 1525.

Yours very truly, Erasmus Schets   30

To the incomparable and erudite Master Erasmus of Rotterdam. In
Basel

1591 / To Jean de Selve   [Basel, c July 1525]

Written as a preface and dedication for Erasmus' *Adversus Petri Sutoris quondam theologi Sorbonici nunc monachi Cartusiani debacchationem apologia* (Basel:
Froben, August 1525), this letter complains not only about the attacks of Pierre
Cousturier (in Latin, Sutor) on recent biblical translations by Erasmus and
others but also against a forged edition of his own *Colloquies*. Jean de Selve
(1475–1529), sieur de Cormières, was first president of the Parlement of Paris,
France's highest court of law, having been in royal diplomatic and judicial
service since the reign of Louis XII. While the French occupied Milan, he was
vice-chancellor of that duchy (1515–20). Although humanists such as Andrea
Alciati and Jacques Lefèvre d'Etaples regarded him as a powerful friend at
court and honoured him with dedications, as first president he was deeply
involved in efforts to suppress heresy, efforts which came to include the

* * * * *

3 Another reference to the peasant uprising of 1525, which developed rather
later in the Austrian lands than in south-western and central Germany and
was still in full swing there during the summer of 1525. Cf Preface, page xi–xii.

attempts by Noël Béda, Pierre Cousturier, and other Paris theologians to condemn Lefèvre and Erasmus as well as Luther. Subsequently, he was involved in the trial and execution of Louis de Berquin. His personal opinion on these specific cases is not known, but Erasmus wrote this dedication seeking his protection at the suggestion of his friend Nicolas Bérault (Allen Ep 1598:2), who was well informed about persons and factions at the French capital. In fact, however, de Selve was not in Paris to act on Erasmus' plea, for he spent most of the second half of 1525 in Spain, negotiating for the release of his captive king. Most of the publications on him concentrate on his work as a diplomat, but for a broader approach see Gordon Griffiths in CEBR III 238–40.

TO THE RIGHT HONOURABLE JEAN DE SELVE, FIRST PRESIDENT OF THE AUGUST PARLEMENT OF FRANCE, FROM ERASMUS OF ROTTERDAM, GREETING

The ancients had a wise saying, most honoured sir, that good laws arise from bad practices.[1] But humanity faces a greater threat if the reverse is true and the worst of practices spring from the best of laws. For what hope of recovery do we have if our remedies turn to poison and the medicine which was designed to combat the disease makes it worse? The only way to prevent this from happening is for the skilled and trusted physician who has prescribed the drug to administer it himself. An excellent law was passed to control irresponsible and defamatory publications, as a beneficial and necessary measure against a serious and growing evil.[2] But human

* * * * *

1591
1 Macrobius *Saturnalia* 3.17.10; cf *Adagia* I x 61.
2 In fact this 'excellent law' was aimed at preventing the spread of the Lutheran heresy. On 18 March 1521 Francis I issued an order commanding the Parlement to supervise the publication of books on religion so that no work would be published without the approval of the faculty of theology. The Parlement registered this edict promptly and quickly set to work suppressing dangerous books. In 1524 it even suspended royal letters patent authorizing publication of 'Paraphrases d'Erasme sur les évangiles de Luc et de Marc' unless the book had the faculty's approval – not a very auspicious law for Erasmus to cite in the present context! Cf Roger Doucet *Etude sur le gouvernement de François I dans ses rapports avec le Parlement de Paris* (Paris 1921) 331–3; and Knecht *Francis I* 142–4; but Farge *Orthodoxy* 253–4 concludes that the faculty, not the king, acted first, and that the exact date of the royal action remains unclear. He has more recently established that the king had nothing to do with this law, which was enacted solely by the Parlement, acting at the request of the University of

perversity is turning this valuable measure into a greater evil – unless those who introduced the law will also administer and uphold it. If this is not done, I foresee that a regulation which was introduced to prevent the publication at Paris of anything which failed to meet the standards of your distinguished university and Parlement will inevitably mean that all the best books will be driven out and works like the two which have recently burst forth from the press will be printed with impunity. One of these had the downright impudence to tamper with my *Colloquia*,[3] adding a preface to which my name was falsely attached. In it I am represented as saying about myself whatever the author felt like saying. If you have time to look at the work, you will comprehend the fellow's hopeless delinquency: nothing would hold him back if he felt tempted to set fire to the city or poison someone or commit murder. But if you don't have the time, you can easily find out the sort of work it is by looking at the *Catalogue* of my writings, which I am enclosing along with this.[4] The name of the author is known and there is no mystery about the printer. Both profit by their misdeeds.

Since this piece of effrontery turned out well, Pierre Cousturier[5] burst on the scene with a book of his own. 'But of that I shall not say another word.'[6] If an experienced critic like yourself cannot infer from my *Apologia* what the work and its author are like, then the book itself will give you a full portrait of the man, like a reflection in a mirror. It has not escaped me that some theologians are satisfied with what they learned when they were young and have such a deep dislike of languages and literature that nothing pleases them which has any connection at all with polite letters. They have armed themselves with hundreds of titles and innumerable theses, and if these fail them, they feel free to invent new doctrines, as this fellow Cousturier is doing. Anyone with so many snares and with the attitude to criticism which Cousturier has, could even build a specious case against St Paul in a thousand places. A law which curbs the godless notions of schismatics and incurable heretics is excellent. But some people are perverse in the extreme; they are enslaved by their private passions, and so they use

* * * * *

Paris. See his 'Early Censorship in Paris: A New Look at the Roles of the Parlement of Paris and of King Francis I' *Renaissance and Reformation / Renaissance et Réforme* ns 13/2 (1989) 175–6.

3 Cf Ep 1581 n59.

4 Erasmus probably sent the much expanded list of his writings published at Basel by Froben in September 1524, *Catalogus novus omnium lucubrationum Erasmi Roterodami.* For this text in its earlier and later forms, see Ep 1341A.

5 Cf Ep 1571 n10.

6 Horace *Satires* 1.1.121

medicine intended for the sick in order to destroy the healthy and with the
cauterer's iron they leave a raw wound on sound flesh; they would do more   45
for their reputations if they read the works of modern writers with an open
mind and gave languages and literature a friendly invitation to become
partners with themselves. I cannot imagine that any of the theologians at
Paris would be so biassed against the liberal arts as to approve of
Cousturier's bacchanalian raving. All the more reason, then, to punish   50
severely those who are making a mockery of an excellent law. If they can
do whatever they please and go scot free, this is the sort of book which
Paris will give us. On the other hand, if someone stands up to defend
himself against an obvious slander or attempts to publish something which
might be of use to the scholarly world, then we shall see the full force of   55
the law and the censors will be at their posts. In every assembly the chicanery of the few is generally more than a match for the good sense of the
many. There is no surprise when weight of numbers defeats the better
cause; but here it is often a minority of the worse which defeats a majority
of the better. Unless the princes, with their sense of justice and fair play,   60
help humanists to resist the stubborn and malicious attacks of these men,
polite learning will soon be crushed and those disciplines in whose success
alone they are interested will collapse along with it.

The death of that most distinguished man, François Deloynes,[7] has
robbed the world of learning of a great patron and defender. If fate had not   65
taken King Francis from us for the time being,[8] I would not have wearied
your ears with this tale of woe; I would have gone to the great champion
of the Muses himself and begged his help against the onslaught of the
barbarians. In the meantime it will fall to you and to men like you to support the cause of learning and by just measures to control the unjust behav-   70
iour of the Cousturiers of this world. For letters from many scholars have
convinced me that you possess unique gifts of intellect, learning, and judgment, surpassed only by the excellence of your character and the courtesy
of your manner. With talents such as these, you are lending no ordinary
distinction to that venerable Parlement, over which you have deservedly   75
been appointed to preside. But if you accept this task, not only will you

* * * * *

7 Cf Ep 1571 n1.
8 Francis I was captured at the battle of Pavia, 24 February 1525, and his release
   from captivity did not occur until 17 March 1526. He had generally favoured
   Erasmus, Lefèvre, and other reformist humanists, and during his long absence
   their enemies in the university and the Parlement were vigorously pursuing
   measures against them.

give your support to the most honoured fields of learning, but you will also
help to promote the reputation of theology, which is now discredited in the
eyes of many people because of the unfair and ill-considered judgments of
an unstable minority. We know the burden of prejudice which the whole   80
priesthood bears because of the shortcomings of a few. We know of the
unmerited sufferings of good monks because of the scandalous behaviour
of some of their members. So no one will have done more for the standing
and influence of theologians than the man who suppresses these noisy
troublemakers, who are no theologians, but sores and cancers on the whole   85
profession of theology. And there is no action which sane and honest theologians will applaud more justly.

I should have had a more auspicious reason for getting in touch with
a great man like yourself, but my present concern was thrust upon me by
Cousturier, an inauspicious bird if ever there was one! Farewell.   90

1592 / To Gianfrancesco Torresani   Basel, 5 August 1525

Although Erasmus had been publishing with Johann Froben in Basel for a
decade, he had carefully maintained his earlier connection with the press of
Aldo Manuzio and Andrea Torresani (Asulanus) of Asola. The latter was the
father of Gianfrancesco and had been the partner (as well as father-in-law) of
Aldo. One of Karl Harst's tasks during his business trip to Italy in 1525 was
to offer the text for a new edition of Erasmus' *Adagia* to this famous Venetian
firm, which had published an important early edition in 1508. As this letter
suggests, the press, which since Aldus' death in 1515 was under the control
of Torresani, was too busy to undertake it; and the new edition was printed
by Froben in February 1526. Despite Erasmus' remark here about Andrea
Torresani's kindness, he and his son had developed the reputation of being
less interested in scholarship and more interested in money than their
deceased partner Aldus. They were also notoriously brusque in their relations
with their scholarly authors. As the tone of this letter indicates, Erasmus knew
both Torresani rather well. He had in fact lodged in the elder's house at
Venice in 1508. His relations with them were civil but not intimate. On Gianfrancesco, the present recipient, cf Ep 212:3n. This letter was first published by
Pierre de Nolhac in his *Erasme en Italie* 2nd ed (Paris 1898).

Cordial greetings. I thought I would earn your gratitude if I sent you a
revised copy of my proverbs. I was not forced to do this through any lack
of printers; I did it partly out of devotion to you, since your letters have
often expressed some concern on this score, and partly from self-interest,
since I hoped your press would lend an added splendour to my work. I   5

know that your father[1] shows his kindness more in action than in word.
There is no reason why the present business should not be conducted in a
friendly spirit. If it is not to your advantage to publish, send the manuscript
back, at no cost to yourself – although it was at my expense that it was sent
to you. I know that any disingenuousness in your treatment of me would   10
be out of keeping with your usual courtesy and with the respect which I
deserve of you. And if this were your intention (which I cannot believe to
be the case), there is no way I could be taken in. I have a second copy,
containing the same revisions, to which I could add whatever I wished, and
I have a printer who is always at my disposal.[2] But if you will deal with   15
me in good faith, I guarantee that you will have no reason to complain of
bad faith on my part.

Farewell. Give my best wishes to your father, your brother,[3] your
nephew Manuzio,[4] and the rest of my friends.

Basel, 5 August 1525   20

To the learned Master Gianfrancesco Asulanus. In Venice at the metal-
workers bridge

1593 / To Krzysztof Szydłowiecki   Basel, 14 August 1525

This letter was published as the dedication to Erasmus' *Lingua* (Basel: Froben,
August 1525), a treatise on the power of the human tongue for good and evil
which has attracted little attention in modern scholarship but was reprinted
several times in its own century and translated into German, Dutch, and
Spanish. Spanish editions were especially numerous and influential until the
work was finally placed on the Index in the second half of the century. Cf F.
Schalk in ASD IV-1 226 and Elaine Fantham in CWE 29 253–4. Krzysztof Szyd-

* * * * *

1592
1 Andrea Torresani; cf introduction.
2 Johann Froben of Basel. In fact, as Erasmus states here, one of the reasons why
  he offered the Torresani the revised *Adages* was that they had complained in
  1523 about Froben's monopoly of publishing the profitable revised editions of
  that work. Cf Ep 1349 introduction.
3 Frederico Torresani (d 1561), a younger son of Andrea, less active than
  Francesco in the Asolani printing firm.
4 your nephew Manuzio] Probably Paolo Manuzio (1512–74), the ablest of Aldo's
  sons, who was still a youth but eventually shared in the management of the
  Aldine-Asolani press. Since he and his Torresani cousins did not agree well,
  in 1539 they liquidated the firm and Paolo then printed in his own name.

Krzysztof Szydłowiecki
Miniature from the so-called 'Liber Genesaeos familiae Schidloviciae'
by Stanislaus Samostrzelnik
Courtesy of the Institute of Art, Polish Academy of Sciences

łowiecki (1467–1532) was a high-ranking nobleman and close adviser to King
Sigismund I of Poland. Although chiefly active in diplomacy and internal administration, he used his great wealth to become an important patron of
literature and art. Erasmus probably made this dedication at the urging of Jan
Łaski, a young Polish nobleman and humanist who later became an important
Protestant leader but at this period was a devoted Erasmian and spent six
months of 1525 living as a guest in Erasmus' house at Basel. Szydłowiecki
promptly arranged for the republication of *Lingua* (Cracow: Hieronymus Vietor
1526) and sent valuable gifts of gold to Erasmus (cf Ep 1698). The present
translation differs in a few particulars from that printed in CWE 29.

TO THE ILLUSTRIOUS KRZYSZTOF SZYDŁOWIECKI, PALATINE AND
PREFECT OF CRACOW, CHANCELLOR OF THE KINGDOM OF
POLAND, FROM ERASMUS OF ROTTERDAM, GREETING
Distinguished sir, distinguished for more than the glory of your line, the life
of mankind is beset on all sides by so many great misfortunes that when   5
Homer compared our lot with that of all the different kinds of living creatures, he concluded that 'there is no creature more miserable than man.'[1]
Silenus judged it best never to have been born, or, once born, to perish at
the earliest possible time.[2] Pliny thought that no greater or more generous
gift was given by the gods to man than shortness of life, and that no one   10
was denied the power to end that life, if he so decided.[3] According to
Lucian, Pythagoras (whose soul is supposed to have changed its abode
repeatedly and to have entered into the bodies of creatures of every kind,
men and women, bipeds and quadrupeds) admitted that he lived a much
happier life as a frog than as a king.[4] All this may sound absurd, but it   15
would not be far from the truth, if that heavenly teacher of wisdom had not
convinced us that everlasting happiness is laid up for those who have
placed all their hopes of bliss, from stem to stern,[5] as it were, in him. So
powerful is this hope that, even in the greatest misfortunes, it preserves and
sustains the joy which belongs to a soul at peace with itself, especially since   20

* * * * *

1593
1 *Iliad* 17.446–7; *Odyssey* 18.130–1.
2 Attendant of the god Dionysus. The story is told by Cicero in *Tusculanae
  disputationes* 1.114; cf Pliny *Naturalis historia* 7.4 and Plutarch *Moralia* 115B–E.
3 *Naturalis historia* 2.27, 7.168.
4 Lucian *Gallus* 15–27; *Vera historia* 2.21
5 Cf *Adagia* I i 8; Cicero *Ad familiares* 16.24.1.

it always has that wonderful and miraculous talisman that turns all the gall of this life into honey.

Since man, being composed of body and soul, is troubled by two kinds of affliction, wise men have always sought to know whether the ailments of the body or those of the soul are worse; and the answer they have given is that ailments of the soul have more terrible consequences.[6] Yet common opinion is far from agreeing with this view. There are few indeed who do not think it worse to suffer from dropsy than from avarice. Similarly it is considered a greater blessing to have a splendid physique than a mind enriched with fine learning and noble qualities. We cannot be surprised that men who put the body before the soul also make inverted judgments about what is good and what is bad. Antiquity counted some three hundred varieties of disease besides accidents and deformities;[7] to this number new and previously unknown diseases have been added, and continue to be added every day in a sort of guerrilla war against the science of medicine. But who could count the ailments of the soul? I wish it were only in number that they surpassed the ills of the body, but, alas, they have the advantage in many other respects as well. For in the first place it is the better part of us which they harm. Then physical illnesses only make men sick, but diseases of the soul make us evil and wretched as well, because they come from within ourselves. Again there are some physical illnesses which do not entail acute pain, like consumption. But would you say that the physical pain of dropsy or fever surpasses the mental torment which is caused by the craving for money, or rampant lust, or jealousy, or envy? Moreover illnesses of the body often bring relief to the troubles of the mind, whereas moral failings are generally accompanied by physical problems too. We are more apprehensive about physical ailments which are not only disagreeable, but carry a stigma as well; but all moral ailments act like this: for not only do they rob the mind of its calm, but they bring shame to the sufferer.

Doctors think that there is no type of illness more dreadful than that which robs the patient of his capacity to understand his trouble. The sufferer from gout who keeps complaining of his troubles and has the doctor called in is easier to cure than the lunatic or the lethargic. The latter thinks he is sane, the former assaults the doctor who wants to help him.[8] Almost all sicknesses of the mind are like this: the worse the illness is, the less will

* * * * *

6 See, eg, Plutarch's essay *Animine an corporis affectiones sint peiores* in *Moralia* 500A–502A; Maximus of Tyre *Orationes* 7.
7 Pliny *Naturalis historia* 26.9
8 Horace *Satires* 2.3.30 records this of the lethargic patient.

the sufferer accept the doctor's help. These ailments, too, differ among themselves. It is far easier to heal self-indulgence, lust, extravagance, and all the less complicated mental illnesses – if I may call them that – than to cure ambition, envy, selfishness, and hypocrisy. You will see many people who could never be charged with fornication or drunkenness, but who are totally   60 immersed in self-love and measure everything by this yardstick. If someone opposes them, there is no type of revenge they will not resort to, and their abominable desires are covered up with a mask of fine-sounding names. Nothing is more destructive or more difficult to cure than this type of man.

The mind can pass judgment on the ailments of the body, but this is   65 impossible in the case of illnesses of the mind, because we are damaged in the very part which enables us to judge. What remedy then could you apply to help the man who calls his insatiable acquisitiveness 'taking thought for the future' or his envy 'a passion for honour,' or who gives the name of 'prudence' to blind self-love and covers up a compulsive scurrility with the   70 label of 'frankness'? We might add that the man whose feet are crippled with gout is still sound in eye and ear, but a single moral ailment corrupts the whole mind. Again, a man troubled with the stone is free of other diseases. But there is no moral sickness which does not bring with it a whole regiment of vices.   75

Furthermore, if we should estimate the seriousness of a disease by the danger of infection, then, if we believe Pliny, old men are immune from the plague;[9] nor does the plague spread at random, but arises in the south and generally travels westward.[10] Some illnesses do not affect children and others pass over the female sex; some attack the ruling class and spare the   80 common people – such as eczema.[11] Some diseases affect only particular ages, or even districts. Leprosy[12] and *gemursa*[13] quickly died out when they crossed over into Italy. England did not experience the deadly sweat-ing-sickness[14] until thirty years ago, and it is a scourge which does not

* * * * *

9 *Naturalis historia* 7.170
10 Ibidem
11 Ibidem 26.7–8
12 Ibidem
13 Pliny ibidem describes this disease, which has not been identified, as a growth between the toes.
14 This febrile disease, characterized by profuse sweating, rapid onset, and frequent fatalities, was epidemic in northern Europe, but especially in England, during the fifteenth and sixteenth centuries. Often known as 'the English sweat,' it first appeared in England in 1485, and the last of the six recorded epidemics was in 1578. Only the fourth outbreak, in 1528–9, seems to have

generally pass beyond the limits of the island. All these diseases have their   85
particular territory and their particular seasons and tend to attack certain
persons and even certain parts of the body. But plagues of the mind spare
neither rank nor sex nor age and are restrained by no boundaries, but
sweep the earth with unimaginable speed. Nor do they yield place to one
another in turn, as plague and quinsy and whooping cough break out one   90
at a time. But each moral weakness is responsible for another, like the links
in a chain, and once they have set in, it is not easy to be rid of them.

Suppose someone asked which disease of the body should be accorded
the first place. In my opinion the prize will fall easily to that disease of
unknown origin which has stalked every region of the earth for many years   95
now, though there is no settled convention about its name. Most men call
it the French, but some the Spanish pox.[15] Is there any plague which has
traversed the various regions of Europe, Asia, and Africa with equal speed?
Does any penetrate more deeply into our veins and organs, or persist more
doggedly or defy more stubbornly the skill and treatment of the doctors?   100
Is any disease more contagious or responsible for more cruel torments?
Psoriasis is not harmful except for the disfigurement of the skin, and it
admits of cure.[16] Eczema covers first the face and then the rest of the body
with an ugly scaling rash, but there is no pain and no risk to life, although
it is true there is no cure except one which is worse than death.[17] But this   105

* * * * *

spread widely to the Continent, and then only in lands bordering on the North
and Baltic seas. Dr John Caius published a thorough description of the sickness
as he encountered it while practicing medicine at Shrewsbury in 1551. It has
not been certainly identified with any disease now known. Cf OED²; *Black's
Medical Dictionary* (31st ed) 820.

15 Erasmus refers to the current debate over the disease syphilis, which some
contemporaries regarded as a new disease brought from America to Spain by
the crews of Columbus' expedition of 1492, spread thence to Naples by Spanish soldiers, and then spread to the rest of Europe by French troops. Other
contemporaries (including his learned acquaintance Dr Niccolò Leoniceno)
thought it to be just a new epidemic of an old disease. This question is still
debated among historians of disease, with some scholars arguing that syphilis
is a mere clinical variant of yaws, pinta, bejel, or other less serious diseases of
the skin. See Alfred W. Crosby, jr *The Columbian Exchange* (Westport, Conn
1972) 122–64; R.E. McGrew *Encyclopedia of Medical History* (New York 1985) sv
'syphilis.' Many of the relevant documents are printed in Charles Clayton
Dennie *A History of Syphilis* (Springfield, Ill 1962) 3–71.

16 Pliny *Naturalis historia* 26.2

17 Pliny *Naturalis historia* 26.2–3, reports of eczema that the only cure was the use
of caustics, successful only if 'the flesh was burnt through right to the bones';
this may well be the cure 'which is worse than death.' As for syphilis,

scourge brings in its train all the terrifying aspects of other illnesses: disfigurement, pain, infection, the risk of losing one's life, and a treatment that
is both difficult and extremely unpleasant; and no matter how successfully
it is controlled, it suddenly breaks out again, like gout.

Finally, if anyone were to consider diseases of the mind, and ask   11
which had the greatest power to harm, I would not hesitate to give this
unrewarding award, this prize which no one prizes, to the affliction of an
unbridled tongue. This plague is neither new nor simple in nature, but
includes all the diseases of the mind. No generation has ever been so sound
in morals that it did not complain of this affliction. Some fevers and plagues   11
never die out, but erupt from time to time like a flood and rage more
violently than before and over a wider region, threatening the human race
with annihilation. In the same way we can now see how this deadly sickness of a malicious tongue has infected the whole world with its awful
venom, pervading the courts of princes, the homes of commoners, theologi-   12
cal schools, monastic brotherhoods, colleges of priests, regiments of soldiers,
and the cottages of peasants, and so great is the force of the onslaught that
it threatens the total ruin and destruction of the liberal arts and of good
morals, and civic harmony and the authority alike of the leaders of the
church and the princes of the realm.   12

When the scourge, of which I spoke a moment ago, first began to
spread, our initial reactions were torpid, and even now we are not awake
to the danger of infection, although sufferers from leprosy, a less serious
illness, are isolated from human contact. But, faced with an even greater
threat to human society, we have done nothing so far to control the reckless   13
frenzy of men's tongues and we are still doing nothing. Meanwhile the
sickness grows worse each day and is passing beyond cure. There are some
who, like incompetent doctors, have merely aggravated the disease by their
ill-advised treatment. Bishops who combined Christian prudence and
knowledge of the gospel with an attitude of moderation should have made   13
this matter their special province. We can see what has been achieved so far
by branding, mutilation, and imprisonment. As for my own contribution,

* * * * *

although other treatments were tried, the only truly effective treatment
involved use of an unguent containing mercury, documented in use at Verona
as early as 1496, and evidently applied to the lesions characteristic of the
secondary stage. Use of this highly toxic heavy metal was painful. Patients
suffered loss of hair, abdominal pains, and loosening of the teeth. Thus many,
such as the humanist Ulrich von Hutten, preferred the illness to the torture of
the treatment. See R.E. McGrew, as in n15.

although I do not possess the authority, learning and wisdom which the gravity of the malady requires, in my distress over the general calamity which has befallen the Christian world, I am offering such palliatives as I am able. If the disease cannot be eradicated completely, it is my hope that by these means it may at least be weakened. 140

I have heard from the honourable Jan Łaski[18] that there is still much of that old-fashioned morality among your people – I might say in poetic terms that Astraea, in her flight from the world,[19] seems to have left her last footprints in your land. I understand that it is enjoying great prosperity, thanks to the wise government of that virtuous and watchful ruler, Archbishop Jan Łaski,[20] who in our decadent age is reviving the example of the bishops of old. I find these reports easier to believe, having experienced in my informant an honesty and self-discipline such as I have rarely met before in any other man. If, as I think, this general scourge of a malicious tongue has not yet reached your own dear Poland, then I thought I might celebrate your good fortune with this composition; but if some trace of the infection has spread to you, my gift will serve as an antidote. 145 150

* * * * *

18 This young Polish nobleman and humanist (1499–1560), nephew and namesake of the archbishop of Gniezno and primate of Poland, had travelled and studied in Italy and at Vienna and had accompanied his elder brother Hieronim to France in 1524. The family group (including another brother, Stanisław) visited Erasmus at Basel on their way west. After study at Paris, where he became close to the reformist circle centered around Marguerite d'Angoulême and Lefèvre d'Etaples, Jan returned to Basel in the spring of 1525 and spent six months as a paying guest in Erasmus' household. The young Polish humanist and the elderly Erasmus became close friends, and Jan persuaded Erasmus to make the present dedication to the chancellor of Poland. Upon his return to Poland, he became the center of Polish Erasmianism. Eventually attracted to the Reformation, he ended his career as a minister of the Reformed church at Emden, which was a formative influence on early Dutch Calvinism. The article by Maria Cytowska in CEBR II 297–301 summarizes recent scholarship and cites both Polish and western studies.
19 Goddess of justice and the last of the gods to leave the earth at the close of the golden age; cf Virgil *Eclogues* 4.6; *Georgics* 2.473–4; Ovid *Metamorphoses* 1.149–50.
20 Uncle (1455–1531) of the younger Jan Łaski, archbishop of Gniezno and primate of Poland from 1510 to his death. Unlike his nephew (whose career in the church he actively promoted), he remained rather cool towards Erasmus despite the latter's many expressions of friendship, though the aloofness seems to have been more due to politics (he was committed to an anti-Hapsburg foreign policy and perceived Erasmus as their client) rather than to any objection to Erasmus' religious opinions or humanistic learning.

It was the Jan Łaski whom I mentioned a moment ago who encour-   155
aged me to publish this work under the auspices of your name. He has
never ceased to speak most enthusiastically about your great natural gifts
and outstanding qualities. As a result I too have been filled with admiration for your merits, and feel I must congratulate both you and the whole
kingdom of Poland upon your excellence as a minister of affairs. The   160
person who inspired this dedication is quite young in years, but he is
mature in character and old in judgment. He is too shrewd a witness to be
deceived; and claims which are advanced with such persistence and enthusiasm cannot be invention. Indeed if you will be kind enough to accept a
poor creature like myself into your circle, I shall count myself fortunate to   165
have you as friend or patron. I feel no embarrassment about this request,
for the friendship of such men as you has always seemed to me the greatest factor in human happiness. Yet it is not for ourselves that we seek the
favour of princes, but for the cause of piety and learning, which are now
everywhere endangered by the factious feuding of certain individuals and   170
would collapse altogether if they were not propped up by the authority
and loyalty of men like you. I would cut a sorry figure indeed if I were
still seeking offices and benefactions for myself, when I am so soon to
leave this life. Such gifts are mere burdens; they weigh a man down when
he is preparing his soul to take flight and cannot follow him when he is   175
gone. If I have been of any help to the humanities or the Christian faith by
my studies, or by the good men whom my exhortations have aroused, then
this will be my prize and I shall gladly take it with me as provision for the
journey.

But I have kept you too long from the *Lingua* itself. I fear there are   180
places where a discriminating man like yourself might hope to see a clearer
arrangement. But the material is of immense variety, and in trying to touch
on every aspect and to combine the sacred with the profane, I have found
it difficult to avoid confusion, all the more so since I had no leisure to
polish all the material which I have brought together. Farewell.   185

Basel, 14 August 1525

1593A / To the Reader   [Basel, end of August 1525]

Though this has the form of a letter, it is really a set of errata added to fol av
of the first edition of *Lingua* (Basel: Froben, August 1525). It obviously was
composed in haste just before the book was put on sale. It must have been
written after the dedication (Ep 1593, dated 14 August 1525), and probably
between that date and Epp 1602 and 1603, both of which are dated 28 August
and report that Erasmus has 'sent off' his *Lingua*. The letter reflects Erasmus'

rather chaotic method of working on the final stages of a book, since he admits that his own manuscript contained many additions and extra slips of paper, so that he attributes the blame for the listed errors to himself rather than to the printer. This letter does not appear in the English edition of *Lingua*, CWE 29 249–412, but it is reproduced photographically from the first edition in the revised modern edition of the Latin text of *Lingua* by J.H. Waszink, ASD IV-1A (Amsterdam 1989) 4–5, though not in the earlier publication of *Lingua* in the same series, ASD IV-1 (Amsterdam 1974).

ERASMUS OF ROTTERDAM TO THE READER, GREETING

On reading over the work as soon as it came off the press, I discovered a number of errors which should not be blamed on the printers so much as on the state of my manuscript, which, because of additions and extra slips of paper, was so blurred and tattered that I myself could hardly make out 5 the final text. But I give the proper readings now. It will not be difficult for anyone to number his own copy: the front side of letter b should have the number 1 and the reverse should be 2, and so on for the rest of the sheets, each being assigned two numbers.

Page 5 (that is, b3), line 7: read *Atticae*.   10

Page 17, line 13, *ut incautius*: delete *ut* and move it to the next line before the word *dolore*.

Page 23, 6 lines from the end: for *damnum* read *iacturam*.

Page 37, 8 lines from the end: for *leporum* read *luporum*.

Page 61, line 8: for *Archidamus* read *Archidamidas*.   15

Page 68, 10 lines from the end: read *discurrere*.

Page 91, line 7: for *Antiochus* read *Antigonus*.

Page 99, 3 lines from the end: The quotation is from a poem of Homer which appears differently in *Odyssey* 19, namely in the form: ἔξω δ' ὡς ὅτε τοι στερεὴ λίθος 'ἠὲ σίδηρος.[1] I had followed Plutarch, who in his *De nu-* 20 *gacitate* cites the line as I gave it;[2] from which I conclude that either he suffered a lapse of memory or quoted the same sentiment in different words from some other passage in Homer.

Page 109, line 11: for *furiarum una* read *furiarum vice*.

Page 140, line 4: read *quantam*.   25

* * * * *

1593A
1 Homer *Odyssey* 19.494
2 Referring to one of the *Moralia*, Περὶ ἀδολεσχίας 506A, more commonly known by the Latin title *De garrulitate*.

Page 152, line 6: read *veritas dei*.

Page 161, line 3: read *animum*.

Page 172, line 113: read *dii tui*

Page 213, line 2: read *sexies mille*.

Page 233, 7 lines from the end: for *Caius* read *Octavius*.   30

Page 256, line 4: read *regerit*; also 4 lines from the end: read *Aristaeneto*.

Page 285, line 5: for *ineptius* read *civilius*.

Page 291, line 3: read κενοφωνιας.

Page 329, line 8: read *infantili*.

1594 / From Leonard Casembroot   Padua, 23 August 1525

This letter from a young Flemish friend who was studying law at Padua refers
to Erasmus' unsuccessful offer of the manuscript for a new edition of his
Adagia to the Venetian printer Andrea Torresani of Asola (cf Ep 1592). It
expresses the disappointment, even anger, felt by Erasmus' private courier,
Karl Harst, and also by Erasmus' friends at Venice and Padua, at Torresani's
lack of interest. It also demonstrates the admiration felt by educated young
Netherlanders for Erasmus, and it documents his continuing contact with other
intellectuals in and near Venice. Casembroot (1495–1558) was a native of
Bruges, where he had taught Latin and Greek. No later than 1525 he had
reached Padua, where he supported himself by tutoring three sons of Guillaume de Moscheron, a merchant of Bruges, while he pursued his doctorate
in law. He probably visited Erasmus at Basel *en route* to Padua. Allen Ep 1594
introduction suggests that he may be identified with the Leonard who appears
in Epp 1208 and 1352. After completing his doctorate, Casembroot returned to
Bruges (1527–8), where he had a successful career in civic administration.
While still in Italy he sought and got Erasmus' help in finding patrons. Cf de
Vocht *Literae* Ep 55 introduction. This letter survived in a Leipzig manuscript
which was first published by Förstemann and Günther in 1904. Erasmus'
reply, friendly but critical of Casembroot's bragging about his sexual exploits
in Italy, is Ep 1626.

My dear Erasmus, my dear, dear Erasmus, greetings. Your man Karl was
here with that thoroughly delightful letter of yours;[1] we gave him a special
welcome, the sort of welcome which no one has received since we came to

* * * * *

1594
1 No such letter is extant.

Italy. As for the help you asked for in connection with the publication of the
Adagia, some Italian trickery has been at work and so I cannot send you the   5
glorious hymn of triumph which you might have expected and which our
hard work justified. In spite of the most strenuous exertions on our part, all
our plans were defeated by typical Asulan treachery (I might almost have
said 'Asinine treachery'!) and their treachery was matched by their effrontery.[2] Yet we left no path unexplored which promised any hope of success.   10
Soon after receiving your letter, I rushed off to Venice with Karl, where it
was only with the greatest difficulty that we managed to get an interview
with Francesco Asulanus after four or five days. It seemed to amuse him to
give us the slip every time we turned up, or, what was worse, to say he
was not at home when we knew from his own voice that he was. But I did   15
not tear myself away from Karl until, with the timely support of Thomas
Lupset,[3] we agreed on a contract, by which Asulanus undertook to begin
work on the edition within a fortnight.

Karl set off for Rome, expecting to find on his return that much of the
work (which he had brought with him to Venice) would already have been   20
set up. Of course we did not relax our efforts in the meantime. Thomas
Lupset, being on the spot, continued to press our man to keep his promise,
and I can tell you there were sharp exchanges on both sides. Giambattista
kept a watchful eye on the affair and let no opportunity slip by.[4] I too

* * * * *

2 On the reputation of the Torresani for crass commercialism and lack of sympathy for scholarly authors, cf Ep 1592 introduction.
3 On his early life and study under Erasmus cf Ep 270:69n. After taking his MA
   at Oxford in 1521, he went to Padua, where he tutored Thomas Winter, illegitimate son of Cardinal Wolsey. The two of them resided in the household of
   Reginald Pole there. At this time he was one of four Englishmen who were
   working for the Asulani press on the *editio princeps* of Galen in Greek, which
   came out in five volumes in 1525. Hence he was well placed to help Harst and
   Casembroot make contact with Francesco Torresani. On the importance of the
   Galen edition see Gerhard Baader 'Die Antikerezeption in der Entwicklung der
   medizinische Wissenschaft während der Renaissance' in *Humanismus und
   Medizin* ed Rudolf Schmitz and Gustav Keil (Weinheim 1984) 61, and Nikolaus
   Mani 'Die griechische Editio princeps des Galenos (1525), ihre Entstehung und
   ihre Wirkung' *Gesnerus* 13 (1956) 39.
4 Giambattista Opizzoni (documented 1509–25), a physician at Venice who was
   active in the reform of medicine both through observation and through the
   linguistic and textual study of classical authors, was the central figure in the
   Aldine-Asolani edition of Galen. Hence he was a valuable contact for Erasmus'
   young foreign friends who were pressing the Torresani to bring out a new
   Aldine edition of Erasmus' *Adagia*.

rushed over from my place in Padua to do my part. But there is no need to   25
go on. We all wasted our time. Francesco Asulanus treated us with haughty
disdain and on several occasions, when challenged, he replied, 'Stop bother-
ing me! Erasmus will be well done by. He is a close and intimate friend of
mine, whom I have known for many years.' Nevertheless he did take notice
when we said that if he did not give us some evidence of his good faith to   30
dispel our mounting suspicions, he would not be able to boast of Erasmus'
friendship much longer. Now two months later Karl has returned from
Rome, like a wolf with his mouth open, as the saying goes.[5] We trot off
again to see Asulanus. It seems that the last thing you should have expected
was your *Adagia*! What were we to do? We asked for the copy back and   35
gave it to *le grand médecin* Giambattista[6] to keep safe until you indicate to
Asulanus himself and to us what you want done.

It seemed that there was also some sort of nervousness about your
familiar colloquies, which were *suspects d'hérésie*.[7] What an age it is we live
in! Here in Italy we observe things to which, with our native innocence, we   40
can never get accustomed. Of course we are nothing but observers, for how
could we experience things which are so utterly loathsome to us. Not that
we reject everything Italian: there are melons and watermelons and figs and
many varieties of similar fruit which are wonderfully refreshing. Then there
are *les charmes des femmes* which are admirable *pour lutter au lit et pour la*   45
leonardogenèse.[8] (I think you will recognize your own joke.)[9] If justice is not
done to your opinion of me, at least it won't be my fault! I only wish it
were as easy to make ducats as it is to produce bastards!

But no more joking. Let me tell you about my personal arrangements.
Six of us, all from Flanders, have rented a house together. Italian lodgings   50

* * * * *

5 A proverb indicating desire and frustration. See *Adagia* II iii 58.
6 This letter is full of Greek phrases used in an effort to be clever and stylish,
   much the way certain modern English writers use French phrases. Hence some
   of these Greek phrases are here turned into French. The Greek is also used to
   cover (or call attention to) indiscreet remarks.
7 Another example of the use of Greek phrases to veil meaning. For a report of
   charges of heresy against the *Colloquies* at Louvain, cf Ep 1296:23, and for
   Erasmus' own description of such charges and his defence, Epp 1299, 1300,
   1301.
8 Greek words (here translated as French) are used to cover Casembroot's risqué
   picture of student life in Italy. The expression *leonardogenèse* is an invented
   Greek word, and the phrase means 'for making babies' (literally, 'for begetting
   little Leonards').
9 Allen Ep 1594:43n suggests that this refers to the letter mentioned in the
   second sentence.

are not as a rule very comfortable. In addition to myself there are three de
Moscherons,[10] the fifth is Willem van Schoonhove,[11] the son of Cornelis,
a lawyer at Ghent, who, I know, is a great friend of yours; the sixth is Karel
de Beuckelaer of Antwerp,[12] whose uncle is also a Beuckelaer of Antwerp;
he too holds the rank of canon and is a close friend of yours. We look after   55
ourselves and our life here is very agreeable, except that the high cost of
living is a heavy burden both for ourselves and for our patrons. Everything
else is just as we would wish. The gardens attached to the house are
a veritable shrine of Pomona[13] which would be the envy of any *grand
seigneur*.   60

I return to the report which your friend Karl gave us. I wish that this
unpleasantness would persuade you to make the journey yourself. Fortune
would become my favourite goddess if she favoured my prayers with such
an answer. But I greatly fear that the opposite will happen because I want
it so badly.[14] Apart from Willem van Schoonhove, who is a medical stu-   65
dent, the other five of us have decided to work on civil law. In doing so, I
was influenced by the wishes of my patron, who believes that this is the
best course for his own children; being compliant by nature, I readily
accepted his advice, partly because it was with this in mind that my patron
had presented me with the income from a living, amounting to eight Flem-   70
ish pounds per year,[15] and partly because I had myself begun to hope that
I might rise in the world by this route. I was not put off, as so many are, by

* * * * *

10 At this time Casembroot was employed as tutor to three sons of the Bruges
merchant Guillaume de Moscheron. Later in 1525 the father unexpectedly
appeared at Padua and withdrew his sons from Casembroot's care. Loss of
these pupils left him in a difficult financial situation, and in Ep 1650 he begged
Erasmus for help in finding support in the household of Reginald Pole, who
was then studying at Padua.
11 Willem van Schoonhove (documented 1525–7), son of Cornelis, the fiscal
advocate at Ghent, studied medicine at Padua and later at Montpellier.
Erasmus knew the father (Ep 1214).
12 He is known only from this letter, but his uncle Nicolaas de Beuckelaer (d
1549), canon of the collegiate church of Notre Dame at Antwerp, was an
associate of Erasmus' deceased friend Jérôme de Busleyden.
13 Roman goddess of the fruit of trees
14 Cf *Adagia* III x 60.
15 Latin *pensione librarum Flandricarum octo annua*. Presumably in livres gros
Flemish. See CWE 1 322–3, 328, 347; CWE 8 349–50.

talk of the 'incomprehensibility of the language' and of the use of 'specious
rhetoric in the defence of injustice' and a thousand other gibes of that sort
which are regularly trotted out against the legal profession; this was less   75
important to me than the excitement I felt when I saw the success and (let
me say it even though philistines burst with envy!) the triumph of literary
studies, which you and a small band of likeminded souls have defended so
vigorously; for no branch of studies and no aspect of life will remain
untouched by this influence. I swear to God that my only aim is to gain a   80
place in the world of affairs so that, whatever position I may achieve, I may
be able to place at the service of the public all that I have learned from
study or reflection or experience.

Now you know my ambitions. How they will turn out, I leave to God,
who knows men's hearts. In the meantime may I ask you for a favour?   85
When you next write to Master Lupset or Richard Pace,[16] who is now
ambassador to the patrician government of Venice, please do me the honour
of some brief word of commendation. I would like to ask you to do the
same when you write to others, but I don't want to appear too much of a
nuisance. Pietro Bembo[17] is here and Reginald Pole,[18] a relative, it is said,   90
of the king of England, also Becichemo,[19] who holds a public appointment

* * * * *

16 This Italian-educated English humanist, a friend of Erasmus since they met at
   Padua in 1508, had served as secretary to King Henry VII and as ambassador
   in Germany and at the papal curia, and at this time was English ambassador
   to Venice. At the end of this summer, however, he became seriously ill and by
   November had returned to England. For his earlier life see Ep 211:53n; for
   more on his illness see Epp 1595 n4, 1624 n3.
17 Although Erasmus probably heard reports of this brilliant Venetian humanist as
   early as his residence at Venice in 1508 (cf Adagia II i 1), he confessed in his reply
   to Casembroot (Ep 1626) that he knew him only by reputation and from some
   of his publications. Finally in 1529 he wrote to Bembo (Ep 2106), initiating an
   epistolary friendship that lasted for the rest of his life. In 1525 Bembo was living
   in his villa near Padua, engaged in classical and vernacular literary studies.
18 Cf n10 above and Ep 1627 introduction.
19 Marino Becichemo (c 1468–1526) of Shkodër (Scutari), often called Scodrensis,
   son of a Venetian agent at Shkodër in Albania, fled when the Turks conquered
   his native town in 1478 and was educated at Brescia. He became known as a
   teacher of the classics at several places, including Venice, and from 1517 taught
   rhetoric at the University of Padua. Erasmus never met him, but in a letter of
   1519 (Ep 1016) claimed familiarity with his commentary on book 1 of Pliny
   Naturalis historia. Indeed, Erasmus' letter, dated 2 October 1519, was the preface to the 1519 Paris edition of Becichemo's commentary printed by Pierre
   Vidoue and edited by Nicolas Bérault. On his classical scholarship see CTC IV
   352–6.

in classical literature. At Venice there is Giambattista Egnazio[20] and countless others. O what men these are! How I should like to make my way into
such company! You see I do have a little ambition! But why should this
embarrass me? Is not honour a godlike thing?[21] Every day, as a result of   95
your kindness to me, I discover how important it is to have won the favour
of the great.[22] To whom should I credit such good fortune as I now enjoy
except to that divinity which first brought you and me together? The magic
of your name would be enough by itself to make anyone feel blessed. What
a thrill I get whenever I hear it said, 'That man is a friend of his.' O my   100
dear Erasmus, beloved soul, whom I can never honour and respect as you
deserve, how I should like to throw my arms around your waist and kiss
your saintly head and drink in your honeyed words! Remember that
Leonard is your most faithful admirer, almost your worshipper, and that as
long as he remembers he is a man, he will never forget what Erasmus has   105
done for him, for it is by your help that he is the man God wishes him to
be.

I shall not weary you with excessive chatter if I repeat this one request,
that you forgive me for the unhappy outcome of my efforts to secure the
publication of your *Adagia*; for your man Karl and all of us who interested   110
ourselves in the matter have earned this indulgence for our hard work. It
is now up to you to consider how to deal with Asulanus' tricks. Whatever
you suggest, I promise to carry out with all the speed and energy and
attention I am capable of. All the members of our household wish me to
convey to you their respectful good wishes. Georgius Agricola,[23] a young   115

* * * * *

20 Unlike some of the scholars mentioned by Casembroot, Giambattista de'Cipelli
   (1478–1553), known as Egnazio, was quite familiar to Erasmus, who in a
   preface of 1513 (Ep 269) and in *Adagia* II i 1 acknowledged him as one of the
   circle of scholars in the shop of Aldo Manuzio who in 1508 helped him find
   classical texts for the famous Aldine edition of the *Adagia*. Born and educated
   at Venice, Egnazio was a noted teacher, editor of texts, author, and orator and
   seems to have remained on considerably better terms with Erasmus than many
   of the latter's former Venetian associates. Cf J.B. Ross in RQ 29 (1976) 536–57.
21 'But this ... godlike thing': this is a Greek iambic line which remains unidentified.
22 Horace *Epistles* 1.17.35
23 Agricola (1494–1555) is most famous as the author of a treatise on mining, *De
   re metallica* (1556). He studied medicine at Leipzig and several Italian universities, receiving a doctorate from one of them before returning to Germany and
   Bohemia in 1526. He was one of a number of young foreign scholars who
   assisted Giambattista Opizzoni in editorial work on the Greek edition of Galen
   (cf n3 above). Although he was an admirer of Erasmus at this time, there was

man who is as attached to you as anyone, joins us in sending greetings. He is responsible for correcting the text of Galen at the Asulani press. Please give my fond regards to your friend Algoet, who is a countryman of mine.[24] May you be long spared, renowned Erasmus, to serve this age of ours.

      Padua, 23 August 1525

      Your affectionate friend, Leonard Casembroot

      To Master Erasmus of Rotterdam, the greatest scholar in the world. In Basel

120

1595 / From Thomas Lupset   Padua, 23 August 1525

For Lupset's early life and connection with Erasmus at Cambridge in 1513, see Epp 270:69n, 271; for his current activities in Padua cf Ep 1594 n3. The pretentious and even turgid Latin style, which this translation attempts to mirror, may be due in part to his embarrassment, not only because of his failure to correspond regularly but also because of his thoughtless mishandling of private papers of Erasmus which had been left in his custody in 1516, including Erasmus' rough draft of the *Julius exclusus*, the scandalous satire against Pope Julius II whose authorship Erasmus always denied. Even though Erasmus denied that he remained angry (Ep 690), their relations seem to have been somewhat strained (Epp 431, 664) despite Lupset's active support of Erasmus during his conflict with Edward Lee (Epp 1053, 1083). One particular significance of this letter is that it represents Erasmus' epistolary introduction to Reginald Pole, the humanistically educated second cousin of Henry VIII, with whom Lupset was residing. Erasmus responded promptly by writing to Pole, recommending to his favour the young Polish humanist Jan Łaski (Ep 1627). On the whole circle of English students associated with Pole's household at Padua, see George B. Parks *The English Traveller to Italy* I: *The Middle Ages (to 1525)* (Rome 1954) 475–82. This letter was first published by Förstemann and Günther in 1904.

* * * * *

no direct contact until 1529, when a friend sent the manuscript of Agricola's first work on mining, *Bermannus sive de re metallica dialogus* to Erasmus, who arranged for it to be published by Froben (1530) and added his own preface (cf Epp 2216, 2274). Cf Helmut M. Wilsdorf in *Dictionary of Scientific Biography* I 77–9.

24 On Lieven Algoet, Erasmus' servant-pupil and courier, see Ep 1091 introduction.

FROM THOMAS LUPSET TO ERASMUS OF ROTTERDAM, HIS
TEACHER, WITH CORDIAL GREETINGS

Karl Harst,[1] who, as I observed when he was here, is very fond of you and
most attentive to your wishes, brought me your letter.[2] It had all the marks
of your old friendliness towards me; for although I see you suspect me of   5
pride and neglect for not finding someone to take a letter to you, yet the
charge itself seems to prove the constancy of your affection, since, in re-
proaching me for my silence, you imply that the attentions which you want
from me would give you much pleasure and delight. That fills my heart
with such agreeable and welcome feelings that any embarrassment your   10
accusation may have brought me has nearly or completely vanished,
especially since I find considerable comfort in a good conscience: for I
reckon that I have always felt, and continue to feel, such deep respect for
you that nothing has ever been more important to me at any point in my
life than to be known, both to you and everyone else, for the strength of my   15
feelings towards you. I want others to understand and approve the affection
and regard which I have for you as a most kindly and learned teacher, and
I also hope that every day you will become increasingly happy at having
treated me so well. So if, as a correspondent, I do not appear to have come
up to your expectations or fulfilled my own obligations, you should   20
attribute this to the scarcity of couriers. I can swear that up to now I have
met no one who was setting out to the remote and distant spot where you
live. You must not suppose that this situation came about from any forgetfulness on my part or pride over some new success. Do you really think
that any forgetfulness, unless it deprived me of all powers of thought,   25
would be great enough to blot out the undying memory of your services to
me? Every day I realize more fully what these mean to me and each day I
appreciate them more fully. So it is not possible that I should ever forget
you.

So you think it was pride that made me treat you as a person of no   30
importance. I do not want, Erasmus, to tell you to your face what a great
man you are, showing you to be more venerable and distinguished than the
pope, to say nothing of the whole band of cardinals; nor do I want to reveal
the real nature of my own talents or the wretched state of my fortune. It is

* * * * *

1595
1 On Erasmus' secretary and confidential courier for important foreign missions
   like his current one to Rome and Venice cf Ep 1575 n2.
2 Not extant. Obviously it must have scolded Lupset for failing to write.

enough if I make one point clear: whatever advances I may make in fortune   35
or position, I shall always proclaim without equivocation that I could never
have hoped for such success if I had not enjoyed your friendship in the past
and listened to your counsel and advice. In fact, Erasmus, my delightful
friend – if I may reply in a serious vein to your amusing remarks – if I were
a cardinal, you would be my pope, and if I were pope, I would treat you,   40
second only to Christ himself, with every reverence and respect. So there is
no possibility that success will ever dim the affection in which I hold your
name. Perhaps I seem more long-winded on this point than the subject
warrants; but no words of mine can express how much I want you to accept
this apology without reservations and to recognize that, whether I speak or   45
keep silent, I am truly your most devoted servant and that my feelings for
you are as strong as those the most grateful student could ever feel, or
ought to feel, for the best of teachers, or the most devoted son for his
father.

I should feel obliged to write at great length about the disgraceful   50
behaviour towards you of Francesco Asulanus,[3] if your man Karl were not
in a better position to give you a fuller account than I could in a letter; not
only was he involved in the whole transaction, but he suffered much hard-
ship and unpleasantness in the course of it. I should also have to tell you
about myself and about Richard Pace[4] and Reginald Pole,[5] but you will get   55
a better account from Karl when you see him.

I believe that Pole is not so well known to you; so I want to say, à
propos of his affection and regard for you, that the grandest compliment
which anyone could utter about anyone will be inadequate to express the
kind and generous feelings which this man has for you. I have long had   60
clear and convincing evidence of this, both from my daily conversations
with him and whenever we come into contact with men of rank. For
although you, Erasmus, may not be aware of it, you are on trial everywhere
throughout this region and you stand in great need of defenders. Pole
always takes your side and no one could plead for you with more enthusi-   65
asm and energy. His words are enhanced and seasoned by wide learning,
graceful wit, and remarkable dignity, as well as by unusual restraint and

* * * * *

3 Francesco Torresani of Asola; cf Ep 1592 introduction.
4 English ambassador to Venice; cf Epp 211: 53n, 1594 n16, 1624 nn2 and 3. The
   unidentified illness mentioned later in this letter compelled Pace to resign his
   ambassadorship and effectively ended his career. He left Venice in early
   October and was in London by 17 November.
5 See introduction to this letter and Ep 1627 introduction.

honesty which win the admiration of all who hear him. Even as a young
man he showed great promise and integrity; now he has not only fulfilled
the expectations of his friends, but far surpassed everyone's hopes. Con-   70
sider, Erasmus, (and no one could appreciate the point better than you)
what it means for this young man, who is still in his twenty-fifth year, to
have made a careful study of all the surviving works of Aristotle, working
under the most distinguished teachers, chief among whom were Latimer,[6]
Linacre,[7] and Leonico;[8] and not only to have read and reread all the writ-   75
ings of Plato, but to have built on this foundation a calm steadiness of mind
and character which remains sure and unchanging in face of all the hazards
and assaults of chance and nature; and through his intimate acquaintance
with this divine philosopher to have learned never to say an unkind word
about anyone and not to be irked by the insults of others; and on top of all   80
this to have demonstrated unmistakably his excellence in all the liberal arts.
There can be no doubt of it, Erasmus: he is a *rara avis*.[9]

If you look at Pole, you will find, quite apart from his learning, that
he is a man of matchless courtesy, great natural kindliness, exceptional
ability and judgment, and such honesty of character and behaviour that the   85
purity of his life shines out like a beacon, putting all others into the shade.
Since I am writing to a philosopher, I shall pass over certain petty and
unimportant facts about him, the splendour of his family and the long line

* * * * *

6 On William Latimer cf Ep 207:25n and Parks *The English Traveller to Italy* 456,
  467–70.
7 On Thomas Linacre cf Ep 118:27n and Parks *The English Traveller to Italy*
  455–61, 491.
8 Niccolò Leonico Tomeo was the first lecturer at Padua officially appointed to
  teach Aristotle from the Greek text (1497). Although he left to teach Greek at
  Venice in 1504, he seems to have returned to Padua after a few years and was
  definitely re-established there by this time. On his career cf Ep 1479 n70. Although most of his scholarly publications were translations from Ptolemy,
  Proclus, Theophrastus, and above all Aristotle, Erasmus in *Ciceronianus* (ASD
  I-2 668 / CWE 28 418) regarded him as a Platonist. Erasmus had a high opinion
  of Leonico's moral character and piety, contrasting his religious sincerity with
  the questionable faith of many other Italian humanists; cf Epp 1479:196–200,
  2443, 2526. Leonico seems to have been especially close to his English pupils,
  dedicating books to Pole, Tunstall, and William Latimer. He is often confused,
  and was even confused by contemporaries, with another Italian scholar whom
  Erasmus admired, the physician Niccolò Leoniceno.
9 *Adagia* II i 21

of his ancestry. He is related by birth to our invincible king,[10] who holds
him equally dear for his impressive learning. There is no one in fact to   90
whom our most honoured king seems more attached than Pole: certainly he
always mentions his virtues in the most flattering and complimentary terms
and with the clearest demonstration of his deep personal affection for him.
I earnestly beseech you, illustrious Erasmus, to cherish this man Pole and
hold him among your special friends, because he is the noblest, the most   95
learned, the most accomplished of young men, the glory of your beloved
England, someone who loves and honours you – in a word because he
deserves your friendship. How warmly he and Pace commended you in a
letter to the datary,[11] you will find out from Karl, whose loyalty and devotion to you may have been unproven in the past, but I can testify that there   100
is no one in your household who would have taken greater pains with the
commission you gave him.

   As for your book of proverbs,[12] you should know that we deposited
it for the time being with Giambattista,[13] an honourable fellow and a physician by profession; he will keep it until you inform Francesco himself   105
clearly and in writing what your wishes are and whether you want him to
publish the book. There is no need to be worried about Giambattista's
honesty: I have known him all his life and I have no fears that your opinion
of me will suffer on his account. Indeed it would not be wrong to describe
him as someone very like our friend Latimer.   110

   Pace asks me to give you his best wishes. Recently he has been suffering miserably from almost unrelieved insomnia, which has its origin in the
worrying responsibilities which he bears, and these are brought about in
turn by the shocking circumstances of our times. I am very much afraid of
what the outcome will be. I dread a more serious and terrible fate than that   115
which death would bring. So I urgently beg you to remember in your
prayers to God this kindly man, who is an old and faithful friend of yours.
Farewell.

   Padua, 25 August 1525

       * * * * *

10 Through their mothers, Elizabeth of York and Margaret Pole, daughter of
   George, duke of Clarence, Henry VIII and Reginald Pole were second cousins.
11 Gian Matteo Giberti was datary under Pope Clement VII. Cf Epp 1443A introduction, 1589 n2, 1589A.
12 The manuscript for an enlarged edition of *Adagia*, which Karl Harst had
   brought to Italy to be offered to the press of Andrea Torresani of Asola and
   which Erasmus' Paduan and Venetian friends vainly pressed Torresani to
   publish. Cf Ep 1592 introduction.
13 Cf Ep 1594 n4.

Within the past few days I have received from the royal palace several   120
consecrated rings, about whose effectiveness you have more knowledge and
experience than I.[14] I want to share them with you: so I am sending two
golden ones with the courier. Please give my regards to Rhenanus, whose
kindness I shall never forget,[15] and also to Froben[16] and Glareanus.[17]
Farewell again, most learned master.   125

All Italy is trembling because of a rumour that the emperor is
coming.[18] Rome is hardly big enough to hold the emperor and the pope
at the same time. If the emperor is on his way, the pope will leave the City,
which will be in keeping with his characteristic clemency. Perhaps the seat
of the church will be in Venice for a while. Extraordinary things are hap-   130
pening in England, which I am sure many people have written you about.
There is a young man called Winter who is treated as affectionately by our
most reverend lord as if he were his own legitimate offspring.[19] He has

* * * * *

14 Allen Ep 1595:113n identifies these as rings blessed by the English king and
   supposedly possessing medicinal value. The following Christmas, Erasmus
   gave one of these two rings to the wife of Erasmus Schets, the Antwerp merchant who was acting as Erasmus' financial agent in England and the Netherlands. Cf Epp 1654, 1671.
15 On Beatus Rhenanus, who was Erasmus' closest editorial collaborator through
   most of his work with the Froben press, see introductions to Epp 327, 594.
   Lupset must have experienced his 'kindness' while visiting Erasmus in Basel
   en route to Italy in 1523, a visit that this letter and Ep 1360 make probable but
   not absolutely certain.
16 Johann Froben, the great Basel printer, whose press brought out all of Erasmus' most important publications in the middle and later part of his life; cf Ep
   419 introduction.
17 On Henricus Glareanus cf Ep 440 introduction. He was not only the ablest
   Swiss Latin poet and a major writer on musical theory and geography but also
   a successful teacher in several cities. At this period he resided in Basel.
18 Whatever the source of this particular report may have been, the Italian
   powers, and especially the papacy and Venice, were terrified over what the
   emperor might do to them after his crushing defeat of the French at Pavia on
   24 February 1525. Cf Francesco Guicciardini History of Italy trans Sidney
   Alexander (London 1969) 346–7 (book 16, I); Edward Armstrong The Emperor
   Charles V (London 1902) I 160–2; but Karl Brandi The Emperor Charles V (London
   1939) 223–9 minimizes the Italians' terror and emphasizes the emperor's
   indecisiveness and the ability of his Italian antagonists to recover their confidence after the initial shock of the French defeat.
19 Thomas Winter was the illegitimate son of 'our most reverend lord,' Cardinal
   Thomas Wolsey, who took care to have him carefully educated in England and
   at Louvain and then sent him to study at Padua, where Lupset was serving as
   his tutor. Both Allen Ep 1361:11n and J.A. Gee The Life and Works of Thomas
   Lupset (London 1928) 105–7 conclude that Winter accompanied Lupset on his

already been honoured with some notable preferments and has acquired an
income of 7,000 ducats.[20] We hear that he is soon to marry the daughter   135
of the Earl of Essex,[21] but, unless I am mistaken, only after resigning his
ecclesiastical benefices.

Here the only criterion of scholarly excellence is the imitation of
Cicero, and there is no higher praise possible than to be counted a plagiarist
of Cicero.[22] All of Longueil's works which he left complete have now been   140
published; they are greatly admired in Italy.[23] I gave Karl a volume to take
to you so that you can judge for yourself. There are some remarks about
you in his letters. When you read them, don't pay Longueil the compliment
of letting yourself be upset by his words. Farewell once more.

To that consummate theologian and excellent man, Master Erasmus of   145
Rotterdam, my most respected teacher. In Basel

1596 / To Noël Béda   Basel, 24 August 1525

> This is a second reply to Béda's stern and threatening letter of 21 May (Ep
> 1579). As this letter explains, Erasmus' first reply (Ep 1581) was sent on 15
> June but never made it beyond Strasbourg for want of a courier and was
> returned to its author in Basel. This much shorter and rather conciliatory letter,
> contrasting to the sharp rebuttal of Béda's charges offered in the first one, was

* * * * *

trip to Padua in 1523, but Thomas F. Mayer *Thomas Starkey and the Commonweal*
(Cambridge 1989) 46–8 argues that there is no evidence of any close connection
between Lupset and Winter until 1525.

20 Latin *septena ducatorum milia*. If the Venetian gold coin itself is meant, a coin
with virtually the same pure gold content (3.56 g) and value as the Florentine
florin (currently worth 6s 8d gros Flemish), then a sum amounting to £2,333
6s 8d gros Flemish, or about £14,737 tournois, or exactly £1,575 sterling – a
very substantial sum indeed. From 1517, however, the term 'ducat' came to
mean specifically the silver-based Venetian money-of-account worth 6 lire 4
soldi Venetian; and the gold coin itself was henceforth generally known instead as the zecchino (from *zecca* 'the mint'). See CWE 1 314; CWE 8 350.

21 Anne (d 1571), only child of Henry Bourchier, second earl of Essex, did not in
fact marry Winter, but rather William Parr, the future Earl of Northampton.

22 This was an issue between Erasmus and those humanists whom he labelled as
Ciceronians. Ciceronianism was especially strong in Italy, but the Belgian
humanist Christophe de Longueil (Longolius) was regarded as the archetypal
Ciceronian and was the target of much of Erasmus' criticism in his *Ciceronianus*
(1528). On this issue see Ep 914 introduction and A.H.T. Levi's introduction
to the *Ciceronianus* in CWE 28.

23 A posthumous collection of his works, including an account of his life by
Reginald Pole, was published at Florence in 1524 by the firm of Filippo di
Giunta. On Longueil himself cf Ep 914 introduction.

then sent along with the first. In his own publication of this correspondence, Béda included the present letter and omitted the earlier one with the excuse that this one retracted it. Cf Allen VI 147, giving a long quotation from Béda's *Apologia adversus clandestinos Lutheranos* (Paris: Josse Bade, 1 February 1529) in which the Paris theologian presents his own interpretation of Erasmus' response. He brusquely dismisses the earlier letter, in which Erasmus 'defended his errors,' but includes the present letter, written 'in a far milder style.' Erasmus printed both of his replies in his *Opus epistolarum*.

TO THE MOST ACCOMPLISHED MASTER NOËL BÉDA, MY
HONOURED AND RESPECTED FRIEND, CORDIAL GREETINGS
Distinguished sir, I wrote a reply to your letter and sent it to Strasbourg with instructions that it be taken to you from there. But when no one suitable could be found to deliver it, it was returned to me. The present 5 courier I have hired out of my own pocket, so that he may bring me back your *Annotationes*. I knew I had read Augustine on our Lord's Sermon on the Mount,[1] but could not remember how carefully. But as soon as I began to read it again, as you advised me to do, I found I had completely covered the margins with notes in my own handwriting. Moreover in my *Annota-* 10 *tiones* on the fifth and sixth chapters of Matthew I cite this work frequent-ly.[2] So I am surprised you suspect me of not having read it. Augustine wrote these chapters in a most elegant and careful style, but he was only a priest at the time and not yet very familiar with theological writings, although he had already made some successful experiments in commenting 15 on Holy Scripture. He himself made many corrections in the work, and there are some passages which need a kind and indulgent reader. This was the reason I did not worry greatly if occasionally I disagreed with him. I have almost finished rereading the whole thing without noticing any dan-gerous lapses in my own work. I do not have Gerson in my own library, 20

* * * * *

1596
1 For the Latin text, CCL 35 or PL 34 1229–1308. English translations: *Select Library of Nicene and Post-Nicene Fathers* [first series] VI 1–63; *The Fathers of the Church* XI 19–199; or *The Works of Aurelius Augustine, Bishop of Hippo* ed Marcus Dods, 15 vols (Edinburgh 1872–1934) VIII 1–132.
2 LB VI 25–40. Erasmus does indeed cite Augustine's commentary frequently, beginning with his very first note on Matthew chapter 6. His citations from Augustine deal mainly with textual issues. He also cites other works of Augustine and many other patristic authors in these notes on Matthew.

but I shall buy a copy or borrow one from somewhere.[3] You see how ready
I am to learn, if I find a good teacher to put me right.

Men are blessed with different talents and do not travel by the same
road towards that felicity which is their ultimate goal. I believe I have
always done what you and your colleagues are doing, though in a different   25
way. And if this disastrous storm had not blown up, the efforts which I
made to revive the study of languages and letters and to renew an interest
in the ancient Fathers and the sources of Scripture would not have been
entirely fruitless. But since I see that nothing can be written these days
without offending someone, I have decided to be quiet and devote all my   30
energies to revising what has already been published and cannot therefore
be recalled, so that my work will be as free as possible from anything which
might cause the slightest offence. Anyone who will be kind enough to help
me in this plan will earn my deepest gratitude. If in the next edition I seem
too hesitant about altering those passages which people found offensive, I   35
am ready to be a harsher critic of my own work than Augustine was of his.
Only don't look for the knot in the bullrush:[4] only the more important
errors need be pointed out. You will find me neither reluctant to explain
and defend my views, nor too gentle with myself when corrections have to
be made. Some doctrines are controversial, for example, 'that the pope is   40
superior in authority to an ecumenical council'; some are enigmatic and
imperfectly understood, like the argument 'on not translating the Holy
Scriptures into the vernacular'; some are so complex that they raise many
worrying problems. It does not seem wrong to discuss these matters, with
the idea either of finding a fuller and better solution or of removing the   45
difficulty and confirming the accepted view. We should also take into
account the needs of the times. I wish people would take the trouble to read
my work more carefully. I am sure you will do so with an open mind.

I did not wish to burden my man with too heavy a load of books, but
I am sending you a list of all my writings.[5] To the third edition of my *New*   50
Testament I have added several new *Apologiae*,[6] which you will be able to

* * * * *

3 Béda's letter had urged Erasmus to read the works of this Paris theologian of
   the early fifteenth century on a number of issues on which they disagreed (cf
   Ep 1579:185–90, and especially Allen's note at Allen line 160). In his earlier
   reply to Béda, Erasmus appeared much less willing to take Béda's advice and
   flatly expressed his preference for patristic authors over the scholastics.
4 *Adagia* II iv 76
5 The reference is to Erasmus' letter to Johann von Botzheim, *Catalogus omnium
   lucubrationum Erasmi Roterodami*, probably in the revised edition of 1524,
   printed in CWE as Ep 1341A.
6 Allen Ep 1597:45n observes that this is misleading, since the addition of the

skim through easily. I have replied to Zúñiga's *Conclusiones* and 'articles.'[7]
I consider myself a Catholic, not just because I have no quarrel with the
pope or the emperor or Ferdinand or with those bishops whom I know, but
because there is no one whom the Lutheran faction hates more than me. But   55
if it is my fate to be attacked from both sides, I shall try nonetheless to be
found acceptable in the eyes of Christ. I am preparing myself as best I can
for the day of his judgment. May He keep you safe and well, honoured sir
and brother.

Basel, St Bartholomew's day 1525   60
Erasmus of Rotterdam in his own hand

1597 / To Germain de Brie   Basel, 25 August 1525

On this well-connected French humanist see Ep 569 introduction. Erasmus
published the letter in his *Opus epistolarum*.

ERASMUS OF ROTTERDAM TO GERMAIN DE BRIE OF AUXERRE,
GREETING
How fortunate, how very fortunate you are, my dear de Brie, to have kept
to the garden of the Muses and never set foot in the thorny wasteland of the
theologians! How I would envy you this peaceful existence, if you were not   5
so dear to me that I count your blessings my own! In these times it is not
safe to write whether what one says is true or false, and there is a strange
and sinister agreement among the rabbis.[1] In attempting to change everything, Luther is destroying everything, and his wrong-headed efforts to

* * * * *

Apologiae was to the second edition (1519) of his New Testament, not the third
(1522), though the added sections were retained in the third edition.
7 Erasmus' replies were *Apologia respondens ad ea quae Iacobus Lopis Stunica*
taxaverat in prima duntaxat Novi Testamenti aeditione (Louvain: Dirk Martens,
September 1521; NK 2851); *Apologia adversus libellum Stunicae cui titulum fecit,*
Blasphemiae et impietates Erasmi and *Apologia ad prodromon Stunicae*, printed
together in a collection of Erasmus' works (Basel: Froben 1522); and *Apologia*
ad Stunicae conclusiones, printed together with Stunica's *Conclusiones* in Erasmus' *Exomologesis* (Basel: Froben 1524). On Stunica, or Zúñiga, see Ep 1128 n2;
H.J. de Jonge, introduction to ASD IX-2, especially 13–49; and Rummel I 145–77,
II 126–7.

1597
1 Commonly used by humanists as a derogatory term to designate the conservative theologians, whom they accused of conspiring to suppress 'good letters'
– that is, humanist studies.

secure our liberty have made us slaves twice over. I think I had not com-   10
pletely taken leave of my senses when I refused to go to France in spite of
inducements of every kind; for I could see what was going to happen.
Comforting rumours are circulating here of a reconciliation between the
kings which will be as solid as diamonds. I should like to think the rumours
were true, but whenever I consider *la mentalité de l'empereur et de l'Espagne*,[2] 15
I fear it may not be so.

Here a cruel tragedy is being acted out; what the *dénouement* will be,
I do not know.[3] It seems to me that the world is sinking into a state of
Scythian barbarity, with the total ruin of all liberal studies. For me the game
is already over.[4] Now I hand on the torch to those of you who are in the   20
prime of life. The old champions of the Muses are dying off everywhere:
Longueil, who wrote a wonderfully polished oration against Luther, which
I have here, has passed away at Bologna;[5] Battista Casali died recently at
Rome,[6] Linacre in England[7] and Deloynes near you;[8] Dorp has passed
away at Louvain:[9] he had the courage to declare his support for liberal   25

* * * * *

2 This translation uses French to mark Erasmus' stylish use of a Greek phrase
  in the original letter. Allen Ep 1597:12n suggests that Erasmus' pessimistic
  remarks about Charles V and about Spain may reflect both his own exasper-
  ation over the imperial government's failure to pay his promised pension and
  his suspicion that the mendicant orders had too much influence over the
  emperor; as regards Spain, it reflects his disdain for Spanish admiration of
  military glory: Allen refers to *Moriae encomium* (ASD IV-3 130; LB IV 448E):
  'Hispani bellicam gloriam nulli concedunt.'
3 A reference to the German Peasants' War, which had reached its peak in late
  spring and early summer but was still producing unrest in regions near Basel.
  Cf Preface, pages xi–xii.
4 Literally, 'My life has shot all its arrows'; cf Aristophanes *Plutus* 34.
5 Christophe de Longueil had died on 11 September 1522 at an early age, and
  de Brie was one of a number of French humanists who commemorated his
  death in verse. Cf Ep 914 introduction.
6 On this influential Roman humanist and canon of St Peter's at Rome, cf Epp
  1270A, 1479, 1603. The death here reported must have been quite recent; but
  since Erasmus had just recently had his agent Karl Harst at Rome, he would
  have been rather up-to-date on news of the curial humanist community.
7 This famous English humanist and physician had died on 20 October 1524. Cf
  Ep 118:27n.
8 On this influential patron of humanism at Paris cf Epp 494 introduction, 1571
  n1. He had died not long before 27 July 1524.
9 Maarten van Dorp was Erasmus' most reliable supporter among the theologians of Louvain. He died on 31 May 1525. For Erasmus' expression of sorrow
  at this news, see Ep 1584; cf Epp 491 introduction, 1585.

studies at a time when all the philistines were foaming at the mouth. Perhaps this opposition was the cause of his death. I mentioned Deloynes'
name in a little work which will reach you soon,[10] although your own
most elegant verses have hallowed the memory of this fine man for all time.

I have engaged the courier at my own expense so that he may bring   30
me back letters from my friends.[11] You can safely entrust whatever you
write to him. I send you my best wishes. Let me know how you are getting
on.

Basel, the day following St Bartholomew's day 1525

Please give Budé my kindest regards – if I don't get time to write to   35
him.[12]

1598 / To Jean de Selve   Basel, 25 August 1525

This letter accompanied the presentation copy of Erasmus' *Apologia* against
Pierre Cousturier (Petrus Sutor), which he dedicated to de Selve. Cf Ep 1591
introduction. As Erasmus feared, the recipient was still in Spain negotiating
for the release of King Francis I from captivity. Erasmus printed the letter in
Opus epistolarum.

ERASMUS OF ROTTERDAM TO JEAN DE SELVE, FIRST PRESIDENT
OF THE PARLEMENT OF PARIS, GREETING
Distinguished sir, I am sending you a little book, which is a reply to the
fanatical inanities of Pierre Cousturier.[1] Nicolas Bérault is responsible for
my dedicating it to you.[2] He encouraged me to do so by describing your   5
remarkable qualities in several of his letters to me. I cannot understand how
works of this sort can be printed in Paris with impunity, especially with the
authorization of the Parlement and the approval of the theologians – unless

* * * * *

10 In his *Adversus Petri Sutoris ... debacchationem apologia* (Basel: Froben, August
   1525); cf Ep 1591.
11 Erasmus' use of a specially hired courier at this period to carry letters to
   France is also mentioned in Epp 1599, 1601, 1618, 1620; Ep 1618 makes it clear
   that this person was not one of his *famuli* or secretaries, who often acted as
   couriers.
12 In fact Erasmus did write him a short letter on this same date: Ep 1601; on the
   great French Hellenist cf Ep 403 introduction.

1598
1 Cf Ep 1571 n10.
2 On him see Epp 925 introduction, 1571 n15, 1579.

the preface misrepresents the situation. I know that such decisions are generally taken by one or two persons, with the rest following their lead as if it were no business of theirs. It would be hard to imagine a greater knave than the fellow who produced a travesty of my *Colloquia*.[3] Yet no one took any notice. The author, however, is not unknown. He is a Dominican, called Lambertus Campester. The printer's name is Pierre of the Great Bite.[4] The fact that these men have not been punished is an invitation to others to try something worse. A book has appeared at Antwerp, written by some Dominicans, but under a pseudonym.[5] It is the most tasteless, stupid, dishonest, barefaced, scatterbrained thing you could imagine.

It is perverse behaviour of this sort which is bringing the whole order of monks into general disrepute. In Germany many convents and monasteries have been savagely plundered.[6] Some councils are more moderate. They have expelled only those who took their vows elsewhere, and have prohibited the admission of novices. They have abolished the right to supervise nuns and to preach except in one's own monastery. In short, the monks can do nothing without the permission of the authorities. Their aim seems to be to turn the monasteries into parishes. For they believe that these scheming battalions, with their arsenal of privileges, can no longer be tolerated.

I would have written at greater length, but I was not certain if you had returned from your mission to Spain. I commend to you the cause of humane letters – and remember me too, if you think I have made any contribution in this field. Farewell.

Basel, the day following St Bartholomew's day 1525

1599 / To Louis de Berquin   Basel, 25 August 1525

Erasmus with much justification felt that the acts of his enthusiastic but injudicious followers often exacerbated his own difficult relations with conservative

* * * * *

3 On this falsified edition of the *Colloquia* and the probable culprit, Lambertus Campester, cf Epp 1341A:307–412, 1581 n59.
4 An allusion to the publisher of the false *Colloquies*, Pierre Gromors. Cf Ep 1581 n60.
5 Cf Ep 1571 n14.
6 This is a general reference to the suppression or close regulation of monasteries by city governments during the German Reformation, and more particularly to violent incidents that occurred during the Peasant War. Many examples are related in Franz, eg 201, 260–1. On the Peasant War, see Preface, pages xi–xii.

critics like the Paris theologians. Berquin was one such follower, and in this letter Erasmus attempted to persuade him to abandon his plans to translate and publish in French works by Erasmus on controversial topics. He also begged Berquin to avoid direct confrontation with the theologians and open legal challenges to their authority, actions which would cause difficulties not only for Berquin but also for Erasmus. All in vain: despite Berquin's influence at court, his aggressive habits eventually led to his execution as a relapsed heretic in 1529. Erasmus published this letter in his *Opus epistolarum* just a few months after the execution, no doubt being eager to show that he had urged moderation on his young admirer. On Berquin cf Ep 925:17n.

I am sure that you meant well, my learned Berquin, when you did what you did, but, by translating my books into the vernacular and submitting them to the judgment of the theologians, you are increasing the burden of resentment against me, which is already heavy enough.[1] I know that there

* * * * *

1599
1 Erasmus learned of these translations, if not from Berquin in a letter that has been lost, then certainly from his antagonist Noël Béda, who at the end of a menacing letter dated 21 May 1525 (Ep 1579) informed him that on the preceding day the theological faculty had condemned three of his works in French versions which Béda believed to be the work of Berquin. These translations were *Declamation des louenges de mariage*, *Brefve admonition de la maniere de prier*, and *Le symbole des apostres*. Brigitte Moreau *Inventaire chronologique des éditions parisiennes du XVIe siècle* III 250 (no 316) attributes these works (published without name of place or publisher and without date) to the Paris printer Simon Du Bois and dates them 1525, apparently and plausibly assuming that the faculty condemned printed texts, not works in manuscript. On the other hand, the condemnation of *La complainte de la paix* by the faculty on 1 June involved a text that was probably not printed until 1531 or 1532. For the record of the faculty actions, see Farge *Registre* 96 (94A) and 97 (95A). On the attribution of the three texts published in 1525 to the printer Simon Dubois (or Du Bois), see Emile V. Telle's 'Introduction' to his edition of Berquin's *Declamation des louenges de mariage* (Geneva 1976) 106–9. On the attribution of Berquin's *La complainte de la Paix* to the press of Pierre de Vingle at Lyons and to the period 1531–2, see Emile V. Telle's 'Introduction' to his edition (Geneva 1978) of the text, pages 1 and 69–72, though Telle argues (pages 70–72) that there probably was an earlier edition by Dubois in 1525. The translation was believed to have perished until a copy was discovered in the Houghton Library of Harvard University. See James E. Walsh 'The *Querela Pacis* of Erasmus: The "Lost" French Translation' *Harvard Library Bulletin* 17 (1969) 374–84. In June a fourth French translation from Erasmus, *La complainte de la paix*, was also condemned. Despite these condemnations, some French printer, probably Simon Dubois of

are many honest, good-hearted men among the theologians, but the spiteful- 5
ness of the few often defeats the moderation of the many. I have a natural
abhorrence of controversy, and now because of my age and health I desire
peace even more, while I make myself ready for that day which cannot now
be far off. I see the world embroiled in a deadly conflict; I see the theologians and their opponents carrying their quarrels to the point of utter 10
lunacy. Since I know there is nothing I can do to help, I keep quiet and look
after my own affairs, commending Christ's church to him, for he alone
knows how to bring good out of the rash purposes of men. Perhaps, my
dear Berquin, you will serve your own interests better, if, once an old
quarrel has been put to rest, you refrain from stirring it up again. Our dear 15
friend Papillon has been taken from us,[2] and Deloynes before him.[3]

Here a bloody play is unfolding; what the outcome will be I do not
know. We are stuck here, shut off from the world; how safe we are, God
only knows. I believe the king's sister[4] has already set off for Spain.
Rumours fly, promising a golden age, but so far I see no evidence that it is 20

* * * * *

Paris, in October 1525 published the first three of these texts; and about 1531–2
another printer, probably Pierre de Vingle of Lyon, published the fourth.
Erasmus had already pointed out to Béda (Ep 1581) that he knew Berquin only
through correspondence and that the translator might have put things into the
vernacular text that were not in the original Latin. Although it is certain that
Erasmus had no first-hand knowledge of Berquin's translations of his works,
his suspicions about interpolations were justified. Margaret Mann Phillips
Erasme et les débuts de la Réforme française (1517–1536) (Paris 1934) 131–40 shows
that the preface of the *Brefve admonition* had been taken from a letter by Guillaume Farel, a radical French Evangelical whom Erasmus detested (cf Epp
1342A n305, 1477A, 1538 n7, 1548 n3, 1640 n5); also, that its companion piece,
Le symbole des apostres, contained interpolations from a text by Luther known
to have been owned by Berquin, while the *Declamation des louenges de mariage*,
which was published separately, contains substantial added material lacking
doctrinal significance and apparently added by the translator in order to
display his classical erudition and to make the literary references in the original more explicit for the information of readers not learned in the classics. For
other references to these interpolations, see Farge *Registre* 96 n44. Although
these anonymous editions (anonymous, that is, except that each of them
claimed to be a translation from Erasmus) were suppressed, a few copies
survived; and they have been edited with introduction and notes by Emile V.
Telle (Geneva 1976, 1978, and 1979).

2 Antoine Papillon (d 1525) was a member of the Grand Conseil at Paris and a
protégé of Marguerite d'Alençon, sister of the king and the leading patron and
protector of reform-minded French humanists, including Berquin.

3 Cf Ep 1571 n1.

4 Marguerite d'Alençon. Cf Ep 1615 introduction.

coming and I would not dare put my forebodings down on paper. So you will not expect me to deal with any of the matters you raised in your long letter, now that there has been a dramatic change in the situation.

I have engaged this young man at my own expense to carry my letters and bring yours back in return. If there is anything going on which I ought   5
to know about, write to me. Farewell, dear friend.

Basel, the day following St Bartholomew's day 1525

1600 / To François Dubois   Basel, [c 25 August] 1525

François Dubois of Amiens (c 1483–1536), elder brother and teacher of Jacques Dubois, who later became a famous professor of medicine at Paris, was himself a teacher of humanities at several colleges in Paris. His *Progymnasmata in arte oratoria* (1516) became a widely used textbook of rhetoric, and he also published other works on oratory and poetics. From 1516 he frequently assisted the printer Josse Bade of Paris with editions of classical authors, especially Cicero. Although his scholarly work was of no lasting significance, Erasmus thought well of him. Only this and one other letter (Ep 1677) survive, but the tone used in both letters is familiar, and Erasmus regularly included his name in complimentary lists of French humanists (cf Epp 1407, 1713). In Allen Ep 2874:163 Erasmus claims that he met Dubois at Louvain, an event that must be dated before October 1519. Erasmus included this (and most of this cluster of letters to French correspondents) in his *Opus epistolarum*.

ERASMUS OF ROTTERDAM TO FRANÇOIS DUBOIS, GREETING
You are showing me up, my dear François, by sending me two or three letters – and long letters too.[1] You would be right to complain that this is not the courtesy which you praised so highly, but let me tell you that even cardinals are sometimes treated as I am treating you now, not through any   5
indolence on my part, but for want of leisure. In any case I like and admire your warm and open nature.

How far I am responsible for the progress of the humanities, I do not know. But I do know that I get little thanks for my pains from certain people, though I attribute this in large measure to the dreadful turmoil   10
through which we are passing. Those who can watch as spectators are fortunate indeed. But look at me: at an age when I should be enjoying peace

* * * * *

1600
1 These, like all of Dubois' letters to Erasmus, are lost.

and quiet, I am hauled off to the gladiatorial arena to kill or be killed, or
perhaps I should say, to cut someone's throat and have my own throat cut
at the same time.[2] The world is undergoing a strange metamorphosis. It is   15
unfortunate for me that my old age falls in such a period. So far as one can
see, it will all end in a state of Scythian barbarity. I am already weary of the
race, and now hand on the torch to Bérault[3] and de Brie[4] and to you and
men like you. Deloynes has left the world of literature the poorer for his
passing;[5] Papillon too has recently been taken from us.[6]   20
    You will say that this is poor compensation for your letter, not just
because it is short and yours was long, but because yours was beautifully
polished and this is quite uncouth. If you look only at what is on the page,
this is no answer to your letter. But if you consider the feelings which
accompany it, then my feelings are a true response to yours and always will   25
be. It seems that those who are filled with a love of fine literature don't
usually get on with the theologians, and conversely the theologians are not
very sympathetic to more humane fields of learning. The ancient quarrels
of great princes are often settled by a marriage; I wish some damsel would
appear who could join both sides in mutual good will and that both kinds   30
of learning would flourish with increasing vigour. Now, while they shout
insults at one another, all forms of learning crumble and decay. Farewell.
    Basel, 1525

1601 / To Guillaume Budé   Basel, 25 August 1525

This is the letter which in Ep 1597 Erasmus said he might not have time to
write. His major theme appears to be the striking contrast between the apparent stability of Budé's scholarly career and the insecurity and controversy that
dogged his own career. He included it in his *Opus epistolarum*. On Budé, the
most famous French humanist of his generation, see Ep 403 introduction.

ERASMUS OF ROTTERDAM TO GUILLAUME BUDÉ, GREETING
You must be the darling of the gods, my learned Budé, to be able to main-

* * * * *

2 Defeated gladiators had their throats cut. The Latin verb used here (*iugulare*)
  means both 'to cut the throat' and 'to ruin a reputation,' and Erasmus is
  playing on this double meaning.
3 Cf Epp 925 introduction, 1571 n15, 1579:133–4
4 Cf Epp 212:2n, 620 introduction, 1597.
5 Cf Epp 1571 n1, 1597 n8
6 Cf Ep 1599 n2.

tain a peaceful existence amid all this deadly turmoil. The different roles in
this drama pass from one actor to another.[1] In the first act we had the
rumpus over the humanities.[2] Here Reuchlin played his part and your   5
humble servant contributed something too.[3] Then the plot turned to the
subject of faith. Here Luther had the chief part as the leading actor in a
bloody drama. There were parts also for the kings to perform. The king of
the Danes is now in exile,[4] and your king, I am sorry to say, is a guest of
Spain.[5] Recently nobles and peasants made their appearance on the stage.   10

* * * * *

1601
1 In this extended figure of speech, the various acts of the drama are the controversies over humanism, with Reuchlin and Erasmus himself playing the
   leading roles; the Reformation, with Luther as the leading actor; the international wars of the decade, with the exiled Danish king and the captive French
   king playing the leads; and the rebellions of the knights and the peasants in
   Germany. Other examples of Erasmus' liking for this figure of speech based
   on the theatre are Epp 737:5, 742:24, 754:6, and Ep 1437:1.
2 Erasmus appears to claim that the various conflicts between humanists and
   their scholastic critics amounted to a general confrontation and not just a series
   of scattered incidents, and that he himself was a major participant in the
   confrontation. For a persuasive scholarly statement of the contrary view, see
   James H. Overfield *Humanism and Scholasticism in Late Medieval Germany*
   (Princeton 1984).
3 Although the best recent scholarship concludes that the real issue in the
   famous controversy between Johannes Reuchlin and the Cologne theologians
   was not antihumanism but antisemitism, and that most leading humanists
   (Erasmus included) held aloof from the struggle, Erasmus here explicitly
   associates Reuchlin (as well as himself) with controversy over the role of
   humanism. In the long run, the conflict did impress many other humanists also
   as an attempt by ultra-conservatives to persecute the most distinguished of the
   older German humanists because of his scholarly interests. Although Erasmus
   had intervened privately at Rome in favour of Reuchlin (Epp 333, 334), his
   own desire to remain uninvolved and his own not-so-latent antisemitism are
   evident in many of his letters about the affair, such as Epp 694, 1167:82–114.
   For the argument on antisemitism cf Overfield *Humanism and Scholasticism*
   247–97 (chapter 7) and the same author's earlier 'A New Look at the Reuchlin
   Affair' *Studies in Medieval and Renaissance History* 8 (1971) 167–207.
4 Cf Ep 1228 n6. King Christian II's authoritarian policies and the failure of his
   attempt to regain control of Sweden led in 1523 to a rebellion by the Danish
   nobles that drove him permanently from his throne. He spent the first several
   years of his exile in the Netherlands, seeking military and financial support
   from his brother-in-law, the emperor Charles V.
5 Francis I was captured at the battle of Pavia on 24 February 1525 and not
   released from captivity in Spain until 17 March 1526.

The plot was decidedly bloody. Now the situation is becoming serious again. What the *dénouement* will be, I do not know. I rejected the idea of going to France – and with good reason. I saw that something unpleasant was brewing. But remaining here does not keep me out of serious danger. Nor is there any place to which I can retreat for safety; and if there were, the state of my health requires that I take things easy. All this time I, a man of sixty, am compelled to enter the arena and do battle with a host of fiends, to kill others or be killed myself in the encounter.[6] 15

The courier is very dependable. I hired him at my own expense. Give him a letter for me and let me know how you are. You will hear the rest of my news from Bérault.[7] Farewell. 20

Basel, the day following St Bartholomew's day 1525

1602 / To Jan Antonin   Basel, 28 August 1525

Jan Antonin of Košice (c 1499–c 1549) was born in what was then northern Hungary and studied at Cracow (BA 1517) and at Padua, where he received a doctorate in medicine. He then spent several months in Basel, where he became a fast friend of Erasmus and was invited by the city authorities to establish his practice. When he left in November 1524 to return to Hungary, Erasmus regretted his departure, claiming to have benefited much from his remedies (Epp 1512, 1564). In 1525 he settled in Cracow, where he became personal physician to bishops Piotr Tomicki and Piotr Gamrat and to King Sigismund I, and where he also became close to local humanists. He was active in promoting Erasmus' reputation in Poland, putting him in touch with important figures like Alexius Thurzo (Ep 1572) and Piotr Tomicki (Ep 1919). He also conducted an active correspondence with both Erasmus and Bonifacius Amerbach and wrote or edited several literary and medical works, including the preface to an edition of Erasmus' *Lingua* (Cracow: Hieronymus Vietor 1526). Erasmus included this letter, which is the first part of their correspondence to survive, in his *Opus epistolarum*.

* * * * *

6 An obvious thematic (but not verbal) reminiscence of the gladiatorial simile used in the preceding letter (Ep 1600:13–14).
7 For his biography, see Epp 925 introduction; for his role as a reliable contact for Erasmus in Paris at this period, see Ep 1571 n15, Epp 1579:132–4.

ERASMUS OF ROTTERDAM TO JAN ANTONIN,
PHYSICIAN, GREETING

After the note you sent me from Frankfurt[1] I have had nothing from you
in the way of a letter. The book which I dedicated to the treasurer at your
request[2] was given to my man Karl[3] to take to Innsbruck. From there I   5
know it was sent to Buda with a letter from me.

We were disturbed by a rumour blowing in this direction that the
present dreadful turmoil has even reached your part of the world, bringing
serious danger and financial loss to the treasurer.[4] If the story is true, the
news saddens me for many reasons: first I am sorry that that excellent man   10
has suffered unjustly; then I realize that your patron's misfortunes must
affect you too; and finally the dedication which I made to him will perhaps
be no more welcome than music at a time of mourning. But war produces
many absurdities. I hope your next letter will bring better news.

From now on your humble servant will be speechless, since he has   15
parted with his *Tongue*.[5] I hope things have improved in your part of the
world so that I don't have to call you back here. But even if they got worse,
I would hardly dare to encourage you to return because of the disturbances
here with their ominous portents of trouble to come. I shall be glad to hear
how things are going and how well you are getting on.   20

Basel, 28 August 1525

1603 / To Willibald Pirckheimer   Basel, 28 August 1525

By this time, the eminent Nürnberg patrician and humanist had become
disillusioned with Luther as a religious reformer but still hoped for a religious

* * * * *

1602
1 Not extant, but probably written shortly after Anton left Basel in November
   1524
2 Erasmus had dedicated his translation of Plutarch's *De non irascendo* and *De
   curiositate* to Alexius Thurzo, treasurer and adviser to King Louis II of
   Hungary.
3 Karl Harst, Erasmus' secretary and frequent courier. See Epp 1215 introduction, 1575 n2.
4 The misfortune here mentioned was probably Alexius Thurzo's forced resignation as treasurer the preceding April. In fact the Hungarian ruler found his
   services (and his willingness to advance cash) indispensable and restored him
   to office in July 1526. The reference may also imply a more general lament
   over the growing danger from the Turks.
5 A reference to his recent publication of his treatise *Lingua* (Basel: Froben,
   August 1525)

Title-page of the *Apologia* of Godefridus Ruysius Taxander
Centre for Reformation and Renaissance Studies, Victoria University, Toronto

renewal without violence and disunity. Hence he would have shared the
position taken here by Erasmus, deploring extremism and violence by both
sides. Erasmus never published this letter, which was first made public in
Pirckheimeri Opera (1610).

Cordial greetings. Because my voice is always raised in support of moderate
policies, some accuse me of timidity and others of collusion with the followers of Luther. Both sides are now fighting tooth and nail to protect their
own, and far from conceding any of the territory which they hold by right,
they are even pushing beyond the positions they have already occupied. So   5
we have reached the point where God alone can calm this tempest in the
affairs of men. No place remains untouched by this deadly evil.

They say the archbishop[1] has been thrown out of Hungary.[2] Cardinal
Campeggi has returned to Italy,[3] and Ennio, the bishop of Veroli, has departed also.[4] The archbishop of Salzburg is under siege.[5] Here the   10

* * * * *

1603
1 László Szalkay (1479–1526), son of a cobbler, rose to high political and ecclesiastical office at the court of Hungary and in 1524 became archbishop of Eszter-
gom (Gran) and primate of Hungary. He was himself a humanist and a patron
of humanists. During two national diets held in 1525 because of the political
and military crisis, he came under attack for his greed, corruption, and accu-
mulation of wealth; but the report that he had been forced to flee the country
proved false. He remained in the service of King Louis II and like his master
was among those slain in the Turkish victory at Mohács on 29 August 1526.
2 The Latin word in Allen Ep 1603:8, *profligatum*, literally means 'utterly cast
down' or 'overcome' and conceivably might be stretched to cover a meaning
like 'has been thrown out of.' But if the reading were emended to the
postclassical *profugatum*, it would make better sense in this context: 'has fled.'
In most medieval and Renaissance scripts, *profugatum* would be almost indis-
tinguishable from *profligatum*.
3 The cardinal was papal legate to Germany, Hungary, and Bohemia in 1524–5
and spent the first half of 1525 in Hungary, trying to organize resistance to the
Turks. Pope Clement VII had recalled him to Italy in July. Cf Ep 1552 introduction.
4 Ennio Filonardi, papal legate in Switzerland, left Zürich for Constance in 1522
because of the growth of Protestantism in the former city. In 1525 he established himself at Chur in the Graubünden, a region allied with the Swiss but
independent of the confederation. Cf Ep 1282 introduction.
5 Cardinal Matthäus Lang, prince-archbishop of Salzburg since 1519, had already
suppressed a rebellion by the townsmen of his capital city against his authoritarian rule in 1523 and in June 1525 had to take refuge in his citadel against
an occupation of the city by peasants that was joined by local townsmen and

princes and the peasants have taken up arms again, each side threatening the annihilation of the other. The men of Basel tried to settle matters and prevent bloodshed, but their efforts were in vain.[6] Ferdinand is in Württemberg; he is expected in Freiburg, but I don't know if he will arrive.[7]

There is a fairly large town in Brabant, with a considerable population,   15
called 's-Hertogenbosch.[8] The people of the town expelled all the Minorites and Dominicans. Margaret, the emperor's aunt, is now besieging the place. Some people have ventured to preach outside the city walls at Antwerp, and the citizens were not too scared to flock to hear them in spite of all the proclamations of the emperor and Margaret and the authorities.[9] And so   20
the whole city is now seething with an ominous excitement. Guards are on

* * * * *

by miners from the mountain districts. After a temporary settlement in the autumn of 1525, the archbishop's harsh ways caused another uprising in 1526, when he was again besieged in Salzburg's citadel; but in July 1526 he crushed the rebellion and imposed stringent conditions. Cf Ep 549:52–3n, and on the general course of the German Peasant War, Preface, pages xi–xii.

6 The city government of Basel had adopted a remarkably conciliatory and generally successful policy of negotiating with the rebellious peasants of their own rural districts in 1525 and vainly tried to persuade the Austrian regency council at Ensisheim to treat with the remaining bands of rebels and avoid bloodshed. Cf Franz 140, 148, and Paul Burckhardt *Geschichte der Stadt Basel* 2nd ed (1957) 10–13. Erasmus, living in Basel and closely linked to influential citizens, was well informed on peasant disturbances in the vicinity and sympathetic to the moderate policy of the city government.

7 Archduke Ferdinand, younger brother of the emperor, had been acting as regent of the hereditary Hapsburg possessions in Germany since 1522, including the scattered lands of Vorderösterreich (the Vorland, or Anterior Austria), such as the Breisgau and Alsace. At this time these territories also included the duchy of Württemberg, which had been occupied by Hapsburg troops since they and the Swabian League expelled Duke Ulrich in 1519. The expectation that Ferdinand would come into the Breisgau (presumably at the head of an army) is not surprising, since unlike Basel, the Austrian regents at Ensisheim had adopted a policy of harshly repressing peasant rebels in their district.

8 This city in northern Brabant experienced popular violence against the religious orders in June and July 1525; but the governor, Margaret of Austria, sent troops which suppressed the uprising in early August. Although heretical religious ideas may have played some part, the expulsion of the mendicant orders appears to have been motivated chiefly by popular resentment at their insistence on continued exemption from municipal taxation at a time of economic difficulties. Cf James D. Tracy *Holland under Habsburg Rule, 1506–1566* (Berkeley 1990) 149.

9 In July and August, an Augustinian friar named Nicholas and the pastor of the village church in Melsen preached Lutheran doctrine outside the walls of Antwerp, causing much excitement.

duty night and day. Once the people of 's-Hertogenbosch have been taught a lesson, I fear there will be an attack on Antwerp. Both towns are wealthy. The splendour of the prize will be a temptation to the princes: such is their greed for plunder that even the flimsiest excuse is sufficient.   25

In my native Holland several people have been condemned for heresy.[10] They will be treated severely. Hulst, who was disarmed some time ago, has now been armed again by the emperor. He was the only layman to be a ringleader in the Inquisition.[11] A large majority among the population of Holland, Zeeland, and Flanders are familiar with Luther's teaching   30 and have conceived an implacable hatred of the monks. So now we shall go to war to defend the monks, although many of them are evil men, and if they are victorious, it will spell disaster for decent people everywhere. Already they are beginning to show their teeth.

Lambertus Campester, an itinerant Dominican, has produced a travesty   35 of my *Colloquies* at Paris.[12] The Carthusian Pierre Cousturier has attacked me in an utterly silly pamphlet, also published at Paris.[13] I wrote a reply, which I would not have done, if it had not been clear from the French title-

* * * * *

10 The first execution for Lutheran heresy in the Netherlands took place at Brussels on 1 July 1523, when two Augustinian friars from Antwerp were burned. In the following two years there were many arrests and a few executions at various places. Many of the victims were clergymen. See P.J. Blok *History of the People of the Netherlands*, 5 vols (New York 1898–1912; repr New York 1970) II 309–11; R.R. Post *Geschiedenis van Nederland*, Deel II: *Middeleeuwen* (Amsterdam 1935) 433–5; L.-E. Halkin and A.L.E. Verheyden *Algemene geschiedenis der Nederlanden*, Deel IV: *De Bourgondisch-Habsburgse monarchie 1477–1567* (Utrecht 1952) 255–6.
11 On Frans van der Hulst cf Ep 1345 n8 and Tracy *Holland under Habsburg Rule* (n8 above) 153–5. Although a layman, Hulst took special interest in the pursuit of heretics, being deeply involved in 1521–2 in the prosecution of Erasmus' humanist friends Cornelius Grapheus and Jacob Proost, in close association with Erasmus' most unrelenting critic among the Louvain theologians, the Carmelite Nicolaas Baechem of Egmond (Egmondanus). In 1522–4 he headed a secular inquisitorial commission appointed by the emperor and given broad discretionary powers. During his prosecution of Cornelis Hoen, another Erasmian with strong Evangelical sympathies in 1523, Hulst not only disregarded Hoen's privileged position as a member of the Council of Holland but even forged documents to be used in the prosecution. This excess caused the governor, Margaret of Austria, to demand his resignation; and contrary to Erasmus' report here, he never again held a powerful office.
12 Cf Ep 1581 n59.
13 Cf Ep 1571 n10.

page[14] that the work was printed by authority of the faculty of theology. At Louvain there is a nest of Dominicans of the most villainous kind.[15] Vincentius, a man whom nature intended for the galley or the plough, but who is now a doctor of theology, wrote an attack on me several years ago. To get permission to publish, he set off to see his vicar-general. That man absolutely forbade him to do any such thing. So he held his peace, though with some difficulty. Now at last the work has appeared. A more uncouth, tasteless, ignorant, dishonest, impertinent, crack-brained production you could not imagine! Four people had a hand in it. Vincentius contributed his own brand of poison. Cornelis of Duiveland was responsible for the greater part of it. A third man embellished it with several flourishes of his own. Godefridus Taxander is given credit for the whole work. To all these things the theologians of Louvain turn a blind eye. Latomus has published three volumes, in which I am the target of some remarkable sophistries.[16] Oecolampadius wrote a reply. They tell me the title is *Elleboron*.[17] I have not seen it yet. I am afraid this turmoil may spread to Italy sooner than the pope imagines. While all this goes on, we fail to recognize the manifest signs of the wrath of God, who is calling us to repent; but though warned, like the Egyptians, by so many plagues, we do nothing to amend our lives.

In many places the monks have been harshly treated. But, since many of them are insufferable, there was no other way to bring them to their senses. They are protected by so many privileges and exemptions, and have such strength of numbers. Some cities are adopting quite lenient measures.[18] Those who can show reason why they wish to change their way of life are permitted to leave; they are provided with a living allowance from the resources of the monasteries themselves, as a sort of stipend for their chronic idleness, even in cases where they brought nothing with them

* * * * *

14 Cf Ep 1581 n62.
15 Cf Ep 1571 n14. The three names that follow (Vincentius, Cornelis of Duiveland, and Godefridus Taxander) are related to this 'nest of Dominicans.'
16 Cf Epp 934, 1571 n5, and on his 'three volumes,' Ep 1581 n58, which also demonstrates that Latomus' open attacks on Oecolampadius were obliquely but recognizably aimed at Erasmus, though they avoided use of his name.
17 On Oecolampadius' earlier career cf Ep 324:30n. By this time, he was the leader of the Reformation party in Basel. His work *Elleboron, pro eodem Iacobo Latomo* (Basel: Andreas Cratander, 18 August 1525), reprinted and refuted Latomus' *De confessione secreta*.
18 What Erasmus is describing, with apparent though tacit approval, is the suppression of the monasteries by many Swiss and German cities.

when they arrived. Those who took their vows elsewhere are ordered to depart; they are not permitted to establish daughter houses in other places according to their usual custom. They may not accept novices to fill a vacant place except with the consent of the authorities. They are banned from the oversight of nunneries. They may not preach outside their own 70 monasteries, and only at regular hours. Where there is a general desire for a change of religious practice, permission is granted. Those who do not wish to do so must nevertheless take an oath of allegiance to the authorities in all matters pertaining to the interests of the state. By these means they reckon they will either have no monks at all or monks who are more sober 75 in their behaviour. Empty monasteries will be turned into parishes or schools. In future no one under thirty-six years of age will be allowed to take perpetual vows, as they are called. Every effort will be made to turn them into good pastors. If that happens, the number of monks will not be large. A few monasteries will be left, but only those which are famous or 80 are situated outside the walls of a city or perhaps I should say, deep in the country, where manual labour will provide brisk physical exercise. They believe the present infinite variety of religious orders should be abolished completely. They are opposed to annual assemblies, or 'chapters' as they are called, and also to dispensations, which the monks abuse so that they can 85 sin with impunity. Instead they will be made subject to their bishops and to the magistrates, as other priests and laymen are.

Whether this is a justifiable policy or not, I do not propose to discuss for the moment. But at least the tyranny of evil monks will be controlled with less turmoil, and action will be taken to prevent good monks, and 90 especially young men, from giving themselves over in future to this kind of slavery. Policies introduced as a result of popular clamour generally turn out badly. The fact that everyone may change his way of life as he pleases leaves the door open for wicked men to act immorally. We would secure the best results if things were under the control of the pope and the 95 bishops. Certainly the important thing at present is for the authority of the magistrates to prevent disorder and to assist good men without giving evil men a licence to sin. I wish we could all be true monks, that is, men who are dead to this world. But it seems the world cannot endure these scheming hordes of provocateurs much longer. And al- 100 though the looting of monasteries by the peasants seems a monstrous crime, this is the fate to which the depravity of these men has brought us, since no laws could reform them and they are blind to their own shortcomings.

You had written earlier about the cup which the bishop of Olomouc 105

sent me as a gift, but you did not mention it in your recent letter.[19] It was
a present for me and had a personal inscription on it. But since Beatus had
received a letter from the bishop which mentioned the sending of a golden
goblet[20] and Velius[21] had said something similar, while I had heard nothing and there was no reason why the bishop should send me anything, I   110
gave the cup to Beatus, suspecting that Koberger had made a mistake in the
name.[22] If you know anything about this, please write. I have not yet seen
your *Ptolemy*, but I shall make a point of getting a copy.[23] I can find no
one here who knows how to make an alabaster cast.[24] So I should have
preferred the original to remain with you. I have sent off my *Tongue*;[25] so   115
you will have to admit from now on that your friend Erasmus is speechless!

I have had some considerable relief from the stone since I began
mixing my wine with water boiled with liquorice root. Still my poor old
body is growing thinner and more desiccated every day. Soon, I am afraid,
I shall shuffle off this mortal coil and emerge in a new form, like a cicada.   120
Martin Dorp has gone before me. Linacre died in England, Longueil at
Bologna, Battista Casali at Rome, and François Deloynes, a great patron of
the humanities, at Paris.[26] Here the rain has fallen continuously for a month
and a half; and as if it was not enough to be drenched with the rain from

* * * * *

19 On the cup cf Ep 1557:27–32, and on the bishop, Stanislaus Thurzo, Ep 1242
   introduction. Neither of the letters here mentioned by Erasmus is extant.
20 Beatus Rhenanus had been promised a gilt cup as a reward for dedicating to
   Bishop Thurzo his *Autores historiae ecclesiasticae* (Basel: Froben 1523), and
   Caspar Ursinus Velius at Vienna had received it and promised to forward it
   to Erasmus for delivery. Cf Ep 1557:27–32.
21 On the Silesian humanist Caspar Ursinus Velius, who was now teaching at
   Vienna, cf Epp 548:5n, 6n, 1557 introduction.
22 The Nürnberg publisher Johann Koberger frequently forwarded letters for
   Erasmus. Erasmus appears to assume that he was also responsible for incorrectly engraving Erasmus' name onto the cup which Bishop Thurzo sent for
   Beatus. Erasmus may not have expected a present for himself at this point, but
   in February he had dedicated his edition of Pliny *Naturalis historia* to Bishop
   Thurzo; cf Epp 1544, 1557 n11.
23 Pirckheimer's translation of Ptolemy *Geographia* (Strasbourg: Johannes Grienin-
   ger, 30 March 1525) long remained the standard Latin version.
24 Allen Ep 1603:101n thinks that this is a reference to Erasmus' continuing efforts
   to obtain copies of the medal made by Quinten Metsys in 1519. Cf Allen Ep
   1408:29n, and Ep 1092 (where the medal is reproduced in CWE 7 260).
25 One of many punning references to the very recent publication of Erasmus'
   Lingua; cf Ep 1593 introduction.
26 This list of humanist friends who were recently deceased appears also in Ep
   1597:22–5. Longueil died at Padua.

heaven, the nobles and peasants are lined up for battle, to drench them-   125
selves in each other's blood.

Give my regards to Dürer,[27] who has no equal in Apelles' art.[28]
Greet Paulus Ricius too:[29] today I used the pill which he recommended
with excellent results. I take only half the dosage, but it moved my bowels
with no discomfort. I am looking forward to receiving your letter and also   130
the portrait of myself from Dürer's most accomplished hand. Farewell.

Basel, 28 August 1525

You will recognize the hand of your friend, etc.

To the most illustrious Willibald Pirckheimer

1604 / To Francesco Minuzio Calvo   Basel, 31 August 1525

On the early career of the recipient, who by this period was established as a
printer in Rome, see Ep 581:33n. He had moved to Rome about 1519, working
as an editor for Eucharius Silber; and about 1523 he established his own shop.
In 1524 he succeeded Silber as printer to the Holy See. In 1535 he moved his
business to Milan, where he died in 1538 (cf Allen Ep 3032:581n). Erasmus
published this and the following letter in his *Opus epistolarum*, no doubt in
order to demonstrate his excellent connections at Rome.

ERASMUS OF ROTTERDAM TO FRANCESCO CALVO, ROMAN BOOK-
SELLER, GREETING

I want to thank you on behalf of the general cause of learning for the
attractive books your house has already given us; we eagerly await the
others which you have promised. The bearer of this letter is an excellent   5
fellow who was in the employ of Froben for some time.[1] I wanted you to

* * * * *

27 Both Erasmus and his Nürnberg friend Pirckheimer admired the great Nürn-
    berg artist, who is regularly mentioned in this correspondence. See for example
    Epp 1536, 1558, 1560.
28 The association of Dürer with the name of the great Greek painter Apelles is
    a commonplace of this correspondence, for example Epp 1536:3, 1558:41–3.
29 Cf Epp 548:16n, 1558 n10.

1604
 1 This and the following letter were both carried to Rome by the same courier,
    a Frenchman who had worked for some time for the Froben press. Allen Ep
    1605:17n suggests that he may have been Anianus Burgonius of Orléans, who
    accompanied Jan Łaski during his six-month residence with Erasmus in 1525
    (cf Allen Ep 1502:8n). If so, he must have preceded Łaski to Italy, since Łaski
    left Basel about 5 October 1525 in the company of Erasmus' regular confiden-

get to know him in the hope that you could make use of his services. I find
Bishop Sadoleto's book delightful;[2] but when I contemplate the golden river
of his eloquence, I realize how muddy and shallow my own little stream is.
In future I shall try to fit my style to the model he has provided. I pray that   10
Mercury may bless and prosper all your efforts.[3] Farewell.

Basel, 31 August 1525

1605 / To Pierre Barbier   Basel, 31 August 1525

Pierre Barbier (d December 1551 or January 1552) was an employee of the Louvain printer Dirk Martens in 1513, when Erasmus first met him; but he rose
to positions of considerable importance as secretary to Jean Le Sauvage,
chancellor of Burgundy and of Spain, and then to Cardinal Adriaan of Utrecht,
regent of Spain for King Charles I (later the emperor Charles V). Adriaan's
election as pope in 1522 catapulted Barbier to a position of great influence, and
he became the central figure among Erasmus' friends in Rome. After the
pope's death in 1523, Barbier entered the service of Girolamo Aleandro, where
he continued to be useful to Erasmus. Evidently Erasmus did not yet know
that Barbier had left Rome in April 1525 to enter the service of Charles de
Lannoy, viceroy of Naples. For earlier contact with him cf Ep 443. Erasmus
included the letter in his *Opus epistolarum*.

ERASMUS OF ROTTERDAM TO PIERRE BARBIER,
GREETING

It seems your friendship for me is cooling off, since you do not reply to my
letters. My friendship for you, however, will never die. You are always
promising mountains of gold. Well then don't rob me of my annuity, as you   5
seem to be planning to do, and don't make me regret having placed my
complete confidence in you.[1] I have no doubts about your honesty, but I

* * * * *

tial courier, Karl Harst. In return for his delivery of these letters, Erasmus
commended the bearer to the patronage of both recipients. If he was Bur-
gonius, his experience working for Froben must have been a valuable qualifica-
tion for Calvo, a bookseller and printer.
2 A commentary on Psalm 50, printed by Calvo this same year. Cf Ep 1586
introduction.
3 The Roman god of commerce. Erasmus was well aware from his own experience that publishing is a commercial undertaking.

1605
1 Barbier had devised the complicated financial and legal arrangements which

do fear your naïveté may lead you astray; it is an all too common failing of yours.

My feelings for Aleandro are a mixture of affection and suspicion.[2]   10
Certain people who feed him with false suspicions are turning him against me. He is one thing behind my back and another to my face. So you would be well advised not to blurt out anything in his presence which would not be in keeping with our friendship or could sharpen his hostility towards me. My poor body is gradually failing and growing drier and weaker. I   15
predict that the time is not far away when I shall shuffle off this mortal coil and spring forth in a new form, just like a cicada, soaring into the purer and freer air to sing a happier song in praise of Christ. Then you can have the Courtrai annuity for yourself. But in the meantime it would be cruel indeed to starve your poor friend Erasmus to death.   20

The Frenchman who is delivering this letter lived for some time with Froben.[3] He seems to me an honest man. At Rome he was made a subdeacon, but could go no further because he has no title.[4] He wants either to be freed of his obligations or allowed to proceed. I shall not trouble you with

* * * * *

converted the prebend at Courtrai which the Burgundian court had granted Erasmus in 1517 into an annuity, thus freeing Erasmus from the obligation to reside and perform clerical functions at Courtrai. But these arrangements required that the annual payments from the purchaser of the prebend, Jan de Hondt, should pass from de Hondt to Barbier and only then to Erasmus, a complex procedure further complicated by the fact that Barbier himself retained some interest in the revenues. This arrangement occasioned frequent delays in the delivery of revenues to Erasmus, who always suspected (incorrectly, it seems) that Barbier was cheating him. After 1530, Barbier's personal financial problems and his dispute with de Hondt led to a total suspension of payments and to considerable bitterness on Erasmus' part. Bietenholz in CEBR I 94 provides a useful survey of this arrangement.
2 Although Erasmus had become a close friend of Aleandro at Venice in 1508, their subsequent relations were uneven, as Erasmus here states. For a survey of their relationship from about 1520, see Ep 1553 n9. Cf Epp 1581 n52, 1582 n8.
3 Cf Ep 1604 n1.
4 In medieval canon law, a candidate for ordination to the rank of deacon or priest was required to have a *titulus* or affiliation with a specific church, partly to ensure that he had a parish connection but mainly to ensure material support. Cf NCE X 726–7. A member of a religious order (such as the young Erasmus) could count his order as his *titulus*. Since the subdiaconate imposed the obligation of celibacy, Erasmus' messenger, a secular cleric, hoped to be released from that obligation if he could not be advanced to the diaconate and the priesthood.

a recommendation, but if there is anything you can do for him, I am sure   25
you will be assisting a good man. Farewell, distinguished patron. My letter
to Hovius will give you the rest of my news.[5]

Basel, 31 August 1525

1606 / To Polidoro Virgilio   Basel, 5 September 1525

On this Italian humanist and historiographer to Henry VIII of England, see Epp
531:456n and 1175 introduction. Despite a certain tension over the issue
whether the first edition of Erasmus' *Adagia* was published before or after
Virgilio's *Proverbiorum libellus* (1498), the two men remained on friendly terms.
Even though Virgilio (whose collection was indeed the earlier) retitled later
editions of his book *Adagiorum liber*, Erasmus put aside his suspicions and
magnanimously encouraged his friend Froben to print a new edition of it,
which is referred to in the first sentence. Erasmus published the present letter
in his *Opus epistolarum*.

ERASMUS OF ROTTERDAM TO POLIDORO VIRGILIO, GREETING
Polidoro, my honoured friend, your works have been printed in a most
elegant and handsome edition.[1] Froben would like to know the terms of the
contract since he expects nothing but chicanery from X. That schemer will
reap the profits for himself and play Froben for a fool.[2] It does not matter   5

* * * * *

5 This letter is not extant. For Johannes Hovius, who worked for Erasmus at
  Basel and Louvain from about 1518 to about 1523 but was now living at Rome,
  see Epp 857 introduction, 867:189n, 1387 n3, and Ep 1575:5.

1606
1 This was a combined edition of two of Virgilio's works, *Adagiorum liber.
  Eiusdem de inventoribus rerum libri octo*. Froben had already published these two
  works in 1521 and 1524 and again in the summer of 1525, but although
  Erasmus pleaded the case for a new edition, Froben expressed doubts about
  the market for such a book at a time when it seemed that buyers wanted only
  works by Luther. Cf Ep 1494. Erasmus had also claimed credit for persuading
  Froben to publish the first combined edition of these works in 1521; cf Epp
  1175:124–30, 1210.
2 A reference to the international bookseller Franz Birckmann, who had been
  involved in the negotiations for a re-edition of Virgilio's works. He had long
  had close business relations with the Froben firm, and Erasmus frequently
  used his services to obtain books and to transmit funds and letters, but neither
  man thought him to be honest. Cf Ep 258:14n and more recently Epp 1388,
  1437, 1488.

greatly to me personally, except that Froben is the finest man I have ever set eyes on and I wish him well. Moreover it was on my prompting that he undertook the task. I should also like to see him well treated so he will be more enthusiastic in the future about considering other treatises of yours. Certainly you will always be able to rely on me to promote your good name   10
since you have been so kind to me.

As for what you tell me about More, I think you should not take it seriously. If for one reason or another he was offended, any resentment he may feel will be slight.³ It is not his way to dwell on insults, even insults that are serious. I have written to him, however, not to reconcile the two of   15
you, but to strengthen your mutual friendship. For since you honoured me with your friendship some time ago, it is only fair that we share our friends in common, and this is something I fervently desire. If I find a courier whom I can trust, I shall write at greater length.

Here a cruel and bloody tragedy is being played out. The peasants are   20
rushing to their deaths. Everyday there are fierce battles between them and the princes; the fighting is so close that we are within earshot of the guns and cannons and can almost hear the groans of the dying. You can guess how safe we are in this place! It is a terrible disaster, and it is spreading with remarkable speed into every region of the world. Cardinal Campeggi   25
left Hungary for fear of the troubles. The archbishop was thrown out. The cardinal-archbishop of Salzburg has been under siege for some time. The bishop of Veroli, who was papal nuncio, was afraid to remain in Switzer- land.⁴ There have been several outbreaks at Cologne.⁵ The situation in Brabant is becoming worse. The princes know nothing but the usual rem-   30
edies. I am afraid they may exacerbate the problem, but Christ, our great master-craftsman, is alone able to bring some good out of this deadly tempest.

Some people won't let my quarrel with Lee sink into oblivion,⁶ but

* * * * *

3 There is no record of a quarrel between Virgilio and Thomas More.
4 'Cardinal Campeggi ... bishop of Veroli': this catalogue of disasters is repeated from Ep 1603:8–12.
5 Popular disturbances, directed largely against the special privileges of the clergy, troubled the city through the spring and summer of 1525.
6 The attack on Erasmus published in 1525 by four Louvain Dominicans under a pseudonym was dedicated to Erasmus' old antagonist Edward Lee; cf Ep 1571 n14. Erasmus was particularly unhappy about the rekindling of this old animosity because Lee had already begun the rise to favour at the English court that ultimately led to his appointment as archbishop of York in 1531. Late in 1525 Henry VIII sent him as ambassador to Spain.

keep rubbing the scar on the old wound.[7] I know that, with your usual   35
kindness, you will try to maintain what you call in your letter 'the quiet
enjoyment of our common friends.' Farewell.

    Basel, 5 September 1525

1607 / From Paul Volz   [Sélestat], 5 September 1525

> For the earlier career of Paul Volz, abbot of the Benedictine monastery at
> Honcourt (Hugshofen), see Ep 368 introduction. He had been strongly
> attracted not only to Erasmian humanism but also to Lutheranism; but he had
> remained in the monastery, engaged in literary studies and in close touch with
> the humanist circle at nearby Sélestat. In 1525 rebellious peasants destroyed
> the monastery and he lost not only his many unpublished works but also his
> place of residence. After first taking shelter in Strasbourg, he went to Sélestat
> in early August to seek help; but the regional Austrian authorities at Ensis-
> heim denied him aid because of his well-known sympathy for Luther. In 1526
> he moved to Strasbourg, where he openly embraced the Reformation and
> became a preacher. At this juncture, still uncertain of his future course, he was
> asking Erasmus to help him find some source of support. Erasmus always
> remained warmly favourable to Volz despite his defection from the Roman
> church. Erasmus never published this letter, which was first edited by För-
> stemann and Günther in 1904 from a Leipzig manuscript.

Cordial greetings. My dear Erasmus, I think you have already heard what
happened to me and to my beloved monastery. My neighbours and even
those who claim to be my protectors have stripped me of everything, and
I have nothing left except the clothes which cover me and a pocket edition
of the New Testament. Now I can truthfully claim with the philosopher that   5
'everything I own I carry with me.'[1] But I have never been interested in
money and have always been content with little. This, however, is not the
only misfortune which has befallen me: for the man who was given charge
of the monastery told me, when I was returning recently from Strasbourg
after my first visit in a period of four years, that orders had gone out from   10

* * * * *

7 *Adagia* I vi 80

1607
1 A saying of Bias, quoted in *Adagia* III iv 62

the councillors at Ensisheim[2] not to give me a cent from the revenues of the monastery and to make sure that I was not provided with lodgings or food or drink at our house in Sélestat, because, as he put it, I was 'a member of the Lutheran sect.' I wrote to the councillors to complain, and Master Ulrich of Rappoltstein[3] etc. also wrote on my behalf. I received a reply, a copy of which is in the hands of our mutual friend, Beatus, along with an account of the whole affair.[4] I did not want to burden you with all the trivial details and to encroach upon your spare time with my silly litany of complaints, for your time is sacred and already fully occupied. But when you have a moment, you may, if you wish, hear the story from Beatus. All I ask is that, just as I was commended to you, you commend me to anyone whose advice or assistance could help and protect me, for I have done no harm to anyone and need support because of my health and advancing years.

In the meantime I am staying at Sélestat, existing as best I can. Sapidus, who provides me with food and clothing, sends you his very best wishes.[5] With the restoration of the old ritual, Wimpfeling[6] came to life

* * * * *

2 Ensisheim was the seat of administration for the westernmost Austrian possessions on the Upper Rhine, known collectively as Vorderösterreich or the Vorland (Anterior Austria), and including the Breisgau, the Sundgau, and most of Upper Lorraine, and at this period also the confiscated duchy of Württemberg.

3 Graf Ulrich (d 1531) was the descendant of a family of Alsatian knights who held several estates near Sélestat. A pupil of Ulrich Zasius at the University of Freiburg, he secretly sympathized with the Reformation. His father, Graf Wilhelm, was the governor of the Austrian Vorland.

4 Cf BRE 241. Beatus Rhenanus was interested not only as a friend of Volz and a close collaborator in Erasmus' scholarly work for the Froben press but also as a native of Sélestat who always maintained close connections with his native city and in 1527 returned there from Basel to spend the last two decades of his life.

5 On Sapidus (Johann Witz) see Ep 323 introduction. Witz had been immensely popular and successful as headmaster of the famous Latin school at Sélestat. His humanistic interests linked him closely with the humanistic group centered around Jakob Wimpfeling, but unlike the group's leader, he became a follower of Luther. In August 1525 the official restoration of Catholic ceremonies in the city forced Sapidus to resign his position as schoolmaster. Late the following year, he moved to Strasbourg, where he continued his work as teacher, humanist, and writer. He was an especially close friend of Volz and Erasmus.

6 The conservative humanist and priest Jakob Wimpfeling, despite his efforts to correct abuses in the local church, firmly opposed the spread of the Reformation in his native city. Hence he would have been pleased with the official action to restore Catholic ceremonies which led to Sapidus' resignation. On him cf Ep 224 introduction.

again, though he now uses three legs instead of two.[7] I have been reading
your friend Cousturier,[8] a cobbler who does not stick to his last;[9] I was
amused at the effrontery of a swine like that trying to teach Minerva a
lesson,[10] and at the good sense and appropriateness of your reply; you   30
answered the fool according to his folly, so that he may not seem wise in
his own conceit.[11] Although I find it hard to tolerate troublemakers like
that, I cannot help feeling some pleasure because these people always elicit
from you a valuable, if reluctant, response. Farewell. My love to you, which
I pray you will reciprocate.   35

      5 September 1525
      Your friend, Paul Volz, former abbot
      To that consummate doctor of sacred letters, Master Desiderius
Erasmus of Rotterdam, my friend and beloved brother in Christ. In Basel

1608 / To Nicolas Coppin and the Theologians of Louvain

Basel, 6 September 1525

> Erasmus here lodges formal complaint with the highest authorities of the
> University of Louvain against the *Apologia in eum librum quem ab anno Erasmus
> Roterodamus de confessione edidit ... Eiusdem libellus quo taxatur ... liber de carnium
> esu ...* published under the pseudonym Godefridus Taxander. This was an
> attack on his own *Exomologesis sive modus confitendi* and his *De esu carnium*. On
> this book and the group of Dominican theologians who published it see Epp
> 1571 n14, 1582 introduction. Nicolas Coppin, who had twice served as rector
> of the University of Louvain and held a chair of theology there, was chancellor
> of the university. On him see Ep 1162 n18. Erasmus included this letter in his
> *Opus epistolarum.*

ERASMUS OF ROTTERDAM TO NICOLAS OF MONS, DEAN AND
CHANCELLOR OF THE UNIVERSITY OF LOUVAIN, AND THE OTHER
THEOLOGIANS, GREETING
Esteemed brothers, the publication of such an ignorant book pains me as

* * * * *

7 That is, he uses a walking-stick – an echo of the famous riddle of the Sphinx.
   Wimpfeling, who belonged to an older generation (born in 1450) suffered
   declining health from the time of his return from Strasbourg to Sélestat in 1515
   down to his death in 1528, and often pleaded inability to travel as an excuse
   for not visiting his friends in other cities.
8 Cf Ep 1571 n10.
9 A pun on the Latin form of Cousturier's name, Sutor, which means cobbler.
10 For the proverb 'The sow teaches Minerva,' see *Adagia* I i 40.
11 Prov 26:5

much for your sake as my own. From a letter which was intercepted and   5
sent to us from England I now know who are responsible for this mad
production.[1] Credit is given on the title-page to Godefridus Taxander, but
Cornelis van Duiveland wrote most of it. Many passages were taken from
a book which Vincentius had written attacking me. And there was also a
contribution from someone called Walter. I collected seventy manifest lies   10
in the work, short though it is. What will intelligent scholars think when
they read such stuff? With the encouragement of the pope and the kings, I
am waging war, at some risk to my own life, against the Lutheran faction,
a faction which is no less defiant than it is powerful. Yet your people are
stirring up all this unpleasantness for me. I was preparing something which   15
might have checked a part of the trouble, but it was not safe to publish it
unless I moved house, and this has not so far been possible because of my
health and scholarly obligations, and is now ruled out by this murderous
revolution,[2] even if nothing else stood in the way.

I cannot describe to you how bad things are in Germany. But, consid-   20
ering the present circumstances, I have kept a clear conscience, as a Christian should who lives in expectation of that final day, which in my case
must be close at hand. We pursue the same ends, you and I, though by
different paths. But if this is the way I am treated by those whose cause I
am supporting with all my strength, why should I expose myself to the fury   25
of the other side? Perhaps you expect this evil can be suppressed by puni-
tive measures. I wish some way had been found to settle it. But I see no
solution unless unusual remedies are applied to an unusual malady. If my
advice had been taken at the start, we might perhaps have avoided the
present state of anarchy. But what use is the surgeon's knife or branding   30
iron when fever has already spread throughout the body? The disease is
now in the veins, and unless it is purged by drugs, there is no hope of
recovery. If the disease is suppressed, it will break out again after an inter-
val and the danger will be greater. Ferdinand began to employ violent

* * * * *

1608
1 Erasmus' correspondence shows that he only gradually pieced together information on the identity of the anonymous group of Dominican theologians
  responsible for the *Apologia*. Allen Ep 1608:2n speculates that the intercepted
  letter may have been written by or to his English antagonist Edward Lee, to
  whom the pseudonymous *Apologia* was dedicated.
2 The German Peasant War, which was not entirely suppressed in all regions
  until late in 1525 or even early in 1526, made travel hazardous. See Preface,
  pages xi–xii.

remedies,[3] then changed his mind. If the emperor were here, perhaps he 35
would do the same.

I am not saying these things to support the followers of Luther or the
mob who are now in open revolt, but in the interests of public peace. I have
written certain things which are offensive to Egmondanus;[4] but whatever
may have happened in the past, if he will desist, I shall forget everything. 40
This is the most honourable course for both of us: for me, because I must
soon stand before the judgment-seat of Christ, and for him because he has
taken on the role of theologian and monk; and perhaps it will not be long
until he follows me – who knows, he may even go before me.[5] I live at
peace with the pope, and with the emperor and Ferdinand, and with cardi- 45
nals and kings and bishops of the true faith. Only with Egmondanus and
Vincentius is it impossible to make peace. I am battling against all the
followers of Luther with no prospect of a truce. I thought it was enough to
be attacked on one flank. Heresies and schisms I cannot abide, just as I
cannot hate the humanities. Nevertheless I am not automatically opposed 50
to anyone who lacks a taste for good literature, provided he does not
denounce those who do. I have said it many times and I repeat it now: if
you find anything in my books which rightly offends your ears or mind,
point it out and I shall change it and thank you for your pains. What keeps
us apart is words, not sentiments. It was the same in the case of the Stoics 55
and Peripatetics.[6] I am prepared to put aside all personal rancour, as I

* * * * *

3 For Archduke Ferdinand's aggressive attitude during the early stages of the
Peasant War, see Balan *Monumenta* I 155, 162, 169 and Franz 90, 106.
4 On this vociferous and intractable Carmelite theologian and critic of Erasmus,
cf Ep 878:15n. After seeking vainly to silence him through appeals to the rector
of Louvain in 1520 (Ep 1153) and even a personal confrontation that same year,
Erasmus had published a refutation of his attacks on the second edition of the
New Testament, *Apologia de loco 'Omnes quidem'* (Basel: Froben 1522) and
openly ridiculed him in the colloquies *Apotheosis Capnionis* (English title: 'The
Apotheosis of That Incomparable Worthy, John Reuchlin') and Ἰχθυοφαγία
(English title: 'A Fish Diet'), and also in many letters of this period. The English titles of the colloquies are from the translation by Craig R. Thompson
(Chicago 1965), which remains the standard English text until his revised
edition appears in CWE.
5 In fact both Erasmus' Carmelite enemy Egmondanus and his Dominican critic
Vincentius Theoderici died in 1526, preceding him by a decade.
6 For the idea that these two ancient philosophical schools agreed in substance
though not in words, see Cicero *Tusculanae disputationes* 4.6; cf *De finibus*
4.3–20, 56–7, 72.

would if I were going to die today. If there are some among you who reject
this offer of peace, this letter will at least acquit me before the judgment-seat
of Christ. Farewell.

Basel, 6 September 1525   60

1609 / From Noël Béda   Paris, 12 September 1525

A reply to Epp 1581 and 1596, treated together because they reached Béda
together. Considering the date of their receipt, therefore, Béda's reply was very
prompt. On him, see Ep 1571 introduction. Béda published this letter in his
own *Apologia adversus clandestinos Lutheranos* (1529).

TO THE MOST LEARNED MASTER DESIDERIUS ERASMUS OF
ROTTERDAM, MY GREATLY BELOVED AND RESPECTED FRIEND,
GREETING
I believe it was the work of divine providence, dearly beloved and most
learned brother and master, that no courier was available to deliver your   5
first letter when you wished. If it had come by itself, I would have nothing
to say in reply, judging silence the most appropriate response. I am not
competent to answer the various and almost innumerable arguments which
you included in that letter. It was, unless I am mistaken, very largely a
waste of effort. It arrived, however, with a second letter in which you   10
appear to have answered many of the questions contained in the earlier one;
so, placing my trust in God, I have decided to send you this brief note by
way of reply. You will see, dear brother, that your letter prompted and
encouraged me to do what I would otherwise not have done, to write with
true Christian frankness all that I judged expedient for your salvation. I only 15
wish the Lord had made it possible for us to talk these matters over face to
face. You would then realize, I think, that it is your happiness which I
desire. Thanks be to God, who gave you grace to speak with a gentler voice
when you wrote that second letter in your own hand.

Dear brother, if the letter which you sent to the bishop of Basel[1] con-   20
cerning the interdiction on the eating of meat etc was approved by Ludwig

* * * * *

1609
1 A reference to Erasmus' *Epistola apologetica de interdicto esu carnium* (1522); cf
Ep 1581 n100. The bishop, a firm friend and patron of Erasmus and other
humanists at Basel, was Christoph von Utenheim (cf Ep 598 introduction).

Baer,[2] after, as you tell me, he had read it twice, my response is not simply
to say 'Unless I am mistaken, this man has acted most unfortunately'; rather
I assert it as an unalterable article of truth, that he and anyone who is of the
same opinion have gone pitifully astray and have misled you in no small   25
degree. I shall see that he is given a warning by our friend Master Gervasius,[3] to whom I have passed on your good wishes. One could hardly
claim that those who give you such advice when you seek their opinion are
showing much concern for your salvation or for your peace of mind or
good name. For, as the saying goes, counsel misjudged hurts him who gives   30
it most.[4] I wish that work had never issued from your pen – and you were
an old man, too, when it appeared. It is not hard to see how good a Catholic you were when you wrote that work, that is, how close you were to the
holy traditions and practices of the church, and how dangerous your words
were for the morals of Christian people. The answer to that question is   35
clearer than the light of noonday. I am pained, deeply pained, that in
putting forth this and other similar views, you have given Luther's followers something to cast in your teeth: they will say, 'We hold you bound
by your own writings, since you agree with us on many points.' I beg you,
do what you can to defend yourself from such a charge; and enlighten and   40
edify the world with your wisdom, rendering to God and your neighbour
what is their due.

I think you misread my letter, since you say that it was at my urging
that you went back to St Augustine's discussion of our Lord's Sermon on
the Mount.[5] I am sure I never mentioned that work, though I am aware   45

* * * * *

2 Baer was not only Basel's leading scholastic theologian but also a top-ranking
  graduate of Béda's own theological faculty at Paris, and hence Erasmus regularly used his approval in defence of his own orthodoxy. On him cf Epp 488
  introduction, 1571 n6.
3 Gervasius Wain of Memmingen (c 1491–1554) studied at Paris, probably under
  Ludwig Baer at the Collège de Sainte-Barbe, then at Freiburg (1511–3) under
  Johann Maier von Eck, and finally returned to Paris, where he held many
  college and university offices and in 1522 completed his doctorate in theology.
  From about this period, however, he was often absent, being increasingly
  drawn into political and diplomatic service to the king of France. He remained
  close to Baer, to whom he dedicated a publication in 1519, as well as to Beatus
  Rhenanus and Wolfgang Capito, and was well known to Erasmus, who sent
  him greetings via Béda in Ep 1581. Some direct correspondence between them
  also survives, beginning with Ep 1884.
4 A Greek proverb found in Hesiod *Works and Days* 265–6 and translated by
  Aulus Gellius 4.5.5; cf *Adagia* I ii 14.
5 Cf Ep 1596 n1.

that it is as you describe. What I was talking about was St Augustine's twenty-eighth sermon on the words of the Apostle[6] as well as certain other books and letters of the same Augustine, all of which he published when he was already well grounded in theology. I admit that, because the courier was in a hurry, I dictated my letter too hastily and it was copied out too rapidly by my secretary; I do hope that, in these discussions, there will be no silly misunderstandings between us as a result of the actions of my secretary or anyone else.

You will find herewith my comments on some of your writings. I offer them to you in the name of God. Some are concerned with doctrines of the faith, others with general principles of conduct, some with your own behaviour, since in discussing your own and other people's writings you have not always maintained a moderate tone. Let me say that my purpose in sending you these is not to irritate or annoy you, but to do what little I can to assist you in the task which you mention in your second letter. When you examine them, you will see where it was that you wrote about translating Ezekiel and the Song of Songs[7] etc. You should not think, my dearest friend, that I am more critical of you than it is fair to be, etc. Josse Clichtove will tell you from his own experience that, in matters of faith or in matters which bear in some way upon the faith, when I believe I have something useful to say, I spare no one and speak my mind without holding anything back; yet he and I are now such close and trusted friends that he will not publish the slightest thing, unless it has first received my scrutiny (for whatever that is worth).[8] Pierre Cousturier knows this too,[9] but perhaps you do not.

You will have further proof on this point if the Lord permits the publication of the notes which I appended to the dialogues of a countryman

* * * * *

6 The annotator has been unable to trace this reference.
7 Cf Epp 1579:174, 1581:834–5.
8 Cf Ep 594:15n. Clichtove had been a close follower of the humanist Lefèvre d'Etaples in the early years of the century and had even defended him publicly against attacks by Béda; but by 1521 he had broken with him and formally retracted the position on Mary Magdalen that he had taken in support of Lefèvre. For Clichtove's retraction and the statement he made on this issue by order of the theological faculty, see A. Clerval (ed) *Registres des procès-verbaux de la faculté de théologie de Paris* I (1505–23) (Paris 1917) 296, 299–301. He had never been a particular admirer of Erasmus and had opposed Erasmus' views on clerical celibacy and other issues since 1519, though he did not publicly attack Erasmus by name until publication of his *Antilutherus* in 1524.
9 Cf Ep 1571 n10.

of yours, Christiaan Masseeuw,[10] supporting the sacred decrees of Jerome and Gelasius against the defenders of Origen.[11] The nature of the argument did not allow me to spare even you, although, as the Lord our God knows, I undertook the task reluctantly. The point which involves you is this: in the reply which you made to Latomus[12] in your *Apologia*, you credit Adamantius[13] with what in my opinion he does not deserve and you deny to Jerome and Augustine, those great luminaries of the church, much that the church believes to be their due. Since this trumpeting of the praises of Origen by Erasmus, whom I love in the Lord with all my heart, ran counter to my own purpose, I tried to weaken that position as far as was possible in a brief discussion amounting in all to a single sheet of paper, and I did my best to preserve a moderate tone. If the work is published, there should be no difficulty about getting a copy. But if publication is not permitted – and the decision has been in the hands of the Parlement now for three years[14] – then let the outcome be what it may: I commit it wholly to the providence of God. At any rate this may console you for the

75

80

85

* * * * *

10 This member of the Brethren of the Common Life (1469–1546), a native of Warneton near Comines, was a teacher at the Collège des Bons Enfants at Cambrai. His dialogues attacked the *Apologia* which the Paris theologian Jacques Merlin added to his edition of the works of Origen (Paris: Josse Bade 1512) to defend the orthodoxy of that Greek church Father. The dialogues were submitted to the Paris faculty of theology in January 1522, with Béda pressing hard for a formal condemnation of Merlin's *Apologia* and also for permission to publish Masseeuw's dialogue as well as his own refutation of Merlin. See Farge *Registre* 19 (19A) and 139 (156A) for evidence of the conflict. Contrary to the hope that Béda here expresses, litigation by Merlin in the Parlement of Paris succeeded in blocking publication of these attacks on him. On Merlin, one of the few Paris theologians who managed to withstand direct attacks by Béda, cf Allen Ep 1763:59n, and Farge *Biographical Register* 325–31 (no 343).
11 While Pope Gelasius I was only peripherally involved in the controversies over the orthodoxy of Origen, St Jerome shifted from being an admirer to being an outspoken foe of Origen (and of his contemporary supporter Rufinus). Cf NCE VIII 873–4 and X 773–4.
12 Cf Ep 934 introduction.
13 That is, Origen. What Béda finds objectionable is the contrast between Erasmus' praise for Origen's understanding of Scripture (eg, LB IX 97) and his occasionally critical remarks in the *Apologia* about opinions held by Jerome and Augustine (and other patristic and scholastic authorities).
14 On the litigation over Christiaan Masseeuw's attack on the *Apologia* for Origen by the theologian Jacques Merlin, see Walter F. Bense 'Noel Beda and the Humanist Reformation at Paris, 1504–1534' (unpublished PhD dissertation, Harvard University, 1967) 289–97, 416–23. Cf n10 above.

difficulty you experience in Paris in getting your *Paraphrases* or other writings approved for publication. If you would like to see my work, just ask me and I shall send it to you with that same charity which I show you in   90
other matters. I beg you, good brother, in the name of Christ, keep the promise which you made and penned with your own hand, and consider, I beseech you, what squabbles and endless bickering you are provoking by responding as you did in your first letter to the fraternal criticism and advice which I wished in all charity to offer you.   95

So in future when someone writes to you or against you, if he does so without good reason, my advice is to treat him as a fool and make no reply. But if his argument is convincing, and he is interested in your salvation and in purging your works of error (and there is much in them which needs the file, as you will realize if you read my annotations with an unprejudiced   100
mind, as you tell me you intend to do), then take his criticism as a gift from heaven and if courtesy demands a reply, do so in a few words. 'There is no easier way to make the truth crystal clear,' says the saintly Bernard, writing on the subject of advocates in the first book of his treatise to Eugenius, 'than to put the case simply and succinctly.'[15] I wish, dear brother and master,   105
you could observe for yourself how eager I am to see you. If you did, you would consider me your friend – I do not just think so, I am sure of it – for I see the dangers which threaten you more clearly than my own, although I have read few of your works and only because I was provoked to do so by public clamour. In fact I have never owned or read your *Annotationes*; I   110
have only seen the passages mentioned in the articles which I chose to discuss.[16] If my little notes seem somewhat insignificant to you – and I have no right to hope that you will be influenced by my opinion against the judgment of wiser men – send them to the bishop of Rochester,[17] whom I consider an outstanding theologian, or give them to other men of similar   115
ability, and say to them simply: 'Here are some extracts which a friend of mine has taken from my books and sent to me in Christian admonition; he

* * * * *

15 *De consideratione* 1.10, in *Opera omnia*, ed J. Leclercq, H. Talbot, and H.M. Rochais (Rome 1957–78) III 408:20–1; cf PL 182 740C.
16 A remarkably good example of a practice of the Paris conservatives that infuriated Erasmus and other humanists, namely, to judge a book on the basis of a number of isolated sentences extracted from it, without ever reading the book itself
17 John Fisher, a conservative theologian but also a friend and patron of Erasmus. Cf Ep 229 introduction. In Epp 1571 and 1581, Erasmus had vainly cited Fisher's favour as *prima facie* evidence that Béda's attacks on his orthodoxy were unfounded.

claims that most people would find them unacceptable. Like other men, I am blind in my own concerns. I beg you etc.'

If you will do this, I shall begin in the Lord to have great hopes for 120 you. I would not want to claim that each and every one of the propositions which I am sending should be utterly condemned. Many perhaps could be easily explained. All I want to do is to pass them on to you so that in your wisdom you will have a chance to consider them with the help of good and learned men. They contain, however, not a few statements which should by 125 no means be accepted. 'Bring all things to the test,' say the Scriptures, 'and hold fast that which is good.'[18] Farewell dear master and brother, whom I cherish and love with all my heart.

From my cell at Montaigu, 12 September 1525

Your friend, who remembers you before God in his prayers, Noël Béda 130

1610 / To Noël Béda [Basel, September] 1525

This letter is not a reply to the preceding one. It is undated, but the contents indicate that it must be from about this period. Allen Ep 1610 introduction, on the basis of other letters between these two men, suggests 24 August (Ep 1596) as the earliest possible date and 21 October (Ep 1642) as the latest possible date. The visit to Besançon to which it refers occurred more than a year earlier, in the spring of 1524. Erasmus included it in his *Opus epistolarum*.

ERASMUS OF ROTTERDAM TO NOËL BÉDA, GREETING
I gather from a letter which Pierre Richard[1] wrote to Ludwig Baer[2] that a nasty rumour has reached you about my departure from Besançon[3] and that Richard believes it to be true. That does not surprise me and certainly ought not to surprise you. Nevertheless I shall not let him remain any 5 longer under a misapprehension, for I am sure he is an honest man who has made an innocent mistake.

This is the story of my departure from Besançon. I shall tell it as it

* * * * *

18 1 Thess 5:21

1610
1 This Paris doctor of theology (documented c 1506–1554), a native of Moulins, was a contemporary of Ludwig Baer at both the Collège de Sainte-Barbe and the Sorbonne, and hence likely to correspond with Baer about happenings within the theological faculty, including discreditable rumours about Erasmus.
2 Cf Epp 488 introduction, 1571, 1581.
3 After 14 April and before 8 May 1524; cf Ep 1440 n4.

happened, without inventing or omitting anything. Ferry de Carondelet,[4] brother of the archbishop of Palermo[5] and archdeacon of the church at Besançon, had written frequently to invite me to visit him; in fact he wanted me to move in with him if that appealed to me. The good weather and the fresh beauty of the world in springtime made the prospect more inviting. So at last I mounted my horse and travelled to Porrentruy,[6] with the idea of paying my respects on the way to that venerable old man and model of all the virtues, Christoph, bishop of Basel.[7] In spite of his affectionate welcome I could spare him only one day; he would not let me leave, however, until I promised a longer visit on the way back. I gave him my word and set out, accompanied by my servants and by Thiébaut,[8] pastor of Porrentruy, Richard,[9] chaplain to the Reverend Father Nicolaus,[10] coadjutor to the bishop, and Father Ferriot,[11] a priest from the same town. After Clerval[12] we also had the company of a guest from the public inn.

When we were not far from Besançon, we met a priest, who had been escorting a lady and who now joined our party too. When I saw that he wanted to move ahead, I suspected Thiébaut of having revealed my name. I ordered the priest to come back and told him not to spread the rumour that I was on my way until I wished it known. We had spent many hours on horseback that day; the heat had been intense and I knew how exhausting those throngs of well-wishers could be. So I hoped to devote the night to the restoration of my poor old body. I lay down for a while before dinner. At nightfall dinner was served. In the middle of the meal the archdeacon's official came in,[13] accompanied by another man from the archdeacon's household. They expressed their pleasure at my arrival, and told

* * * * *

4 Cf Ep 1350 n6.
5 Jean Carondelet; cf Ep 803:12n.
6 From about 1519 this small town in the Jura was the usual residence of Christoph von Utenheim, bishop of Basel.
7 See Ep 598 introduction.
8 Biétry; see Ep 1391 introduction.
9 This letter is the only trace of this chaplain.
10 Nikolaus von Diesbach; cf Ep 1258 n17.
11 Georges Ferriot, a native of Porrentruy, was, together with Biétry, a priest of the Confrérie Saint-Michel there, and is attested in *Die Matrikel der Universität Basel* ed Hans Georg Wackernagel 5 vols (Basel 1951–62) I 227.
12 A small town, now in eastern France, approximately half-way between Erasmus' previous stop, Porrentruy, and his destination, Besançon.
13 Guillaume Guérard; see Ep 1534 n9.

us that the archdeacon was away on a visit to his abbey,[14] but had left
instructions with his servants that, if I arrived in his absence, the whole   35
house should be available to me until he himself hurried back. A message
was sent to the archdeacon informing him of my arrival. The same message
was also sent, without my knowledge, to the official of his Lordship, the
archbishop of Besançon; he too was out of town.

The following day two men arrived; one of them was a doctor of laws   40
whom I had once known at the emperor's court;[15] the other was a magistrate from the town and a relative of the archdeacon. They hovered around
the door for a long time, until I asked who they were and what they
wanted. I was told that they had come to pay their respects, but were
reluctant to address me, not wishing to be a nuisance. I asked that they be   45
invited in and we exchanged greetings. A little later, after hearing the office,
I went to the home of the archdeacon's official, intending to lie low there
until the archdeacon arrived. But immediately I had a visit from François,
the treasurer of the chapter and a young man of noble birth and exceptional
gifts.[16] He greeted me most courteously: you could see he was a person of   50
great liveliness and enthusiasm. I ordered a light meal to be prepared, but
with specific instructions that nothing except chicken be served and that no
one else be admitted. I did this out of consideration for my health. No one
else arrived except Thiébaut, my companion on the road, and Désiré,[17] a
learned and pious man, who was a canon in the church there. We had   55
dinner at the treasurer's house: only the official and Thiébaut were present.
While we were having dinner, the master of the school arrived,[18] and after
dinner the cantor of the church.[19]

The next day we visited part of the city and had lunch at the home of
the archdeacon's proctor, Antoine.[20] The treasurer was there and the offi-   60

* * * * *

14 In addition to being archdeacon of the chapter of Besançon, Ferry de Car-
   dondelet was commendatory abbot of Montbenoît, where he was active in
   restoring and expanding the buildings.
15 Allen Ep 1610:37n conjectures that this was Petrus Phoenix of Dôle, the probable recipient of Ep 1956.
16 François Bonvalot; cf Ep 1534 n10.
17 Désiré Morel; cf Ep 1534 n11.
18 Antoine Bercin (c 1490–1538), canon of Besançon; see Ep 2138 introduction.
19 The name of this person is not known.
20 At the home of this officer, who is not otherwise identified, occurred Erasmus'
   slighting remark during a servant's extended chain of invocations before dinner, one of which included a blessing in the name of 'beata viscera Mariae
   Virginis.' This incident, according to Erasmus, was being unjustly used at Paris

cial and Thiébaut and a priest whom I scarcely knew, but who seemed very attached to me. In the meantime the archdeacon had arrived and also the archbishop's official. The archdeacon tried to drag me off to have dinner with the official who had just returned. I pleaded fatigue and obliged the archdeacon to dine with me at the home of his own official.   65

By now the news of my visit had spread everywhere. The magistrate sent over a large supply of wine and oats as a gesture of respect. We had lunch at the archdeacon's: this time there was a larger number of guests: both officials were present along with Désiré, one or two of the canons, and the magistrate who had been the first to welcome me. There was a succession of gifts from   70
different people, special fish and Hippocratic wine,[21] but none of these were any use to me. We passed two or three days like this, with no dinner-parties except at the home of the archdeacon and the archbishop's official, who lived nearby. And although I kept complaining that, unless these dinner-parties were shorter and simpler, it would be the end of me, I nevertheless fell in with   75
their wishes, until I realized that an attack of phlegm was coming on, an ailment with which I am all too familiar.

The magistrate wanted to organize a great banquet in my honour, and would have done so, had I not protested that I was critically ill. All this time the canons were doing what they could to honour me. They made   80
arrangements for me to have a double prebend and promised I could hold it in perpetuity; to this they added a house and a sizable sum of money. The magistrate offered me an annuity of a hundred crowns.[22] I replied that, if I accepted all their gifts, this would not increase the debt I already owed them. In any case the only reason I had come to Besançon was to visit   85
my old friend the archdeacon. If I had known beforehand that he was going to be in his abbey, I would not even have come to Besançon. Moreover if I had to live there, I would prefer their good will to their benefactions because I was content with the little wealth I had and valued my indepen-

* * * * *

to suggest that an irreverent remark by him had scandalized those in attend-
ance. Cf Epp 1642:75–7; Allen Ep 1679:93–103, 1956:24–35.
21 Refers to wine carefully strained through a bag known as 'Hippocrates' sleeve' and hence thought to be of better quality. OED[2] sv 'hippocras' indicates that it can also mean a wine flavoured with spices.
22 Latin *centum coronatos annuos*. For the reasons noted in Ep 1434 n3, these 'crowns' were probably *écus d'or au soleil*, the French gold coin that displaced the *écu à la couronne* in 1475, and was now worth 40s tournois in France and 76d gros in the Hapsburg Netherlands (CWE 8 350). Thus this annuity would have been worth £200 tournois, or £31 13s 4d gros Flemish, or £21 7s 6d sterling.

dence more than money. On several occasions they invited the young choristers and the rest of the singers to sing for us and cheer our spirits.

By now the illness had gradually worsened to the point where, if I wanted to survive, I had to refuse all invitations to dinner. For three or four days I had my food in the bedroom. Lunch consisted of an egg and a small helping of chicken, cut very fine, and instead of wine I had water warmed with sugar. I did not talk even with the archdeacon, for the state of my health made it necessary to take precautions. At last when the worst of the fever had abated somewhat (for this too was part of the illness), I began to make preparations for departure; I did not want to remain in bed there and be a nuisance to people whom I did not know. I was sure the illness would last a long time, as it usually does. So when I felt strong enough to carry on a conversation, I asked someone to fetch the closest of my friends and I expressed my gratitude to them. The archdeacon had been called away on business, but on leaving he had given careful instructions for his home to be completely at my disposal.

The following day I ordered the horses to be got ready and I made it clear that I wished to avoid a large escort. When I left my room, three or four men had come in to pay their respects, one of whom was a Franciscan theologian. I mounted my horse. When I left the gate of the house, I met, among others, Master Antoine, dean of Montbéliard and canon of Besançon,[23] who greeted me most affectionately. As I passed the house of the archbishop's official, he was there himself seated on a mule and the treasurer was with him. Despite my protests, they insisted on accompanying me through the middle of the town and went with me for as much as two miles. The horse I was riding was no magnificent beast, but it suited me well enough. The official kept pressing me to get up on his mule; he wanted me to take his servant with me so that he could bring the animal back. I had great difficulty in putting him off. Eventually I reached Basel without offending anyone or taking offence, except that, because of my ill health, I had inconvenienced the friends whom I wanted to please, and could not enjoy the company of those for whose sake I had made the journey.

Now you have the whole story exactly as it happened, with not a syllable of additional embellishment. But in case I leave the impression that I am concealing something, I shall also tell you about the rumours that followed my departure. Someone wrote to Thiébaut from Montbéliard to tell

* * * * *

23 Antoine Montrivel of Besançon (d 1534) held prebends at both Besançon and Montbéliard and was of considerable importance in ecclesiastical administration.

him of a rumour which some people were circulating (I don't know who they were), to the effect that, when I left Besançon, I was on bad terms with everyone. I wondered what this embarrassing situation could be; so I asked Thiébaut to make inquiries. He did so and discovered that there had been 130 some itinerant Lutherans at Besançon when I was there – these people, you know, are to be found everywhere. They had taken offence at my *Spongia*, which had just recently appeared, because I had attacked Hutten, the great defender of the gospel; so they had begun to attack me like gibbering idiots (they were Germans), and it was they who were responsible for spreading 135 this rumour, which has absolutely no foundation. Later Thiébaut came to Basel. I fished around to find out what was going on. He replied that it was only the ravings of some sniveling nonentities who had spread those rumours among their vulgar friends. Shortly afterward Thiébaut went to Besançon and without any difficulty obtained a commission from the arch- 140 bishop on my recommendation. On his return I asked him what had been going on. He told me it was nothing except the ranting of one or two boorish Lutherans. I questioned my servants and those who had accom- panied me to see if they had had a disagreement with anyone. They denied talking to anyone except those miserable Lutheran vagabonds. In the present 145 state of things I cannot go anywhere without many people getting excited over rumours and I cannot leave without attracting a large escort, which is something I find particularly trying. And amid all the conflicting interests, there will inevitably be people who will spread nasty stories about me. But such rumours, being without foundation, fade away quickly. Could any- 150 thing be more hurtful than an evil tongue? In no age has that scourge ever been more powerful than our own. Anyone who could elude the tooth of slander would be a fortunate man indeed, and no person of distinction could do so in these times.

Since this is the truth and I can prove it with many witnesses, I cannot 155 understand what people mean when they talk about 'the things that hap- pened to Erasmus at Besançon.'[24] Nothing happened to me except what I have told you. Your expression shows clearly that someone with a vicious tongue has acquainted you with that false and wicked rumour. There is

* * * * *

24 This whole passage is puzzling, as is Erasmus' eagerness in subsequent letters (Epp 1679, 1956) to provide further exculpatory details about his visit to Besançon, especially since no surviving letter of Béda makes accusations against Erasmus except for displeasure at Erasmus' impatient remarks about an excessively long dinner invocation. Cf Béda's cool reaction in Ep 1642:73–9, a letter which appears to postdate this one.

nothing strange or remarkable in that. But it ill befits a theologian to take   160
notice of such things, or if he takes notice, to mention it in a letter as sure
and certain fact.

In the year 1525

1611 / To Willibald Pirckheimer   Basel, 20 September 1525

This brief note to the eminent Nürnberg humanist was first printed in *Pirck-heimeri opera* (1610).

Cordial greetings, most honoured Willibald. I am delighted that you are
well. I sent a letter by Froben,[1] whom I expect to bring a letter from you.
No corner of the world can escape this present turmoil. Where this gospel
will lead us, I do not know. For me at any rate it has brought nothing but
disaster, so far as this world's happiness is concerned. I am sorry about   5
Ceratinus.[2] I was afraid he would forget the advice he was given and
embarrass his supporter. So it is with most of those who profess the new
gospel. But Christ will reconcile all things to himself. This young man[3]
brought me your letter; he is remarkably modest and unassuming. Give my
greetings to Dürer[4] and the doctor.[5]   10

Basel, the eve of St Matthew 1525
To the honourable Willibald Pirckheimer, councillor of Nürnberg

1612 / From Michel Boudet   Mussy, 20 September [1525]

Boudet (1469–1529), bishop of Langres, was an influential figure at the French

* * * * *

1611
1 Probably Ep 1603, dated at about the time when Froben would have been
   departing for the Frankfurt book fair.
2 On this Dutch humanist cf Ep 622:34n. Erasmus had played an active role in
   getting him appointed professor of Greek at Leipzig (cf Ep 1561 n3) and was
   naturally disappointed when he left after only a few months. Apparently Duke
   George of Saxony became dissatisfied with him when he was accused of trying
   to conceal his status as a priest (in fact he was not ordained until 1527), and
   Erasmus here concluded that his Protestant sympathies were the cause for the
   brevity of his tenure at Leipzig.
3 Not identified
4 Erasmus regularly sent greetings to the famous Nürnberg artist in his letters
   to Pirckheimer.
5 Paulus Ricius; cf Ep 548:16n. He was probably already acting as physician to
   Archduke Ferdinand, in whose service he eventually was raised to noble rank.

court and a patron of Guillaume Budé and many other French humanists. He
was interested in theological studies, especially Greek patristics. He became
bishop in 1511 and almoner to Queen Claude in 1516. In 1523 he was one of
three bishops appointed by the king to scrutinize (in a pro-humanist sense) the
investigation of the works of Erasmus, Lefèvre d'Etaples, and Berquin undertaken by the Paris theological faculty at the urging of Noël Béda. This letter
acknowledges Erasmus' gift of a copy of his *Lingua*. Despite its warmth and
the distinguished rank of the writer, Erasmus never published it; it was first
printed by Förstemann and Günther in 1904.

When you sent me your *Tongue*, most learned Erasmus, you revealed your
heart – at least that part of it which was open to view. The tongue is indeed
a great index of the heart. You honoured me with your tongue and presented me with your *Tongue*. How, then, shall I respond to all your
kindnesses? We shall honour you not simply for a golden tongue that has   5
brought you universal renown for grace of language and grandeur of
phrase, but because your tongue is truly divine. For when you plunged into
the fountains of Holy Scripture, such an abundant stream of never-failing
water flowed from your lips that the whole Christian world is refreshed by
it and made fertile and fruitful. I pray that God may fulfil for our leaders   10
the noble prayer which you offered in the concluding paragraph of your
Tongue,[1] and that he may ordain for you a long and happy life crowned
with success. If there is anything you desire, I shall do all that so dear and
agreeable a friend deserves. Farewell.

    From my palace at Mussy on the eve of St Matthew   15
    Your friend, Michel, bishop of Langres
    To that great scholar, Erasmus of Rotterdam

1613 / From Juan Luis Vives   Bruges, 20 September 1525

On this prominent Spanish humanist see Ep 927 introduction. At this period
Vives was living part of the time in England, where he was close to the royal
court and its circle of humanists, and part of the time in Bruges, where he had
married in 1524. The letter reflects the belief of Erasmus' friends in the Nether-

* * * * *

1612
1 Erasmus concludes the *Lingua* with a prayer that the leaders of church and
  state be granted a powerful tongue and the people a docile heart (CWE 29 412
  / ASD IV-1 370 / LB IV 752F).

Juan Luis Vives
Collection Duque del Infantado
Photo: MAS

lands that he was about to return there in order to secure payment of his imperial pension. It also illustrates Vives' importance as a source of political and other news from England. It was first published in Vives' *Opera* 2 vols (Basel: Nicolaus Episcopius 1555) II 970.

VIVES TO ERASMUS

I shall not write at great length because I don't know if you are already off on your travels. There was a rumour abroad that you had already reached Cologne by the first of September. That rumour faded, but a second sprang up, inspired, it is claimed, by a letter from your own hand, that you will be 5 here by the first of October. I pray that whatever you decide turns out well for you. I wrote a reply to your last letter and gave it to Pieter Gillis.[1] I am sure it reached you, at least during the recent Frankfurt fair.

If Froben has decided against publishing my *Opuscula*,[2] I wish he would return them. I hear that printing has begun on the Augustine.[3] 10 Please let me know for certain if this is so. If it is, I shall send Froben a few revisions to my commentary on the *City of God* – they are quite brief, covering no more than three sheets in all.

* * * * *

1613
1 Cf Epp 184 introduction, 1541 introduction. Although no longer in charge of Erasmus' financial affairs, Gillis still was helpful in transmitting letters from the Netherlands to Erasmus in Basel.
2 There is no evidence that the Froben press published such an edition, which appears to have been proposed by Froben's associate Franz Birckmann (cf Ep 1513 n17). His *Opuscula varia* were published at Louvain by Dirk Martens (NK 2172), probably in 1520; and Peter Schoeffer of Strasbourg brought out a different collection, *Opuscula aliquot vere catholica*, in 1521. The context does not make it quite clear whether the proposed edition was to be a reprint of the Louvain edition, of the Strasbourg edition, or of other works.
3 At Erasmus' urging, Vives edited St Augustine *De civitate Dei*, with an extensive commentary, published by Froben in 1522. Although Erasmus had a generally high opinion of Vives' scholarship, he was sharply critical of this edition, complaining that the excessive length of the commentary was hurting sales (Epp 1531, 1889). Despite the offer here made by Vives to send a few emendations for use when his edition was incorporated into the projected collection of all of Augustine's works, when volume 5 of that collection came out in 1529 under Erasmus' general editorship, Erasmus had made some textual changes on his own and had omitted *all* of Vives' commentary and prefaces. Vives' name appeared only on the title-page.

There is news that England has made peace with France.[4] I think this is the best possible time for you to visit your old friends again. As for my own plans, I shall not go to England before next year. The bearer of this letter is a merchant from Genoa[5] who has a very high regard for you and is most anxious to meet you. I hope we shall soon see you here in good health and spirits: it would be to your advantage to come. Farewell.

20 September 1525

1614 / To Otto Brunfels   Basel, [September ?] 1525

> This chilly letter is a reply to a letter now lost, in which Brunfels attempted to heal the breach caused by his defence in 1523 of Ulrich von Hutten against Erasmus' *Spongia*. Cf Ep 1405 introduction and Ep 1406, which contains the text of Brunfels' remarkably candid attack on Erasmus. Both the Hutten incident and Brunfels' open adherence to Lutheranism ruled out a return to the earlier close friendship between the two men, but henceforth they did maintain civil relations, and Erasmus included this letter in his *Opus epistolarum*.

ERASMUS OF ROTTERDAM TO OTTO BRUNFELS, GREETING
What a fantastic notion to have entered your head! Pierre Cousturier, who was once a theologian at the Sorbonne and is now a Carthusian at Champagne in France, wrote a violent polemic against me, in which he asserted that all new translations were heretical and blasphemous and that the classical languages and liberal studies generally were the root of all evil.[1] I wrote a reply, though I was careful to confine my strictures to the man himself; indeed I would not have replied at all if the book had not been dedicated to the faculty of theology at the Sorbonne and published with the approval of the theologians of Paris. I have no intention, however, of attacking you; on the contrary I have repeatedly written to a man of considerable learning and eloquence, who, my friends tell me, is preparing a reply to your polemic against me, and I have implored him by all that is sacred, if

* * * * *

4 Negotiators for England and France signed a definitive treaty on 30 August (LP IV, part 1).
5 Allen Ep 1613:16n surmises that this was Lazarus a Parentibus, to whom Erasmus addressed a letter in 1527 (Ep 1818).

1614
1 On this ultra-conservative Paris critic of Erasmus, cf Ep 1571 n10, and Ep 1591, Erasmus' preface to his *Adversus Petri Sutoris ... debacchationem*.

he has not yet begun to write, not to do so, and if he has begun, to tear up whatever he has written, if he wishes to please me and keep me as his friend. I only wish you had developed that aversion towards 'female tantrums,' as you call them, before you published that pamphlet, and that you had allowed yourself to be guided by good sense instead of by men who seek advancement for themselves at the cost of the discomfiture of others. I wish too that Hutten had paid more attention to my letters – I wrote to him several times in a most friendly spirit and tried to warn him that the publication of such a book would damage both our reputations and provide a spectacle which would be greeted enthusiastically by certain blockheads among the enemies of letters.

As for your willingness to forget all your disagreements with me, I see no reason to feel under any obligation to you, at least not on that score. For I never did you any injury, and I had a very different opinion of you before you revealed your true nature in that pamphlet. You would serve your own interests better if you abandoned that fierce spirit of yours for true Christian gentleness and moderation. Even the conciliatory letter which you sent me is full of threats.[2] You did not even manage to avoid abuse, and all because of an unfounded suspicion which arose from the mere mention of the name Cousturier and of a man of the Carthusian order. Ordinary common sense would have told you that you ought to have got a grip on the facts of the case before resorting to threats and vilification. I have never rejected any man's friendship and I have never given anyone cause to hate me. But it is difficult to remain on friendly terms with people who are so tetchy and truculent. You promise to adopt a more Christian attitude: when you show evidence of it, you will have my felicitations. As for your friendly offices, I neither court nor spurn them. You will be a good enough friend to me when you have learned to be a friend to yourself. The only service I want from you is that you stop damaging the reputation of others. This is all you can do. It is not a hard request which I make of you, especially in the present circumstances. Farewell.

Basel, 1525

1615 / To Margaret of Angoulême   Basel, 28 September 1525

At this date, Margaret (1492–1549), sister of King Francis I of France, was not yet queen of Navarre, but rather the recently widowed spouse of Charles, duke of Alençon. The 'storm of troubles' to which Erasmus refers in the first

* * * * *

2 Not extant; cf introduction.

Marguerite D'Angoulême
Bibliothèque Nationale, Paris

sentence included not only this bereavement but also the death of her sister-in-law Queen Claude in 1524, and most especially the defeat and capture of her adored brother at the battle of Pavia in February. Margaret had been carefully educated and was a major patron (indeed, *the* major patron) of humanists and other literary figures at court. She had come under the influence of the reformist bishop of Meaux, Guillaume Briçonnet, and the humanist Jacques Lefèvre d'Etaples. Strongly inclined to mystical spirituality from her youth, she became an influential protector of French evangelicals as well as humanists, though she was never fully committed to the incipient French Reformation. Despite Erasmus' admiration for her and one other recorded attempt (Ep 1854) to initiate a regular correspondence, she replied only indirectly and held aloof from him, apparently because she thought his approach to religion too rationalistic and too little sensitive to the need for grace. The standard biography is Pierre Jourda *Marguerite d'Angoulême, duchesse d'Alençon, reine de Navarre (1492–1549)* (Paris 1930). Erasmus included this letter in his *Opus epistolarum*.

ERASMUS OF ROTTERDAM TO MARGARET, QUEEN OF NAVARRE,
GREETING

The admirers of your great virtues have urged me often in their letters to write something which might console your Highness at this time when you are buffeted by such a storm of troubles. So when the bearer of this letter[1]   5
unexpectedly appeared, a man both learned and distinguished, and I discovered that he was travelling directly to Spain, but had to rush off without delay, I debated with myself whether it would be better to say nothing at all or jot down a brief informal note. In the end the warm feelings which I have for you overcame my shyness and timidity; for I have long admired   10
and revered the many splendid gifts with which God has endowed you: learning of which even a philosopher might be proud, chastity, self-control, a devout nature, an indomitable strength of will, and a remarkable contempt for all transient things. Who would not admire such qualities in the sister of a mighty king, qualities which are rarely to be found among priests and   15
monks? I would not mention these things if I were not certain that you impute nothing to your own strength, but ascribe all praise to the Lord, who is the giver of every good gift. So it is more to congratulate than

* * * * *

1615
1 Not identified here, but probably Pierre Toussain (cf Ep 1559 introduction). The letter was intended to follow Margaret to Spain, where she had gone to negotiate for the release of her brother.

console you that I have taken up my pen. I know how bitter is the disaster which has befallen you. But in this world nothing is so terrible that it can shake a soul whose anchor is truly fixed on that immovable rock, which is Christ Jesus.

You may wonder how it is that I know you when I have never set eyes on you; but many who have never had the good fortune to see your Highness know you from your portrait. In my case letters from some honest and learned men have given me a much clearer picture of your mind than any painter, with all the colours of his palette, could provide of your person. There is no reason to doubt my good faith. I praise and esteem you for what I know you to be: I do not flatter you because of your position. I have nothing in mind except mutual friendship. I have long been a friend of his most Christian Majesty, or rather I returned his friendship, since it was he who took the initiative and encouraged me in so many ways to be his friend. So I cannot help but revere in the Lord such a brave and noble woman as yourself. I owe the emperor not just my support, but my allegiance – and I have more than one reason for feeling as I do: in the first place I was born in his realm, and secondly many years ago I was sworn in before him as a councillor. Yet I wish his victory had been won over the Turks.[2] What rejoicing there would have been throughout the world if the two greatest monarchs on the earth had made peace and joined their arms to repel the assaults of the enemy on Christ's kingdom. That was the prayer which burned so fiercely in our hearts. But it was our sinfulness, I believe, which blocked the way: God did not judge us worthy of such grace.

Thus far I have been unable to give the emperor my wholehearted congratulations on his victory, splendid though it may have been; but there is every hope that soon you and your beloved France may have as much reason as the emperor to rejoice in this terrible upheaval, however it may have come about. For this is the way of that great designer who guides with unseen hand the destinies of men: often when all seems lost, he turns our defeats into glorious victory. My hope is based first and foremost on the clemency of God, who hears our prayers and, I believe, has already begun to show his mercy towards us; but I am encouraged also, in part by the character of the emperor, whose gentleness equals or surpasses the greatness of his fortune, and in part by the wonderfully accommodating spirit of his most Christian Majesty. Indeed, I feel confident that already a solid and binding agreement has been made between them.

* * * * *

2 The smashing victory of the imperial army over the French at Pavia the previous February, leading to the captivity of King Francis I

These hopes of mine were fortified by the letter which your Highness
sent to the eminent Polish Baron, Jan Łaski,[3] when you were preparing to
set out for Spain. He is living with me in the same house and we share all
things in common by virtue of our friendship. Not only does your letter
make it clear that the cruel blows of fate have not broken your spirit, but   60
it contains some encouraging remarks which have eased our worries. If we
are not deceived in these hopes, then we shall have reason to congratulate
the whole Christian world, not just the emperor and yourselves.

Now I must beg your pardon on two grounds, first for taking the
liberty of writing uninvited to such an exalted lady as yourself, and second-   65
ly for writing in haste, a liberty which an ordinary citizen would scarcely
allow himself when writing to a close friend. But I felt so convinced of the
wonderful generosity of your spirit that any uneasiness which I had on this
score was banished from my mind. May the Lord Jesus keep you safe and
make you abound in him with the true riches of his blessing!   70

Basel, Michaelmas eve 1525

1616 / To Claudius Cantiuncula   [Basel, c September 1525]

A response to a letter (now lost) in which the Metz humanist and jurist urged
Erasmus to write in opposition to Oecolampadius' recent work on the Eucharist (see n4 below). On Cantiuncula cf Ep 852:85n. He taught civil law at Basel
from 1518 to 1524, when he moved back to Metz, probably because of the
growth of Protestantism at Basel. By the time of this letter, he was probably
already established at Vic-sur-Seille in the service of the absentee bishop of
Metz, Cardinal Jean de Lorraine, and he later served as a high-ranking official
for Duke Antoine de Lorraine and King Ferdinand I. Erasmus included this
letter in his *Opus epistolarum*.

ERASMUS OF ROTTERDAM TO CLAUDIUS CANTIUNCULA, DOCTOR
OF LAWS, GREETING
How I envy you your good fortune in having the leisure to write letters like
that! I don't even have time to read the letters I receive. There is no doubt
about it, my dear Cantiuncula, everything you write is striking and impres-   5
sive and shows a fine command of language. You would be the perfect

* * * * *

3 The young Polish humanist, unlike Erasmus himself, had formed close personal ties to Margaret and the intellectual and spiritual circles around her. He
   probably received her letter during the six months of 1525 that he spent living
   with Erasmus at Basel. Cf Epp 1341A n319, 1593 n18.

orator if only your theme were not wholly impracticable and ill-founded.
Perhaps the strength of your feelings and your immense enthusiasm for the
cause have carried you away, and you have therefore come to believe that
what you are so eager to see done is easy to do; or perhaps you are so   10
blinded by affection for me that you take me for an elephant[1] when I am
nothing but a fly. Do you really believe that there is nothing which I do not
know? Both sides believe – and their belief is well founded – that there is
nothing which I *do* know. Can I accomplish by myself what the emperor,
the pope, and whole multitudes of theologians cannot accomplish? Will the   15
world accept me as its sole authority, when even the theologians' dogs piss
on me as they pass? You appeal to me to end the schism, as if that conflagration had not been out of control for a long time now. You reproach me
for my silence, as though I had never dared to raise my voice against these
tragic evils which engulf the world, or never tried to settle the conflict on   20
fair terms – and all without success, though not without danger to myself.

I had begun something on the Eucharist before your letter arrived.[2]
But I have so little free time that I have not yet read your letter through
myself, though Count Łaski[3] read it aloud to me after lunch. Oecolampadius' book also remains unread through lack of time.[4] What you   25
seem to have in mind is that I should take on the responsibility of pro-
nouncing judgment on the whole issue, regardless of the fact that both sides

* * * * *

1616
1 *Adagia* I ix 69
2 If this is true, Erasmus never completed such a work. Oecolampadius' book on
  the Eucharist was an important early statement of what came to be known as
  the Sacramentarian position, and this and other religious differences had
  created tension between him and Erasmus. In reality, from about this period,
  though Erasmus continued to criticize Oecolampadius in private letters, he
  carefully refrained from public criticism of his former friend. Allen Ep 1616:17n
  conjectures that Erasmus' failure to continue his own work on the Eucharist
  was part of a private agreement between him and the Basel Protestant leaders,
  Pellicanus and Oecolampadius, whereby each side refrained from open attacks
  on the other. In any case, writing on such a delicate subject would have been
  risky for his relations with Catholics as well as Protestants.
3 Jan Łaski, who was living in Erasmus' house at this period. Cf Ep 1615 n3 and
  the other citations given there.
4 *De genuina verborum Domini 'Hoc est corpus meum' iuxta vetustissimos authores
  expositione liber* (n p, n pr, but probably Strasbourg, no later than mid-Septem-
  ber 1525). Cf Ernst Staehelin *Das theologische Lebenswerk Johannes Oekolampads*
  Quellen und Forschungen zur Reformationsgeschichte XXI (Leipzig 1939) 276–7
  and [Ernest] Gordon Rupp *Patterns of Reformation* (Philadelphia 1969) 25.

are attacking each other like gladiators and each is racked by internal conflict. Suppose I had the time, suppose also that I did not lack the knowledge necessary for so important an issue, what hope of success can you   30
hold out before me? Shall I come down on the side of the theologians? But which theologians, those north or south of the Alps? Or shall I give my support to the other side? But to whom, to Luther's followers or Zwingli's[5] (for I hear that Karlstadt has decided on a retraction)?[6] Or should I play the impartial judge and settle the dispute by avoiding both extremes? But what   35
am I likely to accomplish by that? Shall I not suffer the usual fate of those who try to interfere between implacable foes – to be clobbered by both sides?

That is all I can say for the present in response to your eloquent appeal. It reflects a nimble mind and a fluent tongue, which I respect and   40
admire; as for your misunderstanding of my position, I take it in good part as kindly meant. But I wish you had chosen some other subject on which to exercise your pen. For this is the kind of praise which is heaped on me by those who want to see me destroyed. We can talk about the rest whenever you wish, but come in the afternoon; for this is the only time I can set   45
aside for my friends. Farewell.

†1526†

1617 / From Lucas Bathodius   Strasbourg, 1 October 1525

On the author of this appeal for a bowdlerized Erasmian version of the plays of Terence, see Ep 883:15n. The letter survived in manuscripts at Leipzig and Strasbourg but was not published until the edition by Förstemann and Günther in 1904.

TO MASTER ERASMUS OF ROTTERDAM, GREETING
I do not know, most learned Erasmus, if the prayers of the uneducated will carry any weight with you, but I am putting shame aside and venturing to

* * * * *

5 The split between Luther and Zwingli over the presence of Christ's body in the Eucharist had become evident by late 1524. Cf Mark U. Edwards, jr *Luther and the False Brethren* (Stanford, California 1975) 82–4.
6 Andreas Karlstadt had sought reconciliation with Luther by June 1525, perhaps even earlier, and by late that month had secretly come to live in Luther's house at Wittenberg. On 25 July he signed a partial recantation of his Sacramentarian eucharistic opinions (cf Edwards *Luther and the False Brethren* 74–80), but their accord later broke down, and in 1529 Karlstadt fled from Saxony, spending his last years as professor of Old Testament at Basel.

thrust myself upon you, though a man of your eminence is doubtless occupied with more important things. I do not wish to plead for myself, for I   5
have been called to another kind of ministry, namely to the care of the poor,
which will not leave me much time in future for literary pursuits. I approach you rather on behalf of young Christian students, for whom I want
to provide a sound and effective training in the Latin language. I am aware
that in your book entitled *De ratione studii*[1] you argued that students should   10
be initiated into Latin and that the presentation should be not just scholarly
but kind and affectionate; nevertheless some of the authors mentioned in
that work as suitable for presentation to the young and innocent do not
meet Christian standards of moral purity.[2] However fine they may be in
other respects, they are likely to cause frequent offence unless something is   15
supplied to counteract their influence. They may be excellent as models for
correct speech and useful for ordinary conversation, but their subject-matter
is too indecent, not to say silly, to be fit and proper reading for students at
this stage; their very excellences, in my opinion, make these works all the
more harmful, no matter how exquisitely decorated the package may be. (I   20
hope, most learned sir, you will pardon an ignoramus!) Of all these writers
I have noticed that Terence has the unique capacity to supply everything
which a child needs in order to acquire an elegant and fluent command of
the spoken language, but is so full of passages of the kind which I have
mentioned that, unless you rob the comedy of all its grace, the child will not   25
grasp the meaning without risk of harm. We know what happens: the
student learns to fall in love with girls rather than with literature. So what
begins as an interest in literature, because of the poor judgment of the kind
of schoolmaster of whom this age has more than enough, ends in moral
depravity.   30

* * * * *

1617
1 This guide to literary and linguistic studies, first published in an unauthorized
  and incomplete edition of 1511, received a corrected and authorized edition in
  1512, followed by two more that year and many others thereafter. On the   35
  complex history of its publication, see Ep 66 introduction and the introduction
  by Jean-Claude Margolin in ASD I-2 89–96.
2 Erasmus' book recommends the study of specific Greek and Latin authors; and
  among the latter, Terence is the most highly recommended (ASD I-2 115–6 /
  CWE 24 669 / LB I 521). Later on in the text, Erasmus explicitly deals with how   40
  a good teacher should guide a class in reading Terence. He is by no means
  insensitive to moral questions involved in teaching these texts, but he shows
  no inclination to bowdlerize them as Bathodius here suggests.

You are the only person I can think of who can supply what is needed to cure this disease: each of the comedies will have to be clothed with more respectable episodes, and salacious scenes replaced with something more uplifting.[3] That you have the ability to do this is amply proven by the great works of learning which you have left us; that you should also have the will 35 is the prayer of every young scholar, as it is my own; that you have an obligation to act is something which your Christian conscience will tell you. Good men have long been convinced that you, who are the sole champion and restorer of the ruined house of literature, were born for such a task. Farewell.   40

Strasbourg, 1 October in the year of our redemption through Christ 1525

Lucas Bathodius, deacon in the church at Strasbourg

To the most illustrious Master Erasmus of Rotterdam, the greatest champion of the greatest literature   45

1618 / To Michel Boudet   Basel, 2 October 1525

A reply to Ep 1612 but, unlike it, published by Erasmus himself in his *Opus epistolarum*. Despite the promise implied here that he would write against Oecolampadius' opinion on the Eucharist, it is likely that Erasmus had no intention of completing and publishing whatever work on that subject he may have begun. Cf Ep 1616 nn2 and 4.

ERASMUS OF ROTTERDAM TO MICHEL BOUDET, BISHOP OF
LANGRES, GREETING
Reverend bishop, the letter you sent me, brief in expression but remarkable in the force of its ideas, showed me how sober and lively your mind is and what unusual powers of judgment it possesses. Now that I have sent off my 5 *Tongue*,[1] I have become more tongue-tied than I used to be; so I have begun to practise the laconic style – and I have your example to guide me. These days one would have to be born of the white hen to write without offend-

* * * * *

3 In other words, the text must be altered to eliminate morally questionable passages.

1618
1 Erasmus' recently published treatise, *Lingua*. Ep 1612 was Bishop Boudet's acknowledgment of the author's gift of a copy.

ing somebody.[2] I only wish it were possible to keep silent. But a new doctrine has raised its head, that there is nothing in the Eucharist except bread   10
and wine.[3] Johannes Oecolampadius has made the notion difficult to refute
by buttressing it with so much evidence and so many arguments that even
the elect are likely to be led astray.[4] I must put aside the lute and take up
the sword or it will appear from my silence that I am casting my vote on
their side like some humble back-bencher.[5] I am very pleased that my   15
Lingua has found favour with so distinguished a person as yourself. But
what was the point in showering so many gold pieces on the courier?[6] He
was not a servant of mine, but someone whom I hired for four crowns[7] to
carry letters back and forth.

The bearer of this letter is a young man called Pierre Toussain.[8] He   20
comes from a good family in his own country, has a generous nature, and
is learned beyond the common run. He is passionately interested in Greek,
but all such studies are moribund here. He is not asking for anything. I only
wanted you to get to know him. On some other occasion I shall show my
gratitude for your generous interest in me, which goes beyond anything I   25
deserve. May the Lord keep your Excellency safe.

Basel, 2 October 1525

* * * * *

2 To be born of the white hen is proverbial for good luck; cf *Adagia* I i 78.
3 The new 'Sacramentarian' interpretations of the Eucharist, expressed by Karlstadt, Zwingli, and (most recently) Oecolampadius
4 Matt 24:24. This passage subtly implies Erasmus' private conviction that scriptural evidence supporting some kind of spiritual rather than corporeal presence of Christ in the Eucharist was very strong.
5 Literally, 'Lest I seem by remaining silent to cast a vote on foot.' The phrase
   'to cast a vote on foot' is classical, but its origin is uncertain (see Gellius 3.18).
   The phrase came to refer to junior senators of inferior rank, who habitually
   avoided speaking out on controversial issues. Cf *Adagia* I x 79.
6 Cf Ep 1597 n11.
7 Latin *quatuor coronatis*. Undoubtedly the French gold *écu au soleil*, and thus a
   sum worth £8 tournois or £1 5s 4d gros Flemish. See Epp 1434 n3, 1545 n6,
   1610 n22, and CWE 8 350.
8 Cf Ep 1559 introduction. This is a good example of Erasmus' willingness to
   promote the careers of promising young scholars despite their attraction to the
   opinions of Protestant theologians (in this case, Oecolampadius) with whom
   he disagreed.

1619 / To Guillaume Budé   Basel, 2 October 1525

In recommending the bearer of this letter, Pierre Toussain, to Budé, Erasmus
was placing him in the hands of France's greatest Hellenist. The reference to
Budé's 'kicking a man when he is down' apparently refers to a lost reply to
Ep 1601 in which Budé must have jested with Erasmus over the long list of
calamities enumerated in that letter and must have suggested that Erasmus
would have done better if he had accepted the royal invitation to settle in
France. On Toussain, see Ep 1559 introduction. Erasmus published this letter
in his *Opus epistolarum*.

ERASMUS OF ROTTERDAM TO GUILLAUME BUDÉ, GREETING
Budé, my honoured friend, you are indeed a cruel fellow! You kick a man
when he is down instead of consoling him in his distress. You reproach me
for delays and hesitations and procrastinations. A man can bear his misery
better if it is not his own doing, but arises from the injustice of fate. At any   5
rate I congratulate you on your great good fortune in having time to yourself: I hope one day your time will be completely your own so that your
happiness may be complete.
      The bearer of this letter is a young man of good family called Pierre
Toussain. He has great ability and a generous nature and I expect splendid   10
things of him. He is passionately interested in Greek, but at Basel only
Glareanus teaches Greek,[1] and poverty prevents him from doing justice
either to himself or to students of this calibre. I am sure you will be
delighted by this young man's qualities and, if I know your good heart, you
will do all that one might expect from a great prince of letters, even without   15
anyone asking you. Farewell.
      My friend Toussain will tell you the rest of my news.
      Basel, 2 October 1525

            * * * * *

1619
 1 On this scholar, whom Erasmus regarded as the outstanding Swiss humanist
   of the day, see Ep 440 introduction. From 1522 to 1529 he lived and taught in
   Basel. This letter reflects the disruption of university study throughout German-speaking lands by the early Reformation, which initially turned many
   young men against all academic pursuits, even humanistic studies. This caused
   a sharp decline in enrolments at Basel and hence greatly reduced Glareanus'
   income from student fees. See Otto Fridolin Fritzsche *Glarean: Sein Leben und
   seine Schriften* (Frauenfeld 1890) 44–5; Mark Sieber 'Glarean in Basel' *Jahrbuch
   des Historischen Vereins des Kantons Glarus* 60 (1963) 69; Edgar Bonjour *Die
   Universität Basel* (Basel 1971) 111.

1620 / To Noël Béda　　　　　　　　　Basel, 2 October 1525

A reply to Ep 1609 and a further item in the outwardly polite but intensely
hostile correspondence with the ultra-conservative syndic of the Paris faculty
of theology. On this exchange cf Ep 1571 introduction. The two letters mentioned in the opening sentence are Epp 1581 and 1596. Béda himself published
this and most of the letters of this correspondence in his *Apologia aduersus
clandestinos Lutheranos* (1529), adding an introduction (the Latin text is
excerpted in Allen VI 180) that accused Erasmus of being unwilling to recant
his errors in spite of his claims to the contrary. Erasmus also published it the
same year in his *Opus epistolarum*.

TO THE MOST ACCOMPLISHED THEOLOGIAN, MASTER NOËL BÉDA,
MY MOST RESPECTED BROTHER, CORDIAL GREETINGS
I am very glad that that long-winded letter of mine was not delivered by
itself, since it seems to have hurt your feelings. I wrote it with you only in
mind and I was so convinced of your generous nature that I was sure you　　5
would not resent my frankness – or 'bluntness,' if that is how you would
prefer to put it. You are right when you say that timely advice is the first
obligation of friendship, but friends should recognize this obligation as
mutual. A man as erudite as you may need no advice from me; nevertheless
even a vegetable-grower has often said things which are very apropos.[1]　　10
Moreover conscientious advice, even if it fails of its purpose, should be
applauded since it shows a desire to help. I am delighted to have the annotations which you were kind enough to send. I wish you had also sent me
a list of the points which you found so offensive in my letter to the bishop
of Basel,[2] and also the copy of the book which you are trying to have　　15
published. The courier was absolutely reliable. I had hired him personally
at a very fair wage for this very purpose. Still, whatever you have
addressed to Konrad,[3] the bookseller here, will reach me safely. It is important that anything you send be covered with a wrapper and tied with

* * * * *

1620
1 *Adagia* I vi 1.
2 His *Epistola de esu carnium*; cf Ep 1274 n7 and the text with introduction by
　Cornelis Augustijn in ASD IX-1 1–50.
3 Konrad Resch, at this period one of the official booksellers to the University
　of Paris, also active in Basel, and because of this business connection especially
　useful for transmitting letters between the two cities. Cf Ep 330:15n.

string and sealed. That does not require much effort. I find your secretary's   20
hand difficult to read, but I manage.

It would save you some trouble if you confined your criticisms to
points of Christian doctrine and to errors which you regard as inexcusable.
In your first point you criticize something which you have inferred from my
words, namely that not all letters ascribed to Paul are indisputably Paul's.[4]   25
I see no reason why you should find fault with this, unless you suppose the
letters to the Laodiceans and the letters to Seneca are indisputably Paul's.[5]
But supposing you twist my words to apply to the Epistle to the Hebrews,
if you read the *Apologia* which I wrote many years ago in response to
Jacques Lefèvre,[6] you will not be able to deny that many orthodox critics   30
have had serious doubts about the authorship of that epistle.[7] Up to this
point there has been no authoritative statement from the church which
forbids us to have doubts in this matter – unless whatever is read in church
under Paul's name is automatically Paul's. But many other things are read
in church about which it is legitimate to have doubts. Nevertheless, even on   35
this point, if it is not too much trouble to mark the passage, I shall be
obliged to you; and if you will be good enough to tell me in a word or two
what it is which troubles you about it, I shall regard it as a twofold kindness.

* * * * *

4 On the authorship of letters (both scriptural and non-canonical) commonly
  ascribed to St Paul, see Bentley 159–60. Erasmus' challenge to the Pauline
  authorship of the apocryphal Epistle to the Laodiceans and the letters supposedly exchanged between Paul and the philosopher Seneca offended the French
  humanist Jacques Lefèvre d'Etaples, who had included them in his edition
  (1512) of St Paul's letters. Even more controversial, because it affected a canonical book of Scripture, was Erasmus' note in his *Annotationes* disputing the
  attribution of the Epistle to the Hebrews to Paul. That attribution had been
  widely doubted in the early Western church, and Hebrews was definitively
  incorporated into the Latin canon only in the late fourth and early fifth centuries. It was then generally accepted until Erasmus challenged it. The Council
  of Trent (1546) persisted in upholding the traditional attribution.
5 Cf preceding note and Ep 325:78–81.
6 Cf n4 above and Ep 597:37n.
7 A number of patristic authors doubted the attribution of Hebrews to Paul,
  notably Origen and Tertullian, though Béda would not have accepted these
  two as orthodox witnesses. Cf *The Interpreter's Bible* 12 vols (New York 1951–7)
  XI 581–3. But both in his *Annotationes* to the New Testament (LB VI 1023–4) and
  in his *Apologia ad Fabrum*, Erasmus also cited doubts about this attribution
  from St Jerome and St Augustine. He also observed that St Ambrose produced
  a commentary on every other letter of Paul except Hebrews, an argument that
  he admitted was only suggestive, not conclusive.

Baer[8] tells me that he read that letter[9] a second time after it had been   40
issued by the printers and had marked several passages, but all were so
insignificant as to trouble none but the most prejudiced reader. I asked him
to read it a third time and he promised to do so. You write very angrily
about 'counsel most dire.' How good or bad the counsel was does not
matter. What is clear is that I did not reject even harsh criticism from theo-   45
logians when they happened to give such advice. Everyone here knows that
Baer is an honest man. Even now I cannot suspect him of deception. As for
his learning, even if I am not capable of judging it myself, you yourselves
have already judged him by ranking him first in his year. Nor can I see
what help that letter is to the Lutherans. Luther's teachings were already   50
carrying all before them. Here, because of the influence of certain
troublemakers who scorned and despised the established practices of the
church, meat was being eaten, wives married, and many other things contrary to the ordinances of the church were taking place. I wrote that letter
to counter this reckless and seditious behaviour, and not without effect.   55
First of all it produced an uproar against me from the Lutherans, who
should have been wildly enthusiastic if the letter is favourable to their
cause. I express my strong support for celibacy, though if you consider how
monks and priests live their lives these days, especially in Germany, it
would be better to be lenient and allow the remedy of marriage. How few   60
people there are in the world who fast! How many eat meat whenever they
please! I believe more people will fast as they should if the practice is
encouraged rather than prescribed. Nevertheless I do not wish to see any
of these things changed except on the authority of the church. Such a
change is not in conflict with the teaching of the Fathers; it does remind us,   65
however, that the treatment must be varied to suit the changing character
of the age. If this is not acceptable to the princes of the church, then the
Lutherans have no reason to gloat, since I hold that no changes should take
place unless the permission of the church is first obtained.

But I must conclude, or you will be bored once more with my long-   70
windedness, although in a court of law more time is usually allowed the
defence than the prosecution. It is easy to launch an accusation, but long
speeches are necessary for the defence. You have no difficulty in persuading
me to trust you, though if it is true that Baer's advice turned out so badly,
can anyone be safely trusted? You swear that you will not deceive me, but   75

* * * * *

8 Ludwig Baer, professor of scholastic theology at Basel, and a close friend of
  Erasmus. See Epp 488 introduction, 1571 n6.
9 His *Epistola de esu carnium*. Cf n2 above.

I fear you could deceive yourself. I once had a higher opinion than I now
have of the theologians of the Sorbonne, believing that I could safely trust
every one of them and not just one here and there. I always liked Josse
Clichtove,[10] though he would have acted more fairly if, in defending Dio-
nysius,[11] he had made Valla the main target of his attack since it was he   80
who first put forward that opinion. But don't think that I cannot accept such
criticisms as these. As for Pierre Cousturier,[12] if he had so much faith in
you, why were you unable to persuade him to drop the publication of a
book like that, or, if he published it, to adopt a more moderate tone? For I
have never read anything that can match it for ignorance and lack of bal-   85
ance. I wrote a reply to the fellow at the urging of my friends, and I have
never regretted anything more than the trouble I wasted on that. His book,
I am told, is scorned by every honest and learned man, and would be so
even if no one had written a reply. You advise me not to answer such
works: I only wish your advice had arrived in time! But it should have been   90
directed to him in the first place: he should have been told not to make
such a wild and unseemly attack upon his neighbour; believe me, this sort
of thing does nothing but harm to the good name of theology.

Karlstadt has now stirred up a bigger fuss than we have ever seen: he
has persuaded people that there is nothing in the Eucharist except bread   95
and wine.[13] Zwingli supported the proposition in a series of publica-

* * * * *

10 Cf Ep 594:15n, and Rummel II 73–9. Early in his career, Clichtove had been
    closely associated with Jacques Lefèvre d'Etaples and had defended him
    against critics on the Paris theological faculty, but subsequently he had public-
    ly retracted some of his opinions in the face of attacks by Béda – exactly what
    Béda now demanded Erasmus must do. After his defection from the humanist
    cause, Clichtove became critical of Erasmus, and in his *Antilutherus* (1524)
    attacked him for challenging the authenticity of Dionysius the Areopagite and
    for his opinions on fasting, clerical celibacy, and monastic vows, though
    without mentioning him by name.
11 The false attribution of the works of this anonymous Neoplatonist author of
    the sixth century to an Athenian philosopher converted by St Paul (Acts 17:34)
    had first been seriously challenged by Lorenzo Valla in his annotations on the
    New Testament, which Erasmus discovered in manuscript and published in
    1505. The traditional attribution was stubbornly defended not only by conser-
    vatives like Béda but also by reforming humanists like Lefèvre, who were
    attracted not only by the strongly Platonic cast of his thought but also by the
    further error of thinking the author identical with St Denis, first bishop of
    Paris. Gallican patriotism as much as orthodoxy was involved.
12 Cf Ep 1571 n10.
13 Like Luther, Erasmus incorrectly regarded Andreas Karlstadt as the source of
    all the radical eucharistic views that had been recently published by Zwingli

tions.[14] Recently Oecolampadius has followed suit with such conviction, such eloquence, and so imposing a structure of argument that, unless God prevents it, even the elect[15] could be led astray. The city here is wavering, but I have hopes that it will recover. So I am compelled to put everything 100 else aside and descend into the arena, although I am not up to so arduous a task. If the book reaches you, you will understand that it is time for all of you to get your ammunition ready: what we need now is not propositions, but persuasive argument.[16] I would have sent the book, but I only have one copy and it is not on public sale here. Farewell, my brother in Christ, 105 whom I hold always in respect.

Basel, 2 October 1525
Erasmus of Rotterdam, by his own hand

* * * * *

at Zürich and by Oecolampadius at Basel; his recent visits to both Zürich and Basel made this opinion seem plausible. On him see Epp 911:61n, 1616 n6.

14 During the period 1523–5 Zwingli had developed his Sacramentarian or symbolic view of the Eucharist and had begun expressing it in letters and publications. His open letter to Matthew Alber, written in November 1524, widely circulated in manuscript, and printed in March 1525, clearly expressed his substantial (but not total) agreement with Karlstadt on this question. Also in March 1525 he published an influential book, *De vera et falsa religione*, which clearly rejected transubstantiation and emphasized the spiritual aspects of communion. Its chapter on the Eucharist was also separately published in German as *Vom Nachtmal Christi*. But the first really clear statement of 'Zwinglian' doctrine on the Eucharist was his *Subsidium sive coronis de eucharistia*, which appeared in August 1525. Though directed against Catholic conservatives in Zürich, it was interpreted at Wittenberg as anti-Lutheran. His first unmistakable pronouncement was a German-language paraphrase (not a mere translation) of the *Subsidium*, *Ein klare Underrichtung vom Nachtmal Christi*, which did not appear until February 1526. A long and bitter public controversy with Luther and his followers ensued, leading to a permanent split that created separate and rival branches of Protestantism. See G.R. Potter *Zwingli* (Cambridge 1976) 287–342, especially 288–300; Ulrich Gäbler *Huldrych Zwingli* (Philadelphia 1986) 131–5; and W.P. Stephens *The Theology of Huldrych Zwingli* (Oxford 1986) 218–39.

15 Cf Matt 24:24.

16 A humanist rhetorician's blow at the theological method upheld by Béda and other scholastic theologians who proceeded by extracting propositions or articles from the writings of heretics but did not (in Erasmus' opinion) provide effective and persuasive arguments that could be used against the heretics in real situations where the faith was threatened, as for example in Basel, which 'is wavering' in its adherence to traditional religious beliefs and practices

1621 / To Pierre Barbier   Basel, 3 October 1525

On the recipient see Ep 1605 introduction. Erasmus published this in his *Opus epistolarum*. The concluding portion well expresses his frustrated sense of being assaulted from the conservative side at the very time when he was struggling to uphold the traditional faith against heretical attacks.

ERASMUS OF ROTTERDAM TO PIERRE BARBIER, GREETING

Noble patron, I sent my man Karl[1] to Rome but, since you were away, he brought back the letter which I had addressed to you; so here it is now along with the enclosed. Please, please send me the certificate of non-residency[2] as soon as you can: if you don't, Jan de Hondt[3] tells me that we shall both be in trouble. I am surprised at your slackness in this matter, and this is not the first time either. As for my imperial pension,[4] there is no hope of it unless I return. Everything is expensive here, and I have absolutely no prospect of making any money. You are always promising mountains of gold from Paria:[5] please send me then at least one little lump! I know what a talented person you are; so use your eloquence to build up the friendship between Aleandro and myself.[6] I admire the man's erudition

5

10

* * * * *

1621
1 His courier to Italy, Karl Harst. Cf Ep 1575 n2.
2 Cf Epp 1094 n6, 1605 introduction. See next note.
3 Cf Epp 1094 introduction and n6, 1605 introduction and n1. De Hondt, Barbier, and Erasmus were involved in complex legal and financial arrangements resulting from Erasmus' resignation of a canonry at Courtrai in favour of de Hondt in return for a pension; and the legal validity of the arrangement depended on Barbier's submitting each year the certificate of non-residency, which he apparently had not provided.
4 In the preceding decade, while in the service of the Burgundian chancellor Jean Le Sauvage, Barbier had shared in his master's efforts to secure payment of a pension promised Erasmus by the government of the Netherlands, often referred to as the imperial government.
5 Gerlo's note on the French text of this letter sees a reference to Paros, which in antiquity was famed for marble, not gold. The reference must rather be to the South American diocese of Paria (cf Epp 913:6n, 1225:375–6, 391–4). It is also an example of their frequent teasing of Barbier about his benefice in the Spanish Indies, which utterly disappointed his hopes of drawing a great income from the new colonies. In the Latin text of Ep 1225, line 350, Erasmus gives a first-declension feminine singular form, *Paria*, rather than the form used here, *Pariis*.
6 Barbier had been in the service of Girolamo Aleandro, and Erasmus did not

and regard his abilities very highly, but the world is full of mischievous
tongues which are ready to douche everything with cold water.[7] I have just
sent my *Tongue* out into the world, so from now on your friend Erasmus   15
will be speechless.[8] I sent a copy to my friend Hovius.[9] At letter *n* near the
bottom of the recto of the last page, you should read *milia talentorum* for
milia ducatorum.

When Karlstadt[10] was in hiding in these parts, he distributed some
pamphlets, written in German, in which he maintained that nothing was   20
involved in the Eucharist except bread and wine. Several people were
persuaded at once. His views have now been supported by Zwingli in a
series of publications.[11] Four years ago a Dutchman made the same point
in a letter which has now been published, though without the author's
name.[12] When Oecolampadius[13] preached this same doctrine here day   25
after day, he made many people angry, even those who were not hostile to
Luther. At last he has produced a book, so carefully written and so buttressed with argument and supporting evidence that even the elect could be
led astray.[14] The book, however, has not been printed here and is not on
public sale.   30

I am now being pressed to enter the arena, much against my natural

* * * * *

yet know that in April he had left Rome to enter the service of Charles de
Lannoy, the imperial viceroy of Naples. He was keenly aware of Aleandro's
thinly veiled hostility to him, and no doubt hoped that this mutual friend
could patch things up.

7 *Adagia* I x 51
8 Erasmus' treatise *Lingua*, published in August. Erasmus liked to pun on the
name of the work.
9 On Johannes Hovius, a former secretary of Erasmus who was then living at
Rome, cf Epp 857 introduction, 867 189n, 1387 n3, Ep 1575 n4.
10 Cf Epp 911:61n, 1616 n6, 1620 n13.
11 Cf Ep 1620 n14.
12 Cornelis Henricxzoon Hoen by 1521 had produced his *Epistola tractans coenam
Dominicam*, which his countryman Hinne Rode circulated among reformers in
Germany and Switzerland. It influenced Zwingli, who published it (probably
at Zürich) in 1525. Cf Ep 1358 n7.
13 Cf Ep 1616 introduction and nn 2 and 4. As Erasmus suggests at the end of
this paragraph, because the Basel city council sought to prevent publication of
books that undermined religious calm, Oecolampadius had his book printed
abroad, probably at Strasbourg. Erasmus repeatedly praised the learning and
effectiveness of this book, even though he deplored its rejection of authoritative dogmas of the church. Cf Ep 1636.
14 Matt 24:24

inclination.[15] And while I am engaged on this, to the detriment of my own affairs and even at the risk of my life, those for whom I am fighting continue their attacks on me from different quarters in a series of vicious pamphlets. Latomus read aloud three short works at Louvain, in which I   35 was the constant target of his abuse.[16] True, he omitted my name, but that meant nothing since he quoted me verbatim. Later he published these works with all their remarkable sophistries. At almost the same time another attack on me appeared in print, full of incriminations and scurrilous abuse, which goes beyond anything you could imagine for stupidity, incompetence, and   40 dullness.[17] Credit for this production was shared among several Dominicans. It is ascribed to an empty-headed fool called Godefridus Taxander. The printer was Cornelis of Duiveland. Vincentius added some rubbish of his own from an attack on me which he had composed some time ago but had been forbidden to publish by the vicar-general. A man called Walter   45 contributed some flowery passages from the treasure-house of poetry. When the deed was done, they scattered in different directions, Vincentius to the shades below. I am not imagining all this; I was sent a copy of the letter which Cornelis wrote to Lee – for it was to Lee that this splendid production was dedicated – and it proves that what I am saying is true.[18] Pierre   50 Cousturier,[19] who was once a theologian at the Sorbonne and is now a Carthusian monk, has published a work at Paris which is nothing but a furious diatribe against translators and liberal studies generally. I wrote a reply and now regret having paid the scoundrel so handsome a compliment.

See that you line your pockets with gold and amass enough loot for   55 both of us! I was very keen to be off to Italy, since the stone is treating me more gently at present, but there were complications which could not be resolved. In the meantime winter has crept up on us and is now approaching with increasing speed. Farewell.

Basel, 3 October 1525   60

* * * * *

15 By Claudius Cantiuncula, among others. Cf Epp 1616, 1636.
16 Cf Ep 1581 n58.
17 On this scurrilous and anonymous attack published under the pseudonym Godefridus Taxander by a group of four Dominicans associated with Louvain, and on the names of Cornelis of Duiveland, Vincentius, and Walter, whom Erasmus identified as the real authors, see Ep 1571 n14.
18 The attack by 'Taxander' was dedicated to Erasmus' troublesome English antagonist, Edward Lee (cf Ep 765 introduction, and many letters of the years from 1518 onward, especially Epp 897, 936).
19 Cf Ep 1571 n10.

1622 / To Hieronim Łaski   Basel, 3 October 1525

A reply to a lost letter in which Erasmus seems to have been promised the gift of a horse. The recipient is the elder brother of Jan Łaski, who had spent the past six months as a paying guest in Erasmus' house at Basel and who was now moving on to Italy and then back home to Poland at the insistence of his father. On the recipient see Ep 1242 n5. Erasmus included the letter in his *Opus epistolarum.*

ERASMUS TO HIERONIM ŁASKI, BARON OF POLAND, GREETING
Distinguished sir, about that horse you promised to send – it would not matter if you sent Cyllarus[1] or Pegasus,[2] you could not turn a snail into a horseman; and, now that your brother has left,[3] I don't imagine you will send your man here simply because of the horse. I suppose your letter was 5 written before the decision was taken to ask your brother to return. Since his company brought me more pleasure than almost anything else in life, I am naturally very distressed by his leaving. His delightful companionship almost gave me a new lease on life. I could not have asked heaven for anyone more congenial to my own temperament; or, it would be truer to 10 say, he has the sort of temperament which enables him to get on with everyone. Some things ease the pain which I feel: first, the blow was not entirely unexpected since I always felt that the time would come when he would be suddenly taken from me; secondly, I have been no stranger to the perversity of fate, for no sooner does a piece of good luck come my way 15 than fate snatches it from me, while anything unpleasant that happens clings relentlessly and cannot be removed or shaken off. He was prevented from reaping the full benefit of his stay with me by the unremitting burden of the scholar's life. We kept making plans, but some unforeseen obligation always intervened to frustrate our efforts. His own preference was to con- 20 tinue to enjoy the quiet life of the Muses; but Plato thought the wise man should be carried off, even against his will, to serve the interests of the

* * * * *

1622
1 The horse given by Juno to Castor or to Pollux; cf Virgil *Georgics* 3.90; Suidas sv 'Cyllarus.'
2 The famous winged horse of Bellerophon; cf Ovid *Metamorphoses* 4.785, 5.262.
3 Jan Łaski, the future Protestant leader. He left Basel just a few days after the date of this letter, accompanied by Erasmus' secretary Karl Harst. Cf Ep 1593 n18.

state.[4] So I should offer my congratulations to Poland instead of feeling
sorry for my personal loss.

I am delighted, indeed I feel it a real triumph, that my *Tongue* has not   25
disappointed our distinguished friend, the lord chancellor.[5] You will not
be surprised if from now on you find Erasmus without a tongue! I pray
some gracious deity may rescue your Highness from the tangle in which
you say you have become enmeshed.[6] I know what a real Hercules you are,
but one thing I have learned from long experience, that it is never safe to   30
despise an enemy, however weak he may appear. Farewell.

Basel, 3 October 1525

1623 / To Giambattista Egnazio   Basel, 3 October 1525

Egnazio, a prominent Venetian humanist, was well known to Erasmus (cf Epp
269:56n, 1594 n20). He was drawn into the efforts of Erasmus' secretary Karl
Harst and several of Erasmus' young admirers then living in Venice and
Padua, such as Leonard Casembroot and Thomas Lupset, to persuade Andrea
Torresani of Asola to issue an enlarged Aldine edition of Erasmus' *Adagia* (cf
Epp 1592, 1594, 1595). He had tried to calm the anger of Erasmus' young
friends over Torresani's unwillingness to undertake this new edition; and
Erasmus here explains to Torresani his own motives in proposing a new
Aldine edition, obviously attempting further to quiet the furore raised by his
overzealous young admirers. Erasmus included this letter in his *Opus episto-
larum*.

ERASMUS OF ROTTERDAM TO GIAMBATTISTA EGNAZIO
Cordial greetings, my good and learned friend. I am sorry you were put to
such trouble over that silly affair of mine. I was not worried about the
publication of the *Adagia*, since I could always rely on Froben here to do the
job. Francesco had written to me several times complaining that I never sent   5

* * * * *

4 *Republic* 519C–520F
5 Ep 1593 is Erasmus' dedication of his treatise *Lingua* to Krzysztof Szydłowiecki, chancellor of the kingdom of Poland. The latter had evidently sent
   his thanks in the lost letter from Hieronim Łaski to which this is a reply.
6 Just what 'tangle' Erasmus has in mind is unclear, but at this period Hieronim
   Łaski was deeply involved in the troubled factional politics of the kingdom of
   Hungary, in which he would soon be a leading partisan of the native nobility's
   favourite for succession to the throne, the anti-Hapsburg (and pro-Turkish)
   John Zápolyai.

him any of my works.[1] So I offered him my book of *Adages*: it had first
seen the light of day at the Asolani press and I hoped it might be reborn
there if the arrangement suited him. If not, he was to return the copy by the
same messenger who delivered it. There was no need for more than a word
or two from either side.   10

I have sent my man Karl back again;[2] I want him to bring me the
commentaries of Chrysostom on the Acts of the Apostles.[3] Would you be
kind enough to see that I am not cheated? You can do this by asking an
expert to examine the manuscript to ensure it is complete and has been
accurately copied. Jan Łaski who brings you this letter is Polish; he belongs   15
to a family which is distinguished in his own country, and is likely to make
a name for himself in the near future; he is a man of spotless character,
more brilliant than gold and precious stones.[4]

The complete Jerome has now been printed again.[5] I corrected many
errors which had escaped me before. There are still a few difficulties which   20
I could not conquer. One of these is in the preface which he placed before
the translation of Ezekiel, about *phagoloedori* and *seneciae*.[6] If you have any
ideas, let me know. I could add a note at the beginning or end, since the
work is not due to appear for several months. I know you care nothing for
personal glory, but I shall make it my business to see that a kind act is not   25
robbed of its proper reward.

I am sorry that Ambrogio of Nola is dead,[7] a loss both to us and to
the world of learning. But we must all die some day, and he had a long and

* * * * *

1623
1 Francesco Torresani of Asola, son and business associate of Andrea, who
   directed the Aldine press
2 Karl Harst, Erasmus' courier to Italy; cf Epp 1592, 1594, 1595.
3 This involves a Greek manuscript of St John Chrysostom, evidently for sale in
   Padua and desired by Erasmus for his patristic and biblical studies.
4 When young Łaski left for Italy in the company of Erasmus' courier Harst,
   Erasmus provided him with letters such as this one commending him to
   influential Italian acquaintances.
5 Erasmus' revised edition of the works of St Jerome, replacing his edition of
   1516, began appearing in July 1524, and the first eight volumes had appeared
   by this time; a ninth and final one came out in February 1526, along with a set
   of pages that were bound in at the beginning of volume I.
6 This problem concerning the preface to Jerome's Ezekiel and the terms *phagoloedori* and *seneciae* had baffled Erasmus and Paul Volz in 1515. Cf Ep 372:5–21.
7 Ambrogio Leoni, a noted physician and translator of Greek texts in the circle
   of Aldus at Venice; cf Ep 854.

untroubled life and made a good end. May God have mercy on him and
grant him eternal rest with the souls of the faithful departed. Farewell.   30
     Basel, 3 October 1525

1624 / To Thomas Lupset   Basel, [c 4 October] 1525

> This reply to Ep 1595 consoles Lupset for the failure of his efforts to persuade
> the Venetian printer Andrea Torresani of Asola to bring out a new Aldine
> edition of Erasmus' *Adagia*, assuring him that the efforts of Erasmus' courier
> Karl Harst to exert pressure on Torresani had far exceeded the author's
> designs. Cf Epp 1592, 1594, 1595, 1623. Erasmus included this in his *Opus*
> *epistolarum*.

ERASMUS OF ROTTERDAM TO THOMAS LUPSET, GREETING
Should I thank you now, my dearest Lupset, for your loyal efforts on my
behalf, as if what you did was something new? I was not worried about the
publication of my *Proverbs*. But how typical of my friend Karl to kick up a
cloud of dust over something of no importance! I wanted the commentaries   5
of Chrysostom on the Acts of the Apostles, but he chose to return empty-
handed.[1] The lad isn't very strong and seems unfit for any kind of hard
work. I have now arranged for him to return on horseback. You could help
by seeing that the book is not damaged or full of errors. I hope our friend
Pace has recovered by now.[2] A plague on all those diplomatic comings and   10
goings! He was intended by nature for the service of the Muses. I am afraid
les plaisirs de l'amour may be responsible for a good part of his trouble.[3]
     Philippus Melanchthon is seriously ill: he has the same problem with

* * * * *

1624
1 Cf Ep 1623 n3.
2 Richard Pace, English ambassador at Venice. Cf Epp 1594 n16, 1595 n4.
  Erasmus regards Pace's important diplomatic missions to Italy and elsewhere
  as a regrettable distraction from his scholarly interests.
3 The Latin text expresses this in Greek and clearly implies that Pace's illness
  was syphilis. The early symptoms were fever and insomnia, and after his
  return to England he manifested a mental instability that led to his being put
  into custodial care. His modern biographers Frank Manley and Richard S.
  Sylvester in their edition of Pace's *De fructu qui ex doctrina percipitur* (New York
  1967) ix–xii and Jervis Wegg *Richard Pace, a Tudor Diplomatist* (London 1932;
  repr 1971) 260–6 describe the symptoms and show that the disease ended his
  promising political career but do not hazard a guess concerning the nature of
  his ailment.

insomnia, I am told.[4] When Duke Frederick was dying,[5] he left him a legacy of 1,000 gold florins.[6] Luther has taken a wife, a very pretty girl from   15
the distinguished family of the von Boras, but apparently without a
dowry.[7] She abandoned the veil several years ago. Luther himself has
yielded to the pleas of the brethren and abandoned the philosopher's cloak
and beard.[8]

Thomas Grey[9] and his youngest son are staying with me. He tells me   20
that nothing revolutionary is happening in England. People are restrained
by fear. The peasant uprising has been settled after a fashion, but we are
dealing with a hydra, and when one head is cut off, others grow in its
place. Great efforts are being made at reform, but I see no sure prospects of
peace.   25

How lucky you are to be able to take your ease in the gardens of the
Muses without a care in the world! At an age when most men are retiring,
I am being forced to take on the role of gladiator, or rather to enter the
arena with wild beasts, to fight single-handed against a multitude, and to
go out unarmed against those whose weapons are not just tooth and claw   30
but poisoned darts. I have thrown down the gauntlet to Luther, whom men
describe as a 'wild boar.'[10] He has already prepared a riposte. I cannot

* * * * *

4 Although Luther's close associate was in chronic ill health and had suffered
   from insomnia so severely in 1524 that some days he was unable to teach, at
   this particular time he must not have been in especially poor health since he
   had just agreed to go to Nürnberg and help the city council found a new
   school (Melanchthon *Briefwechsel* CR 1, nos 348, 349).
5 Frederick the Wise, electoral prince of Saxony and Luther's protector during
   the early Reformation, died at Lochau on 5 May 1525.
6 Latin *mille florenos aureos*. Probably Rhenish or Electoral gold florins (Rheingulden), currently valued at 57d gros Flemish; and if so, a sum worth £237 10s
   0d gros Flemish, or £160 6s 4d sterling, or exactly £1,500 tournois. See Epp
   1362 n2, 1651 n5. If, however, these were Florentine florins, that sum would
   have been worth £333 6s 8d gros Flemish (CWE 8 350).
7 Luther's marriage to Katharina von Bora took place on 13 June, though the
   public celebration was delayed until 27 June so that Luther's parents and other
   guests from outside Wittenberg could attend.
8 Probably meaning that he no longer wore his monastic habit
9 See Ep 58 introduction. During their long friendship, Grey visited Erasmus at
   Louvain in 1518 (Epp 768, 777, 817, 827) and now during another trip to the
   Continent had come with his youngest son to visit Erasmus in Basel. Virtually
   nothing is known about him except for his occasional appearance in Erasmus'
   correspondence.
10 Cf Ep 1576:8–9, citing Ps 79:14. The 'gauntlet,' of course, was Erasmus' *De
   libero arbitrio* (1524), directed against Luther.

understand what he has in mind by holding it back so long.[11] When Karlstadt was here, he secretly distributed several pamphlets written in German,
and convinced many people that there is nothing in the Eucharist but bread   35
and wine.[12] That heresy caught on everywhere with the speed of fire running towards naphtha.[13] Huldrych Zwingli published two books in support of this view.[14] Now Oecolampadius has also joined in, with a book
which is so thorough and so full of ingenious arguments that anyone who
wishes to answer him will have his work cut out.[15]   40
    I am being thrust into the debate, though brawling is the last thing in
the world for which I have a natural aptitude. But no matter what I do, I
am still considered a Lutheran and continue to be the target of vicious and
defamatory pamphlets. Latomus issued three at the same time, though he
shrank from mentioning my name.[16] It is all very urbane, but his wit is   45
slyly aimed at me. As for his treatment of the subject itself, it is feebler than
I would wish to see or expected – for I am on the same side as he is. Four
Dominicans, Vincentius, Duiveland, Godefridus, and Walter, have secretly
collaborated on the production of a book which is full of the most scurrilous
abuse and surpasses anything you could imagine for incompetence and   50
stupidity.[17] Then there suddenly appeared in Paris a work by Pierre
Cousturier, who was once a 'rabbi' at the Sorbonne and is now a Carthusian
monk.[18] He writes in a fury of rage. I replied, but now repent of my
trouble. So far they have published nothing against Luther except lists of
questionable doctrines,[19] but they publish whole books attacking me. They   55

* * * * *

11 Luther had proceeded quite deliberately in preparing his response to Erasmus'
   De libero arbitrio, putting other, more pressing matters first. Not till 25 September 1525 did he himself admit in a letter that he was fully engaged in writing
   his refutation (WA-Br 3 582 [no 926]). The work was not completed till November and not published until December 1525.
12 The radical reformer Andreas Karlstadt had indeed visited Zürich and Basel
   late in 1524, and both Erasmus and Luther incorrectly regarded this visit as the
   source of the Sacramentarian ideas expressed by Zwingli and Oecolampadius.
   Cf Ep 1620 n13.
13 Cf Pliny *Naturalis historia* 2.235.
14 On the emergence of Zwingli's Sacramentarian interpretation of the Eucharist,
   cf Ep 1620 n14.
15 Cf Ep 1616, nn2 and 4.
16 Cf Ep 1581 n58.
17 See Ep 1571 n14 and the subsequent letters there cited, especially Ep 1603.
18 Cf Ep 1571 n10.
19 Cf Ep 1620:103–4 for a similar suggestion that the scholastic theologians who
   opposed Luther produced useless lists of questionable doctrines rather than

make it abundantly clear how much greater is their dislike of the humanities than of Luther. This is the thanks I get for defending their camp against
the enemy and risking my own neck in the process.

The man accompanying my friend Karl is called Jan Łaski.[20] He is a
Polish count who belongs to a family distinguished in his own country.   60
Before long he is likely to be given important responsibilities. Besides being
a man of uncommon erudition, he has such pleasant manners and is so
warm and friendly that as a result of his company I am finding my youth
again and taking a renewed pleasure in living. But consider the malevolence
of fortune: when something unpleasant occurs, it clings for ever and cannot   65
be shaken off; but when something good happens (which is a *rara avis*),[21]
it is snatched away almost before there is time to sample its delights.

A person of high rank[22] asked me to produce something for your
illustrious queen on the obligations of marriage. They say she was much
taken by the book which I published comparing a virgin with a martyr.[23]   70
Vives dedicated to her his 'Virgin, Wife and Widow.'[24] So I am surprised
she is looking for something more. Nevertheless I shall fall in with her
wishes when I have done with this battle over the Eucharist.

After his lengthy wanderings Karlstadt has returned to Wittenberg; he
has recanted and been received back into the church there.[25] That's evan-   75
gelical mercy for you! Farewell.

1525

* * * * *

effective arguments that would persuade the people to uphold the traditional
religion.
20 Cf Epp 1593 n18, 1622 n3, 1623 n4.
21 *Adagia* II i 21; cf Persius 1.46, Juvenal 6.165.
22 Erasmus' friend and patron Lord Mountjoy. Cf Ep 1727, the dedication of the
work that resulted, *Institutio christiani matrimonii* (Basel: Froben, August 1526),
dedicated to the English queen, Catherine of Aragon.
23 His *Virginis et martyris comparatio*, written at the request of the Benedictine
nuns of Cologne and printed in 1523 and again in 1524, had caught the attention of the English queen and had led to her request for a work on matrimony.
Cf Ep 1346 introduction.
24 The humanist Juan Luis Vives had become close to Queen Catherine and
dedicated to her his *De institutione foeminae Christianae* (Antwerp: Michaël
Hillen 1524; NK 2167).
25 See Ep 1616 n6 on Karlstadt's return to Wittenberg and temporary recantation
of his radical opinions.

1625 / To Christoph Truchsess   Basel, [4 October 1525]

This letter to a highly placed young German nobleman who was studying in
Padua illustrates Erasmus' ideal of an aristocracy devoted to learning rather
than war and pleasure. Erasmus published it in his *Opus epistolarum*.
Christopher Truchsess von Waldburg (c 1509–35) was the son of a councillor
of Archduke Ferdinand of Hapsburg and had a brother who later became a
cardinal and bishop of Augsburg, while another member of his family com-
manded the army of the Swabian League. Though he had studied at Tübingen
and was now studying in Italy, he chose a military career in the service of
Ferdinand and the emperor Charles V. Although the date as printed in Erasmus' own *Opus epistolarum* (1529) is clearly 1524, Allen redated it to 1525 on
the basis of Truchsess' reply (Ep 1649), a text founded on the original autograph letter which survived at Leipzig. The latter text is far more likely to be
accurate than the shaky memory of Erasmus four years later when he was
preparing his collected correspondence for publication.

ERASMUS OF ROTTERDAM TO CHRISTOPH TRUCHSESS, BARON OF
WALDBURG, GREETING
My distinguished young friend, my man Karl[1] brought me an unexpected
gift from Italy and nothing could have given me greater pleasure; it was a
portrait of yourself,[2] taken from the life, and painted, so to speak, with a   5
verbal brush. It was so well done that he filled my heart with love and
admiration for your virtues: it was just as though I had seen you face to
face. Wise men rightly condemn those who are rich in the gifts of fortune
but totally impoverished in the things of the mind, those who excel in
physical beauty but have minds unadorned by any virtue, and those who   10
take pride in their family tree but have no better claim to nobility than the
portraits of their ancestors; but there is more reason to condemn those
whose clothes and homes are sumptuously adorned but whose minds are
barren through idleness and neglect, those whose fair appearance cloaks a
mind made squalid by its sins, those whose moral frailty blackens and   15
dishonours the memory of their ancestors. By the same token we should
praise those who have so enriched and refined and embellished their lives

* * * * *

1625
1 Karl Harst, Erasmus' trusted courier to Italy
2 From the context, not a painting but Harst's own verbal description of
   Christoph

with true wealth and unfading splendour that that quality which ordinary
people regard as the very essence of nobility is least evident in them. Such
is your character: may he to whom we owe every real blessing preserve and   20
fortify it always.

There is a great deal of resentment today against the humanities[3] and
now the aristocracy are beginning to feel the sting of the same viper. But all
this prejudice will turn to admiration if we have many men like you. Moderate success always invites envy; but when we see youthfulness allied with   25
modesty, wealth devoid of ostentation, noble birth free of pride, and moral
integrity joined to more than ordinary learning, such qualities vanquish all
envy. We see many excellent men shine like stars in Britain's firmament,[4]
and new men are constantly appearing who seem likely to put the glory of
their elders in the shade – though it would be nearer the truth to say that   30
they will brighten, not obscure, the glories of the past. In Germany there is
perhaps not yet the same cause for congratulations; yet some glorious
blooms have already appeared which offer great hopes of splendid things
to come. I would congratulate you personally, dear Christoph, on the qualities of your mind, but I see many young men among the German nobility   35
running with you in the same race to earn the same applause, so I ought
now to congratulate the whole of Germany. I trust that as time passes your
example may spread to more and more. When our aristocracy spends its
time on the great books of antiquity rather than on dice and cards, when it
embraces the virgin Muses instead of harlots, when it finds its pleasure in   40
the most sacred laws and in the teachings of philosophy and not in war and
pillage, then it will be truly eminent, truly noble, worthy of distinction and
respect. Nothing is more attractive than virtue,[5] but it gains an added grace
and beauty if it is commended to the world by the blessings of fortune. I
should have liked to write at greater length to encourage you, though you   45
are running a good race on your own,[6] but because of the demands of my
work I could scarcely find time even for this. Do all you can so that each

* * * * *

3 The letter's only reference to the upheaval then going on in German society,
  which included both a rejection of higher learning (not only scholastic but also
  humanistic) by many young German enthusiasts for the gospel, and the violent
  attacks on aristocratic privilege by the peasants in the spring and early summer of 1525. On the Peasant War, see Preface, pages xi–xii.
4 Erasmus frequently marvelled at the flourishing condition of humanistic
  studies in remote England, mentioning especially Colet, Grocyn, Linacre, and
  More. Cf his praise of English learning in Epp 118, 965.
5 Cicero De natura deorum 1.121
6 Cf Adagia III viii 32.

day you will have less need of encouragement from anyone, and I, who
applaud your virtue, will have more cause to rejoice at your success. Farewell.   50
    Basel, †1524†

1626 / To Leonard Casembroot   Basel, 4 October 1525

> This reply to Ep 1594 was written not only to console Casembroot and Eras-
> mus' other young friends at Padua and Venice for the failure of their attempt
> to persuade Andrea Torresani to publish a revised Aldine edition of the
> *Adagia*, but also to admonish him to put aside the gastronomic and sexual
> delights of Italy, about which he had bragged in his letter, and to concentrate
> on the true riches available in Italy, its sources of humanistic and legal learn-
> ing. It also served as a letter of reference for Erasmus' friend and recent guest,
> Jan Łaski. Erasmus published it in his *Opus epistolarum*.

ERASMUS OF ROTTERDAM TO LEONARD CASEMBROOT, GREETING
My dear Leonard, in that awful fuss over the *Adagia* which upset you all so
badly,[1] I recognize the master touch of my friend Karl.[2] He can always be
counted on to raise a cloud of dust, no matter how trivial the circumstances.
My *Adagia* are now being printed at the Froben press. That will keep me   5
here for the moment; otherwise I should rush off to visit you in the company of this Polish count, Jan Łaski.[3] He is a learned young man, but not
arrogant, aristocratic and well-to-do without being supercilious, and he has
such warm, friendly, and charming manners that the pleasure of his company has nearly restored my youth, just when I was wasting away under   10
the strain of illness, overwork, and the blows of my detractors.
    What is this I hear? So you have developed a taste for Italian canta-
loups and water-melons?[4] I am afraid you may soon be jealous even of the
donkeys![5] When you are better acquainted with the delights of Italy, you
will agree that it has greater things to offer than melons. But, my dear   15

* * * * *

1626
1 See Epp 1593 introduction, 1594 introduction.
2 Karl Harst, Erasmus' courier. Cf Ep 1575 n2.
3 Cf Epp 1593 n18, 1622 n3.
4 See Casembroot's enthusiastic praise of Italy's fruits, Ep 1594:43–4.
5 Although it sounds aphoristic, this phrase does not appear in the *Adagia* or in
  the standard dictionaries of proverbs.

Leonard, let me jog that good memory of yours[6] and remind you that you did not set out for Italy to populate the place with bastard children,[7] but to ravish its cultural riches so that some day you might endow your own dear Flanders with the spoils. Your business now is with the Muses and the Graces: how well they accord with the goddess of Cyprus is something you should reflect on.[8] Your native Bruges has always produced men of great ability, like the great men of Athens. But you have been given such gifts that even among the talented you stand out as the favourite of fortune. Naturally we have formed high hopes of you, and you have confirmed those hopes by the success of your studies so far. Now that you have moved to Padua, the richest and most famous emporium of learning, you can easily imagine that your friends are expecting nothing ordinary or second-rate from you; and unless I am a poor judge of your abilities, I have no doubt that, however high our expectations, you will surpass them all by the lively business you will do in the markets of learning. There will be no shortage of men to produce those *petits Léonards:*[9] it will be your task – and it is a task worthy of your special genius – to use your learning for the benefit of Flanders to bring into the world a large family of disciples who will resemble you in the purity of their character and in their remarkable learning and eloquence.

I wish I could pass on these thoughts to you in that garden of yours. Not that I envy you for having it, but it is a pity we cannot share it together. Your decision to take up the study of civil law has my full support for many reasons, particularly because it is as remote as it could be from the wrangling of the theologians. It is this which is responsible for the present ferment, so that I have almost come to hate learning of every kind. I also think you have a natural aptitude for the study of politics. Be kind to all those young friends of yours. Whether you do as I request or not, remember me kindly to them (as I am sure you are doing without being asked) and urge them in my name to live up to the expectations of their family and their country and do justice to the learning and devotion of their teacher.

* * * * *

6 Cf *Adagia* I ii 12.
7 A reference to Casembroot's boasting about his sexual exploits in Italy; cf Ep 1594:45–6.
8 Aphrodite (the Roman Venus), goddess of love and fertility, was believed to have been born on the coast of Cyprus; and that island was especially noted for worship of her. Homer (*Iliad* 5.330) refers to her as 'the Cyprian.'
9 This translation uses the French phrase to reflect Erasmus' humorous and rather affected use of Greek terms, responding to the similar use of Greek in Casembroot's letter. Cf Allen Ep 1594:43n.

Your catalogue of names tore at my heart.[10] Lupset has always been a part of my very being.[11] Pace[12] has long been as close a friend as Pylades was to Orestes.[13] Pietro Bembo's great abilities are known to me both by repute and through his writings.[14] Lupset sent me a pen-sketch of   50
Reginald Pole,[15] which was so good a likeness that no Apelles[16] could improve upon it. Becichemo's name I have learned for the first time from your letter.[17] I have had a long and close association with Giambattista Egnazio; he is a man of great learning and integrity, warm-hearted and truly loyal to his friends.[18] How lucky you are to be able to enjoy such   55
delights. Think of me on the other hand, bound to my treadmill by age, poor health, and some strange evil genius![19]

I should like to continue this nonsense, but I must write to others. Karl plans to return here; so load him up with letters. Farewell.

Basel, 4 October 1525   60

I wonder if you will be able to read this hurried note, but you are familiar with my scrawl.

* * * * *

10 See Ep 1594:86–92.
11 Thomas Lupset; see Epp 270:69n, 1594 n3, 1595
12 Richard Pace; cf Epp 211:53n, 1594 n16, 1595 n4, 1624 nn2 and 3.
13 In classical Greek mythology, Orestes and Pylades were a proverbial example of friendship. Their story was most widely diffused in the dramatic works of Aeschylus (*The Libation-Bearers*), Sophocles (*Electra*), and Euripides (*Electra, Orestes,* and *Iphigenia in Tauris*).
14 See Epp 1594 n17, 2106.
15 See Ep 1627 introduction.
16 Conventionally regarded as antiquity's greatest painter, and hence a term used to designate any painter of great talent, as in Ep 1536, where it is applied to Albrecht Dürer.
17 Perhaps a slip of memory, since Erasmus provided a letter of endorsement (Ep 1016) which was printed in an edition of Becichemo's *In C. Plinium praelectio* compiled by his friend Nicolas Bérault (Paris: P. Vidoue for K. Resch 1519), and this letter subsequently appeared in his edition of his own *Epistolae ad diversos* (Basel: Froben 1521). But it is not at all certain that he had actually seen the Paris edition. Furthermore, in his letter Erasmus refers to Becichemo only by his nickname (Scodrensis), drawn from his place of birth, and may never have connected that name with the name Becichemo. Cf Ep 1016 introduction and n8, and on Becichemo himself, Ep 1594 n19.
18 See Ep 1594 n20. Erasmus consistently maintained the high estimation of Egnazio's learning and character here expressed and repeated it for all to read in his *Ciceronianus* (ASD I-2 668–9).
19 *Adagia* I i 72.

1627 / To Reginald Pole   Basel, 4 October 1525

Pole (1500–58), second cousin of Henry VIII, was educated by the Carthusians
at Sheen and at Magdalen College, Oxford, where Thomas Linacre and
William Latimer were his teachers. Although early destined for the church and
generously provided with benefices because of his relationship to the king, he
was also deeply moved by the classical and reformist elements in English
humanism. In 1521 he asked the king to send him to Padua for further study.
There he studied under Niccolò Leonico Tomeo and became a close friend to
the French humanist Christophe de Longueil, the Venetian humanist Pietro
Bembo, and his fellow countryman Thomas Lupset. The latter's warm praise
of him in Ep 1595 was the occasion for the present letter. Pole remained at
Padua from 1521 to the winter of 1526–7, and his wealthy household was a
center of support for young humanists. He also came under the influence of
the evangelical spirituality of his Italian contemporaries, although his personal
contact with the leading evangelical reformers, Contarini, Priuli, and Carafa,
did not begin until his second period of residence in Italy, starting in 1532.
From 1527 he found residence in England increasingly difficult because of his
dislike of the royal divorce. After his return to Italy in 1532, his opposition to
Henry's break with Rome became open. In 1536 he entered the service of Pope
Paul III, who made him a cardinal. He became one of the leading moderate
Catholic reformers. After the restoration of Roman jurisdiction by Queen Mary
I (1553–8), he returned home as papal legate and became archbishop of
Canterbury. On his activities in Padua at this period see George B. Parks *The
English Traveller to Italy* I: *The Middle Ages (to 1525)* (Rome 1954) 475–82;
Dermot Fenlon *Heresy and Obedience in Tridentine Italy: Cardinal Pole and the
Counter Reformation* (Cambridge 1972) 24–7. Erasmus included this letter in his
Opus epistolarum.

ERASMUS OF ROTTERDAM TO REGINALD POLE OF ENGLAND,
GREETING
Most honoured sir, Thomas Lupset sent me a letter with a full-length portrait of you, which was so well done that I could not know you better if I
had lived with you in the closest intimacy for many months. A painter   5
represents the physical features of his subject; we learn much about a man
through our ears; but the inner qualities of the mind, which are the most
precious by far, can only be known from long familiarity. That part of
Lupset's letter was indeed a great comfort to me. For in these sorry times
I am delighted to see a new generation of men arise who are able to defend   10
and promote the cause of literature and religion. I am not going to sing
your praises now: I only wish to congratulate you on having received from

Reginald Pole
By an unknown artist, 16th century
Biblioteca Ambrosiana, Milan

a benevolent God such signal gifts; he of his goodness will preserve these
blessings in you and increase and enhance them always. Lupset is very fond
of you, as his eloquent tribute shows, for it breathes such a wonderful spirit   15
of friendliness that it makes me love you too. We marvel when a magnet
attracts iron to itself. But is there anyone so iron-hearted as not to be
attracted and captivated by such a harmonious blend of diverse talents in
a single soul?

If my man Karl[1] had returned sooner, perhaps I would be with you   20
now. I could not hope to find a better travelling companion or guide than
this Polish baron, Jan Łaski,[2] whose company has given me such happiness
recently, just as his departure wrings my heart. You will like him, I am
sure, since he has much in common with yourself. You will not find in him
the least trace of pride despite a long line of distinguished ancestors, great   25
honours, and even greater promise for the future, a rich vein of talent, and
learning which far exceeds the common run. You have men around you
whose company would make me young again: Richard Pace,[3] a friend like
Pylades to me,[4] Thomas Lupset,[5] whom I have always loved like a son
and now cherish as a patron, Leonard Casembroot,[6] a man of sterling   30
character and deep learning, who is certain one day to take his place among
the famous, and you above all, my dear Pole. But it is my fate to be tied to
this place. For what can I blame for this but fate?

Since I cannot enjoy your company, it would be pure delight to prolong this chat by letter, but I have three couriers to load up on the same   35
day.[7] One is off to France, another to Brabant; the third is my good man

* * * * *

1627
1 Karl Harst, the courier who carried Erasmus' letters to and from Italy in this
period
2 The young Polish humanist was the bearer of this and other letters of about
this date. The letters also served as valuable introductions to Erasmus'
acquaintances in Italy, both Italian and foreign. Cf Epp 1593 n18, 1622 n3, 1623
n4, 1626 n3.
3 Cf Epp 1594 n16, 1595 n4, 1624 nn2 and 3.
4 Mythological figure symbolizing enduring friendship; cf Ep 1626 n13.
5 Cf Epp 1595, 1624.
6 Cf Epp 1594, 1626.
7 Pierre Toussain (see Ep 1559:9) carried Epp 1615, 1618–20 to France; the second
was probably Lieven Algoet (see Ep 1091 introduction), who was no longer in
Erasmus' service but who still occasionally carried letters between Basel and
the Low Countries; the third was Karl Harst, the person most frequently
mentioned as a courier at this time because he served as Erasmus' confidential
agent for business with Italy.

Karl, whom you entertained so well that he is eager to visit you again. Please forgive this foolish and muddled note, which I have not even had time to reread. Farewell.

Basel, 4 October 1525   40

1628 / To Gianfrancesco Torresani   Basel, 5 October 1525

This letter, which Erasmus never published and which remained unprinted in the Vatican Library (MS Reg Lat 2023 f 159) until published by Pierre de Nolhac *Erasme en Italie* 2nd ed (Paris 1898) 110, is an attempt to mend Erasmus' relations with the father and son Andrea and Gianfrancesco Torresani. On the ill will generated among Erasmus' friends by Andrea's decision not to bring out a new Aldine edition of Erasmus' *Adagia*, see Epp 1587, 1592, 1594, 1595, 1623, 1626. In his letters Erasmus consistently takes the position that he had never been especially eager to have his work republished at Venice and that his agent Karl Harst and his friends had promoted the proposal far more zealously than he had intended.

Cordial greetings. I wrote some time ago in reply to your letter. Froben is publishing my book of *Adages*. Karl, the man who brought my manuscript to you, will pick it up, as I instructed him to do. The publication of Galen is causing much excitement in the scholarly world.[1] As for my own work, my dear Francesco, I have always relied on the services of Froben, since I   5
found no one who was more suitable. But I feel the same enthusiasm for your press as for literature itself, about which my feelings are very strong indeed, and literature owes more to your press than to anyone else. If an opportunity arises to make my feelings clear, I shall show you that this is not mere talk.   10

Please give my kind regards to your father Asolano[2] and to your brother and the rest of the family. I shall write to the physician Baptista,[3] if I have a spare moment. Farewell.

Basel, 5 October 1525
Your friend, Erasmus   15

* * * * *

1628
1 On this important first edition of the Greek text of Galen's works, see Ep 1594 n3.
2 Andrea Torresani of Asola, who now controlled the former Aldine press
3 Giambattista Opizzoni; cf Ep 1594 n4.

To the excellent Master Francesco Asolano, who is as dear to me as a brother. In Venice

1629 / To Andrzej Krzycki   Basel, 5 October 1525

Erasmus had many admirers among the ecclesiastical and intellectual elite of Poland; and as in this case, his contact with many of them was established through the family of Jan Łaski. Andrzej Krzycki (1482–1534) was the nephew of Piotr Tomicki, vice chancellor of Poland and bishop of Cracow. He studied at Bologna (1498–1503) under the humanists Antonio Codro Urceo and Filippo Beroaldo the Elder. After his return to Poland, he rose rapidly, both within the church and in the service of King Sigismund I, and by this time he was not only secretary but also a close adviser to the king. He was a skilled and prolific Latin poet, noted especially for his gift for epigrams. In 1522 he became bishop of Przemyśl, a diocese which he later changed for Plock (1527) and eventually Gniezno (1535), the primate's see. Though an enthusiast for humanistic learning and at first inclined to sympathize with some of Luther's ideas, he quickly became an outspoken foe of the German reformer, producing both tracts and poems against him. His role in negotiating the treaty (1525) which led to the transformation of Prussia into a secular and Lutheran duchy was based entirely on political considerations, not religious sympathy. The writings referred to in this letter are related both to his opposition to Luther and to his part in the Prussian settlement. Allen VI 194 quotes a letter of Krzycki to Stanislaus Hosius which shows the delight caused by receipt of this letter from Erasmus; and an active correspondence ensued, though only one of Krzycki's letters survives (Ep 1652). On his career, especially as a Latin poet, see Harold B. Segel *Renaissance Culture in Poland* (Ithaca, NY 1989) 191–226. Erasmus included this letter in his *Opus epistolarum*.

ERASMUS OF ROTTERDAM TO ANDRZEJ KRZYCKI, BISHOP OF
PRZEMYŚL
Cordial greetings, my Lord Bishop. When the illustrious Baron Stanisław Łaski[1] passed this way, he showed me a book of yours[2] in which you hurl

* * * * *

1629
1 A younger brother of Hieronim and Jan Łaski. After his visit to Erasmus at Basel he entered the service of Francis I, sharing the king's captivity at the battle of Pavia. He was soon released and later in 1525 accompanied Margaret of Angoulême to Spain to negotiate for the French king's release.
2 Probably his *In Luterum oratio*, which was published in a volume of prose and

your infantry and cavalry against the army of the Lutherans. Recently his 5
brother (and a true brother he is, since they are so alike) showed me your
Epistle,[3] which sets out a record of events along with some verses thrown
in for good measure. I realized from this that your Lordship has spent many
profitable hours in the garden of the Muses, not to mention the gymnasia
of the rhetoricians and the holy of holies of the theologians, and that you 10
have been generous enough to cast a glance at my works too, typically
Dutch though they be.

Since you have set an example which is rare these days among our
bishops, I am sending you as a gift a book[4] by the Reverend Father Cuthbert Tunstall, bishop of London in England,[5] who has lately left on a 15

* * * * *

verse by him and several friends, *Encomia Luteri* ὡς ἐκ τρίποδος (Cracow:
Hieronymus Vietor 1524). In it, he refers to Erasmus' published criticism of
Luther. He also wrote a number of other verse and prose works attacking
Luther.

3 There are several possible identifications of this work. Allen Ep 1629:5n identifies it as Krzycki's *De negotio Prutenico epistola* (Cracow: Hieronymus Vietor
1525), a defence of Poland's agreement to the transformation of Albert of
Brandenburg, grand master of the Teutonic Knights, into a secular duke of
Prussia, an act which led both to the secularization of an ecclesiastical principality and to the triumph of Lutheranism in the region. Krzycki's reply in Ep
1652:87–9 implies that he himself was puzzled by Erasmus' reference but had
concluded that his *De negotio Prutenico epistola* was the work which Erasmus
had seen. Harold B. Segel *Renaissance Culture in Poland: The Rise of Humanism,
1470–1543* (Ithaca, NY 1989) 219–21 seems to imply that the *Epistle* mentioned
here might have been one of his poems on the pro-Lutheran riots against the
local ruling class staged by the German population of Gdansk in January 1525.
The difficulty with this identification is that Erasmus' words show that the
passages of verse were only incidental insertions into a text which he labels an
epistle. According to Theodor Wotschke *Geschichte der Reformation in Polen*
(Leipzig 1911) 16, the book *Encomia Luteri* also contained, among other items,
a letter which savagely vilified Luther. But again there is a difficulty with such
an identification: the work here mentioned is presented as something quite
distinct from the one previously mentioned. Since Erasmus' text indicates that
the *Epistle* came into his hands by way of his house guest Jan Łaski and not
from Stanisław Łaski, it might also refer to a work of Krzycki edited by
Franciscus Bachiensis and published at Rome in 1524, *Epistola Andree Crucii et
edictum regis Polonie in Martinum Luterum*. In any case, the identity of the
precise text Erasmus had in mind remains obscure and apparently was obscure
to Krzycki himself.

4 *De arte supputandi* (London: Richard Pynson, 14 October 1522; STC 24319). This
was the first book on arithmetic printed in England and was reprinted several
times in Paris and Strasbourg. Allen Ep 1629:12n notes that Krzycki wrote
directly to Tunstall expressing his admiration of this book.

5 Cf Ep 207:25n. Educated in Italy and a close friend of Erasmus, Tunstall was

mission to the emperor Charles. He is a man whose life is beyond reproach, equally at home in both Greek and Latin, and knowledgeable in all the liberal arts. I knew you would be delighted to see that this kind of bishop is becoming gradually more common. I had also something else in mind. Just as I had found in Tunstall an incomparable patron, so I hoped to make   20
use of the opening which presented itself to find a place in your circle too. I know I shall be loved more faithfully by both of you, if you are joined by mutual friendship and good will, cemented by similarity of character and common interests.

I have written this in a great hurry, while our distinguished friend   25
Jan[6] is getting ready to mount his horse. His departure is a mortal blow to many here, myself included; everyone who shared his company will miss him sorely when he leaves. I wish your Lordship well.

Basel, 5 October 1525

1630 / To Jacobus Apocellus   Basel, 9 October 1525

Apocellus (d 1550), born near Bruchsal in southwestern Germany, matriculated at Heidelberg in 1509 and by 1515 was in Rome, where he made his career in curial service, chiefly as an official of the confraternity of Germans resident in Rome, Santa Maria dell'Anima. He was interested in humanistic studies and owned a number of Greek manuscripts. Erasmus' letter commends to him one of Apocellus' own kinsmen who was travelling to Rome. The letter was printed in the *Opus epistolarum*.

ERASMUS OF ROTTERDAM TO JACOBUS APOCELLUS, GREETING
Honoured sir, if you think it impertinent of me to write to you when we are such strangers to one another, you can assign a good share of the blame to your cousin Justus.[1] He pressed me with all his usual eloquence and even

* * * * *

not only a bishop but also an experienced diplomat. His mission to the imperial court in Spain kept him there from April 1525 until late January 1526 and was related to the captivity of Francis I of France.
6 Jan Łaski, who had been living in Erasmus' house at Basel and was now leaving for Italy and thence back home to Poland

1630
1 Justus Diemus of Bruchsal was apparently unknown to his kinsman Apocellus and carried recommendations from both Erasmus and Beatus Rhenanus (BRE 249). Though well received at Rome, he found the climate unbearable and returned to Germany, where he entered the service of Johannes Fabri in the

induced others to back him up, so that I could not refuse what he asked.   5
But if you are willing to pardon his audacity and my weakness, I shall be
glad that this happy chance has increased the list of my friends. Your cousin
seems cut out for the management of affairs. He has a ready tongue and a
polished style, and his shyness is so nicely under control that it does not
obscure what he has to say. He will be a great man one day, if you continue   10
to give him your backing. Farewell.

Basel, 9 October 1525

1631 / To Paolo Bombace   Basel, 9 October 1525

On the recipient see Ep 210 introduction. Since first meeting Erasmus at
Bologna, Bombace had become one of his firmest friends among the curial
humanists, and increasingly he functioned as a mediator between Erasmus and
those at the curia who suspected him of being a Lutheran. The specific purpose of this letter was to congratulate Bombace on his appointment as secretary to Pope Clement VII the preceding year. Bombace died in 1527, a casualty
of the sack of Rome by the imperial army; and his library was destroyed at the
same time. Erasmus included this letter, which documents his close relations
with an influential member of the papal curia, in his *Opus epistolarum*.

ERASMUS OF ROTTERDAM TO PAOLO BOMBACE, GREETING
Greetings to you, Croesus, or would you prefer to be addressed as Midas![1]
But seriously, my dear Bombace, I am delighted by this rise in your for-
tunes[2] and even more by your good health; I can now hope that my dear
friend will have a long and vigorous old age. The kindness with which you   5

* * * * *

household of Archduke Ferdinand. Sometime before a letter of 14 August 1527
from Stephanus Martialis to Friedrich Nausea, he had drowned.

1631
1 Both Croesus (c 560–46 BC), the last king of Lydia, and Midas, a legendary king
  of the Phrygians, were proverbial in ancient literature for their wealth, the
  former because he really was the king of a prosperous state and was associated
  with the introduction or reform of coinage, the latter because of the myth that
  by the power of a Silenus whom he captured, he was given the power to turn
  everything he touched into gold. Erasmus also refers to this story in *Adagia* I
  vi 24 (CWE 32 18–19), 'The riches of Midas,' where the story is that Midas in
  return for his hospitality to the god Bacchus was promised one wish and hence
  prayed that whatever he touched would turn into gold.
2 Bombace was appointed secretary to Pope Clement VII on 5 September 1524.

received my man Karl pleases me;[3] that same occasion showed me how
warmly your patron, the cardinal,[4] feels towards me, and this pleases me
too. You know I could hardly believe you before. I have had no time to
write; so you must be my substitute for a long letter to him. I tried again
in the early autumn to visit Italy, but the couriers were late in returning and   10
winter came upon us earlier than usual.[5] Farewell, mighty patron.
    Basel, 9 October 1525

1632 / To Fridericus Nausea   Basel, 9 October 1525

For Nausea's career see Ep 1577 introduction. At this time he was in Bologna
and in a letter now lost had announced his intention of visiting Basel, probably in connection with his attempt to take up his appointment as cathedral
preacher at Frankfurt-am-Main, which the triumph of the Reformation in that
city made it impossible for him to hold. He did visit Erasmus early in 1526;
cf Epp 1632, 2906. He was already gaining recognition as a defender of
Catholicism in the press, and by the end of the decade (1529), when Erasmus
published this letter in his *Opus epistolarum*, his outspoken defence of traditional religion had helped him to develop excellent connections with the
Hapsburg court in Vienna. Unlike many Catholic apologists, Nausea remained
a strong defender of Erasmus' reputation; and his *In magnum Erasmum Roterodamum nuper vita defunctum monodia* (Cologne: Johannes Gymnicus 1536), a
eulogy published shortly after Erasmus' death in 1536, attributes to Erasmus
a divine mission to restore religion.

ERASMUS OF ROTTERDAM TO FRIDERICUS NAUSEA, GREETING
I was delighted by the book you sent,[1] and even more by the letter,[2] which

* * * * *

  3 Karl Harst, Erasmus' secretary who carried most of Erasmus' letters to Italy at
    this period.
  4 Bombace had been secretary to Cardinal Lorenzo Pucci from 1513 until his
    appointment as papal secretary. See Ep 860 introduction, Ep 1411 n14.
  5 Erasmus had made plans to go to Italy in the autumn of 1522, but ill health
    prevented him from getting farther than Constance. See Ep 1315 introduction.

  1632
  1 In 1524 Nausea had published a book urging Erasmus to become directly in-
    volved in political efforts to end the religious divisions of Germany (cf Ep 1577
    n1). The book here mentioned is probably his *Ad ... Carolum V ... pro sedando
    plebeio in Germania ... tumultu* (Vienna: n pr 1525; repr Venice: L. Lorius 1525)
    dealing with the Peasant War.
  2 Not extant, but probably a reply to Ep 1577

was a work of art. It was not all those eulogies which delighted me, though
you passed them out with a generous, or rather a prodigal, hand. In fact I
could not have brought myself to read them, had I not realized that they   5
came from a very warm heart and a mind deeply prejudiced in my favour.
But may I ask you, my dear Nausea, to search out some other subject in
future on which to exercise your pen?

I have written to Cardinal Campeggi on your behalf.[3] It was only a
short note, but there was no need for more and I had no time to write at   10
greater length. If you come here, you will see that the agony in the countryside has eased and is closer to a cure. The blood-letting has brought the
fever down.[4] The rest of our news can wait till you come, which I hope
will be soon. Till then, my dearest Nausea, farewell.

Basel, 9 October 1525   15

1633 / To Daniel Mauch   Basel, 10 October 1525

This letter, with its scandalous (and erroneous) gossip that Luther's wife gave
birth to a child only a few days after her wedding, was published by Erasmus
himself in *Opus epistolarum*, but with the paragraph about Luther omitted. The
complete text was published in 1602 by Justus Baronius, probably from the
original manuscript. Allen VI 198 in upholding the authenticity of the suppressed portion observes that Erasmus told the same story in Epp 1653 and
1655 but chose not to publish those letters. Daniel Mauch of Ulm (1504–67)
was educated at Heidelberg, Tübingen (BA 1523), Cologne, Vienna, and Erfurt
and later studied law at Louvain before taking his doctorate in both civil and
canon law at Pavia in 1536. When Cardinal Campeggi came to Hungary on his
legation in 1524, Mauch attached himself to the service of his principal secre-

* * * * *

3 This letter to the cardinal is lost, but since Nausea had spent 1524–5 in his
   service, accompanying him on his travels as legate to Germany, Hungary, and
   Bohemia, it could hardly have been a mere generalized reference and most
   likely had to do with support for Nausea's appointment in Frankfurt. Campeggi in fact had actively solicited support for that appointment, writing letters
   to Archduke Ferdinand, the Frankfurt city council, the bishop of Strasbourg,
   Theoderich Zobel (vicar to the archbishop of Mainz), and Lorenz Truchsess of
   Mainz in his behalf. See Nausea's *Epistolarum miscellanearum ... libri X* (Basel:
   Iohannes Oporinus 1550) 31–4.
4 That is, the bloody suppression of the Peasant War, which had reached its
   peak in the spring and summer of 1525 but was now over in most regions. On
   the peasants' uprising, see Preface, pages xi–xii. In the medicine of the time,
   blood-letting was the remedy for fever: cf Celsus *De medicina* 2.10.6.

Martin Luther and Katharina von Bora
From the workshop of Lucas Cranach the Elder, 1529, detail
Kunstmuseum, Bern

tary, Floriano Montini, and in this way entered the cardinal's household. In 1525–7 he accompanied Montini on a papal embassy to Muscovy, and in 1531 he entered the service of George of Austria, bishop of Bressanone. In 1542–4 he worked as advocate in the imperial court at Speyer and then took holy orders and became a canon of the chapter at Worms, where for many years he headed the chapter school.

Cordial greetings. To be loved, my good Daniel, and not to love in return – wild beasts would hardly act like that! You love Erasmus, whom you know from his books; so I love Daniel in return, who has revealed himself in his kind and modest letters. It was said of Daniel that he was a 'man greatly desired.'[1] Is it strange, then, that you, a man desired, should desire   5
Desiderius? But what is this you are telling me? When others are leaving the courts of the mighty because of a desire for a quiet life, you have fled from the storm into the court, as though it were a peaceful haven! Nausea is always the same: wherever he goes, he sings my praises, making me out as great a man as his extravagant love for me convinces him that I am. That   10
was a delightful letter of Montini's,[2] but I doubt if I have time to reply at present.

    Will you pass on to Montini some delightful news? Luther has put aside the philosopher's cloak and taken a wife (may heaven bless and prosper the event!). She is an attractive young lady from the distinguished   15
family of the von Boras, twenty-six years old, but dowerless, who abandoned the life of a vestal some time ago. And in case you should have any doubts that the marriage was blessed by heaven, a few days after the singing of the wedding hymn the new bride gave birth to a child![3]

    Montini finds something funny in this bloody crisis;[4] but it sent about   20

* * * * *

1633
1 Dan 10:11
2 Not extant. On Montini see Epp 1552 introduction, 1578.
3 Although Erasmus' information on the supposed pregnancy of Katharina von Bora was untrue, he was well informed on her identity and background. Her marriage to Luther took place on 13 June; cf Ep 1624 n7. By the following March Erasmus had learned that the news of the bride's pregnancy at the time of their marriage was false and corrected the error in a letter (Ep 1677) to the Paris humanist François Dubois.
4 That is, the Peasant War. Allen Ep 1633:17n suggests that Montini's letter, which is lost, may have played on two similar Greek words, *crisis* (meaning crisis) and *chrisis* (chrism). Erasmus, who experienced the excitement and suffering in country districts near Basel, obviously found these events less amusing. On the peasants' uprising, see Preface, pages xi–xii.

100,000 peasants into the world of Orcus. The worst is over now, and
Nausea will find, if he comes here, that the illness has become much more
treatable. Farewell, and be my friend. You must do so if you are as fond of
Nausea as you say.

Basel, 10 October 1525   25

Best regards to Montini

Your friend, Erasmus of Rotterdam

To Daniel Mauch of Ulm, a young man of great promise, in the household of his Eminence Cardinal Campeggi. At Rome

1634 / To Alberto Pio   Basel, 10 October 1525

Erasmus had long been uneasy about reports that influential persons in the
Roman curia and elsewhere in Italy were accusing him of being the source of
Luther's errors, even of being secretly in collusion with him. This uneasiness,
connected with his justified feeling that Girolamo Aleandro was privately
circulating similar charges, focused on Alberto Pio, prince of Carpi. Already
in a letter of 31 August 1524 he hinted at this enmity, though he did not
openly mention Pio's name (Ep 1479 n57). In May 1525 he complained to Celio
Calcagnini, a mutual friend, that Pio was slandering him at Rome (Ep 1576:
46–9). Despite Calcagnini's reassuring reply (Ep 1587), Erasmus was convinced
that the rumours were true and decided to confront Pio by writing directly to
him. This letter opens an exchange of letters and publications which brought
out into the open a group of curial humanists who accused Erasmus of prima-
ry responsibility for the religious upheaval in Germany. Pio was the most
overt such opponent; Aleandro was the other major figure, though he circulated his views only in secret (cf Epp 1553 n9, 1581 n52, 1582 n8, 1605 n2). The
controversy with Pio continued down to, and even after, Pio's death. Erasmus
had good reason to be alarmed, for Pio was highly influential both among
scholars and among ecclesiastical and governmental officials, not only at Rome
but also in Paris and elsewhere. The present letter is a remarkably candid
account of Erasmus' own perception of the relation between humanism and
the Reformation, all the more remarkable as it was addressed to a person he
knew to be hostile. He frankly admits that at first he sympathized with Luther
and hoped that his actions might lead to true reform. He also bluntly charges
that the real cause of the religious upheaval was the worldliness and corruption of many of the clergy and the oppressiveness and arrogance of certain
theologians and monks. He believes that these obscurantists were really
fighting against the revival of humanistic studies and that they consciously
sought to get the upper hand by falsely identifying the humanist cause with
the cause of Luther. He also implies that persons living at Rome had no idea

of conditions in Germany or of the pressures faced by German Catholics and so had no right to criticize them.

Alberto Pio (1475–1531) was a scion of the ruling family of the principality of Carpi, but by this time he had been driven into permanent exile at Rome and had lost his lands because he had supported the French against the emperor. He had also had a major career as a diplomat, representing at different times the marquis of Mantua, the emperor Charles V, and the king of France. His intellectual credentials were at least as formidable as his political and social ones. His mother was a sister of the famous Giovanni Pico della Mirandola, who after the death of the boy's father became his guardian and chose Aldo Manuzio, the humanist and publisher, as his tutor. When Aldo began his printing career at Venice, Alberto Pio may have been one of his financial backers. Pio also studied at Ferrara under the philosopher Pietro Pomponazzi and was a close friend of Calcagnini, Pietro Bembo, Jacopo Sadoleto, and Ludovico Ariosto. Thus his connections at Rome and throughout Italy created the danger that he would turn the humanist intellectuals and the officials of the Roman curia decisively against Erasmus. Unlike Calcagnini and other Italian friends of Erasmus, Pio seems not to have been impressed at all by Erasmus' open break with Luther; and in his subsequent publications, he attempted to prove that Erasmus' opinions were essentially identical with Luther's and to demand that at the very least Erasmus must acknowledge his guilt and must publicly recant the errors in his books.

Pio's reply to this letter has the form of a letter but is really a treatise, *Responsio accurata et paraenetica, Martini Lutheri et asseclarum eius haeresim vesanam magnis argumentis et iustis rationibus confutans*, and is dated 14 May 1526. Although not published until early in 1529, it circulated in manuscript. In a letter of September 1526 (Ep 1744), Erasmus reported having received a copy from the author and complained that it was being handed about at the curia. Although most of its criticisms struck Erasmus as unfair, what really infuriated him was the author's determination, even in the title, to associate him with Luther. Nevertheless, although he eventually wrote a letter to Pope Clement VII (Ep 1987) protesting against the circulation of both this book and an anonymous tract which he correctly attributed to Aleandro, he did not write a response until he learned in a letter from Louis de Berquin (Ep 2066) that Pio, having fled to Paris after the sack of Rome, was now planning to publish his earlier attack. On 28 December 1528 he again wrote directly to Pio (Ep 2080), excusing his failure to write earlier on grounds of uncertainty where to find Pio after his flight from Rome, and begging him not to publish. The letter was too late, for Pio's book came off the press of Josse Bade in Paris on 7 January 1529. Erasmus thereupon produced (in only ten days, he claims) his own *Responsio ad epistolam paraeneticam Alberti Pii*, a treatise of eighty pages which Froben published in March. This edition included the present letter. Although Erasmus remained civil, Pio was neither mollified nor convinced. He set to work producing an extensive reply, at which he continued to work until his death on 7 January 1531. His secretary, Francesco Florido Sabino, saw this book through the press: *Tres et viginti libri in locos lucubrationum variarum D. Erasmi Rotterodami* (Paris: Josse Bade, 9 March 1531). This book attempted to demonstrate in great detail the accuracy of Pio's charges. Although some friends urged Erasmus not to reply since the author was dead, he regarded the accusations as too serious to pass unanswered. His reply, *Apologia adversus rhapsodias Alberti Pii*, was published by Froben in July 1531. Myron P. Gilmore 'Erasmus and Alberto Pio, Prince of Carpi' in *Action and Conviction in Early Modern Europe: Essays in Memory of E.H. Harbison* ed Theodore K. Rabb and Jerrold E. Seigel (Princeton 1969) 313 called it 'one of the most savage compositions Erasmus ever wrote'; it accuses Pio of lies, misquotations, and distortions, and excuses him only to the extent that he was probably senile and accepted uncritically false materials provided by others. This was Erasmus' last public word in the affair, but one of those whom Erasmus had named as having provided Pio with falsified materials, Juan Ginés de Sepúlveda, wrote an *Antapologia* (Rome: Antonius Bladus 1532) denying any share in it and defending Pio's good character and intentions though not necessarily endorsing all of his accusations. Cf Rummel II 123–8. This time Erasmus chose not to reply, except in a polite private letter (Ep 2701) which initiated a reasonably friendly correspondence that continued down to Erasmus' death. The present letter was included in the prefatory materials of Pio's original *Responsio* (1529), but with many errors. Erasmus reprinted it with corrections in his own *Responsio* (also 1529), and it appeared again in Pio's posthumous *Tres et viginti libri* (1531). The extensive literature on this controversy is surveyed by Bernuzzi and Deutscher in CEBR III 88, to which add Chris L. Heesakkers in *Erasmus of Rotterdam* ed Jan Sperna Weiland and W.T.M. Frijhoff (Leiden 1988) 79–87, Silvana Seidel Menchi 'Alcuni atteggiamenti della cultura italiana di fronte a Erasmo (1520–1536)' in *Eresia e riforma nell'Italia del Cinquecento: Miscellanea* I (DeKalb, Illinois 1974) 71–133, especially 73, 89–90, and Rummel II viii, 115–23; in the older literature, cf Friedrich Lauchert *Die italienische litterarische Gegner Luthers* (Freiburg im Breisgau 1912).

TO HIS ILLUSTRIOUS HIGHNESS ALBERTO PIO, PRINCE OF CARPI, CORDIAL GREETINGS
Men of high birth should show a generous heart, and those who have been blessed by fortune have no cause to envy anyone. Friends of long standing who know you well are full of praise for the exceptional kindliness of your nature, which extends even to those who have done little to deserve your

support. So I cannot understand what can have entered your head to make you turn against Erasmus. I hope you will pardon the frankness of my remarks. Possibly there is some confusion over names: I know how danger- ous it is to trust rumours of this kind. So, if anything like that has hap-   10 pened, please consider this letter as not meant for you.

We hear the same story from many visitors from your part of the world, that there is a certain prince of Carpi at Rome, a good scholar and a man of influence among the cardinalate, who takes every opportunity to denounce Erasmus openly as no philosopher and no theologian, and as   15 someone who lacks any solid learning.[1] I get the same message from many of my correspondents, whose letters all point in the same direction.

I am not troubled, and never have been, when someone says things about me which I frankly admit, both in conversation and in print, to be true; on the other hand nobody upsets me so much as those who heap false   20 and invidious praises on my head. If I ever put myself forward as a great theologian or philosopher, I would deserve to have my lion's skin stripped from me.[2] But I make no great claims for myself and promise only what I can deliver, without setting myself up above others or undermining anyone else's reputation; why then, I wonder, should someone of good family and   25 uncommon learning, that is, someone so blessed by fortune that he might feel contempt, rather than hate, for these apelike nonentities from the world of learning, stoop to belittling Erasmus; for I have always worshipped and venerated men like you, and, far from envying my equals, I delight in praising my inferiors in every way I can. In the subjects which I have   30 tackled, I think I have acquitted myself tolerably well, especially if you bear in mind that I am a barbarian writing for barbarians.[3] I have not so far dealt with any subject which requires a deep knowledge of philosophy, except the problem of free will.[4] This I took up reluctantly and in response

* * * * *

1634
1 Cf Ep 1576:46–9, where the report of the accusation is framed in exactly the same way: 'as no philosopher and no theologian, and as someone who lacks any solid learning.' But the really serious accusation, that Erasmus is to blame for the religious upheaval in Germany, does not appear until the fourth para- graph.
2 The reference is to the story of the Cumaean donkey who dressed himself in a lion's skin but was eventually unmasked. Cf *Adagia* I iii 66; I vii 12.
3 An obvious reference to the Italian practice of belittling all northern Europeans as 'barbarians'
4 A reference to his own *De libero arbitrio* directed against Martin Luther

to many requests. I treated it as simply as I could, and if my work was   35
deficient in learning, I do not think it lacked respect for the faith. So what
is to be gained, I ask you, if a great man like yourself persuades us that
Erasmus is a mere beginner in these noble fields of learning? There are
many people in this category who nevertheless claim the rank of scholar.
You would have been better employed unmasking those (and they are to be   40
found everywhere in our schools) who teach young people nothing and
make them believe they know everything.

When someone makes a personal judgment about my abilities, my
writings, or my style, I accept the criticism without protest. But the story
which this prince likes to repeat every time the cardinals give a dinner-party 45
or scholars have a meeting – this I find more disturbing, for he tells them
that all our present troubles began with Erasmus.[5] This story is entirely
without foundation, but could anyone have thought of a more damning
indictment if I had poisoned both his parents? When the opening scene of
the Lutheran tragedy began to unfold, to the applause of nearly the whole   50
world, I was the first to urge my friends not to get involved, for I could see
that it would end in bloodshed. And since certain people were putting it
about, presumably with the idea of attracting others to their cause, that I
was sympathetic to Luther, I published several books in which I made it
clear that I never had, and never would have, any truck with Luther.[6] I   55
advised Luther himself to be careful how he treated the gospel message,[7]
so that no one could accuse him of yielding to ambition or spite, and to see
that the whole thing did not end in civil strife. I even used threats to discourage Froben from publishing anything of Luther's. He did not publish
his work, though that meant a considerable financial loss, for he preferred   60
to take my advice rather than serve his own interests.[8] In Germany and
Switzerland all lovers of the humanities were enthusiastic supporters of

* * * * *

5 Here, not the charge that Erasmus was deficient in learning, is the crux of the
  dispute. Such charges had been made before (cf Ep 1341A:1145–6), but generally by persons like Noël Béda whom Erasmus despised and whose opinions
  he could belittle as the result of their ignorance of 'good letters.' But Pio was
  an influential member of the very innermost circles of Italian humanism, as
  also of curial society. To be attacked (and at Rome itself) by such a man as the
  source of Luther's heresies was both offensive and dangerous. That is why
  Erasmus pursued this issue so doggedly.
6 For example, De esu carnium, Spongia, and Catalogus omnium lucubrationum (the
  latter is Ep 1341A)
7 See Epp 980, 1127A.
8 See Epp 904:20n, 938:1, 1033:52–5, 1143 n6, 1167:305–7, 1195:143–4.

Luther at the beginning. With a few exceptions, I turned all of them from my devoted friends into the bitterest of foes.[9] On the one side I had the theologians, who, because of their hatred of the humanities, were doing everything possible to push me into a sect which they themselves believed should be condemned out of hand; on the other side I had the Lutherans, who were working in the same direction through wheedling, trickery, threats, and abuse, though their ultimate aim was different from that of the theologians. Yet in spite of this no one has yet been able to move me a finger's breadth from membership in the church of Rome. You would not be so totally unsympathetic to my attitude if you understood what so many of the regions of this country feel and what the princes are planning to do, or if you realized what trouble I could have caused, had I wished to put myself at the head of this movement. But I chose instead to expose myself, naked and unarmed, to attack from both sides rather than lift a finger in support of a sect which the Roman church does not recognize.

But 'Luther drew his inspiration from my books.' Luther himself stoutly denies it. In what he says about me and in his writings he takes the same position as the prince of Carpi, namely that I know no theology, apparently because I agree at no point with his own teaching. But let us suppose that he did derive something from my writings. Should I be held accountable for that, any more than Paul and Augustine, whose works he is fond of quoting in support of his point of view? Certainly when I was writing those works of mine, I had no idea that such a commotion would arise.

Some people say: 'Why did you not oppose this evil the moment it first appeared?' Because, like many others, I thought Luther was a good man, sent from God to reform the evil ways of men – though even then some of his ideas offended me and I spoke to him about them. Moreover, the world was full of universities, and I could see that Luther's fantasies were gaining a surprising amount of support not only among ordinary people, but among princes, bishops, and even a number of the cardinals; so would it not have been sheer effrontery for an ordinary citizen like myself to fly in the face of such general support?

If I may speak freely, I shall tell you what was the original source of

* * * * *

9 Erasmus must have in mind persons like Oecolampadius and Pellicanus in Basel, Zwingli in Zürich, and Eobanus Hessus in Erfurt. In all of these cases, a warm, affectionate friendship was chilled (though not quite so completely destroyed as Erasmus' words here suggest) solely because of religious disagreement.

this disaster, at least as I understand it. It was the blatantly godless lives of some of the clergy, the arrogance of certain theologians, and the tyrannical behaviour of some monks – these were the things which brought such a storm of troubles upon us. When I say this, I should not like my strictures on the wicked to reflect upon the reputation of the good; nor should my general remarks be construed as an insult to any particular order. The first battles were against the study of languages and of Latin literature. I supported such studies in so far as their inclusion might further and support traditional learning, not, as the saying goes, 'to push the old professors off the bridge.'[10] I thought they might serve Christ's glory; I did not want to bring the old paganism back to the modern world. Then, when the outcome of the battle was still in doubt, some monks turned the issue into a question of faith. This was a convenient target, which suited their purpose. I am sure you have heard of the sorry business concerning Reuchlin.[11] From that time on, the resentment which scholars felt against the monks was more bitter. Soon, when the war between the devotees and enemies of the Muses was still raging at its fiercest, Luther came on the scene. Immediately the monks began to connect the supporters of the humanities with the Lutheran affair, hoping in this way to destroy both at the same time. So between the obstinacy of the one faction, with its steady decline from bad to worse, and the prejudices and untimely clamour of some of those on the other side, things have gradually sunk to their present sorry state.

That is the whole story, just as it is, without any embroidery. If the rumours I have heard are true, I must ask you to revise your view of the case and stop saying things like this which are dangerous to me. If on the other hand the rumours are false, please pardon my intrusion upon your Excellency's time with this mournful litany. I wish you every success and happiness.

Basel, 10 October 1525
Erasmus of Rotterdam in haste, with his own hand

1634A / From Benedetto Giovio   [Como, summer? 1525]

This letter is undated but must precede 7 October 1525, the date of Ep 1635,

* * * * *

10 A variant on the proverb, 'to throw the sexagenarians off the bridge'; cf *Adagia* I v 37.
11 This passage shows that Erasmus regarded the attack on Reuchlin as aimed at humanism in general. Modern scholarship has questioned this widespread opinion; cf Ep 1601 n3.

which is Erasmus' reply. It was long believed lost but was discovered in a manuscript of the Biblioteca Ambrosiana of Milan and published by Ida Calabi Limentani in *Acme* 25 (1972) 5–37. Aloïs Gerlo assigned it the number 1634A and published it in an Appendix to volume VI of his French translation of the correspondence, but it must be several weeks or even months earlier than Ep 1635. Chronologically, therefore, it should appear earlier in this volume, probably with the letters for June or July. In a preface to the manuscript in which it was found, Giovio explains that he collected several minor works with a view to publication, but the collection never appeared. Limentani includes this preface in her edition.

Benedetto Giovio (c 1471–c 1545) is much less well known than his younger brother Paolo, who became bishop of Nocera and a papal diplomat but is best known for his historical writings, especially his *Elogia* of famous contemporaries. Unlike his much-travelled brother, Benedetto spent his life in his native Como, though he did travel to Milan to perfect his Greek pronunciation under the tutelage of Demetrius Chalcondyles. He practised law and was active as a translator from Greek and Latin, as a poet, as an expert on Vitruvius, and as an historian. His principal historical work, published posthumously, was a history of Como; and his strong sense of local patriotism is also reflected in an unpublished commentary on the preface of Pliny *Naturalis historia*, where he begins by proving that Pliny was a native of Como and not of Verona (cf CTC IV 356–8). Giovio's purpose in writing this letter was to seek the opinion of Erasmus, whom in the preface to his manuscript he called 'without doubt the greatest scholar of our time,' on a number of textual questions, especially a difficult passage in the New Testament, John 8:25. But his local patriotism breaks through when he proudly informs Erasmus of a local inscription concerning Pliny (Limentani 27; now CIL V 5263) and seeks his opinion on the meaning of an abbreviation. At some later date, an unknown person has gone through the manuscript and systematically obliterated all references to Erasmus, substituting the less theologically sensitive name of Guillaume Budé.

BENEDETTO GIOVIO TO ERASMUS OF ROTTERDAM, CORDIAL
GREETINGS
A relative and fellow townsman of mine, Paolo Benzi,[1] not only urged and

* * * * *

1634a
1 Limentani pages 28–9 n129 observes that Benzi is documented at Como from 1516 to 1554 as a local official and that a tax record of 1537 lists him and a brother as owning property and business interests at Como and at Rome. The

prodded me, but actually forced me to send you these words of greeting, unpolished though they may be – as indeed all my letters are. I have long been aware what a great and distinguished man I would be disturbing if I obeyed his orders, for as Jupiter reigns on the heights of Olympus, so you command the heights of letters and of every branch of learning. So I felt embarrassed and could not work up the courage to send you anything in the way of a letter; you see I did not have the effrontery[2] to imagine it would be proper for me to exchange pleasantries with you. But he broke down my resistance. What changed my mind was his mentioning your good nature and genuine humanity, a quality which is evident also from the great monuments of your genius which you have left us. No one, no matter how insignificant, is driven from your door or from that inner sanctum where you tend the Muses. How could you scorn or despise, because of its lack of wit, any clumsy attempt which I might make at writing, when you have already produced so many pages and so many volumes for the benefit of everyone, and on every subject under the sun, so that everyone has access to you and may question you about anything without causing you offence? There can be no doubt that you are the Varro of our time.[3] In his day he filled the Roman world with countless 'hebdomads,'[4] covering grammar, logic, poetics, history, and all the other branches of the humanities. He then tackled theology, and, according to Augustine, treated the gods in the most

* * * * *

relationship mentioned by Giovio must have been through his mother, Elisabetta Benzi. The manuscript also contains three words which the later censor has rendered completely illegible and which Limentani (page 28) surmises may have expressed the connection between Erasmus and Benzi on which Benzi relied when he encouraged Giovio to write to Erasmus.

2 Cf *Adagia* I viii 47: *Faciem perfricare. Frontis perfricatae* (the etymological sources of 'effrontery'). Cf Quintilian 11.3.160, and Pliny *Naturalis historia* 1 preface 4.

3 Marcus Terentius Varro (116–27 BC), reputed 'the most learned of the Romans (Quintilian 10.1.95),' is now known for his *De re rustica libri III*, the most important Roman treatise on agriculture, and his *De lingua Latina*, which survives only in part but is a major source not only for the meaning of Latin terms but also for ancient usages and customs, both civil and religious. His *Antiquitates rerum humanarum ac divinarum*, of which only a few fragments survive, described Roman political and religious institutions and was the chief basis of his fame in ancient times, being a major source for St Augustine's *De civitate Dei*. His other works, also lost, included a collection of seven hundred biographical sketches of Greeks and Romans, the *Imagines* or *Hebdomades* here mentioned.

4 Cf preceding note. His works were arranged in groups of seven. Gellius (3.10.17) says that by age seventy-eight, he had completed seventy such 'hebdomades.'

minute and penetrating detail.[5] When he was in his eightieth year, to   25
everyone's surprise, he turned to agriculture, that 'unique consolation of old
age,' as Cicero later described it,[6] and wrote a detailed account of the subject. I do not propose to go through the incredibly long list of your own
writings, but you have accompanied Varro *pari passu*, as the saying goes, so
that as long as Greek and Latin literature last, you will be regarded as   30
undoubtedly the most learned and prolific of authors.[7] To provide a more
elegant translation of the teachings of our faith as found in the New Testament and then to elucidate them in the form of a paraphrase – that was a
task which required not just courage, but a well-stocked mind; what you
write comes from experience, you give us the fruit of your own observa-   35
tions. It was no doubt this undertaking of yours which stirred up such
resentment against you from our celebrated experts. This is why I venerate
you – if it is proper for a Christian to bow down, like a Persian, before
another human being![8] If I could have my wish, I would like to possess the
flow of speech and the concise elegance which my fellow townsman Plinius   40
Caecilius displays when he writes in praise of one of his friends;[9] then I
could praise you as you deserve and do my best to save you from the
jealous hand of oblivion.[10]

To conclude, I should like to ask you about a few problems which
trouble me, since I have little experience in these scholarly matters. For since   45

* * * * *

5 St Augustine cited Varro frequently, especially on Roman religion, in *De
civitate Dei*; see, for example, 6.3.2.
6 *De senectute* 51
7 Giovio employs two Greek adjectives, πολυίστωρ 'of wide learning,' and
πολυγραφώτατος 'prolific.' For the first, cf Pliny *Naturalis historia* 36.79 and
Suetonius *De grammaticis* 20; the second adjective is applied to Varro by Cicero
Ad Atticum 13.18.
8 A reference to the Persian practice of *proskynesis* or prostrating oneself in the
presence of the king. The Greeks regarded the custom as barbarous and de-
grading (eg Herodotus 8.136), and many ancient authors recounted the story
of Alexander's attempt to adopt it and the opposition of the philosopher
Callisthenes (eg Arrian 4.10–12; Quintus Curtius Rufus 8.5.6–12; and Plutarch
Alexander 54). On the whole issue see J.R. Hamilton's commentary on the latter
passage and Ernst Badian *The Cambridge History of Iran* 5 vols (Cambridge
1968–85) II 457–9. Giovio's text here uses the Greek term: προσκυνεῖν.
9 Giovio (correctly) claims Pliny's nephew, author of the *Letters*, as a native of
Como like his uncle, author of *Naturalis historia*.
10 Pliny *Letters* 3.5.4

my earliest years I have worked on legal documents[11] and produced, like other notaries, quite unliterary letters.[12]

First, how is it possible to defend the reading in John's Gospel[13] *Principium qui et loquor vobis* taking *principium* in the nominative case, as Augustine does,[14] when the Greek text reads τὴν ἀρχήν? A host of com-   50
mentators have disagreed over this phrase, as is clear from the *Aurea catena*.[15] Giovanni Maria Cattaneo,[16] in discussing a passage in Pausanias

* * * * *

11 Benedetto worked as a lawyer and notary in Como.

12 A phrase used by Pliny the Younger *Letters* 1.10.9 to describe those letters that he wrote not for literary purposes but as part of his duties as a treasury official.

13 John 8:25. The Greek text of this passage has been much disputed and may be corrupt. It is difficult to find a suitable meaning for the accusative phrase τὴν ἀρχήν 'the beginning.' The Vulgate translation *principium* increases the ambiguity, since it could be either nominative or accusative. If nominative, the meaning would presumably be: '[I am] the beginning, who speak also to you.' The reader needs to be aware that both in this letter and in Erasmus' reply (Ep 1635), Giovio and Erasmus have three different texts (each with variants) in mind when they discuss this difficult passage in the Gospel of John: the Greek text, the Vulgate Latin, and Erasmus' new Latin translation. Their discussion moves from one text to the other without much warning.

14 *In Iohannis Evangelium tractatus* CXXIV: *Tractatus 38* CCL 36 344. Giovio is wrong about Augustine. He took *principium* as accusative with the sense '[believe that I am] the beginning ...'

15 *Catenae* 'chains' of the Bible are commentaries consisting of short excerpts from the Fathers or other ancient writers, strung together like links in a chain. They were important in the Middle Ages and remain so today since they preserve much patristic commentary, and even readings of the biblical text, that would otherwise be unknown. In the Greek tradition, such *catenae* go back to the late fifth century. *Catenae* in Latin go back to the Carolingian period and reached a peak in the high scholastic period (twelfth and thirteenth centuries), especially in the *Catena aurea* of St Thomas Aquinas. (Cf NCE III 244–6, art 'Catenae, biblical.') The patristic citations given by Aquinas from Augustine, Bede, and Chrysostom certainly do not resolve the confusion that troubles Giovio. See *Catena aurea* ed Angelico Guarienti (Turin 1953) II 45 (section 6).

16 A contemporary of Giovio and Erasmus, with date of death variously given as 1529, 1519, 1530. A native of Novara and a physician at Brescia, he became secretary to Cardinal Bandinello Sauli. He produced several translations from Greek to Latin, commentaries on Pliny the Younger and Plutarch, and some original works of poetry and prose, but neither Mario Cosenza *Biographical and Bibliographical Dictionary of the Italian Humanists* 2nd ed, 5 vols (Boston 1962) II 946–7, V 124 nor George B. Parks (CTC II 215–20) gives any trace of notes on Pausanias.

about the rhinoceros,[17] holds that οὐδὲ ἀρχήν is equivalent to *omnino* [altogether] or *prorsus* [absolutely]; this passage is cited by Angelo Poliziano in his *Miscellanea*,[18] who translates οὐδὲ ἀρχήν as *ne initio quidem* [not even   55 at first], which, *pace* Poliziano, does not make sense. Cattaneo's understanding of the phrase was accepted by a German commentator in his notes on this Gospel;[19] he claims that the Greek writer Nonnus[20] takes the same view in his metrical paraphrase of the Gospel. I brought this up because you translated the phrase as *in primis*, which does not seem logical.   60

I also thought that the name 'Iohannes' could be spelled with an aspirate in the middle, since we often put an *h* between two vowels, as in *traho, veho, mihi*; and in old texts we find *incoho*.[21] It is true that the Greeks pronounce the word without an aspirate; nevertheless I see no reason to follow them in the case of a foreign, that is a Hebrew, word. This word is   65 derived from the Hebrew *Hen*, written with the letter *cheth*, which, according to Jerome,[22] is pronounced as a double aspirate; the sound is so emphatic that the translators of the Septuagint represented it not just with an aspirate, but with the Greek letter.

Since I have mentioned Pliny, I must tell you that we have a very old   70 marble tablet in a mutilated state which bears the following inscription: C. PLINIO L.F. O.V.F. CAECILIO SECUNDO COS. AUG. CURAT. TIBER. ET. RIP.[23] The

* * * * *

17 9.21.1, a description of the rhinoceros
18 The great Florentine Hellenist, in his *Liber miscellaneorum* c 56 in *Opera* (Lyon 1539) page 611
19 Limentani 26 n111 conjectures that the reference is to some commentator excerpted in whichever *Aurea catena* Giovio had in mind; she rejects Allen's hypothesis (Allen Ep 1635:33n) that this is a reference to the prose commentary on Aratus by Germanicus Caesar.
20 Nonnus *Paraphrasis sancti evangelii Iohannis* 61–3 ed A. Scheindler (Leipzig 1881) 91–2. Nonnus of Panopolis (fl 5th cent) was a representative of the late Alexandrian school of Greek epic. In addition to this metrical *Paraphrasis*, also known as *Metabole*, he composed a work, *Dionysiaca*, about the adventures of Bacchus. The Greek text of the *Paraphrasis* had been published at Venice by the press of Aldus Manutius in 1501. A Latin translation by Christoph Hegendorf appeared from the press of Johannes Secerius at Hagenau in 1528. Neither Giovio nor Erasmus seems to have known the text at first hand. Nonnus' more famous poem *Dionysiaca*, which later became an important source for study of classical mythology, was not published until 1569 (Antwerp: Christoph Plantin) but existed in manuscript in the Laurentian library at Florence, and Poliziano cited it in his widely used collection of classical essays, *Miscellanea*.
21 The alternative form is *inchoo*, but ancient grammarians preferred *incoho*, and this spelling is supported by several early inscriptions.
22 *Commentarii 4 in Hieremiam* CCL 74 182; cf *Epistola ad Titum* PL 26 630.
23 The inscription (CIL V 5263) reads: 'To Gaius Plinius Caecilius Secundus, son

rest has been destroyed. Apart from the three letters O.V.F. everything is easy to understand: for Plinius Caecilius was consul and augur and curator of the banks and channel of the Tiber. These three letters occur more fre- 75 quently in inscriptions from Como than perhaps has been realized. Valerius[24] thought they stood for *omnibus viris fecit* [he acted for all men], but this interpretation does not make sense. When I put the question to Andrea Alciati of Milan,[25] a great expert not just in law but in all the liberal arts, he suggested that the letters stand for *omnium votis factum* 80 [approved by a general vote]; he thinks we should understand them of the public adoption of Caecilius Plinius by his uncle,[26] but this interpretation will not suit all passages. The letters occur less frequently in written texts. I have noted two examples in Julius Frontinus' *De aquaeductibus*,[27] but I could not puzzle out what they mean. If you have a better idea, please 85 make me a fellow initiate in the mystery. Farewell.

1634A / Appendix

This is the preface of Benedetto Giovio to the collection of his lesser works,

* * * * *

of Lucius, of the Ufentine tribe, consul, augur, curator of the Tiber and its banks.' In ancient Rome, citizens of Como were enrolled as Roman citizens in the Ufentine tribe. It was this tribal designation, OVF (which he transcribed by mistakenly adding a period after each letter) that Giovio could not understand. His (and others') speculative decipherment was completely off the mark. Cf Limentani 27, 34–36.

24 Limentani (27 n117) cites a work called *Notae iuris* or *De iuris notarum*, but the reference is not to be found in modern editions of Valerius Probus. Perhaps the citation is to a work which circulated under that title in the sixteenth century under the name of Probus but was not authentic. Limentani (35 n160) also attributes the solution *omnibus viris fecit* to a number of fifteenth- and sixteenth-century publications on the meaning of Roman inscriptions.

25 Cf Ep 1250 introduction. That this distinguished Milanese jurist could not resolve Giovio's puzzle with anything better than another conjecture shows clearly how little even the best classical scholars understood the nature of Roman inscriptions. According to Limentani 32, Alciati published this conjecture in his *Collectanea*.

26 The younger Pliny was adopted by his uncle. Alciati interpreted the abbreviation (as he incorrectly expanded it) as referring to a particular form of adoption, *adrogatio*, which in early times required a public act. But this requirement had been dropped long before Pliny's time.

27 The abbreviation here discussed, OVF, does not appear in modern texts of Frontinus *De aquis urbis Romae*. Limentani 27 n120, suggests a confusion with 'cos. V.F.' at 2.100, 104, 106, 108, where cos. stands for *consul* and V.F. stands for *verba fecit* 'made a report.'

Farrago suorum lusuum, which he prepared with a view to publication but never published. It includes the preceding letter. It survived in manuscript copies at Milan and Como and was published, along with the letter itself, by Limentani 24.

Preface to Benedetto Giovio's 'Farrago'

It was Desiderius Erasmus of Rotterdam,[1] without doubt the greatest scholar of our time and the flower among all cultivated men, who caused me to risk my reputation by publishing this collection of trifles, such as it is; my aim was to avoid being enrolled through a copyist's error in the wrong city! I preferred to hazard whatever literary reputation I might have rather than be falsely credited with belonging to a noble city to which I have no claim and to possessing a skill in medicine which I have never attained. If I were a native of Seriphos,[2] I would not think it proper to bask in the false glory of being called an Athenian, nor would I want to pass myself off as a lawyer when I am a legal clerk. In that volume of learned correspondence which Erasmus published lately, I appear by some accident, in the heading of a letter addressed to me, as a citizen of Milan and a physician. The mistake arose, I think, from the fact that my letter was lost, having been given to Beatus Rhenanus[3] to read, and also because there is some confusion with my fellow citizen Francesco Cigalini,[4] who is a medical man with a keen interest in the humanities. Erasmus had also written to him in reply to an erudite letter of his on questions of theology. This work of mine is not the sort of thing which should reach Erasmus' hands. Remember, Lucilius did not wish to be read by the scholarly Persius, but preferred the less learned Laelius Decimus.[5] All I intend by publishing these pieces is to show the reader of Erasmus' books

* * * * *

1634A
1 In the original manuscript, a later hand has obliterated Erasmus' name and inserted 'Guilelmus·Budaeus.' Cf Limentani 6, 9, and also her Table I, a photocopy of the defaced opening page.
2 An island of the Cyclades group. Plato (*Republic* 339B) and Cicero (*De senectute* 8) preserve a famous retort of Themistocles: 'I would not be so distinguished if I came from Seriphos, nor would you, if you came from Athens.'
3 At this period Erasmus' close collaborator on his editions of biblical, patristic, and classical texts for the Froben press was still spending most of his time in Basel, with frequent short trips to his native town of Sélestat, where in 1527 he established his permanent residence.
4 On this humanist physician of Como, a friend of both Giovio and Erasmus, see Ep 1680, which is the letter of Erasmus to which the present text refers.
5 Cicero *De oratore* 2.25

that I have, so to speak, been brought back from exile and restored to my native land.

1635 / To Benedetto Giovio   [Basel, ? October] 1525

This is a response to the preceding letter. On Giovio and the circumstances of this exchange, see the introduction to Ep 1634A. Erasmus here responds only to a very narrowly defined portion of Giovio's inquiry about the meaning of a passage from the Gospel of John (8:25), specifically the phrase τὴν ἀρχήν, on which Giovio had cited the opinions of the humanists Giovanni Maria Cattaneo and Angelo Poliziano. Those authors, however, had been dealing with a passage in Pausanias on the rhinoceros, not with the meaning of the phrase in the Gospel of John. Erasmus here explicitly replies that a sound scholar like Poliziano (*Miscellanea* ch 56 in his *Opera* [Lyons 1537–9] I 611) would have understood the Greek phrase in Pausanias but that that usage is not relevant to the scriptural passage. He replies even more vaguely to Giovio's inquiry about the aspirate in the middle of the name 'Iohannes'; and he does not respond at all to Giovio's request for help in deciphering the inscription referring to Pliny the Younger. The letter also contains a brief statement (Allen lines 8–10) of Erasmus' view of his own role in fostering the spread of humanistic studies from Italy into Germany and the Low Countries. Erasmus published it in his *Opus epistolarum*.

ERASMUS OF ROTTERDAM TO BENEDETTO GIOVIO OF MILAN, GREETING

I would not refuse the handsome compliment you pay me on my 'humanity' – so characteristic of your own humanity – if my health and the remorseless burden of my work and, what is almost worse, the obligations   5
of my correspondence allowed me to demonstrate my 'humanity' by helping those I would like, or ought, to help. No one will now find anything odd in the old proverb about making an elephant out of a fly,[1] since, if it pleases the Muses, you are trying to turn a real Dutch dumpling like me into another Varro.[2] For what have I in common with him except perhaps   10
my years and my voluminous writings?[3] I had fair success in Germany in

* * * * *

1635
1 *Adagia* I ix 69
2 That is, an authority for the meaning of Latin terms and for knowledge of ancient usages and customs, civil and religious. Cf Ep 1634A n3.
3 Erasmus used a Greek term which would be transliterated into Latin as *poly-*

arousing interest in languages and polite letters, and the applause which greeted my efforts was not entirely grudging (remember, the show was not intended for Italian ears); but then there was this sudden and disastrous upheaval, which, with its controversies and senseless disputes, began to   15
throw everything into confusion, and has now reached the point where human blood flows in torrents.[4] For, to mention nothing else, it is hard to imagine how anyone could avoid being saddened when peace is extinguished over so large an area of the world. The blow would be easier to bear if the downfall of the guilty did not involve so many innocent people.   20
Meanwhile everyone is grabbing what he can for himself – as when a fire breaks out in a public place.

I worry that some of the princes may take advantage of our present misfortunes to impose a tyranny of their own. There are people whom the world has long found it difficult to tolerate and whom it is always trying   25
to get rid of. What was originally a small band of honest men, like the Aeginetans,[5] is now a horde of reprobates who have taken control of the whole world; they have mixed with ordinary people; they have invaded the seats of authority and infiltrated the courts of princes; if you try to punish one of them, the battalions close ranks. It is they who are at the root of the   30
present tragedy because of their hatred of liberal studies.[6] They now churlishly insist that our troubles are the result of an interest in languages and letters, and they find princes whom they can convince that this is true. They raise an outcry against me as the originator and standard-bearer of these innovations, a charge which I neither can nor wish to repudiate entirely. I   35
can only hope that some divinity will check their imperious pride and unbridled arrogance. I see death and starvation hanging over the humanities and all those who practise them.

* * * * *

graphia. Cicero *Ad Atticum* 13.18 uses the corresponding Greek adjective in reference to Varro's prolific writing. Cf Erasmus' *Ciceronianus* (LB I 1013D / CWE 28 425 and n709) for another instance of the same usage, which he also applies to St Jerome in Allen Ep 1451:69.

4 A reference to the violence and instability associated with the spread of the Reformation in Germany. The reference to 'human blood' in line 17 shows that he has in mind particularly the Peasant War of 1524–5, which by this date had been ruthlessly suppressed in most regions. On the uprising, see Preface, pages xi–xii.

5 *Adagia* II v 61

6 A sharply negative reference to the monastic orders, especially the mendicants, who are presented here as a movement which was good and well-intentioned at its beginnings but has now become corrupt and insupportably oppressive, especially because of the orders' hostility to the growth of humanistic studies

But it is time to put an end to this tale of woe, which has gone on too long. I have not seen a copy of Nonnus[7] or of the German commentator[8] anywhere. I never doubted that οὐδ' ἀρχήν[9] is used in Greek for 'quite' or 'altogether.' I have seen it used in this way in more than one passage and I cannot imagine that Poliziano[10] was unaware of this. He must surely have found the meaning he gave it in a good Greek author or assumed that it was a Greek idiom; this is something which the old scholars did not hesitate to do. But I don't think that τὴν ἀρχήν is parallel to this expression. For a thing which has not even been begun is not happening at all τὴν ἀρχήν – though once in Gregory of Nazianzus I find: Σὺ δὲ οὐδὲ ὁμῇ τὴν ἀρχήν,[11] but it is not used there without the negative. I am not aware of any instances of τὴν ἀρχήν without the negative except in John. But if he is right to use τέλος [finally] for what comes last, then he is also right to use τὴν ἀρχήν to indicate the first of several points. I wonder if you have seen the third edition of my New Testament.[12] In it I discuss these matters in somewhat greater detail.

As for the spelling of certain words, this is a subject on which I never argue, especially where the words in question have been spelled differently by different authors or at different periods. The most acceptable spelling, however, is clearly that which best reflects the origin of the word, except when this runs counter to established usage. I should prefer *adfero* to *affero*, though I could not bring myself to write *herpyllum* for *serpyllum*.[13]

* * * * *

7 See Ep 1634A n20.
8 Cf Ep 1634A n19.
9 Erasmus' rather involved argument aims at demonstrating that although the Greek phrase mentioned by Giovio can indeed mean 'not at all,' and while Poliziano must have known this fact and so must have had some authority for translating the phrase in Pausanias as 'in the beginning,' the phrase οὐδ' ἀρχήν is negative and must be distinguished from the positive expression τὴν ἀρχήν. The meaning 'at all' is possible only with a negative, and even the passage from Gregory of Nazianus contains a negative earlier in the sentence. The negative usage is logical because a thing which has not even begun (the literal meaning of τὴν ἀρχήν) is not happening at all. Without the negative expression, however, this idiomatic sense would not emerge. So, he seems to have concluded, τὴν ἀρχήν can never mean 'at all' since it lacks a negative, and in the passage of John being discussed, it must mean 'at first' or 'firstly.' Thus John's usage of τὴν ἀρχήν is justified and clearly parallel to his quite unremarkable use of τέλος 'end' in the sense 'finally.'
10 See the preceding note and Ep 1634A n18.
11 *Sermo in Paschua* 17
12 *Annotationes in Novum Testamentum*, sv John 8:25.
13 *Adfero* was the original form of this compound verb, which became *affero* by

What you said about antiquities pleased me; it also delighted several
scholars to whom I showed your letter because of the reference. Beatus
Rhenanus[14] was especially pleased; he is a man of broad learning, with a
particular interest in this sort of thing. As for myself, I do not have time for
the intellectual pleasures which such alluring subjects bring. The mention   65
of Alciati[15] in your letter cheered me up no end. He is that rare thing, a
man who combines varied and uncommon learning with exceptional judgment and remarkable openness of mind. Some day he will be a great orna-
ment to scholarship and to his country – if there is any match at all between
his abilities and his fortune. Farewell.   70

    1525

1636 / To the Town Council of Basel   [Basel, c October 1525]

Earlier in 1525, Erasmus' former disciple and colleague Johannes Oecolampadius, now the leading figure in the Protestant movement at Basel, published
at Strasbourg *De genuina verborum Domini 'Hoc est corpus meum' iuxta vetustis-*
simos authores expositione liber, a powerful defence of the Zwinglian or Sacramentarian viewpoint on the presence of Christ's body in the Eucharist (cf Ep
1616 nn2 and 4). Although Oecolampadius had been circumspect enough not
to publish the work in Basel, the city council was alarmed by such a publication by a leading local clergyman and professor and invited Erasmus and three
other influential residents (Ludwig Baer, Bonifacius Amerbach, and Claudius
Cantiuncula) to evaluate it. The following text may represent only the opening
sentence of Erasmus' cautious reply. The rest appears to be lost, though the
contemporary report by Amerbach, endorsed by Baer and Cantiuncula, survives in manuscript at Basel and has been published by Alfred Hartmann (AK
III 89–90, no 1066). This letter implies that Erasmus himself found Oecolampadius' opinion persuasive but felt constrained by the authority of the church to
reject it.

Cordial greetings. Right honourable lords of the council, at the request of
your excellencies I have read Johannes Oecolampadius' book *De verbis coenae*
Domini. In my opinion the work is learned, well written, and thorough. I
would also judge it pious, if anything could be so described which is at

* * * * *

assimilation in classical times. Erasmus connects *serpillum* 'thyme' with the
Greek verb *herpo*, but Pliny (*Naturalis historia* 20.245) relates it to the corresponding Latin verb *serpo*.
14 Cf Ep 1634A Appendix n3.
15 Cf Epp 1250 introduction, 1634A n25.

variance with the general opinion of the church, from which I consider it   5
perilous to dissent.

1637 / To Conradus Pellicanus   Basel, [c 15 October 1525]

This angry letter, written in Erasmus' own hand, is an example of the painful
divisions between Erasmus and many of his closest followers when those
followers adhered to the Reformation. What especially galled Erasmus was the
tendency of his former close friends to associate their heretical opinions with
his own real or alleged beliefs. This issue already appears in Ep 1538 to Oecolampadius. On the Eucharistic issue, he had already shown his uneasiness
with the Sacramentarian views of Andreas Karlstadt the previous year in a
letter to Melanchthon (Ep 1523). Only about a month previously, he had
responded to a letter of Claudius Cantiuncula that urged him to write in
opposition to Oecolampadius' book *De genuina verborum Domini*, claiming that
he had already begun writing 'something on the Eucharist' but refusing to
commit himself to completion of a book which would only cause him to be
attacked by all sides (Ep 1616:22–38). The present letter is a prime example of
Erasmus' willingness to defer to the tradition and authority of the church. His
principal complaint against Pellicanus was that he was using opinions that
Erasmus had expressed only in private to close friends in order to claim his
authority in support of the Sacramentarian position. The break with Pellicanus
initiated by this letter was painful both because of their close association in
scholarly work for the Froben press and because Pellicanus' modest, gentle,
and irenic personality was deeply appealing to Erasmus.

Conradus Pellicanus (Konrad Kürschner, 1478–1556) of Rouffach in Alsace
was educated at Heidelberg and Tübingen and in the Franciscan order, which
he entered in 1493. His Franciscan teacher at Tübingen, Paulus Scriptoris,
aroused his interest in philological learning and was also the earliest source
of his critical evaluation of scholasticism. In 1499 he began the study of
Hebrew and in 1501 completed his pioneering Hebrew grammar, *De modo
legendi et intelligendi Hebraeum*, first published in 1504 as an appendix to Gregor
Reisch's *Margarita philosophica*. In 1502 he became lecturer in theology in the
Franciscan monastery at Basel, where he soon became a scholarly collaborator
of the Amerbach/Froben press and a friend of the reform-minded bishop,
Christoph von Utenheim. Both connections drew him close to Erasmus from
1515, and he assisted with Erasmus' great editions of St Jerome and other
patristic authors. His willingness to allow the Franciscan monastery, of which
he was guardian, to become a center for Reformation propaganda in Basel did
not mar his closeness to Erasmus in the early years. In 1523 the city council
appointed both him and Oecolampadius as professors of theology. What

Conradus Pellicanus
Portrait by Hans Asper, 1540
Kunsthaus, Zürich

caused the break with Erasmus was reports that he claimed that Erasmus privately shared his Sacramentarian views on the Eucharist. The result was the present letter, which produced an enduring break despite Pellicanus' letters justifying his beliefs and pleading for continued friendship (Epp 1638, 1639). Erasmus felt betrayed (Ep 1640) and possibly suspected Pellicanus of responsibility for publication of their correspondence, which appeared in two small pamphlets, anonymously printed and undated, but probably of 1526, *Expostulatio ad quendam amicum admodum pia et christiana Erasmi Roterodami* and *Epistola D. Erasmi Roter. cum amico quodam expostulans*. A personal interview failed to end the dispute, and Erasmus renewed his accusations in August 1526 (Ep 1737) and again in an undated letter written shortly after 18 March 1527 (Ep 1792A; Allen Ep 1644 but now redated). After these letters, there was a total break in communication for nearly a decade. Pellicanus, who had moved to Zürich in February 1526, never abandoned hope of a reconciliation and always claimed to be a disciple of Erasmus. Finally in 1535 he wrote a letter urging an end to their estrangement (Ep 3072); and on 25 June 1536, just a few days before Erasmus' death, he called on Erasmus while passing through Basel and spent three hours with him. In addition to the two rare pamphlets of 1526 mentioned above, the present letter, but not Pellicanus' two replies, appeared in Erasmus' *Opus epistolarum* (1529). Allen Ep 1637 introduction also mentions an edition of this letter in a volume published by Thomas Murner (without place or date, but about April 1526), *E. Roterodami de sacrosancta synaxi et unionis sacramento corporis et sanguinis Christi ad amicum expostulatio.*

ERASMUS OF ROTTERDAM TO CONRADUS PELLICANUS, GREETING
Cordial greetings. The power of the gospel does not destroy the moral law, but fulfils it.[1] You must be aware that to betray the secrets of a friend is not just immoral but completely contrary to every decent human feeling. Even after the breakup of a friendship, anyone who reveals secrets which   5
were confided to him as a friend is treated with contempt; and men of better instincts cannot bring themselves to attack their bitterest enemies with news they gathered in the confidence of an earlier friendship. I always thought that you at least were the sort of person to whom I could safely entrust a secret, and it was you I chose to hear the secrets of my inmost   10
thoughts. So I cannot understand what made you broadcast about me things I never said or thought.[2]

* * * * *

1637
1 Matt 5:17
2 Concerning his personal opinion on Christ's presence in the Eucharist. Cf introduction.

A short time ago, in a confidential talk with a young man of excellent character,[3] you intimated that my views on the Eucharist were the same as yours. He might well have carried this poison back with him to his own   15
country but for the lucky chance that the subject came up when we were together. I am far from certain that he may not even now have some linger-ing suspicions about me. At first, as I listened, I imagined your views were no different from those which you are accustomed to profess in my pres-ence. You used to condemn anyone who dared to proclaim that there was   20
nothing in the Eucharist except bread and wine; and this was where I always thought you stood – until our last meeting,[4] when, like someone possessed and changed into a new person, you revealed unequivocally what you really felt in your heart.

Now that you have begun to profess this doctrine openly, you are   25
spreading the story that you and I agree. And you broadcast these remarks so widely that a popular misconception has arisen about me, for which hardly anyone doubts that you are responsible. I am sure that in writing to your friends you say the same thing. But I have never agreed with you, not even with your earlier opinion, when you thought one should teach that the   30
body of Christ is indeed present in the mass, but how it is present was an issue best left to God, who knows all things. My comment on your position at that time was that it was too simple; all the complex puzzles of theology could be evaded if Christians could dissent from anything which had been established on the authority of councils and supported by every church and   35
nation throughout the centuries. I have always said that nothing could induce me to accept the position you have taken, especially since the Gos-pels[5] and the apostolic Epistles[6] speak so clearly of the 'body which is given' and the 'blood which is shed,' and since it accords wonderfully well with the ineffable love of God for all mankind that he should have wished   40
those whom he redeemed with the body and blood of his Son to be nour-ished in some ineffable way by that same flesh and blood and to receive as a pledge the comfort of his mysterious presence, till he returns in glory to be seen by all.

These considerations would incline me more to the position of the   45
Catholic church, even if nothing were laid down on one side or the other.

* * * * *

3 Jan Łaski, Erasmus' young Polish admirer, who had spent six months living in Erasmus' home and had left the city about 5 October. See Ep 1593 n18; cf Ep 1640:7–8.
4 There seems to be no previous mention of this meeting.
5 Matt 26:26–8, Mark 14:22–4, Luke 22:19–20
6 1 Cor 11:23–5

You can imagine what an uproar there would be if I were rash enough to declare there is nothing in the Eucharist except bread and wine. When I am with my learned friends, especially if the weaker brethren are not present, I am accustomed to speak freely whatever the subject of discussion may be; I do this to raise a question, sometimes to try out a new idea, occasionally just for the fun of it. Perhaps I am more naïve about this than I ought to be. But I shall plead guilty even to a charge of murder, if any man has ever heard me express the opinion, either seriously or in jest, that there is nothing in the Eucharist except bread and wine or that the real body and blood of our Lord are not present there, a view which some people are now defending in print. No! May Christ himself deny me his mercy if such an idea ever lodged in my mind! If some fleeting thought did ever enter my head, I rid myself of it at once by remembering the inestimable love of God for us and reflecting on the words of Holy Scripture. Even Luther himself, whom you set above all schools and popes and authorities and councils, was constrained by the evidence of Scripture to profess what the Catholic church professes, though he is not reluctant as a rule to express dissent.[7]

I know what little respect you and your friends have for the councils of the church. For myself I do not condemn the Roman church, least of all when it has all other churches on its side. Paul believes we should close our ears even to an angel if it preaches any other gospel.[8] It was the church which persuaded me to believe in the gospel and it was from the same teacher that I learned to interpret the words of the gospel.[9] Hitherto, along with all other Christians, I have always worshipped in the Eucharist the Christ who suffered for me, and I see no reason now to change my views. No human argument could make me abandon what is the universal teaching of Christendom. For those five words : *In principio creavit Deus coelum et terram* [In the beginning God created the heaven and the earth][10] mean more to me than all the arguments of Aristotle and the rest of the philosophers, by which they seek to show that the universe had no beginning.

What reasons do these friends of yours adduce that I should accept so

* * * * *

7 A reference to Luther's insistence on the real presence of Christ's body in the Eucharist (though not on the doctrine of transubstantiation). This insistence was now becoming a divisive issue between Lutherans and Swiss theologians such as Zwingli, Oecolampadius, and Pellicanus.
8 Gal 1:8
9 Cf Augustine *Contra epistolam Manichaei quam vocant fundamenti* 1.5; PL 42 176: 'I would not believe the Gospel, unless the authority of the church compelled me to do so.'
10 Gen 1:1. Erasmus does not count the preposition and copulative as 'words.'

unorthodox and subversive a doctrine? Their arguments are nothing but
straw: 'once and for all he took upon himself flesh, that it might not be an
offence'; 'the apostles did not revere or worship it.' We are told to be spiri-   80
tual, as if the presence of his body were an offence to the spirit. It is indeed
flesh, though perceived by none of our senses; and yet it is also a pledge of
God's love towards us, bringing us the consolation of hope. The word of
God is on my side. We are told: 'This is my body which is given for you,
this is my blood which will be shed for you.' Where do these people read: 85
'This is not my body, but a symbol of my body, this is not my blood, but
a symbol of my blood?' Then, when they find themselves tied in knots, they
try to show with the help of other passages that a word for a thing can
stand for the symbol of the thing, though even here they cannot make a
clear and convincing case. We say of a picture, 'This is Hector who killed   90
Patroclus,' but everybody knows that it is not the real Hector who is in the
picture. But whatever Christ says exists, must be real.

But supposing they are right, what weight are we to attach to an
argument like this: 'These words can be interpreted in this way, therefore
they *must* be interpreted in this way'? And what do they gain by citing so   95
many authorities from the past? No matter how much they twist and distort
and misrepresent what those men have said, they cannot adduce a single
passage which states plainly that the body and blood of our Lord are not
present. They urge us to partake of the body and blood of our Lord in a
spiritual sense, but what is remarkable about such advice? For this is to   100
recommend something which is more effective when we partake of both
body and blood; to accept the material elements without it is to invite
damnation. Tell me, have they shown me any reason why I should forsake
a belief which the Catholic church has taught and practised for so many
centuries?   105

You know that I do not fully agree with Luther on any point except
when, with all too much justice on his side, he attacks the immorality of the
world. Am I then, because of Karlstadt, who has already renounced his own
beliefs, to remove myself from communion with the Catholic church?[11] If
I had confessed to you as a friend that I had been guilty of theft or some   110
lewd act, would it not be entirely contrary to all the laws of friendship to
blurt out my confession even to a single person and so risk bringing trouble
on your friend? But now, when you are spreading far and wide the most
serious charge that could be made against me, something which, for all the

* * * * *

11 Cf Epp 1522, 1523, 1616, 1620, 1621, 1624; the latter, lines 74–5, reports Karlstadt's return to Wittenberg and submission to Luther on this issue.

freedom of my tongue, I never uttered nor conceived in my mind, what   115
name are we to give to such behaviour towards a friend who shares the
same gospel? Was it to convince others of a doctrine you had lately come
to believe that you chose to misappropriate the authority of my name? I ask
you, in Christ's name, is this what the gospel teaches, that you should
invent so odious and unchristian a charge against your friend with the   120
object of inducing others to join a new sect, as if there were not enough
sects already? If what you assert is the true faith, have you no way of
making it credible except by the absurd fiction that Erasmus believes what
you believe? If my authority means so much to you, why does it count for
nothing in all those many cases where we disagree? You have no place for   125
the authority of prelates or councils, and so, as you are always saying, your
mind is in a constant state of flux; my mind, on the other hand, has been
kept firm thus far by the universal agreement of the Catholic church. If you
have come to believe that there is nothing in the mass except bread and
wine, I would rather be torn limb from limb than believe what you believe;   130
and I would suffer any fate rather than depart this life with such an awful
sin upon my conscience.

I am not using violent language to build a case: my protest is fully
justified; the facts themselves are dramatic enough. If you possess a single
ounce of the spirit of the gospel, you will clear up the infection you have   135
spread with these idle rumours. Blurt out to the whole world, if you like,
anything I ever said in private conversation, whether drunk or sober, in
earnest or in jest; but I shall not let you say that I conceived or shared such
a belief as this, which never passed my lips nor entered my head. So may
I never be separated from the presence of Christ! Amen.   140

Basel, †1526†

Erasmus of Rotterdam, with his own hand

1638 / From Conradus Pellicanus   [Basel, c October 1525]

This and the following letter are both replies to Ep 1637, exculpating the
author from Erasmus' charge that he had unethically betrayed their friendship.
But it is also an open defence of the Sacramentarian interpretation of the
Eucharist, flatly denying that his theological position maintains that there is
nothing in the Eucharist except bread and wine. Shrewdly, Pellicanus focuses
not on the 'realness' of Christ's presence in the consecrated elements but on
the high-scholastic doctrine of transubstantiation, which Erasmus found repug-
nant and could accept only because the institutional church had affirmed it as
part of Catholic dogma at the Fourth Lateran Council in 1215. This letter
appeared in *Epistola D. Erasmi Roter. cum amico quodam expostulans*, the second

of the two anonymously published pamphlets (probably dating from 1526) mentioned in Ep 1637 introduction. Erasmus did not include it in any of his own collections of his correspondence, and it seems not to have been published again until Allen included it in his edition (1926).

THE FIRST LETTER TO ERASMUS FROM HIS FRIEND

Erasmus, my learned friend, I shall let no earthly danger rob me of the sacred gift of your friendship, most unworthy though I was to receive it. However cruel fortune or the stars may be, I shall never betray, nor have I ever betrayed, a secret committed to my trust, no matter what the circum-   5
stances may have been. I shall continue to love and honour you as my teacher,[1] even if you turn against me (which the Lord forbid!); for the respect and loyal affection which I have for you, my great and worthy friend, will be no less warm and stable than the feelings I have always demonstrated throughout my life for all those others whom I admitted to   10
my friendship.

I have never said or thought that 'there is nothing in the Eucharist except bread and wine.' On the contrary I have repeatedly condemned this view wherever I went and tried to refute it with serious arguments, as I can prove from numerous witnesses. You yourself have heard me say the same   15
thing, and this is still my firm and unwavering conviction today. Moreover I have never heard such views from your lips, nor have I ever believed that you held them; in fact I know you took a different view in all your *Paraphrases*. So how could I have spread such a damaging story about you in anything I wrote or said, as you allege? You could not have borrowed the   20
idea from me (though if I had ever suggested such indebtedness, the very suggestion would be an impertinence on my part), and similarly I could not have adopted the notion from you (though this has a more modest ring about it), for the fact is that neither of us believes it. Nor could I have broadcast a doctrine which never entered my head. I have always believed,   25
and still believe, that it is the body of the Lord and his most holy blood which we receive in the mass. That is the clear message of the Gospels and the apostolic Letters, which it would be anathema to disbelieve. I say again what I said before: I wish there had been no investigations or discussions or explanations of the why and wherefore of that great and holy mystery   30
except those which have come down to us in the words of Scripture and

* * * * *

1638
1 Cf Ep 1637 introduction.

those which the ancient Fathers of the true faith, the trusted pastors and
Doctors of the church, have bequeathed to us in their writings. Everything
which I or any good Christian needs to know about the holy mystery of the
sacrament will be found in the account which you have given in all your   35
Paraphrases, based on the works of the holy Doctors of the church and
presented with great and ample learning and careful scholarship. When I
read these works, I often kissed the book and expressed my enthusiastic
approval; if the defence of the truth which they contain should ever bring
you into danger (which God forbid), I should want to share that danger   40
with you, even if it meant death itself.

    I agree with you completely that, as you put it in your letter, 'it
accords wonderfully well with the ineffable love of God for all mankind,
that he should have wished those whom he redeemed with the body and
blood of his Son to be nourished in some ineffable way by that same flesh   45
and blood and to receive as a pledge the comfort of his mysterious presence
until his glorious return.' There is nothing which I should want to add to
these words of yours. For you are wise enough to stop there and do not
claim that the blood of the son of God must be present in some physical,
carnal, real, and substantial sense, with its own corporeal substance, though 50
invisible to our eyes. You speak instead of an 'ineffable way' and a 'mysterious presence' which is a pledge of his consolation until we meet him face
to face in his glory. Suppose I were condemned to death and shut up in a
dark prison: if someone arrived from the emperor with a letter and an
official document releasing me from sentence of death, and if a seal were   55
affixed to it with the emperor's own ring, signifying his kindness and
clemency and securing my escape from these grave perils, and if all this
took place before my eyes while I watched in great excitement and believed
that what I was witnessing was truly happening, would I not consider the
emperor present indeed and bow before him and count myself truly fortu-   60
nate that he was there? Would this most gracious prince not be present in
the truest sense if he made me so deeply grateful, filling my mind and heart
and spirit with a new and unexpected joy and offering and granting me the
gift of freedom? But what would happen, what would I gain if he withheld
his mercy, but stood there before me silently in the dark prison? You can   65
hardly doubt I would rather have the emperor alive and well in Spain but
present through his ring as the sure symbol of his mercy, than standing
with me in the prison, silent, unseen, and speechless.

    If this seems to you too simple, too easy to grasp, too close to the
ordinary way of speaking as we find it everywhere in Scripture or in the   70
common usage of mankind, do you think I shall be influenced by the
authority of councils whose records I have never read? I believe that for a

thousand years the churches and the peoples of those times accepted this
doctrine without question, as it was preached to them by pious and orthodox bishops;[2] the doctrine was committed to writing at the time and pre-   75
served until our day, and now, with the invention of printing, it is available
everywhere for anyone to read; certainly it is easier to see such documents
now, to examine them and get to know them than it could have been in the
past for the doctors of Paris or, three hundred years ago, for their bishop,
Peter Lombard.[3] The same is true of many other topics which, thanks to   80
you and other scholars, the learned world has come to know and understand much better. This is not to say that no one ever knew what we now
know from our study of the early Fathers. But what the men of Paris could
not have known because of the difficulties of the times and the shortage of
books, their children today, or should we say their bastard children, flatly   85
refuse to learn, preferring to hold on to their native ignorance. They would
rather be blind leaders of the blind,[4] considering their own beliefs as the
first principles of the faith; since many of these beliefs are so obviously
false, a sensible man may well have doubts about the rest.

But if a man cannot trust in Christ our Lord, or sincerely believe that   90
he was redeemed and saved by the body and blood of Christ, the Son of
God, offered once and for all upon the cross, unless he receives anew the
actual body of Christ impanated in the bread and his blood transub-
stantiated from the wine and is able to touch them physically; if he was not
satisfied with the emperor's personal seal, which surely must mean more   95
to him than a mere ring of gold, if he is not content with the grace which
he experiences, but must have the emperor present, even if it be only in
some ghostly form, invisible and therefore open to doubt; if this is what he
wants, then let him hold whatever view he pleases and teach what he can
prove, but let him not compel me to accept a doctrine which, for more than   100
a thousand years, the true Fathers of the faith knew nothing of or, if they
knew it, never taught their people (of these two possibilities, the first would

* * * * *

2 Pellicanus thus adopts a common Protestant opinion, that the faith and practice of the church remained fundamentally sound until the Gregorian reform
of the eleventh century laid the foundations of papal power and the emergence
of dialectical theology (scholasticism) in the eleventh and twelfth centuries
eclipsed the influence of the patristic theologians.
3 The *Book of Sentences* of Peter Lombard (1095–1160), bishop of Paris, had long
been the standard text for the teaching of theology in the universities, and
most of the major scholastic theologians produced commentaries on all or part
of it.
4 *Adagia* I viii 40

convict them of ignorance and the second of hypocrisy and disrespect for
the faith). Let him consider how he is to escape the frightening tangle of
problems which transubstantiation poses and the countless difficulties which   105
are associated with it. He should consider also the Jewish converts who are
awaiting baptism: how will he convince them, or try to convince them, from
the canon of Holy Scripture to believe any such doctrine as this; or let him
try, if he can, to achieve the same end without the help of Scripture. Certainly I have never been able to do this, nor would I presume to do so   110
today, though I once sat under an eminent scholar with whom I studied all
the relevant arguments on this issue.[5] Moreover I have lectured four times[6]
in various schools on the fourth book of the *Sentences*,[7] though without
being able to satisfy myself, to say nothing of my audience, on all points.

I cannot remember precisely what else I wrote in my letter. I did not   115
have time to make a copy. I know there were some barbed remarks about
individuals, all regrettably true. Just as soon as I have a moment to myself,
I shall finish what I have to say. Please don't be offended by all this. Farewell.

1639 / From Conradus Pellicanus   [Basel, c October 1525]

> A second reply to Ep 1637, printed in *Epistola D. Erasmi Roter. cum amico
> quodam expostulans*, the second of two undated pamphlets that reproduced
> some of the letters exchanged in this controversy. See Ep 1637 introduction.
> Unlike its predecessor, which concentrates on answering what Pellicanus
> regards as Erasmus' misunderstanding of his position on the Eucharist, this
> letter undertakes the defence of the Sacramentarian position, arguing that this
> position, and not transubstantiation, was the prevailing doctrine of the church
> until the twelfth and thirteenth centuries. It includes a substantial defence of

* * * * *

5 Paulus Scriptoris of Weil der Stadt (d 1504) was guardian of the Franciscan
   house at Tübingen when Pellicanus was sent there in 1496. He encouraged
   Pellicanus' study of Hebrew. Sometime after 1499 he was suspended as guardian because of his opinions on the Eucharist, and in 1501 he was transferred
   to Basel. He died while on a special assignment from the bishop of Basel to
   reorganize a Benedictine monastery in Alsace. Pellicanus, his favourite student,
   later thought his eucharistic doctrine similar to that of Luther. He was also the
   teacher of Johann von Staupitz and Johannes Eck.
6 Pellicanus in his *Chronikon* ed Bernhard Riggenbach (Basel 1877) 26, 39, 44
   refers to his lectures on the *Sentences* at Basel in 1502, Rouffach in 1508, and
   Pforzheim in 1512.
7 Book 4 of Lombard's *Book of Sentences* dealt with the sacraments.

Martin Luther (but not of his Eucharistic doctrine, which Erasmus in Ep 1637: 60–3 had interpreted as identical with that of the Roman Catholic church), and it bluntly criticizes scholastic theology along lines remarkably reminiscent of Erasmus' own earlier attacks on scholasticism. It also directly questions the authority of the Fourth Lateran Council (1215), which had made the doctrine of transubstantiation a dogma of the Catholic faith (Concilium Lateranense IV, cap 1, in Mansi XXII 982). Needless to say, Erasmus never incorporated this letter or its predecessor into any collection of his own correspondence, though his own action in allowing manuscripts of the correspondence to circulate among his close friends may have been the origin of one or both of the unauthorized pamphlets (cf Ep 1640 n9). More surprisingly, despite its apologia for the Eucharistic doctrines of Zwingli and Oecolampadius, Pellicanus never reprinted it after the original (and very scarce) edition of 1526, and it remained virtually unknown until the appearance of Allen VI in 1926.

Greetings. You were very kind, my dearest Erasmus, about the defence I sent you, in which I sincerely and honestly expressed what I thought, and you chose not to renounce your friendship for me, for which I am grateful and only wish I could offer you something in return; nevertheless I cannot hide certain thoughts which occurred to me when I reflected on that stern   5 letter of yours, thoughts which the Holy Spirit put into my mind, though I am just a simple man without eloquence, more eager to advance God's glory than capable of making it a reality. It is not that I expect you to learn something from me that you did not know already, nor that you have any need of a counsellor; for you think more deeply than I do about these and   10 other problems, and you do everything you can to work them out for the glory of Christ, so as to be in a position to convince others on whose shoulders the burden of responsibility rests. My aim is different: it is that a great man like you should learn from someone as insignificant as I am (and you know me inside out[1] and are aware of my slight ability with words and   15 even slighter capacity for action) what might be said and done by those who are wiser, more learned, more zealous, and more eloquent than I. Truth is strong in itself, and even the eyes of the blind, if they have not been totally destroyed, may be illumined with at least the blurred image of its splendour. What it hides from those who are greedy for position and gold,   20

* * * * *

1639
1 Literally 'inside and on the skin'; cf *Adagia* I ix 89.

it can reveal to the weak, if they are simple and devout, even to those who belong to the mass of the laity.

I hope, if you have time to spare, you will be good enough to read this letter. You yourself have a fine command of language, and yet you put up with my stammering for hours at a time, treating me with great kindness   25
and civility and graciously sending me on my way as your friend. You do not expect from me, I know, a polished style, nor at my age can I hope to change my way of speaking. I come now, after these preliminaries, to that part of your letter where you are concerned with some ruling of the church on one side or the other. I dearly wish I could have seen long ago, and   30
could have available now, the proceedings of the Lateran Council, which was held, if I remember correctly, in the reign of Innocent III in the year of our Lord 1215; I should like to read the arguments and grounds for belief advanced by the Fathers concerning the doctrine of the Eucharist, if indeed they advanced any. The discussions of the council on the conception of the   35
Blessed Virgin Mary survive here in our monastery at Basel, along with other records of the same council, carefully copied in the notary's hand.[2] One can still read the arguments used against the Arians, as they were written down by the Fathers at the time and published. As for the book written by Pope Innocent,[3] who is said to have been a theologian at Paris,   40
and at whose instance the definition was perhaps given, informed readers must be aware what modern scholars think of it. The tractate of Thomas Aquinas is read in church, but so sadly and wretchedly corrupted that it is an embarrassment to listen to it.[4] The *De sacramentis*, which is published

* * * * *

2 But there is no trace of the doctrine of the Immaculate Conception in the canons of the Fourth Lateran Council (Mansi IV 982–1067); and modern Catholic scholarship, while maintaining that the roots of that doctrine go back to apostolic times, concedes that it did not begin to attract much attention from theologians until several decades after that council. Duns Scotus (c 1264–1308) appears to have been the first theologian to present a widely accepted theological defence of the doctrine. See NCE VII 378–82.

3 Innocent III (1160–1216, elected 1198), the pope who summoned the Fourth Lateran Council, studied at Paris and Bologna. Although his own theological works are in general not of great importance, his work on the Eucharist, *De missarum misteriis* (formerly known as *De sacro altaris mysterio libri sex*; PL 217 763–916) had appeared in three editions quite recently (Paris 1518, Oléron 1518, Rouen 1520) and so was still part of current theological literature when the eucharistic controversies of the Reformation broke out in the early 1520s.

4 Among the *Opuscula* attributed to Aquinas are at least two texts on the Eucharist. The first, *De sacramento eucharistiae secundum decem predicamenta*, which is probably the text also known as *De quidditate sacramenti* and *De corpore Christi*,

under the name of Ambrose,[5] is generally considered in the same light as   45
the *De vera et falsa poenitentia*, which, by a dangerous deception, is wrongly
ascribed to Augustine.[6] These two books, by the fearful judgment of God,
misled Gratian[7] and other leading scholars in the church just when the
Paris theologians were beginning to take on Aristotelian airs,[8] deceiving the
see of Rome and the universities as well.   50

    Today some men are not afraid to say that, if we refuse to believe that
these books are the work of Ambrose and Augustine, they in turn will not
accept the Gospel which we read today as Matthew's or John's. This is not
an argument, but insufferable blasphemy, profane and silly talk. The writings of holy bishops, extending over a thousand years, can now be read and   55

    * * * * *

    was published under the latter title at Cologne in 1473 (Proctor 1092). A
    second eucharistic title, *De venerabili sacramento ad mandatum Urbani papae*, also
    appears among the collected works of St Thomas, such as the *Opera omnia*
    (Rome 1572) endorsed by Pope Pius V. The authenticity of these texts is ques-
    tionable, and the present reference does not specify just which work Pellicanus
    has in mind.
  5 Pellicanus had questioned the authenticity of *De sacramentis* as early as 1509,
    and several of the Protestant reformers had rejected it, though Erasmus includ-
    ed it in his edition of Ambrose (Basel 1527) without comment. The text (book
    4 chapter 5 paragraph 23) seems clearly to imply a change of substance
    brought about by the words of consecration (PL 16 463:23 / CSEL 73 56). Mod-
    ern scholarship remains divided about its authenticity: but Faller (CSEL 77
    6*–49*) argues at length in favour of Ambrose's authorship, while McGuire
    (NCE I 375) leaves at least a shadow of a doubt, and Largent *Dictionnaire de
    théologie catholique* ed A. Vacant 15 vols (Paris 1899–1950) I¹ 946 regards it as
    a mere imitation of his *De mysteriis* written by an unknown hand in the fifth
    or sixth century.
  6 *De vera et falsa poenitentia*, though contained in PL 40 1113–1130 and accepted
    as genuine by Gratian and Peter Lombard, is now universally held to be of
    later date and was already so regarded by Migne in the nineteenth century.
    The author is unknown. The popular Benedictine author Johannes Trithemius
    had already noted that the book could not be by Augustine because in chapter
    17 it cites him as an authority: *De scriptoribus ecclesiasticis* (Basel: Johannes
    Amerbach 1494) fol 24.
  7 This supposititious work of Augustine is cited in Gratian's *Decretum*, secunda
    pars, causa 33, distinctio 3, c 4 (part of his *Tractatus de penitencia*), which
    appears in *Corpus iuris canonici* 2nd ed, ed Aemilius Friedberg 2 vols (Leipzig
    1879; repr Graz 1955) I 1211.
  8 The reference is to the development of mature scholastic philosophy and
    theology during the thirteenth century, heavily influenced by the recovery of
    the works of Aristotle at the beginning of that century. Erasmus himself had
    been repeatedly and openly critical of the various systems of systematic theol-
    ogy that developed from that beginning.

readily located with the help of indexes. Almost all of these had been printed before Karlstadt began to raise such a fuss over this question, and few thought the matter should be kept hidden from devout and pious men. As for Luther's knowledge of Scripture and of languages,[9] I do not set him above all universities, popes, and councils. You will find men in these institutions today who are perhaps more learned than Luther – I hope it may be so. But I should like to avoid such odious comparisons.[10] That he wrote more substantial works than all those which have emerged so far from the universities, that in knowledge of languages and of Scripture he outshines everyone who has lived within the past three hundred years or more, this is something which the writings of both parties will amply demonstrate, and those who come after us will judge, when sectarian preju- dice has, at least partly, cooled. To speak for myself, I have derived more profit from your works and from Luther's, which I have used to good effect for almost seven years now, than from the works of all those others, which I pored over for twenty-seven years at the cost of much greater effort. I have no doubt now that all that time was wasted, and my labours of the past seven years corroborate this judgment.

This Luther is a man whom I still respect and admire, but I use discre- tion when I read his writings and I weigh what he says, as I do with every author. As for the violence of his language and the character of his style, I put these down to temperament, nationality, the man, his zeal, the flesh. God even turns such things to his own glory, and reserves the spotless purity of truth for his word alone. The same may be said of you: you have some peculiar opinions which spring from your civility and natural gentle- ness; you know that certain people are critical of these, just as I feel strongly about some of Luther's ideas because I am not fired with the same zeal. We admit that the prophets and apostles made progress in morals and faith; why then shall we deny to Luther what we necessarily and deliberately concede to ourselves? Luther confesses that with time and self-discipline he made progress. Should one be surprised, then, if with the passage of time he might also change his opinion about this human tradition concerning the nature of Christ's body in the sacrament of the Eucharist? I have no doubt that the worthy Fathers of the ancient church were totally ignorant of many of the theses of the Paris school, including the doctrine of the transubstanti-

* * * * *

9 Erasmus in Ep 1637:60–3 had cited against Pellicanus Luther's well publicized hostility to the Sacramentarian opinions of Zwingli and other leaders of the Reformation in Switzerland and south-western Germany.
10 Cf Ep 1565 n2.

ation of bread into the body of Christ; this was forced upon us at the
Lateran Council without the authority of Scripture as a most puzzling article
of faith. That they attempted to pass even worse proposals than this is clear
from the brief and scattered references to this council compiled from the
records of the time. It is evident that there has always been opposition to   95
this doctrine from good and learned men, but these were crushed by forces
more powerful than themselves and suffered the penalty of death and
condemnation, though they were never convicted by Scripture or by any
solid argument, as the surviving history of those times attests. On the other
hand none of the Parisians during all this period ever had the courage to   100
face death for his beliefs or even to suffer the loss of the poorest benefice.

Nothing in your letter annoyed me so much as the two assertions you
make about Luther: first that he is always ready to dissent from the Catholic
church, and secondly that I know there is not a single doctrine on which
you and Luther agree. Do you really believe, good sir, that a church which   105
is based on human traditions, philosophical dogmas, and mercenary laws
could be truly Catholic or would deserve the name? Such, we know, were
many of the assemblies of the past, to which came bishops, monks, and
masters of theology, schooled in the teaching of their idol Peter Lombard.
The decrees which were passed in certain councils were a reflection of the   110
ignorance, sycophancy, greed, and vanity of men like these, for they knew
nothing of the spirit of truth and had no concern for public honour. Consider as an example the Lateran Council under Julius the soldier.[11] Although
they admitted again and again that the reform of the church was necessary,
they took every means in their power to thwart it. The councils of our own   115
day and of our fathers' day and those which have met within the past four
hundred years show us what such councils were like, what confidence they
inspired, how far they served the church and in what ways. Yet these are
the bodies whose authority you want to defend, even perhaps to the point
of making it a crime to take issue with them or dissent from their views on   120
matters of faith and morals. Yet it is clear from the word of God, as almost
all learned and pious scholars agree, that these councils were mistaken and
in not a few cases contradicted the earliest councils of the Fathers of the
church. These dangerous heretics are prepared to deny and denigrate the

* * * * *

11 A reference to the Fifth Lateran Council (1512–17) summoned by Pope Julius
    II. The phrase 'Julius the soldier' was an oblique reproach to Erasmus, who
    had frequently expressed opposition to the militaristic career of Julius II and
    who despite his denials was widely (and correctly) regarded as the author of
    the antipapal satire *Julius exclusus*.

sacred texts and apostolic writings – something which no arch-heretic has   125
dared to do from the time of the sufferings of our saviour Christ, that is, to
discount the gospels and exalt to equal status the writings of the doctors
and the legends of the saints. They can thus say they will not believe the
Gospel if we do not believe Augustine[12] and the bishop of Rome. We
know that the bishop of Rome was ignorant of Scripture (unless the stories   130
told about him are false); he was a man more suited to war and temporal
rule than to the elucidation of the canon of Scripture and, if we may judge
from other men of that sort, he is likely to have been surrounded and
abetted by people like himself.

I doubt if there was ever a general council which was celebrated with   135
more dignity, pomp and energy than the one which took place here in
Basel.[13] The discussions were long and detailed and all were recorded and
preserved. And what authority has it enjoyed? Although the men of Paris
defended it strenuously until recently, they have lately allowed it to sink
into oblivion and expire, for fear of losing their privileges.[14] Bring together   140
from our own time primates, archbishops, bishops and abbots along with
learned doctors from the schools, Béda, Cousturier, Duchesne, Latomus,
Egmondanus, Baer, Gebwiler,[15] and others of the same standing from
throughout the Christian world, discuss with them the Holy Scriptures, and
see what conclusions they will reach about those doctrines and interpreta-   145
tions which you claim to be authentic and what view they will take of the
faith and practices of the church. Let us see if the true, Catholic, apostolic
church is able to agree with them and if such men can prove their point
with arguments drawn from human tradition or from the apostolic and
canonical writings, or whether they will say in the end, with the theologians   150
of Paris: 'This is what we want; this is what we say; we settled this point
long ago; this is what we teach, and the world and the church must believe
it.'

* * * * *

12 Cf Ep 1637 n9.
13 Despite its claims to supreme authority in the church, the Council of Basel
   (1431–49) ended in failure, being unable either to maintain its claim to
   superiority over the pope or to effect a thoroughgoing reform of the church.
14 The University of Paris had been one of the principal centres of conciliarism,
   the opinion that a general council is the supreme authority in the church,
   throughout the period of the Great Schism (1378–1417) and well into the later
   fifteenth century, but enthusiasm for conciliar authority had declined there.
15 'Béda ... Gebwiler': a list of contemporary scholastic theologians, the first three
   from Paris, the next two from Louvain, and the last two from Basel. Ludwig
   Baer was a close friend of Erasmus; most of the rest were hostile.

We do not measure the authority of a council by the titles and revenues which are derived from its primatial sees and archbishoprics and   155
abbacies, or from the opinions of our fine masters of theology. Theologians
often turn out to be stupider than a log and sodden with wine, as though
they had just come from one of their collegial dinners. We have never seen
emerge from such councils any evidence of true religion, or anything which
might nurture a genuine piety, but we have seen great increases in income,   160
exemptions, privileges,[16] new benefices, and monasteries. Look at the offspring which the Lateran Council and its successors produced for the
church! It was there that the mendicant orders were established and
endowed with privileges, and grew in a very short time to include so many
thousands of monasteries, and filled cities which had previously been free   165
of such people, though Christianity had flourished for a thousand years and
the privilege of mendicancy and the unscriptural idleness of monks had
been unknown until that time.[17]

These, Erasmus, are the councils of the Fathers which you commend
and from which Luther feels free to dissent. God forbid that he should reject   170
those holy councils which based their precious teachings securely on the
word of God and established laws which were to prove useful for the
reformation of the church. The Fathers did not come to these councils in the
vain spirit of this world; they did not seek their own interests, or fight for
honours for themselves; they gave no thought to primacies or income, but   175
ardently desired the glory of God alone; they cared only for the advancement of the church in faith and morals, and listened to the voice of the Holy
Spirit speaking to them from the pages of Scripture, not from the traditions
of ordinary men.

You say I am well aware that you never agreed with Luther complete-   180
ly on any point of doctrine. I do know you always disliked Luther's passionate nature and the unbridled ferocity of his style and you were offended
by his 'subversive teaching,' as you like to describe it, whatever the doctrine
in question may have been. Of course I too have always regretted these

* * * * *

16 The Latin is *libertatum*, a word which in medieval usage had much more the
   sense of a set of legally enforceable privileges than the modern sense of an
   abstract set of human rights, 'liberty.'
17 The Lateran Council here mentioned is the Fourth (1215), not the recently
   concluded Fifth (1515). Although the mendicant orders were contemporary
   with the Fourth Lateran Council, the council forbade the founding of new
   orders, and Pope Innocent III, who authorised the mendicants, circumvented
   this legislation by advising St Dominic to use the Augustinian rule for his new
   order.

things in the man; I wished he had a kindlier pen and that, when he spoke   185
the truth, he sounded more like a man who was speaking the truth; for
many of his ideas could have avoided the resentment they caused and been
accepted more readily by a greater number of people if, by changing a few
words here and there, he had expressed the same sentiments more temper-
ately in a different style. This, as I recall, often came up in our conversa-   190
tions. But this criticism apart, I never doubted that wherever Luther disagreed with the schoolmen and our learned friends in Paris, his views are
to be found in the writings of the good Fathers of the church; in fact nearly
all of them are in what they call the *Glossa ordinaria*.[18] But the sophists of
the Sorbonne thought it beneath them to read such things, wrapped up as   195
they were in their texts of Aristotle, and satisfied with Peter Lombard and
his articles of belief,[19] which were supported by the authority of their own
bishop.

As for those errors which arose from abuses within the church, I
believe – and the opinion is shared by all your friends and even by your   200
opponents – that Luther has said nothing which is not implied in your own
writings, though you are more subtle and restrained and keep the argument
more on a general level without, however, beating about the bush. But even
if you had kept silent, the whole world was ready to protest against such
practices in no uncertain terms. As for the rest of his teaching, where it is   205
not concerned with the sacraments, or with indulgences, masses, immun-
ities, excommunications, and primacy, if you disagree with Luther, this will
not make the Romans angry with Luther or grateful to you. On many points
you differ very little from Luther, though you always write less offensively.
This leaves your views on the Eucharist, which Zwingli and Oecolampadius   210
will deal with some day, if you try sniping at them with the same arguments.

The story which your dishonest informers are telling you, that Karlstadt has changed his position, is nothing but lies, even if he did in fact
suggest, perhaps out of deference to Luther or to fill his own belly, that he   215

* * * * *

18 A traditional set of glosses, or explanations of specific words of the Bible,
   drawn largely from patristic and early medieval sources, which had accumu-
   lated during the twelfth and thirteenth centuries. The person chiefly responsible for bringing most of this collection together is now thought to be Anselm
   of Laon (d 1117).
19 The reference is apparently to the standard medieval textbook of theology, the
   Book of Sentences (*Sententiarum libri quattuor*) compiled by the Paris theologian
   Peter Lombard (c 1095–1160), whose subsequent authority was enhanced by
   his becoming bishop of Paris towards the end of his life.

had not yet made up his mind on the matter and did not want to lay down the law on his own authority.[20] I only wish he had never touched the subject at all. These people are abusing your simple, trusting nature and bringing disgrace upon your head, as they are constantly setting traps to damage the reputation of other honest men and to impede their progress. 220 It is for this purpose that they dress up false charges as true, attacking even godly men, who are doubtless their brethren and innocent of any wrong. If only you could have brought yourself to trust me, who have always thought better of you and tried to convey this opinion to others, you would have discovered what habitual liars they are. They lied frequently about 225 Zwingli[21] and they lied about the worthy brethren of Strasbourg[22] who are full of zeal for Christ's glory (they mock the very word 'brother,' being themselves unworthy of the name). It is the same in the case of our friend Oecolampadius,[23] a man of spotless character, whose close attachment is a blessing to you and works to the glory of God.   230

I do not blame you for all the other charges you thought it proper to bring against me for reasons which I cannot understand; instead I blame those vipers whose names are known to the Lord and whom you are too inclined to trust. You know they are lovers of this world and of its riches, but they cannot serve both God and Mammon[24] and, being rich, can no 235 more embrace the gospel than a camel can pass through the eye of a needle.[25] If they possess a grain of Christian piety or Christian faith, let them come forward, let them meet together and explain the basis of their faith. Let them help their brothers in peril, who call upon them so often and whose death they mourn with false tears. Let them succour the church by 240 which they are so sumptuously fed and for whose protection they solemnly swore to form a wall of defence. But for them it is enough if they have their pride, the money they amassed, their graded honours, and a reputation for learning, which they never demonstrate. But if they continue as before, I hope for their own good they will be brought low and forced to change 245

* * * * *

20 But in fact he had; cf Ep 1616 n6.
21 The Zürich reformer Huldrych Zwingli was the first major Protestant leader to enunciate what came to be known as the 'Sacramentarian' doctrine of the Eucharist.
22 This term was often used at the time to refer to the leaders of the Reformation at Strasbourg, such as Jakob Sturm, Matthäus Zell, Martin Bucer, and Wolfgang Faber Capito.
23 See Ep 1636 introduction.
24 Matt 6:24; Luke 16:13
25 Matt 19:24

their lives; that they will come to their senses and realize that, now that the
word of God flashes its message to the faithful in every tongue, Christ's
gospel and his glory have returned to the earth. If they refuse to rejoice in
this, they will discover that their portion is with the Antichrist and with
those who descend into the pit.[26] From such a fate may the Lord, by his   250
grace, be pleased to preserve them and mercifully lead them to know his
truth and to despise the world. I pray the Lord you will not attack me in
future with so uncharacteristically harsh a pen; I am your friend and have
not earned such treatment at your hands. Please believe that the painful
suffering which this letter has caused me arises from my concern about the   255
dangers which threaten both our friendship and the truth. Farewell, and
please don't take this too much to heart.

1640 / To Conradus Pellicanus   [Basel, c October 1525]

> A reply to Ep 1639. Like Ep 1637 but unlike Pellicanus' two intervening letters,
> this letter was published in Erasmus' *Opus epistolarum*, no doubt because he
> wanted to advertise his flat rejection of Sacramentarian theology. Although the
> identity of the recipient would in any case have been obvious to anyone who
> was well informed about current controversies, Erasmus chose to reveal the
> identity of the addressee in 1529 when he published the letter in his *Opus
> epistolarum*.

ERASMUS OF ROTTERDAM TO CONRADUS PELLICANUS, GREETING
I cannot understand why you wanted to waste your time and try my
patience on letters like that, so pointlessly verbose and *mal à propos*.[1] You
talk well but write badly; so if you have anything to say, keep it in future
till we meet. I was half ready to believe you, but now you are reviving all   5
my old suspicions. You admit you are sympathetic to Karlstadt's point of
view[2] and you cannot deny that you told my Polish friend that you and I
think the same way.[3] If the charge were true, I would have reason to complain that you violated the laws of friendship; but since it is completely

* * * * *

26 Ezek 26:20, 32:18–30.

1640
1 Literally, 'uncongenial to Dionysus,' that is, not to the point; cf *Adagia* II iv 57
  and Cicero *Ad Atticum* 16.13.1.
2 That is, what Erasmus regarded as an extreme Sacramentarian position. Cf Ep
  1616 n6.
3 Jan Łaski; cf Epp 1593 n18, 1637 n3.

false, it is hard to think of a more shocking injury you could have done me. 10
You threaten me with Zwingli's pen: do you think I would be afraid to face
ten Zwinglis, if my heart were in it? And what do you mean by my 'disgrace'? Would I suffer disgrace if I hesitated to oppose the decrees of the
Catholic church? Are you going to tell me what I may and may not write?
Am I not to be as free as Luther? If I know Luther, he will attack you 15
people with all the force at his command. Or do you think that no one here
will turn his pen against you? If what you are doing is of God,[4] it will be
strengthened in the struggle; if not, then it is a pious duty to fight against
impiety. But what is the point of all these threats? The apostles used persuasion: do you want to compel us to accept your gospel? 20

Suppose I had no intention of writing: you could not have chosen a
better way to drive me to it than by spreading the rumour that I am on
your side and warning me not to take up my pen. Your friend Farel[5]
dropped a similar lie into the ear of an English acquaintance of mine,[6] to
the effect that I had the right ideas, but did not have the courage to speak 25
up. He has the audacity to implant such a story in people's ears when he
knows full well what a bitter conflict there has been between himself and
me on almost every aspect of Luther's teaching. What Farel means by 'the
right ideas' is what popes and emperors call 'heresy.' So you think Luther
does not dissent from the Catholic church? When I find a better church than 30
the one I belong to, I shall stop calling this one 'Catholic.' But I have not
found such a church.

I hoped that some good might come from the strong medicine we have
been taking, but I can find nothing good to say of the results so far and I
dislike remedies which are worse than the disease. How much human blood 35
has already been shed! In Holland the carnage is terrible; there are men
there who are better at burning their victims than arguing a case, and soon
the killing will spread everywhere else. But this is only the beginning of our
troubles.[7] The emperor is about to make peace with France. But no treaty
will be concluded among the princes except on condition that Luther's 40
faction is stamped out, and the emperor will not feel he is really emperor
unless he brings that about. I would rather gloss over ten vaguely worded

* * * * *

4 A verbal reminiscence of Acts 5:39
5 The correspondence contains many instances of the mutual antipathy between
  Erasmus and the outspoken French Protestant exile Guillaume Farel. On his
  life see Ep 1341A n305, and cf Epp 1477A, 1489 n11, 1496 n31, 1510 n4.
6 Perhaps Thomas Grey, who visited Basel about this time. Cf Allen Ep 1624 n9.
7 Matt 24:8

articles than give occasion for such a dreadful tragedy. I cannot ordain what
Christ ought to do. If he has resolved to punish us in this way for our
impiety, he is the Lord, let him do what he wishes. If he needed me as his   45
helper and instrument, he would breathe his inspiration into my heart, as
once he inspired Pharaoh and Cyrus and Nebuchadnezzar.[8]

You regret that my letter was made public.[9] I would prefer that had
not happened, but I have some consolation in the fact that it gives the lie
to the tales you have been spreading about me. That was something you   50
should have undertaken yourself, although the letter did not have your
name on it. In future don't send me such long-winded letters. Write to
Baer,[10] if you want to, and to Luther himself.[11] Come here and I shall
listen to your reproaches, threats, and scoldings to your heart's content.
Farewell.   55

†1526†

1641 / To Conradus Goclenius   [Basel, c October 1525]

Goclenius (d 1539) was professor of Latin at the Collegium Trilingue at Louvain from 1519 and proved to be an outstandingly successful teacher as well
as a thoroughly trustworthy (and fully trusted) friend of Erasmus. Cf Ep 1209
introduction.

ERASMUS OF ROTTERDAM TO CONRADUS GOCLENIUS, GREETING
This letter is for Thomas Grey,[1] whom I count among my Pyladean

* * * * *

8 Three instruments of God's purpose, mentioned respectively at Exod 1:8–23,
  Ezra 1:1–11, and 2 Kings 25:1–22.
9 Ep 1637. See also Allen Ep 1674:36–41, which reveals that Erasmus himself
  showed copies of his correspondence with Pellicanus to a few close friends,
  who in turn allowed the texts to circulate in manuscript. Erasmus here claims
  that these copies did not name Pellicanus as the recipient, though his identity
  must have been obvious to any well-informed person. Subsequently, when
  Erasmus published his own letters (but not Pellicanus' two replies) in 1529, he
  did name the recipient. The private circulation in manuscript may well have
  been the origin of the two unauthorized and anonymously printed pamphlets
  mentioned in Ep 1627 introduction.
10 Ludwig Baer, Paris-trained professor of theology at Basel, a Catholic colleague
  of the two Evangelical professors appointed in 1523, Oecolampadius and
  Pellicanus himself. On him see Epp 488 introduction and 1571 n6.
11 Despite his other heresies, Luther was sharply critical of the Sacramentarian
  position.

friends.[2] If he settles at Louvain, please give him good advice on where to
find a suitable place for his son. I don't suppose there would be room for
him at the college.[3] It will work out better, I think, if you recommend him   5
to some reliable person who takes two or three promising young students
for private instruction. Farewell.

1642 / From Noël Béda   Paris, 21 October 1525

This reply to Ep 1620 continues the extended and chilly exchange of letters
with the syndic of the Paris theological faculty, which Erasmus had inaugur-
ated in April (Ep 1571). Béda published it in his *Apologia adversus clandestinos
Lutheranos* (Paris 1529); Erasmus never included it in any of his own collections
of his correspondence.

TO THE MOST LEARNED ERASMUS OF ROTTERDAM, OUR GREATLY
BELOVED AND RESPECTED FRIEND
Greetings, brother and master. I see I must confine my reply to selected
points in your letter. So it will be brief. But whether your letter was long or
short, a man of your learning could write nothing which, so help me, would   5
make me sad on your account. The very title of the letter to the bishop of
Basel[1] and the three subjects which you deal with there[2] must offend every
godly man of learning – at least that is how I feel. You will understand this
more readily if you read that work of Clichtove's which he called the *Antilutherus*[3] (the reference is to book 3, chapter 1, paragraph 3). It is not diffi-   10
cult to guess from this what he felt about your *Epistola*, although he did not
mention the author's name when he wrote; but in another work of his,[4]

* * * * *

1641
1 Cf Epp 58 introduction, 1624 n9. Grey and his son were leaving Basel for
   Louvain, where the son planned to enroll.
2 In classical mythology, the close friendship between Orestes and Pylades was
   proverbial, so that a Pyladean friendship would be an enduring one.
3 No doubt the Collegium Trilingue, founded by the will of Jérôme de Busleyden, where Erasmus had been one of the founding trustees and Goclenius was
   now professor of Latin.

1642
1 A reference to Erasmus' *De esu carnium*; cf Ep 1581 n100.
2 Ie, mandatory fasting, observance of saints' days, and clerical celibacy
3 Josse Clichtove *Antilutherus* (Paris: S. Colinaeus, 13 October 1524). Cf Epp
   594:15n, 1620 n10.
4 Clichtove's *Propugnaculum ecclesiae* (Paris: S. Colinaeus 1526), which directly

which we hope will appear before the first of February, he treats the subject
more directly, though with his usual restraint. As for your suggestion that
I note only those passages in your writings which have a bearing on the   15
Christian faith etc, it is now too late: what I have written I have written.[5]
I have taken up my position, but I assure you that I marked nothing in your
work which was not important to your salvation – and therefore worth
considering on that account – or a matter of faith. If by this expression,
however, you mean I should neglect everything which is not contained in   20
some collection of divine utterances or that everything else is unimportant
for salvation, you are in serious error; for it is just this concession which is
allowing countless people to do enormous damage to the church, and that
rascal Luther shelters behind the same doctrine.

As for the rest of our disagreements, I shall not argue with you any   25
longer. I have done my duty as a friend. I don't think I said that I could not
make a mistake. God forgive me if I ever made such a sweeping and arrogant claim. For, although I can say with confidence that I have no intention
of deceiving anyone, yet I cannot be absolutely certain that someone will
not be led astray. I do not think your writings have led me astray; I only   30
hope that those who approve of them have not been led astray, and that
you have not been deluded by their extravagant praise.

What you think, or once thought, of the theologians of the Sorbonne
is of no great importance. The faculty will survive.[6] Like myself, you will
soon be treading the path which all human flesh must tread[7] – and I hope   35
it will lead you to eternal bliss! I venture to suggest, my esteemed brother,
that if the circle of theologians whom you call the 'men of the Sorbonne'
had not attacked the errors of our time as well as those old errors which
were condemned long ago but are now enjoying a revival, Christian theology would have fallen into a worse state than it has. The fact that some   40
people speak ill of them does not bother these theologians. They are not
afraid of the tongues of the Lutherans or of the lovers of novelty, for they

* * * * *

criticizes Erasmus' *De esu carnium* and *Encomium matrimonii*. The book did not
appear so promptly as Béda hoped, for the colophon is dated 18 May 1526.
5 John 19:22. Béda here informs Erasmus that he has finished his *Annotationes*
against Erasmus and Lefèvre d'Etaples, published the following year: *Annota-
tionum Natalis Bede ... in Jacobum Fabrum Stapulensem libri duo, et in Desiderium
Erasmum Roterodamum liber unus ...* (Paris: Josse Bade, 25 May 1526).
6 Erasmus had declared (Ep 1620:76–86) that his own trust in the Paris faculty
of theology had diminished because of the behaviour of many of its members,
including Clichtove and Pierre Cousturier (and, by implication, Béda himself).
7 Josh 23:14, 1 Kings 2:2, Gen 6:13

are closer to purity of faith than those men are, however bitter the anger
they feel at present. Moreover they are well thought of by all Catholics in
France. So don't worry about their reputation in the future, but consider   45
carefully in your own mind how suspect a man's faith must appear if he
shows himself hostile towards theologians, who are simply doing their duty
when they devote themselves to the examination of new doctrines and, by
censoring various articles, warn the faithful of their real import. If you are
unaware of this, you will find enlightenment in Jean Gerson (part 1, number   50
14, letter v).[8] The judgments of the thoughtless lover are blind: I hope you
will realize how very true this is.

I do not imagine the readers of your *Apologia in Sutorem* will be any
kinder to you than they were to him;[9] for whatever others may have
thought – and there were different opinions on the subject – his references   55
to you and Lefèvre were excessively arrogant and sarcastic. May the good
and merciful Lord grant us all his pardon. I sent the man a friendly note
of protest when he wrote in a letter 'As soon as it became known to me
etc.'[10] There is no reason why anyone should be upset that the work
came out with the consent of the faculty. For it is not our practice in these   60
cases to examine a writer's style, only his doctrine.[11] If I had seen it before it appeared, it would not perhaps have come out in precisely this
form.

Finally you will put us in your debt if (as you said at the tail-end of
your letter) you stand up to those enemies of religion with their show of   65
Greek and their interest in the ancient tongues (you call them 'liberal
studies'). These people have reached such a point of madness that they are
sacrilegiously trying to remove Christ, as he is found in the sacrament, from
the church, which is his bride. Nothing you could do would meet with a

* * * * *

8 *Considerationes 12 de pertinacia* no 7, in his *Oeuvres complètes*, ed Palémon
   Glorieux (Paris 1965) VI 166. For the alphabetical method of citing Gerson, and
   also Erasmus' own reserved attitude toward him as a theological authority, cf
   Ep 1579 n42.
9 On the *Apologia* see the introduction to Ep 1591, the dedicatory epistle to the
   first edition.
10 Béda's Latin here closely paraphrases the Latin in the preface of Cousturier's
   De tralatione Bibliae. On that work, which attacked the biblical translations and
   editions of both Erasmus and Lefèvre d'Etaples, cf Ep 1571 n10.
11 Perhaps this is an accurate definition of the faculty's conception of its duty, but
   it also (and no doubt intentionally) implies the opinion of Béda and others that
   Erasmus and his kind were mere rhetoricians, qualified to judge matters of
   style but not matters of doctrine.

kinder reception from Catholics. May the Lord grant you strength to chal-   70
lenge these ungodly men. Amen.

Paris, 21 October 1525

I did not intend to speak about what you did, or saw done, on your
visit to Besançon, for I have discovered a hundred times how unreliable
rumours are. But if what I was told is true, that during the saying of grace   75
you protested when you heard the words 'the blessed womb of the Virgin
Mary' etc, which were added in accordance with pious custom – if that is
true, then your behaviour troubles me deeply, since you are placing yourself
in a perilous position.[12] Do steer clear of that sort of thing, I beg you.

1643 / From Mercurino Gattinara   Toledo, 28 October 1525

> On Gattinara, the imperial chancellor and the emperor's most influential
> adviser, see Ep 1150 introduction. From his youth Gattinara had favoured
> humanistic studies, and since they first met in 1520 he had warmly supported
> both Erasmus' scholarly work and his efforts at religious reform within the
> structure of the existing church. Repeatedly, Erasmus turned to him for help
> in getting payment on his imperial pension and in compelling his critics at
> Louvain to stop their open attacks on his orthodoxy, sometimes seeking his
> help through subordinates like Jean Lalemand (Ep 1554), sometimes approach-
> ing him directly for help, and usually with success (cf Epp 1700, 1747, 1757,
> 1784A). The present letter remained unpublished in a rough draft at Madrid
> (MS Est 18, gr I 5 f 21) and was first published by A. Helfferich, *Zeitschrift für
> historische Theologie* N F 23 (1859) 596.

Cordial greetings, most distinguished sir. Nothing could have given me
greater pleasure or delight than the letter you sent me on the Feast of St
Matthew the apostle.[1] It was delivered later than perhaps you would have
wished, but was no less welcome on that account. It brought me the news

* * * * *

12 For the incident here mentioned, which gave rise to rumours that Erasmus had
   spoken irreverently at a public occasion while visiting Besançon in 1524, cf Ep
   1610, Allen Epp 1679:93–103, 1956:24–35. Erasmus was extremely sensitive
   about this matter and repeatedly offered explanations to prove that he had not
   spoken irreverently and that what he said had not given offence. Clearly, as
   this letter shows, Béda did think that Erasmus had spoken irreverently.

1643
1 Not extant, but no doubt contemporaneous with Epp 1553 and 1554

I was greatly hoping for, that you have publicly declared yourself Luther's   5
enemy and have not just begun to attack his pestilential doctrines, but have
already made no small impression. I pray the gods may bless your efforts
every day.

There is only one thing which worries me, that you suffer so much
from the stone. But you know what misery this life is; and since it must be   10
endured, there is certainly no escaping its bitter moments. One thing must
give you very great comfort, that you may hope for praise in your lifetime
and glory when you are dead. These are two great blessings in the life of
man which can make up for whatever other misfortunes befall.

The emperor was very willing to grant your requests,[2] both for the   15
payment of your annuity and for action to be taken against your critics. I
enclose the letter which he commissioned for this purpose.[3] Carry on with
your plans: I have long been convinced of their importance both for religion
and the state; and don't be afraid of anyone, for there is nothing which is
more to be feared than one's own conscience, and if this is at peace, what-   20
ever happens afterwards must be counted gain, not loss. You will always
have me to protect your interests and your honour and I shall not let you
down. Farewell.

Toledo, 28 October 1525

Yours as ever, Mercurino Gattinara, chancellor   25

To the most distinguished Master Erasmus of Rotterdam, who is like
the best of brothers, etc. In Basel

1644 / To Conradus Pellicanus

On the basis of internal evidence, this letter has been assigned a new date and
appears as Ep 1792A in volume 12.

1645 / To Maximilianus Transsilvanus   Basel, 8 November 1525

This letter to one of Erasmus' most highly placed friends in the administration
of Margaret of Austria in the Netherlands is yet another effort to secure
payment of his imperial pension. In his introduction to the Latin text, Allen

* * * * *

2 Requests for payment of the promised imperial pension and for action to
 silence Erasmus' relentless critics among the theologians at Louvain
3 Not extant, but the order silencing the theologians met with sullen obstruction
 (cf Epp 1690, 1747, 1815), and renewed, extremely blunt intervention by Gattinara was necessary; cf Ep 1784A.

(VI 1645) quotes a manuscript from Madrid which shows that shortly after receiving this letter Maximilianus did act to advance Erasmus' interest. On him see Ep 1553 introduction. Erasmus printed this letter in *Opus epistolarum*.

ERASMUS OF ROTTERDAM TO MAXIMILIANUS TRANSSILVANUS,
SECRETARY TO THE EMPEROR, GREETING

Most honoured Maximilianus, I have now received a copy of the letter which you say you sent from 's-Hertogenbosch.[1] I never got the earlier one. How much I appreciate the warm and friendly feelings which your letter 5 conveys to me, dear Maximilianus. I am not worried about the pension. I know how insatiable the court always is – it is just like a leaky jar. I realized all along that what you suspect has happened would happen; for I know what those monsters are like. I am sorry for the court as well as for the university.[2] They have been carrying on like this for a long time. They 10 are well aware themselves that I have nothing to do with any clique and this makes them mad. They have read my *Spongia*, which is outspoken enough, and my *De libero arbitrio* too.[3] If they were here, they would be able to appreciate what friendly remarks the Lutherans are making about me! And of course they have read those books by Hutten[4] and Otto[5] 15 which make their opinion of me very clear. On top of that, if any trouble breaks out here, I shall be the first to be attacked. But these people will try anything without shame or scruple if it damages the cause of genuine learning. I see our civilization moving inexorably, as though impelled by the hand of Fate, into a state of Scythian barbarism. Since I cannot help, I shall 20 do the one thing I can, keep my conscience pure and unsullied and try to win Christ's commendation. I shall shortly send you my personal servant,

* * * * *

1645
1 Not extant
2 Louvain, where Erasmus found many hostile and outspoken critics despite efforts by his friends in Brussels and in Spain to silence them
3 Both his *Spongia adversus aspergines Hutteni* (1523) and his *De libero arbitrio* (1524) against Luther were, in the opinion of Erasmus but not of his conservative critics, clear proof that he was not a supporter of the Lutheran heresy.
4 Hutten's public attacks on Erasmus for failing to support Luther culminated in his *Cum Erasmo Roterodamo, presbytero, theologo Expostulatio* (1523), to which the *Spongia* was a reply.
5 Otto Brunfels took up the cause of the deceased Hutten against Erasmus, publishing *Pro Ulricho Hutteno vita defuncto ad Erasmi Roterodami Spongiam responsio* (Strasbourg: Johannes Scotus 1524). Cf Ep 1405 introduction.

whom I trust completely.[6] I shall give him a letter dealing most fully with a number of different points. In the meantime I wish my dear Maximilianus every happiness, as he deserves.   25

Basel, 8 November 1525

1646 / To Jan of Heemstede   Basel, 8 November 1525

Jan Symons of Heemstede, a Carthusian of Louvain, had written Erasmus a letter (not now extant) about the premature death of Maarten van Dorp, their mutual friend and Erasmus' one reliable supporter on the Louvain theological faculty. Almost alone of the monastic orders, the Carthusians maintained friendly relations with Erasmus (cf Ep 1196 n58). In a letter of 1530 (Ep 2353) Heemstede referred to Erasmus as 'my most esteemed teacher,' though whether this refers to formal study under Erasmus (presumably at Louvain, where he took his MA degree in 1520) is uncertain. Correspondence between the two men continued down to 1533, when records of Heemstede cease (cf Epp 1837, 1900, 1994, 2771). Erasmus included this letter in his *Opus epistolarum*.

ERASMUS OF ROTTERDAM TO JAN OF HEEMSTEDE OF THE CAR-
THUSIANS AT LOUVAIN, GREETING
No sooner was your letter delivered than someone appeared who was on his way to Brabant; so I am sending you an epitaph which I composed on the spur of the moment, though it cost me some effort. I hope you won't   5
think poorly of it – unless Conradus Goclenius[1] regards it as unsuitable. If it is unsatisfactory, I shall send you another, more carefully worked over. For I too consider Dorp's memory as something sacred.[2] His early death, which has robbed us of his many talents and cut short such bright hopes, ought to make me very sad, but ours is an age when no decent man can   10

* * * * *

6 Karl Harst, his secretary and courier, whose name appears repeatedly at this period as the bearer of letters and a trusted confidential agent

1646
1 On him cf Ep 1209 introduction. Although Erasmus originally had not favoured his appointment as professor of Latin at the Collegium Trilingue in Louvain, by this time he had formed a high opinion of his ability, an opinion reflected here and in several other letters.
2 After some wavering in the early years, Dorp had become a reliable supporter of Erasmus' scholarship from about 1516. Thus the regret expressed in this letter and the annexed epitaph was no doubt sincere.

live a happy life, and, even if this were the best of times, there could be no greater happiness than to dwell with Christ.

I was overjoyed to hear about that splendid man, Father Jan of Delft.[3] It is remarkable how, in spite of infirmities of body, his spirit always triumphs, sound and unimpaired. Please give him my sincere and affectionate good wishes. I shall not allow van Dorp's memory to perish, if there is anything my writings can do. Remember me to the worthy members of your community: I pray they may have every blessing in Christ.

This is your letter, my beloved friend, no longer than the epitaph, but the secretary was in a hurry.

Basel, 8 November 1525

EPITAPH[4]
Maarten van Dorp has left his earthly home.
Now Holland mourns for its departed son;
Theology laments a light snuffed out;
The saddened Muses and the Graces fair
Weep for their mighty champion who is gone;
Louvain has lost, alas, its radiant star.
'O Death' it cries, 'cruel and awful death,
Full of injustice and malevolence,
Thus prematurely do you fell the tree
While still it flowers, and rob us of our hopes
And of his gifts, leaving our prayers
Forever unfulfilled?' But no! Cease, cease
These impious cries. He is not dead, but lives.
He has been rescued from this evil world
And all the endowments of his soul are safe.
Our lot it is to mourn, his to rejoice.
The earth now holds his body in its care,
That body which once lodged his pious soul

* * * * *

3 This Carthusian monk (d 25 May 1530) may have studied at Cologne in 1463 before entering the order. In 1495 he was sent to Louvain to found a new convent there, becoming its first prior in 1504, a position he held until 1525, when he resigned because of advanced age. In 1521 he fulfilled his goal of having the monastery incorporated into the university. Erasmus' warm sentiments reflect his excellent relations with both the individual and the Carthusian order.
4 First printed in Erasmus' *Ciceronianus* (Basel: Froben, March 1528), with only one minor textual variation.

But when we hear the call of the last trump,
Earth will unseal the tomb and give us back
The body of our friend, its sacred trust.

1647 / From Erasmus Schets   Antwerp, 9 November 1525

On the recipient see Ep 1541 introduction. This letter shows Schets' eagerness
to assist Erasmus, especially by using his own extensive business connections
to help him secure payment and easy transfer of his pensions from England
and the Netherlands. Like most of the letters dealing with Erasmus' finances,
this letter remained unpublished, though carefully preserved among Erasmus'
papers at Basel, until publication by Förstemann and Günther in 1904.

Cordial greetings. I wish you would send me more frequent bulletins about
your health than you have done up to now. That would make me feel better
and set my mind more at ease, for I cry out for news because of my love
and admiration for you and the warm esteem in which I hold you, though
you may be scarcely aware of how I feel. A month ago I received your   5
letter,[1] informing me that you had written to Canterbury about the payment of your pension. In the meantime I have not been idle myself; I wrote
to my friend Alvaro,[2] who, as a favour to me, quickly agreed to take the
matter in hand; he said he would be delighted to have the opportunity to
serve you, for you are considered, and rightly considered, a giant among   10
men. He tells me that the archbishop of Canterbury was not in London, but
that he spoke to the man in charge of his financial affairs.[3] The official
indicated that a payment of twenty pounds had already been made to you
from another source, but a second payment of ten pounds would shortly be
made to Alvaro himself.[4] As soon as Alvaro receives it, he will let you   15

* * * * *

1647
1 Not extant, but probably an answer to Ep 1590, which shows that Erasmus
  relied on Schets' assistance to secure payment of his annual pension from the
  parish of Aldington in England
2 Cf Ep 1590 n2.
3 Allen Ep 1647:9n surmises that this was Thomas Bedyll, secretary for many
  years to Archbishop William Warham. He was frequently involved when any
  problem arose over payment of Erasmus' pension. Alternatively, but less
  plausibly, Allen speculates that the person may be the unnamed major-domo
  (oeconomus) whom Erasmus greeted in a letter of 1520 to Bedyll (Ep 1176:20).
4 Latin pensionem librarum viginti. Sums in pounds sterling (CWE 1 330); £20

know. In the meantime I suggest you write and tell me what you want done with the money. There is nothing within my powers or capabilities that I would not do to further your interests and promote your honour and glory.

You give me no hope of your return. I wonder what you will decide to do now that the bloodshed is over. We do not expect you now because of winter and the cold weather. But unless you build up our hopes for the coming summer, your friends and I will be plunged into despair. In the meantime, best wishes and every success.

Antwerp, from my business office, 9 November 1525

Your devoted friend, Erasmus Schets

Here is a postscript to inform you of some new developments. I have just received a letter from Spain, from which I learn that the emperor paid a hurried visit to the French king, who was unwell.[5] At the meeting there was nothing but the greatest courtesy, goodwill and amity on both sides. When all their personal staff had withdrawn, they had a conversation lasting two hours which was bright with the promise of peace and concord. They say that the emperor's marriage[6] with the sister of the king of Portugal will be celebrated and will take place sometime next Christmas. I don't know what will happen to us as a result of the rejection of the king of England's daughter.[7] May God make all things turn out for the best! Farewell once more.

To that incomparable scholar, Master Erasmus of Rotterdam. In Basel

1648 / From Johann Matthäus Schad   Padua, 19 November 1525

This little-known provost of the cathedral chapter at Constance was closely

* * * * *

sterling would then have been worth about £29 12s 6d gros Flemish or about £187 3s tournois. See also Ep 1651 n3.
5 During his captivity at Madrid after the battle of Pavia, Francis I fell gravely ill (September 1525), a crisis that precipitated this hurried visit by the emperor on 18 September. See Knecht 187.
6 To Princess Isabella of Portugal. The wedding took place in Seville on 10 March 1526.
7 A marriage treaty betrothing Charles V to the five-year-old Princess Mary was signed in 1521 and had been confirmed by a gift from the princess early in 1525, but the advantage of a dynastic connection with Portugal caused Charles to abandon this commitment to Mary, who many years later became the wife of his son Philip II. See D.M. Loades Mary Tudor: A Life (Oxford 1989) 22.

related to Cardinal Matthäus Lang and had studied at Tübingen and Louvain before continuing his education at Padua. He is first documented by his matriculation at Tübingen in 1515 and last documented as the recipient of a book dedication by Johannes Cochlaeus in 1546. The letter survived in a manuscript at Wrocław (MS Rehd 254.134) and was first published in L.K. Enthoven (ed) *Briefe an Desiderius Erasmus von Rotterdam* (Strasbourg 1906).

Greetings. I realize, most learned sir, what a great responsibility I am assuming when I write to one who is universally considered one of the wonders of the world, not just for his incredible learning but also for all his other intellectual gifts. For no one, I feel certain, would have the effrontery to compare himself with Erasmus. It is because of Erasmus' remarkable   5
learning that our native Germany, once a boorish and unlettered place, has now burst forth with such splendour and vitality that it will soon be ready to enter the lists with the Muses of Italy.[1] All this is making the Italians jealous of the great glory which our country has won – for with typical arrogance they think of all nations but themselves as barbarians; neverthe-   10
less they are ready to admit that the Muses have moved from Parnassus and Helicon and under your inspiration have spread the glories of learning throughout our land. For we see among us a constant stream of scholars reaching a remarkable maturity and emerging from your school, as though they were descending from the Trojan horse, resplendent in every branch   15
of learning. For when our beloved Germany was in a state of paralysis, with nothing on its mind except carousing and drunkenness, and buried, so to speak, in the slumbers of Endymion,[2] you brought us to life with your immortal works, and now there is hardly an intelligent young man among us who does not think he should devote himself to the refinements of the   20
Muses. So it is not easy to say how much Germany owes to you. Certainly whatever learning she has gained, must certainly be credited to you; for as a people we seem predisposed to recognize those who have helped us on our way.
It is not my intention to continue this eulogy any further, partly   25

* * * * *

1648
1 The correspondent's strong identification with both humanism and Germany appears in this passage, and he associates Erasmus with a revival of high culture in Germany that makes even the arrogant Italians take notice.
2 In classical mythology, Endymion was a strikingly beautiful young man who sleeps forever, remaining deathless and ageless. Cf Apollodorus 1.7.5.

because your fame is already known beyond the heavens,[3] and partly because I think, as the historian says about Carthage, that it is better to be silent altogether than say too little.[4] But I have this one request to make, that you pardon my impertinence and brashness in daring to trouble a great literary phoenix like yourself with my clumsy letter and my foolish wits.[5]   30
It is because of your celebrated virtues that, though we have never met, I am not just an admirer of yours but feel a very deep devotion to you. Moreover the kindness which you show all students emboldens me to set aside all modesty and send you this letter in the hope of being admitted to your friendship, if you judge me worthy. Farewell, and may you live as   35
long as Nestor!

Padua, 19 November 1525
Johann Matthäus Schad, provost of Constance
To the excellent theologian, Master Erasmus of Rotterdam

1649 / From Christoph Truchsess   Padua, 20 November 1525

A reply to Ep 1625 but, unlike it, not published until 1904, by Förstemann and Günther, on the basis of a Leipzig manuscript.

Nothing could have pleased me more than your letter, dear Erasmus, my erudite and accomplished friend. From it I learned of the remarkably gener- ous tribute which our friend Karl paid me,[1] and I received your good words of fatherly advice, urging me to aim not only for moral betterment but for progress in the liberal arts. You are afraid that the humanities, which   5
are coming to life under your guidance everywhere in Europe, may be packed off to the antipodes by Philistines. Even Italy, which was once rightly called the refuge of the Muses, is now harbouring people who want to drive talented young men away from the noblest form of learning by the bitterness of their invective. Recently a well-known lawyer[2] stood up in a   10

* * * * *

3 Virgil *Aeneid* 1.379
4 Sallust *Jugurtha* 19
5 The Latin phrase is *rudi Minerva*, a variant of the more familiar *crassa Minerva*; cf *Adagia* I i 37.

1649
1 Karl Harst, who at this period served Erasmus as secretary and courier and in 1525 made two important trips to Italy, where he must have met Truchsess
2 The identity of this person is unknown, but clearly he was upholding the traditional medieval approach to legal studies (*mos italicus*) against humanist-

crowded hall in Bologna and without a blush made an attack upon the
Muses (I quote his actual words): 'Keep away, gentlemen, from the humane
arts, as you would from a painted harlot'; with this sort of talk he worked
on the minds of the students until they preferred the Bartolists[3] to Servius
Sulpicius[4] and Sorbonists[5] like Cousturier[6] to Chrysostom.[7] Cicero rightly   15
dismissed men like these as 'pettifoggers,' illiterate pedants who lack a
sound general education.[8] So, most learned Erasmus, do not take it too
much to heart when men like Cousturier turn up their arrogant noses[9] at
you; all the servants of Apollo will put up a spirited fight on your behalf.
Farewell, the darling of our age!   20

* * * * *

inspired critics who wanted to discard the accretions of medieval commentary
and base legal scholarship on the ancient sources, an approach to the study of
law which had come to be called *mos gallicus*. Cf Guido Kisch *Humanismus und
Jurisprudenz: Der Kampf zwischen mos italicus und mos gallicus an der Universität
Basel* (Basel 1955).

3 Ie, followers of traditional medieval jurisprudence, one of whose greatest
figures was Bartolus of Sassoferrato (1313–57), professor at Perugia

4 Servius Sulpicius Rufus, a great Roman jurist who served as consul in 51 BC
and is celebrated by Cicero in his ninth *Philippic*. Although none of his many
legal works survives, he is credited with devising the methodical treatment of
law followed by later generations of Roman jurisconsults. For Cicero's praise
of him as the greatest figure in Roman law, cf *Brutus* 151–6.

5 Although the Sorbonne was only one of several Paris colleges in which theology was taught, popular usage (though never official university documents)
sometimes used the term as equivalent to the entire faculty of theology, and
the usage has persisted into modern times. Erasmus himself used the term
loosely and in a polemical sense (eg Ep 1620:77), a habit for which his antagonist Noël Béda implicitly reproved him (Ep 1642:37). On the history of this
usage, see Farge *Orthodoxy* 3–4.

6 On him see Ep 1571 n10. He appears frequently in letters to and from
Erasmus, treated as an incompetent but dangerously malevolent buffoon, the
very personification of all that was wrong with traditional scholastic theology
and theologians.

7 St John Chrysostom (349–407), patriarch of Constantinople and Doctor of the
universal church, was one of the most admired patristic theologians, especially
noted for his homiletic commentaries on Scripture and his eloquent preaching.
Erasmus had edited and translated several of his works, including in this very
year his *De sacerdotio*. In the present context, he represents Erasmus' ideal of
the proper theologian, deeply engaged with Scripture and committed to
pastoral care, in contrast to Cousturier, who is presented as representing an
arid and useless theology.

8 *De oratore* 1.236

9 Erasmus' Latin phrase is *nasum suspendunt*, a variant on Horace's *naso suspendunt*; see *Satires* 1.6.5, 2.8.64.

From the city of Antenor,[10] 20 November 1525

Truly your most devoted friend, Christoph Truchsess, Baron von Waldburg

Deliver to[11] the most learned of men, Master Erasmus of Rotterdam, a friend beloved as a father. In Basel   25

1650 / From Leonard Casembroot   Padua, 23 November 1525

A reply to Ep 1626. The translator has continued the practice, begun in Ep 1594, of using French to render Casembroot's self-consciously 'clever' use of Greek words and phrases. On Casembroot see Ep 1594 introduction. This begging letter remained unpublished in a Leipzig manuscript until edited by Förstemann and Günther in 1904.

Cordial greetings, mighty Erasmus, in every way *le plus désiré des hommes!*[1] I got your letter – but why do I call it a 'letter,' when it was a pearl to be treasured for all time? It was delivered by that illustrious and worthy gentleman, Baron Jan Łaski,[2] a man whom Nature intended to be a blessing to other countries besides Poland. No one who has had the good fortune to   5 meet him and experience even briefly the charm of his personality will be surprised that, as you put it, you became young again through the pleasure of his company. A short time ago we listened to your eloquent *Tongue,* which is dedicated to his brother;[3] in fact we not only listened, but allowed it to penetrate into the inner recesses of our hearts. Please God we may   10

* * * * *

10 The mythical founder of the city of Padua; cf Virgil *Aeneid* 1.242–8.
11 The address in Latin ends with the puzzling letters *c r,* which Allen Ep 1649:23n suggests may stand for *curato reddendas,* and which are so translated here. Allen also suggests that the manuscript might be read *c t,* the writer's initials.

1650
1 Casembroot's Greek term is one of his own coinage, ἐρασμιώτατε. The translation makes a parallel play on Erasmus' Christian name, Desiderius.
2 See Ep 1341A n319, Allen Epp 1593 n18, 1622 n3, 1627 n2.
3 Erasmus' treatise *Lingua* was published at Basel in August 1525, but it was dedicated to the grand chancellor of Poland, Krzysztof Szydłowiecki, not to Jan Łaski's brother Hieronim (who did, however, receive the dedication of Erasmus' *Modus orandi Deum* in 1524). Cf Epp 1502, 1593. Casembroot's mistake about the dedication probably rests on failure to distinguish between the two dedications and also on the fact that Jan Łaski is twice mentioned in the dedication to Szydłowiecki.

profit from it as the earnestness of our efforts deserves! I cannot measure
my gratitude, even at a personal level, for such a work; but at least I shall
try to express it in the only way I know you care about – by making my
whole way of life a witness to the power of your book and by expressing
it in my conduct. Heaven protect us! We have been living in a dream world   15
as far as our salvation is concerned: we have gone utterly astray from stem
to stern,[4] as the saying goes. Yet what evils attend us if we ignore this
philosophy and what felicity if we practise it! Ears which are not charmed
by the music of so sweet an instrument must have no hope of salvation:
they are worse than Boeotian. But, as the old proverb goes, bellies have no   20
ears,[5] and music will have no effect on them. I believe it would be easier
to train the ears of a Midas, though his were the ears of an ass.[6]

O how much pleasure it would give me to use my tongue, or, failing
that, my pen, to celebrate the marvels of your *Tongue*! But your tongue has
warned me against the folly of pursuing pointless ends. And, after all my   25
eulogies, I might hear someone say, 'Does anyone really disagree?' Then, a
short time ago, just at the height of my excitement, your high-minded letter
arrived, which affected me like the lash of a whip added to the prick of the
spur. These painful jabs have sent me hurrying into the race 'for propriety
and obligation.'[7] But another master stands over me with a sharper lash,   30
Hunger, an acknowledged master of his art; so intolerable and unexpected
are his threats that I am forced to seek your protection once more against
his tyranny, since you were kind enough to protect me from it some time
ago. It is in your strength and yours alone that I place my confidence that
the tyrant will soon lose his power, never to raise his head again.   35

You will wonder where all this is leading. Let me tell you. I have
parted company with my friends the Moscherons.[8] It was through no fault

* * * * *

4 *Adagia* I i 8
5 *Adagia* II viii 84
6 One of the legends about this legendary king of Phrygia tells how Apollo
  punished him for preferring the music of Pan to that of Apollo by transform-
  ing his ears into ass's ears. See, for example, Ovid *Metamorphoses* 11. 173–93.
7 Two technical terms of Stoic ethics, cited here in Greek. The distinction is
  between what is absolutely required, a matter of obligation (Cicero calls it
  'perfectum officium rectum,' or κατόρθωμα) and what is an ordinary duty, a
  matter of propriety (Cicero calls it 'commune officium,' or καθῆκον, or in the
  second passage cited, 'decorum,' or πρέπον). Cicero explains these terms and
  their meaning in *De officiis* 1.8 and 93.
8 Casembroot had been tutoring three sons of a wealthy Bruges merchant at
  Padua; cf Ep 1594 introduction.

of mine that I know of – and those with whom I live say this too. If this were not the case, how could I have the gall to pester you with my woes? The problem (not to be too uncivil about it) was the incompatibility of our interests. Master Guillaume de Moscheron spent three days with us, leaving on the thirteenth of November, and although he kept it a dark secret for a long time, he eventually made his intentions known just before he left. Evidently he wanted to separate me and his children, two of whom were devoted to literary studies and the rest to commerce. He decided to leave the pair who were interested in literature without the protection of a tutor. He gave no reason for this action except that his expenses were too onerous. He thanked me, but that was all.

So Leonard, who hardly deserved such a fate, is left high and dry, almost destitute, abandoned in Italy far from his home, his relatives, and friends, and just when the frosts of winter are approaching and before he has been in the country very long. A case indeed of the gelding at the gate!⁹ But do not expect from me a tragic diatribe against fate and fortune and the changing morals of the times; somewhere there should be an example of stubborn courage holding firm. What I must now do is hunt out a little bit of luck, just enough to soften somehow the cruel blows of that terrible tyrant, Hunger, if not to banish it completely. For no ordinary pain could tear me away from Italy, which I love so dearly. We have had our little joke about melons and bastards and about *la lutte au lit* and bringing into the world some *petits Léonards*.¹⁰ The main reason for leaving my dear Flanders, in other respects an admirable country, was the conflict I experienced there between *l'intempérance* and *mon désir d'apprendre*.¹¹ I could have had a prebendaryship (as they call it) at St Donatian's, but it seemed preferable to exchange it for an annuity of twenty-four ducats,¹² which I still

40

45

50

55

60

65

* * * * *

9 Proverbial for someone who suffers discouragement at the start, like the gelding which stumbled at the gate; *Adagia* I v 78
10 Casembroot uses Greek (here suggested by the use of French) to refer back to his bragging about his sexual exploits among the Italian women (Ep 1594: 45–8), for which Erasmus had sharply rebuked him (Ep 1626:30–1).
11 *l'intempérance ... mon désir d'apprendre*] Again, Casembroot uses Greek words (τὸ ἀκρατές and φιλομαθία), this time to suggest that the conflict between intemperate habits and his desire to become learned had already been a problem while he lived in Flanders.
12 Latin *quatuor et viginti ducatorum*. At current exchange rates (6s 8d gros Flemish), an annuity worth exactly £8 gros Flemish, or £5 8s 0d sterling, or about £50 10s 6d tournois.

70

75

receive. You see I am not out for any kind of plunder except to plunder the classics, and this is something which you yourself encourage.

But why these petitions and tales of woe when I am writing to a friend who is as influential as he is generous, that is, someone who is both able and willing to help? But if I may make a suggestion, you know that the young Englishman, Master Reginald Pole,[13] whose distinction does not rest solely on his family tree, lives here. If I could have a complimentary recommendation which would allow me to find a place in his household, perhaps just to dine without charge at his table, I would ask for nothing more. My own youthful vigour would do the rest. Or perhaps you could recommend me to someone else in one of the universities. I am told that, among others at Bologna, there is a grand countryman of ours who is bishop of Arras and son of the lord of Roeulx;[14] that would suit me well too. I do not know his name. Your man Karl,[15] who is with us here, will be able to suggest other possibilities.

But it would surpass all our hopes of happiness if we could see you here too sometime. You would find a home with a lovely garden at your disposal, and there won't even be any charge, for the old arrangement has come to an end, and I have already paid the landlord a year's rent. I swear to you we would sing you a fine wedding song here to celebrate your marriage to the charming Hebe, now that you have sent a writ of divorce to that wretched creature Old Age.[16] To bring this to a conclusion, my dearest Erasmus, let me say that I am your most devoted servant. If you know of anything which I could do, just say the word. You will find me ready to serve you whether that means going to India or the distant Garamantes.[17] May the peace of Jesus soften the wrath of your critics and make

5

10

15

20

25

* * * * *

13 See Ep 1627 introduction. Erasmus twice mentioned Casembroot favourably in letters to Pole (Epp 1627, 1675), but Casembroot did not manage to become a member of Pole's household at Padua.

14 Eustache de Croy (1502/3–1538), younger son of a nobleman of Hainaut, Ferry de Croy, lord of Roeulx, chamberlain to Philip the Handsome and to Maximilian I, governor of Artois, and knight of the Golden Fleece. The son matriculated at Louvain on 13 September 1521, being already apostolic protonotary; in 1523 he became bishop of Arras but went to Italy instead of taking charge of his diocese.

15 Karl Harst, Erasmus' courier to Italy at this time, mentioned repeatedly in letters to and from there

16 Both *Hebe* and *Old Age* are in Greek. The Greek word *hebe* means both 'youth' and 'goddess of youth.'

17 An ancient people of the most remote inland portions of eastern Libya, mentioned by Herodotus 4.174, 183; Virgil *Eclogues* 8.45; Pliny 5.5, 43; Isidore

all things serene. Farewell, mighty Erasmus, and don't forget your friend Leonard.

Padua, 23 November 1525

Your good friend, Leonard Casembroot

To Master Erasmus of Rotterdam, the most accomplished scholar in   95
every field of learning

1650A / From Gian Matteo Giberti   Rome, 27 November 1525

This reply to a lost letter of Erasmus (probably written contemporaneously with Epp 1621–35, according to a plausible conjecture by Allen) comes from one of Erasmus' firmest supporters at the papal curia. On Giberti, papal datary and a close adviser to Pope Clement VII, see Ep 1443A introduction. Rather surprisingly, considering its demonstration of support by a highly placed curial official, Erasmus never published it. It survived in the Vatican Archives (MS Particolare 143, f 122), from which Allen edited it for his volume VI (1926).

TO ERASMUS

Reverend sir, etc. Your most recent letter filled me with joy three times over; for it let me know that my services to you had been welcome,[1] that you had found relief from the pain of the stone, and that you were writing a new work to refute a new falsehood of the heretics.[2] No news could have   5
delighted me more, especially that last announcement that you are planning to defend the majesty of the Holy Eucharist against these modern Titans.[3] So from the depths of my heart I thank Almighty God for having restored you to us safe and sound, and for not permitting the poison which threatens us to be stronger than the antidote which protects our holy religion; but I   10

* * * * *

Etymologiae 9.2.125; Pomponius Mela 1.23, 45; Strabo 17.3.19, 23; and several other ancient historical and geographical authors. In short, the southernmost people of North Africa known to the ancients.

1650A
1 Probably Giberti's efforts, not fully successful, to use papal authority to silence open attacks on Erasmus by Louvain theologians. See Epp 1481, 1506, 1589A.
2 Erasmus' lost letter must have mentioned his plan, later abandoned, to write in opposition to Oecolampadius' Sacramentarian book *De genuina verborum Domini*. See Ep 1616 nn2 and 4.
3 The Titans attacked the gods and are thus frequently used in antiquity as a symbol of impiety. The parallel here is the Protestant reformers' attacks on the doctrine and authority of the church.

thank him most of all because he wanted you alive at this hour, that we might have your learning and eloquence, and your authority too, as a defence against those who impiously deny God. Do keep it up, for you give us hope. Fight on, and strike at the foe with your pen: their ranks have been diminished by the sword, but they still support, and add to, their former   15
blasphemies. I shall be with you and your friends as I have always been; I shall do what I can to let Jacques Lefèvre know, if I am approached by his agents, that your support was no less significant than his own merits.[4]

Rome, 27 November 1525
To the Reverend and most respected Master Erasmus of Rotterdam   20

1651 / From Erasmus Schets   Antwerp, 3 December 1525

> This letter is a follow-up to Ep 1647 and like it deals chiefly with Schets' efforts to facilitate payment of Erasmus' English pension and transfer of the proceeds to him at Basel. It remained unpublished among Erasmus' papers at Basel until published in Allen VI (1926).

Cordial greetings. I wrote you quite recently – a month ago or thereabouts. I wonder if you received my letter. I hope you did. I explained what my friend Alvaro de Castro[1] wrote from England about the payment of your pension. He has now written a second letter to say that, as my agent acting on your behalf, he has received from the archbishop of Canterbury[2] one   5
hundred and thirty-eight and a half *écus d'or*,[3] which is the equivalent of

* * * * *

4 This letter is the only evidence that Erasmus intervened at Rome in behalf of his fellow humanist Lefèvre, who had fled to Strasbourg (October 1525) for fear of prosecution by conservative leaders in the Parlement and the Paris faculty of theology. These had acted to suppress the reformers working for the bishop of Meaux at a time when Lefèvre's chief protector, King Francis I, was held captive in Spain.

1651
1 Cf Ep 1590 n2.
2 William Warham. On his role in assuring Erasmus an income from England, see Ep 1583 n1.
3 Latin *centum triginta octo cum dimidio scutos aureos (qui triginta librarum sterlinarum pertingunt summam)*. For the current French *écus d'or au soleil*, then worth 40s or £2 tournois and 6s 4d gros Flemish, see CWE 1 315–16, 336; CWE 8 350; and Epp 1434 n3, 1545 n6. A sum of 138.5 *écus au soleil* was thus officially worth £277 tournois and £43 17s 2d gros Flemish; and, by the rate of exchange employed in these notes for the year 1525 (£1 gros = 13s 6d sterling), equal to just over £29 12s 0d sterling – close enough, with casual rounding in this correspondence, to thirty pounds. See also Ep 1647 n4; and n5 below.

thirty pounds sterling.[4] I shall fish around for a way of having this sum transferred here to me. Please let me know where you would like the money sent. Perhaps you have friends on the spot who could transmit the *écus* to you in cash, or you might prefer to have one hundred and eighty- 10 four gold florins instead,[5] which is the official exchange for the afore-mentioned sum in *écus*. If you like, I shall pay over the whole amount to your friends, after showing them your letter to me. If this is not possible, however, and you so instruct me, I shall arrange to have the money delivered to you at Basel through my agents after the next Frankfurt fair, so that 15 eventually it will reach you safely without being eaten into. Remember that Alvaro de Castro has promised Canterbury to produce a receipt from you; he asked me to request it from you and to have it sent. Please see that my friend's obligations are properly discharged.

A businessman from Basel, called Martin Lompart,[6] is staying with us. 20 I have asked him to take you a jar of preserved fruit from Barbary – it is really a delicious syrup known as 'succade'; he has promised to deliver it safely.[7] I hope you will be pleased to accept it as a gift. It will be an unusual treat in Basel, I am sure; no matter how little you take, I think you

* * * * *

4 See note 3 above.
5 Latin *centum octuaginta quatuor florenos in auro*. Simple arithmetic proves that these must be Rhenish florins (Rheingulden), since these 184 florins are stated to be equal in value to the 138.5 *écus au soleil* in n3. Though the Rhenish florin, unlike the French *écu*, was not officially rated in the August 1521 coinage ordinance for the Hapsburg Netherlands (CWE 8 350), this florin's value can still be deduced from that same ordinance, which, like all such ordinances, slightly undervalued foreign gold coins in relation to domestic coins. The *écu au soleil*, with 3.296 g fine gold, was officially valued at 76d gros; the Rhenish florin, if maintaining its original, full 1490 weight, with 2.527 g fine gold, should have been worth 58.5d: ie 76 × (2.527/3.296) = 58.5. If, however, that Rhenish florin had lost about 2.5% of its weight from the 1490 standard, through circulation, it would have enjoyed a market exchange rate of about 57d gros Flemish in 1525. Thus 184 florins × 57d = £43 14s 0d gros, which is very close indeed to the value of 138.5 *écus au soleil* indicated in n3 (ie £43 17s 2d gros Flemish). As an alternative calculation to prove the same point: 138.5 *écus* × 76d gros Flemish = 10,526d gros, and thus 10,526/184 florins = 57.2d gros, as the estimated value for the Rhenish florin.
6 This little-known merchant is also mentioned in Epp 1658, 1671, 2511. He appears to have managed the Antwerp office of the Basel banker Jakob Lompart, whom Schets (Ep 1658) identifies as his brother.
7 Since the preserved fruit known as succade (documented in OED as early as 1463) contained spices and oranges, the Latin *fructuum Barbaricorum* probably means 'fruit from Barbary,' the North African coast, which then produced citrus fruits and still does.

will find it effective against dryness.[8] But since you are an expert in all   25
these things, I need not go into details about its merits. That would be
giving lessons to Minerva![9]

I see that your *Tongue* has appeared and has reached us here. I have
not read it yet because I have been swamped by business from all quarters,
but I am about to try it now. How I would like to see the seven so-called   30
penitential Psalms spring forth from that fountain from which your *Paraphrases* come![10] I am afraid the people mumble them with their lips without comprehending them in the spirit in which they were sung by the
servant of God.

Farewell, dear Erasmus. There are Erasmian resources here which you   35
must not allow to go idle; all they want is to serve you.

Antwerp, 3 December 1525
Yours sincerely, Erasmus Schets
To the incomparable scholar, Master Erasmus of Rotterdam. In Basel

1652 / From Andrzej Krzycki   Cracow, [20] December 1525

This letter, which survived in two manuscripts (Kórnik MS 243, f 109 and Cracow
MS 44, f 1) and was first published in Allen VI (1926), is a delighted response to
Ep 1629 and is the only surviving part of Krzycki's half of an extensive corre-
spondence. Erasmus' reply is Ep 1753. On Krzycki see Ep 1629 introduction.

ANDRZEJ KRZYCKI, BISHOP OF PRZEMYŠL, TO ERASMUS OF
ROTTERDAM
I received your letter, most learned Erasmus, also the book by the Reverend
Father Cuthbert Tunstall, bishop of London,[1] which you sent at the same
time, both most welcome gifts for a host of reasons. But one reason stood   5
out beyond the others: for, although I am destined to continue the study of

* * * * *

8 Since Schets' Latin was poor, he may think that *siccitas* means 'thirst,' as Gerlo
    assumed in his French translation of this letter; but 'dryness' also has medical
    connotations, such as dryness of skin, in sixteenth-century usage.
9 *Adagia* I i 40; cf Cicero *Ad familiares* 9.18.3; *Academica* 1.18.
10 A wish previously expressed in Schets' first letter to Erasmus, Ep 1541. Begin-
    ning with a commentary on Ps 1 dedicated to Beatus Rhenanus in 1515,
    Erasmus produced commentaries or other expositions on several psalms (now
    collected in LB V) but never dealt with any of the seven Penitential Psalms (Pss
    6, 31, 37, 50, 101, 129, and 142 in the Vulgate numeration).

1652
1 On Bishop Tunstall and his book on arithmetic see Ep 1629, nn4 and 5.

theology, the humanities bring me such delight that I am unable to tear
myself away from them and cannot help stealing time from theology and
the never-ending distractions of business to devote to the humanities instead. We have never met face to face, and yet I have long felt impelled to   10
love and admire you deeply as the chief exponent and champion of these
studies in our day and of that ancient and more enlightened theology.
Everyone here who professes a devotion to literature knows how much I
treasure your wonderfully learned and elegant works, though you yourself
may choose to call them 'typically Dutch.' There is no doubt that they can   15
stand comparison with any of the classics, Greek or Latin, and that is not
just my opinion; it is an opinion shared by the whole world. As soon as a
work of yours appears, I insist on possessing it for myself, I set my humble
(and truly Scythian) Muses to sing its praises, and I have the work printed
in this country.[2] Until now I have had no opportunity to declare the undy-   20
ing affection and devotion which I feel for you without making you or your
friends suspicious that I want to make myself immortal through your
works, when in fact I am the least ambitious of men. Many people, even
those who have no claim to it, seem to have it as their sole ambition to win
your praise – though to be praised by Erasmus, even undeservedly, could   25
be seen as the very pinnacle of glory. But when you yourself actually made
the opening and decided to offer me your love, you can imagine what
delight and comfort your letter brought me; all I wanted was some sign of
recognition – I never dreamed of winning your affection.

Need I say much about the book? You could not have sent me a more   30
appropriate or helpful gift. I used to think that calculation and accountancy
were more for businessmen than bishops, and I dare say I have never asked
any of my treasurers or officials for a statement of accounts. I had forgotten
the lesson which our great lord and master, Christ, seems to want us to
learn when he shows us great men and heads of families working on their   35

* * * * *

2 Some of Erasmus' works had already been printed in Cracow: *Querela pacis* in
  1518; *Colloquiorum formulae* in 1519; *De conscribendis epistolis, De constructione,*
  De copia, and *Paraclesis* in 1523; *Precatio dominica, Modus orandi Deum,* and a
  second edition of *De conscribendis epistolis* in 1525 (Allen Ep 1652:17n). Since
  these Polish imprints are scarce in western libraries (none is listed in the
  National Union Catalogue or in the printed catalogues of the British Library and
  the Bibliothèque Nationale), the annotator has been unable to determine
  whether Krzycki had a role in publication of these editions. He was, however,
  a canon of Cracow cathedral from 1512, and even after becoming bishop of
  Przemyśl in 1522, was active both as a royal adviser and as a talented writer
  of humanist Latin poetry.

accounts with their servants and stewards.[3] But when you sent me this book – a great man's gift of a great man's work – you sprinkled cold water (as the expression goes) on my awful lethargy.[4] Either of you could easily persuade me to make up my accounts or to dance a jig in the market square for that matter. So with such great men to encourage me, I shall prepare 40 myself to adopt a new practice for the rest of my life, especially since I am still at an age when it is neither embarrassing nor difficult to learn new things or change one's mind or habits. And yet I am afraid that my duties and responsibilities at court may interfere not only with keeping accounts, but with all my other interests, for, alas! I seem cut out for that sort of life 45 alone. I have often tried to pluck myself from these waters, to be free for myself and for my humble literary efforts, but the closer I get to the harbour, the further some mysterious gale drives me out to sea. So, my dear Erasmus, if you want to know what my life is like, I toss and tumble miserably on this sea, not because I am bewitched by these illusory honours 50 which enslave other men, but partly out of regard for the wishes of my family and partly through the kindness of my prince.[5] Just how generous he is, you may judge from the bishopric he conferred on me when nothing was further from my thoughts; and when I present him with some of my literary bagatelles, he carries them with him and keeps them in his private 55 case. It is in this respect alone that a poetic gnat like myself can claim comparison with the divine Homer.

To return now to your letter, you write that his excellency Stanisław Łaski[6] procured for you a copy of the little book[7] which I wrote against the Lutherans. He was prompted, I have no doubt, by the friendship which 60 we have for one another and perhaps by a desire to demonstrate our religious orthodoxy. But it embarrasses me nonetheless that such a trifling work, which has somehow leaked out[8] against my will, should have found its way to a distinguished man like yourself. You know, my dear Erasmus, that in this age there is hardly a nook or cranny anywhere which is not filled 65 with critics and quibblers, and you know how much trouble is caused for honest men, even those of the highest rank, by such hornets or beetles, or

* * * * *

3 Matt 18:23, 25:19
4 *Adagia* I x 51: *Frigidam aquam suffundere* 'sprinkling with cold water,' ie, 'rousing to action.'
5 Sigismund I, king of Poland from 1506 to 1548, a patron of Renaissance culture; Krzycki was his secretary and close adviser.
6 Epp 1341A n320, 1629 n1
7 Ep 1629 n2
8 Cf Cicero *De oratore* 1.94.

whatever they are. Since I defended all your ideas and even defended some
of Luther's earlier notions when he seemed to be on the right lines,[9] I could
not escape these people's furtive stings, and there was no shortage of   70
troublemakers to invent stories and carry them even to the pope. What
moved me to anger was the foulness of Luther's language when he made
his offensive and impudent attacks on everything we hold sacred and on us
bishops individually; such insults not even the most worthless and impudent cur could dream up, much less hurl at others, without feeling guilty   75
or blushing for shame. It was easy to guess what the source was like which
produced such a torrent of mad abuse; so I published that little book, for
what it is worth, partly out of pain and partly to stop the mouths of my
critics. But that represented only my light-armed troops: in the meantime
I drew up the strongest possible force in heavy mail in case he should try   80
to strike back. But when, after the second printing of my book in Rome, he
had not uttered a word, perhaps because he thought it ill suited to his
dignity and moderation, I marched my troops back to camp. I thought it
better not to tangle with men of that sort whose minds are filled with
nothing but blind rage and slanderous abuse. Defeat, I thought, was more   85
honourable than victory.

I cannot think what you meant by that second work of mine, when
you refer to a letter 'setting out the whole history of the affair,' unless the
sad tale of events in Prussia[10] has reached you. That was a personal letter
written to a friend;[11] despite my vigorous protests, it was immediately   90
published by the illustrious Baron Krzysztof Szydłowiecki, palatine and
chancellor of this kingdom,[12] a man who is very fond of both of us. All
this, my dear Erasmus, does not justify the praise you give me for my
familiarity with the Muses and with the art of rhetoric. But whatever my
work may be, I am delighted that it has been the means of bringing us   95
together in friendship and good will. It is my earnest wish that we nourish
and strengthen this friendship with mutual affection and respect.

My dear Erasmus, although you may think of us as the 'distant Sar-

* * * * *

9 Krzycki was an enthusiastic supporter of humanistic ideas of church reform
  and so found some of Luther's early criticisms attractive, but at an early date
  he turned against Luther's extremism and wrote against him on several occasions.
10 Cf Ep 1629 introduction and n3.
11 To Giovanni Antonio Buglio (Puglione), a Sicilian baron active in this time as
  a papal diplomat in Poland and Hungary
12 On this powerful figure see Ep 1593 introduction.

matians,'[13] we are not ignorant of the storms which grip your own land
of Germany. Is it not truly astonishing how the greatest things always   100
collapse upon themselves? How many kingdoms and empires have fallen
at the zenith of their power? Is it not clear to all that this is what is happening to Germany, a land which is rightly thought to surpass all others in its
military discipline, the glory of its cities and palaces, its trade, its men of
talent, and its scholarly renown. But what a sudden storm has come upon   105
you, threatening everything with shipwreck, so that not even in the anchor
of religion is there any cause for hope; and so shocking and cruel has been
the blow that one cannot speak of it without tears.

Surely some injured power is bringing this about.[14] The folly of fighting against such odds is clear even from the fables of the poets, to say   110
nothing of the record of history. That you, my dear Erasmus, the glory of
our age[15] and the prince of learning, should live in this Babylon with all
its mad confusion, in this primeval swamp of vice and error, seems a tragic
shame. What can you do in such a place where no one listens to your sound
advice? So leave this scene of turmoil without delay and 'snatch yourself,   115
I beg you, from the flames.'[16] I cannot think of anything more beneficial
to yourself or to the cause of learning than for you to move here as soon as
you can. Our country, as you know, has people of both German and Polish
stock, but there are others here too who have been happy to settle with us,
even though they consider their own country the most blest and fortunate   120
in the world. We have a prince whose virtue, wisdom, kindness, piety, and
achievements could not be praised too highly. We have a senate possessed
of great wisdom, and princes as versed in letters as in arms. We have men
of no mean talent; we have a noble temple of the Muses, and, if Erasmus
comes, we shall also have the Frobens. As for the invitation and the terms,   125
I shall make sure that they do justice to your true worth. Just say you will
come and tell us what you want us to do. Please do not say you are old and
weak; the air here is so bracing that you will soon appreciate its rejuvenat-
ing powers; and as for our beverages, they have such excellent qualities
that, even after using them for a short period of time, you will be able to   130
say farewell to the stone. So don't delay, consider what you will do and let

* * * * *

13 A nomadic people of antiquity living between the Don and the Danube; hence,
   a people thought of as very remote.
14 The Latin is part of a hexameter line but not identifiable as a quotation from
   a known classical or modern work.
15 Cf Horace *Odes* 2.17.4.
16 Virgil *Aeneid* 2.289

us know as soon as possible. Accept my best wishes, dear Erasmus, and return the affection which your true friend Krzycki feels for you.

Cracow, December 1525

1653 / To Nicolaas Everaerts   Basel, 24 December 1525

> This letter to the Lord President of the Council of Holland, a friend of long standing and an active promoter of humanistic church reform, was first printed by Pierre Bayle in his *Dictionnaire historique et critique* 2nd ed (Rotterdam 1702) I 649, and again by Jean Leclerc in LB (no 781). The original letter also survives in the British Library, MS Egerton 1863 f 2. On the recipient, see Ep 1092 introduction.

Cordial greetings, my lord president. The squabbles of comedy usually end with a marriage, at which point a sudden calm descends on the whole scene. Nowadays the tragedies acted out by our princes often have the same ending: and though it may bring little joy to the people, it is still better than war (you will remember the man who would rather be fleeced than sold   5
into slavery).[1] It looks as though the tragedy of Luther will end in a similar way. He has married a wife, a religious like himself. Evidently the marriage began under good auspices, for within a fortnight of the singing of the wedding hymn, the bride went into labour.[2] Luther is now becoming more moderate. There is nothing so wild that it cannot be tamed by a wife.   10
    I am doing all I can to persuade both sides to conclude a fair peace and put an end to these senseless wars. How far have I got? About as far as those who try to part a pair of armed and angry drunks and are beaten up by both sides for their pains. I think you have read my *Apologia* against Cousturier.[3] Who would have expected to find such a stupid creature   15
lurking among theologians and Carthusians? And yet this monster has his

* * * * *

1653
1 Fabricius, the Roman hero in the war against Pyrrhus, supported a corrupt candidate for the consulship because of his military skill, preferring, as he said, to be fleeced rather than to be sold into slavery; Cicero *De oratore* 2.268.
2 On this scandalous and untrue rumour see Ep 1633 n3.
3 Erasmus repeatedly denounced Cousturier as the most shamefully incompetent as well as the most malevolent of his antagonists at Paris. On his first *Apologia* against Cousturier's attacks, published in August 1525, see the letter of dedication, Ep 1591. On Cousturier himself see Ep 1571 n10.

admirers among the theologians. If Josse Clichtove's[4] superstitious books are on sale in your part of the world, please read his *Antilutherus* book 3, chapter 1, section 3. Béda told me in a letter that the passage refers to me.[5] If that is so, surely everyone can see that there is not a grain of sense in that lousy head of his. And yet it is wretches like this that Luther has armed against us! I see no end to it all, unless some *deus ex machina* appears to unravel the plot. The Lutheran faction has never been more arrogant, and the other side, far from giving an inch, tightens the old chains more tightly every day. They now have a new theory, which is utterly absurd, that it is the ancient languages and the humanities that are the cause of all our present woes. They have already won converts among several of the princes.

Since I cannot be with you in any other way, I send you my greetings by letter. We have lost van Dorp before his time.[6] Here considerably more than 100,000 peasants have been killed, and every day priests are arrested, tortured, hanged, decapitated, or burnt at the stake. I do not deny that a remedy is necessary, however bitter. We Germans are better at punishing wrongdoing than preventing it. My best wishes for every happiness to yourself, your wife, and your children.

The bearer of this letter is Frans van der Dilft, who once lived in my house.[7] He is a young man of good family and courteous manners. I should like you to get to know him.

Basel, Christmas eve 1525

Yours truly, Erasmus of Rotterdam

In haste, with his own hand

Don't be too critical: I did not have time to read it over.

To the distinguished authority on canon and civil law, Nicolaas Everaerts, president of Holland. In the Hague

1654 / To Erasmus Schets   Basel, 24 December 1525

This is a response to the good-hearted efforts of Schets (cf Epp 1647, 1651) to

* * * * *

4 On him see Epp 594:15n, 1620 n10.
5 See Ep 1642:9–10.
6 Erasmus sincerely mourned the premature death of Maarten van Dorp, who was his most reliable and most influential defender on the Louvain theological faculty. Cf Epp 1584, 1585, 1597, 1603, 1646.
7 See Ep 1663 introduction. After studying at Basel and living in Erasmus' household there, Dilft returned to his native Antwerp, carrying this letter.

arrange a smooth and cost-free transfer of Erasmus' revenues from his English
ecclesiastical pension through Schets' business connections in London and
Antwerp. Schets' reply is Ep 1671. Like nearly all of Erasmus' financial correspondence, this letter remained unpublished for centuries, being first published in Allen VI (1926). Allen based his text on the original manuscript in the
British Library (MS Add 38512 f 11).

Greetings. I am most grateful, my dearest Schets, for your kind offer of
assistance. Here is the whole business in a nutshell. I am sending Karl
Harst,[1] whom I regard both as trusted friend and trusted servant; he will
pick up in England whatever my pension may amount to. You know I get
nothing from the emperor; my only reward from him is to be sprinkled   5
with the holy water of the court. Whatever Karl receives, he will deposit
with your friend Alvaro.[2] Please write and give him careful instructions to
have the money transferred through your good offices at the least possible
cost to me. You know the ins and outs of this business, being an expert in
such matters. If you have a friend who plans to go to Frankfurt, I should   10
like him to take the money to my good friend Johann Froben, the bookseller, and make sure that this is done with the least loss to myself.[3] I
realize of course that it is impossible to avoid a penalty altogether. Please
make the payment to Froben in gold. You are wise in these matters and
know what currency involves the least expense. I think it is crowns.[4] If you 15
have nothing to suggest, then hold on to the money in a safe place until I
let you know what I want done. Pieter Gillis has some money belonging to

* * * * *

1654
1 The bearer of this letter, having completed two important and confidential
  trips to Italy in 1525 in pursuit of Erasmus' concerns, spent the early part of
  1526 serving Erasmus in England and the Netherlands.
2 Cf Ep 1590 n2; also mentioned in Epp 1647, 1651.
3 A good example of how Erasmus relied on the travel of his Basel publisher
  (and close friend) to the international book fair at Frankfurt in order to effect
  transfer of funds from abroad.
4 Latin *in coronatis*. See Epp 1434 n3 and 1545 n6. Erasmus is evidently discussing an actual purchase of gold coins – the French *écus au soleil* – to be sent to
  Froben, and not payment by a bill of exchange.

me.[5] He is interested in other things and financial matters are not his strong suit; he would rather not act as banker for other people. I have instructed Karl to collect all that Pieter Gillis is holding and bring it to me, unless his brother Frans can pay over the whole amount to Johann Froben at the next fair without inconveniencing himself.[6] If this is not possible, he should give it to Karl Harst, and he will carry out my orders. Could I ask you to give half an hour to Pieter Gillis to help him with the calculations? It is not that I distrust him, for there is not a more honest man alive; but he does not apply himself to matters of this sort, for he has a mind which was made for higher things.

Also I should like you to buy me a roll of Dutch linen, not too fine, but close-woven and smooth, and about eighty or ninety ells long. Frans Gillis, Pieter's brother, will be happy to take it in his baggage to Frankfurt and deliver it to Froben. Your wife will be able to help with this. See that a careful note is made of how many ells it measures, and after the outside measurements have been written down, have the whole parcel sealed; ask that a thread be included equal in length to an Antwerp ell.

I am sending your wife a gold ring, blessed by the king of England himself;[7] I am afraid I have nothing else to offer at present. Tell her to be more careful with it than she was with the little gift of the unicorn.[8] Farewell.

Basel, Christmas eve 1525
To the honourable Master Erasmus Schets. In Antwerp

1655 / To Frans van Cranevelt   Basel, 24 December 1525

This letter, written the same day as the preceding one and no doubt sent with

* * * * *

5 Until the emergence of Schets as Erasmus' most reliable financial agent in northern Europe early in 1525, Gillis had handled most of Erasmus' financial affairs in England and the Netherlands. The present letter represents a closing of that account. Some (but according to Erasmus not all) of the money due was transferred to Froben at the spring fair at Frankfurt in 1526 by Gillis' brother Frans, who appears to have been a merchant active in foreign trade. Cf Epp 1681, 1682, 1696.

6 See preceding note. A few lines further on, Erasmus also arranges for Frans Gillis to transfer to Froben at Frankfurt an order of fabric to be bought for him at Antwerp by Schets with the assistance of his wife. Frans is known only from this correspondence.

7 Cf Ep 1595 n14.

8 Apparently Schets' wife had somehow lost an earlier (and surely rarer) gift of unicorn's horn, which she much regretted.

the same courier, Karl Harst, begins by repeating the same inaccurate and scandalous tale about Luther's marriage that opened Ep 1653 to Nicolaas Everaerts; cf Ep 1633 n3. On Cranevelt, a distinguished Dutch humanist and admirer of Erasmus, see Ep 1145 introduction. The original manuscript survived at Louvain and was first published in De Vocht *Literae* 469–72 (no 172).

Cordial greetings. All the ups and downs of comedy usually end in marriage. It looks as though the Lutheran tragedy will end in the same way. He has taken a wife who was once a vestal virgin. The marriage has been a great success, as you can guess from the fact that, a few days after the singing of the wedding hymn, the new bride gave birth to a child. If you 5 have a moment to spare, Karl will show you a good likeness of the bride and groom.

That book by 'Taxander' was produced, as its title page suggests, by four Dominicans with no sense of shame.[1] Godefridus is given credit for it, but Cornelius Taxander wrote the text. Walter Ruys contributed a few 10 gems and Vincentius van Haarlem, to whom I addressed my letter of protest, added some filth of his own which he had tried to spew forth several years ago, but had been prevented by his vicar-general.[2] That wretch of a Dominican who botched my *Colloquies*[3] has just robbed his own guardian, a protonotary, at Lyons, and made off with three hundred crowns.[4] He 15 fled, but they pursued him and caught him drinking with a party of whores.[5] The cowl was useful to him on that occasion, for otherwise he would have hanged.

But you will get a better account of these things from my faithful friend, Karl Harst, who intends to return here, and also from Frans van der 20

* * * * *

1655
1 On this pseudonymous attack on Erasmus, which he eventually identified as the joint product of a group of Dominicans associated with the theological faculty of Louvain, whose names follow, see Ep 1571 n14.
2 See Ep 1582 n1.
3 On this forged edition of Erasmus' *Colloquies* by Lambertus Campester see Ep 1581 nn59 and 60.
4 Latin *coronatos trecentos*. For the reasons noted in Ep 1434 n3, these 'crowns' were probably *écus d'or au soleil*, the French gold coin that displaced the *écu à la couronne* in 1475, and was now worth 40s tournois in France and 76d gros in the Netherlands (CWE 8 350). Thus this sum would have been worth £600 tournois, or exactly £95 gros Flemish, or £64 2s 6d sterling.
5 Erasmus offers no evidence to support this scurrilous charge.

Dilft.[6] I have never met anyone more kindly or warm-hearted than this young man. He greatly admires your scholarship and wants to be commended to you and to make your acquaintance. Farewell, distinguished sir. In haste.

    Christmas eve, 1525   25
    Your friend, Erasmus of Rotterdam
    With his own hand
    To the right honourable Master Frans van Cranevelt, member of the Council of Mechelen. In Mechelen

1656 / To Robert Aldridge   Basel, 25 December 1525

> Erasmus' work on a revised version of his earlier Froben edition of the works of Seneca (1515) led him to address his former pupil at Cambridge, Aldridge, who was now senior proctor in that university. He needed someone to collect variant readings from manuscripts he knew to exist at King's College and Peterhouse. Unfortunately, not only did circumstances cause a delay in the collation of the manuscript and then in the transmission of the variant readings to Erasmus by Thomas More, but also the parchment manuscripts which Erasmus remembered seeing at Cambridge and from which he expected much useful material seem to have been missing from the library of King's College (cf Ep 1766, which is Aldridge's reply, and Epp 1797, 2040). Thus despite his good will, Aldridge was able to contribute little to the revised Seneca, published at Basel in 1529. Aldridge (c 1495–1556) studied at Eton and King's College Cambridge and spent six months under the personal tutelage of Erasmus there. He served as his interpreter during the pilgrimage to the shrine of Our Lady of Walsingham which is reflected in the famous colloquy *Peregrinatio religionis ergo* 'A Pilgrimage for Religion's Sake' (cf ASD I-3 479–80). He had been headmaster of Eton (1515–21) but then returned to Cambridge and took a bachelor's degree in divinity before moving to Oxford in 1530, where he took the DD degree. His rise to influence in the church began in 1528 and culminated in 1537 when he became bishop of Carlisle. He actively supported the royal supremacy but was a conservative who resisted the reforms of Edward VI and was active in suppressing heresy under the Catholic restoration of Mary I. Erasmus published this letter in *Opus epistolarum*.

* * * * *

6 Cf Epp 1653 n7, 1663 introduction. These favourable remarks to an influential man like Cranevelt make this letter function as a valuable letter of recommendation.

ERASMUS OF ROTTERDAM TO ROBERT ALDRIDGE OF ENGLAND,
GREETING

If you remember our former friendship and are still the sort of man you were
in those old days, perhaps you would be able to do me a favour: it would
not involve you in any expense. There is a parchment manuscript of the   5
works of Seneca in King's College. I once made a large number of notes from
it in my own copy. I entrusted the publication to a German friend whom I
considered perfectly reliable.[1] In my absence he acted most irresponsibly
during the printing of the work, then to avoid being caught, he did away
with the greater part of the original. I must do something to atone for this   10
shameful business. So I am asking you, my dear Aldridge, to get hold of that
volume of Seneca's works in the Froben edition, and ask a few people whom
you can trust to write any variants in the margin. Then send the volume with
the annotations to Thomas More,[2] who will see that it is passed on to me.
As for the *Quaestiones naturales*,[3] I know the work has been published. I shall   15
complete the collation of it myself. Seneca is worth this much trouble. You
share our common debt to the cause of letters; to me you owe nothing except
such obligations as arise from our mutual regard. I shall reimburse you to the
last cent for anything you spend on this business and I shall also make sure
that, in doing me this good turn, you do not feel you are planting a barren   20
field. Please do this as soon as you can. Give my regards to my old friends
Fawne, Humphrey, Vaughan, Garret, and the booksellers Johann Siberch and
Nicolaas.[4] May peace and happiness be yours.

* * * * *

1656
1 The reference is to Wilhelm Nesen, to whom Erasmus had entrusted materials
  prepared for a revised edition of the works of the rhetorician Seneca, materials
  which Nesen seems to have lost. Cf Ep 1341A:443–63 and nn101, 104, and Ep
  1257:6–10 and nn3–5.
2 This letter and Epp 1766 and 1797 show that despite the long hiatus in their
  surviving correspondence (from Ep 1220 in June or July 1521 to Ep 1770 of 18
  December 1526), Erasmus and More remained in touch.
3 An edition of this work of Seneca had been published by Matthaeus
  Fortunatus (Venice: Aldus, February 1523), a Hungarian student at Padua, with
  a text based on Erasmus' edition of 1515 but with many corrections which
  Erasmus not only accepted in his revised edition of 1529 but generously
  acknowledged on the title-page and in the dedication of his book.
4 These friends from Erasmus' period of residence in Cambridge (August 1511
  to February 1514) are John Fawne, Humphrey Walkden, John Vaughan, the
  Dutch-born bookseller Garret Godfrey (with whom Erasmus may have resided
  during part of his stay in Cambridge), and the itinerant booksellers Nicolaas
  Spierinck and Johann Siberch. Erasmus had known Siberch in the Netherlands,

Basel, Christmas Day 1525
There are some very old manuscripts at Cambridge, especially at   25
Peterhouse. Do what you can to help me – and Froben too. You will not
find me ungrateful for anything you do.

1657 / To Simon Grynaeus   Basel, 26 December [1525]

Although this letter bears no clear indication of year, Allen (VI 244) argues
plausibly in favour of 1525. The occasion appears to have been a letter of self-
introduction from Grynaeus which does not survive. Grynaeus (c 1494–1541)
had been a fellow student of Philippus Melanchthon in the Latin school at
Pforzheim and after prior study at a university that has not been identified,
matriculated at Vienna in 1511. Opposition to his religious opinions forced him
out of his first job as director of a grammar school in Hungary. He matriculated at Wittenberg in 1523 but the following year accepted a chair of Greek
at Heidelberg despite the opposition of his faculty colleagues to his religious
views, which reflected the influence of Zwingli and Karlstadt. He remained
there until 1529, when he was called to teach Greek at Basel. Despite his
adherence to the Reformation, he remained on good though not intimate terms
with Erasmus. He already had a substantial reputation as a classical scholar,
capped by his spectacular discovery in 1526 of five lost books of Livy. He
became an active associate of the Froben press and participated in several
classical and patristic editions. He directed the reorganization of Tübingen as
a Protestant university (1534–5) and in 1536 became professor of New Testament at Basel. This letter was published by Oporinus at Basel in 1556 as part
of an annex to the second edition of Grynaeus' commentary on Book VIII of
Aristotle's *Topica*.

ERASMUS OF ROTTERDAM TO SIMON GRYNAEUS, CORDIAL
GREETINGS
You stand higher in my regard, my dearest Grynaeus, because your varied
intellectual gifts are set off by a remarkable modesty. This type of person
has always held a peculiar, I might almost say, a fatal fascination for me. I   5
am afraid, however, that if you look too closely at me, I shall sink greatly
in your estimation, but I shall consider the loss amply repaid if I can have
the pleasure of your company and your conversation. As soon as you can
do so conveniently, please pay us a visit – you will be not just a delightful,

* * * * *

and in 1521 he founded the first press in Cambridge. For Aldridge's report on
transmission of these greetings, see Allen Ep 1766:116–19.

but a welcome guest. In the meantime if there is anything I can usefully do   10
to enhance your reputation or promote your interests, lack of enthusiasm
on my part will be the last thing to stand in the way: you can be certain of
that.

   This is all I can manage for now. I have competed with you in *gri-*
bouillage and I think I have won! Farewell, my friend, most dear to my   15
heart.

   Basel, the feast of Stephen, the first martyr

TABLE OF CORRESPONDENTS

WORKS FREQUENTLY CITED

SHORT-TITLE FORMS

INDEX

WORKS FREQUENTLY CITED

This list provides bibliographical information for works referred to in short-title form in this volume. For Erasmus' writings see the short-title list, pages 409-12. Editions of his letters are included in the list below.

AK	*Die Amerbachkorrespondenz* ed Alfred Hartmann and B.R. Jenny (Basel 1942–)
Allen	*Opus epistolarum Des. Erasmi Roterodami* ed P.S. Allen, H.M. Allen, and H.W. Garrod (Oxford 1906–58) 11 vols and index
ASD	*Opera omnia Desiderii Erasmi Roterodami* (Amsterdam 1969–)
Balan *Monumenta* I	*Monumenta reformationis Lutheranae, ex tabularis secretioribus S. Sedis 1521–1525* ed Pietro Balan (Regensburg 1884)
Bataillon (Fr)	Marcel Bataillon *Erasme et l'Espagne: Recherches sur l'histoire spirituelle du XVIe siècle* (Paris 1937)
Bataillon (Sp)	Marcel Bataillon *Erasmo y España: Estudios sobre la historia espiritual del siglo XVI* trans Antonio Alatorre, 2nd ed (Mexico 1966)
Bataillon 1991	Marcel Bataillon *Erasme et l'Espagne* rev ed 3 vols, text by Daniel Devoto, ed Charles Amiel (Geneva 1991) (This revised posthumous edition is now the standard text.)
Bentley	Jerry H. Bentley *Humanists and Holy Writ: New Testament Scholarship in the Renaissance* (Princeton 1983)
Bierlaire	Franz Bierlaire *La familia d'Erasme* (Paris 1968)
Blickle	Peter Blickle *The Revolution of 1525: The German Peasants' War from a New Perspective* trans and translators' introduction by Thomas A. Brady jr and H.C. Erik Midelfort (Baltimore 1981)
BRE	*Briefwechsel des Beatus Rhenanus* ed Adalbert Horawitz and Karl Hartfelder (Leipzig 1886; repr Hildesheim 1966)
CCL	*Corpus christianorum, series latina* (Turnhout: Brepols 1954–65) 176 vols
CEBR	*Contemporaries of Erasmus: A Biographical Register of the Renaissance and the Reformation* ed Peter G. Bietenholz and Thomas B. Deutscher (Toronto 1985–7) 3 vols

CIL   *Corpus inscriptionum latinarum* (Berlin 1862–1936) 16 vols
                               and supps

CR   *Philippi Melanchthonis opera quae supersunt omnia* ed C.G.
                               Bretschneider et al *Corpus Reformatorum* 1–28 (Halle
                               1834–60; repr 1963)

CSEL   *Corpus scriptorum ecclesiasticorum latinorum* (Vienna
                               1866–)

CTC   *Catalogus translationum et commentariorum: Mediaeval and
                               Renaissance Latin Translations and Commentaries, An-
                               notated Lists and Guides* ed Paul Oskar Kristeller et al
                               (Washington, DC 1960–)

CWE   *Collected Works of Erasmus* (Toronto 1974–)

DBI   *Dizionario biografico degli Italiani* (Rome 1960–)

De Jongh   Henri de Jongh *L'ancienne Faculté de Théologie de Louvain au
                               premier siècle de son existence (1432–1540)* (Louvain 1911;
                               repr Utrecht 1980)

DSB   *Dictionary of Scientific Biography* (New York 1970–80) 16
                               vols

Farge *Biographical*   James K. Farge *Biographical Register of Paris Doctors of
                               Theology, 1500–1536* Pontifical Institute of Mediaeval
                               Studies, Subsidia Mediaevalia 10 (Toronto 1980)

Farge *Orthodoxy*   James K. Farge *Orthodoxy and Reform in Early Reformation
                               France: The Faculty of Theology of Paris, 1500–1543,*
                               Studies in Medieval and Reformation Thought 32
                               (Leiden 1985)

Farge *Registre*   James K. Farge ed *Registre des procès-verbaux de la faculté de
                               théologie de l'Université de Paris de janvier 1524 à Novembre
                               1533.* (Paris 1990)

Ferguson *Opuscula*   *Erasmi Opuscula: A Supplement to the Opera omnia* ed
                               Wallace K. Ferguson (The Hague 1933)

Förstemann/Günther   *Briefe an Desiderius Erasmus von Rotterdam* ed J. Förstemann
                               and O. Günther, XXVII. Beiheft zum *Zentralblatt für
                               Bibliothekswesen* (Leipzig 1904; repr Wiesbaden 1968)

Franz   Günther Franz *Der deutsche Bauernkrieg* 4th ed (Darmstadt
                               1956)

Herminjard	*Correspondance des réformateurs dans les pays de langue française ... tome premier 1512–1526* ed A.-L. Herminjard (Geneva/Paris 1866; repr Nieuwkoop 1965)
Knecht	R.J. Knecht *Francis I* (Cambridge 1982)
LB	*Desiderii Erasmi Roterodami opera omnia* ed J. Leclerc (Leiden 1703–6; repr 1961–2) 10 vols
Limentani	Ida Calabi Limentani 'La lettera di Benedetto Giovio ad Erasmo' *Acme* 25 (1972): 5–37.
LP	*Letters and Papers, Foreign and Domestic, of the Reign of Henry VIII* ed J.S. Brewer, J. Gairdner, and R.H. Brodie (London 1862–1932) 36 vols
Mansi	*Sacrorum conciliorum nova et amplissima collectio* ed Giovanni Domenico Mansi, (Paris 1901; repr Graz 1960–1) 53 vols
NCE	*New Catholic Encyclopedia* (New York 1967–79) 17 vols
NK	Wouter Nijhoff and M.E. Kronenberg (eds) *Nederlandsche bibliographie van 1500 tot 1540* ('s Gravenshage 1923–61) 3 vols
OED²	*The Oxford English Dictionary* 2nd ed, 20 vols (Oxford 1989)
Opus epistolarum	*Opus epistolarum Des. Erasmi Roterodami per autorem diligenter recognitum et adjectis innumeris novis fere ad trientem auctum* (Basel: Froben, Herwagen, and Episcopius 1529)
Pastor	Ludwig von Pastor *The History of the Popes from the Close of the Middle Ages* ed and trans R.F. Kerr et al, 6th ed (London 1938–53) 40 vols
Pirckheimeri opera	*Bilibaldi Pirckheimeri ... opera politica, historica, philologica, et epistolica* ed Melchior Goldast (Frankfurt 1610; repr Hildesheim/New York 1969)
PL	J.P. Migne ed *Patrologiae cursus completus ... series latina* (Paris 1878–90) 222 vols
PW	*Paulys Real-Encyclopädie der classischen Altertumswissenschaft* ed Georg Wissowa 24 vols
Rogers	*The Correspondence of Sir Thomas More* ed Elizabeth Frances Rogers (Princeton 1947)

RQ   *Renaissance Quarterly*

Rummel   Erika Rummel *Erasmus and His Catholic Critics* 2 vols
                          (Nieuwkoop 1989)

STC   *A Short-Title Catalogue of Books Printed in England, Scotland,
                          and Ireland and of English Books Printed Abroad, 1475–1640*
                          comp A.W. Pollard, G.R. Redgrave et al, 2nd ed rev, 3
                          vols (London 1986–91)

TRE   *Theologische Realenzyklopädie* ed Gerhard Krause, Gerhard
                          Müller et al (Berlin 1977–   )

de Vocht CTL   Henry de Vocht *History of the Foundation and Rise of the
                          Collegium Trilingue Lovaniense 1517–1550* 4 vols, Humani-
                          stica Lovaniensia 10–13 (Louvain 1951–5)

de Vocht *Literae*   *Literae virorum eruditorum ad Franciscum Craneveldium
                          1522–1528* ed Henry de Vocht, Humanistica Lovaniensia
                          1 (Louvain 1928)

WA   *D. Martin Luthers Werke, Kritische Gesamtausgabe* (Weimar
                          1883–   )

WA-Br   *D. Martin Luthers Werke: Briefwechsel* (Weimar 1930–78) 15
                          vols

SHORT-TITLE FORMS FOR ERASMUS' WORKS

Titles following colons are longer versions of the same, or are alternative titles. Items entirely enclosed in square brackets are of doubtful authorship. For abbreviations, see Works Frequently Cited.

Acta: Acta Academiae Lovaniensis contra Lutherum *Opuscula* / CWE 71
Adagia: Adagiorum chiliades 1508, etc (Adagiorum collectanea for the primitive form, when required) LB II / ASD II-4, 5, 6 / CWE 30–6
Admonitio adversus mendacium: Admonitio adversus mendacium et obtrectationem LB X
Annotationes in Novum Testamentum LB VI
Antibarbari LB IX / ASD I-1 / CWE 23
Apologia ad Caranzam: Apologia ad Sanctium Caranzam, or Apologia de tribus locis, or Responsio ad annotationem Stunicae ... a Sanctio Caranza defensam LB IX
Apologia ad Fabrum: Apologia ad Iacobum Fabrum Stapulensem LB IX
Apologia adversus monachos: Apologia adversus monachos quosdam hispanos LB IX
Apologia adversus Petrum Sutorem: Apologia adversus debacchationes Petri Sutoris LB IX
Apologia adversus rhapsodias Alberti Pii: Apologia ad viginti et quattuor libros A. Pii LB IX
Apologia contra Latomi dialogum: Apologia contra Iacobi Latomi dialogum de tribus linguis LB IX / CWE 71
Apologiae contra Stunicam: Apologiae contra Lopidem Stunicam LB IX / ASD IX-2
Apologia de 'In principio erat sermo' LB IX
Apologia de laude matrimonii: Apologia pro declamatione de laude matrimonii LB IX / CWE 71
Apologia de loco 'Omnes quidem': Apologia de loco 'Omnes quidem resurgemus' LB IX
Apologia qua respondet invectivis Lei: Apologia qua respondet duabus invectivis Eduardi Lei *Opuscula*
Apophthegmata LB IV
Appendix respondens ad Sutorem LB IX
Argumenta: Argumenta in omnes epistolas apostolicas nova (with Paraphrases)
Axiomata pro causa Lutheri: Axiomata pro causa Martini Lutheri *Opuscula* / CWE 71

Carmina: poems in LB I, IV, V, VIII / CWE 85–6
Catalogus lucubrationum LB I
Ciceronianus: Dialogus Ciceronianus LB I / ASD I-2 / CWE 28
Colloquia LB I / ASD I-3
Compendium vitae Allen I / CWE 4
Conflictus: Conflictus Thaliae et Barbariei LB I
[Consilium: Consilium cuiusdam ex animo cupientis esse consultum] *Opuscula* / CWE 71

De bello turcico: Consultatio de bello turcico (in Psalmi)

De civilitate: De civilitate morum puerilium LB I / CWE 25
Declamatio de morte LB IV
Declamatiuncula LB IV
Declarationes ad censuras Lutetiae vulgatas: Declarationes ad censuras Lutetiae
 vulgatas sub nomine facultatis theologiae Parisiensis LB IX
De concordia: De sarcienda ecclesiae concordia, or De amabili ecclesiae concordia
 (in Psalmi)
De conscribendis epistolis LB I / ASD I-2 / CWE 25
De constructione: De constructione octo partium orationis, or Syntaxis LB I / ASD
 I-4
De contemptu mundi: Epistola de contemptu mundi LB V / ASD V-1 / CWE 66
De copia: De duplici copia verborum ac rerum LB I / ASD I-6 / CWE 24
De immensa Dei misericordia: Concio de immensa Dei misericordia LB V
De libero arbitrio: De libero arbitrio diatribe LB IX
De praeparatione: De praeparatione ad mortem LB V / ASD V-1
De pueris instituendis: De pueris statim ac liberaliter instituendis LB I / ASD I-2 /
 CWE 26
De puero Iesu: Concio de puero Iesu LB V / CWE 29
De puritate tabernaculi: De puritate tabernaculi sive ecclesiae christianae (in Psalmi)
De ratione studii LB I / ASD I-2 / CWE 24
De recta pronuntiatione: De recta latini graecique sermonis pronuntiatione LB I /
 ASD I-4 / CWE 26
Detectio praestigiarum: Detectio praestigiarum cuiusdam libelli germanice
 scripti LB X / ASD IX-1
De taedio Iesu: Disputatiuncula de taedio, pavore, tristicia Iesu LB V
De vidua christiana LB V / CWE 66
De virtute amplectenda: Oratio de virtute amplectenda LB V / CWE 29
[Dialogus bilinguium ac trilinguium: Chonradi Nastadiensis dialogus bilinguium
 ac trilinguium] Opuscula / CWE 7
Dilutio: Dilutio eorum quae Iodocus Clithoveus scripsit adversus declamationem
 suasoriam matrimonii
Divinationes ad notata Bedae LB IX

Ecclesiastes: Ecclesiastes sive de ratione concionandi LB V / ASD V-4
Elenchus in N. Bedae censuras LB IX
Enchiridion: Enchiridion militis christiani LB V / CWE 66
Encomium matrimonii (in De conscribendis epistolis)
Encomium medicinae: Declamatio in laudem artis medicae LB I / ASD I-4 / CWE
 29
Epistola ad Dorpium LB IX / CWE 3 / CWE 71
Epistola ad fratres Inferioris Germaniae: Responsio ad fratres Germaniae Inferioris
 ad epistolam apologeticam incerto autore proditam LB X / ASD IX-1
Epistola ad graculos: Epistola ad quosdam imprudentissimos graculos LB X
Epistola apologetica de Termino LB X
Epistola consolatoria: Epistola consolatoria virginibus sacris LB V
Epistola contra pseudevangelicos: Epistola contra quosdam qui se falso iactant
 evangelicos LB X / ASD IX-1
Epistola de esu carnium: Epistola apologetica ad Christophorum episcopum
 Basiliensem de interdicto esu carnium LB IX / ASD IX-1

Euripidis Hecuba LB I / ASD I-1
Euripidis Iphigenia in Aulide LB I / ASD I-1
Exomologesis: Exomologesis sive modus confitendi LB V
Explanatio symboli: Explanatio symboli apostolorum sive catechismus LB V /
    ASD V-1
Ex Plutarcho versa LB IV / ASD IV-2
Expositio concionalis (in Psalmi)

Formula: Conficiendarum epistolarum formula (see De conscribendis epistolis)

Hyperaspistes LB X

In Nucem Ovidii commentarius LB I / ASD I-1 / CWE 29
In Prudentium: Commentarius in duos hymnos Prudentii LB V / CWE 29
Institutio christiani matrimonii LB V
Institutio principis christiani LB IV / ASD IV-1 / CWE 27

[Julius exclusus: Dialogus Julius exclusus e coelis] *Opuscula* / CWE 27

Lingua LB IV / ASD IV-1A / CWE 29
Liturgia Virginis Matris: Virginis Matris apud Lauretum cultae liturgia LB V /
    ASD V-1
Luciani dialogi LB I / ASD I-1

Manifesta mendacia CWE 71
Methodus (see Ratio)
Modus orandi Deum LB V / ASD V-1
Moria: Moriae encomium LB IV / ASD IV-3 / CWE 27

Novum Testamentum: Novum Testamentum 1519 and later (Novum instru-
    mentum for the first edition, 1516, when required) LB VI

Obsecratio ad Virginem Mariam: Obsecratio sive oratio ad Virginem Mariam in
    rebus adversis LB V
Oratio de pace: Oratio de pace et discordia LB VIII
Oratio funebris: Oratio funebris in funere Bertae de Heyen LB VIII / CWE 29

Paean Virgini Matri: Paean Virgini Matri dicendus LB V
Panegyricus: Panegyricus ad Philippum Austriae ducem LB IV / ASD IV-1 / CWE
    27
Parabolae: Parabolae sive similia LB I / ASD I-5 / CWE 23
Paraclesis LB V, VI
Paraphrasis in Elegantias Vallae: Paraphrasis in Elegantias Laurentii Vallae LB I /
    ASD I-4
Paraphrasis in Matthaeum, etc (in Paraphrasis in Novum Testamentum)
Paraphrasis in Novum Testamentum LB VII / CWE 42–50
Peregrinatio apostolorum: Peregrinatio apostolorum Petri et Pauli LB VI, VII
Precatio ad Virginis filium Iesum LB V
Precatio dominica LB V

Precationes LB V
Precatio pro pace ecclesiae: Precatio ad Iesum pro pace ecclesiae LB IV, V
Psalmi: Psalmi, or Enarrationes sive commentarii in psalmos LB V / ASD V-2, 3
Purgatio adversus epistolam Lutheri: Purgatio adversus epistolam non sobriam
    Lutheri LB IX / ASD IX-1

Querela pacis LB IV / ASD IV-2 / CWE 27

Ratio: Ratio seu Methodus compendio perveniendi ad veram theologiam (Me-
    thodus for the shorter version originally published in the Novum instru-
    mentum of 1516) LB V, VI
Responsio ad annotationes Lei: Liber quo respondet annotationibus Lei LB IX
Responsio ad collationes: Responsio ad collationes cuiusdam iuvenis
    gerontodidascali LB IX
Responsio ad disputationem de divortio: Responsio ad disputationem cuiusdam
    Phimostomi de divortio LB IX
Responsio ad epistolam Pii: Responsio ad epistolam paraeneticam Albert Pii, or
    Responsio ad exhortationem Pii LB IX
Responsio ad notulas Bedaicas LB X
Responsio ad Petri Cursii defensionem: Epistola de apologia Cursii LB X / Allen
    Ep 3032
Responsio adversus febricitantis libellum: Apologia monasticae religionis LB X

Spongia: Spongia adversus aspergines Hutteni LB X / ASD IX-1
Supputatio: Supputatio calumniarum Natalis Bedae LB IX

Tyrannicida: Tyrannicida, declamatio Lucianicae respondens LB I / ASD I-1 / CWE
    29

Virginis et martyris comparatio LB V
Vita Hieronymi: Vita divi Hieronymi Stridonensis *Opuscula* / CWE 61

Index

Aachen 94

Accius (fr 168) 68n

Accolti, Benedetto, of Florence, archbishop-elect of Ravenna 203 and n

Achilles. *See* Zeno

Adam 197

Adamantius. *See* Origen

Adrian VI (Adrian of Utrecht), former
professor of theology at Louvain,
pope 37n, 97n, 137n, 172n, 203
intro; defends Erasmus against
critics xix, 52 and n, 56, 137, 144,
172 and n, 181 and n, 204n; encourages Erasmus' biblical scholarship
100, 141 and n, 149n, 157; respects
Erasmus as a theologian 131 and n;
advises Erasmus to preserve good
relations with the Louvain theologians 141n; assesses Erasmus'
opinions 149 and n; approves of
the *Enchiridion* 160; regent of Spain
258 intro. *See also* Pigge, Albert;
Lee, Edward; Baechem, Nicolaas

Aeginetans 341

Aerts, Jan, prior 35

Aeschylus, *Philoctetes* (fr 250) 186n,
(fr 176) 189n; *The Libation-Bearers*
313n

Aesculapius 67

Africa 219, 384n, 386n

Agesilaus, king of Sparta 190 and n

Agricola, Georgius: sends greetings to
Erasmus 229–30; *De re metallica*
(1556) 229n; corrects the text of
Galen for the Asulani press 230;

Erasmus arranges for Froben to
publish the *Bermannus sive de re
metallica dialogus* (1530) 230n

Akragas. *See* Phalaris of

Albania 228n

Alber, Matthew: letter to, from
Zwingli printed in 1525 298n

Albert of Brandenburg, cardinal-bishop of Mainz: Erasmus writes Ep
1033 to, excusing Luther 144 and n

Albert of Brandenburg, grand master
of the Teutonic Knights: becomes
the first duke of Prussia 319n

Albert of Saxony, first rector of the
University of Vienna 153 and n

Albertine. *See* George, duke of Saxony

Albertus Magnus 153n

Alciati, Andrea, of Milan, jurist 209
intro; *Collectanea* 338 and nn;
praised by Erasmus 343

Alcibiades, trial of 79

Alcmene 195n

Aldington, parish in Kent 175n, 375n

Aldridge, Robert, bishop of Carlisle:
assists Erasmus in locating a manuscript of Seneca xxi; career 397
intro

– letter to 398–9

Aleandro, Giambattista 180n; Erasmus criticizes 38 and n, 39

Aleandro, Girolamo, archbishop of
Brindisi, papal nuncio: enmity
towards Erasmus xiii, xx, 37n, 38,
53n, 300n, 326–7 intro; and
Barbier 37 and n, 258 intro, 299n;

Baechem, Nicolaas, of Egmond
(Egmondanus), O Carm, Louvain
theologian 360; attacks Erasmus 52
and n, 56, 61n, 139 and n, 143–4,
144n, 172, 181, 203 intro, 253n,
266n; silenced by Adrian VI 52n,
56, 172 and n, 181 and n; and Ferdinand of Hapsburg 54 and n,
144n, 181; ridiculed by Erasmus
139n; attacked by Erasmus 172n;
Erasmus desires peace with 266;
predeceases Erasmus 266n
Baer (Ber), Ludwig, professor of theology at Basel 98n, 128, 162 and n,
268n, 360 and n, 366 and n; Erasmus praises 12 and n; assists Erasmus in preparing the second edition of the *Novum Testamentum* 98;
assists Erasmus in preparing the *De
libero arbitrio* 98n; petitions the
curia 128 intro; asks Erasmus to
send greetings to Pucci 130;
advises Erasmus on the first edition
of his *Novum Testamentum* 139;
preeminence at Paris 141; reads
and approves of Erasmus' *Epistola
apologetica de interdicto esu carnium*
158–9, 158n, 267–8, 268n, 296 and n;
and Richard 272 and n; evaluates
Oecolampadius' *De genuina verborum Domini* 343 intro. *See also*
Oecolampadius, Johannes; Pucci,
Antonio
Baltic, sea 219n
Bamberg, Camerarius at 25. *See also*
Camerarius, Joachim
Baraninas: St Jerome's Jewish teacher
78n
Barbaro, Ermolao, of Venice: scholarship of 27; *Castigationes Plinianae*
(1492–3) 27n; translates Themistius'
commentary on Aristotle's *De anima*
73 and n; praised by Calcagnini
198 and n. *See also* Calcagnini, Celio
Barbary 386 and n
Barbier, Pierre xix, 299; letter to (Ep
1621) xiiin, xviii and n; and
Erasmus' prebend at Courtrai 37

and n, 258–9 and n, 299 and nn;
leaves for France with Aleandro 37
and n; Erasmus' suspicions of
37nn; conveys Adrian of Utrecht's
encouragement to Erasmus 141 and
nn; admires Erasmus 141n; career
258 intro; holds a benefice in the
Spanish Indies 299n; leaves Aleandro to serve Lannoy 299–300n. *See
also* Aleandro, Girolamo; Lannoy,
Charles de
– letters to 258–60, 299–301
Barlandus, Adrianus, professor of
Latin in the Collegium Trilingue
176 intro, 177n; reports Dorp's
death to Erasmus 176n
– letter to 176–7
Basel: Erasmus in xi, xii, xiii, xiv, xx,
41, 55n, 236 intro; and the Peasant
War xi, 177n, 179 and n, 240n,
252n, 281n, 325n; the Reformation
party in xii, 77n; the bishop of xv,
15n; Jan Łaski lives with Erasmus
in xiv, 216 intro, 221n, 257n, 288n,
320n; Protestant leaders and Protestantism in xvii, 7 intro, 10n, 11n,
108n, 287 intro, 288n; Erasmus'
letters (Epp 1539, 1636) to the town
council at xviii and n, xxii, 11–16,
343–4, 360 and n; and the suppression of monasteries xviii; Erasmus
praised by Oecolampadius as pre-
eminent among the learned men
of 9n; Farel expelled from 11n,
36n; and the Waldshut affair 18; Ep
1539 to the Town Council of xxii,
11–6, 360 and n; Schets transfers
Erasmus' revenues to xxii, 19 intro,
208 intro and n, 385 intro, 386;
Paumgartner forwards letters to
Erasmus at 20 and n; the College
of Saint Leonard surrenders property to 35 and n; Erasmus alarmed
by the religious changes in 36
intro; and Ep 1542 58 intro; Amerbach, the famous printer in 57n;
Erasmus meets Velius in 62 intro;
Toussain returns to 76 intro; Cera-

lation into, of the *Paraphrase of St John's Gospel* 45 and n; sects in 48; decline of faith in 49; Michiel Gillis travels between Spain and 51 and n; Erasmus dislikes stoves in 52; Amerbach's reputation in 57; the *Enchiridion* translated into 62; Velius returns to 63 and n; cure for kidney stone in 68; Pirckheimer's influence with, princes 75; Harst reports on the religious situation in 111n; hostility towards Erasmus in 112, 116; Erasmus attacks Lutherans in 113; Nausea and several, leaders seek to enforce the edict of Worms against Luther 115n; translation of Scripture into 126, 159; social unrest in, paralleled with religious unrest in Meaux 126n; Erasmus' loss of respect in 133; declining authority of, theologians 142–3 and n; nominalism in, universities 153nn; decline of scholarship in 176 intro, 176–7, 310n; Rivulo brings Barlandus news from 177; difficult for Erasmus to attack Luther while living in 178n; *De libero arbitrio* reaches Pistofilo from 186; popularity of Luther in 192; deleterious impact of Luther upon 194; Calcagnini's thoughts on the uprising in 200; the spread of the peasant uprising in 209n; translation of the *Lingua* into 214 intro; Pace is ambassador to 228n; Agricola returns to 229n; Erasmus, Reuchlin and the persecution of the older, humanists 247n; Hapsburg possessions in 252n; dire state of affairs in 265; Lutherans attack Erasmus 277; decline of university study in German-speaking regions 293n; immorality of monks and priests in 296; translations and paraphrases of Zwingli's eucharistic writings 298n; Karlstadt's pamphlets in 300, 307; Truchsess and scholarly revival in 310; the, popu-

lation of Gdansk stage pro-Lutheran riots 319n; Diemus returns to 320n; Nausea urges Erasmus to involve himself in the political efforts to end religious division in 322n; Erasmus charged with responsibility for the upheavals in 326 intro, 329n; source of support for Luther 330; commentator on St John's Gospel 337 and n, 342; Erasmus credited with reviving the humanities in 340 intro, 377 and n; the Reformation in 341n, 358n. *See also* Campeggi, Lorenzo; Emser, Hieronymus; Erasmus, original works: *Enchiridion*; Faber, Johannes; Ferdinand of Hapsburg; George, duke of Saxony; Hoogstraten, Jacob of; Karlstadt, Andreas; Luther, Martin; Montini, Floriano; Peasant War; Pirckheimer, Willibald; Pistofilo, Bonaventura; Resch, Konrad; Rode, Hinne; Santa Maria dell'Anima; Velius, Caspar Ursinus; Zwingli, Huldrych

Gerson, Jean, Paris theologian, *De laude scriptorum* (*De scriptoribus ecclesiasticis*), *De communione laicorum sub utraque specie*, *Collectorium super Magnificat, tractatus octavus* 126 and n; works published by Petit and Regnault (1521) 126n; Erasmus expresses cautious admiration for 126n, 134; Erasmus urged to read 133 and n, 151, 238n; valued by the Paris theologians for theological insights 151n; authority of 153; Erasmus promises to buy a copy of the works of 237–8; *Considerationes 12 de pertinacia* 369 and n

Geryon 189 and n

Ghent. *See* Algoet, Lieven; Schoonhove, Cornelis van

Giberti, Gian Matteo, datary to Pope Clement VII xix, 204 and n, 206 intro, 234n, 384 intro; encourages Erasmus to oppose Luther 205n;

portrait of 207 *illustration*; seeks to
silence Erasmus' critics 384n
- letter to Hezius xxii, 206, 208
- letter from 384–5
Gillis, Frans 395 and nn
Gillis, Michiel: carries Erasmus' letters to Spain 51 and n
Gillis, Pieter, replaced by Schets as
Erasmus' financial agent xxii, 19
intro; reports on Erasmus'
health 20; business relations with
Erasmus 37 and n, 394–5, 395n;
sends books to Cornelis of Bergen 84; conveys letter from Vives
to Erasmus 281 and n. *See also*
Bergen, Cornelis of; Schets, Erasmus; Vives, Juan Luis
Giovio, Benedetto 332–3 intro, 335nn;
exegesis of St John's Gospel 336–7
and nn, 340 intro, 342n; preface to
Farrago suorum lusuum 338–9 intro,
339–40
- letter from 333–8
- letter to 340–3
Giovio, Paolo, bishop of Nocera,
Elogia 333 intro
Giunta, Filippo di, Florentine publish-
er: publishes Longueil's collected
works and biography (1524) 236n.
See also Longueil, Christophe de;
Pole, Reginald
Glapion, Jean 183n. *See also* Halewijn,
Joris van
Glareanus, Henricus (Heinrich Loriti
of Glarus), Swiss humanist: Lupset
sends greetings to 235 and n;
teaches Greek at Basel 293 and n
Glaucus, Greek hero 62 and n
Glossa ordinaria, the scholastic gloss to
the Vulgate Bible 100n, 362 and n
Gniezno, primatial see of 318 intro.
See also Krzycki, Andrzej; Łaski, Jan
Goclenius, Conradus (Conrad
Wackers), professor of Latin at the
Collegium Trilingue 366 intro,
367n, 373 and n; assists Erasmus
and Lips in editing the works of St
Augustine 34 and nn, 35; urged to

buy the *Paraphrases* for Lips 35n;
Erasmus warns, against trusting
Franz Birckmann 82n; consulted by
Erasmus on Ceratinus' candidacy
for the chair of Greek at Leipzig 83
and n; opinion of Erasmus' epitaph
for Dorp 373. *See also* Birckmann,
Franz; Ceratinus, Jacobus Teyng;
Dorp, Maartin van; Lips, Maarten
- letter to 366–7
Godfrey, Garret, Dutch bookseller
398 and n
Goldast, Melchior: publishes Ep 1568
in *Pirckheimeri opera* (1610) xxii, 3
intro, 92 intro. *See also* Pirckheimer,
Willibald
Golden Fleece, Order of the 60 intro
Goliath: denotes Luther 42. *See also*
Israelites, David.
Goths: denotes those who attack the
humanities 103
Gouda 165n. *See also* Winckel, Pieter
Gran. *See* Szalkay, László
Grapheus, Cornelius, humanist friend
of Erasmus: prosecuted by Hulst
253n. *See also* Hulst, Frans van der
Gratian, Italian Camaldolese monk,
medieval canonist: compiled the
Concordantia discordantium canonum
(*Decretum*) 118 and n; Erasmus
urged to read 125, 151; *Causa* (22.1)
125n; view of the *De vera et falsa
poenitentia* 357n; *Decretum* (*Tractatus
de penitencia*) 357 and n
Graubünden. *See* Switzerland
Grebel, Conrad: and the Waldshut
affair 17n. *See also* Waldshut
Greek, Greeks: necessary for the professor of, at Leipzig to oppose
Luther 43n; Velius teaches, at
Vienna 62 intro; pun on *Enchiridion* 62n; philosophers condemned
the flute 63n; reference to Hephaestus 64 and n; Linacre translates,
medical and scientific works 68n;
advance of the study of 71; loss of
sense of, in Latin translations 72–3;
Erasmus recommends Chrysostom

159 and n; partisans of, welcome
attacks against Erasmus 162;
Taxander accuses Erasmus of teaching 164n; *Rationis Latomianae confutatio* (1521) 164n; Erasmus, and
monastic dress 164 and n;
Latomus' polemic against 173 and
n; Erasmus must live in the Low
Countries and not Germany to be
able to write freely against 178n;
and Dorp 181–2; Calcagnini attacks 186 intro, 186–95; accused of
reviving the errors of Hus 188n;
Erasmus viewed as a counterweight
to 194; Erasmus criticized by both
the opponents and disciples
of 194–5; Giberti encourages Erasmus to oppose 205n; condemned
by Paris theologians 210 intro;
Longueil orates against 240; Berquin interpolates a text by, into the
Le symbole des apostres 244n; role in
the Reformation 247 and n; Pirckheimer is disillusioned with 249
intro; teaching known in Holland,
Zeeland, and Flanders 253; increased demand for works by 260n;
Volz's sympathy for 262 intro; Witz
becomes a follower of 263n; Erasmus undecided between, and
Zwingli 289; eucharistic teachings
of 289n, 300, 348 and n, 349, 354n,
355 intro, 366n; Karlstadt reconciled
with 289n; irrepressible spread of
teachings 296; regards Karlstadt as
the source of radical eucharistic
views 297n, 307n; marries
Katharina von Bora 306 and n;
Erasmus challenges 306; prepares a
response to Erasmus' *De libero
arbitrio* 307n; objections of the scholastic theologians to 307 and n;
scholastic theologians prefer, to the
humanities 308; and Krzycki 318
intro, 319n, 390 and n; Erasmus
publishes criticism of 319n; marital
scandal surrounding 323 intro, 325
and n, 392 and n, 396 and intro;

portrait of, and Katharina von Bora
324 *illustration*; hostility of, towards
Erasmus 331; humanists' support
for 331; Erasmus' early support
for 331; monks attack, and the
supporters of the humanities 332;
defended by Pellicanus 358, 361–2;
opposes Sacramentarian views of
Zwingli 358n; rejects conciliar
authority 361; and the schoolmen
362; criticized by Béda 368
– Lutherans, Lutheranism: heretics
burned xiv n, 253n; Geldenhouwer
defects to the 31n; Erasmus fears a,
victory 32; Erasmus viewed as a 44
intro, 79, 112, 117, 204, 251, 307, 321
intro, 372n; Aleandro and the, crisis
53n; spread of, influence alarms
Erasmus 55; Botzheim and 58;
Erasmus' suspicion of 77, 331;
ubiquitousness of 77; and criticisms
of the clergy 91; Cousturier criticizes, reformers 99n; Erasmus asserts his opposition to the 161–2;
Erasmus fears physical attack by
179; hatred of Erasmus 239, 372;
doctrine preached outside Antwerp 252n; Volz attracted to 262
intro, 263; Erasmus at war with
the 265; offended by the *Spongia*
277; Brunfels' adherence to 282
intro; and Erasmus' *Epistola de esu
carnium* 296; Prussia becomes a,
duchy 318 intro, 319n; attacked by
Krzycki 319, 389–90; pro-Lutheran
riots in Gdansk 319n; tragedy 330;
eucharistic teaching 348n; not
feared by the Paris theologians 368;
accused of arrogance 393
Lycian. *See* Proclus
Lydgate, *Hors, shepe and Gosse* (526)
89n
Lydia 321n. *See also* Croesus
Lyons 396; the Poor Catholics (Poor
Men) of 148n. *See also* Vingle,
Pierre de; Waldensian
Lyra, Nicholas of, OFM, medieval
exegete 100 and n

This book

was designed by

ANTJE LINGNER

based on the series design by

ALLAN FLEMING

and was printed by

University

of Toronto

Press